Strategic Planning Process

The International Library of Management
Series Editor: Keith Bradley

Titles in the Series:

Performance Evaluation
Walter C. Borman

Public Sector Management
Sir John Bourn

Decision Science
Derek Bunn

Training and Development in Public and Private Policy
Peter Cappelli

Internal Auditing
Andrew Chambers

Takeovers
A. Cosh and A. Hughes

Ethics and Management
Thomas Donaldson

Group Management
Connie Gersick

Career Development
Douglas T. Hall

Power and Politics in Organizations
Cynthia Hardy

Industrial Relations: Institutions and Organizational Performance
Morris M. Kleiner

Strategic Planning Process
Peter Lorange

Management of Non-profit Organizations
Sharon M. Oster

Organizational Sociology
W. Richard Scott

Concepts of Leadership
Jeffrey A. Sonnenfeld

The Manager as a Leader
Jeffrey A. Sonnenfeld

Organizational Psychology
Philip Stone and Mark Cannon

Managerial Economics
Stefan Szymanski

Organizational Theory
A.W.M. Teulings

Management of Marketing
Vikas Tibrewala

International Management
Rosalie L. Tung

Management of Change and Innovation
Bengt-Arne Vedin

Management Accounting
Richard M.S. Wilson

Marketing Controllership
Richard M.S. Wilson

Strategic Cost Management
Richard M.S. Wilson

Management Buy-outs
Mike Wright

Strategic Planning Process

Edited by
Peter Lorange
President
IMD – International Institute for Management Development

Dartmouth
Aldershot · Brookfield USA · Singapore · Sydney

© Peter Lorange, 1994. For copyright of individual articles please refer to the Acknowledgements.

All rights reserved. No part of this publication may be reproduced, stored in a retrieval system, or transmitted in any form or by any means, electronic, mechanical, photocopying, recording, or otherwise without the prior permission of Dartmouth Publishing Company Limited.

Published by
Dartmouth Publishing Company Limited
Gower House
Croft Road
Aldershot
Hants GU11 3HR
England

Dartmouth Publishing Company
Old Post Road
Brookfield
Vermont 05036
USA

British Library Cataloguing in Publication Data
Strategic Planning Process. –
(International Library of Management)
I. Lorange, Peter II. Series
658.4

Library of Congress Cataloging-in-Publication Data
Strategic planning process / edited by Peter Lorange.
  p. cm. — (The International library of management)
  Includes bibliographical references and index.
  ISBN 1-85521-350-8
  1. Strategic planning. I. Lorange, Peter. II. Series.
HD30.28.S73447 1994
858.4'012—dc20

93-33571
CIP 1

ISBN 1 85521 350 8

Printed in Great Britain by Galliard (Printers) Ltd, Great Yarmouth

Contents

Acknowledgements ix
Series Preface xi
Introduction xiii

PART I CORPORATE-WIDE STRATEGIC PLANNING

1. Balaji S. Chakravarthy and Peter Lorange (1984), 'Managing Strategic Adaptation: Options in Administrative Systems Design', *Interfaces*, **14**, pp. 34–46. 3
2. Richard G. Hamermesh and Roderick E. White (1984), 'Manage Beyond Portfolio Analysis', *Harvard Business Review*, pp. 103–9. 17
3. John C. Camillus and Deepak K. Datta (1991), 'Managing Strategic Issues in a Turbulent Environment', *Long Range Planning*, **24**, pp. 67–74. 25
4. Daniel G. Simpson (1992), 'Key Lessons for Adopting Scenario Planning in Diversified Companies', *Planning Review*, **2**, pp. 10–17, 47, 48. 33
5. Paul J.H. Schoemaker and Cornelius A.J.M. van der Heijden (1992), 'Integrating Scenarios into Strategic Planning at Royal Dutch/Shell', *Planning Review*, **2**, pp. 41–46. 43
6. A. Steven Walleck, J. David O'Halloran and Charles A. Leader (1991), 'Benchmarking World-Class Performance', *The McKinsey Quarterly*, pp. 3–24. 49
7. Robert J. McLean (1990), 'Memo to a CEO: Planning for Value', *The McKinsey Quarterly*, pp. 75–81. 71
8. Benjamin B. Tregoe and Peter M. Tobia (1991), 'Strategy Versus Planning: Bridging the Gap', *The Journal of Business Strategy*, **12**, pp. 14–19. 79

PART II STRATEGIC PLANNING AT THE BUSINESS LEVEL

9. Balaji S. Chakravarthy and Peter Lorange (1991), 'Adapting Strategic Planning to the Changing Needs of a Business', *Journal of Organizational Change Management*, **4**, pp. 6–18. 87
10. Balaji S. Chakravarthy (1987), 'On Tailoring a Strategic Planning System to Its Context: Some Empirical Evidence', *Strategic Management Journal*, **8**, pp. 517–34. 101
11. Henry Pankratz (1991), 'Strategic Alignment: Managing for Synergy', *Business Quarterly*, **55**, pp. 66–71. 119

12	Thomas S. Robertson and Hubert Gatignon (1991), 'How Innovators Thwart New Entrants into Their Market', *Planning Review*, **19**, pp. 4–11, 48.	125
13	Simon Majaro (1992), 'Strategy Search and Creativity: The Key to Corporate Renewal', *European Management Journal*, **10**, pp. 230–8.	135
14	Walter Schaffir and David Moore (1989), 'The Myths of Strategic Planning', *Strategic Direction*, pp. 1–2.	145
15	Anil K. Gupta (1987), 'SBU Strategies, Corporate-SBU Relations, and SBU Effectiveness in Strategy Implementation', *Academy of Management Journal*, **30**, pp. 477–500.	147

PART III IMPLEMENTATION PROCESSES AND STRATEGIC PLANNING

16	William Sandy (1991), 'Avoid the Breakdowns Between Planning and Implementation', *The Journal of Business Strategy*, **12**, pp. 30–3.	173
17	R. Malcolm Schwartz and Frank A. Petro (1985), 'The Role of Systems in Implementing Strategy', *Outlook*, **9**, pp. 46–51.	177
18	Peter Lorange, Johan Roos and Peggy Simcic Brønn (1992), 'Building Successful Strategic Alliances', *Long Range Planning*, **25**, pp. 10–17.	183
19	Chris Voss (1992), 'Successful Innovation and Implementation of New Processes', *Business Strategy Review*, **3**, pp. 29–44.	191
20	Steven J. Heyer, Daniel H. Marcus and Reginald Van Lee (1988), 'Making Strategy Work: The Team Approach', *Outlook*, **12**, pp. 17–23.	207
21	Jon R. Katzenbach and Douglas K. Smith (1992), 'Why Teams Matter', *The McKinsey Quarterly*, pp. 3–27.	215

PART IV THE HUMAN RESOURCE DIMENSION IN STRATEGIC PLANNING IMPLEMENTATION

22	Peter M. Senge (1992), 'Mental Models', *Planning Review*, **20**, pp. 4–10, 44.	243
23	Peter M. Senge (1990), 'The Leader's New Work: Building Learning Organizations', *Sloan Management Review*, pp. 7–23.	251
24	Kathryn Rudie Harrigan and Gaurav Dalmia (1991), 'Knowledge Workers: The Last Bastion of Competitive Advantage', *Planning Review*, **19**, pp. 4–9, 48.	269
25	Paul Evans and Peter Lorange (1989), 'The Two Logics Behind Human Resource Management', in P. Evans, Y. Doz and A. Laurent (eds), *Human Resource Management in International Firms: Change, Globalization, Innovation*, Macmillan, **8**, pp. 144–61.	277
26	D.E. Hussey (1991), 'Implementing Corporate Strategy: Using Management Education and Training', *The Best of Long Range Planning*, pp. 73–82.	295
27	Morgan W. McCall Jr. (1992), 'Executive Development as a Business Strategy', *The Journal of Business Strategy*, **13**, pp. 25–31.	305

PART V APPENDIX – STRATEGIC PLANNING TECHNIQUES: SUMMARY ARTICLES

28 Yoram Wind and Vijay Mahajan (1981), 'Designing Product and Business Portfolios', *Harvard Business Review*, **59**, pp. 155–65.   315
29 Nandini Rajagopalan, Abdul M.A. Rasheed and Deepak K. Datta (1992), 'Strategic Decision Processes: An Integrative Framework and Future Directions', in P. Lorange, B. Chakravarthy, J. Roos and A. Van de Ven (eds), *Implementing Strategic Processes: Change, Learning and Co-operation*, Basil Blackwell: Oxford, pp. 274–312.   327
30 James L. Webster, William E. Reif and Jeffrey S. Bracker (1989), 'The Manager's Guide to Strategic Planning Tools and Techniques', *Planning Review*, **17**, pp. 4–7, 12, 13.   367

Name Index   373

Acknowledgements

The editor and publishers wish to thank the following for permission to use copyright material.

Academy of Management Journal for the essay: Anil K. Gupta (1987), 'SBU Strategies, Corporate-SBU Relations and SBU Effectiveness in Strategy Implementation', *Academy of Management Journal*, **30**, pp. 477–500.

Basil Blackwell Limited for the essay: Nandini Rajagopalan, Abdul M.A. Rasheed and Deepak K. Datta (1992), 'Strategic Decision Processes: An Integrative Framework and Future Directions', in P. Lorange, B. Chakravarthy, J. Roos and A. Van de Ven (eds), *Implementing Strategic Processes: Change, Learning and Co-operation*, Basil Blackwell: Oxford, pp. 274–312.

Business Quarterly for the essay: Henry Pankratz (1991), 'Strategic Alignment: Managing for Synergy', *Business Quarterly*, **55**, pp. 66–71.

Faulkner & Gray Publishers, New York for the essays: Benjamin B. Tregoe and Peter M. Tobia (1991), 'Strategy Versus Planning: Bridging the Gap', *The Journal of Business Strategy*, **12**, pp. 14–9; William Sandy (1991), 'Avoid the Breakdowns Between Planning and Implementation', *The Journal of Business Strategy*, **12**, pp. 30–3; Morgan W. McCall Jr. (1992), 'Executive Development as a Business Strategy', *The Journal of Business Strategy*, **13**, pp. 25–31. Reprinted with permission.

Harvard Business Review for the essays: Richard G. Hamermesh and Roderick E. White (1984), 'Manage Beyond Portfolio Analysis', *Harvard Business Review*, pp. 103–9. Copyright © 1984 by the President and Fellows of Harvard College. All rights reserved. Yoram Wind and Vijay Mahajan (1981), 'Designing Product and Business Portfolios', *Harvard Business Review*, **59**, pp. 155–65. Copyright © 1981 by the President and Fellows of Harvard College. All rights reserved.

The Institute of Management Science for the essay: Balaji S. Chakravarthy and Peter Lorange (1984), 'Managing Strategic Adaptation: Options in Administrative Systems Design', *Interfaces*, **14**, pp. 34–46.

McKinsey & Co. Inc. for the essay: Jon R. Katzenbach and Douglas K. Smith (1992), 'Why Teams Matter', *The McKinsey Quarterly*, pp. 3–27. This article is excerpted from *The Wisdom of Teams: Creating the High-Performance Organization*, Boston 1993 and is reprinted by permission of Harvard Business School Press. Copyright © 1992 by McKinsey & Co. Inc.

Macmillan Limited for the essay: Paul Evans and Peter Lorange (1989), 'The Two Logics Behind Human Resource Management', in P. Evans, Y. Doz and A. Laurent (eds), *Human Resource Management in International Firms: Change, Globalization, Innovation*, Macmillan, **8**, pp. 144–61.

Simon Majaro (1992), 'Strategy Search and Creativity: The Key to Corporate Renewal', *European Management Journal*, **10**, pp. 230–8. Copyright © Simon Majaro.

MCB University Press for the essay: Balaji S. Chakravarthy and Peter Lorange (1991), 'Adapting Strategic Planning to the Changing Needs of a Business', *Journal of Organizational Change Management*, **4**, pp. 6–18.

The McKinsey Quarterly for the essays: A. Steven Walleck, J. David O'Halloran and Charles A. Leader (1991), 'Benchmarking World-Class Performance', *The McKinsey Quarterly*, pp. 3–24; Robert J. McLean (1990), 'Memo to a CEO: Planning for Value', *The McKinsey Quarterly*, pp. 75–81.

Oxford University Press for the essay: Chris Voss (1992), 'Successful Innovation and Implementation of New Processes', *Business Strategy Review*, **3**, pp. 29–44.

Pergamon Press Limited for the essays: John C. Camillus and Deepak K. Datta (1991), 'Managing Stategic Issues in a Turbulent Environment', *Long Range Planning*, **24**, pp. 67–74; Peter Lorange, Johan Roos and Peggy Simcic Brönn (1992), 'Building Successful Strategic Alliances', *Long Range Planning*, **25**, pp. 10–17; D.E. Hussey (1991), 'Implementing Corporate Strategy: Using Management Education and Training', *The Best of Long Range Planning*, **6**, pp. 73–82.

The Planning Forum for the essays: Daniel G. Simpson (1992), 'Key Lessons for Adopting Scenario Planning in Diversified Companies', *Planning Review*, **2**, pp. 10–17; Paul J.H. Schoemaker and Cornelius A.J.M. van der Heijden (1992), 'Integrating Scenarios into Strategic Planning at Royal Dutch/Shell', *Planning Review*, **2**, pp. 41–46; Thomas S. Robertson and Hubert Gatignon (1991), 'How Innovators Thwart New Entrants into Their Market', *Planning Review*, **19**, pp. 4–11, 48; Kathryn Rudie Harrigan and Gaurav Dalmia (1991), 'Knowledge Workers: The Last Bastion of Competitive Advantage', *Planning Review*, **19**, pp. 4–9, 48; James L. Webster, William E. Reif and Jeffrey S. Bracker (1989), 'The Manager's Guide to Strategic Planning Tools and Techniques', *Planning Review*, **17**, pp. 4–7, 12, 13.

Peter M. Senge (1990), 'Mental Models', in *The Fifth Discipline*, by Peter M. Senge. Copyright © 1990 by Peter M. Senge. Used by permission of Doubleday, a division of Bantam Doubleday Dell Publishing Group Inc. Also in *Planning Review*, **20**, 1992.

Sloan Management Review for the essay: Peter M. Senge (1990), 'The Leader's New Work: Building Learning Organizations', *Sloan Management Review*, pp. 7–23. Copyright © 1990 by the Sloan Management Review Association. All rights reserved.

John Wiley and Sons Limited for the essay: Balaji S. Chakravarthy (1987), 'On Tailoring a Strategic Planning System to Its Context: Some Empirical Evidence', *Strategic Management Journal*, **8**, pp. 517–34. Reproduced by permission of John Wiley and Sons Limited, UK.

Every effort has been made to trace all the copyright holders, but if any have been inadvertently overlooked the publishers will be pleased to make the necessary arrangement at the first opportunity.

Series Preface

The International Library of Management brings together in one series the most significant and influential articles from across the whole range of management studies. In compiling the series, the editors have followed a selection policy that is both international and interdisciplinary. The articles that are included are not only of seminal importance today, but are expected to remain of key relevance and influence as management deals with the issues of the next millennium.

The Library was specifically designed to meet a great and growing need in the field of management studies. Few areas have grown as rapidly in recent years, in size, complexity, and importance. There has been an enormous increase in the number of important academic journals publishing in the field, in the amount published, in the diversity and complexity of theory and in the extent of cross-pollination from other disciplines. At the same time, managers themselves must deal with increasingly complex issues in a world growing ever more competitive and interdependent. These remarkable developments have presented all those working in the field, whether they be theorists or practitioners, with a serious challenge. In the absence of a core series bringing together this wide array of new knowledge and thought, it is becoming increasingly difficult to keep abreast of all new important developments and discoveries, while it is becoming ever-more vital to do so.

The International Library of Management aims to meet that need, by bringing the most important articles in management theory and practice together in one core, definitive series. The Library provides management researchers, professors, students, and managers themselves, with an extensive range of key articles which, together, provide a comprehensive basis for understanding the nature and importance of the major theoretical and substantive developments in management science. The Library is the definitive series in management studies.

In making their choice, the editors have drawn especially from the Anglo-American tradition, and have tended to exclude articles which have been widely reprinted and are generally available. Selection is particularly focused on issues most likely to be important to management thought and practice as we move into the next millennium. Editors have also prefaced each volume with a thought-provoking introduction, which provides a stimulating setting for the chosen articles.

The International Library of Management is an essential resource for all those engaged in management development in the future.

KEITH BRADLEY
Series Editor
The International Library of Management

Introduction

Any corporation faces a number of challenges – or dilemmas – when it comes to developing strategies. These may involve difficult choices regarding setting priorities, trade-off decisions with respect to resources committed to the future versus today's 'fire fighting' to achieve the bottom-line results, decisions whether to pursue a strategic initiative through a greenfield, joint venture or acquisition-based approach, and so on. Strategic management literature is abundant with analytical models for developing strategies, both at the corporate level and within the various business units of a firm. These models often provide the stimulus to firms in conceptualizing both strategy setting and strategy implementation. However, such analytical models are not much help when it comes to involving the members of an organization as a whole, to secure their understanding and commitment which provide a practical delineation of a realistic strategy within an organization.

It is important that strategic planning processes be employed within organizations with a degree of formality, particularly if these organizations are beyond a certain size and complexity. Strategic planning processes, together with strategic analyses, provide complementary sources of support in forming and implementing workable strategies.

The following four typical dilemmas, often faced by corporations, all lend credence to the rationality of employing strategic planning processes.

In a given situation a corporation and its management have to make sure that a certain part of available resources (funds, people, etc.) will be employed *today* in order to achieve the operating bottom-line results necessary to keep the organization going. It must, *also* today, employ resources to make sure that preparations are made for the future, for instance by opening new markets and carrying out research and development for new products. Thus, there must be a balance between the extent of resources to be allocated today for use today, as opposed to those allocated today for future use.

Corporations typically have problems maintaining this balance in a reasonable manner. Rather, unexpected crises, launching of special projects and responding to short-term pressures all tend to lead to fire fighting, so that systematic implementation efforts when it comes to longer-term strategies, are disrupted, or, at worst, not carried out. A strategic planning process can help the organization cope with and manage this tension in a more explicit and productive manner.

A second dilemma has to do with the organization's willingness and ability actually to search for new opportunities, to look for new ways of doing things and to discover new processes. This is in contrast to following approaches and procedures which have worked in the past. Most organizations tend to follow an incremental extension of what is tried and tested, rather than breaking loose and looking at the future in a more open-ended manner. Strategic planning processes can help the organization put pressure on itself, helping to justify more radical thinking and allowing the firm to free itself from the trap of extrapolating too much from the past. Without the self-imposed pressure put on the organization through a strategic planning process, it can be much harder to make this happen.

A third dilemma has to do with the fact that, while an analytically-developed strategy can have many strengths and merits, it will typically mean relatively little to those members of an organization who have not been directly involved in its conception. Thus, a broader part of the organization may not understand the strategy, and there may be a lack of 'ownership', with little commitment in terms of motivation and willingness to give it a good try. This can be avoided by a more participative planning process which ensures broader engagement in a bottom-up manner within the organization. Such a participative planning process also allows top-down viewpoints to be presented, creating a dialogue or interaction between the various stakeholders within the firm. Gradually, the strategic process can facilitate the narrowing down of options, so that particular ones are agreed upon; thus the strategic choices made should ultimately be recognized as meaningful by the members of the organization in a broader sense.

A final dilemma has to do with the fact that, while an analytical strategy may have a 'right' or 'wrong' profile, in reality any organization may be much more concerned with attempting to build up *incremental* knowledge about how well a strategy works, thus improving on it over time through organizational learning. In order for this to happen, a process of strategic control to stimulate incremental change must be in place. A strategy will be ineffective if there is no strategic planning/control process available which allows for this incremental improvement through organizational learning.

All of these dilemmas call for a proper strategic planning process to complement the strategy paradigms and analytical approaches that are in the competitive strategy literature as well as in the industrial economics literature. This volume provides a number of essays that outline the basics of such a strategic planning process approach.

Strategic planning was a very prominent feature both in the literature and in corporate practice from the mid-1960s into the 1970s. The comprehensive book from this period, *Top Management Planning* by Steiner, represents a good example of strategic planning, also labelled long-range planning or corporate planning.[1] The approach fell into relative disrepute after time, first, because much of it inherently tended to be based on extrapolative types of exercises, both quantitatively and qualitatively and, second, because the proposed strategies tended to lack any theoretical underpinning. At present, however, the pendulum is swinging back.[2] There is now a growing realization that *both* strategic analysis *and* strategic processes are needed; the two complement one another.

In the present book, we have attempted to collect a number of typical recent works within the strategic planning process area. Needless to say, the selection cannot be totally representative. The field is burgeoning, both from a practitioner-oriented viewpoint[3] and from an academic-research perspective.[4] We have, however, attempted to select works that have interest both for the practitioner and for practitioner-oriented researchers. We also feel that it is an advantage, rather than otherwise, to include selections that perhaps are not so well-known. By making these works available we hope that fresh insights can follow and a strengthened perspective be achieved.

In the following paragraphs, we highlight some of the major themes covered in each of the four sections of the book, as well as in the Appendix. We also refer explicitly to seminal thoughts and contributions of some of the authors included. It is, however, beyond the scope of this Introduction to review all of the chapters that the reader finds herein: such an overstructuring would indeed be dysfunctional.

Part I deals with corporate-wide strategic planning. Such strategic planning processes consider the firm as a whole: how to set an overall strategic plan for a complex, typically multi-divisional firm attempting to pursue a multi-business strategy. Such a planning activity must help top management provide energy and vision into the strategic thinking of the many parts of the firm. The planning process must be a top-down 'pumping station' in this respect, channelling energy, drive and urgency into the strategic thinking of the various divisions.

Furthermore, as every modern manager is aware, the strategic planning process must adapt to an increasingly complex environment which may differ from one division of the firm to another. This in turn calls for 'local' bottom-up responses. The essays presented here take this into account. For instance, in Chapter 3 Camillus and Datta present a framework for dealing with strategic issues in a turbulent environment by integrating conventional Strategic Planning Systems and Strategic Issues Management Systems. Hamermesh and White (Chapter 2) move us away from the classical portfolio analysis of the firm to provoke consideration of other issues involved in the decision process, while Walleck, O'Halloran and Leader (Chapter 6) indicate how to benchmark world-class process performance in order to judge one's own company against competing corporations.

The corporate planning process must also allow for a corporate-wide search for opportunities. Perhaps the most effective way to ensure this is by including executives who are close to the marketplace where the opportunities arise. These executives typically spot opportunities more readily and signal them through the planning process, so that a better strategy can emerge. 'Memo to a CEO' addresses this subject through McLean's advice on planning for value (Chapter 7). He offers three basic conditions for incorporating a focus on value, the first being to set up practical decision guidelines and processes that focus management action. The second is management's understanding of what drives shareholders, while the third is management evaluations, incentives and reward systems that encourage decision making.

It is important, however, that the overall custodian of the corporate-wide planning process is the chief executive officer and his/her close associates. All chief executive officers face a number of pressures which need responses so that not only the firm, but also the CEO, can succeed. Some of these pressures are structural in nature, having to do with maintaining the appropriateness of the overall portfolio mix within the firm. Others are more short term or financial in nature, relating to the basic shorter-term survival of the firm, such as takeover threats, problems of dissension from one's own stockholders, weakened support from financial institutions, etc. All in all, the strategic planning process must allow top management to focus its energy when interacting with the organization. This means manoeuvring between the various types of pressures – finding meaningful trade-offs and balances in such a way that all the stakeholders involved support the strategy chosen, as far as can be accomplished. This is discussed by Chakravarthy and Lorange in Chapter 1. Chapter 5 on strategic planning at Royal Dutch/Shell outlines probably one of the best examples of how a large firm has successfully integrated a comprehensive strategic planning process, and how scenarios are extensively used to involve the whole organization.

Part II deals with strategic planning processes at the business level within the firm. Partly, the challenge here is for executives to assess the attractiveness of a particular business, possibly along a certain quantitative dimension such as its growth potential, as well as perhaps more fundamentally in terms of understanding the longer-term opportunities that a particular business segment might provide. Thus, the business executives in question must be able to identify opportunities and develop a sense of how to take advantage of such 'windows', thereby generating a more innovative 'leap-frogging' strategy.

Another issue that typically needs to be resolved at the business level involves assessing the strengths of one's organization in advance of pursuing the various types of business opportunities at hand. A measure of these strengths can be achieved by looking at one's market share, thereby perhaps getting a better feel for cost differentials. More fundamentally, the quality of one's organization can be assessed along a number of other dimensions to see how well it performs relative to others; this type of 'benchmarking' can ensure realism. The ability to mobilize resources internally to maximize opportunities that have been identified is also critical.

A third issue central to the business level area has to do with developing links between closely related business units, so that synergies can be articulated within such a 'business family' context. Chakravarthy and Lorange, as well as Pankratz, discuss how a strategic planning system can facilitate the pursuit of different businesses at the Strategic Business Unit level. They further discuss how to tailor the system to different business 'contexts', in the sense of environmental complexity and distinctive competencies (see Chapters 9, 10 and 11). Robertson and Gatignon (Chapter 12) indicate how innovators can thwart new business pursuits, while some myths about the difficulty of achieving synergies through the strategic planning process are tersely outlined by Schaffir and Moore in Chapter 14.

The contributions in this section thus emphasize the importance of understanding that planning at the business level must be creative and forward-oriented. It must also be based on a good understanding of business realities – as opposed to being too remote or theoretical.

Part III deals with the implementation of strategic planning processes in terms of developing the necessary momentum to accelerate plans. Issues in this context include how members in an organization cooperate across organizational boundaries, and also how teams are set up so as to pursue particular implementation projects, keeping in mind that innovative plans almost always imply relatively new tasks for team members. These chapters also point out that approaches to joint ventures can be used when striving for more effective implementation. One reason is the existence of many similarities between in-house implementation planning involving many parts of a firm and alliance work involving external partners. Good strategic alliance practices can thus represent a valuable source of learning for in-house strategy implementation.

A broad discussion of most of these issues is dealt with by Lorange, Roos and Simcic Brønn in relation to forming strategic alliances (Chapter 18). Here we are introduced to the cooperative initiatives necessary for creating a network: from the initial, relatively loose rudiments required during the creation of an alliance, all the way to completion, which is manifested by a formal network specifying each party's roles. The subject of team-work is thus critical in terms of strategy implementation; this is covered very well in the selections constituting Part III. An important theme in today's business environment, Katzenbach and Smith provide an excellent overview of why teams, as opposed to groups, are essential for achieving organizational performance (Chapter 21).

Part IV deals with human resources – the firm's most precious strategic asset – and how this most critical resource forms part of strategic planning activities. In this context, the question of human resource management is central. How should one 'allocate' this strategic resource? How can one develop a better understanding of organizational learning, so that plans indeed are implemented more and more effectively through the appropriate delineation of organization members in team settings that allow the *organization* to learn? How can processes be put in place to 'make good become even better'?

D.E. Hussey looks at the link between corporate strategy and management training and education, powerful weapons for implementing strategy, but unfortunately too often ignored (Chapter 26). On the other hand, Harrigan and Dalmia indicate that 'savvy' firms *are* learning how to train their 'knowledge workers', those the authors identify as being key problem-solvers, innovators and masters of process (Chapter 24). The entire organization as a learning entity seems to be the emerging challenge for executives; it is not just a matter of training managers, but training the organization. Senge gives us a good introduction to this relatively new concept which he believes will be a key to any organization's gaining competitive advantage in the future (Chapter 22).

Part V is provided as an Appendix of survey readings which hopefully will be of practical interest to many readers but which do not fit into any of the four basic state-of-the-art subject areas described above. These three chapters provide surveys of a number of common techniques which relate to practising strategic planning. The reader can refer to them as overviews of what is available and then follow up with more detailed study of background articles, along with those in this volume.

Webster, Reif and Bracker offer us a manager's guide in the form of a framework for evaluating 30 strategic planning tools and techniques (Chapter 30). Also provided is a list of the 12 most frequently used techniques and recommended sources for further reading.

Much of the discussion in strategic processes deals with the 'portfolio of the firm'. In Chapter 28, Wind and Mahajan outline how portfolio models for planning strategy are constructed, giving readers a broader understanding of what researchers mean by this term. The authors also give key characteristics of nine portfolio models and offer some suggestions on how to choose the most appropriate model for a firm's particular portfolio analysis.

An excellent review and synthesis of past research on strategic decision processes are provided by Rajagopalan, Rasheed and Datta (Chapter 29). The authors have developed a framework for clarifying the determinants and outcomes of strategic processes, based on a critical review of the body of available empirical research. For readers who may want to delve further into this area, particularly researchers, this essay is perhaps a good starting point. Further, the authors suggest several useful directions for future research, giving a glimpse of the wave of new thinking that is emerging in strategic processes.

Hopefully, this volume will provide a useful and up-to-date approach to the subject of strategic planning processes. Taken as a whole, the essays reprinted here represent an impressive body of knowledge regarding how strategic planning processes can make a difference when trying to ensure the long-term success of a firm. Such managerially-focused strategic planning processes will receive more and more attention in the years to come, particularly given the complexity of the modern transnational corporation. Indeed, in using this volume, the intelligent corporation will have to hand an important resource for gaining competitive advantage.

Notes

1 G. Steiner (1969), *Top Management Planning*, New York: Macmillan.
2 B. Chakravarthy and P. Lorange (1991), *Managing the Strategy Process: A Framework for a Multibusiness Firm*, Englewood Cliffs, NJ: Prentice-Hall.
3 *Journal of Long-Range Planning*, Oxford: Pergamon Press, edited by Professor Bernard Taylor, provides an excellent source for state-of-the-art practitioner-oriented strategic planning approaches.
4 P. Lorange, C. Chakravarthy, J. Roos and A. Van de Ven (eds) (1992), *Implementing Strategic Processes: Change, Learning and Cooperation*, Oxford: Basil Blackwell.

Part I
Corporate-Wide Strategic Planning

Managing Strategic Adaptation: Options in Administrative Systems Design

BALAJI S. CHAKRAVARTHY

The Wharton School
University of Pennsylvania
Philadelphia, Pennsylvania 19104

PETER LORANGE

The Wharton School
University of Pennsylvania
Philadelphia, Pennsylvania 19104

The challenge for strategic planning is to provide a proper trade-off between the short-term and long-term interests of the firm. Four alternative administrative arrangements have been used to make these trade-offs in multibusiness firms. The key distinction between the models is the level within the organization at which these trade-offs are made. Several contextual factors influence the choice of a model for the firm.

Strategic planning seeks to ensure the continuous adaptation of the goals and strategies of a firm to the changes in its environment. Successful adaptation is possible only if managers expend some of the current financial and human resources of their firms in building strategic positions with future payoffs. This "adaptive" managerial focus [Lorange 1980] requires slack resources, that is, surplus contributions provided by the stakeholders of the firm beyond the inducements paid to insure their cooperation [Barnard 1968]. Slack resources can be generated only by paying careful attention to the firm's efficiency. This "integrative" managerial focus [Lorange 1980] is, therefore, a necessary complement to the "adaptive" managerial focus.

Corresponding to these two focuses are two distinct processes in strategic planning. The first process, *adaptive generalization*, aims at preparing the firm for strategic responses to future environments; whereas the second process, *adaptive specialization*, seeks to fine tune the strategies of the firm for better fit with its current environment [Chakravarthy 1982]. While the design of planning systems either for adaptive generalization or adap-

ADMINISTRATIVE SYSTEMS DESIGN

tive specialization is well understood [Lorange and Vancil 1976], little attention has been paid to systems that simultaneously focus on both of these processes. Long term survival of the firm clearly demands a balanced attention to both processes. An overcommitment to adaptive specialization can compromise the future of the firm [Hayes and Abernathy 1980], and an overindulgence in adaptive generalization can lead to a severe profit crisis in the short run.

Adaptive generalization in a multibusiness firm focuses more on its long run strategy, that is, the future businesses that the firm should participate in. It is concerned with entry into new businesses both through internal development and through acquisitions and mergers. Adaptive specialization, on the other hand, concentrates more on the near term. It seeks to fine tune the competitive strategies pursued by each business currently in the firm's portfolio, so as to maximize the firm's financial return. We seek to explore where and how adaptive generalization and adaptive specialization are managed within the diversified firm.

We first describe the four basic models that have been successfully used to manage strategic adaptation in multibusiness firms. The administrative systems used in each model are then contrasted in some detail, concluding with a discussion of the circumstances under which each of the four models may be best suited to a firm's context.

Model One: Centralized Strategic Planning

In this model, top management and corporate staff assume responsibility for all new strategic moves, while business-unit managers focus on implementing the business strategies approved by top management. The business-unit manager's role in strategy formulation is limited to proposals for fine tuning current strategies. Acquisitions and mergers are often the preferred route for entering new businesses. Consequently, new business decisions are typically centralized. Adaptive specialization is the predominant thrust at the business-unit level, and adaptive generalization at the corporate level.

Centralized strategic planning is generally used by single business or dominant business firms [Rumelt 1974]. In such firms, the CEO, with the help of close associates at the corporate headquarters, may be able to understand the nuances of each of the firm's businesses. Interestingly, this model is also used by some firms which diversify into businesses unrelated to their current product, market, or technology domains, because their existing businesses have limited opportunities for growth. The International Telephone and Telegraph Company under its former CEO, Harold Geneen, may be classified as such a Model One company.

With centralized strategic planning, goal setting is generally top down in nature and not overly participatory. Risk taking is centralized and the CEO thus has tremendous influence in shaping the firm's strategy. While Model One can be very effective in the hands of a strong and brilliant CEO, as was the case at ITT [Kotter, Schlesinger, and Sathe 1979] under Geneen, it does have a few drawbacks.

CHAKRAVARTHY, LORANGE

Current operations in a Model One firm are run as efficiently as possible, so as to provide predictable cash surpluses for the corporate level's use in its acquisition attempts. Consequently, it is possible for obvious opportunities at the business-element level never to get the attention they deserve. Moreover, executives running these businesses can easily become disenchanted, being little more than caretakers of their businesses.

The success of the model also hinges on such outside factors as the general health of the stock market, the cost of acquisitions, and societal acceptance of a corporation's right to make acquisitions and divestitures.

Model Two: Decentralized Strategic Planning

In Model Two firms, adaptive generalization is delegated to lower levels of management, often the business level and occasionally even the functional level. New business ideas typically originate in such firms as a response to a functional "discrepancy," for example, a capacity utilization problem, loss of market share, or unfulfilled research and development aspirations. A strategic response is shaped by the functional manager in consultation with his business unit manager. The proposal is then sent up to top management for approval. The role of top management is largely one of managing the structural context that encourages such bottom-up strategic decision making [Bower 1968].

In sharp contrast with Model One, each business unit is encouraged to seek profitable new opportunities in its immediate environment. In this decentralized model, as long as each business element provides reasonable returns top management rarely interferes with its decisions.

In reality, this model rarely exists in its pure form. Typically business elements are aggregated into clusters or "business families" [Lorange 1980]. The clustering seeks to exploit synergies among business elements through the utilization of joint facilities, such as in manufacturing, research and development, or selling, and through the pursuit of a range of businesses that complement each other in the marketplace. Thus, each business family might generate resources from its more mature business elements to fund the development of other new business elements within the same family [Lorange 1980]. The corporate management delegates the responsibility for resource balance and risk management to the business family managers. Some adaptive generalization may, however, be pursued at the corporate level, through transfer of resources between business families and through selective acquisitions or divestitures.

Like Model One, Model Two is also a popular model with firms seeking diversification. However, there are several important distinctions. More emphasis is typically placed in Model Two on related diversification, that is, products, markets, and technologies allied to the current operations of the company. Internally generated strategic ideas are valued much more in Model Two than in Model One. The CEO relies primarily on a bottom-up process of decision making. The obvious advantage of Model Two is that several layers of management are involved in the strategic decisions of the firm. The firm's

ADMINISTRATIVE SYSTEMS DESIGN

future is not predicated upon the brilliance of the "One Big Brain," but rather shaped "by a lot of smaller brains," working in concert over an extended period of time [Hunt 1966].

The CEO in a Model Two firm actively seeks the participation and consensus of his division managers on strategic decisions affecting their divisions, a decision process very similar to that used by the Japanese [Pascale and Athos 1981]. In contrast with Model One, both the corporate level and the business level have responsibility for adaptive generalization. Further, a richer set of adaptive options are actively pursued, that is, both internally generated and acquisitions-related ones.

A good example of a Model Two company seems to be the Dexter Corporation [Christensen et al. 1982]. Each division at Dexter was a "tub standing on its own bottom." Consequently, the company claimed several advantages: (1) low corporate overhead, (2) no problems of cross-subsidization among divisions, (3) "a hell of a lot more interesting life" for people in the division, and (4) better decisions because they were made closer to the marketplace.

Model Three: Decentralized Decision Making Guided by Corporate Portfolio Planning

Model Three is an extension of Model Two. While adaptive generalization is decentralized just as it is in Model Two, it is guided by a corporate level portfolio plan [Wind and Mahajan 1981]. Moreover, all business families in Model Three are not expected to focus as fully on their own self-renewal as was the case in Model Two. A typical business family in a Model Two context would be encouraged to pursue a wide diversity of businesses that might lie anywhere in the life-cycle continuum from an emergent to a mature business. The business family's own mature elements would have provided a significant part of the resource base required to support the emerging businesses. In contrast, in a Model Three firm, most of a business family's business elements would be relatively homogeneous. A business-family may either have a dominant goal of adaptive specialization or adaptive generalization, depending on the placement of the business family's "gravity point" within the portfolio. An important implication, therefore, is that relatively larger fractions of strategic resources will have to be reallocated *between* families in Model Three than in Model Two. While in Model Two each business family plays a critical role in resource allocation, in Model Three it is primarily the corporate level that allocates resources. Model Three is popularly referred to as portfolio planning.

A potential advantage of portfolio planning is the relatively clear-cut clustering of business elements, either around needs for adaptive specialization or adaptive generalization [Henderson 1979; Wright 1974]. For example, the administrative systems for a mature business family may include design features that are conducive to adaptive-specialization: a hierarchical organizational structure, tight linkages between plans and budgets, appraisal focused on short term performance, and rewards based on performance against budgets. In contrast, an emerging business-family may benefit from administrative systems that encourage adaptive generalization: nonhierarchical organizations, loose linkages between plans and budgets, performance appraisal based more on contribution to long term goals, and rewards based on the introduction of new products or the capture of new markets. While a more evenly balanced set of business elements may be desirable if each business-family has to be given an opportunity for self-renewal, administering such a "full-scale dual focus" is difficult. Corporate managers may, therefore, deliberately choose to create business families that are relatively narrowly focused. Adaptive specialization and adaptive generalization can then be balanced by assembling business-families with different focuses in the corporate portfolio. The Norton Company is one of several companies that use Model Three [Brandt 1981].

Despite the growing popularity of portfolio-planning among Fortune 500 firms [Haspeslagh 1982], it has several limitations that undermine its usefulness for strategic adaptation [Chakravarthy 1983]. The most important of these are:

(1) Static design: A portfolio configuration is but a snapshot in time. An emerging business-family can become, in time, a growth business-family. That, in turn, will eventually mature and may even degenerate. Administrative systems must, therefore, be designed not only to reflect the "adaptive" or "integrative" needs of a business-family at each stage of its evolution, but must also be sensitive to such needs during the transition from one stage to the next. Thus, a manager entrusted with an emerging business-family, requiring an "adaptive" administrative focus, may also have to provide it with an "integrative" focus. This blend of focuses would be required to move the business-family to the next stage in its evolution, that is, the growth stage. Model Three firms cannot, therefore, shy away from the need to provide a dual administrative focus in certain contexts. The dual focus can, in fact, stimulate the evolution of a business-family in an intended direction. This proactive use of administrative systems does, however, require extraordinary managerial insight and vision.

(2) Labelling: Managers in a portfolio-planning company typically run the risk of being typecast [Haspeslagh 1982]. The administrative mission assigned to a manager is often confused with his role in the company; for example, managers who are assigned administrative missions that require the milking or divestment of a business are likely to be considered as performing a lesser role than those assigned the task of managing growth businesses. While clearly not the intent of portfolio planning, it can be the cause of a managerial caste system within Model Three companies.

Model Four: The Dual Focus

In response to some of the administrative difficulties with Model Three, dual structure arrangement has evolved in recent years. This approach does not require the creation of tight consistent clusters of administrative arrangements that focus predominantly either on adaptive specialization or generalization. The organization is linked both through a strategic and an operating structure, the

ADMINISTRATIVE SYSTEMS DESIGN

former helping in adaptive generalization and the latter ensuring adaptive specialization [Lorange 1983].

Adaptive generalization is managed through the strategic structure, which is the basis for determining the objectives for each competitive segment of the firm and the various strategic programs that need to be undertaken in order to achieve the chosen strategic objectives. The strategic structure, however, is not a permanent structure, but more like a "lens" for how the corporation elects to view its environment. This "strategic lens" can be changed whenever required by the environment.

The operating departments receive their "desired" strategic signals through the operating structure, articulated through line items in their budgets. This more stable, semipermanent operating structure thus deals with the implementation of strategies and day-to-day operating tasks. The link between the strategic and the operating structures is in the delineation of roles that each operating department and executive plays in executing a given strategic program. A set of strategic roles are thus assigned to each operating manager, together with the specific resources required to carry out these roles over and above ordinary day-to-day duties.

A major benefit of the dual structure is that the "adaptive" focus of the business elements as well as the entire business-family can be adjusted without simultaneously undertaking massive changes in the operating organization structure. A relatively stable operating structure is useful in pursuing "integrative" goals. This approach might be especially helpful in process industries such as chemicals or electronics. The operating structure can be designed around the manufacturing processes, while the strategic structure can focus on product-markets.

Adaptive generalization and specialization become parallel concerns in Model Four. Managers can be urged to look beyond self-renewal of a business-element or business-family to the optimal exploitation of all opportunities available to the firm and synergies across all business elements. In companies that use the dual structure, such as Texas Instruments, it is not uncommon for an operating manager to work on strategy problems outside his division's operating scope [Lorange and Vancil 1977].

Administering the Four Models

Strategic adaptation can be managed then through four distinct models (Table 1), and each requires a unique set of administrative systems:

(1) Organization structure: Model One uses a hierarchical structure, with each operating manager assigned the responsibility of improving operating efficiency. Model Two also uses a hierarchical organization and, as in Model One, managerial roles are generally undifferentiated within the organization, although each manager is also asked to focus on adaptive generalization for the business element or business family that he manages. In Model Three, depending on the placement of the business within the corporate portfolio, each manager can be assigned a differentiated role, but normally no more than one role. In contrast, Model Four expects each manager to assume at least two

CHAKRAVARTHY, LORANGE

	Locus of Initiative for Strategic Adaptation	
	Adaptive Generalization	Adaptive Specialization
Model One	Initiative rests largely with the CEO. Little involvement of business unit and divisional managers.	Business unit and divisional managers encouraged to improve operating efficiencies and to fine tune existing strategies, with the concurrence of the CEO.
Model Two	Strategy shaped in the divisions. CEO approves these strategies. Some corporate initiatives on acquisitions and mergers.	Initiative rests primarily with the divisions, but under the close scrutiny of the CEO.
Model Three	Strategy shaped jointly by CEO and the division managers. Initiative of the latter high if managing an "emerging" or "growth" business family, low otherwise.	High initiative encouraged in divisions with "mature" businesses and in "growth" businesses that are maturing, with close monitoring by the CEO.
Model Four	High initiative at all levels of management, facilitated by the strategic structure.	High initiative at all levels of management, helped by the operating structure.

Table 1: The initiative for adaptive generalization and adaptive specialization is encouraged at different levels in the four models.

major roles — one for adaptive generalization and the other for adaptive specialization. Moreover, these roles have to be discharged through a matrix-like structure, wherein a manager often will have two bosses. There is one important difference between this type of dual structure and a typical matrix organization: while a matrix structure implies *permanence* in the dual relationships, Model Four explicitly assumes that the strategic dimension is temporary and changing, and has a rapidly shifting and evolving "matrix" relationship with the stable operating dimension.

(2) Planning systems: The planning system of a company can be distinguished [Lorange 1980] along the following dimensions: (a) focus of planning, that is, is the process top-down or bottom-up? and (b) time spent on the three planning cycles, that is, does the firm spend more time on setting long-term objectives, or on drawing up medium-term programs to meet these objectives, or on short-term budgeting for the upcoming year? Model One uses a top-down focus, with heavy time-emphasis on the third or budgeting cycle. Objective setting and strategic programming, the two cycles that commonly precede budgeting are typically less emphasized. In Model One, operating managers are largely preoccupied with the refinement of existing strategies and not invited to brainstorm on radically new strategies. An entirely separate staff group at the corporate level supports the adaptation by acquisition strategy. In Model Two, by contrast, top management does spend more time interacting with divisional managers in the objective-setting cycle, exploring several objectives for the firm and goals for the divisions. However, since each division is expected to be a

ADMINISTRATIVE SYSTEMS DESIGN

"tub standing on its own bottom," there is not much pressure at the corporate level to allocate resources across divisions. Strategic programming, an important step in strategy implementation that focuses on resource allocation, is largely delegated to the divisions. As long as budgets generated in a bottom-up fashion meet the corporate objectives, divisional managers have a lot of leeway in selecting strategies for their businesses. Model Three often emphasizes all three of the three cycles referred to earlier: negotiation of goals between the corporate and divisional managers in the objective-setting cycle; negotiation between these two and the business-unit managers on the strategic programs required to implement the chosen goals; and budgeting the resources required to implement the approved strategic programs. This sequential-negotiated process of planning translates all long-term goals eventually into short-term actions through the budgets assigned to various managers.

While Model Four may also use the three cycles described above, there is less rigidity with regard to sequencing these cycles at various periods in the financial year. Rather, ongoing attention is paid to all three cycles, even though, for reasons of administrative convenience, only a few select business-families may be reviewed at a time. However, the strategic resource allocation process in Model Four is frozen at periodic intervals in order to: evaluate the overall corporate portfolio that emerges from such an incremental allocation of resources, and reaffirm resource commitments made to managers between periodic reviews.

(3) Performance measurement and reward system: Model One uses the profit center or investment center to assign responsibilities to its operating managers. Each investment center manager is measured frequently on his ROI performance and rewarded accordingly. While Model Two also bases its performance appraisal on the ROI criterion, it does so predominantly at the level of divisional managers, that is, business-families. The measurement of performance below this level is heavily based on the divisional manager's perceptions of a business element's contributions to divisional goals. Since the division is the unit of analysis, poor profit performance by some business elements may be tolerated if their activities are expected to contribute to long-term growth of the division. Managers of such a business often share in the success of the overall division and earn a reward, determined at the discretion of the divisional manager. In Model Three, the long-term and short-term goals are clearly delineated and assigned to separate business elements or families. Performance appraisal and rewards are tailor-made based on the business' placement in the corporate portfolio. Finally, in Model Four, each manager is evaluated explicitly in two modes: the long-term or strategic mode and the short-term operating mode. While salary increments and bonuses are rewards for good performance in the latter mode, promotions and equity participation are rewards for good performance in the former mode.

Summary: In contrasting the four models, the complexity of their administrative systems seems to increase as one

CHAKRAVARTHY, LORANGE

	Structure	Systems
Model One	Hierarchical: Decentralized profit centers with vertical communication.	Top down planning. Emphasis on budgeting. Frequent monitoring of profitability targets. Rewards based on short-term performance.
Model Two	Hierarchical: Decentralized business families with lateral communication within families and none across.	Bottom up planning. Emphasis on objective-setting and budgeting cycles and not on strategic programming. Rewards based on profitability of business family, with some tailor making within families.
Model Three	Hierarchical: Decentralized business families with lateral communication within "emerging" and "growth" business families; vertical otherwise.	Goals negotiated between CEO and divisional managers. Sequential attention to all three planning cycles. Rewards based on tailor-made growth or profitability targets, depending on divisional mission.
Model Four	Matrix: Dual responsibility for adaptation and integration at all levels. Lateral and vertical communication.	Goals negotiated. Objectives, programs and budgets not set by a formal calendar, but by a selective scrutiny of divisions. Performance in the operating and strategic structures measured and rewarded separately.

Table 2: The organization structure and management systems used with the four models evolve in their complexity as one moves from Model One to Model Four.

progresses from Model One to Model Four (Table 2). This does not imply however, that the more complex the administrative design the better it is for strategic adaptation; that is, that Model Four is superior to Model One. Several contingencies influence what administrative design is best suited for a particular firm.

Criteria for Model Selection

The choice of a model will depend on the context of the focal firm. Some important contextual factors are:

(1) Strategic context of the firm: The portfolio and financial pressures experienced by the firm have an important bearing on model choice. Portfolio pressure refers to the severity of imbalances in the firm's business portfolio. If a firm has limited diversification, for example, and most of its businesses are fast maturing, it experiences high portfolio pressure. Even in diversified firms as the gravity point of the firm's portfolio starts drifting toward the mature or declining business quadrant portfolio pressure starts building. Financial pressure on the other hand is a function of investor dissatisfaction with the firm's overall profitability and the riskiness of its financial and operating leverages. Depending on the portfolio and financial pressures experienced by the firm, one of the four models proposed may be the most appropriate (Figure 1).

High portfolio pressure calls for a strategy of diversification. Both Models One and Two can be useful in such a context. The former is especially suited to unrelated diversification and the latter to re-

ADMINISTRATIVE SYSTEMS DESIGN

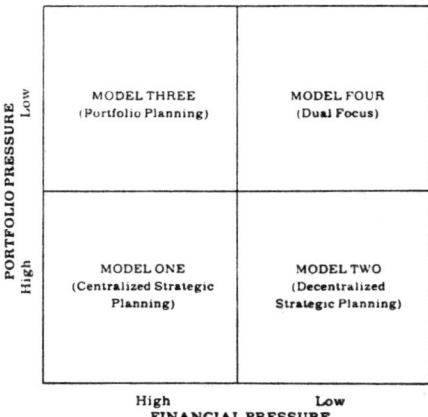

Figure 1: A contingency view of managing strategic adaptation: The choice of an administrative model most appropriate to the firm would depend on the portfolio and financial pressures experienced by it.

lated diversification. Moreover, if financial pressure is also concurrently high, Model One is to be preferred. The financial performance of a firm using Model One is more predictable than one using Model Two. Besides, the top-down planning focus of Model One would be required to ensure that the scarce financial resources of the firm are carefully invested.

When portfolio pressure is not high, either Model Three or Model Four may be appropriate. Portfolio pressure may be low either because a firm has high diversity and good balance in its portfolio, or because the gravity point of a firm's limited portfolio falls within the emerging or growth business quadrant. Several high technology firms belong to the latter category. Model Four is most appropriate in these cases, because dual focus is possible only when there are interdependencies among the businesses in a firm's portfolio. When the diversity in a firm's portfolio increases, Model Three is perhaps the more appropriate administrative model. Furthermore, Model Three is to be preferred if the financial pressures on the firm are high. In such a context, the firm has to rely more on internally generated funds to fuel its expansion. Portfolio planning is a useful administrative model for deciding which businesses to grow and which to harvest. The internal transfer of funds from one business to the other minimizes the need for external funds.

(2) Management style: Another important factor that influences model choice is the compatibility of the model with the CEO's leadership style. Administering each of the four models discussed requires very sophisticated but different leadership styles. In Model One, for example, the general manager makes virtually all the major strategic decisions. While he may draw upon the help of a powerful staff and may also seek the counsel of his line managers, he alone makes the final choice. In Models Two and Three, the general manager uses his power of approval as a way of influencing strategic decisions. However, unless divisional managers are motivated to bring forth effective new strategies, there will be little for a general manager to choose from. The general manager must, therefore, orchestrate the firm's administrative systems to encourage a steady flow of strategic ideas from the business-unit level. Perhaps the key leadership skill in Models Two and Three is not so much personal brilliance in making unerring strategic decisions, but rather, the ability

to manage decision premises [Simon 1976]. Manipulation of administrative systems to influence managerial mind-sets is the key general management challenge.

The general manager in Model Four faces the added challenge of motivating his managers to produce two very different behaviors concurrently: an "integrative" orientation for the operating structure and an "adaptive" focus for the strategic structure. Moreover, since adaptation and integration are pursued by each manager, they can be balanced only very indirectly. As in a matrix organization [Davis and Lawrence 1976], general managers in a Model Four organization must be skillful at managing the locus of relative power. The composition of key committees can be used, for example, to signal shifts in focus desired by top management. A relatively strong staff representation in strategic decisions may signal a bias towards an "adaptive" focus. Conversely, a strong line dominance of the committee may indicate a greater emphasis on "integration." Together with the more substantive changes in adminstrative systems, managing decision premises in a Model Four organization requires subtle and symbolic intervention.

Without the CEO's strong commitment to the planning model, it cannot function effectively. The "De-Geneening" of ITT [Colvin 1982] or the recent reorganization of the planning process at Texas Instruments [Uttal 1982] must be viewed from this perspective. ITT seems to be moving away from a Model One system towards a Model Three orientation, perhaps in keeping with the management style of its new CEO, Rand Araskog. Similarly, modifications to the Model Four orientation at Texas Instruments, with a greater emphasis on vertical communication, may reflect the desires of J. Fred Bucy and Mark Shepherd to influence the company's strategies more directly.

(3) Skill level and orientation of business-unit managers: Models Two and Four, for example, expect business-unit managers to take a lot of initiative in new business development. Such a system of bottom-up idea generation will, however, work only in certain contexts. Take for example, the case of a well-known manufacturing company that tried a predominantly bottom-up participative approach when it first wanted to diversify out of its maturing businesses. After a year's trial, it had to modify its approach, facing the painful admission that most of the ideas gathered were no better than suggestion-box quality. Unless the business-unit managers have the requisite skills to develop new businesses and are oriented to look beyond their current businesses, a bottom-up planning process will be quite ineffective.

It may be quite appropriate in certain contexts, therefore, to seek either limited participation (Model One), or selective participation by a few business-unit managers (Model Three) in new business development.

(4) Cultural setting: The cultural setting of a firm is another important factor in choosing a planning system. In certain firms managers may consider it a "loss of face" to revise a strategy that they had helped shape [Hamermesh 1977], or they may be reluctant to offer new ideas for fear they may fail. A Model Two or Model

ADMINISTRATIVE SYSTEMS DESIGN

Four cannot be supported by such a firm. Both these models require a cultural setting that encourages risk taking and is tolerant of failures.

Because changing a firm's culture is at best a slow and difficult process, it is important to ensure that the model chosen fits the firm's culture [Deal and Kennedy 1982].

Conclusions

The strategic context of the firm is perhaps the most important contingency that should influence model choice. Four distinct contexts were described, each requiring a different administrative arrangement (Figure 1). The organization structure and systems best suited to each model are summarized in Table 2. Important as this fit between strategy, structure and systems is, the choice of an administrative model cannot be restricted only to such analytic criteria. Management style, skill level of business-unit managers and the cultural setting of the firm were highlighted as other important contingencies.

Each structure-systems combination calls for a distinct leadership style, which may or may not be in keeping with the personality of the encumbent CEO. The CEO, being the architect of strategic change, must be comfortable with the chosen administrative model. It is the responsibility of the board, therefore, to ensure when choosing a new CEO that his style will be compatible with the anticipated changes in the structure and systems used by the firm.

Likewise, the culture of the firm or the skill level of its business-unit managers may also be mismatched with the needs of the planning system. Without the support of these "softer" management systems it would indeed be difficult for the firm to successfully adapt to its changing strategic context [Peters and Waterman 1982]. Moreover, the mobilization of these support systems needs a longer lead time than the relatively straightforward modification of the firm's organization structure and formal planning systems. The CEO must ensure, therefore, that employee orientation and skills appropriate to future strategic contexts are systematically nurtured even though there may be no immediate payoffs from such initiatives.

References

Barnard, Chester I. 1968, *The Function of the Executive*, Harvard University Press, Cambridge, Massachusetts.

Bower, Joseph L. 1968, *Managing the Resource Allocation Process*, Harvard University Press, Cambridge, Massachusetts.

Brandt, Steven C. 1981, *Strategic Planning in Emerging Companies*, Addison-Wesley, Reading, Massachusetts pp. 124-155.

Chakravarthy, Balaji S. 1984, "Strategic self-renewal: A planning framework for today," *Academy of Management Review*, Vol. 9, No. 3 (July), forthcoming.

Chakravarthy, Balaji S. 1982, "Adaptation: A promising metaphor for strategic management," *Academy of Management Review*, Vol. 7, No. 1 (January), pp. 35-44.

Christensen, C. Roland, et al. 1982, *Business Policy: Text and Cases*, Richard D. Irwin, Homewood, Illinois, pp. 717-744.

Colvin, Geoffrey 1982, "The De-Geneening of ITT," *Fortune*, Vol. 105, No. 1 (January 11), pp. 34-39.

Davis, Stanley and Lawrence, Paul 1977, *Matrix*, Addison-Wesley, Reading, Massachusetts.

Deal, Terrence E. and Kennedy, Allan A. 1982, *Corporate Cultures*, Addison-Wesley, Reading, Massachusetts.

Hamermesh, Richard 1977, "Responding to divisional profit crises," *Harvard Business Review*, Vol. 55, No. 2, pp. 124-130.

CHAKRAVARTHY, LORANGE

Haspeslagh, Philippe 1982, "Portfolio planning: Uses and limits," *Harvard Business Review*, Vol. 60, No. 1 (January-February), pp. 58-73.

Hayes, Robert H. and Abernathy, William J. 1980, "Managing our way to economic decline," *Harvard Business Review*, Vol. 58, No. 4 (July-August), pp. 67-77.

Henderson, Bruce D. 1979, *Henderson on Corporate Strategy*, Abt Books, Cambridge, Massachusetts.

Hunt, Pearson 1966, "Fallacy of the one big brain," *Harvard Business Review*, Vol. 44, No. 4 (July-August), pp. 84-90.

Kotter, John P., Schlesinger, L. A., and Sathe, V. 1979, *Organization: Text, Cases and Readings*, Richard D. Irwin, Homewood, Illinois, pp. 271-310.

Lorange, Peter and Vancil, Richard 1976, "How to design a strategic planning system," *Harvard Business Review*, Vol. 54, No. 5 (September-October), pp. 75-81.

Lorange, Peter and Vancil, Richard F. 1977, *Strategic Planning Systems*, Prentice-Hall, Englewood Cliffs, New Jersey, pp. 338-361.

Lorange, Peter 1980, *Corporate Planning: An Executive Viewpoint*, Prentice-Hall, Englewood Cliffs, New Jersey.

Lorange, Peter (forthcoming), "Organization structure and process: Implications for effective strategic management" in Guth, William, ed., *Handbook of Strategic Management*, Warren, Gorham and Lamont, New York.

Pascale, Richard T. and Athos, Anthony G. 1981, *The Art of Japanese Management*, Simon and Schuster, New York.

Peters, Thomas J. and Waterman, Robert H., Jr. 1982, *In Search of Excellence*, Harper and Row, Cambridge, Massachusetts.

Rumelt, Richard 1974, *Strategy, Structure, and Financial Performance of the Fortune "500,"* Harvard University Press, Cambridge, Massachusetts.

Simon, Herbert A. 1976, *Administrative Behavior*, The Free Press, New York.

Uttal, Bro 1982, "Texas Instruments," *Fortune*, Vol. 106, No. 3 (August 9), pp. 40-45.

Wind, Yoram and Mahajan, Vijay 1981, "Designing a product and business portfolio," *Harvard Business Review*, Vol. 59, No. 1 (January-February), pp. 155-165.

Wright, Robert 1974, *A System for Managing Diversity*, Arthur D. Little, Cambridge, Massachusetts.

[2]

Manage beyond portfolio analysis

Richard G. Hamermesh and Roderick E. White

The nature of a business unit's relationship to headquarters can have as much effect on its performance as its competitive position and the industry's environment

The approach is as old as borrowing from Peter to pay Paul. If one of your divisions is not growing as quickly as it ought to, you take cash from a healthy, stable unit to fund the growth. Often this strategy works, but many times it doesn't. The reason it may not work, the authors of this article claim, is that in applying the strategy derived from portfolio analysis, managers may overlook a key variable in the unit's performance, namely, the relationship that exists between headquarters and the business unit. In studying the relationships that 12 organizations' headquarters have with their divisions (a total of 69 business units), the authors found that the administrative arrangements concerning the degree of autonomy a business unit has, how line responsibilities are structured, and how the unit's incentive compensation program is designed have as much effect on its performance as market share and cash flow considerations. The authors urge managers to spend as much time defining what the correct relationships ought to be – which varies depending on the competitive strategy of the division and whether the unit is in a stable or a dynamic environment – as they do conducting portfolio analyses and deciding on build, hold, or harvest strategies.

Mr. Hamermesh is associate professor of general management at the Harvard Business School, where he conducts research on how strategies are formed in large diversified organizations. This is his fourth HBR article, and the topic will be reported on more fully in his forthcoming book Making Strategy Work, *to be published by John Wiley & Sons. Mr. White is assistant professor at the School of Business Administration, University of Western Ontario. This article is based on some of the work he did while completing his doctorate at the Harvard Business School.*

Several years ago, a company lay at the door of bankruptcy. Following the best available advice, management had targeted a few of its divisions for rapid sales growth. To encourage growth and entrepreneurial behavior, corporate management granted these divisions considerable latitude to conduct their business and rewarded their executives for growth. Meanwhile, the company used the remaining divisions to produce the cash to fuel the growth of their sister units. It tightly controlled these cash-generating divisions and tied their managers' small bonus incentives to stringent cost-reduction goals.

During the first few years this approach seemed to work splendidly. Sales and earnings rose dramatically while the growing divisions introduced new products at a rapid rate. Then problems began to emerge.

First, key personnel in the cash-producing divisions began to resign with greater and greater frequency. During their exit interviews the executives revealed that they felt no confidence in corporate management's commitment to these divisions.

Second, the growing divisions evinced disturbing signs of loss of control: high inventory levels, high warranty costs, and frequent complaints about new products began to depress sales and particularly earnings. Compounding this problem, some key managers in the growth divisions, many of whom had been richly rewarded for their prior accomplishments, resigned when headquarters started to ask probing questions about their activities.

Eventually, the company's profits turned to losses, and, in an attempt to rectify the situation, the board of directors brought in new management.

This case is neither extreme nor uncommon. It illustrates that the way corporate management interacts with its operating divisions can have a major impact on those divisions' performance. Despite awareness of this, many top managers have difficulty knowing what stance to take with their divisions, and many times they set up inappropriate relationships.

Two main causes lie behind these misguided actions. First, many managers have been seduced by corporate portfolio strategies that focus their attentions on market share and cash flow objectives.[1] In many instances, top managers have accepted this orientation without considering their divisions' competitive strategies or seeing whether market share and cash flow objectives provide a meaningful basis for building the relationship between headquarters and the business units.

Second, when corporate managers do turn to the question of how to structure relationships with their operating divisions, they find few existing guidelines. The advice they uncover tends to be very general, such as "closely control mature divisions," "create an entrepreneurial atmosphere in growth divisions," or (even more glib) "match a manager's personal orientation or style with operating strategy."

But this advice doesn't tell a manager how much autonomy to give different divisions, how large a bonus payment is appropriate, or how reporting relationships between key functions and shared departments should be structured. In looking at how the corporate management of 12 multibusiness companies structure these relationships with 69 of their business units, we tried to answer these questions. (See the accompanying insert for a description of our methodology.) In the following pages we present the results of our research.

Study methodology

This study is made up of a subset of the PIMS (profit impact of market strategies) research base. Twelve PIMS member companies agreed to supply us with organizational information about 69 of their business units. No more than 8 businesses came from any one company. To the existing PIMS data base, which primarily included each unit's industry, market characteristics, competitive position and measures of performance we added organizational information.

We collected the organizational data in late 1979. Performance, market, and competitive data were four-year averages. Although we present the data in cross-tabular form with cell averages in this article, we conducted the analysis using multiple regression, with performance (either ROI or sales growth) as the dependent variable and the aspects of organizational context as independent variables. In order to control for their effects, we included measures of market factors and competitive position in the right-hand side of the equation. A comparable type of control was used for the data reported in this article. Unless otherwise noted, the performance results reported have been adjusted to remove the linear effects of real market growth and relative market share. Using multiple regression, we found that the relationships reported in this article had a confidence level greater than or equal to 95%.

What's behind business unit performance

Profitability is of course the end result of a complex set of market, competitive, and organizational interrelationships. An important but difficult task for practitioners, consultants, and business researchers is to distinguish the effects of these different relationships.

Earlier explanations of performance have focused on only one or two of these factors. We think that the situation is more complicated than that, and in our research we considered the effects all of them have on business unit performance. While an industry's environment and a business's competitive position within the industry as well as the competitive strategy the business employs to take advantage of the aforementioned factors together determine a business's performance potential, our notion is that the business will realize that potential *only if it is appropriately organized* to exploit its strategic position and to deal with its competitive environment.[2]

Although common measures for important industry characteristics, competitive position, and strategy are available, there is less understanding of those aspects of corporate-business unit relationships that influence performance, namely the organizational and administrative arrangements between the corporate office and the business unit. We refer to these as the unit's organizational context.

We studied the following three aspects of business unit organizational context:

1   **Autonomy,** or the degree to which business unit managers can make decisions independent of other parts of the company, especially the corporate head office.

2   **Line responsibility,** or the degree to which business unit managers have direct and complete responsibility for key functions (sales, marketing, manufacturing, engineering, and so forth) or share responsibility for some of these with other unit managers.

3   **Incentive compensation,** or the percentage of the business unit general manager's total cash compensation attributable to the unit's performance.

What makes a successful relationship...

Although we did not uncover any easy or precise ways of structuring corporate-business unit relationships, we did isolate those situations where organizational context has the greatest effect on performance and those factors that are the most important in structuring these relationships. Specifically, we found that organizational context does affect performance and that the business unit feels these effects the most when it competes in a dynamic, changing industry. The organizational context has less effect on (and is frequently mismanaged in) business units competing in stable, slowly changing industries.

Previous research on business unit performance that considered only the industry environment and competitive position variables has explained a large part of the variance in return on investment (ROI) among business units.[3] Our research, which used fewer industry and competitive position variables but which included measures of organizational context, explains a comparable amount.[4] (Even though we did not consider such important administrative variables as the person who manages the business unit or the subtle import of day-to-day communications between corporate and business unit managers, the organizational context is still of great significance.)

In fact, we found that corporate managers can have as much impact on a business unit's performance by attending to its administrative ties to headquarters as they can by managing according to detailed strategic portfolio analyses. Moreover, executives can affect the organizational context more easily than they can the competitive and environmental conditions confronting that unit.

Despite the close relationship that organizational context has with performance, however, it is important to recognize that no simple, dominating association between any of the elements of organizational context and performance holds for all business units. Any executive who looks for one best level of autonomy, incentive compensation, or line responsibility will be disappointed. If, however, the executive takes the environment in which the business unit operates and its competitive strategy into account as well, then he or she will find that different relationships between headquarters and business units do have significant connections with business unit performance.

To determine the effect of these relationships on performance, we split the business units in our study into two groups – those in dynamic environments with frequent product introductions, sweeping technological changes, and fluctuating market shares between competitors; and those in stable environments, which have the opposite characteristics.

...in dynamic environments

For those business units that compete in dynamic environments, we found that the kind of relationship the unit has with headquarters has a significant impact on performance. *Exhibits I* and *II* show, for example, that in stable environments a business unit's level of autonomy has little impact on either sales growth or ROI. But for business units in dynamic environments, high autonomy is associated with rapid sales growth, while low autonomy is associated with much higher ROI.

Judging from our experience, we think these findings make sense for two reasons. First, managers of units competing in dynamic environments have so many options to choose from that when corporate managers get involved they will inevitably influence the units' strategies and, ultimately, performance. Second, business unit managers given much autonomy tend to pursue sales opportunities rather than profitability. To ensure that sales growth is balanced with profitability, corporate management may have to step in and tighten the reins a bit.

The amount of line responsibility unit managers have also carries a strong correlation with the business unit's performance. As *Exhibits III* and *IV* show, in dynamic markets business units that share responsibility for key functions have sales growth roughly equivalent to, but profitability higher than, that of business units having direct line responsibility for sales, marketing, manufacturing, and engineering. In dynamic environments shared responsibility for functions pays off. For business units in stable environments, the opposite relationship exists. Higher sales growth and profitability result when reporting relationships are self-contained within the unit.

---

1 In a recent HBR article entitled, "Portfolio Planning: Uses and Limits," January-February 1982, p. 58, Philippe Haspeslagh estimated that as of 1979, 45% of the *Fortune* "500" industrial companies had introduced portfolio planning to at least some extent.

2 See our article, "Toward a Model of Business Unit Performance: An Integrative Approach," *Academy of Management Review,* 1981, vol. 6, p. 213.

3 Sidney Schoeffler, Robert D. Buzzell, and Donald F. Heany, "Impact of Strategic Planning on Profit Performance," HBR March-April 1974, p. 137.

4 Roderick E. White, "Structural Context, Strategy and Performance," unpublished doctoral dissertation, Harvard Business School, 1981.

Again sifting through our experience, we think that one reason this situation occurs may be that in a changing market units share functional responsibilities so that the competencies of the entire company can be applied flexibly to meet the numerous opportunities a dynamic environment presents, even though it takes extra time and effort for business units to coordinate functions. The sharing process may lead to a cross-fertilization of ideas and allow each unit to have access to costly functions, such as engineering and sales, that otherwise may not be justified for units facing a shifting market.

Because organizational context can have such an impact on the performance of business units competing in dynamic markets, the implications for corporate managers are great. Rather than taking a hands-off stance toward growth businesses, as management in our opening example did, corporate managers need to carefully consider the influences that the organization itself has on business units facing dynamic environments. Precisely because some environments change so rapidly and the range of outcomes that business units can achieve in these environments is very wide, the organizational context surrounding these business units can have a strong influence on the results they achieve and on whether the business units achieve fast growth or high ROI. At General Electric, for example, corporate managers actually oversee growth businesses and spotlight the performance of venture managers.

...in stable environments

Corporate managers in both dynamic and stable environments need to pay attention to the organizational arrangements between business units and headquarters. But whereas our data suggest that direct involvement in business decisions has a significant positive impact on the profitability of businesses in dynamic environments, whatever effect it has on the results of business units in stable environments may be negative (see *Exhibits I* and *II*). In our view, stable environments provide clear signals to the managers of business units. Because the range of feasible competitive strategies and performance outcomes for these businesses is narrow and changes little, too much corporate attention is unnecessary and can prove counterproductive.

Our opening example illustrates that when top management involves itself too much with business units in stable environments, it can cause problems. In this case, management tightly controlled these businesses and targeted them to produce high cash flows. Eventually the businesses lost their competitive edges in their markets. In discussing these

Exhibit I   **Sales growth according to degree of autonomy and the volatility of the business environment**

	Autonomy Low	Autonomy High	Number of observations
Total sample	4.9%	9.0%	69
Business units in dynamic environments	5.9%	12.0%	35
Business units in stable environments	3.7%	6.8%	34

Exhibit II   **ROI according to degree of autonomy and the volatility of the business environment**

	Autonomy Low	Autonomy High	Number of observations
Total sample	23.0%	18.2%	69
Business units in dynamic environments	23.3%	14.3%	35
Business units in stable environments	22.7%	20.9%	34

Exhibit III   **Real sales growth according to the structure of reporting relationship and the business environment**

	Reporting relationship for key functions Shared	Self-contained	Number of observations
Total sample	5.9%	7.2%	69
Business units in dynamic environments	8.7%	6.1%	37
Business units in stable environments	3.2%	8.1%	32

Exhibit IV   **ROI according to the structure of reporting relationship and the business environment**

	Reporting relationship for key functions Shared	Self-contained	Number of observations
Total sample	20.3%	21.5%	69
Business units in dynamic environments	22.2%	18.4%	37
Business units in stable enviornments	18.5%	25.8%	32

issues with managers, we found that such situations are not unusual. In what we have labeled "self-fulfilling prophecy of portfolio management," the decision to harvest a business for cash leads to tighter controls and less autonomy, which leads to lower morale in the business unit, which leads to worse performance and the resignations of key managers, and possibly the eventual disposition of the business unit. But this pattern can be broken. To get the results they desire, corporate managers don't have to restrict the autonomy of businesses in stable environments.

Top managers also have difficulty establishing the appropriate incentive compensation for managers of business units competing in stable environments. Even though the managers in our sample indicated that their incentive compensation was based on measures such as profits, residual income, and return on investment, *Exhibit V* shows that for businesses in both stable and dynamic environments, higher levels of incentive compensation are related to lower average return on investment.

This unexpected relationship is particularly strong for business units in stable environments. As *Exhibit V* illustrates, the managers of these businesses who received high bonuses had an average ROI of only 17.4%, eight percentage points less than their counterparts who got lower bonuses. While it is possible that higher levels of base compensation may offset lower levels of incentive compensation, our findings suggest that although many top managers talk about rewarding the managers of mature, cash-cow businesses with high incentives based on cash flow and return on investment, they do not translate these ideas into meaningful action.

None of the exhibits, of course, shows what is cause and what is effect. But as *Exhibit VI* illustrates for this sample, high sales growth and high ROI are, understandably, both necessary for large bonus payments. Executives of business units with low growth in sales but *high* ROI, however, received the lowest level of incentive compensation: on average, only 8.6%. On average, managers of units with high sales growth were rewarded well regardless of the return generated. Clearly, the connection between incentive compensation and business unit performance is not easily explained and we suspect often mismanaged, especially for units facing stable environments.

Exhibit V   **ROI in relation to incentive compensation and the business environment**

Return on investment

	Business-based incentive as a percentage of total compensation		Number of observations
	Low	High	
Total sample	23.5%	18.5%	65
Business units in dynamic environments	21.9%	20.0%	32
Business units in stable environments	25.7%	17.4%	33

Exhibit VI   **Cash bonus in relation to sales growth and profitability***

		Real sales growth	
		Low	High
ROI	Low	12.3%	15.5%
	High	8.6%	22.7%

*Cell averages are cash bonuses as a percentage of total compensation.

Exhibit VII   **Generic business strategies**

		Relative price position	
		Low	High
Relative cost position	Low	Pure cost	Cost and differentiation
	High	No competitive advantage	Pure differentiation

Exhibit VIII   **Impact of organizational context and generic business strategy on ROI***

Strategy	Autonomy		Responsibility for key functions	
	Low	High	Shared	Self-contained
Pure cost	37.9%	17.9%	40.7%	20.5%
Pure differentiation	20.9%	23.0%	12.3%	25.3%
Cost and differentiation	31.6%	29.5%	29.1%	32.0%
No competitive advantage	9.7%	-1.6%	1.7%	7.8%

*This exhibit uses unadjusted ROI data.

Unit strategy & organizational context

In considering how managers relate their business units' strategies to the organizational contexts they establish, we find that market share and cash flow objectives based on build, hold, or harvest portfolio strategies do not provide a useful guide to how corporate managers ought to structure their relationships with their units. On the other hand, an understanding of the business unit's *competitive* strategy can provide corporate managers with guidelines.

Of course, all business units end up generating or consuming cash and gaining, holding, or losing market share. But it is important not to regard these variables as if they comprise a strategy but rather to see them as the result of strategic actions. A group vice president of a large industrial company illustrated the difference when he said:

"Two of the divisions that report to me are in very sluggish industries. In one case, we have been able to develop more original strategies, we have the employees all fired up, and we're making a good return. But I have had to fight to keep the corporate planners from giving their view of the situation. In the other division, the view from the top that has permeated the unit is that it is a cash-generating division and should be squeezed. I feel we could do some original things there to improve our competitive position, but it's impossible to get anyone in the division very excited to try something new. Eventually, we'll probably sell or liquidate the division."

In his book *Competitive Strategy,* Michael Porter argues that the essence of strategy is the creation of sustainable competitive advantage.[5] Managers can achieve this advantage in one of two basic ways: by establishing an overall low-cost position or by effectively differentiating the product and charging a premium price for it. As *Exhibit VII* demonstrates, these approaches can result in several possible generic strategies. With a pure cost strategy, the business has a low-cost position and low price. Its key competitive advantage is its cost position. On the other hand, managers of businesses with a pure differentiation strategy are able to command a premium price but also incur higher costs. Naturally, the most desirable, but hardest to achieve, position is to have both cost and differentiation advantages. For example, Caterpillar Tractor has a low-cost position but also has differentiated its product on the basis of reliability and after-sales service and parts-supply operations.

Our research suggests that corporate administrators can enhance performance by tailoring the organizational context to the business units' competitive strategy. *Exhibit VIII* illustrates that for businesses with pure cost strategies, low autonomy is related to much higher ROI.

For a pure cost strategy to be successful, managers typically must pay attention to operational details, relentlessly pursue productivity improvements and reduction of defects, centralize purchasing, and standardize components. To carry out these kinds of activities, managers have to direct their attention to the internal aspects of their units, primarily to the production and engineering functions. When the division has low autonomy and top management is in strong control and involved, its managers have the support and impetus they need to keep them focused on the necessary tasks.

In contrast, with an externally oriented differentiation strategy, because business unit management is closer than top management to the customer and the market, corporate involvement can contribute little to a unit's success. (See *Exhibit VIII*.)

The strategy of the division also determines how line responsibilities should be structured. As *Exhibit VIII* shows, business units that have pure cost strategies and also share line responsibilities with others have much higher ROIs than units that have self-contained functions. As we have discussed, sharing costly functions helps minimize overall costs.

The gap in portfolio analysis

In sum, a strong relationship exists between the organizational and administrative structures surrounding a business unit and its performance. In recent years, planners have zealously applied sophisticated strategic planning techniques to the problems of managing multibusiness companies. These techniques focus exclusively on industry and competitive conditions as the determinants of business unit performance and on market share and cash flow objectives. While we do not dispute the importance of factors such as competitive dynamics, market share, and cash flow, some corporate executives have watched these variables exclusively and ignored the important relationship between organizational context and business unit performance. Also, executives can affect the context far more easily than they can competitive and environmental factors.

---

5 Michael E. Porter, *Competitive Strategy: Techniques for Analyzing Industries and Competitors* (New York: Free Press, 1980).

Our research suggests that rather than focusing exclusively on portfolio management variables, one of corporate management's principal roles is establishing an appropriate organizational context for each of its business units, and that the character of each business's environment and strategy must condition the design of its organizational context.

Given the limited size of our sample and the complexity of the phenomenon, managers need to apply our specific findings with caution. But to our minds, what is more important than any of the individual relationships we uncovered is the overall finding that the appropriate design of organizational contexts requires that top managers be sufficiently aware of the affairs of their business units to appreciate and understand the market conditions they face and the competitive strategies they are trying to implement.

When managers design organizational contexts in light of these considerations, they can anticipate the impact of the contexts on business unit performance. Even the most sophisticated of strategies can fail if corporate managers pay insufficient attention to the organizational and administrative variables in the performance equation. And questionable strategies can produce acceptable results when corporate executives organize and implement them appropriately.

Managing Strategic Issues in a Turbulent Environment

John C. Camillus and Deepak K. Datta

A major shortcoming of conventional Strategic Planning Systems (SPS) is their lack of sensitivity in coping with changing environments. On the other hand, Strategic Issues Management Systems (SIMS), which has been recently developed to respond to 'weak' signals and turbulent environments, lack some of the visionary, enduring, motivational qualities of the SPS. This article describes how the SPS and the SIMS can be integrated so as to complement their individual strengths and mitigate their respective weaknesses. A process that can promote this integration is proposed.

Organizations, over the last decade, have felt the impact of unprecedented environmental uncertainty and how they cope with this increasing dynamism and turbulence will probably be the most important determinant of their future success or failure. More than ever, businesses need to be more sensitive and responsive to such environmental changes; not doing so can prove extremely costly, even jeopardizing their very existence. Strategic planning provides only a partial answer, with traditional planning systems often being criticized for their lack of sensitivity and inability to deal with the discontinuities and crises that arise in a dynamic and turbulent environment.[1] Organizations face a continuous barrage of stimuli, and repeated instances of corporations encountering strategic crises that could have been anticipated and defused but were not, has led to strong reservations about the ability of conventional strategic planning systems (SPS) to manage strategic change.

An alternative that has emerged in the 1980s has been termed as Strategic Issues Management,[1,2] processes and systems which are designed to be flexible, sensitive and action-oriented in order to minimize the probability of encountering strategic surprises. Proponents of Strategic Issues Management systems (SIMS) argue that these systems have the potential to play a critical role in management's efforts at formulating effective strategies. Unfortunately, as noted by the Emerging Issues Group at AT & T in their report 'The Context of Legislation', issues are not always obvious or easily identifiable and analysing them can, therefore, prove to be an uphill task. However, it is important that such analyses be done because it is only through such an analysis that considerations pertinent to corporate decisions can be drawn, making today's decisions more effective and tomorrow's decisions easier.

While both SPS and SIMS have their relative advantages, operating the two separately does have potential drawbacks. A more desirable alternative involves the reconciliation and integration of the two systems, with the SPS design being modified to overcome its shortcomings by incorporating aspects of SIMS. Moreover, such an integration is important to provide the needed convergence in terms of the actions taken due to the SPS and SIMS since one cannot function independently of the other. Ideally, effecting this integration should not detract from or change the fundamental purposes of either the SPS or the SIMS but should indeed be a move towards enabling them to meet their expected roles more powerfully. A mutually supportive and, hopefully, synergistic relationship between the two systems is clearly desirable and possible.

Our objectives in this article are to facilitate and promote this needed integration by modifying the design of the SPS to accomplish what the SIMS has been developed to do. The resultant integrated system incorporates the advantages of the conventional SPS without the shortcomings to which the SIMS was intended to respond.

Strategic Planning and Strategic Issues Management Systems

A strategic planning system can be viewed as a set of

John C. Camillus is Associate Dean and Professor at the J. M. Katz Graduate School of Business, University of Pittsburgh. Deepak K. Datta is Assistant Professor of Business at the University of Kansas.

organizational task definitions and procedures for ensuring that pertinent information is obtained, forecasts are made, and strategic choices are addressed and evaluated in an integrated, internally consistent and timely fashion. It deals primarily with the effort directed to the development of a purpose, the design of strategies and implementation policies by which organizational goals and objectives can be accomplished.[3] Specifically, the strategic planning activity in an organization should help executives address some basic questions about the organization, such as, 'What have been our business objectives?' or 'What has been or will be our business?' or 'What should we do to ensure that objectives are achieved?'. Potentially significant payoffs are associated with the adoption of strategic planning as evidenced by the findings of empirical research. Although the evidence is somewhat mixed, studies by Thune and House,[4] Krager and Malik[5] and Welch[6] among others have found that companies which engaged in formal strategic planning outperformed those that did not.

While the design of the SPSs adopted by organizations vary, there is a basic commonality of factors and a typical, stylized SPS framework would consist of the following activities:

☆ Environmental Analysis

☆ Defining Goals and Objectives

☆ Internal Analysis (Evaluating Strengths and Weaknesses)

☆ Formulation and Evaluation of Alternative Strategies

☆ Strategy Selection

☆ Operational Plans and Implementation

☆ Performance Evaluation and Feedback

A characteristic feature of the SPS is that the planning cycle is repeated at pre-specified intervals, the frequency of which would depend on factors such as the nature of the business, industry characteristics (including the extent of competition), and the degree of environmental uncertainty or turbulence faced by the firm. However, it must be understood that comprehensive planning processes in complex organizations typically cannot effectively be carried out more frequently than every 3 to 5 years. Overly frequent repetition of comprehensive planning processes can be undesirable and counter-productive, resulting in ritualistic 'form-filling' exercises rather than sensitive and creative activities.[7] On the other hand, as Hayes[8] points out, environmental volatility and changes (e.g. those brought about by the recent Iraq–Kuwait conflict) result in significant deviations from forecasts, making the elaborate strategies based on such forecasts obsolete. In such cases, rigid plans have the undesirable effect of reducing a company's flexibility, resulting in missed opportunities. The appropriate form of planning in such circumstances is 'responsiveness planning',[9] designing and using a system than can quickly detect deviations from the expected and respond to them effectively.

Like strategic planning, strategic issues management is a process of constructive adaptation to discontinuity. SIMS can be defined as a set of organizational procedures, routines and processes devoted to the perceiving, analysing, and responding to strategic issues.[10] They are designed to be flexible, sensitive and action oriented with the objective of reducing the probability of strategic surprises; particularly in terms of the negative impact of unanticipated events.

The SIM process can generally be identified by the following components:[11]

☆ Continuous monitoring of the environment;

☆ Identification of issues;

☆ Assessing issues, judging their likely impact and establishing priorities;

☆ Planning strategy and tactics for handling issues in accordance with assigned priorities; and

☆ Implementing tactics and planning activities.

SIMS can facilitate the realization of an organization's objectives by helping it anticipate and respond to changes in its external environment. For example, Bank of America uses strategic issues management to account for unexpected and unanticipated environmental events that might otherwise be ignored. A major objective of its issues management activity is the detection of weak signals of change in the environment, changes which might later have a significant impact on the organization.[12] Most strategic issues are triggered by threats or opportunities which originate outside the organization; they can be defined as developments which in the judgement of strategic decision makers are likely to have significant impacts on the organization's present and/or future strategies.[13]

Large organizations find it necessary to monitor and analyse a wide range of issues they consider relevant—such issues being in the areas of demographics, values/lifestyles, resources, technology, public attitudes, government policies and economic trends. Not surprisingly, firms (particularly multinationals) have started viewing issues management as being important and are more willing to commit additional resources to such activity.[14] However, most organizations are still not sure how issues can be managed or how issues management can be integrated with the planning process. While the issues management group is often an integral part of the strategic planning unit, organizations such as Atlantic Richfield Co., United Airlines, Union Carbide and Allstate Insurance have separate issues management units which work closely with their respective corporate planning units.[15] Archie Boe, CEO of Allstate (1972–1982), for example, created a Strategic Planning Committee in 1977 and an Issues Management Committee in 1978 with interlocking memberships. The Issues Management Committee was chaired by a vice-president who was also a member of the Strategic Planning Committee.[16] In addition, the approaches of organizations to the identification and analysis of issues vary considerably. In E.I. DuPont de Nemours, for example, issues management is the responsibility of the senior management while in other companies the function is delegated to staff analysts.[17] An unfortunate outcome of the popularity of SIMS is that it is often seen as a panacea by its proponents, with the result that many of its limitations are often ignored. Operated independently of the SPS, SIMS can suffer from a lack of focus and also result in substantial resources being expended without realizing the corresponding benefits.

SPS—SIMS Differences

A prerequisite to developing an integrated framework is an appreciation of the important differences between SPS and SIMS. The following differences have particular significance for the systems designer:

(1) Most SPSs are based on *periodic* activities, while SIMSs by their very nature, have to be *continuous* in character. An SPS usually involves a process of scanning, analysis and strategy formulation that is normally repeated at pre-set intervals. SIMS, by contrast, is *event* rather than *time-triggered* and, consequently, is a constantly ongoing process.

(2) The conventional SPS tends to respond to 'strong' signals, while SIMS is intended to pick up 'weak, not so obvious' signals.

(3) As a corollary of (1) and (2) above, the SPS focuses on issues *directly relatable* to the organization itself, while the SIMS presumably is receptive to issues having less direct or immediate effects on the corporation. Furthermore, executing the SPS itself may become somewhat narcissistic in character in that the planning process may become the superordinate goal.

(4) The output of SPS is typically characterized by a *vision* of what the organization would aspire to be; the SIMS in contrast endeavours to ascertain the *pragmatic consequences* of identified issues to focus actions which will reduce the negative impacts of and/or exploit the opportunities offered by strategic discontinuities.

(5) The orientation of the SPS towards the existing organization and the emphasis on enacting a predetermined process normally results in analysis and outputs that are significantly influenced by *existing* structure and power relationships. In contra distinction, the task forces envisaged by Ansoff[1] and King and Cleland[18] orient the SIMS to *nontraditional* modes of thought and action.

(6) Finally, given the goal orientation suggested in (4) above, the SPS would be biased towards a 'goals-means' sequence in strategy formulation. The SIMS, however, given its *ad hoc*, essentially reactive character, would inherently be limited to a 'means-goals' sequence. The paucity of related information that is characteristic of 'weak' signals would reinforce this intrinsic orientation of the SIMS.

Given the above differences, we can now examine their implications from the viewpoint of systems design.

Implications for Systems Design

From the six differences that have been identified it is evident that both SPS and SIMS have features that need to be incorporated into an integrated framework. If we take up each of the differences, the related integrated systems design directions can be deduced.

First, the SPS is typically a time-triggered activity and its periodic character makes it an inadequate mechanism for dealing with an environment characterized by abrupt discontinuities and 'weak' signals.[1] To avoid strategic surprises and to promote aggressive, proactive strategies rather than defensive or reactive ones, it is imperative that environmental scanning of a more continuous nature be performed during the interim between the strategic planning cycles. Such scanning would generate a continuous inventory of strategic issues which need to be analysed and appropriate action responses developed. An example of a continuous issues identification programme is the highly successful TAP (Trend Analysis Program) of the American Council of Life Insurance which helped its member companies by anticipating legislative resolutions, sensitizing executives to changing public needs and enunciating issues (as formulated by a creative elite) before they reached the public agenda, thereby allowing a longer lead time for formulating strategies.

Second, the typical SPS focuses on the existing product-market-technology; a focus which is too narrow given today's business conditions. What is required is a scanning mechanism which attempts to identify discontinuities, even those not obviously and directly related to the existing product-market-technology definition. Such undirected scanning (which seeks to monitor sources of information rather than track particular developments) should increase the probability of picking up weak signals because of its nonconditioned character.

Third, in accomplishing the above two, we must not ignore the visionary character of the SPS. If the strategic visions that presumably emerge from the SPS are transitory and not enduring in character, the systematic translation of organizational aspirations into executive actions and decisions will be typified by confusion rather than coherence. Also to ask fundamental questions on a routine basis will inevitably detract from the creativity and commitment that should characterize the responses. This means that the strategic planning process cannot be a frequent activity and it is probably infeasible and certainly undesirable from a cost-effectiveness point of view to go through the entire planning process to take into account the impact of every strategic issue. The SPS modification (if any) should be only to the extent required by the importance and the impact of the issue concerned and, quite often, it need be only an incremental response.

Fourth, the SPS is organization-focused and it may be desirable to break away from the traditional modes of thought, role relationships and responsibilities. The careful design and use of task forces of a cross-functional, multi-level character may be a possible means of accomplishing this end.

Fifth, the task force approach suggested previously can contribute greatly to the effective implementation of strategic changes. Often strategic planning systems are criticized for their focus on concepts rather than actions, and issue-focused task forces with carefully delineated responsibilities can respond to this shortcoming.

The Proposed Integrative Planning Systems Model

The limitations associated with traditional SPS suggests the need for planning systems that can do more to cope with the increased environmental volatility and complexity that confronts business enterprises today. The proposed Integrative Planning Systems Framework (Figure 1) responds to this need by incorporating the esign considerations mentioned above, and it provides the desired synergistic and mutually supportive relationships between the SPS and SIMS discussed earlier.

Environmental scanning, the first component of the system, is designated in the framework by (A) and (G). Any effective planning process requires a careful monitoring of the organizational environment to enable it to more effectively align its capabilities and resources with threats and opportunities. However, the scanning activity carried out at the beginning of the strategic planning process (as represented by 'A') is of a periodic, more directed nature. Such environmental scanning tends to focus on issues which are viewed as being important in determining the strategic direction of the organization, with the timing of the cycle being determined by the systems designer in the context of the characteristics of the organization and its perceived environment. The rest of the steps of the strategic planning process are represented by (B) through (F). However, as mentioned earlier, while periodic scanning cannot anticipate all potential discontinuities, undirected continuous scanning requires the investment of excessive resources. To make the scanning process cost-effective, we therefore propose a continuous semi-directed scanning (G) in that the key assumptions made during the comprehensive planning activity are monitored in addition to selected sources of potentially important information.

Following environmental scanning, the next step in the suggested framework is one of 'Issues Identification' (H). One can hardly overemphasize the importance of an early identification of the relevant issues, which provides organizations with a longer response time to develop proactive strategies. Strategic issues vary in the extent of information that is available for analysis and in the degree of consistency of that information. Sometimes both the information availability and consistency may be low resulting in significant uncertainty and ambiguity.[19] Also, special effort must be made to identify the 'weak' signals generated by 'fuzzy' environmental issues, the strategic effects of which are difficult to ascertain immediately, but which may have the potential of creating a crisis, if ignored. In addition, identifying issues early in the life cycle provides the opportunity for a thorough analysis of their potential impact on the company and the development of effective solutions before the organizational environment becomes frenetic. Efforts must be made to reduce the effect of individual biases in the identification process—consequently, it might be desirable to have executives involved in the process who do not have direct responsibility for the area being analysed.

Once identified, the issues need to be categorized into (1) those that have adequate clarity for immediate action, and (2) others which lack clarity and need to be closely monitored until a clearer picture emerges (permitting them to be moved over to the 'act upon' category). Alternatively, issues might be found irrelevant and be rejected at this stage. This sorting of the inventory of issues is represented by (I) in the system and is intended to be a continuous process. Once identified and categorized, issues must then be analysed and prioritized (J). The priority of an issue would obviously depend on a variety of factors, namely, the strategic relevance, the estimated cost-effectiveness (as measured by the potential impact of the issue) and the urgency (measured by the time period in which action is to be taken). This step is particularly important because, as Neubauer and Solomon[20] correctly point out, organizations are bombarded with hundreds of bits of information and an effective selection process is a must if the whole exercise is to be meaningful.

The Clarity-Priority matrix of Figure 2 can be

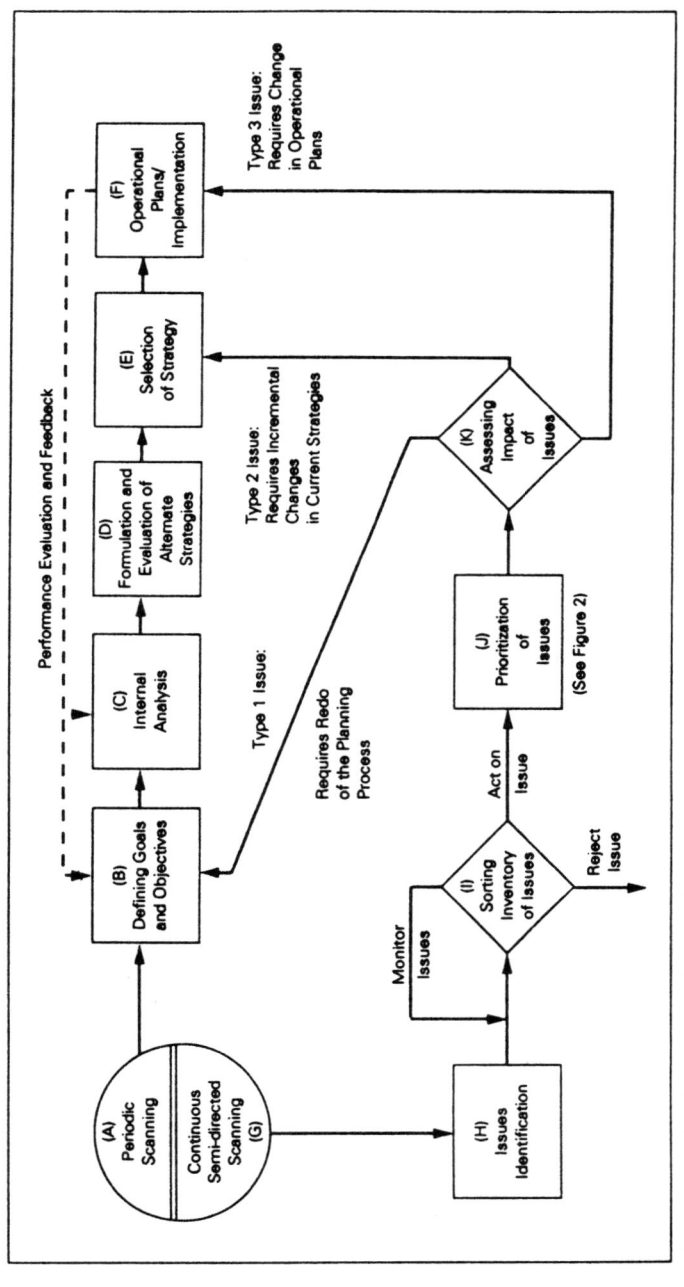

Figure 1. Integrative planning systems framework

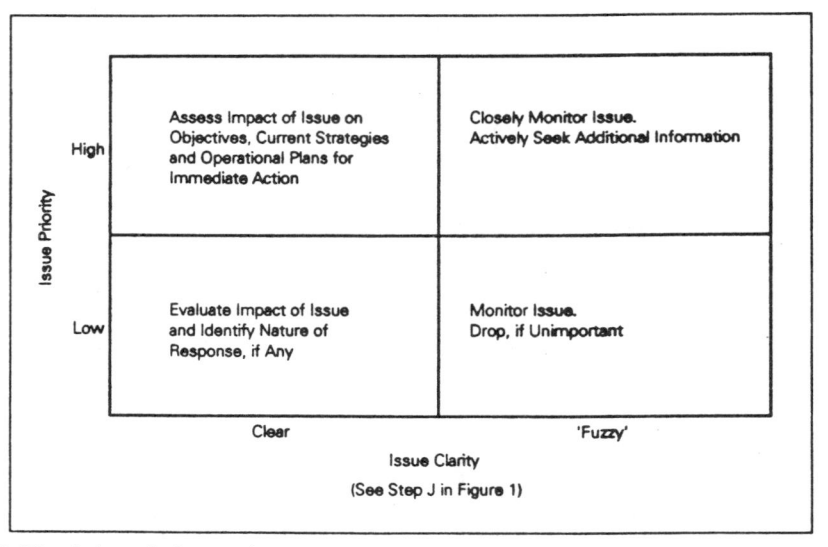

Figure 2. The clarity-priority matrix

especially useful in the sorting and prioritization processes (see step 'J' of Figure 1). The prioritized issues then serve as the input for the next critical step in the whole process, namely, assessment of the impacts of the issues on the outputs of the strategic planning process. Effects on the objectives, current strategies or operational plans are assessed to evaluate the extent to which they need to be modified to incorporate the impact of the issue. This stage requires considerable sensitivity and judgement on the part of those involved and, to avoid the effects of individual biases, is best executed by a group of executives with adequate diversity in terms of their backgrounds, hierarchial levels and functional areas.

The impacts and range of potential actions that need to be taken to address a particular issue can be visualized as falling on a continuum ranging from modest, minor changes in procedures or action plans to radical and dramatic changes.[21] However, for simplicity, we classify issues into the following three types:

Type 1 Issues: These are very major issues that may necessitate a redefinition of objectives and might even require an immediate redo of the comprehensive strategic planning process. Obviously such issues which require an out-of-phase strategic planning process would be very rare. The strategies chosen earlier become obsolete and the entire set of planning activities (B) through (F) needs to be redone. An unexpected major event such as the recent Gulf crisis (following Iraq's invasion of Kuwait) would be an example of such an issue for companies with significant operations in either country. Similarly, an unanticipated regulatory change in an industry would be another example.

Type 2 Issues: These are issues whose impact is not sufficient to require a change in the organization's objectives, but may require a re-evaluation of the current strategies leading to the selection of an alternative or slightly modified strategy. The resulting exercise would be of an incremental nature and in this case changes may need to be made in steps (E) and (F) only. Most issues identified would fall in this category requiring minor changes in the strategic plan. An increase in oil prices which results in automobile manufacturers changing the design criteria for cars would be an example of such an issue.

Type 3 Issues: These are issues that require a change in the organization's operational plans or action programmes. For example, an activity may need to be postponed or accelerated because of the impact of the issue. The fundamental strategic plans, in this case, remain basically unchanged. The delay experienced by Coleco with regard to the introduction of its highly touted 'Adam' computer for Christmas shopping in 1983 (resulting in their competitors making more of their products available in the market) is an example of such an issue.

Salient Features of the Proposed System

The proposed system, an outcome of the integration of SPS and SIMS, has the advantage of being able to retain the positive characteristics of both. It provides strategic direction to the organization in a form similar to the SPS, but it is also responsive to strategic issues (which are continually identified and assessed) by activating necessary changes at the appropriate level.

One of the characteristic features of the proposed

system is the incorporation of semi-directed, continuous environmental scanning for the identification of strategic issues. This would probably necessitate the formation of an environmental scanning unit for the purpose of identifying and doing preliminary analyses of issues. The sources for the identification of issues are many. They include, (1) appropriate literature, technical, industry as well as selected popular journals, (2) special interest groups whose activities might affect the organization, (3) professional associations, (4) organizational members with boundary-spanning roles and, (5) opinion polls. A recent addition to this list has been online databases, the use of which has been growing at a phenomenal pace.[22] These sources need to be continually tapped for a continuous stream of issues that may be relevant to the organization.

As noted earlier, a good published example of the issue identification process is the Trend Analysis Program (TAP) of the American Council of Life Insurance. Close to a hundred publications in the fields of science and technology, social sciences, business, economics, politics and government are reviewed regularly by volunteer monitors for issues that may be relevant. However, such scanning of seemingly appropriate literature, is not the only source of issues. People within the organization such as the CEO, top level executives and managers may themselves be very rich sources of relevant issues. PPG Industries, for example, encourages managers to bring up any important issue that comes to their knowledge by filling up a 'New Issues Alert' form.[23]

In Shell Oil issues identification and analysis is done jointly by senior management and staff analysts (the public affairs group) in consultation with representatives of the operating functions.[13] Staff members prepare an Issue scope paper which outlines the issue and its potential impact on Shell. Issues are reviewed by senior management who help prioritize and categorize the issues into those where immediate action needs to be taken and others which are merely to be followed. In FMC Corporation, a conglomerate with 1989 sales of $3·4bn, issues are identified, analysed and appropriate responses developed by divisional management together with Corporate Development. The issues along with responses are then sent to corporate management for ratification.[24]

Another example of a comprehensive environmental scanning, issue identification and sorting programme was at the Sun Company, a oil refiner that has diversified into other industries. This was accomplished through a 'Future Issues Committee', a free-wheeling group operating in an unstructured fashion.[25] Its members included representatives from the environmental assessment group, an officer from human resources, representatives from government affairs and the vice-chairman of Sun. The committee which met frequently considered a wide range of issues from the very fuzzy to the concrete, which were then assessed and subsequently referred to the policy-making groups in the organization. The concept is similar to that of the formation of a task force as advocated by Ansoff.[1] The scope of such a task group can be expanded to include the responsibility of following up and effecting a change in the strategic plan of the organization if required. Inclusion of a wide range of both operating and staff executives is valuable because of their different perceptions of relevant issues and their possible effects. Obviously, the degree of success enjoyed by the task force is dependent on the extent of co-operation and participation between the various people constituting the task force, a factor which has been stressed by King.[2]

Also, the proposed system ensures that issues which are 'fuzzy' but potentially important are not ignored, thereby reducing the number of crisis situations. Such issues need to be carefully monitored and any strategic or operational plans developed on the basis of an initial assessment of such issues may need to be substantially altered as a clearer, more definite picture emerges. All this points to the importance of contingency planning with alternative strategies and plans being formulated, based on different interpretations of the 'fuzzy' issue and its anticipated development.

Conclusion

An increasingly volatile environment has resulted in executives in most organizations being continuously bombarded by a variety of strategic issues, some providing opportunities and others constituting major threats. There have been several instances where organizations have gained substantial competitive advantage because they were able to identify issues early enough, realize their strategic significance and take specific actions to seize the opportunity. The Conference Board Report[23] mentions among others, the case of two organizations (Whirlpool Corporation and PPG Industries) who, through their environmental scanning programme were able to identify and recognize the significance of key issues which enabled them to take prompt actions making them leaders in their field. On the other hand, there are many instances of companies which have suffered severe losses because of their failure to identify or respond to relevant issues. As aptly stated by the Environment Studies Group at General Electric, '... without proper response, societal expectation of today become the political issues of tomorrow, legislated requirements of the next day and the litigated penalties the day after that'.[23]

The environment of the 1990s promises to be full of potential surprises posing significant challenges for strategic planners. The rapidity of changes taking place in Eastern Europe, the impending changes in Western Europe as EC member countries seek to dismantle trade barriers in 1992, the explosive tensions in the Middle East and the potential for another oil shock all translate into both opportunities and threats for corporations. FMC Corporation's reactions to the recent developments in Iraq and Kuwait provides an example of an organization responding effectively to a crisis. Quick assessment of issues and the development of appropriate responses has not only resulted in FMC avoiding excessive damages but it has also helped the company gear up to take advantage of potential opportunities offered by the crisis.[26]

In addition to the obvious volatility in the global political and economic environment every industry will also need to deal with turbulence in other environmental areas. Particularly important would be the technological environment where rapid changes (e.g. breakthroughs in computer design and technology) impact not only manufacturing but also service industries like banking and financial services.[12] Managers, therefore, cannot just concern themselves with 'static optimization' embodied in the traditional SPS with the hope of developing clear cut and enduring strategies. If one were to draw an analogy, the logic behind strategic planning in the 1990s will be similar to that associated with modern conventional warfare where generals set the strategy and establish the detailed plan of action but, at the same time, continuously monitor the progress of engagement and modify strategies and tactics as and when required.

It is unlikely that strategic planning systems, as advocated in the past, will be adequate in the future; to be effective, organizations need a planning system which is sensitive in detecting and responding to critical issues that surface sporadically. What differentiates the proposed system from the traditional SPS are three important aspects that have been emphasized; continuous scanning to identify key issues; sorting and prioritization of the issues into categories based on the nature of their impact on the SPS; and the formation of task forces dedicated to carrying out the range of activities from scanning to implementation. The proposed 'sensitive systems' framework, in our view, provides executives with a powerful planning and control capability in their efforts to effectively cope with discontinuous and turbulent environments.

References

(1) H. I. Ansoff, Strategic issues management, *Strategic Management Journal*, pp. 131–148, April–June (1980).

(2) W. R. King, Strategic issues management, in W. R. King and D. Cleland (eds.), *Strategic Planning and Management Handbook*, Van Nostrand Reinhold, New York (1987).

(3) J. C. Camillus, *Strategic Planning and Management Control*, Lexington Books (1986).

(4) S. Thune and R. House, Where long range planning pays off, *Business Horizons*, pp. 81–87, August (1970).

(5) D. W. Krager and F. A. Malik, Long range planning and organizational performance, *Long Range Planning*, pp. 60–64, December (1975).

(6) J. B. Welch, Strategic planning could improve your share price, *Long Range Planning*, pp. 144–147, April (1984).

(7) J. C. Camillus, Reconciling logical incrementalism and synoptic formalism—an integrated approach to designing planning processes, *Strategic Management Journal*, 3, July–September (1982).

(8) R. H. Hayes, Strategic planning—forward or reverse? *Harvard Business Review*, pp. 111–119, November/December (1985).

(9) R. L. Ackoff, *A Concept of Corporate Planning*, Wiley-Interscience, New York (1970).

(10) J. E. Dutton and E. Ottensmeyer, Strategic issue management systems: forms, functions, and contexts, *Academy of Management Review*, pp. 355–365, April (1987).

(11) W. L. Renfro, Issue management: the evolving corporate role, *Futures*, 19 (5), 545–554 (1987).

(12) D. E. Raphael, Betting the bank on technology—technology strategic planning at Bank of America, *Long Range Planning*, 19 (2), 23–30, April (1986).

(13) C. B. Arrington and R. N. Sawaya, Issues management in an uncertain environment, *Long Range Planning*, pp. 17–24, December (1984).

(14) D. Nigh and P. L. Cochran, Issues management and the multinational enterprise, *Management International Review*, 27 (1), 4–12 (1987).

(15) T. G. Marx, Strategic planning for public affairs, *Long Range Planning*, 23 (1), 9–16 (1990).

(16) R. L. Heath and K. R. Cousino, Issues management: end of first decade progress report, *Public Relations Review*, 16 (1), Spring (1990).

(17) R. Zenter, Issues and strategic management, in R. B. Lamb (ed.), *Competitive Strategic Management*, pp. 634–648, Prentice Hall, Englewood Cliffs, N.J. (1984).

(18) W. R. King and D. I. Cleland, *Strategic Planning and Policy*, Van Nostrand (1978).

(19) J. E. Dutton, L. Fahey and V. K. Narayanan, Towards understanding strategic issues diagnosis, *Strategic Management Journal*, 4, 307–323 (1984).

(20) F. Neubauer and N. Solomon, A managerial approach to environmental assessment, *Long Range Planning*, April (1977).

(21) J. E. Dutton and R. B. Duncan, The creation of momentum for change through the process of strategic issue diagnosis, *Strategic Management Journal*, 8, 279–295 (1987).

(22) A. Rasheed and D. K. Datta, Strategic environmental scanning using online databases, *Proceedings of the 1986 Annual Meetings of the Decision Sciences Institute*, pp. 621–623 (1986).

(23) J. K. Brown, *The Business of Issues: Coping with the Company's Environments*, The Conference Board Report No. 758 (1979).

(24) S. Early, Issues and alternatives: key to FMC's strategic planning systems, *Planning Review*, 18 (3), 26–33 (1990).

(25) E. A. Weiss, How the Sun Company Addresses the Future Business Environment, Speech Given at the Public Affairs Council's Workshop on Forecasting and Managing Issues, May (1978).

(26) R. Johnson, FMC's quick reaction shows how one firm deals with Iraq crisis, *Wall Street Journal*, 16 August (1990).

Key Lessons for Adopting Scenario Planning in Diversified Companies

By Daniel G. Simpson

The head of planning for a Fortune 500 consumer products company summarizes the lessons managers must master for successful scenario planning in diversified companies.

Management literature has no shortage of theories on how to improve an organization's strategic vision. But most of the techniques are either too general, too intuitive, or too narrow to be useful in a diversified corporation. It is rare when a new technique appears that is proven, practical, and productive. Scenario planning is one that has demonstrated the potential to produce better planning in large, complex organizations.

Like most new techniques, however, it's harder to execute than it first appears. Some of the lessons and pitfalls associated with introducing the scenario process are unique to specific situations, and there's little that can be done to prepare for them. Nonetheless, there's a rather large set of universal lessons that needs to be mastered. This article summarizes some of these requirements for success as well as potential problems a practitioner can expect to encounter while applying the scenario planning process.

Background: What Is Scenario Planning?

Scenario planning is the process of constructing alternate futures of a business' external environment. The goal is to learn to use these alternative futures to test the resiliency of today's action plan.

The best rationale for scenario planning is articulated by Catherine Bateson, currently a professor at George Mason University, in a new book on corporate responsibility, *The Nissan Report:* "Any organism acts not in response to external reality but in response to an internally constructed version of that reality after it has passed through a series of filters. Human beings filter through what we call attention and on the basis of what we call relevance." These filters are critically important to successful management since it is impossible to digest all the information available. The main question addressed by scenarios is whether a corporation's established filters are blocking important information that will be either valuable or harmful if withheld.

Scenario planning originated at Royal Dutch/Shell in London and is most often used by businesses that are extremely sensitive to external factors beyond their control—energy and public utility businesses, for example. For a variety of reasons, the consumer packaged goods industry tends not to be as highly sensitive to its external environment. Initially, I was not convinced that the scenario planning process would be productive in my industry.

I am now convinced. While consumer products companies are less sensitive to the external environment than those in some other industries, that differential is changing. The most powerful agent of transformation is information technology in the distribution channel; however, changes in advertising and media delivery are also occurring. The regulatory environment is becoming an increasingly important

---

Daniel G. Simpson is Director of Corporate Planning for The Clorox Company in Oakland, California.

EXHIBIT 1: Defining the Business Issue

1. Focus on a specific, actionable issue.
2. Focus on an appropriate, actionable issue.
3. Do not generate scenarios on controllable variables.

---

factor as well. The more a business is affected by externally controlled variables, the more the value of scenario planning increases.

The technique of scenario planning is not widely understood. While somewhat descriptive, the word "scenario" elicits all kinds of vague and loosely defined concepts. The most common use of "scenarios" is in financial projections with uncertain outcomes. Long-range planning documents typically include a section called "scenarios," which most often describe alternate outcomes of new product introductions. As a result, scenarios mean different things to different people.

Scenario planning is a very clearly defined technique: It is a disciplined planning methodology that generates a wider view of the external environment. *Webster's* dictionary provides another definition that enriches our understanding: "a plot outline or synopsis of a play or motion picture." Rather than being dry collections of alternatives or probability charts, scenarios are quite literally, stories. That distinction is key to understanding and successfully implementing scenario planning.

When to Use Scenario Planning: Defining the Business Issues

Properly defining an issue, and setting the stage, is critically important to the success of scenario planning. Poor definition at the outset will almost always lead to failure later on, regardless of how well the process is executed in later stages. Three recommendations will help practitioners define the nature of good scenario planning problems (see Exhibit 1).

1. Focus on a Specific, Actionable Issue. One of the most difficult tasks in scenario planning is setting boundaries on the inquiry—defining the issues around which the plays will be written. If the boundaries are too narrow, the scenarios will tend to be only minor variations on a single theme. If the boundaries are too broad, the scenarios lose their significance for the key players—the managers of the strategic business units.

Scenarios must evolve around an actionable issue of significance to the business unit. While learning is an important outcome of scenario planning, ultimately, the right result should be action. Learning is only effective to the degree that it produces action.

Peter Schwartz, President of the Global Business Network and author of a recently published book on scenario planning, *The Art of the Long View*, poses two closely related questions to help define actionability: "What keeps the operating unit managers up at night? What really makes a difference?"

2. Focus on an Appropriate, Actionable Issue. Actionability is necessary but insufficient. Like most planning tools, scenario planning has maximum value only in selected circumstances. An issue for which scenario planning is ideal will have five attributes:

- The external environment can evolve in fundamentally different ways—the outcome is not predetermined.
- The change is out of the control of the business unit.
- The change has the potential to be permanent and structural.
- The optimal actions of the business unit vary greatly, depending on how the environment develops.
- The decisions of the business unit are not easily reversed or undone after the environment becomes clearer.

If the issues in front of the operating business unit fit these criteria, scenario planning is likely to be a very useful and productive process. Examples of good scenario planning issues include major capital projects, investment in alternate technologies for existing or new products, and product positioning.

3. Do Not Generate Scenarios on Controllable Variables. Scenario planning should develop alternate views of uncontrollable variables in the external business environment—not simply lay out alternate outcomes of internal decisions. The resulting scenarios should describe the different environments that shape the playing field where internal decisions will be played out. Variations on the theme of "We do something. It works or it doesn't" are not scenarios. The most frequent example of this approach is a set of alternative outcomes for the launch of a new product. Although generating these alternative outcomes may be very important for financial planning, this is not scenario planning.

Organizational Benefits of Scenario Planning

The ultimate result of scenario planning is taking correct action on an issue critical to the success of the business. However, the business also reaps additional benefits that may extend much farther than the decision at hand (see Exhibit 2).

4. Understanding and Clarifying Perceptions and Assumptions of Key Managers. Group discussion on possible variability in the external business environment often helps crystallize both individual and group thinking. It's naive to assume that the "facts" are consistently perceived the same way by all business managers. Individual assumptions have to be made explicit.

The value of this clarification process cannot be underestimated. As Peter Schwartz pointed out in a recent speech to the San Francisco Bay Area chapter of The Planning Forum:

EXHIBIT 2: Organizational Benefits

4. Understand and clarify perceptions and assumptions.
5. Improve the speed of decision making.
6. Maintain an aggressive, can-do attitude while serving up unfavorable outlooks.

"We make decisions, not based on the real world, but on what each of us believes about the real world." These beliefs are not universal, and some of the most enlightening discussions in scenario building sessions take place when two managers disagree about some element of the future, the present—or even the past.

One useful technique for getting to the root of assumptions— a Japanese practice called "Five Times Why"—was taught to me by Charles Hampden-Turner, author of *Charting the Corporate Mind*. For every assumption, assertion, or belief that becomes the subject of disagreement, ask the people involved why they think their point of view is true. When they offer an answer, ask why that answer is true. By the time you've repeated the process five times, you should get to the real root assumption. Somewhere along the way you may find a statement that can be tested in some logical way.

5. Improving the Speed of Decision Making. Competitive advantage is often a function of speed. Arie de Geus, retired Planning Coordinator for Royal Dutch/Shell, states it even more firmly in his 1988 *Harvard Business Review* article "Planning As Learning": "The ability to learn faster than your competitors may be the only sustainable competitive advantage."

Strategic speed depends in part on the ability to look for and recognize the lead indicators foreshadowing larger changes. Scenarios help to change the threshold of attention by creating a new sensitivity to relevant information—a widened field of perception—so that this expanded range of knowledge can more quickly become part of the thinking process of an organization. A bit of information that might have been regarded as insignificant now becomes crucially important.

Kathy Eisenhardt's award-winning article, "Speed and Strategic Choice" in the *California Management Review*, reinforces the point that building and churning multiple, simultaneous alternatives helps speed decision making. The process of creating alternatives fosters assurance that the best approaches have been considered, and that a fall-back position is always available. Scenarios don't spell out alternatives or options. Scenarios are mental rehearsals for surprising futures as well as opportunities for reaching a consensus on what the implications of the future may mean for operations. The linkages between scenarios, their possible impact on the business, and the lead indicators that help focus information processing is critical.

Managers who learn to apply scenario planning techniques can make good decisions more quickly because they thoroughly understand the relationship between the business and its environment. They "master the clay," to borrow a phrase from Henry Mintzberg's classic "Crafting Strategy" article in the *Harvard Business Review*. This intuitive understanding of the interface between the business unit and the alternate possibilities in the external business environment allows managers who use scenarios to cope quickly and surely with sudden changes in their external environment. By "rehearsing the future" through scenario planning, a business manager is able to successfully adapt instead of just react.

6. Maintaining an Aggressive, Can-Do Attitude While Serving Up Unfavorable Outlooks. One of the less obvious yet important benefits of constructing alternate scenarios is allowing multiple points of view to rise through management communication channels without being prejudged or automatically dismissed. Large organizations have multitudes of very smart and insightful people who care deeply about the business. Behind a number of business failures are individuals or groups who "saw it coming" in time to do something about it but who, for cultural reasons, were unable to clearly articulate their points of view to the key decision makers. Scenario planning allows these alternate and sometimes alarming views to surface without being stigmatized as the product of managers with a defeatist attitude.

The Draft: Choosing the Players

Selecting those who will help build the scenarios is critically important. A variety of management skills are needed on the team (see Exhibit 3).

7. Operating Management Must Take the Lead in the Process. Arie de Geus forcefully articulated this in his *Harvard Business Review* article: "Planning as Learning": "The only relevant learning in a company is the learning done by those people who have the power to act."

Scenario planning must be done by the line managers charged with making the decisions. Even issues that require intensive functional involvement should have some operating management participation. Like most other planning efforts, one of the fastest paths to useless results is to have a planning department or the company's financial community generate the scenarios. The proper role of the scenario planner is one of consultant, facilitator, catalyst, and accelerator of the learning process.

8. Actively Seek and Incorporate Contrarian Views from Outside the Operating Unit. The best scenarios modify current perceptions in fundamental ways. This process is sometimes difficult to ignite without sparks from contrarians outside the operating unit.

While it's true that operating managers know their business better than any one else, this doesn't always mean that they're able to generate excellent scenarios by themselves. The professionals most familiar with the business are also the ones most likely to have developed a single perspective, sometimes even a myopic view, of its external environment. It's not always easy to enter a discovery process when you live a business day-to-day and are emotionally attached to it.

The search for contrarian views should lead in two directions. Find outsiders who bring fresh perspectives or "different mirrors" like the ones Robert Waterman refers to in his book, *The Renewal Factor*. Professional consultants are one obvious source, but others include suppliers, buyers, advertising agencies, and retired experts in related fields.

EXHIBIT 3 : The Planning Team

7. Operating management must take the lead in the process.
8. Actively seek out and incorporate contrarian views from outside the operating unit.
9. Engage a planning leader from outside the business unit.

An often ignored source of input is intelligence and opinion from people inside the corporation but outside the business unit. Large corporations have all kinds of hidden talent within their walls: a first-rate musician who sits in the distribution group; a trained anthropologist in the sales department; a history buff in accounting. Try to find these smart, creative people, and tap them for the scenario workshops.

A wise tip is offered by Peter Schwartz of the Global Business Network: Be unconventional. Get exposed to outrageous opinions that may make operating managers somewhat uncomfortable at first. At the very least this will test the resilience of their thinking. Look for less obvious sources of information. Examples include films, novels, specialized or counterculture magazines from other fields, and remarkable people with completely different experiences.

9. Engage a Planning Leader from Outside the Business Unit. Because the scenario planning process is eminently logical, it seems easy to execute. It isn't. It's hard, especially with the large, multi-functional groups that typically comprise a business unit. Uncertainty about the process, and the complexities of group dynamics make it difficult to try to engage in a scenario planning process without some help from outside the business unit. Ideally, this will be an experienced scenario planner, but it should at least be a strategy expert with group management skills.

A skillful process leader satisfies three needs:

● **Facilitator.** There's a need to perceive and manage the dynamics of the group as a whole, constantly monitoring the delicate balance between individual and group desires.

Scenario planning can stir a wave of uneasiness when it plows uncharted waters or questions an organization's basic beliefs about the external environment. A skilled facilitator should be able to manage both the frame of the discussion as well as the speed at which it proceeds.

- **Consultant.** The scanning "radar screen" of the group may not have the capacity to identify some issues and themes that are potentially important to the organization. In this case, the process leader should be prepared to ask provocative questions and challenge assumptions. While balancing between two roles—facilitator and advisor—the process leader must pay close attention to the individual needs of the key decision makers, both inside and outside the group.

- **Planner.** The planner's role is to keep the group focused on producing germane, adequately detailed alternative views of the external environment. The best process leaders thoroughly understand the discipline of scenario planning, environmental analysis, and techniques for identifying the most important key drivers of the business.

Acquiring this level of expertise probably requires some outside assistance. If planners are unable to hire expert consultants to look over their shoulders, they should pay close attention to the concepts in a growing number of relevant publications. I have listed my personal favorites in the section on Further Reading on Scenario Planning.

Diving In: Process Learnings

The following seven recommendations should be reviewed before initiating the scenario planning process. Since the complete process is complex, the reader should read both case studies and theoretical articles to get a better preview of how it works in practice (see Exhibit 4).

10. Begin the Process with One-on-One Interviews with Key Managers. Pierre Wack of Royal Dutch/Shell, the man most responsible for the development of scenario planning, and author of the "Gentle Art of Reperceiving" articles in the *Harvard Business Review*, is quick to point out that understanding the external business environment is only half of a good scenario planning process. "A good scenario seems to emerge, naturally and miraculously, from an intensely experienced polarity: on one side, a good analysis of the unfolding business environment; on the other side, a clear knowledge of the existing mind-set of managers, which covers their view of the unfolding business environment."

There are all kinds of techniques to try to understand the mindset of key managers, but there's probably none better than the give and take of frank conversation. It's quite effective to begin the strategy-development process with one-on-one interviews with all the relevant managers, using open-ended questions that help map the manager's mind.

11. Identify a Specific Year in Which to Construct Your Scenarios. Lawrence Wilkinson of the Global Business Network counsels that scenarios of the future

---

EXHIBIT 4: Process Basics

10. Begin the process with one-on-one interviews with key managers.
11. Identify a specific year as the setting for your scenarios.
12. Be brutally candid in understanding today's reality—challenge assumptions.
13. Suspend your vision of the business.
14. Identify predetermined elements.
15. Wear bifocals.
16. Do internal reality testing as scenarios take shape.

---

should be framed in a specific year (2000 is quite popular for shorter term scenarios these days). There are two advantages. First, scenarios are best told as stories viewed from that future time. Don't try to construct a tale of the future as it unfolds from today. Instead, tell the story looking back from that future period. The distinction is subtle, but it can prevent some conflicts over the relative likelihood of specific events.

Second, choosing a specific future time period also allows the scenario builders to get a sense of the possible rate of change. But before looking ten years into the future, practice by looking ten years into the past. Because managers tend to focus on day-to-day business operations, they're sometimes blind to the fundamental changes occurring bit by bit over the long haul.

These days, looking back into history is relatively easy, given current technology. The NEXIS service or some of the others on the DIALOG network are useful sources for major news items ten years in the past. Convert your own company's annual reports from ten years ago into a list of key business issues. Call industry associations and check their files. Reach into the storage cabinets and grab the old planning documents, if they're still available. You'll be surprised at the difference between current reality and what was projected in old planning documents. One warning: Do not rely solely on anyone's personal recollections; such memories get rewritten in the light of current events. Make an effort to talk to people who were in the business ten years earlier, but be sure to get some facts together before calling on them.

12. Be Brutally Candid in Understanding Today's Reality— Challenge Even the Most Well-grounded Assumptions. Peter Senge, Director of the Systems Thinking and Organizational Learning program at M. I. T. and author of *The Fifth Discipline*, aptly points out that many corporate strategies fail not from lack of vision but from poor understanding of current reality. Peter Schwartz makes an even more startling statement, which also rings true upon deeper reflection: "We all recognize that the future is uncertain, but it is important to recognize that the past is equally uncertain. We choose the past selectively. The same is true with the present. Scenarios are different images of the past played out into the future. Just as there are many theories of the future, there are also many theories of history."

Scenarios are stories of the future, but they must be rigorously grounded in today's reality if they are to be substantive enough for action. There's more than one way to see today's facts, and a good scenario workshop should focus on alternative views of current reality before venturing too far into the future. Graham Galer, Head of Planning Support at Royal Dutch/Shell and an experienced scenario planner, says: "Some of the best scenarios are not blue-sky explorations of the future, but alternative conceptualizations of what is happening now, with a 'working-out' of the ways these patterns may evolve."

Actively try to disprove assumptions that are perceived by all to be indisputable. Is there any chance that known current reality is not as known as everyone thinks?

13. Suspend Your Vision of the Business. Focusing only on a "single, desirable vision" has at least one significant risk. It tends to reduce the field of vision and sometimes block information that, while not currently relevant, may become so later. Catherine Bateson restates this important issue in a different way: "Many years ago my father [Gregory Bateson] proposed that conscious purpose is not adaptive because such purposefulness leads to partial perception, not of full cybernetic loops but only arcs in those loops."

When operations are driven by a single-minded focus, important perceptions outside the field of vision are discounted. Our construction of reality drifts further and further from the evolving truth, and the organization is led into a major discontinuity. As Peter Senge says, "advocacy in pursuit of a goal becomes so paramount that inquiry and reflective digestion are shortchanged." Suspend your own vison of the future for a time, however deeply held, and think through alternative explanations of today's reality, being brutally candid in doing so.

14. Identify Predetermined Elements. Much of the focus of scenario planning is on critical uncertainties in the external environment, but some elements of the future are actually quite certain and largely fixed. A few variables will not change at all. Others may change, but the change is quite predictable because the drivers are already locked into place—two examples are the U. S. deficit and population demographics. The deficit is a reality that will exist for decades to come because of the complex politics and economics that drive it. How we deal with the deficit may be an uncertainty, but the deficit itself is predetermined. In demographics, the size of the teenage population in the year 2000 is also largely predetermined—these people have already been born. When constructing scenarios, search for some relevant elements that are predetermined and that are common to all possibilities.

Michael Porter offers some practical advice in his book, *Competitive Advantage:* "To identify uncertainties, each element of industry structure must be examined and placed into one of three categories: constant, predetermined, and uncertain. Constant elements of industry structure are those aspects of structure that are very unlikely to change. Predetermined elements are areas where structure will change, but the change is largely predictable. Predetermined trends may well proceed faster or slower, depending on the scenario. Often a variety of structural changes are [shown to be] predetermined if a thoughtful industry analysis is done. Uncertain elements are those aspects of future structure which depend on unresolvable uncertainties. Constant and predetermined structural variables are part of each scenario, while uncertain structural variables actually determine the different scenarios."

> *"Some of the best scenarios are not blue-sky explorations of the future, but alternative conceptualizations of what is happening now."*

Some aspects of the future, which appear on their surface to be a roll of the dice, are in fact largely predetermined. Interestingly, however, group work on what are commonly believed to be predetermined elements sometimes yields the opposite finding. In the process of tying down these elements, it's quite common to discover that a casual list of supposedly predetermined elements gets shorter as they're reviewed under a brighter light. What is first perceived to be predetermined often turns out to be a critical uncertainty. It's important to make the distinction.

15. Wear Bifocals. Effective scenario development requires the constant readjustment of focus between specific actionable issues and the broader world at large—while tracking the interplay between them. To be really insightful, constantly scan your entire field of vision, selectively choosing the elements that are strategically linked. Be both practical and theoretical, short term and long term, focused on the external environment and the internal environment. It is this blend that produces the best thinking, the best learning, and the best actions.

16. Do Some Internal Reality Testing as Your Scenarios Take Shape. As with most management tools, the effectiveness of scenarios is at least partly related to how well they address the concerns of key players in all relevant parts of the organization. Those players need to be convinced that they have some stake in the scenarios—or at least that the process can't be dismissed out of hand.

Don't limit your constituency to the key decision makers involved in the process. Be sure to test the scenarios with other functional groups, as well as with the rest of senior management to make certain they contribute effectively to the change process. Test the waters at several levels of management as the process unfolds. But never give up trying to stretch the boundaries of common perception. While this requires a good deal of patience and tact, it's well worth the effort.

Hitting Bottom: Hazards in the Scenario Planning Process

17. Generating Too Many Alternate Scenarios. The world is a set of endless possibilities. It's all one big system in which everything is connected to everything else, and the number of variables is limitless. It is quite easy to be overwhelmed with possibilities and unnecessary complexity in a scenario planning process. When this happens, frustration and failure are just a step away. (See Exhibit 5)

If you have more than four scenarios, trim the unnecessary ones with Ockham's Razor. [English philosopher William of Ockham, 1285 to 1349, made this point succinctly: What can be done with fewer assumptions is done in vain with more.] Only a few key variables will be significant drivers of your business. Trying to perfectly capture a complex system with all its contingencies requires a model as large and complex as the system itself—an impractical undertaking.

When the scenario process generates more than four scenarios, it's a signal that the business unit is addressing issues that are not crucial to its operations. A fifth scenario isn't always a problem, but it is unusual. Make certain that it adds value. On the other hand, if the unit generates only two scenarios, it's likely to be suffering from a near-sighted vision.

As Pierre Wack cautions: "Scenarios acknowledge uncertainty and aim at structuring and understanding it — but not by crisscrossing variables and producing dozens of outcomes. Instead, they create a few alternatives and internally consistent pathways into the future. Scenarios describe different worlds, not just different outcomes in the same world."

18. Getting Bogged Down in Overly Elaborate Plots. Scenarios are actually quite fun to construct, and it's easy to get energized by the process. That excitement is healthy. But keep a cool head when defining the boundries, and keep each scenario focused on the key decision variables. The value of scenarios is measured not by how interesting or entertaining they are, but by how well they serve management in its decision making. Resist the temptation to use the energy from the scenario process to develop elaborate and intricately woven stories of the future. Build appropriate support for the stories that are created, but don't get lost in detailed data collection in the process.

EXHIBIT 5:
Hazards in Scenario Planning
17. Generating too many alternate scenarios.
18. Getting bogged down in overly elaborate plots.
19. Trying to complete the process too quickly.
20. Do not substitute scenarios for forecasts.
21. Do not generate alternative variations on a single external variable.

By definition, a scenario is an outline of a plot; it should not be a complete script. A scenario should provide only the "Cliff Notes" of the most relevant events.

Another, perhaps more significant risk in elaborately constructed plots is that each individual action in the story is viewed as a prediction. And when some do not become reality, the entire scenario is discredited. SRI's Tom Mandel articulated this problem in a recent Global Business Network publication: "It's not that the [scenario] prediction [will be] wrong but rather that you don't want to undermine the credibility of the scenario itself by tying it too closely to specific events happening." A way to help define the point of diminishing returns is to ask: "Is this particular sub-plot in the story critical to its development? Must it happen for the scenario to prevail?"

19. Trying to Complete the Process Too Quickly. Generating and digesting potential discontinuities in the business environment is hard work and takes time. Don't dawdle and spend years completing a scenario-building process, but do allow enough time to be reflective.

Generating good scenarios usually takes a few months. Using those scenarios in management decisions often requires a few additional months of incubation. Trying to move too quickly tends to result in scenarios that are mere extensions of the present, not fundamentally alternate views of what is possible. Arie de Geus aptly points out in his "Planning as Learning" article in the *Harvard Business Review*: "Hearing, digestion, confirmation, and action: Each step takes time, its own sweet time."

Like some of the other lessons, this one is not a hard and fast rule. The technique of scenario planning can be applied to many circumstances and issues with varying degrees of complexity. It can be used to construct well-documented and substantive stories, but it can also be used to scan the horizon in a relatively quick way. The "full tilt boogie" version of scenario planning will likely take from five to nine months. However, in some circumstances a business unit may want to try scenarios on a smaller, less strategically complex issue. This process can be done in as short a time as a few weeks.

20. Don't Substitute Scenarios for Forecasts. The case for scenario planning is often based on the argument that forecasting has serious weaknesses. The positioning is appropriate—scenario planning does overcome some of the major weaknesses of financial forecasting. Scenarios do broaden horizons and encourage managers to think about multiple options and not just single-line projections. In that regard, scenario planning is a very valuable management tool.

But volume and profit forecasts are also very valuable management tools, and scenario planning is not a substitute for forecasting. Forecasts are quite effective in making resource allocation decisions among multiple business units, and are also important in managing publicly reported financial information. Scenario planning is relatively useless in both areas. Business units need to maintain their forecasting process even while working on scenarios.

21. Don't Generate Alternative Variations on a Single External Variable. Don't fall into the old financial forecasting trap of high/medium/low variations around a single variable. Well-constructed scenarios don't simply adjust the rate of flow—they reconfigure the plumbing.

Business units that operate in a significantly changing environment sometimes view the current source of external change as the single variable upon which to build scenarios. It may be a single competitor who is particularly active at any one moment, it may be a significant change in government regulation or legislative activity, or some other external variable. While this variable may be included in one or two of the scenarios, the full set of scenarios needs to be more multidimensional to be productive.

One of the early warning signs of this problem is the commonly encountered "middle scenario" trap. This occurs when there are three possible alternatives around any single dimension: high, medium, and low. Even the most junior managers can figure out the path of least resistance —go for the middle.

The problem, however, is not that there are three scenarios. Guy Jillings, Head of Strategic Planning at Royal Dutch/Shell in London wisely counsels that three scenarios are often ideal as long as at least one of them is focused on another dimension. The result is not a linear high/middle/low, but rather a three-dimensional cone projection. If your process creates three scenarios, reexamine each one closely to be sure that together they generate a cone and not a linear path.

The Judges Score Card:
Are Your Scenarios Productive?

22. Is Each Scenario Distinct in Fundamental Ways? Good scenarios significantly stretch and sometimes alter current perceptions, and at least one scenario should contain a major discontinuity. Be provocative (see Exhibit 6).

One of the most common problems with a business unit's
Continued on page 47.

KEY LESSONS, *from page 17.*

introductory exposure to scenario planning is that the first set of scenarios will tend to converge in a relatively narrow range. This is particularly likely in consensus cultures where it is risky to offer radical thoughts or opinions.

There is a variety of ways to open people up to a broader perception of change, even in consensus cultures. One of my favorite methods is to resurrect the business unit's long-range plan from five years before. It's instructive to look at the "year five" projections and predictions put together in good faith by some of those very managers who are still predicting only minor variations in the external business environment. The retrospective quickly bolsters what they're learning from their own experience—that the ability to predict the future is a slippery business at best, and the range of its variations is usually wider than expected. The chances that current projections will become reality are quite slim.

EXHIBIT 6: Are Your Scenarios Productive?

22. Is each scenario distinct in fundamental ways?
23. Are scenarios internally consistent?
24. Is each scenario plausible?
25. Do scenarios have memorable names that integrate them into decision making?

There are three other techniques that help expand the range of views around the current business. The first is somewhat obvious: Have various people on the team do individual opportunity and threat analyses of the business. One very useful technique in coaxing those views out of the management team is to ask two questions developed at the Institute for the Future and described in Roy Amara and Andrew Lipinski's book, *Business Planning for an Uncertain Future:*

• Assume for a moment that the future of the business unit develops so badly from the present to the end of the scenario period that there is only one chance in ten that it could have been worse. Describe that future. What events lead to it?

• Assume for a moment that the future of the business unit develops so favorably from the present to the end of the scenario period that there is only one chance in ten that it could have been better. Describe that future. What events lead to it?

The resulting answers will highlight the perceived opportunities and threats on the horizon in the minds of the managers, and will help provide the nourishment to develop a wider field of alternative views.

A second technique to help broaden the alternatives is to view today's reality with the aid of the different "thinking hats" described in Edward de Bono's appropriately titled book, *Six Thinking Hats.* He separates thinking into six different modes, each identified with a colored hat. A white hat focuses thinking on facts, figures, and objective information; a red hat on emotions and feelings. A black hat focuses thinking on logical, negative thoughts; a yellow hat on positive, constructive thoughts. The green hat is for creativity and new ideas; and the blue hat is for process. By consciously switching hats, a group facilitator can redirect thinking and sometimes broaden the bandwidth enough to generate a wider range of possible alternatives.

The third technique is to apply a traditional SEPT analysis: Social, Economic, Political and Technical. If the business unit is stuck on a single variable as the only important driver of the future business environment, classify it as one of the four above and start generating ideas on alternate futures in the other three.

23. Are The Scenarios Internally Consistent? It sounds a bit childish to suggest that scenarios need to be holistic, internally consistent and logically woven, but it's not all that simple to do. A common flaw is neglecting to account for competitors' reactions to both the changes in the business environment and your own business unit's activities. To prevent this type of lapse, ask yourself: "Logically, what will competitors do in this particular scenario? How will their reactions affect our optimal course of action?"

24. Is Each Scenario Plausible? One of the first signs that a manager does not yet understand the scenario process is when he or she asks: "Which one of these futures is the most probable?" It's only a matter of time until a weighted average is created and the old single-line forecast is back. Alternatively, if a single scenario is chosen, it's almost always a "business as usual" story, with only limited departures from conventional wisdom—not a very helpful source of learning.

Pierre Wack articulates this issue with appropriate forcefulness in the *Harvard Business Review:* "The point...is not so much to have one scenario that 'gets it right' as to have a set of scenarios that illuminates the major forces driving the system, their interrelationships, and the critical uncertainties." He elaborates this point further in a Global Business Network publication: "By focusing on the outcome instead of developing an understanding of the forces leading to an outcome, [the scenario planning team] will have a superficial and mechanical impact, and will not change [management] mind-sets in depth."

The actual future often lies in some combination of scenarios. Unswerving loyalty to any single story can be as dangerous as a single-line financial forecast. It's guaranteed to be wrong.

25. Do the Scenarios Have Memorable Names That Help Integrate Them into Everyday Decision Making? To be truly effective, scenarios need to be integrated into the day-to-day decision-making process so they become part of the natural activities of management. One of the secrets of success is to generate provocative yet meaningful scenario titles that create mental pictures all by themselves. The names become a shared language, an effective shorthand, around which all kinds of interesting conversations can germinate. Some planners have borrowed memorable names from old television shows, movies, or books. Even without background information in the industry or the external environment, scenario titles like "The Empire Strikes Back," "Against All Odds," "Star Wars," "Shakedown," "Jeopardy," or "Let's Make a Deal" conjure up the notion of potent changes in the external environment.

Reflections

Scenarios are exploratory learning tools; they are about options. At its heart the ultimate goal of scenario planning is: "to create maneuvering room for management"—well said by Peter Schwartz. Scenario planning can be an extremely effective technique, and when appropriately applied it can have significantly positive effects on your business. The adventure and rewards are well worth the effort. □

Further Reading on Scenario Planning

Books:
- *The Art of the Long View,* by Peter Schwartz (New York: Doubleday Currency, 1990). Before you institute a scenario planning process read this book from cover to cover—twice.
- *Competitive Advantage* by Michael Porter (New York: Free Press, 1985). Chapter 13—"Industry Scenarios and Competitive Strategy under Uncertainty"—provides a good overview.
- *The Fifth Discipline* by Peter Senge (New York: Doubleday Currency, 1990). This book is focused on the art and practice of organizational learning, but much of the material is relevant and some is directly relevant. The material on systems thinking is especially helpful.
- *Six Thinking Hats* by Edward de Bono (Boston: Little Brown and Company, 1985). The author of a number of outstanding books on conceptual thinking, many of de Bono's ideas prove useful as you undertake the scenario planning process.
- *Charting the Corporate Mind* by Charles Hampden-Turner (New York: The Free Press, 1990). This book teaches how to identify and resolve corporate dilemmas. Chapter 6, "Seven Steps to Reconciling Dilemmas Strategically" is especially useful in scenario planning.

Some Landmark Journal Articles:
- Pierre Wack, "Uncharted Waters Ahead," *Harvard Business Review,* September/October 1985 and "Scenarios: Shooting the Rapids," *Harvard Business Review,* November/December 1985.
- Arie de Geus, "Planning as Learning," *Harvard Business Review,* March/April 1988.
- Peter Senge, "The Leader's New Work: Building Learning Organizations," *Sloan Management Review,* Fall 1990.
- Ray Stata, "Organizational Learning—The Key to Management Innovation," *Sloan Management Review,* Spring 1989.
- Kathleen Eisenhardt, "Speed and Strategic Choice: How Managers Accelerate Decision Making" *California Management Review,* 1990.

[5]

CASE STUDY

Integrating Scenarios into Strategic Planning at Royal Dutch/Shell

By Paul J. H. Schoemaker and
Cornelius A.J.M. van der Heijden

*Shell developed a number of new methodologies to make
scenario planning more meaningful to line managers.
It also took steps to integrate the learning that takes place
at the SBU level into the Group Planning System.*

Scenarios have been an important tool for enhancing strategic management at Royal Dutch/Shell since the early 1970s. But in the early 1980s management conceded that Shell was not getting the full benefit of its considerable investment in the scenario process. Part of the problem was that scenario development was an episodic activity—an excursion from the routine planning process. Furthermore, scenario planning was not thoroughly integrated into Shell's Group Planning System, the annual cycle of strategic and business planning (see Exhibit 1). Shell responded to the challenge by developing a number of new methodologies to make scenario planning more meaningful to line managers. It also took steps to integrate the scenario team learning that takes place at the SBU level into the Group Planning System. The new approach features:
- Focused scenarios.
- Competitive positioning.
- Strategic vision.
- Options management.

Integrating these four elements in an iterative process helps managers make practical use of what they've learned from experimenting with scenarios.

First, Shell conducts scenario building and competitive position analysis as parallel activities—both guided by a strategic vision, or elements of one, already in place. Then information and insights gained from these analyses are used to amplify the original strategic vision. After several rounds of this learning process, Shell managers are ready to write a set of strategic options worthy of detailed study. Only after developing the scenarios, the competitive analyses, and the strategic vision are the managers fully prepared to assess the consequences of acting on these options.

Paul J. H. Schoemaker collected insights on Royal/Dutch Shell's planning group in London during a two-year sabbatical from the Graduate School of Business at the University of Chicago. He now heads Decision Strategies International, a Chicago-based consulting firm and is a senior fellow at Wharton's SEI Center for Advanced Studies in Management. Cornelius A.J.M. van der Heijden was Shell's head of scenario planning and internal consultancy and is currently Professor of Business Administration at the University of Strathclyde, Glasgow.

The Components of the Framework

How are these components developed in an individual Shell operating company or sector? As a starting point, assume that a strategic vision exists for the unit, but it has not yet been refined or focused, nor is it shared by the whole management team.

Multiple Scenarios

Scenarios are tools for improving the decision-making process against a background of possible future environments. They should not be treated as predictions capable of influencing the future, but neither are they science fiction stories prepared merely to titillate the imagination. Shell scenarios are focused on:
- Issues and information that greatly concern Shell's decision makers.
- Elements in the environment that are determinable and somewhat predictable.
- Trendbreakers—elements that will affect a system in unpredictable ways, but with understandable dynamics.
- Potential surprises of major significance.

The scenarios benefit the organization by stimulating managers to think together in systematic and disciplined ways. As a result, the team members become more insightful observers of the business environment, capable of recognizing change rather than overlooking or denying it. For complex global issues, multidisciplinary teams are needed to build integrated scenarios.

Step 1: Selecting the Issues. There are a number of elements that each Shell global scenario process has in common. And yet, the process is more art than science—there is no simple formula for generating good, useful scenarios.

In most cases, however, the first step is to select the critical issues that need to be examined. Some issues appear in most Shell scenarios—economic growth, product demand, and energy prices. Others will be added or subtracted as the decision agenda and the external environment change. A major initial challenge for the scenario authors is to anticipate what issues and understandings will be of greatest value several years down the road when the scenarios are in use. Involving the whole management team at this early stage increases the likelihood of eventual success, for it takes the as yet unstructured concerns and anxieties of the team as a starting point.

Step 2: Analyze the Areas of Concern. A detailed analysis of the areas of concern should pinpoint the driving forces, predetermined elements, critical uncertainties, possible discontinuities, and linkages with other areas of the business environment. At Shell the areas of concern usually include energy, economics, social change, the environment, politics, and technology. When emerging areas of concern are investigated for the first time—such as the fall of the Soviet Empire or the passage of the U.S. Clean Air Act—the risks and opportunities have not usually been well articulated. Scenarios can contribute a great deal to the organizational learning process by offering various overviews on these complex issues, and by examining their implications.

Step 3: Organize the scenario around a logical concept. Issues, such as restructured growth or environmentalism, define a scenario and insure that its elements are consistent. These issues also communicate a basic message, such as, growth involves change, or worldwide public opinion is turning "green." This is not just another constraint to reckon with, but rather the onset of an entirely new business environment. However, even at this early stage, quick and dirty quantification can help determine whether a scenario is plausible and internally consistent. The team works to deepen and expand the analysis. One way is to consider the events from the point of view of various key actors. Another way is to refine the quantification. And finally, the communications process takes center stage, since scenarios are useful only if they are well understood by all the stakeholders.

Step 4: Focusing the Scenario. By establishing defined boundaries for the scenarios—in terms of time frames, geographic regions, industries, business sectors, or major projects—the team brings them into sharper focus. Decision makers need to see their concerns reflected in the scenarios, but conceptualized in ways that further new understanding. As another way of bounding the future, Shell teams sometimes investigate antithetical scenarios. To be useful, scenarios that differ sharply from conventional views of the future must be made believable, at least to some degree.

Some traps to avoid. Shell teams are trained not to just write best case/worse case or high/low scenarios. By avoiding the oversimplified thinking that such scenarios engender, Shell managers learn more about the real challenges that complex futures pose. Likewise the scenario-building teams avoid assigning probabilities to scenarios. Indeed, the question of probability is not really appropriate, since Shell's scenarios are not considered business forecasts but rather previews of possible business environments that warrant thinking about in advance.

Competitive Positioning

Competitive positioning is at first a process of understanding all aspects of a business unit's competitive situation. The second step is to devise ways of improving that position. Unlike scenarios, which begin with a global perspective, the focus of competitive positioning is on the microenvironment. Appropriate segmentation of the business is a critical first step. This is a perennial issue for Shell, because a number of its units have grown incrementally to exploit potential synergies between existing businesses and new activities. As a result, Shell is a highly interconnected company with an organizational structure and an accounting system that do not always reflect the activities of segments of its operations. Shell has an intricate internal structure, a high degree of local autonomy, and numerous linkages between business units. These include both business transactions and shared technology.

Shell employs a business segmentation module to identify strategically independent units within the organization. This segmentation might be justified on the basis of the geographical area of operation, features of the customer groups served, types of products or services, or the technology used to produce products. Shell's guideline for segmenting business activities into independent areas of operations is: Does it boost the profit potential and does it improve the competitive focus?

In the oil business, there are plenty of competitors for the profit that can be derived from a barrel of crude. Competitors include suppliers, customers, other producers, and producers of substitute products or services. Even potential market entrants, like shale oil producers, or even energy-saving products (nega-barrels), can be a force to reckon with under some circumstances. Various barriers, such as patents and licenses, protect companies from the forces of competition. Other factors—such as economies of scale, sunk costs, technological know how, customer loyalty, organizational capability, and product excellence create competitive advantage that make the strivings of would-be rivals much more difficult. Shell identifies explicitly what barriers affect major competitors in each business segment. It searches specifically for new business opportunities in areas where its distinctive competencies can be applied to create value for its customers, and thereby acheive a sustainable competitive advantage over potential rivals.

Product/market differentiation is a critical and complex activity. One reason for the complexity is that Shell's offerings have many components— service, trust, financing, and guarantees, to name just a few. In addition to these factors, the differentiation process also examines structural elements, such as technologies, cost structures, organizational design, culture, and distribution systems. By defining ways these differences can be exploited to create customer value, Shell identifies profitable niches where it can systematically outperform its competitors.

The aim of the competitive positioning process is to learn systematically as much as possible about the competitive issues between each Shell business and its rivals. The process looks at both soft analysis, such as a competitor's objectives, capabilities, and personalities, as well as hard data on costs, market share, growth rates, and innovations.

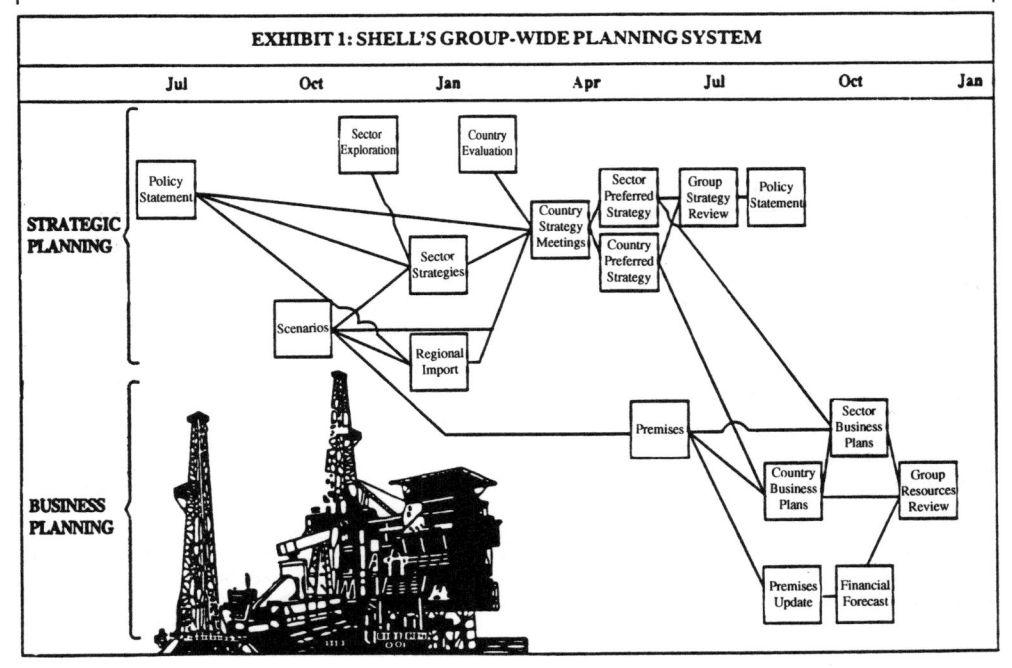

EXHIBIT 1: SHELL'S GROUP-WIDE PLANNING SYSTEM

EXHIBIT 2: A SYSTEM OF FOUR METHODOLOGIES

```
  Competitive                Scenarios
  Position
        ↘                   ↙
              Strategic
               Focus
        ↙       ↓       ↘
  Option Planning
   • Multiple Options
   • Effect of Uncertainty
   • Competitive Implications
   • Explicit Trade-offs
```

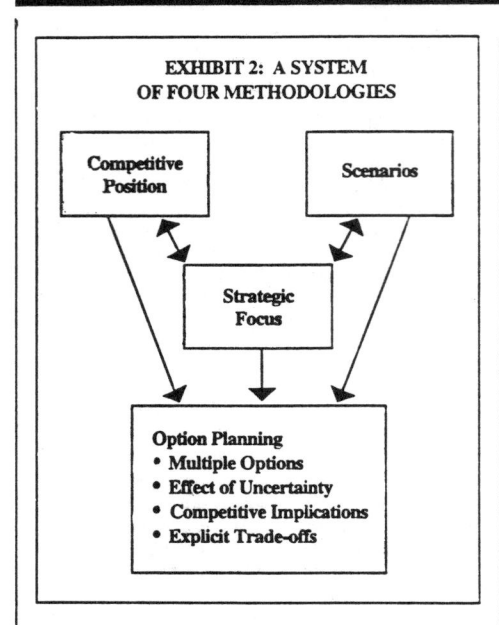

Strategic Vision

After the competitive-positioning and scenario-building processes have deepened Shell managers' understanding of their business' micro and macro environment, the next step is to refine the strategic vision. At Shell, the term strategic vision means insight, not clairvoyance. Performed systematically, the process helps each operating company or sector develop an understanding of what it wants to be in the future, what it can be, and how to reach this goal. Making the vision real requires conviction, creative foresight, and a practical sense of what is feasible.

After defining the vision, Shell managers reassess the strategic focus of the scenarios and competitive analysis. This process sounds complex, but it actually simplifies issues for the business unit decision makers. After agreeing on how a business unit should evolve—that is, what it wants to be and how to get there— Shell managers can focus their attention on the most relevant events, trends, and competitive behaviors. At Shell it typically takes several iterations of the process outlined in Exhibit 2 before a sound strategic focus becomes apparent and accepted. Throughout this process, managers strive for an ever greater understanding of where industries are headed, how technologies are developing, and how society is changing. As a result, Shell managers gain deeper insights into how to identify profit potential, and what moves must be made now to establish a favorable position in the future market.

Like a beacon atop a lighthouse, the strategic vision illuminates the future from a particular vantage point. With this sharply defined perspective, managers can quantify the resources they need for a leadership position in the market with the most profit potential. However, detailed financial analyses are not the primary purpose of the strategic vision process. In Shell's experience, over emphasis on financials at this stage tends to draw attention away from innovative strategic thinking. Shell managers recognize that strategic options represent significant value, like financial options traded at option exchanges. They represent invisible company assests.

Shell's intention during strategic vision development is to reveal the potential of capabilities embedded in the organization which can be strategically organized to produce sustainable competitive advantage in selected businesses. The process requires a search deep in the organization, and depends for success on open communications and creativity motivators. Once articulated, explained, and adopted, this strategic vision then becomes both the guiding perspective and the driving force for several levels of the organization. Such consensus greatly simplifies decision making, often a complex process at Shell.

Options Management

Once Shell managers have developed a strategic focus for a business, they begin the formal process of defining major strategic options and their consequences. Option creation—the fourth methodology—converts everything the planning team learned from developing the scenarios, competitive positioning, and the strategic vision into a unified system that powerfully influences Shell's decision making.

Stage 1: Option Generation. A review of current business assumptions often uncovers some new options. For example, an option may may have been previously dismissed because of internal hurdles and cumbersome decision procedures. Or, an option might have been tainted because it was associated with a previous business failure. By conducting post mortems on ill-fated projects, biases against good strategic options may be uncovered and attitudes changed. Other options emerge from investigating new technologies through joint ventures or experimental projects.

Stage 2: Estimating the Consequences. What are the financial, competitive, and strategic consequences of choosing a promising option? To find out, Shell employs estimation techniques ranging from the intuitive (best guesses) to the mathematical (simulation models based on complex probability distributions). To display the consequences of a number of options, Shell managers use decision trees to show the relationship of sequential decisions and key uncertainties. This is especially useful for displaying the choices in exploration and drilling operations. Monte Carlo simulation is another valuable tool for studying the uncertainty and

EXHIBIT 3: SHELL'S NEW PLANNING FRAMEWORK

Elements, Process, and Context

Culture — History, Emergent Strategy → Strategic Vision, Competitive Position, Business Environment (Scenarios), Option Planning → Communication, Consensus Building, Organization/People → Implementation (Milestones)

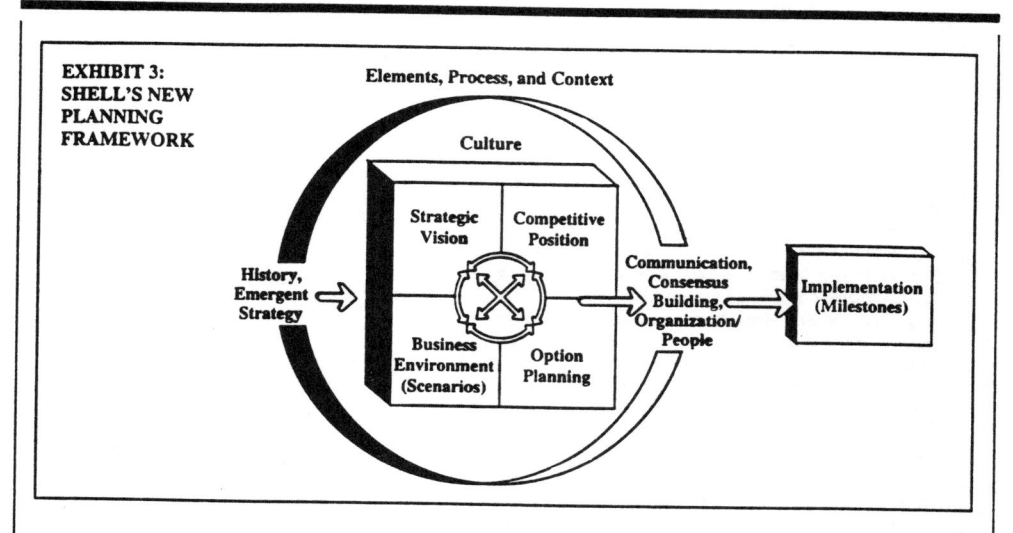

risk of an option. For example, this technique can be employed to look at profit or market share models based on various scenarios.

Stage 3: Selecting Options. When choosing among options, it's critical to select the right decision mechanisms. Shell managers use various quantitative techniques:

• Decision analysis offers a rigorous means of making systematic trade-offs among competing objectives in an uncertain situation.

• Options theory makes it possible for managers to assess the value of avoiding commitments or delaying decisions that are expensive to change.

Stage 4: Option Management. At Shell, strategic options are seen as major company assets requiring careful management.

• Game theory can clarify how opponents would be likely to react to Shell's adoption of a strategic option. For example, Shell has used game theory to review options involving competition for market share through pricing, negotiations with governments, or restructuring of mature industries.

Ultimately, regardless of what technique is employed, the decision to select an option is a matter of judgment. By approaching these decisions as a team, and putting a high value on consensus, Shell benefits from the expertise and experience of all of the members of the group reviewing the options.

Traps to avoid. The option management process can go awry if the group's hidden agenda is to consider just one preferred option and several "straw-man" options. It is also crucial that the process remain apolitical. The various strategic options should be carefully documented and readily available to management at all times. They should not be judged until they are fully analyzed in terms of their financial, competitive, and strategic potential.

Implementation

In the early 1980s Shell's Group Planning consultancy developed an operational program to apply its new conceptual framework. This program used an action-research approach to implementing the program at both the Operating Company and Sector levels. Initially, the Group Planning representatives, acting as internal consultants, had the job of facilitating the process. But lately the local business planners have been encouraged to take on that role.

In the first phase of implementation, which takes about two weeks, planning facilitators interview the local management team about the current strategic vision and the underlying business assumptions. After some discussion, a strategic evaluation of the business situation is made using Shell's conceptual planning framework (see Exhibit 3). This evaluation usually suggests that a more detailed work program is needed. This will constitute phase two. Primarily conducted by the operational group, this second phase can last from three to six months.

Lately, Shell has encouraged Operating Company planners to assume more of the responsibilities formerly assigned to the Group Planning representatives. However, since most Shell line managers assigned to the job of planner had little if any experience using the technologies the process requires, an extensive training program had to be established. Fortunately, operating managers are rotated through the planning job frequently, and as a result, knowledge of the

Continued on next page.

SHELL, *from page 45.*

process and its techniques have moved swiftly throughout the organization.

Shell emphasis, throughout the process, is on team learning. With line executives in charge of both planning and implementation, learning and acting become inextricably linked. When it's time for a performance review of the planning effort, the team is highly motivated to understand the reasons for failure or success. This puts a premium on open communication and discourages defensive behavior. One of the larger aims of the planning process is a broad communication of corporate direction, so that every unit knows where it fits in the total picture. This is encouraged, in part, by concentrating every group's attention on the needs of the current and new customers, or end users of products or services. As more and more of these groups succeed, Shell is increasingly focusing on its managers' need to be recognized and rewarded for all the innovation and risk taking the new planning process requires. ☐

[6]

World-class manufacturing

Benchmarking world-class performance

A. Steven Walleck, J. David O'Halloran, and Charles A. Leader

Competitive analysis is a powerful tool for strategy formulation because it quantifies competitive gaps in cost, quality, and timeliness. But it usually does not provide a deep understanding of the processes and skills that create superior performance. Benchmarking world-class performance within and across industries, however, not only quantifies performance gaps. It also looks beyond discrete product evaluations to compare manufacturing and management processes. Benchmarking establishes how much a company needs to improve to be at world-class levels of functional and cross-functional performance.

- A US manufacturer of electronic circuit card assemblies discovered its total production costs to be four times those of comparable operations at one of the world's best producers. In addition, its quality performance was one-fifth as good, and it spent proportionately twice as much time in nonproductive activities.

- In a similarly eye-opening comparison, a pharmaceutical company found its purity standards were one-tenth as stringent as those of a potential competitor not yet marketing in its region of the globe. Its manufacturing processes were commensurately less capable.

- A third company, a medium-sized auto component manufacturer, found it could reduce its overall manufacturing cycle time from a total of 16 weeks to just 6.5 weeks by applying off-the-shelf techniques. World-class performance, however, meant build-to-order in 3.5 weeks – a goal no direct competitor currently achieves.

Not only in manufacturing but in design processes as well, large performance gaps exist between the best and the average company.

Exhibit 1 Benchmarking your company's design function

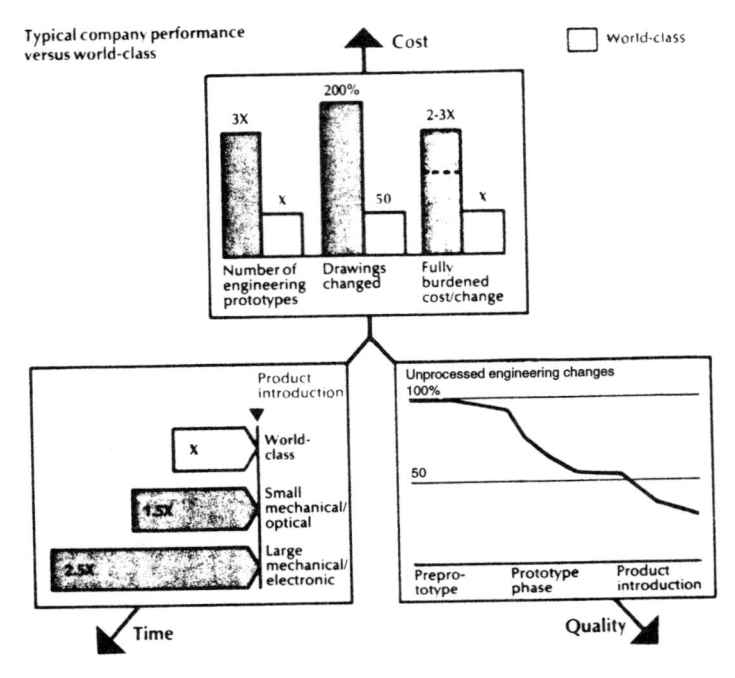

(Figure: Typical company performance versus world-class. Cost bars — Number of engineering prototypes: 3X vs X; Drawings changed: 200% vs 50; Fully burdened cost/change: 2-3X vs X. Time chart — Product introduction: World-class X, Small mechanical/optical 1.5X, Large mechanical/electronic 2.5X. Quality chart — Unprocessed engineering changes declining from 100% at Preprototype through Prototype phase to Product introduction.)

Source: Field visits; McKinsey analysis.

Exhibit I shows the cost, quality, and time gaps between world-class product development and typical industrial company performance.

These are not isolated examples. Wide performance gaps can be found in all industries. Even among the better performers, some companies are much more cost-effective, flexible, and quality conscious than others. Often there are tenfold differences between the best and the average quality or responsiveness in a single industry. Cost gaps of 30 to 50 percent for functionally indistinguishable products are not unusual.

These performance gaps are found not only in industries facing Asian competition, but also in industries whose participants are confined to North America and/or Europe. The best competitors are not just cost leaders. Almost always, they have an advantage in quality and flexibility as well.*

Little progress

Given the galvanizing power of these comparisons, why is it that most companies, even entire industries, do not regularly benchmark their performance against some external standard?

We do not believe it is a lack of awareness. Recent studies on industrial competitiveness have strongly emphasized the power of benchmarking. The MIT Commission on Industrial Productivity, for example, found that "a characteristic of all the best-practice American firms, large or small, is an emphasis on competitive benchmarking: comparing the performance of their products and work processes with those of the world leaders in order to achieve improvement and to measure progress." A criterion of the highly publicized Malcolm Baldridge National Quality Award is the presence of an effective program of external benchmarking.

Why then has there been so little progress? We believe there are three reasons:

1. *The supposed superiority of invention over copying.* Many managers in older industrialized countries have been taught that creative solutions start with blank sheets of paper. Given a new problem, engineers are taught to break it down into simple concepts and first principles, rather than dig out a reference or find a catalogue solution. Our ingrained habit is not to look first to others' experience for answers.

2. *The "We are unique" syndrome.* With few exceptions, businessmen take a perverse pride in the complexities and historical accidents that make their industry and their company different from all others. Confronted by superior practice, most prefer to argue: "That won't work here; our business is different" rather than seek out ways to modify their own company's constraints and adopt a better way.

3. *Moral and legal sanctions against "industrial espionage."* Too much curiosity about another company's practices is suspect, in

---

* Such large cost differentials between companies competing in the same markets would probably surprise theoretical economists. However, even large cost gaps can be offset by less expensive paths to market or by price premiums based on superior service and value, real or perceived, leaving even high-cost producers marginally profitable and low-cost producers far less profitable than they might be.

the United States and even more so in Europe. In Japan, by contrast, a whole industry of "consultants" stands ready to comb public sources, query old-boy networks of friends, and access even dubious information sources for a fee. Prolific, in-depth competitive intelligence is part of doing business in that highly competitive market.

We will try in this article both to bring clarity to the topic of benchmarking and to offer guidelines to those in organizations that want to use it. We will also discuss how benchmarking to world-class standards can stimulate continuing performance improvements within an organization. But first, it will be helpful to review traditional competitive analysis to understand how it is applied most successfully and where it is best complemented by benchmarking.

Competitive analysis

Competitive analysis is one of the most important strategic tools that managers possess. Increased understanding of competitors' strengths and weaknesses through competitive analysis leads to more effective strategy formulation. It is a powerful tool, and it is usually part of a formal planning process.

Conventional competitive analysis is usually conducted as three largely independent streams of analysis that are later integrated and cross-checked to establish a unified picture of what competitors actually accomplish. Reverse product engineering is an important part of most analyses. It highlights effective product designs, their costs, and the process technology necessary to produce them. A thorough financial analysis of publicly available information provides further evidence of competitive cost positions by focusing on total business system economics.

Financial analysis can provide an indication of capacity utilization, illustrate the strengths and weaknesses in alternative paths to market, and highlight differences in the way competitors have decided to concentrate resources. Finally, these exercises are supplemented with field work – interviews with suppliers, distributors, and customers – to fill in gaps in knowledge and to provide tangible illustrations of how different approaches are received in the marketplace.

Competitive analysis is especially useful when top management is faced with a major strategic choice – acquisition or divestiture, make/buy, entry/exit, or business restructuring. Detailed and rigorous competitive analysis has also been used to trigger aggressive internal improvement programs.

- Six years ago a mass data storage device manufacturer set out to reclaim world cost and quality leadership in its industry for the medium- and high-performance segments of the market. Sixty percent cost reductions and tenfold improvements in "plug-and-play" rates were targeted and achieved. Important in building momentum down the line were comparisons of cost, manufacturing throughput time, and quality for each subassembly of a storage unit.

- Four years ago a US auto manufacturer kicked off a program to reintegrate tooling manufacturing and maintenance for stamping dies. Key to the success of the program was the acceptance on all sides, particularly on the part of the UAW (United Automobile Workers), of competitive cost, quality, and turnaround time targets from competitive analysis.

However, competitive analysis often fails to catalyze a successful turnaround program. In many industries competitive gaps are large and well known, and yet the lagging company fails to act.

- Three years ago a European heavy equipment manufacturer commissioned a precise and detailed competitive analysis of its European competitors at both ends of the value spectrum: the low-end producers and the high-performance/high-quality manufacturers. The results were astounding. Even within the European Community, cost gaps of 30 percent for equipment of similar performance were common. Lower factor input costs – cheaper labor or subsidized steel – accounted for one-third of the gap. Better product engineering, process design, and overhead efficiency accounted for the remainder of the differential. However, despite these findings, very little has been done by the company's management to close the performance gap.

We have found that detailed competitive analysis, useful though it often is, can actually delay managers from coming to grips with the root causes of inefficiency, waste, and lethargy, and can even lead a company off in the wrong strategic direction.

For example, stung by the charge that they had ignored competitive inroads in the 1970s, some US automakers made a fetish of competitive analysis in the 1980s. Competitive analysis centers were established, and millions were spent reverse engineering literally every major competitive product in the world. Detailed cost comparisons were made down to the individual stamping, down to the cost of an individual weld spot! Studies were made of competitive process technology, of competitive vehicle design processes, of competitive workforce involvement and supplier involvement programs, and in-depth reviews of competitive organizational design principles were carried out. Management task forces were chartered, joint labor/management study groups were formed, and consultants and academics were employed by the hundreds.

And yet, in the 1990s, a competitive gap still exists. The best US company's vehicle quality – measured in dozens of ways – approaches the best made in Japan. On successful models where capacity is fully utilized, costs are often quite comparable. But now the Japanese have pulled ahead along other dimensions: time to market, the cost of variety, and design innovation. Extensive competitive analysis and all the work Detroit undertook to close the competitive gap were obviously not enough.

We believe there are three faults latent in the nature of competitive analysis, faults that often lead to the wrong action, inaction, or delay.

Prisoner of one's industry

By focusing on one industry, competitive analysis fails to identify potential breakthroughs suggested by the performance of companies in other industries. This makes companies prisoners of their industries. Competitive analysis measures what competitors have already achieved rather than what could be achieved. It focuses an organization on achieving competitive parity, or at best incremental advantage, rather than stimulating new ways of competing that dramatically surpass competitors' capabilities.

Misleading direction

Although competitive analysis does quantify performance gaps, it fails to offer insights into how excellent performance is achieved and sustained. Since it relies mostly on secondary sources of information, competitive analysis usually does not provide first-hand evidence of how the competitive organization structure, roles and responsibilities, skill levels, and management practices, procedures, and motivational approaches work as a system to stimulate improvement. Therefore, the actions competitive analysis suggests can be diametrically opposed to the actions that must ultimately be taken to turn around performance.

A good example of this is the chase for low-cost, offshore labor undertaken by major US manufacturers in the late 1970s and early 1980s, which we now know achieved minimal improvements in productivity. The competitive analysis that led US companies to source offshore, labor-intensive subassemblies offered no hint as to how difficult it would be to integrate product and process design in factories on the other side of the world, or how vulnerable to time-based or variety-based competition a company becomes when its supply chain is strung out around the globe.

Paralysis of analysis

Analysis of direct competitors always raises more questions than it answers, and these are often interesting questions that trigger further study.

Almost always, the competitor to be analyzed is buried in a corporate structure that encompasses noncompeting products and businesses. Almost always, the publicly available information is out-of-date, incomplete, and partially contradictory. And almost everyone in management holds a preconceived and dearly defended notion of competitive strengths and vulnerabilities. These conditions open up the possibility of endless debate over details with very little synthesis and momentum resulting.

Competitive analysis is obviously a useful starting point. However, in many situations analysis of direct competition is not enough to uncover the real scope of the challenge management faces. It can lead to an exhausting and unproductive debate on the validity of the competitive gap identified. And it tends to encourage management to "fight the last war," to develop the capabilities to beat competition as they exist today, rather than as they will exist tomorrow.

Benchmarking

Benchmarking world-class performance starts with competitive analysis, but goes far beyond it. While competitive analysis focuses on product comparisons, benchmarking looks beyond products to the operating and management skills that produce the products. Moreover, while competitive analysis is limited to companies that produce more or less similar products or services, benchmarking studies are free to search out the "best of breed" of a process or skill, wherever it may be found. And unlike competitive analysis, which is usually carried out as a staff exercise, benchmarking any process in depth usually requires the active participation of the line personnel who perform that function in their own businesses. Thus, benchmarking is more than an analytical process; it can be a tool for the encouragement of change.

Some companies that use benchmarking have found that it has become an all-pervasive element of their management culture. For example, 10 years ago, Xerox focused solely on product comparisons – primarily through reverse engineering – to explain Canon's advantage in small copiers. But since then, more comprehensive investigations of several leading Japanese manufacturers in a number of industries led to fundamental changes in how Xerox manages suppliers and develops products. These have been the primary sources of Xerox's now well-known competitiveness.

Motorola, which also uses benchmarking effectively, tries to start every new product, every capital program, and every reform effort with a search for "best of breed" in the world at large. "The further away from our industry we reach for comparisons, the happier we are," comments a senior Motorola executive. "We are seeking competitive superiority, after all, not just competitive parity." Viewed in this way, benchmarking is a skill, an attitude, and a practice that ensures the organization always has its sights set on excellence, not merely on improvement.

Benchmarking can even become a bridge between staff analysis and the design of a line program for achieving continuous performance improvement. Benchmarking can identify what it is that a company needs to be good at, as well as suggest what needs to be done to the support functions and the cross-integrating mechanisms to close the gap. And, through participation in highly structured field visits, line managers can be brought face-to-face with superior operational practice, and satisfy themselves that the benchmarks others achieve are valid and comparable. A properly designed benchmarking exercise thus builds enthusiasm and commitment for change in those line executives who need to be involved for change to take place.

What to benchmark

Most project teams charged with benchmarking world-class performance start in the factory, with the visible and capital- or labor-

Strategic Planning Process

Exhibit II Understanding your company's role in the supply chain, both currently and prospectively

Portion of cost (%)

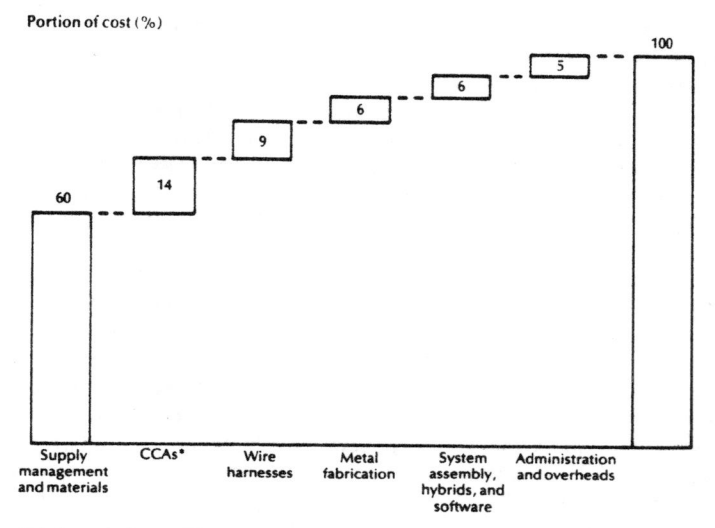

Supply management and materials	CCAs*	Wire harnesses	Metal fabrication	System assembly, hybrids, and software	Administration and overheads	
60	14	9	6	6	5	100

Relative make/buy positions

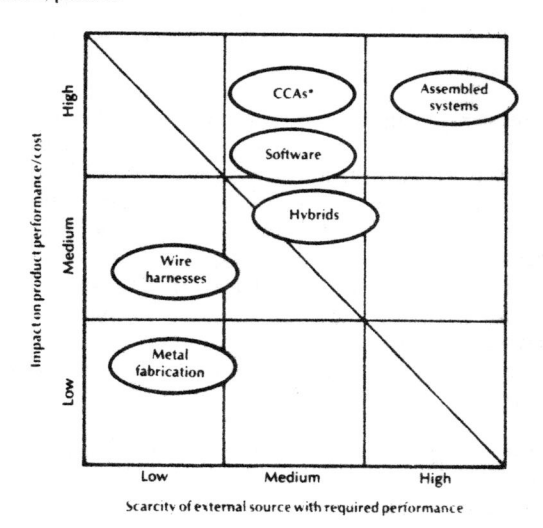

Impact on product performance/cost (Low / Medium / High) vs. Scarcity of external source with required performance (Low / Medium / High)

- High: CCAs* (Medium), Assembled systems (High)
- Medium–High: Software (Medium)
- Medium: Wire harnesses (Low), Hybrids (Medium)
- Low: Metal fabrication (Low)

☐ Make
☐ Buy

*CCAs = Circuit card assemblies
Source: Company data; interviews; McKinsey analysis.

intensive processes they recognize as most similar to their own. This is the wrong way to begin.

The first task of a benchmarking project team should be to define what to benchmark. In most manufacturing companies, value added internally is only a fraction – 40 percent or less – of total cost of goods. And for those components or subassemblies the company does make for itself, external sources are often available (see Exhibit II). Thus understanding your company's own role in the supply chain, both currently and prospectively, should precede the selection of the processes to be benchmarked.

Does your company depend on vendors for half or more of the cost of goods? Then supply management is a more important function to benchmark than any process on your factory floor. How competitive are your suppliers in the world market? How well do you manage the suppliers themselves? And how well do you manage the cross-functional processes that promote excellent supply management – for example, suppliers' involvement in concurrent engineering, integrated logistics management, and strategic make-versus-buy analyses (see Exhibit III)? In most manufacturing companies, superior execution of these functional and cross-functional management processes has a far greater impact on profitability and competitive position than any process carried out on the factory floor.

When benchmarking a complex, cross-functional management activity, it is important to begin with a hypothesis, a pattern of success that the benchmarking team expects to find. This hypothetical success pattern provides a valuable template for structuring discussions and requests for data. For example, material readily available in the public literature suggests that Honda's design process benefits from three strong characteristics: superior individual engineering competence, strong project management skills, and management systems that "frontload" design activities to resolve manufacturing, sourcing, and maintenance issues early in the design process.

A benchmarking team visiting Honda will certainly not have the time or the access to form an opinion of the overall quality of Honda's engineering competence. But they can ask for surrogate measures, many of which Honda is proud to provide, including: average age of a project engineer, 23; number of previous programs worked on by an average engineer, 2.3; and proportion of drawings changed after initial approval, 50 percent.

Exhibit III Defining the management processes to be benchmarked

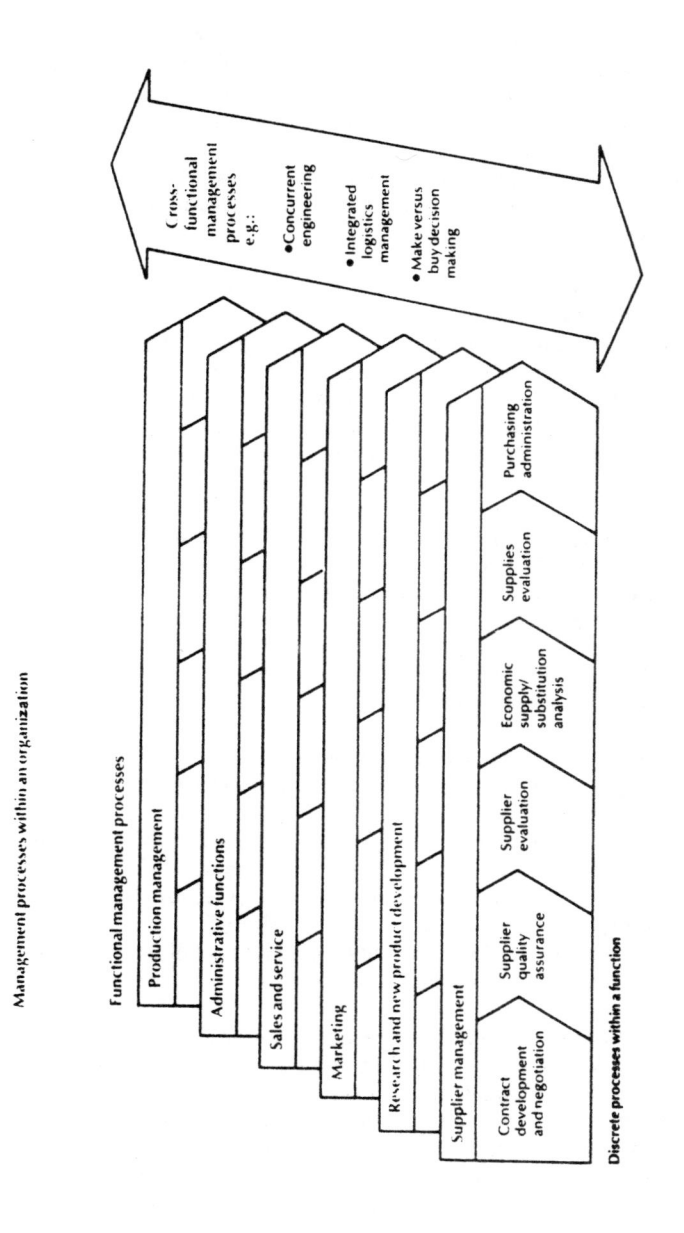

Cross-functional management processes e.g.:
- Concurrent engineering
- Integrated logistics management
- Make versus buy decision making

Management processes within an organization

Functional management processes
- Production management
- Administrative functions
- Sales and service
- Marketing
- Research and new product development
- Supplier management

Discrete processes within a function
- Contract development and negotiation
- Supplier quality assurance
- Supplier evaluation
- Economic supply/substitution analysis
- Supplies evaluation
- Purchasing administration

It is also helpful to let the benchmarking team define the measures they would find most useful, even if some of those measures may not capture the world's best practices. For example, the quality of a company's statistical process control (SPC) program is often listed as a desirable production management benchmark, for which such indices as the number of work stations with consistently plotted X-bar and R diagrams, the proportion of total maintenance done in a preventive, regularly scheduled mode, and the proportion of tooling and gauges regularly recalibrated are suggested as appropriate measures.

But some of the world's most advanced companies have passed beyond this stage to a level of process control where the machines shut down automatically if they make a mistake, rendering these common SPC activities unnecessary. X-bar and R plotting is a waste of time, once process variation is no longer measurable. However, it is often valuable to let the benchmarking team discover these higher levels of performance on their own.

We have found it useful to employ a simple and consistent framework to measure any functional or cross-functional management process (see Exhibit IV). Both inputs and outputs to a managerial process can be measured. Outputs are hard metrics that get the attention of management because they relate superior performance of the process to the company's success overall. Input measures are usually "softer" numbers; they attempt to quantify the "how to" of superior practice.

Often input measures are chosen because they dramatize the difference between one company's operating practice and another's, and not because they represent better practice *per se*. Thus, for example, it is often revealing in Europe to measure the percentage of all purchases made within 100 to 200 kilometers of a company's plants. A high percentage could be the result of a supply base carefully groomed for just-in-time delivery. More frequently it is the result of lethargy, national prejudice, and an unwillingness to take advantage of currency exchange differentials to cut material costs.

We have found that most operational processes can be comprehensively described by understanding a company's approach in five areas: the linkages to *partners'* processes, the *physical configuration* of the process, coordination of *product and process design, people* management, and the use of supporting *procedures and systems*. For each area it is useful to define a relevant management practice and a related, even if indirect, metric.

Exhibit IV Developing hard and soft measurements of management processes

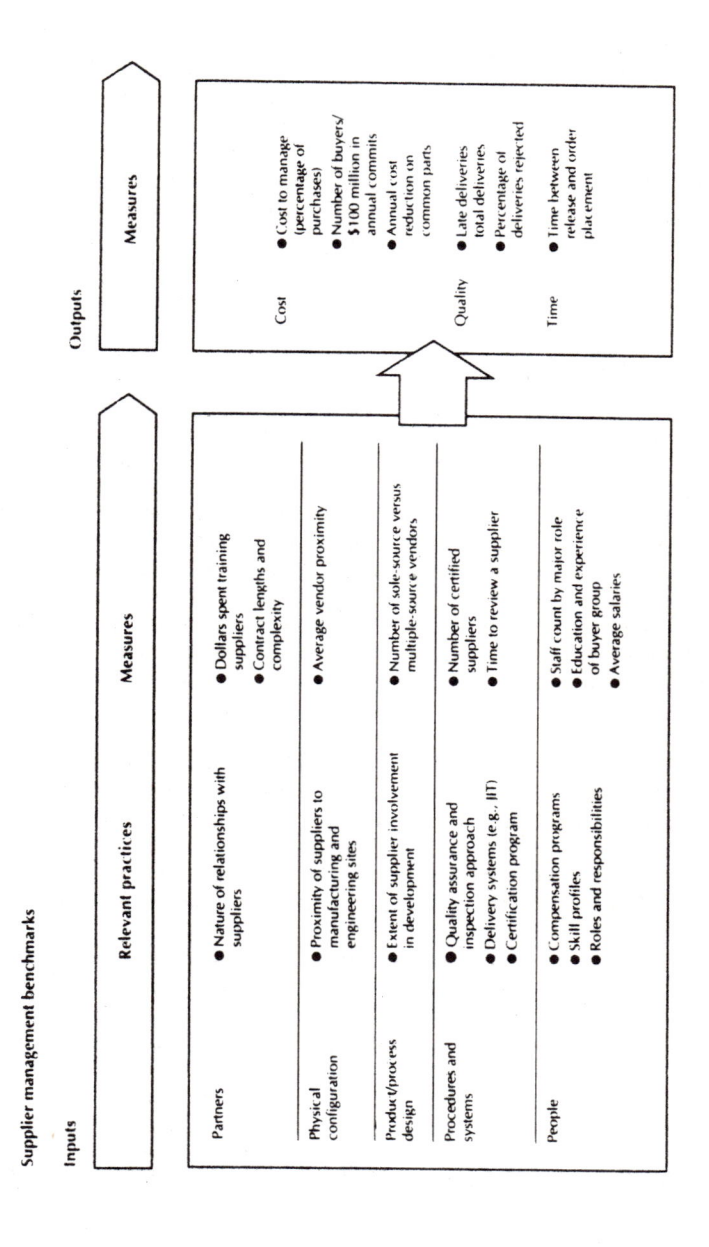

Supplier management benchmarks

Inputs	Relevant practices	Measures
Partners	• Nature of relationships with suppliers	• Dollars spent training suppliers • Contract lengths and complexity
Physical configuration	• Proximity of suppliers to manufacturing and engineering sites	• Average vendor proximity
Product/process design	• Extent of supplier involvement in development	• Number of sole-source versus multiple-source vendors
Procedures and systems	• Quality assurance and inspection approach • Delivery systems (e.g., JIT) • Certification program	• Number of certified suppliers • Time to review a supplier
People	• Compensation programs • Skill profiles • Roles and responsibilities	• Staff count by major role • Education and experience of buyer group • Average salaries

Outputs	Measures
Cost	• Cost to manage (percentage of purchases) • Number of buyers/$100 million in annual commits • Annual cost reduction on common parts
Quality	• Late deliveries total deliveries • Percentage of deliveries rejected
Time	• Time between release and order placement

Of course, some processes influence more costs than they themselves consume. For example, the concept and systems design phases of technical product development consume typically 5 to 15 percent of product lifecycle costs. The most effective product developers understand, however, that these early phases determine approximately 85 percent of lifecycle costs and much of the pricing latitude available to the product. Therefore, these early design phases are the most critical influencers of a product's ultimate financial success or failure. Excellent execution of the early design phases is therefore essential, and benchmarking their performance is more important than detailed examination of seemingly more costly later design stages.

Where to find benchmarks

Usually a few processes can be found that collectively account for the bulk of a company's value added in all its productive and support activities. After specific activities have been selected for comparison, a benchmarking team is still faced with the challenge of where to look for benchmarks. Benchmarking should examine excellent performance in a comparable process, regardless of the industry in which it is found. Setting the criteria for comparability too tightly can reduce the companies to be investigated to direct competitors only, and these may be unwilling to share experiences at the required level of specificity and detail. Setting the criteria too broadly can also be counterproductive, since too many adjustments or "windage factors" will have to be applied to the data eventually collected.

The first issue that typically arises is whether a candidate benchmark process is enough like the company's own to represent a fair comparison. The danger is that such stringent criteria will be applied that the opportunity for learning is severely limited. If the concern for comparability limits the investigation to identical approaches within the same industry, little will be accomplished.

For manufacturing processes, comparable product characteristics are important – for example, product size, production volume, functionality, and the number of levels in the bill of materials. It is usually helpful to define a large set of variance factors that may limit comparability ahead of any field work or plant visits. After a few visits the benchmarking team usually prunes back and simplifies their list of variance factors dramatically, as they see for themselves the essential similarities between fabrication and assembly processes of a given type.

For managerial processes, general characteristics that indicate similarities between industries and the challenges companies face are sufficient to ensure interesting comparisons. Often the most interesting comparisons come from outside one's own industry and technology. Perishable food companies tend to do an excellent job of just-in-time supply chain management, for example, and can often teach dry grocery manufacturers a lot about supply/demand balancing, demand forecasting, production scheduling, and distribution management. Pharmaceutical companies know a lot about production process documentation, record keeping, quality assurance, and batch or time-of-manufacture traceability. In these areas a dry grocery manufacturer could learn from them.

Industries reach different levels of performance for otherwise similar tasks because the factors influencing competitiveness differ across industries. The competitive forces requiring an automotive OEM to be absolutely superb in inventory management are not at work in the pharmaceutical industry, or at least the benefits of strong performance are perceived to have a different value to consumers. But, there is much to be learned from a company that has been forced to approach a task in a fundamentally different manner. In almost every case those companies will have developed creative methods for achieving superior process performance with lower total resource requirements than are typical in industries not similarly challenged.

The more experienced and creative the benchmarking team, the further afield their comparisons range. Some efforts have recognized credible sports analogies for their manufacturing activities, and found themselves visiting NASCAR (National Association of Stock Car Auto Racing) races to measure pitstops as benchmarks for line changeovers, or talking with America's Cup yachting crews as a benchmark for program management. In this field creativity has its own reward.

How to conduct benchmarking

One of the primary benefits of world-class benchmarking is that it offers executives and managers the opportunity to see for themselves how much better a process can be performed. This exposure in case after case has proven to be a strong lever in moving individuals to change – to seek excellence rather than comfort with things that "ain't broke." For some organizations, an understanding of where change may be most resisted reveals where benchmarking is most needed.

Benchmarking visits differ from plant tours

ALTHOUGH most companies send their executives on plant tours, the difference between those and true benchmarking visits is extreme. Four characteristics differentiate the benchmarking process from the disorganized, hands-in-pockets walk-through commonly practised.

- Benchmarking is preceded by in-depth industry and company analysis, so that the benchmarking team knows what to look for. Because of the variety of processes to be examined, the team is highly cross-functional in makeup and consists of executives, managers, and process specialists.

- Benchmarking candidates are selected by careful analysis to facilitate comparisons. Sometimes the most useful visits are not made at the nationally known plants and companies, which tend to be overrun with visitors, but at the smaller companies that are not so well known. Here the managers may be willing to spend more time with guests and be more open about the difficulties they still face. This kind of frank discussion does much to promote learning on both sides.

Searching industry databases and interviews with customers, suppliers, financial analysts, and consultants can all provide candidate companies for benchmarking.

- Agreeing on measurement formats, integrating data and measures from available sources, and splitting the observation tasks for company visits is an essential part of an efficient but comprehensive on-site investigation. A project leader with previous experience can be useful in this staff work. The iterative nature of benchmarking, and syndication of results, revisions, and revisits requires dedicated resources to ensure success.

- Pulling together and interpreting the results is not only the most interesting but also the most difficult task of all and requires a discipline not normally associated with typical plant visit debriefings. It is surprising how much visit participants differ in their assessment of the nature and quality of what they have seen. It is very important to reach a consensus after a benchmarking visit to maximize the learning from each discussion that took place.

A benchmarking exercise first identifies the manufacturing and managerial processes that need to be assessed. It then selects analogous processes in companies which perform them with outstanding results. Finally, it measures in detail how well these processes are performed in these companies.

Since many cost, quality, and time metrics and best practices need to be captured, it is usually more useful to understand a few world-class companies in detail rather than to make a superficial pass through a large number of companies. In advance of even the first visit, a full list of benchmarkable processes and functions should be constructed. Each company visit should be targeted at multiple production and management processes. Even in multi-business, multi-plant companies, up-front effort can pay off in efficiency, since a lot of effort is required to arrange a benchmarking visit or exchange. Hitting a number of topics on a single visit often pays off as well by allowing benchmarking teams to recognize complete patterns of success.

Very early on in this process, most benchmarking teams come to the realization that their own accounting systems provide generally misleading estimates of what production and managerial processes actually cost. It is usually necessary, therefore, for at least some members of the benchmarking team to recast their company's own cost numbers for the processes and activities that are to be benchmarked, in order to understand their own fully burdened costs of the processes they are comparing.

However, the sooner a benchmarking team gets out in the field and begins to conduct interviews, the better.

As a rule of thumb, four to six weeks are necessary to conduct the up-front analysis and project design, as well as to arrange the first field visit. It is usually productive to travel in teams of six to twelve and to examine more than one plant and managerial process on each visit. At least as much time for analysis and evaluation of the visits should be allowed as for the visits themselves. Thus, a comprehensive benchmarking project is at least a four-month project, and first-time projects often take six to nine months.

The most common mistakes benchmarking teams make are to try to gather data on too many topics, schedule too many interviews, and run out of time for analysis of the visits they have made. It is helpful, therefore, to set priorities on the processes to be benchmarked, based on economic importance, future strategic importance, and internal readiness to change (see Exhibit V). A few hours spent giving direction to a manager who is ready for change is often more productive than weeks spent trying to convince a manager of the validity of a comparison he doesn't want to face.

How to evaluate benchmarks

It has been our experience that only a few measures are necessary to comprehensively evaluate the cost, quality, and timeliness of a process. A single measure of total process cost expressed per unit of output achieved is the place to start to define the cost axis. Dollars per unit or per ton produced are adequate for manufacturing processes; fully loaded costs per transaction or per period of time can usually be derived for managerial processes.

Exhibit V Setting benchmarking priorities

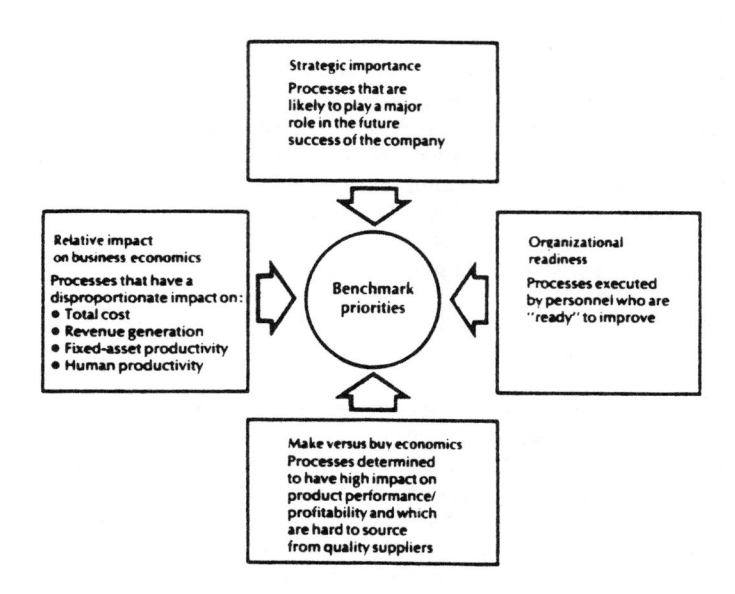

Strategic importance
Processes that are likely to play a major role in the future success of the company

Relative impact on business economics
Processes that have a disproportionate impact on:
• Total cost
• Revenue generation
• Fixed-asset productivity
• Human productivity

Benchmark priorities

Organizational readiness
Processes executed by personnel who are "ready" to improve

Make versus buy economics
Processes determined to have high impact on product performance/profitability and which are hard to source from quality suppliers

Quality measures should capture the errors, defects, and waste attributable to process execution and express them relative to the total output achieved. Since defects tend to cascade down a chain of processes, becoming ever more expensive to correct, and since methods for estimating the cost of non-quality vary extensively, it is usually better to use failure rates rather than failure cost numbers to measure quality performance.

Timeliness indices should be as comprehensive as possible, starting with an initiating event (e.g., a customer places an order, not an order is received) and extending through to the moment a company is paid for results (e.g., funds from the customer's payment are available in your bank). New product development times, for example, should be measured from the hour top management decides to approve a discrete expenditure of funds until the time that customer orders ensure commercial viability of the product. From decision point to pay point a surprising amount of time often leaks out around the edges of a company's visible processes, sometimes more time than the visible processes themselves consume.

Strategic Planning Process

Often the ratio of productive time to total time available is an eye-opening measure of how time is used within an organization. Equipment utilization rates are frequently measured against the rubber yardstick of "available time" or even "scheduled time," not the 8,760-hour year. Human time available to the job is also more variable than one would imagine: in Belgium many manufacturing companies must live with a 1.600-hour working year, after holidays, vacations, guaranteed sick leave, breaks, and so on. The comparable number a few miles eastward, in Germany, can be 1,900. In the United States 2,145 hours are usually available; in Japan 2,250 or 2,300 hours, including Saturdays and voluntary unpaid overtime, are regularly spent on the job.

The proportion of process time that is productive is usually best measured from the point of view of the work in process, whether that be an electronic circuit card assembly or an insurance claim form. Very few productive processes use more than 5 percent of total process time in value-added activities – one indication of the productivity potential available almost everywhere.

In measuring managerial processes, it is sometimes necessary to load each axis – cost, timeliness, and quality – with multiple benchmarks, in order to achieve a comprehensive picture of how another company operates. For example, to measure the supply management function, one company uses an aggregate of 12 metrics (*see* Exhibit VI). Only one of the measures – purchasing cost as a percentage of total goods and services purchases – is a comprehensive measure of purchasing cost efficiency. But it could be argued from this measure alone that spending more on the purchasing function may be bringing savings elsewhere. Unfortunately, the more comprehensive measurement set indicates such is not the case. They found they had:

- A highly fragmented supplier base (34 suppliers/buyer versus 5.3 in a world-class company) whom their buyers hardly knew.

- Extremely cumbersome and time-consuming purchase order approval and acquisition paperwork (six weeks elapsed time from production schedule decision to component orders placed with vendors, versus automated schedule-to-order systems at world-class companies), resulting in twice as many support personnel/buyer.

- Wide ranging vendor lead times (5 to 150 weeks), with over half of all component orders placed inside agreed minimums. As a

Exhibit VI **Comparing supply management capabilities**

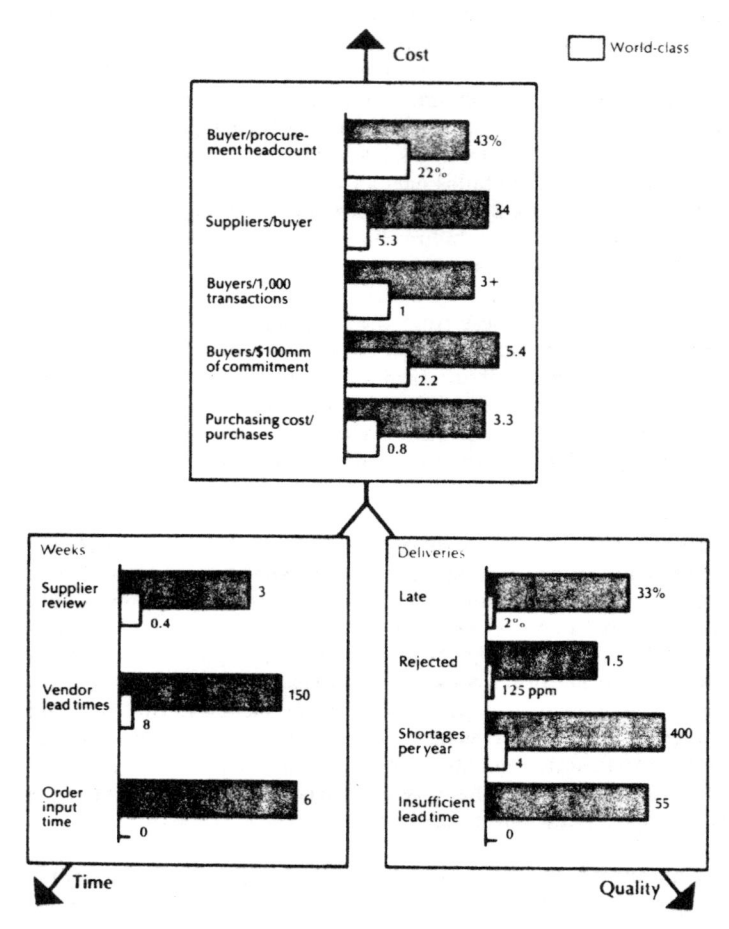

```
                                    Cost ↑            ☐ World-class

        Buyer/procure-          ▓▓▓▓▓ 43%
        ment headcount       □ 22%

        Suppliers/buyer       ▓▓▓▓▓ 34
                            □ 5.3

        Buyers/1,000          ▓▓▓▓▓ 3+
        transactions        □ 1

        Buyers/$100mm         ▓▓▓▓▓ 5.4
        of commitment       □ 2.2

        Purchasing cost/      ▓▓▓▓▓ 3.3
        purchases           □ 0.8
```

Weeks		Deliveries	
Supplier review	3 / 0.4	Late	33% / 2%
Vendor lead times	150 / 8	Rejected	1.5 / 125 ppm
Order input time	6 / 0	Shortages per year	400 / 4
		Insufficient lead time	55 / 0

↙ Time   Quality ↘

Source: Field visits; team analysis.

result, one-third of all incoming materials were late, and parts shortages required shutdowns or rescheduling of assembly about 100 times more often than in world-class operations.

- Very few qualified suppliers and joint quality-assurance programs with suppliers, resulting in incoming parts rejection rates two orders of magnitude away from world-class rates (1.5 percent versus 125 parts per million).

- Three times as many buyers per transaction and nearly three times the number of buyers per 100 million dollars of purchases. This situation was largely the result of ongoing quality disputes, the need to expedite deliveries, and the sheer number of suppliers dealt with.

The aggregate picture that emerges from these 12 supply management benchmarks is not pretty, but it is actionable. Most importantly, the purchasing professionals who returned from the round of face-to-face interviews, where the world-class performance benchmarks were collected, were convinced that there was a lot they could do, quickly, to improve their own performance. And their general management saw and understood, probably for the first-time, how much operating leverage there would be for them in investments that would upgrade the company's supply management capability.

Of course, it should not be assumed that there is only one world-class way to organize and manage a function or a cross-functional activity. Within the same class of process there can be several successful managerial patterns. Certainly field visits will sometimes turn up approaches that can be transferred without change to another company, but for the most part managerial innovation will be required to adapt the important characteristics of successful approaches in ways that best fit a company's own situation. The purpose of benchmarking is to expose managers to new ways of doing things in order to spark creativity in the design of their own processes, not to create efficient copy cats.

* * *

The search for world-class benchmarks is never likely to be over. Companies that use benchmarking regularly find that it is not necessary to ensure the company being studied is absolutely the best in the world. If their performance is sufficiently better than your own company's to make your people disagree about whether the functions or processes can be comparable, then they are probably worth studying.

Benchmarking is a way of involving the organization in looking at best practices outside the company – not only what is possible but how it is done. And it is a way of reaching for quantum-leap rather than incremental performance improvements. Q

Steve Walleck, a Director in the Cleveland office, leads McKinsey's Manufacturing practice and coleads the Operations Effectiveness practice. *Charles Leader* is a Principal and *David O'Halloran* is an Operations Consultant in the Cleveland office. Copyright © 1991 by McKinsey & Company, Inc. All rights reserved.

[7]

Managing value

MEMO to a CEO

FROM: Robert J. McLean   DATE: Spring 1990

SUBJECT: **Planning for value**

The restructuring of your industry during the 1980s was no accident. It occurred despite each of your major competitors having some of the best-developed technical skills and management systems for planning and coordination that existed anywhere. Why? The best explanation is that many participants, flush with cash, went beyond genuinely attractive opportunities to invest in diversification programs that did not make economic sense or increase shareholder value. By failing to adjust their capital and financial policies, they made themselves takeover targets. Apparently, no ROI system – and, equally important, no management incentive system – caused the proper warning bells to ring.

Our earlier discussions have made clear how your own planning processes did not – and do not – necessarily lead to maximizing shareholder value. So what are the requirements for managing your company for value today? In general, they mean that no significant opportunities to create shareholder value in your industry should remain unexploited. In day-to-day terms, they mean that all your managers must make decisions with a careful eye on how they will affect shareholder value. This will not be easy. Traditional measures such as ROI or accounting profits seldom provide adequate guidance. Nor will giving planners PC spreadsheet programs that calculate NPV suffice, where decisions about serving customers in superior ways are not linked to value calculations.

Introducing these sorts of changes – building in a focus on value – will, of course, be difficult. But it can be done - **if** you support it and **if** you help establish the three essential conditions needed to orient managers in the proper direction. These conditions are:

1. The creation of a common understanding among managers of what drives shareholder value.

2. The existence of a set of practical decision guidelines and processes that focus management action on the goal of creating shareholder value.

3. The establishment of management evaluation, incentive, and reward systems that encourage managers to make decisions based on shareholder value.

This memorandum outlines why getting these conditions are critical and how you might move to create them.

Determining the drivers of shareholder value

Shareholder value is a simple notion. It is the value of the returns a shareholder receives from an investment to compensate for investment risk. Shareholders receive returns in three ways: in the form of dividends; from the increased value of equity; or through capital repayments - whether it be by share repurchase programs or capital returns. This is the easy part. What is more difficult to understand and less well known is how shareholders will value the range of management actions and decisions your people will take.

You must understand this if you want your business to revolve around shareholder value. Put simply, you will need to discover what drives shareholder value and then put in place the appropriate management systems so you can measure your performance against these drivers. To do this, you will need to:

- Develop a comprehensive framework for determining what contributes to shareholder wealth. Such a framework must take into account:

  - The NPV of future cash flows.

  - The value of options.

  - The value created by financial restructuring.

  - Corporate center costs.

  - Contingent claims such as unsettled product liability or environment litigation.

- Define a practical and rigorous approach to estimating the shareholder value created by individual projects. This, in turn, will involve:

  - Defining strategies for serving customers that will produce superior cash returns.

  - Forecasting future cash flows for different classes of assets and for different tax regimes.

  - Specifying required rates of return for investments of different risk.

  - Knowing where and how to use option valuation techniques.

  - Estimating the value of different sets of assets to other owners.

- Develop an approach for validating estimates of shareholder value. Here the need is to:

    - Relate market values to internal value measures (the NPV of future cash flows).

    - Determine the consistency of these relationships across markets and over time.

    - Assess how company announcements affect share price.

Developing decision guidelines and processes

Beyond this general shared understanding of what drives value, your managers need a set of practical guidelines to help them make their day-to-day choices, based on value. Each of your business units is constantly making decisions about capital investment, market strategy, market entry, and so on. At the corporate level, you are regularly taking decisions about diversification, foreign exchange risk management, and capital structure. These are all issues that affect your free cash flows and, therefore, shareholder returns. That is why practical guidelines are so important.

To develop them and to integrate them effectively with current management systems, you will have to:

- Identify the types of decisions made by managers of each business unit that influence shareholder value. Here you will need to look at:

    - The types of decisions that get made.

    - Who provides information and on what basis.

- How assumptions are generated.

- Types of uncertainty considered.

• Define the appropriate decision framework and criteria for different types of decisions – the consequences of not investing when others are expected to, or the value of a preemptive move.

• Explain to managers how these systems will work and how they will affect their decision making. These guidelines will be effective only if managers understand both **why** they are being put in place and **how** they will be used – that is, how they will fit in with frequently used reporting measures such as accounting profit and ROE.

The purpose here, of course, is not just to help your people make better individual decisions, but also to help ensure a consistency of approach across your various business units. For example, correctly defining the level of aggregation or disaggregation at which valuations need to be developed will significantly affect the quality of the review process. The most appropriate business unit definition may not be equivalent to an organizational unit or legal entity. Then, too, the most appropriate capital structure for a business will depend on the volatility of its earnings and the tax environment in which it operates. Utilities, for instance, should be more highly levered than global commodities businesses.

Other areas in which consistency of approach will be important include terminal value assumptions and calculations, the choice of real or nominal cash flows and discount rates, and how a benchmark of shareholder value complements reporting measures such as accounting profit and ROE. A consistent methodology means that your planning review processes can be based on an understanding of the key value drivers in each business: volume growth, margins, capital spending (one-off and ongoing), and capacity utilization will all affect the value of different businesses in different ways. This understanding will increase the focus on those management actions that can unlock free cash flows and, therefore, the value of each business unit.

Tailoring incentives and evaluation processes

The incentives any company provides for its managers must encourage them to make decisions based on shareholder value. Similarly, when you look at the performance of an individual business unit, you should assess it on the basis of the shareholder value it has created. But how is this to take place?

We favor adopting performance measures that supplement financial reporting and that focus the attention of business unit managers squarely on value creation. This is made possible by accurately tracking recent performance through value-oriented measures. To get these incentives and evaluation processes in place, you will have to:

- Specify shareholder value measures for each part of your company's business system. This will involve:

  - Adopting change in NPV as an overall measure of group and business unit performance. Value is created only when there is a positive change in NPV. The corollary is that preserving value will rarely provide adequate performance.

  - Developing primary and supporting measures that link actions with customers to how margins are earned and assets are utilized.

- Integrating these measures into a performance measurement system.

- Ensure that values are calculated frequently enough to provide guidance to managers.

- Define the types of incentives that most encourage managers to achieve desired objectives and, conversely, that discourage them from behavior that leads in other directions. To do so involves:

  - Specifying incentives for individual versus team effort and clarifying the nature of risk bearing.

  - Reviewing incentives on a simulated basis and assessing their impact if tried elsewhere.

- Develop an implementation plan for revised accountability and incentive systems.

* * *

Let me stress, again, the importance of upgrading your company's management systems to align them with the objective of enhancing shareholder value. Only if there exist a clear, top-down understanding of the determinants of shareholder value, a set of decision processes consistent with this understanding, and the reporting and reward processes to support it, will you be able to lock in a superior approach to managing value.

Best regards.

Rob McLean is Managing Director of McKinsey's offices in Australia. Copyright © 1990 by McKinsey & Company, Inc. All rights reserved.

Strategy Versus Planning: Bridging the Gap

Benjamin B. Tregoe and Peter M. Tobia

How can a company strike the right balance among strategy, long-range planning, and day-to-day decision making? According to the authors, both long- and short-range planning must be coordinated to effectively implement corporate strategy.

Benjamin B. Tregoe is chairman of the board and Peter M. Tobia is vice-president of Kepner-Tregoe, Inc., a Princeton, New Jersey-based consulting firm specializing in strategic and operational decision making.

In working at the strategic level with senior executives for the past 20 years, we have seen a dominant theme appear: the confusion between strategic thinking and long-range planning. Whenever this confusion exists, a kind of Gresham's law sets in: long-range planning drives out strategic thinking when it is improperly used as a substitute for strategy.

Our aim is not to debunk long-range planning but to show why long-range planning is inadequate for strategy formulation and how both long- and short-range planning can become truly effective instruments for implementing strategy.

To understand the basis for concern with long-range planning, consider two facets that are critical to the survival of any organization: what an organization wants to be, and how it should get there. Although both these facets are integral to long-range planning, they must not be confused.

An organization's future self-definition—what it wants to be—and its planning and operational decision making—how it gets there—are related but separate dimensions. Because what an organization wants to be determines direction, it must be formulated before long-range planning and the day-to-day decision making that follows from such planning.

Unfortunately, strategy has been used rather casually by both management gurus and executives. Consider the terms *financial strategy, human resource strategy,* and *marketing strategy.* Most often, these are decision and planning points that presume an understanding of what an organization wants to be.

Strategy is vision. It is the framework that guides those choices that determine the nature and direction of an organization. These choices relate to the scope of an organization's products, markets, key capabilities, growth, ROI, and allocation of resources.

Why Long-Range Planning Is Not Strategic

Although the distinction between strategy and operational long-range planning

STRATEGY VERSUS PLANNING

is relatively straightforward, it is often misunderstood. There are eight major reasons why long-range planning is not a strategy-setting tool.

☐ Long-range plans are usually based on projections of current operations into the future. Although long-range plans are frequently developed with a recognition of economic, environmental, sociopolitical, and technological changes, such input is used chiefly to determine how expansive or cautious the organization should be about projecting its current operations. These types of input usually are not used as a basis for determining a strategic direction.

As one example, the vice president of operations and a director of a major company had this to say:

"When I came into this position, I had to develop a business plan. I found that the way plans were put together was to use a trend-line approach. The senior people who assembled the plan said that our growth rate for the past several years had been between 4% and 6%, so that should be the type of growth rate in the future. One of our products had averaged 32% growth per year in one geographical area. They just assumed the same growth rate in the future.

"Two things were missing in this straight-lining [of] a variable into the future. There was a technical flaw because a multitude of variables were simply ignored. More important, the plans lacked a long-term sense of direction and value; they didn't address the issue of where we want to go."

Typical example or exception? Whichever, it does illustrate the weakness of long-range planning as a substitute for setting strategy. Long-range planning does not invite managers to think strategically, to think about what the organization should be. Arriving at the future by long-range planning simply does not encourage managers to command their organization's future.

☐ Using the present to predict the future occurs despite many of the writings in the field that urge the establishment of up-front objectives as a part of long-range planning. In fact, many managers do not set objectives that define their future because they lack an approach to assist them.

These managers are forced to build their future on the foundation of the projections rather than on a clear definition of what they want their organization to be. Using this approach, the plans companies make determine their direction, instead of a clear sense of direction determining their plans.

> **66 Many managers do not set objectives that define their organization's future because they lack an approach to assist them. 99**

☐ When long-range objectives do exist to guide planning, they are invariably set in financial terms. Once set, projections for products, markets, and resources are then developed to achieve these objectives. But someone must give attention to the fundamental strategic question: What determines the future scope of the organization's products and markets?

Although every organization has financial objectives around which it plans and measures its operations, few organizations use such objectives as the primary determinant of their product and market scope. When long-range financial objectives are used as the primary guide for long-range planning, they can preempt critical considerations of what determines product and market scope, the resources to be put in place to support that product and market

STRATEGY VERSUS PLANNING

scope, and the expected results to be achieved. Typically, long-range financial objectives are set, plans are formulated, and these key strategic issues are put to rest without ever being examined.

☐ Long-range plans are built up from the lowest levels, where information exists to make projections. These projections from various parts of the organization are consolidated and, in total, become the recommended plan. By the time these accumulated and detailed plans reach the top, there is virtually no opportunity to inject fresh insight about the future. In fact, senior management's ability to modify these plans, except in minor ways, can be severely hampered. If senior managers do not have a clear strategy with which to assess the plans that percolate up through the organization, they become locked into allocating resources on the basis of these plans.

☐ Long-range plans are invariably overly optimistic. This results primarily from the desire of those making the projections at various levels of the organization to do better in their respective areas in the years ahead. This optimism usually exists in the weaker areas of organizations as well as in the stronger ones, thereby blurring distinctions between the two, which are vital for the efficient allocation of resources on a strategic basis.

By the time this optimism reaches senior management, every unit has predicted that given *x* amount of new resources, it will do *y* amount better in the year ahead. This further restricts the freedom of senior management to make changes, because such projections become the prevailing corporate wisdom.

Any changes made that are not purely perfunctory appear as arbitrary and capricious to the rest of the organization. Because the allocation of resources is tied to these optimistic plans, the persuasiveness of strong personalities and the unrealistic goals they guarantee to reach often undermine strategic considerations.

☐ Long-range planning usually begins with assumptions about the environment—the economy, technological change, sociopolitical events—and the organization's strengths and weaknesses. Although this information could have great strategic significance, long-range planning tends to use such data basically as a guide for determining how optimistic or pessimistic to make the long-range product and market projections. This is so because long-range planning is not a process that enables critical data about the external environment to be used for strategic purposes.

> ❝Long-range planning drives out strategic thinking when it is improperly used as a substitute for ● strategy. ❞

☐ Long-range plans are often inflexible. It takes a tremendous amount of work to project three years ahead, let alone five years and beyond. Without a clear strategic framework to define what the organization wants to be, long-range planning is forced to build a composite picture of the organization by projecting every future detail of the business. How else can it arrive at a total view of the organization in the future?

Such effort acts as a deterrent to change; it transforms most long-range plans into Gothic structures of inflexibility. This inflexibility makes it difficult to react to unanticipated changes in the environment and to adjust plans accordingly. The modification of long-range plans usually occurs only when events reach crisis proportions.

STRATEGY VERSUS PLANNING

☐ Long-range planning is really more short-range than anyone cares to admit. Long-range planning theory suggests that planning should project out five years and then recede back to the first year. But how can this be done in the absence of a structured framework for looking ahead five years?

Lacking this structured framework, the sheer force of necessity leads managers to reverse the theory and begin by projecting from the first year. Projections that are farther out are iffy.

Because there is so much work involved, the first year usually gets the most thorough analysis. After all, the manager knows changes can be made in following years; it is only the coming year that cannot be changed—this year becomes the budget. The shorter the time focus, the more easily a manager is locked into constraints of current operations, and the less likely he or she is to be influenced by information of potential strategic significance.

Clearing Up the Confusion

To ensure the proper relationship between strategy, long-range planning, and day-to-day decision making, an organization must be viewed as a continuum. To the left of the continuum is the intuitive, future vision of the organization, which is in the minds of the senior management team. To the right is operations: specific product plans, market plans, and budgets that translate vision into action.

The strategy and operations continuum begins with articulating vision, continues on through integrating strategy and long-range planning, and ends when that vision is an integral part of day-to-day operations. To accomplish this, three broad points along the continuum must be addressed:

- Articulating the vision and formulating a focused, strategic direction.
- Linking that vision to operational plans and budgets.
- Ensuring that the strategy is effectively implemented, maintained, and revised.

Because the first two points bear directly on the strategy-planning relationship, they are explored here in greater depth.

Articulating Strategy

For strategy to be a guide to operational planning and decision making, it must be clear and specific. For example, when senior executives of the worldwide plastics businesses of Dow Chemical Co. met to set strategy, they refused to settle for the usual generalities contained in many strategy statements. Instead, they asked themselves, debated, and finally answered five key strategic questions:

- What is the thrust or focus for future business development?
- What is the scope of products and markets that will—and will not—be considered?
- What is the future emphasis or priority and mix for products and markets that fall within the scope?
- What key capabilities are required to make strategic vision happen?
- What does this vision imply for growth and return expectations?

Executives at Dow Chemical's worldwide plastics businesses knew that the best way to answer the questions was to treat them as an integrated whole. For example, the question about future business development could be answered in several ways. At one extreme, the company could choose to remain focused on its current product offerings and further penetrate existing markets, or it could seek new markets for these products. At the other extreme, its future growth could be tied to new and different products for new markets or customer

66 The modification of long-range plans usually occurs only when events reach crisis proportions. 99

STRATEGY VERSUS PLANNING

groups. How this first question was answered had great significance for the remaining questions.

Dow executives searched for a way to integrate the choices posed by the five questions. The concept that proved to be the decision integrator was termed *the driving force*.

The key to an organization's vision lies in determining what it will sell (its products or services) and to whom it will sell them (its markets or customer groups). In making this determination, we have found that every company has one of eight distinct strategic options available to it. The driving force is the one option that determines the scope of future products and markets along with the product and market emphasis and mix, key capabilities, and growth and return expectations.

In the case of Dow's plastics businesses, senior executives looked at the past driving force and opted for a change. Historically, the strategy had been to build totally integrated petrochemical complexes around the world and become the most significant low-cost producer of large-volume thermoplastics and basic industrial chemicals. The company's historical strategy was driven by low-cost production capability; that approach had worked well for quite a while.

With the oil crisis and increasing cost competition, however, Dow realized it had to reevaluate its historical strategy. It saw the need to differentiate and add value to products and services in the eyes of the customer groups it served and began to move in that direction in the early 1980s. This involved a shift to a products-offered driving force for the worldwide plastics group.

When the five key strategic questions were answered within the framework of the driving force, Dow's plastic businesses had a clear, simple, and specific direction to guide planning, product, and market initiatives throughout the organization.

Linking Strategy to Planning and Budgeting

Dow Chemical took the initial strategic product/market approach just described through a rigorous step-by-step process that addresses more specific questions about products, markets, capabilities, and results:

- What is the most appropriate way to group, classify, or segment products and markets?
- How is relative future product/market emphasis determined?
- For each major change in future emphasis, how valid are the underlying marketplace and competitive assumptions? (These relate to such assumptions as market size and growth, buying motives, and strengths and weaknesses of the product.)
- How are products positioned to meet the requirements of the marketplace and competitive assumptions? (These relate to such requirements as product functions and features, pricing, promotion, and packaging.)
- What capabilities are needed to meet the positioning requirements? (These might include market research, product development, production processes, and sales skills.)
- What are the major product plans needed to achieve the positioning and capability requirements? (These might include end-result objectives, action steps, timing, and accountability.)
- What results can be expected for each product/market project? (These would involve such results as volume growth in revenue or units, ROI, and ROS.)
- What performance measures must be in place to determine whether the action plans resulting from strategy are on track?

When these questions are addressed, an organization has a strategic basis for developing its long- and short-range plans along with product, market, and resource-compatibility projects that respond to the strategic choices it has made. These can then be built into the operating budget.

Lee Shobe, vice-president of sales and marketing for Dow Chemical's US Area Plastics Group, describes the integration between strategy and planning that comes from this approach:

"We evaluate the tactical implications of the strategy. To verify our strategic assumptions about future product and market emphasis, we measure the size of each opportunity, the financial impact, and the degree to which it is competitively satisfied today. We also explore how we could better meet the need. Then, spelling out the positioning requirements closes the loop from a strategic thrust to an operating initiative. When you get through this process, you've got all that is needed to develop a complete action plan.

"The annual plans are the summation of all that is needed for the next year. This puts requests for resources into the [product/market] matrix and allows us to be sure we are putting these incremental resources where the strategic emphasis requires them.

"For example, when the new strategic direction tells us to emphasize polyethylene in microwaveable trays, then we must have a resource plan to back it up. If it isn't there, we're obviously kidding ourselves, either in the strategic element of the plan or on the operational side.

"This entire approach to strategy is ideal for operational planning. It takes away any mystery about linking strategy to action planning."

Conclusion

Strategy and long-range planning and decision making need not be at odds. Wilfried Sander, a general manager of the tractor division of the Varity Corp., located in the United Kingdom, illustrates how strategy and operational planning can be integrated when he describes the planning in his company's purchasing function:

"We developed a five-year business plan for the purchasing department based on the tractor division and purchasing department strategies. Every year we just update the plan, because it doesn't change that much. It may change in the first year, but the overall track of it doesn't change. Then, once each year, we do the annual budget.

"Having been through the company's strategy, the purchasing strategy, and the five-year plan, we develop the annual budget by simply breaking down into 12 months what was in the strategy and five-year plan. Our annual plan is the vehicle for getting our strategy implemented.

"For example, we knew that attacking cost was one of the major ways the purchasing area could support the tractor division's products-offered strategy. A big step in this direction was to establish a cost reduction department, which would manage the cost of the total tractor. We then developed a five-year plan for the new function, outlining the objectives for the department, how it would function and be staffed, and the specific cost reduction targets over the time frame. All this was reflected in the annual plan."

As senior executives and those down the line think carefully about the implications of strategy on product/market categories, positioning, resources, project plans, and financial results, we move toward the right of the strategy and operations continuum, where much of the analyses and conclusions lean more toward operations. Here is where all the operational tools—from long-range planning to budgeting—play a vital role in ensuring that at some point down the road, an organization will realize its goal. ∎

> **"Strategy and long-range planning and decision making need not be at odds."**

Part II
Strategic Planning at the Business Level

Adapting Strategic Planning to the Changing Needs of a Business

Balaji S. Chakravarthy
University of Minnesota, Minneapolis, USA, and
Peter Lorange
The Norwegian School of Management, Sandvika, Norway

This article focuses on how the strategic planning system can facilitate the pursuit of different business missions within a multibusiness firm. In such a firm, the business unit (popularly called the SBU or strategic business unit) is typically the smallest organisational entity that is responsible for strategic decisions.

In recent years, both the popular business press and academia have blamed strategic planning systems for the failure of business units within western multibusiness firms to be innovative and globally competitive (Mintzberg and Waters, 1985; Peters and Waterman, 1982). Implicit in their criticisms is the assumption that a strategic planning system cannot but be *integrative* in its orientation. An integrative planning system is designed to assist the business unit defend its chosen niche and exploit efficiently the opportunities available in that niche. The emphasis is more on process innovation and not on product innovation (Lorange, 1980).

We suggest in this article that the orientation of a strategic planning system is a matter of managerial choice. The system can be designed for several different orientations along the integration-adaptation spectrum. In contrast with an integrative system, an adaptive planning system can assist the business unit discover and consolidate new niches in its chosen environment. The emphasis of the system is on developing new competences and improving the effectiveness of a business unit through product/market innovations (Lorange, 1980).

There is nothing inherently virtuous or unworthy about either an adaptive or integrative orientation; in fact both orientations are appropriate depending on the context of a business unit. What is important for the effective management of a business unit is to ensure congruence between its changing context and the strategic planning system in use.

Although a large number of approaches to the design of strategic planning systems are described in the literature, relatively little emphasis has been placed on how to tailor them to different business contexts (Lorange, 1980). We seek to provide in this article a framework for adapting the strategic planning system of a firm to its business context.

The helpful comments provided by the referees on earlier versions of this article are gratefully acknowledged.

The article is organised into three sections. The first section provides a framework for classifying the context of a business unit and describes the strategic challenge in each of the four distinct business contexts that are identified. The next section discusses the key elements in the design of a strategic planning system. The final section elaborates how the planning system can be tailored to meet the distinct challenges in each business context.

Classifying Business Contexts

The context of a business unit has been classified in the literature in a number of ways. One of the earliest classification schemes was proposed by Bruce Henderson (1979) and his colleagues at the Boston Consulting Group (BCG). They suggested that the context of a business unit can be defined in terms of the attractiveness of its industry segment (as measured by the segment's growth rate) and by the strengths of the business unit in that segment (as measured by the business unit's relative market share). Popularly called the growth-share matrix, this classification scheme was improved on later by General Electric and consulting firms, such as McKinsey and Arthur D. Little (Hax and Majluf, 1984; Rothschild, 1976). Although these later schemes added more measures to the two dimensions of the growth-share matrix, they were, in essence, similar to the BCG matrix. Business strategy is determined in all of these matrices by the position of a business unit in the classification matrix.

A more recent approach, proposed by Michael Porter (1980), challenges the determinism implicit in the above classification schemes. It suggests that within any industry environment, a business unit has several strategic alternatives ranging in competitive scope from broad to narrow and in emphasis from cost leadership to differentiation. For example, in a mature and highly competitive industry such as metal containers, the Crown Cork and Seal Company was able to find an attractive niche by choosing to serve select customers who were more interested in quality products, excellent technical support, and quick delivery of smaller lot size orders rather than in lower price alone (Hamermesh et al., 1977). The company, contrary to the conventional wisdom in that industry, chose to produce only steel cans and not aluminium cans. Even though its market share was low, it was the most profitable firm in its industry.

As in the Crown Cork and Seal example, a creative business manager can unearth attractive opportunities even in mature and declining industries (Hamermesh et al., 1977; Woo and Cooper, 1982). Therefore, it is not industry structure alone that should define the environment of a business unit. In addition, the strategy intended for that business unit must also be considered (see Figure 1). The context of a business unit is shaped by its strategic intent.

Strategic intent is a concise description of the direction in which top management desires that an organisational unit should head in order to survive and prosper (Hamel and Prahalad, 1989). There can be disagreements between top management, divisional managers and business unit managers on what the appropriate strategic intent should be for a given business unit. Figure 1 describes the shared strategic intent that results from the negotiations across organisational levels in the strategic planning process.

Figure 1.
Context, Strategy and Process

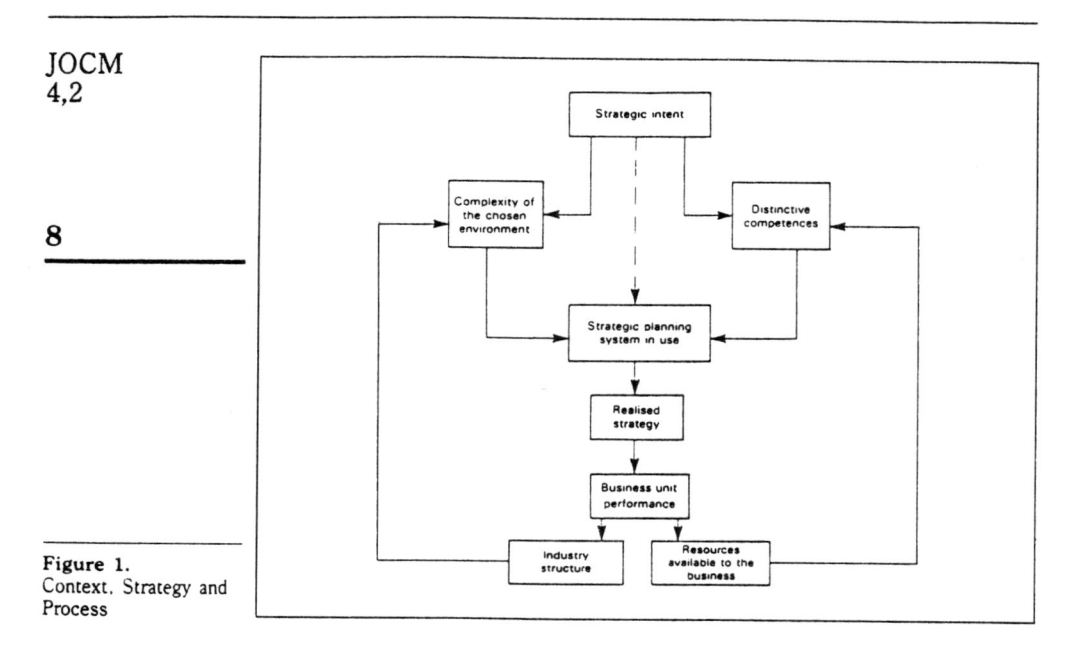

We define the context of a business unit in terms of two dimensions: the environmental complexity associated with its *chosen* industry niche and its distinctive competences in that niche (Figure 1). The framework proposed here is very different from the growth-share matrix and its successors. First, it explicitly recognises the role of strategic intent in shaping the environmental context of a business unit. Second, it suggests that the competitive position of a business unit in its chosen environment should not be measured by its past performance, for example, its market share. Rather, it should be measured by the number of distinct competences that it has to compete with in its chosen niche.

The environmental complexity associated with a business unit is a function of both the heterogeneity and the unpredictability of the stakeholders who confront it in its chosen niche. The stakeholders of a business include its competitors, suppliers, customers, various regulatory bodies, and host communities (Freeman, 1984). The more numerous the stakeholders with whom a business unit must deal, and the less transparent their agendas, the more heterogeneous is the environment that the business unit faces. Additionally, if either the constellation of stakeholders or their agendas keep changing frequently, it becomes difficult for a business unit manager to predict the opportunities and threats in his or her chosen environment with any certainty. The business environment under these conditions is also simultaneously unpredictable.

It is important to note that environmental complexity is as *perceived* by the manager of a business unit. This perception is a function of both the objective characteristics of the niche in which a business unit chooses to operate and the lack of familiarity of its managers with that niche. Therefore, any exploration beyond the niche that a business unit currently operates in can potentially increase environmental complexity, especially if the exploration is in unrelated products and markets. Because industry niche is a matter of choice, it may be asked: Why would a manager choose to operate in a business associated with high environmental complexity? A primary reason for this choice may be the future financial payoffs that the manager sees in the niche. Also, the business unit may not have a better option.

Just as the environment of a business unit cannot be defined without an understanding of the business unit's strategy, similarly the resources available to a business unit cannot be evaluated without considering its strategy. For example, large-scale operational and logistical capacity may be critical to a business unit that seeks to be a cost leader; other competences, such as technological know-how, reputation, and brand name, may be more important to a business unit that aims at being a differentiated player.

Distinctive competences refer to the resources, which are not easily tradable, imitable or substitutable, that a business unit has in support of its strategy (Dierickz and Cool, 1989). The more distinctive competences that a business unit has, the better able it is to defend its strategy from existing and potential competitors (Porter, 1980). Both tangible and intangible resources can contribute to its distinctive competence (Chakravarthy, 1987). The former includes material reserves and operational and logistical capacities; the latter includes technical and managerial know-how, motivation and commitment of employees, and the firm's reputation. Depending on the strategy with which the business unit chooses to compete, one of these sets of resources may lead to distinctive competences for the business unit. As we noted earlier, if the business unit seeks to compete in the low-cost segment, it needs relatively more of the tangible resources; if it wants to be a specialised competitor, it may require relatively more of the intangible resources.

The classification grid proposed in Figure 2 defines four business contexts. The demarcation between the four contexts is intentionally drawn with wavy lines to show that the definition of a business context is influenced significantly by the strategic intent of a business. The contexts are labelled by the primary strategic challenge faced in each: Pioneer, Expand, Reorient and Dominate. Each of these labels has a positive ring to it — implying that no matter what the context, a business unit can perform well if it has a creative strategy. Also, the labels convey the potential for self-renewal in *all* business contexts. In this respect, Figure 2 is very different from the traditional business strategy matrices.

Strategic Challenges in the Four Business Contexts
Pioneer
The most risky of the four contexts is Pioneer, a business context defined by high environmental complexity and few distinctive competences. The environmental flux can present the business unit with attractive opportunities, but it typically does not have the resources to exploit many of them. The primary planning challenge in this context is for the business unit to carve a niche in

Figure 2.
Desired Planning System Characteristics under Different Business Contexts

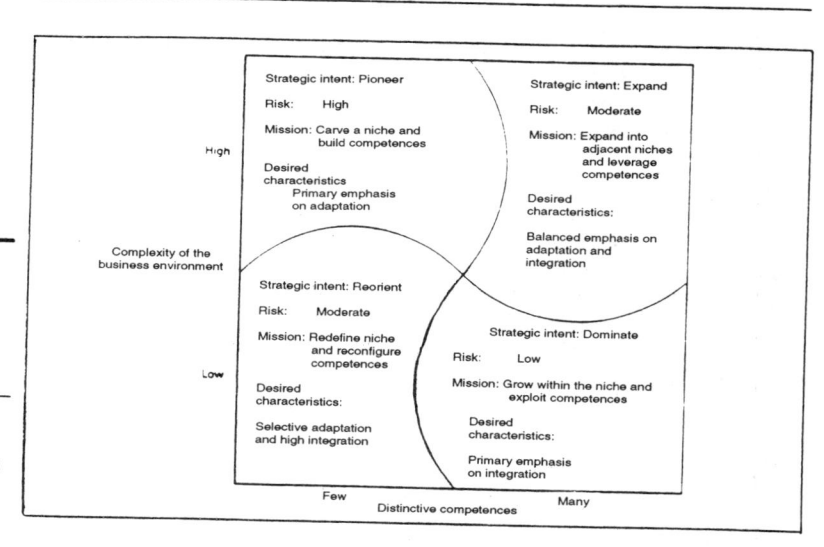

[Figure 2: Diagram showing four business contexts based on Complexity of the business environment (High/Low) vs. Distinctive competences (Few/Many):

- **Strategic intent: Pioneer** — Risk: High; Mission: Carve a niche and build competences; Desired characteristics: Primary emphasis on adaptation
- **Strategic intent: Expand** — Risk: Moderate; Mission: Expand into adjacent niches and leverage competences; Desired characteristics: Balanced emphasis on adaptation and integration
- **Strategic intent: Reorient** — Risk: Moderate; Mission: Redefine niche and reconfigure competences; Desired characteristics: Selective adaptation and high integration
- **Strategic intent: Dominate** — Risk: Low; Mission: Grow within the niche and exploit competences; Desired characteristics: Primary emphasis on integration]

which it can thrive despite its limited resources. Because of the riskiness of the context, it may be prudent to limit the size of the investment placed at risk in this business unit. If the exploration is unsuccessful within those limits, the business unit may have to exit from such a business context. The other major emphasis in this business context should be on building competences. Even a failed exploration offers the potential to help the firm build a new competency. The predominant administrative orientation that is appropriate in this context is that of a Prospector (Miles and Snow, 1978).

Expand

In contrast to the Pioneer business context, the Expand business context is typically less risky. Even though the environmental complexity continues to be high, the business unit manager should have little difficulty in identifying a viable niche because of the business unit's many distinctive competences. The primary challenge for the manager in this context is to expand the business unit's position in adjacent business niches by leveraging its competences in its core niche. The predominant administrative orientation that is desired in this context is that of an Analyser (Miles and Snow, 1978).

Reorient

In a Reorient business context, environmental complexity is low. The stakeholders for the business unit are well identified, and their actions are predictable. But the business unit's relatively small number of distinctive competences prevents it from exploiting this knowledge. The challenge for a business unit manager in such a context is to reorient the business by participating in only the more attractive subsegments of its industry niche. The manager should also attempt to reconfigure the business unit's competences, strengthening those that are relevant to the more focused strategy that is necessary in this context. Here again, the predominant administrative orientation that is needed in this context is that of an Analyser (Miles and Snow, 1978).

Dominate
The Dominate business context is the least risky of the four contexts described in Figure 2. The business unit experiences an environment of low complexity and enjoys many distinctive competencies in it. It has a well-protected niche and experiences stable relationships with its stakeholders in a slowly changing environment. The primary endeavour of the manager in such a context should be to exploit opportunities so that the business unit dominates the chosen niche by growing aggressively and profitably. The administrative orientation that is appropriate to this context is that of a Defender (Miles and Snow, 1978).

Designing the Strategic Planning System
The Critical Design Elements
The relative emphasis on adaptation or integration in a business unit can be altered by manipulating four key elements (see Table I) in its strategic planning system: (1) nature of goal setting, (2) time-spending patterns in planning, (3) the relative importance of the strategic budget to the business unit, and (4) the linkage between the financial plan and the strategic budget.

Direction of Goal Setting
In the first step of the strategic planning process, top management interacts with divisional and business unit managers to finalise corporate objectives and to translate these into goals and strategies at their levels (Lorange, 1980). The nature of the interactions between these various levels of managers can vary from firm to firm. We describe here two distinct types of interactions and discuss their implications for the orientation of a planning system.

In certain business units the goals proposed by top management are not really open to extensive discussion. The meetings between top management and business unit managers are primarily meant for communicating these goals. Such a planning system is more integrative in its orientation. The premise behind top management's behaviour is that no major changes are necessary in the business unit's strategic thrust. Discussions with business unit managers on their goals are brief because past performance data are available to judge how reasonable are the goals imposed from the top.

By contrast, goal setting has to be much more participative and iterative for an adaptive planning orientation. A top-down goal setting process is not conducive to some business units that are expected to search for new opportunities. The managers of these business units must be able to renegotiate at various steps of the strategic planning system the goals that they commit to top management in the objectives-setting step. Denying them the opportunity to do so will force them to set very conservative goals.

Table I. Designing the Strategic Planning System for Integration or Adaptation

Design element	Orientation: Integration	Orientation: Adaptation
(1) Nature of goal setting	Top down	Participative and iterative
(2) Time spending patterns in planning	Relatively more time spent on budgeting	Relatively more time spent on objectives setting and strategic programming
(3) Relative importance of budgets	Operating budget more important	Strategic budget more important
(4) Linkage between the financial plan and budgets	Very tight	Relatively loose

It would clearly be desirable to have a participative and iterative goal-setting process in all contexts. Rich interactions between top management and business unit managers in the objectives-setting step are vital to any business unit. However, one of the scarcest resources in large corporations is top management time. Top management must, as a *minimum*, ensure that the goal-setting process is participative and iterative in those business contexts where it wishes to encourage adaptation.

Time-spending Patterns in Planning
There are three steps in the strategic planning process: objectives setting, strategic programming, and budgeting (Vancil and Lorange, 1975). The goals and business strategies agreed to in the first step get detailed into cross-functional programmes in the next step and are finally translated into budgets in the budgeting step. Depending on the planning orientation it wishes to provide, top management may choose to allocate its scarce time in one of two distinct patterns: a back-end emphasis, or a front-end emphasis.

In some business contexts, top management may choose to have short objectives-setting and strategic programming steps with limited interactions and spend most of its time with a business unit in the budgeting step. This back-end emphasis in planning is not conducive to adaptation but can support integration. Here again, the premise behind top management's behaviour is that the basic strategic thrust of the business unit does not require major change. Although the business unit may need a few new strategic programmes, its main focus is on the efficient implementation of a well-understood strategy. How a business unit details the agreed-upon strategy in its operating budgets is, therefore, critical. The back-end emphasis of top management is aimed at helping business units with this challenge.

If, however, top management wishes to provide an adaptive orientation to the planning system, it must shift its emphasis to the front end of the planning system. The objectives-setting and strategic programming steps would take longer in order to accommodate the large number of interactions and iterations that may be necessary before a new strategic thrust can be shaped for a business unit. Top management involvement throughout this lengthy process is critical for adaptation.

The Relative Importance of the Strategic Budget
In the budgeting step of the strategic planning system, both the strategic budget and the operating budget of a business unit are finalised. The operating budget refers to the budget through which capital investments and expenses required to sustain the current strategic momentum of a business unit are allocated. The strategic budget, on the other hand, is used to allocate the capital investments and expenses required for strategic leap — that is, either to engineer major restructuring of an existing business or to pursue a new business opportunity. It is important to note that the two budgets proposed here are quite different from the capital and expense budgets that are typically assigned to business units (Figure 3).

The capital budget allocates capital resources, and the expense budget provides for human resources, research and development (R&D), and business intelligence gathering expenses. All of these resources — that is, capital investment, working capital, human resources, and technological and business know-how — are required both to sustain current strategic momemtum and to accomplish strategic leap (Lorange et al., 1986). Therefore, unless these resources are clearly earmarked in an operating and strategic budget, respectively, there is the real danger that resources allocated for engineering strategic leap may get diverted to sustaining strategic momentum. Or alternatively, where the business unit is judged on its return on investment, these resources may not be expended as planned due to fear of increasing investment without a corresponding return in the short term. Moreover, a firm's control and incentive systems may encourage such a bias primarily by monitoring and rewarding short-term performance.

Some companies, like Texas Instruments (Vancil, 1972), have indeed followed the approach recommended here, with a clear distinction between the strategic and operating budgets. Although it is preferable to have distinct operating and strategic budgets, it is not a must. What is required, at a minimum, is a careful

	Classification proposed here	
Commonly used classification	*Strategic budget*	*Operating budget*
Capital budget (fixed assets, working capital)	Investments that appear on the balance sheet	
Expense budget (human resources, R&D, business intelligence)	Investments that do not appear on the balance sheet	Expenses

Figure 3. A Typology of Budgets

accounting of investments and expenses under these two budget categories. In the Vick International Division of Richardson-Merrell, for example, resources required to pursue new strategies were allocated to a country budget along with the resources required to sustain the momentum of existing strategies (Vancil and Browne, 1978). However, the resources expended on each strategy were meticulously tracked through distinct work programmes. As long as the monitoring process ensures that resources are expended only on the purposes for which they were budgeted, the absence of a separate operating and strategic budget is not a handicap.

It is obvious that in an adaptive planning system, the strategic budget of a business unit will be considerably more important than its operating budget. The bulk of the resources demanded by the business unit are for either carving a new business niche or building distinctive competences. In an integrative planning system, the operating budget is likely to be more important. Even though the business unit may continue to be the recipient of some funds through the strategic budget, these will be small when compared to the size of its operating budget.

Linkage between the Financial Plan and the Budgets
The fourth design element refers to the tightness of the linkage between the long-term financial plan as formulated in the strategic programming step and the budgets as approved in the budgeting step. A long-term financial plan is prepared for each business unit at the end of the strategic programming step. This plan includes both investments and expenses associated with new strategic programmes, as well as those required for ongoing operations. A long-term capital expenditure and profit plan for the business unit is approved by top management at the end of the strategic programming step, and the strategic and operating budgets proposed in the budgeting step should normally correspond to this plan. When the correspondence is exact, the linkage between the financial plan and the budgets is said to be tight.

However, in the case of a business unit that is developing a new strategic thrust, the planning process cannot artificially be frozen at the end of the programming step. Major environmental changes can occur during the three- or four-month lag between the two steps. The business unit may have to revise its strategic programmes and the associated financial plan. These revisions may often be reflected directly in the strategic and operating budgets proposed by a business unit. The budgets will therefore be at variance from the financial plan that was submitted during the strategic programming step. Unless this "loose linkage" is tolerated by top management, strategic thinking will freeze in a business unit once its financial plan is approved. Such an orientation is not very conducive to adaptation.

The tightness of the linkage between the long-term financial plan and a business unit's budgets can be measured along two key dimensions: content linkage and timing linkage (Shank *et al.*, 1973). Content linkage refers to the commonality between a business unit's long-term financial plan and its budgets on format and content and the precision with which the numbers are presented. The more the commonality that is insisted on, the tighter is the linkage. Timing linkage is tight if the budgets are prepared prior to the financial plan. In such a system planning can be reduced to a mere extrapolation of the budgets.

Adapting the Planning Process to the Context of a Business

In an earlier section we identified four distinct business contexts. Of these, the Pioneer business context needed a predominantly adaptive orientation, and the Dominate business context needed a predominantly integrative orientation. The two ideal types of system configurations described in Table I are tailor-made for these two contexts. We will first describe the strategic planning system appropriate to the Pioneer and Dominate business contexts before addressing the needs of the other two contexts.

Pioneer

Given the high environmental complexity of this business unit, the strategic planning system in use should encourage participative goal setting. Top management may not understand the business context sufficiently to set credible goals in a top-down fashion. Also, the objectives-setting and strategic programming steps should get relatively more of top management's attention than the budgeting step does. As we noted earlier, the primary challenge for this business unit is to discover defensible niches and to develop new competences. The budgeting step is meaningful only so far as the resource limit for such exploration is specified in the strategic budget.

The linkage between the long-term financial plan and the budgets should deliberately be kept loose, so as not to force the business unit manager to implement plans that can rapidly become obsolete.

Dominate

In contrast with the adaptive strategic planning system described above, an integrative strategic planning system is required in a Dominate business context. As we described earlier, this business context is characterised by low environmental complexity and many distinctive competences. The business environment is highly predictable, and the few surprises that it may offer can easily be handled by the business unit, given its many distinctive competences. The goal setting in such a context can be top-down. First, top management has adequate data on the business unit's past performance and a good forecast of its future environment to set goals in a top-down fashion. Second, and most important, by setting difficult but achievable profit goals, top management can induce business unit managers to search for new ways of exploiting their favourable industry niche. The emphasis in the strategic planning system must also shift to the budgeting step. Exploiting current opportunities is the key challenge in this context. Although objectives setting and strategic programming are still important, they do not need to be as long drawn as in the Pioneer business context. This is not to suggest that a business unit in a Dominate business context has no room for innovation but to acknowledge that such innovation will be focused on process efficiencies rather than on new products or services. The link between the business unit's long-term financial plan and its budgets can be tight, as changes in the business unit's environment can be forecast in the strategic programming step with some accuracy.

Expand

In this business context, the business unit has to be simultaneously adaptive and integrative — it needs a system that is a hybrid of the two systems described above.

Given its high environmental complexity, as in a Pioneer context, goal setting in this context should be participative. Top management must also spend more time with this business unit in the objectives-setting and strategic programming steps. In addition, as in a Dominate context, the budgeting step is very important in this context. Because the business unit has a strong position in its industry niche, it should be encouraged to set a challenging operating budget. However, unlike the situation in a Dominate context, the business unit manager should be allowed to renegotiate his or her strategic budget if the manager can show that it is necessitated by changes in the business environment that are outside his or her control and could not have been foreseen.

The link between the financial plan and the operating budget has to be tight if the business unit is to be encouraged to start earning returns on its investments. However, the link with the strategic budget may have to be loose. Both the plan and the strategic budget should be revised periodically if the environmental assumptions made by the business unit in the strategy-making process are subsequently proven to be erroneous.

Reorient

This is a difficult business context to manage because it calls for either a dramatic turnaround or a divestiture (Porter, 1980). There are two distinct processes that must be employed here:

(1) identify products in which the business does not have and cannot build many distinctive competences and divest these as quickly as possible for the best salvage price;

(2) target products that not only have a higher-than-average growth potential for the industry but also ones in which the business can build distinctive competences.

The strategic planning system is thus differentiated within this business context to suit the mission assigned to each product line.

The product lines that are targeted for divestment in a Reorient business clearly require an integrative focus until they are sold. This will help improve the contributions from these product lines. The other product lines may require more of an adaptive focus as the business unit tries to reposition itself in their markets.

Adapting to the Changing Context

The context of a business unit remains invariant only in the medium term. In the long run, its context can change due to both changes in the resources available to the business unit and in the structure of the industry in which it participates (see Figure 1). In fact, sustained superior performance can itself be a destabilising force because of its direct impact on the resources of the business units and its indirect effects on the structure of its industry. These influences can lead to a reassessment of the business unit's strategic intent, requiring in turn a realignment of the strategic planning system.

During its evolution a business unit can experience several of the strategic challenges that were described earlier. For example, Komatsu — the Japanese earth-moving equipment manufacturer — has passed through the Reorient, Dominate and Expand business contexts in its quest to become a dominant global competitor (Bartlett and Rangan, 1985). In the 1960s the company focused on its home market and on smaller machines, while it tried to upgrade its product and process technologies and improve its quality, its strategic intent in that era was clearly Reorient in the face of strong international competition from Caterpillar in its home market. Having successfully built its competences in the 1970s in markets that were relatively simple, as in Eastern Europe and in the Third World countries, its strategic intent in that era was Dominate. But once these niches began to become saturated, the company enhanced its competences further in new product development and entered the more complex European and North American markets in the late 1970s. Its strategic intent had changed to Expand. One can see this evolution as prototypical of any business unit that is engaged in self-renewal, calling for alternate phases of competency building, niche domination and niche expansion. The strategic planning system appropriate to each of these phases is distinct, and failure to provide the necessary process support can abort business self-renewal.

Conclusion

In this article we provided a framework for classifying a business context. The two dimensions of the framework are the complexity of the business unit's chosen industry niche and the business unit's distinctive competences in that niche. In a clear departure from the popular classification schemes in use, our framework recognises that the environmental complexity and the distinctive competences of a business unit can be measured only with reference to its strategic intent. Classifying a business context should not therefore be a mechanical exercise but an important decision process in and of itself. The industry structure in which the business unit participates and its resources do affect its context, but strategic choice can mediate their influence (see Figure 1).

Depending on the positioning of a business unit within the two-dimensional grid that is proposed, its context can be described as Pioneer, Expand, Reorient, or Dominate. These labels are chosen to indicate the primary challenge of the business unit in each of these contexts. The contexts vary in their risk and in the adaptation and/or integration orientation that they demand of the strategic planning system.

We then discussed four key elements of the strategic planning system: direction of goal setting, time-spending patterns in planning, the relative importance of the strategic budget, and the linkage between the financial plan and the budgets. We also examined how these elements can be configured to meet the needs of each of the four business contexts.

Given that the context of a business unit can change over the long run due to: (1) external factors that affect the complexity of its environment, (2) changes in the distinctive competences of the business itself, and (3) modifications in the strategic intent of the business, the strategic planning system in use will also have to be redesigned periodically. Unless this evolution in the planning system is *managed proactively*, the administrative context that is required to support the changing mission of the business unit will be lacking. If strategic planning systems have indeed failed in the past it is because managers have failed to retailor them to the changing context of their business units.

References

Bartlett, C.A. and Rangan, U.S. (1985), "Komatsu Limited", Harvard Business School case 9-385-277, Harvard Graduate School of Business Administration, Boston, MA.

Chakravarthy, B.S. (1987), "Human Resource Management and Strategic Change: Challenges in Two Deregulated Industries", in Niehaus, R.J. (Ed.), *Strategic Human Resource Planning Applications*, Plenum Publishing, New York, pp. 17-27.

Dierickz, I. and Cool, K. (1989), "Asset Stock Accumulation and Sustainability of Competitive Advantage", *Management Science*, Vol. 35 No. 12, pp. 1504-11.

Freeman, E. (1984), *Strategic Management: A Stakeholder Approach*, Pitman, Marshfield, MA.

Hamel, G. and Prahalad, C.K. (1989), "Strategic Intent", *Harvard Business Review*, May-June, pp. 63-76.

Hamermesh, R., Gordon, K.D. and Reed, J.P. (1977), Crown Cork and Seal Company, Inc., Harvard Business School case 9-378-024, Harvard Graduate School of Business Administration, Boston, MA.

Hax, A. and Majluf, N.S. (1984), *Strategic Management: An Integrative Perspective*, Prentice-Hall, Englewood Cliffs, NJ.

Lorange, P. (1980), *Corporate Planning: An Executive Viewpoint*, Prentice-Hall, Englewood Cliffs, NJ.

Lorange, P., Scott Morton, M.F. and Ghoshal (1986), *Strategic Control*, West Publishing Company, St. Paul, MN.

Miles, R.E. and Snow, C.C. (1978), *Organizational Strategy, Structure and Process*, McGraw-Hill, New York.

Mintzberg, H. and Waters, J.A. (1985), "On Strategies, Deliberate and Emergent", *Strategic Management Journal*, Vol. 6, pp. 257-72.

Peters, T.J. and Waterman, R.H. (1982), *In Search of Excellence*, Harper & Row, New York.

Porter, M.E (1980), *Competitive Strategy*, Free Press, New York.

Rothschild, W. (1976), *Putting It All Together: A Guide to Strategic Thinking*, AMACOM, New York.

Shank, J. et al., (1973),"Balance Creativity and Practicality in Formal Planning", *Harvard Business Review*, January-February, pp. 87-95.

Vancil, R.F. (1972), "Texas Instruments Incorporated: Management Systems in 1972", Harvard Business School case 9-172-054, Harvard Graduate School of Business Administration, Boston, MA.

Vancil, R.F. and Browne, P.C. (1978), Vick International Division: Tom McGuire, Harvard Business School case 9-179-068, Harvard Graduate School of Business Administration, Boston, MA.

Vancil, R.F. and Lorange, P. (1975), Strategic Planning in Diversified Companies, *Harvard Business Review*, January-February, pp. 81-90.

Woo, C.Y. and Cooper, A.C. (1982), The Surprising Case for Low Market Share, *Harvard Business Review*, Vol. 60 No. 6, pp. 106-13.

Further Reading

Chakravarthy, B.S. and Lorange, P. (1991), *Managing the Strategy Process*, Prentice-Hall, Englewood Cliffs, NJ.

Hamermesh, R.G. et al. (1978), "Strategies for Low Market Share Businesses", *Harvard Business Review*, Vol. 56 No. 3, pp. 95-102.

Henderson, B.D. (1979), *Henderson on Corporate Strategy*, Abt Books.

Pinchott, G., III, (1985), *Intrapreneuring*, Harper & Row, New York.

ON TAILORING A STRATEGIC PLANNING SYSTEM TO ITS CONTEXT: SOME EMPIRICAL EVIDENCE

BALAJI S. CHAKRAVARTHY
School of Management, University of Minnesota, Minneapolis, Minnesota, U.S.A.

Based on a survey of 111 senior executives this study finds that tailoring a firm's strategic planning system to its context is not a popular practice, despite its presumed importance. Moreover, the lack of fit between a firm's strategic planning system and its context appears to be inconsequential to how managers rate their planning systems. Implications of the findings are discussed.

It has been argued that a well-designed formal strategic planning system (FSPS) must be continuously tailored both to an organization's external and internal contexts (Christenson, 1982; Steiner, 1979). Several scholars (Lorange, 1980; Lorange and Vancil, 1977; Nathanson, Kazanjian and Galbraith, 1982; Newman, 1975; Steiner, 1982) have suggested how such a tailoring should be done. However, there have been very few systematic efforts at empirically testing the validity of these contingency frameworks. This paper attempts to operationalize the notion of fit between a planning system and its context, and seeks to explore whether such a fit is an important determinant of how a planning system is evaluated by the firm's managers.

A CONCEPTUAL FRAMEWORK

The basic framework used in this study is described in Figure 1.

Planning system characteristics

Seven distinct characteristics of a planning system have been discussed in the literature: its emphasis on creativity or control (Camillus, 1975; Lorange and Vancil, 1977; Shank, Niblock and Sandalls, 1973); its reliance on analytical techniques (Grant and King, 1979; Hax and Majluf, 1984); its attention to resource audit (Grant and King, 1982; King and Cleland, 1978); its efforts at environmental scanning (Aguilar, 1965; Fahey and King, 1977; its functional coverage (Hitt, Ireland and Palia, 1982; Snow and Hrebiniak, 1980); the resources provided for planning (King, 1983; Steiner, 1979); and the resistance to planning within a firm (Steiner, 1979).

In a recent empirical study, Ramanujam, Venkatraman and Camillus (1986) found that of the above characteristics the three most significant are resistance to planning within the firm, resources provided for planning, and its emphasis on creativity or control. No planning system can be very effective if it faces resistance or if it is denied sufficient resources. This study focuses exclusively on the third characteristic that addresses the balance between creativity and control orientations in a planning system, and explores how it is tailored to suit the context of a firm.

Received 10 March 1986
Revised 29 August 1986

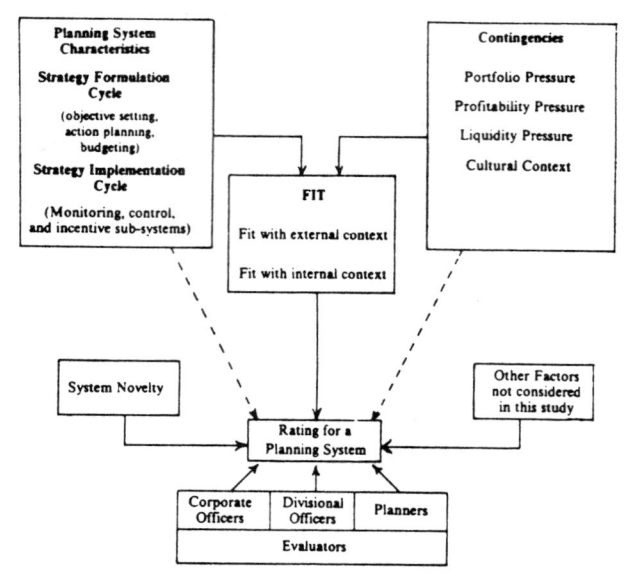

Figure 1. Determinants of the rating for a planning system: the framework used in this study

Balancing creativity and control

Lorange (1980) distinguishes between two orientations in planning: adaptive and integrative. The adaptive orientation nurtures creativity. It helps the firm 'systematically look for opportunities and/or threats in its environment to come up with the best alternatives for the firm to pursue' (Lorange, 1980: 4). An integrative orientation, on the other hand, focuses more on control. It 'facilitates the narrowing down of the options in such a way that a basis can be provided for achieving an efficient course of operation' (Lorange, 1980: 6).

The relative emphasis on adaptation or integration in a firm's strategic planning system can be discerned by analyzing six key elements in its design (Lorange, 1980). Three of these are part of the strategy formulation cycle: direction of goal setting, linkage between action plans and budgets, and whether the corporate planner is a strategist or a catalyst in the planning process.

The three other elements are part of the strategy implementation cycle: frequency with which strategic plans are monitored, the key performance parameters that are controlled, and the criteria used for incentive compensation. Depending on how these six elements are configured within a system, there are four basic ways (Table 1) in which creativity and control can be balanced in multi-business (Chakravarthy and Lorange, 1984).

Type One: centralized strategic planning

In this system, top management and corporate staff assume responsibility for all new strategic moves. Business-unit managers have a very limited role in strategy formulation—that of fine-tuning current strategies. Acquisitions and mergers are often the preferred route for entering new businesses.

Table 1. Four types of strategic planning systems

	Design element	Type One	Type Two	Type Three	Type Four
1.	Direction of goal-setting	Top-down	Bottom-up	Mixed mode (Leaning to top-down)	Mixed mode (Leaning to bottom-up)
2.	Linkage between action plans and budgets	Very tight	Very loose, as long as budgets are met	Loose for some divisions; tight for others	Simultaneously loose-tight for all divisions
3.	Role of corporate planner in strategy formulation	Strategist	Catalyst	Mixed role	Catalyst
4.	Frequency of monitoring strategic plans	Very frequent (once a month)	Frequent (once a quarter)	Very frequent for some, and once a year for others	Infrequent once-a-year review of all plans
5.	Nature of control	Strict adherence to profit budget	Strict adherence to profit budget	Both profit and growth objectives, depending on division	Both profit and growth objectives for all divisions
6.	Criteria for incentive compensation	Standard, universal criteria	Standard, universal criteria	Tailor-made criteria	Tailor-made criteria

Both the strategy formulation and implementation cycles have an integrative orientation in a Type One system. Goal-setting is top-down and the linkage between plans and budgets is very tight. The corporate planner is a strategist, who helps the CEO identify suitable acquisition and merger opportunities. Each business unit is a profit center, and is frequently monitored for its short-term profitability. Incentive systems are typically standardized across all business units and are based predominantly on performance against profit budgets.

Type Two: decentralized strategic planning

In contrast with Type One, in a Type Two planning system business units enjoy greater autonomy in strategy formulation. Typically business units are aggregated into clusters or 'business families' (Lorange, 1980) in order to exploit synergies among them. Each business family is a 'tub that stands on its own bottom', responsible for formulating and financing its own strategies.

The strategy formulation cycle in a Type Two system has an adaptive orientation. Goal-setting is bottom-up, and the linkage between the 5-year plan and budget is loose. Typically such a system is not associated with a corporate planner, and where one exists his/her role is advisory. The emphasis of top management is more on the strategy implementation cycle and not on the strategy formulation cycle. Control is frequent, and the profit targets assigned to each business family are closely monitored. Moreover, incentive systems are uniform across all business families, like in Type One, and tied to their profits.

Type Three: portfolio planning

Type Three is an extension of a Type Two system. It is popularly referred to as portfolio planning. In this system, like in Type Two, business-family managers participate in strategy formulation. However, their autonomy is more restricted. Their strategies have to conform to a corporate level portfolio plan (Wind and Mahajan, 1981). Moreover, all business families in Type Three are not allowed to focus as fully on their own self-renewal as was the case in Type Two. Top management controls resource allocation across business families. Consequently the strategy formulation cycle tends to be more integrative in a Type Three system than in a Type Two.

However, unlike both Type One and Type Two, the strategy implementation cycle in a Type Three system is not integrative for all business families. Depending on the misssion assigned to a business family, the monitoring, control, and incentive stages are tailor-made (Henderson, 1979; Wright, 1974). Thus if the mission is to milk a mature business the strategy implementation cycle will be associated with frequent control, and rewards will be dispensed based on performance against profit budgets. However, if the mission is to grow an emerging business, the control process will not be as rigid, and rewards will be determined more by a business family's market share rather than by its profit performance.

Type Four: dual focus

This planning system has been used in recent years by a few high-technology companies. Firms that use Type Four are linked in a matrix-like fashion both by a strategic and an operating structure, the former nurturing adaptation and the latter ensuring integration (Lorange, 1985).

The strategic structure is used to determine the objectives for each competitive segment of the firm, and to finalize the various action plans that are needed to achieve the chosen strategic objectives. The strategic structure, however, is not a permanent one. The more permanent operating structure deals with the implementation of strategies. Link between the strategic and operating structures is in the assignment of the roles to operating managers for executing a given action plan. Each operating department is thus tied (through the strategic structure) into several temporary supra-project organizations, each of which is responsible for a different strategy.

Business-unit managers enjoy considerable autonomy in both strategy formulation and implementation in a Type Four planning system. The strategy formulation cycle in such a system encourages bottom-up planning, and is loosely coupled with the budgeting process. The role of the corporate planner is that of a catalyst. Plans formulated in the strategic structure are implemented through the operating structure. Monitoring by top management is infrequent. The emphasis is on lateral coordination and self-control. The project team is typically rewarded on reaching various milestones in its plan, and the milestones themselves are adjusted if the context changes. In summary, both the strategy formulation and implementation cycles of a Type Four system are adaptive in their orientation.

Defining key contingencies

Each of the four types of planning discussed above is a valid approach for balancing creativity and control. However, depending on the specific context of a firm one of them may be more appropriate than the others. Two important contingencies that influence this choice are the portfolio and financial pressures experienced by the focal firm (Chakravarthy and Lorange, 1984).

Portfolio pressure varies with the severity of imbalances in the firm's business portfolio. It is a function both of the attractiveness of the industries in which the firm competes, and the intensity of competition in these industries. Thus a firm that participates in predominantly mature and fragmented industries faces very high portfolio pressure. In other words, even as the centroid of a firm's business portfolio starts drifting from the 'star' quadrant in a growth–share matrix to a 'dog' quadrant (Henderson, 1979), the portfolio pressure experienced by it starts building. Financial pressure, on the other hand, is inversely proportional to a firm's profitability and liquidity. If either a firm's profitability or liquidity is below average when compared with that of peer firms, the financial pressure experienced by it is said to be high.

High portfolio pressure calls for a strategy of diversification. Both Type One and Type Two planning systems can be useful in such a context. The former is especially suited to unrelated diversification and the latter to related diversification (Rumelt, 1974). Moreover, if financial pressure is also concurrently high, Type One is to be preferred. In such a context, top managment cannot afford to delegate strategic decision-making to business-unit managers. The top-down planning focus of Type One would be required to ensure that the scarce financial resources of the firm are carefully invested.

When portfolio pressure is not high, either a Type Three or Type Four system may be appropriate. Portfolio pressure may be low either because a firm has high diversity and good balance in its portfolio, or because the gravity point of a firm's limited portfolio falls within the emerging or growth business quadrant. Type Four is most appropriate in the latter case, because dual focus is possible only when there are interdependencies among the businesses in a firm's portfolio. When the diversity in a firm's portfolio increases,

Type Three is the more appropriate planning system. Furthermore Type Three is to be preferred if the financial pressures on the firm are high. In such a context, top managment may not have the luxury of allowing each business family to experiment (and perhaps fail) with radically new strategies. The strategy formulation cycle will, out of necessity, be more integrative.

Finally, the cultural setting of a firm is another important factor in choosing a planning system. In certain firms managers may consider it a 'loss of face' to revise a strategy that they had helped shape (Hamermesh, 1977), or they may be reluctant to offer new ideas for fear they may fail. A Type Two or Type Four planning system cannot be supported by such a firm. Both these systems are associated with an adaptive emphasis in the strategy formulation cycle. They require a cultural setting that encourages risk-taking and is tolerant of failures. In the absence of such an internal context, a Type One or Type Three planning system may be more appropriate.

Evaluating a planning system

Traditional research on planning systems has typically measured the effectiveness of a firm's planning sytem by its financial performance (see Armstrong, 1982 for a review). Many of these studies, however, ignore the long lead time required by a planning system before it can help improve a firm's financial results. Moreover, as Steiner (1982: 37) queries: 'The success of a company is the result of good management, not the planning system *per se*. So, how does one disentangle the effectiveness of a planning system from the capabilities of managers and their staff?'

Some recent studies have highlighted the importance of evaluating a planning system on criteria other than financial performance. The efficiency, adaptability, and ability of a planning system to facilitate decision-making have been identified as important alternative criteria used by managers to evaluate their planning systems (King, 1983; Ramanujam, Venkatraman and Camillus, 1986). King (1983) has further proposed a systematic approach for making such an evaluation more objective. However, his approach is more useful for an internal audit of a planning system rather than as a research instrument for measuring the effectiveness of a planning system. This study used the overall rating given to a planning system by its users as a measure of its effectiveness.

Planning system fit and its evaluation

Planning system fit

If the type of planning system used by a firm is appropriate to its portfolio and financial pressures, it enjoys an external fit. In addition, if the planning system is congruent with the firm's cultural context it also enjoys an internal fit. The external and internal fits enjoyed by a planning system are hypothesized here to have a significant impact on how it is rated by its users.

System novelty

However, it is important to consider the novelty of a system as a moderating variable in the proposed conceptual framework. The introduction of a new planning system or major modification to an existing system can take up to 5 years to be fully operational (Gage, 1982). A planning system that is not operational may not have acquired all of its intended characteristics and consequently may appear misfitted, even though its architects may evaluate it by its intended characteristics.

Other factors

Moreover, as discussed earlier, the two fits referred to above are not the only determinants of a planning system's rating. There are other system characteristics (not analyzed here) that also influence its rating.

Evaluators

Finally, the framework also recognizes that each group of internal stakeholders, like corporate officers, divisional officers, and planners, are likely to evaluate a planning system differently (King, 1983). It is hypothesized that external and internal fits of a planning system will be especially important criteria on which it will be rated by its chief architects—corporate officers and planners in a firm.

RESEARCH METHODOLOGY

The data required to test the above framework were collected through a questionnaire survey. The respondents were senior executives attending a general management program. The Appendix summarizes the key variables surveyed. In addition, the respondents were asked to describe their company culture briefly, and to provide background information on their planning system—such as when it was first initiated and last modified, the number and size of their firm's strategic business units (SBUs), etc.

The sample

A total of 163 executives were surveyed yielding 111 usable responses. All of the respondents came from diversified firms that had more than one strategic business unit (SBU). Firms in the sample represented 42 different industries (four-digit SIC code), and had sales ranging from 50 million to 65 billion dollars. The revenue earned by the largest SBU in the sample firms ranged from a low of 40 million to a high of 15 billion dollars.

All respondents selected were users of a formal strategic planning system (FSPS), and a majority of them (54 percent) were from firms that had used a FSPS for over 5 years. Sixty-seven respondents were line managers, and the rest were planners. Thirty-six of the line managers were from corporate headquarters (corporate officers), and the rest were divisional officers.

Testing the framework

Two major steps were followed for testing the framework proposed in Figure 1:

1. assessing the external and internal fits of a planning system, and
2. evaluating the importance of these fits for how a planning system was rated by its users.

Assessing fits

Based on the questionnaire data, each respondent's planning system was classified into one of the four types described earlier (see Table 1). The details of this procedure are provided in the next section. Similarly, the external context of a respondent's firm was assessed using the questionnaire data, and the planning type appropriate to it was determined using the contingency framework discussed earlier. Thus for each respondent in the data base, two planning systems were inferred: (1) the planning system in use (USESYS) based on the respondent's description of its characteristics; and (2) the planning system appropriate to its external context (REQSYS).

If the contingency framework proposed here is used by firms in the sample then their system in use (USESYS) must match the system appropriate to their external context (REQSYS), and must fit their internal cultural context (CUL). Both of these relationships were explored using a chi-square test of independence. If, for example, USESYS is contingent upon REQSYS then a chi-square test should reject the null hypothesis that the two categorical variables are independent. In other words, a high and significant chi-square would support the hypothesis that the contingency framework proposed here is indeed used by the firms in the sample.

Planning system fit and its rating

It was also hypothesized that the rating given to a planning system (PERF) should be strongly influenced by its fit to its external context (EXTFIT), and its fit to its internal context (INTFIT). EXTFIT is defined as a dummy variable which assumes a value of 1 when USESYS = REQSYS and is 0 otherwise. Similarly, INTFIT is a dummy variable that assumes a value of 1 if the planning system in use (USESYS) is a Type One or Type Three and culture of the firm supports integration, or if USESYS is Type Two or Type Four and the firm's culture supports adaptation. Regression and one-way analysis of variance were used to explore for significant relationships between the external and internal fits enjoyed by a firm's planning system and its evaluation by the firm's managers, moderating for the effects of system novelty.

OPERATIONALIZING THE FRAMEWORK

All the major variables used in the study, and their intercorrelations, are listed in Table 2. The

Table 2. Intercorrelations between variables in the study

Variable Name	Variable Description	V01	V02	V03	V04	V05	V06	V07	V08	V09	V16	V17	V19	V18	V20	V21	CUL	AGE	NOV	PERF
V01	Diversity	1.00																		
V02	Pressure to diversify	0.08	1.00																	
V03	Opportunities for related diversification	0.24**	0.16*	1.00																
V04	Pressure to acquire new business	0.12	0.28***	0.18*	1.00															
V05	Profitability	0.10	0.04	0.34**	0.12	1.00														
V06	Liquidity	0.20**	0.10	0.17**	0.07	0.31***	1.00													
V07	Earnings growth	0.09	0.12	0.37***	0.12	0.74***	0.28***	1.00												
V08	Debt/equity ratio	-0.18*	0.15	0.03	-0.03	-0.10	0.23*	-0.11	1.00											
V09	Market/book ratio	-0.15	0.02	-0.07	0.02	0.02	0.13	0.08	0.31***	1.00										
V16	Nature of goal setting	0.09	0.18*	0.04	0.02	0.12	0.03	0.24***	-0.05	0.14	1.00									
V17	Linkage between plans and budgets	0.07	0.16*	0.03	0.12	0.06	0.11	0.24***	0.12	0.00	0.17*	1.00								
V19	Frequency of monitoring strategic plans	0.12	0.21**	0.08	0.09	0.40***	0.21***	0.44***	0.00	-0.03	0.12	0.26***	1.00							
V18	Role of corporate planner	0.05	0.24**	0.01	0.15	-0.08	0.16	-0.04	0.14	0.02	0.12	0.17**	0.14	1.00						
V20	Nature of control	-0.05	0.10	-0.03	0.14	0.17	-0.05	0.14	0.05	0.00	0.02	0.02	0.20*	0.23**	1.00					
V21	Criteria for bonus computation	0.08	-0.16	-0.07	0.01	0.02	0.23**	0.13	-0.04	0.10	0.00	0.08	0.00	0.04	0.21**	1.00				
CUL	Culture of the firm	0.12	0.07	0.16	0.21*	-0.04	-0.16	0.04	-0.19	-0.22*	-0.09	0.05	0.14	-0.18	0.20	0.03	1.00			
AGE	Age of system	0.04	-0.05	0.05	-0.05	0.06	-0.06	-0.02	0.02	-0.01	0.11	0.03	-0.04	0.00	0.06	-0.04	0.13	1.00		
NOV	Novelty of system	-0.11	0.16	0.03	0.07	-0.20**	0.01	-0.19*	0.22**	0.05	-0.15	0.10	-0.01	0.01	0.02	0.02	-0.07	-0.47***	1.00	
PERF	Rating for planning system	-0.04	0.17*	-0.15	0.10	0.10	0.03	0.13	0.00	-0.20**	0.15	0.29***	0.15	0.07	0.19*	0.14	-0.01	0.02	0.22**	1.00

Spearman correlations: *p 0.10, **p 0.05, ***p 0.01.

significant correlations that were observed were all easily interpretable.

Factor analysis

The variables included in the study corresponded to four distinct classes: portfolio pressure (V01–V04), financial pressure (V05–V09), orientation of the planning system in the strategy formulation cycle (V16, V17 and V18), and orientation of the planning system in the strategy implementation cycle (V19, V20 and V21). Each class of variables was factor-analyzed (using a varimax rotation) to explore whether they could be represented parsimoniously. An eigen value of 1 was used as a cutoff for selecting factors and a variable had to have a factor loading >0.5 to be assigned to that factor. The results of the factor analyses are presented in Tables 3 and 4.

Given the large amount of variance explained by the five factors, and the ease with which they could be interpreted, five new indices were defined:

1. *Portfolio pressure* is an index formed by averaging the scores for a firm's diversity, pressure to diversify, opportunities for related diversification, and pressure to acquire new businesses.

2. *Profitability pressure* is an index formed by averaging the scores for profitability and earnings growth.

3. *Liquidity pressure* is an index formed by averaging the scores for liquidity, debt/equity ratio, and market to book ratio. (Note the scale for debt/equity ratio is the inverse of the other two scales.)

4. Orientation of the planning system in the *strategy formulation cycle* is an index formed by averaging the scores for direction of goal-setting, linkage between plans and budgets, and role of corporate planner.

5. Orientation of the planning system in the *strategy implementation cycle* is an index formed by averaging the scores for frequency of monitoring of strategic plans, nature of control, and criteria for incentive compensation.

The internal consistency of each index was evaluated using Cronback's coefficient alpha (see Tables 3 and 4). All of the indices were of acceptable consistency.

Identifying the type of planning system in use

The two planning indices that were constructed from the questionnaire data were then used to

Table 3. Principal components factor analysis[a] and summary of contextual variables

Variable Description	Variable name	n^b	Mean	S.D.	Range[c] Low	Range[c] High	Portfolio pressure	Financial pressure – Profitability pressure	Financial pressure – Liquidity pressure
1. Diversity	V01	111	3.13	1.09	1	5	0.53		
2. Pressure to diversify	V02	110	2.83	0.97	1	5	0.64		
3. Opportunities for related diversification	V03	109	3.00	1.00	1	5	0.64		
4. Pressure to acquire new businesses	V04	110	2.93	1.00	1	5	0.68		
5. Profitability	V05	111	3.26	1.37	5	1		0.92	0.03
6. Liquidity	V06	109	2.65	1.09	5	1		0.36	0.67
7. Earnings growth	V07	111	3.35	1.23	5	1		0.92	0.05
8. Debt/equity ratio	V08	108	2.46	0.95	1	5		−0.22	0.83
9. Market/book ratio	V09	99	2.65	0.89	5	1		0.07	0.61
				Variance explained			39%	39%	29%
				Cronbach α			0.61	0.91	0.67

[a] With varimax rotation
[b] n varies because of missing observations
[c] All variables use a five-point scale (Appendix 1)

Table 4. Principal component factor analysis[a] and summary of planning characteristics

Planning variable name	Characteristics	n	Mean	S.D.	Range High	Range Low	Strategic planning cycle	Management control cycle
V16	Nature of goal-setting	107	3.44	1.47	5 Top-down	1 Bottom-up	0.69	
V17	Linkage between plans and budgets	108	3.11	1.26	5 Tight	1 Loose	0.76	
V19	Frequency of monitoring of strategic plans	109	2.72	1.55	5 Monthly	1 Yearly		0.65
V18	Role of corporate planner	105	2.70	1.25	5 Strategist	1 Catalyst	0.58	
V20	Nature of control	93	2.71	1.46	5 Profit-dependent	1 Tailor-made		0.80
V21	Criteria for bonus computation	100	3.10	1.53	5 Standard	1 Tailor-made		0.50
					Variance explained		46%	44%
					Cronbach α		0.71	0.56

[a] Varimax rotation

infer the type of planning system used by each respondent. If, for example, the index for the strategy formulation cycle scored above 3, then the strategic decisions of the firm were heavily influenced by corporate managers. This is characteristic of a Type One or Type Three planning system (Figure 2). Further, if the index for the strategy implementation cycle scored above 3, it implies frequent monitoring, standardized-profit-based control and incentive systems. Such a planning system is Type One. A Type Three system, by contrast, requires tailor-made control and incentive systems to suit the mission of each business unit. Similarly, Types Two and Four were inferred from Figure 2. The most popular type of planning system in use was Type Four (44 percent of the sample), followed by Type Three (27 percent of the sample). Types One and Two together represented the remaining 29 percent of the sample.

Identifying the required planning system

External context

The external context of a firm was defined earlier by its portfolio, profitability, and liquidity pressures. If any of these indices was above 3 (on a five-point scale), the corresponding pressure was considered high. This interpretation is consistent with the basic scale for the questionnaire variables, from which these indices were computed. If either profitability or liquidity pressure was high, financial pressure was deemed high.

Depending on the portfolio and financial pressures experienced by a firm, the type of planning system appropriate to it was identified (see Figure 3). For example, under conditions of high portfolio and financial pressures a Type One planning system is the most appropriate. If portfolio pressure is low, but financial pressure is high, then a

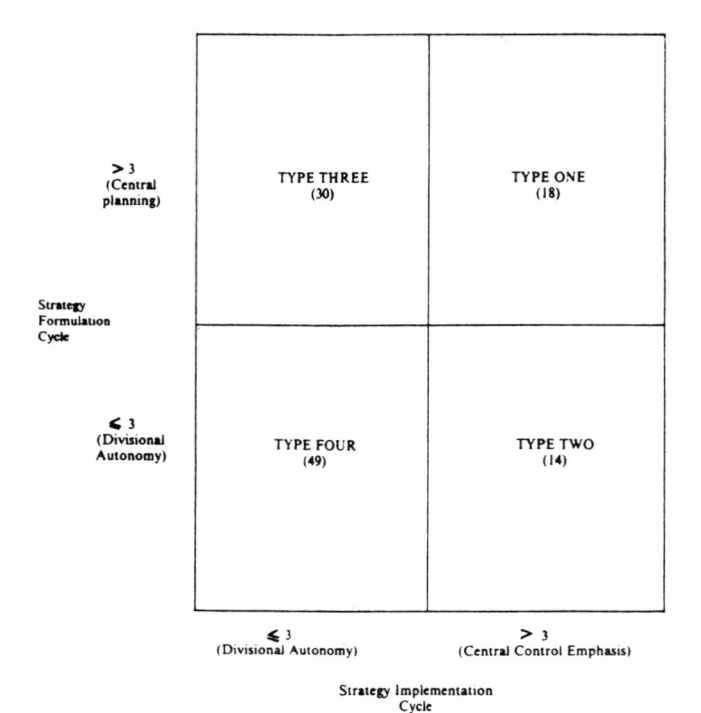

```
                        >3                TYPE THREE          TYPE ONE
                     (Central                (30)                (18)
                    planning)

            Strategy
          Formulation
             Cycle

                       ≤3
                   (Divisional             TYPE FOUR          TYPE TWO
                    Autonomy)                (49)               (14)


                                              ≤3                  >3
                                         (Divisional Autonomy)   (Central Control Emphasis)

                                              Strategy Implementation
                                                      Cycle
```

Figure 2. Planning system characteristics and planning type
Note: Numbers in brackets indicate the number of respondents in each cell

Type Three planning system is to be preferred. The appropriate planning system for the other two contexts in Figure 3 were similarly inferred. However, for a Type Two or Type Four planning system to be chosen there also has to be opportunity for related diversification. Therefore, unless such an opportunity was high (V03>3), a Type One or Type Three system was chosen in their place respectively.

The planning system best suited to a majority of firms was Type Three (49 percent of the sample), followed by Type One (26 percent of the sample), Type Four (14 percent of the sample), and Type Two (11 percent of the sample).

Internal context

The perceptions of the participants on their firm's culture were content-analyzed. Respondents who described their internal environment as myopic, militaristic, autocratic, conservative, or risk-averse, were classifed as having a culture that was supportive of integration in the strategy formulation cycle. On the other hand, if the firm was described as fast, vibrant, loose, risk-seeking, R&D-driven, or creative, it was classified as having a culture that supported adaptation in the strategy formulation cycle. If the culture of a firm is predominantly integrative it can only support

Tailoring a Planning System to its Context 527

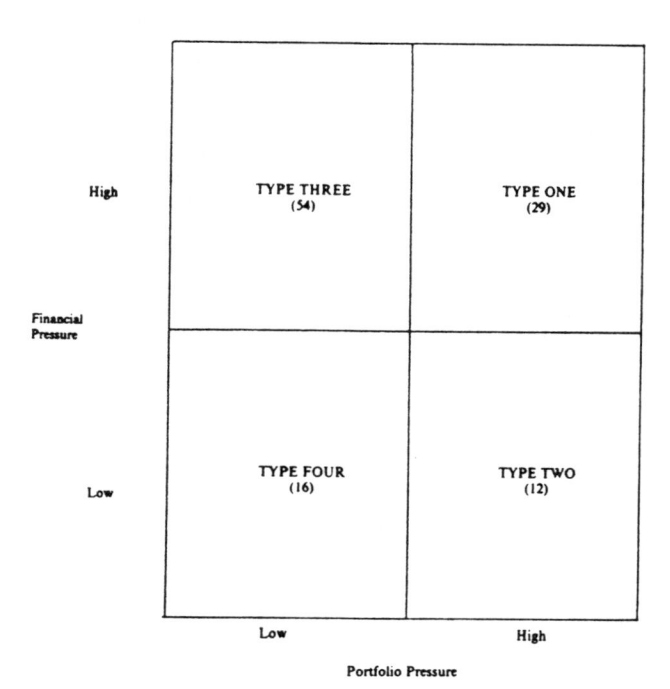

High	TYPE THREE (54)	TYPE ONE (29)
Financial Pressure		
Low	TYPE FOUR (16)	TYPE TWO (12)
	Low	High
	Portfolio Pressure	

Figure 3. A contingency view of balancing creativity and control

Notes: 1. Numbers in brackets indicate the number of firms in the sample whose external context is best described by this cell.
2. In the case of Types Two and Four an additional criterion, i.e. $VO3>3$, had to be satisfied

a Type One or Type Three planning system. On the other hand, if it is predominantly adaptive, it is better suited to a Type Two or Type Four planning system.

It must be noted that nearly half the respondents (47) believed that they did not have an identifiable culture, or felt that they were in a transition from one culture to another. For purposes of analysis a generous assumption is made that such a culture can be molded to suit the needs of any type of planning system. However, the discussion of internal fit in this paper suffers from serious data inadequacy, and is included only for the sake of completeness.

RESEARCH FINDINGS AND DISCUSSSION

System rating unrelated to financial performance

It may be recalled that this study chose not to use financial measures of performance, but instead opted for the rating assigned to a planning system by its users as a measure of its effectiveness. In the sample studied here, managers' ratings of their planning systems showed no significant correlation with the financial performance of their firms. The correlations (Table 2) between system rating (PERF) and profitability ($\rho=0.10$), financial liquidity ($\rho=0.03$), or growth in earnings ($\rho=0.13$) were all insignificant. Though, there was a significant inverse relationship ($\rho=-0.20$) between planning system rating and the pressure to improve a firm's market/book ratio, that relationship was not strong.

It may, however, be argued that the financial pressures reported in the survey are not objective measures of performance. Where financial data were publicly available, the return on sales and market/book ratio (averaged over a 3-year period from 1981 to 1983) of the sample firms were compared with their ratings. A one-way analysis of variance showed no significant relationship between the rating of a firm's planning system and its financial performance.

The above findings support the argument made earlier against the use of financial performance measures to evaluate a planning system. Whereas prior studies have tried to asscociate financial performance with planning system characteristics in the same time period, it is more reasonable to assume a time lag before planning can yield the required financial results. In fact planning should help alleviate the poor financial performance of a firm. The financial performance of a firm is then an important *contextual* variable in the design of its strategic planning system.

Lack of planning system fit

The planning systems of the firms surveyed were for the most part lacking in both external and internal fits.

Only 30 percent of the respondents used a planning system that was appropriate to their external context (Table 5). A chi-square test could not reject the null hypothesis that the type of planning system in use (USESYS) was independent of the system appropriate (REQSYS) to the external context of the respondent's firm.

The internal fit of the planning systems surveyed was also poor. As mentioned earlier, 43 percent of the respondents reported that they had either a transient culture or one that they could easily identify. A chi-square test of independence showed that the systems in use (USESYS) by the rest of the respondents were not aligned (Table 6) to their cultural context (CUL).

Planning system fit unimportant to its rating

Given the high degree of misfit between the planning systems in use and the contexts of the firms surveyed, it would seem surprising that the mean rating of planning systems was as high as 2.83 ($\sigma=0.95$). However, as discussed earlier, the rating of a planning system is influenced by other factors besides fit with its context. But if this fit is to be an important design consideration, it must at least be a significant determinant of the rating a planning system gets.

Table 7 summarizes the relationships that were observed between planning system rating and the external and internal fits enjoyed by it. A one-

Table 5. The fit between FSPS and external context (portfolio and financial pressures)

Required planning system (REQSYS)	Planning system in use (USESYS)				
	1	2	3	4	Total
1	8 (27.6%)	7	7	7	29 (26.1%)
2	3	1 (8.3%)	4	4	12 (10.8%)
3	7	5	14 (25.9%)	28	54 (48.7%)
4	0	1	5	10 (62.5%)	16 (14.4%)
Total	18 (16.2%)	14 (12.6%)	30 (27.0%)	49 (44.1%)	111

$x^2 = 12.49$; (d.f. = 9); not significant at $p = 0.10$.

Table 6. The fit between FSPS and internal context (Company Culture)

Required culture to support FSPS	Prevailing culture			
	Integrative	Adaptive	Transient	Total
Integrative	14	11	23	48
Adaptive	21	18	24	63
Total	35	29	47	111

$\chi^2 = 0.03$; (d.f. =1); not significant at $p = 0.10$.

way analysis of variance showed poor relationship between planning system rating and the external or internal fits that it enjoyed.

Other explanations for system rating

The results of a regression analysis relating the major variables in Figure 1 to the rating of a firm's planning system are shown in Table 8. The external fit (EXTFIT) and internal fit (INTFIT) enjoyed by a planning system were defined earlier as dummy variables, taking the value of 1 when such a fit obtains and 0 otherwise. The characteristics of a planning system were summarized earlier by two indices—the orientations of its formulation and implementation cycles. These indices were further reduced to dummy variables, taking the value of 1 if the cycles were integrative and 0 if they were adaptive (see Figure 2). Similarly, the liquidity pressure was reduced to a dummy variable, 1 if the pressure was high and 0 otherwise (see Figure 3).

There were only three significant correlations among the variables selected for the regression model. The orientation of a firm's strategy formulation cycle was moderately correlated with the orientation of its strategy implementation cycle ($\rho=0.19$), and its internal fit ($\rho=0.32$). The external fit enjoyed by a firm was moderately correlated with the orientation of its strategy formulation cycle ($\rho=0.23$).

The basic model (Model A) was significant but had a low adjusted R^2 of 0.15. This was anticipated, since it was pointed out earlier that the evaluation of a planning system is based on other criteria besides the ones modelled here.

The external fit (EXTFIT) and internal fit (INTFIT) of a planning system were both inconsequential to its rating, and the liquidity pressure experienced by the firm had a minor influence on its system rating. These are consistent with the results reported earlier. The two surprise findings were the importance of a control orientation and novelty to a planning system's rating.

Preference for a control orientation

Model A suggests that if the strategy formulation and implementation cycles of a planning system are integrative, i.e. control focused, they are likely to be rated higher (0.30 and 0.14 respectively) by the firm's managers. This was a surpris-

Table 7. Relationship between external and internal fits and planning system ratings

Rating of planning system	Fit with external context (EXTFIT)		Fit with internal context (INTFIT)		
	(0) Misfit	(1) Fit	(0) Misfit	(1) Fit	Transition
1 (poor)	10	2	3	7	2
2	13	7	6	6	8
3 (average)	33	19	18	11	23
4	20	4	5	6	13
5 (excellent)	1	0	0	1	0
Sub total	77	32	32	31	46
Total	109		109		
F	0.10		0.21		
p	0.75		0.65		

Table 8. Regression models for the evaluation of a planning system

Model	Respondents	Independent variables			System characteristics			R^2	Adj R^2	F
		EXTFIT	INTFIT	Context (liquidity pressure)	Strategy formulation cycle	Strategy implementation cycle	System novelty			
Model A	All respondents	−0.22	−0.11	−0.21*	0.30***	0.14*	0.62***	0.20	0.15	3.89*** (6,96)
Model B	Only planners	−0.16	−0.41	−0.15	0.24	0.14	0.38	0.10	−0.06	0.6 (6,34)
Model C	Corporate officers	−0.81***	0.45	−0.30	0.13	−0.13	1.15***	0.44	0.31	3.42*** (6,26)
Model D	Divisional officers	−0.22	0.05	0.10	0.50***	0.28*	0.43	0.54	0.41	4.23*** (6,22)

***$p < 0.01$; **$p < 0.05$; *$p < 0.10$.

ing finding given that the popular complaint against planning is that it is stifling (*Business Week*, 1984). It is pertinent to note that this preference for a control orientation was not a function of the context in which the planning system operated. If that was the case the two fits, EXTFIT and INTFIT, would have had a significant impact on system rating.

System novelty

The most important determinant of the rating of a planning was its novelty. Novelty measures how recently a planning system has been introduced in the firm, or in the case of a mature system how recently a major modification has been done to it. This is a dummy variable that takes the value 1 if the system was modified (or introduced *de novo*) within the past 5 years: and the value 0 if a system was not modified for the past 5 years. The reason for picking 5 years as a cutoff was explained earlier.

If a new system was introduced, or an old system modified, within the past 5 years, it improved the rating of a planning system by 0.62 on a five-point scale. This could either be attributed to the fad value of a new planning system, or it is possible that the system's novelty was a surrogate variable for the anticipated value of the changes that were being made to it. In other words, changes to a planning system were presumably viewed as eventually improving the fit with its context.

Differences in evaluation criteria

In order to understand better the two findings reported above, the basic model was tested on three different subsamples of respondents: planners, corporate officers, and divisional officers. Two of these models (Model C and Model D in Table 8) were significant, and the associated adjusted R^2s for both subsamples were high.

Interestingly, the external fit (EXTFIT) and internal fit (INTFIT) appeared to be unimportant to planners (Model B). In fact none of the variables used in this study were good predictors of how planners rated their planning systems. This group, being one of the major architects of a planning system, was expected to show more concern for the tailor-making of a firm's planning system.

Model C that modelled the responses of corporate officers showed some surprises as well. It suggested that the most important criterion applied by corporate executives to evaluate their planning systems was novelty. As mentioned earlier, this may be purely faddish, or may in fact reflect inside information about the steady-state characteristics of the new system. The significant and high negative coefficient associated with external fit (EXTFIT) in this model indicates that fit is not the primary criterion that drives the rating of this group.

The criteria used by divisional officers to evaluate their planning systems are modelled by Model D. In this model the only two criteria that were important were whether the strategy formulation and implementation cycles of a planning system had an integrative orientation. This was surprising, given that, of the three groups of executives surveyed, this was expected to show the greatest preference for autonomy in strategy formulation and implementation.

The above findings are, however, preliminary given some important limitations to this study.

Limitations of the study

The first limitation has to do with the survey instrument. A comprehensive questionnaire would have possibly included many more variables than the parsimonious collection used in this study. Since this study was exploratory, a tradeoff was made in favor of a short survey instrument that captured the essence of all variables in interest, over a longer, more tedious, survey. It is, however, possible that the richness of a planning system or its context has not been adequately captured by the survey instrument. Consequently, there may be errors in measuring system fits.

A related problem is that of sample choice. It is difficult to elicit the cooperation of a large sample of managers to any kind of mail survey (Gaedeke and Tootelian, 1976). The attempt by Vancil (1979) in this regard is noteworthy. His study was sponsored by the Financial Executives Research Foundation, and therefore had the enthusiastic support of his respondents—financial executives. This study used a convenience sample of executives, who were similarly 'committed' to the survey. Whereas the reasonably large response ($n = 111$) minimizes some of the bias inherent in such a sampling technique, the results of this survey may not be generalizable.

CONCLUSION

The findings of this study suggest that the lack of fit between a planning system and its internal and external contexts is not a powerful determinant of how it is evaluated by the firm's managers. Consequently, corrective action to remedy any misfits may not be forthcoming. Such a conclusion challenges the popular view, held by scholars and consultants alike, that strategic planning systems must be tailored to their contexts.

An alternate interpretation of the study's findings points to three important issues worthy of further debate:

1. This study showed that tailoring a formal strategic planning system (FSPS) to its context does not appear to be of concern to corporate officers. A recent survey of chief executive officers by Bowman (1986) supports this finding. The design of FSPS was not an important concern of the CEOs surveyed by Bowman. Moreover, FSPS have come in for a lot of criticism of late (*Business Week*, 1984). It is therefore possible that corporate officers in a company pay no more than lip service to the design of formal strategic planning systems, basing their evaluations of the system purely on its novelty (fad value). And yet prior studies (Bower, 1968) have shown that a firm's administrative context has a major influence on its strategic decisions. An improper choice of a planning system can influence strategic decisions in unintended and undesirable ways. The issue then is how to make corporate officers, if not the CEO, care about the design of their firm's FSPS.

2. The lack of concern of planners for tailoring their planning systems was another finding of this study. Is it possible that planners have in fact converted planning into a ritual (*Business Week*, 1984)? Perhaps they are more concerned with endowing it with permanent characteristics rather than adapting the planning process to suit the changing conditions of a firm! The issue then is how to educate planners on the need to keep their planning process adapted to the firm's changing context.

3. The preference of divisional officers for an integrative orientation in both the strategy formulation and implementation cycles was another surprise finding. This would make sense if one were to assume that most incentive systems in use reward divisional officers for their short-term profits than for long-term adaptation. Responses obtained in this study suggest a bias in that direction. Given this bias, divisional managers naturally prefer a planning system congruent with their short-term focus, i.e. one with an integrative orientation in both cyles. The issue then is how can incentive systems be redesigned to provide better balance between short-term profitability and long-term adaptation.

The findings of this preliminary study have obviously to be corroborated by follow-up surveys and clinical studies. It is only then that we can decide whether what is needed is a re-education program aimed at corporate officers and planners, or a revision of the currently popular frameworks for the design of strategic planning systems.

ACKNOWLEDGEMENTS

This paper has benefited from the comments provided by Edward Bowman, Lawrence Hrebiniak, Peter Lorange, and two anonymous reviewers.

REFERENCES

Aguilar, F. J. *Scanning the Business Environment*, Macmillan, New York, 1965.

Anthony, R. N. and J. Dearden. *Management Control Systems*, Richard D. Irwin, Homewood, IL, 1980.

Armstrong, J. S. 'The value of formal planning for strategic decisions', *Strategic Management Journal*, 3, 1982, pp. 197–211.

Bower, J. L. *Managing the Resource Allocation Process*, Harvard University Press, Cambridge, MA, 1968.

Bowman, E. H. 'Concerns of the CEO', *Human Resources Management*, 25(2), Spring 1986, pp. 267–285.

Business Week, 'The new breed of strategic planner', September 17, 1984, pp. 62–67.

Camillus, J. C. 'Evaluating the benefits of formal planning', *Long Range Planning*, 8(3), 1975, pp. 33–40.

Chakravarthy, B. S. and P. Lorange. 'Managing strategic adaptation: options in administrative systems design', *Interfaces*, 14(1), 1984, pp. 34–46.

Christenson, C. J. 'Strategic planning systems from a system science point of view'. In P. Lorange (ed.),

Implementation of Strategic Planning. Prentice-Hall, Englewood Cliffs, NJ, 1982, pp. 25–36.
Fahey, L. and W. R. King. 'Environmental scanning for corporate planning', Business Horizons, 1977, pp. 61–71.
Gaedeke, R. M. and D. H. Tootelian. 'The Fortune '500' List—an endangered species for academic research', Journal of Business Research, 4, 1976, pp. 283–288.
Gage, G. H. 'On acceptance of strategic planning systems'. In P. Lorange (ed.) Implementation of Strategic Planning, Prentice-Hall, Englewood-Cliffs, NJ, 1982, pp. 171–182.
Grant, J. H. and W. R. King 'Strategy formulation: analytical and normative models.' In D. E. Schendel and C. W. Hofer (eds), Strategic Management: A New View of Business Policy and Planning, Little, Brown and Company, Boston, MA, 1979, pp. 104–122.
Grant, J. H. and W. R. King. The Logic of Strategic Planning, Little, Brown and Company, Boston, MA, 1982.
Hamermesh, R. 'Responding to divisional profit crises', Harvard Business Review, 55,(2), 1977, pp. 124–130.
Hax, A. C. and N. S. Majluf. Strategic Management: An Integrative Perspective, Prentice-Hall, Englewood Cliffs, NJ, 1984.
Henderson, B. D. Henderson on Corporate Strategy, Abt Books, Cambridge, MA, 1979.
Hitt, M. A., R. A. Ireland, and K. A. Palia. 'Industrial firm's grand strategy and functional importance: moderating effects of technology and structure'. Academy of Management Journal, 25, 1982, pp. 265–298.
King, W. R. 'Evaluating strategic planning systems'. Strategic Management Journal, 4, 1983, pp. 263–277.
King, W. R. and D. I. Cleland. Strategic Planning and Policy, Van Nostrand Reinhold, New York, 1978.
Lorange, P. Corporate Planning: An Executive View Point, Prentice-Hall, Englewood Cliffs, NJ, 1980.
Lorange, P. 'Organization structure and process.' In W. D. Guth (ed.), Handbook of Business Strategy, Warren, Gorham and Lamont, Boston, MA, 1985.

pp. 23.1–31.
Lorange, P. and R. F. Vancil. Strategic Planning Systems, Prentice-Hall, Englewood Cliffs, NJ, 1977.
Nathanson, D. A., R. K. Kazanjian and J. R. Galbraith. 'Effective strategic planning and the role of organization design,' In P. Lorange (ed.), Implementation of Strategic Planning, Prentice-Hall, Englewood Cliffs, NJ, 1982, pp. 91–113.
Newman, W. H. Constructive Control: Design and Use of Control Systems, Prentice-Hall, Englewood Cliffs, NJ, 1975.
Ramanujam, V., N. Venkatraman and J. C. Camillus. 'Multi-objective assessment of strategic planning effectiveness: a discriminant analysis approach', Academy of Management Journal, 29(2), 1986, pp. 347–372.
Rumelt, R. P. Strategy, Structure, and Econonic Performance, Harvard University, Graduate School of Business Administration, Division of Research, Boston, MA, 1974.
Shank, J. K., E. G. Niblock and W. T. Sandalls, Jr. 'Balance creativity and practicality in formal planning', Harvard Business Review, 51,(1), 1973, pp. 87–95.
Snow, C. C. and L. G. Hrebiniak. 'Strategy, distinctive competence and organizational performance', Administrative Science Quarterly, 25, 1980, pp. 317–336.
Steiner, G. A. Strategic Planning: What Every Manager Must Know, Free Press, New York, 1979.
Steiner, G. A. 'Evaluating your strategic planning system.' In P. Lorange (ed.), Implementation of Strategic Planning, Prentice-Hall, Englewood Cliffs, NJ, 1982, pp. 37–46.
Vancil, R. F. Decentralization: Managing Ambiguity by Design, Dow Jones-Irwin, Homewood, IL, 1979.
Vancil, R. F. and P. Lorange. 'Strategic planning in diversified companies', Harvard Business Review, 53(1), 1975, pp. 81–93.
Wind, Y. and V. Mahajan. 'Designing a product and business portfolio'. Harvard Business Review, 59(1), 1981, pp. 155–165.
Wright, R. A. A System for Managing Diversity, Arthur D. Little, Cambridge, MA, 1974.

APPENDIX: VARIABLES SURVEYED IN THE QUESTIONNAIRE

Variable name	Variable Description	1	2	3	4	5
V01	Diversity	Very low				Very high
V02	Pressure to diversify	Very low				Very high
V03	Opportunities for related diversification	Poor				Excellent
V04	Pressure to acquire new businesses	Very low				Very high

534 B. S. Chakravarthy

		1	2	3	4	5
V05	Profitability	Very high				Very low
V06	Liquidity	Very high				Very low
V07	Earnings growth	Very high				Very low
V08	Debt/equity ratio	Very low				Very high
V09	Market/book ratio	Very high				Very low
V16	Nature of goal-setting	Bottom-up		Mixed mode		Top-down
V17	Linkage between plans and budgets	Very loose		Loose–tight		Very tight
V18	Role of corporate planner	Catalyst		Mixed		Strategist
V19	Frequency of monitoring strategic plans	Infrequent (1 or more year's lapse)		Modest (quarterly)		Very frequent (monthly)
V20	Nature of control	Adaptive		Mixed mode		Integrative
V21	Criteria for bonus computation	Subjective, multiple criteria		Fixed criteria changing weights		Standard universal formula
PERF	Evaluation of planning system	Poor				Excellent

Henry Pankratz
Chairman
Ernst & Young
Management Consultants

INTRODUCTION

Strategic Alignment: Managing for Synergy

In this period of tough economics and survivalist thinking, it may be inspiring to remember 1983. After a rocky start to the decade and an abysmal 1982, the sun began to poke through again. At first, the casualties were counted; the failed, the jobless and even the homeless.

But the spring of 1983 was like the archetypal spring of all ages. Seeds began to germinate, both literally and figuratively. It was a time to reconsider investment of capital and effort. It was a time to evaluate management needs for a growth environment.

In the spirit of the day, Arthur Young International (now Ernst & Young International) and several corporate sponsors decided to commission a landmark management study. The Alfred P. Sloan School of Management at the Massachusetts Institute of Technology was asked to undertake a five-year multimillion dollar research program to forecast the impact of information technology on business management in the decade we have just entered. Appropriately, the project was called Management in the 1990s.

The conclusions were published in 1989.[1] While there were few outright surprises, the findings were illuminating and enlightening. A key finding was that alignment of strategy, business structure and information technology is a key management concept for the '90s. Although strategic planning should remain important, strategic management – adapting to changing circumstances – is expected to be the discipline of the future.

Henry J. Pankratz is an Executive Partner of Ernst & Young and chairman of the firm's management consulting practice, with headquarters in Toronto. He is a Fellow of the Institute of Chartered Accountants of Ontario and a Certified Management Consultant. Over the last 10 years he has had extensive involvement with Canadian universities and is currently a member of the Advisory Council for the Faculty of Commerce and Business Administration at the University of British Columbia.

The Concept of Strategic Alignment

Hence, the management theory called Strategic Alignment was born. It argues that a highly-defined business strategy, even when married with a complementary information technology strategy, can only succeed when organization strategy and culture is supportive and financial/balance sheet strategy fits as well. To achieve optimum results, in other words, these four key areas must develop a functional fit.

That is not where it ends, however. If these above-mentioned strategies could also fit the organizational structures and processes connected with their implementation, that is, a strategic fit, the organization could benefit from enhanced performance.

Movement toward functional fit and strategic fit creates synergy that makes the organization more than just the sum of its parts. Managing the organization toward functional fit and strategic fit is strategic management. A model of strategic alignment (Figure 1) has been developed to help illustrate the concept and establish the parameters of strategic management.

The model identifies the four main areas where an organization makes choices: business, information technology, organization and culture, and finance as related to the balance sheet. Organized sets of choices form functional strategies, represented by the top horizontal row of the model. However, the organization also makes a corresponding set of choices, mindful of its structures and processes, to form strategies of execution. These strategies are represented by the bottom row of the model.

Many organizations have traditionally concentrated on activities within functional disciplines and their structures. The theory of strategic alignment contends that, in the 1990s, the fit or alignment between functional areas and structures will become as important to success as the functions themselves. The model illustrates this notion of functional/structural cross-alignments with arrows connecting each box with all others, on both the (upper) functional strategy and (lower) execution strategy levels.

The Importance of Strategic Alignment

Strategic alignment does not just examine challenges and opportunities in a static state; it recognizes they exist in a dynamic state. Factors like anticipation of technological breakthroughs, for example, and perspectives on markets and new products adopt new importance when the objectives are constantly in motion. Strategic alignment projects a relatively static process such as strategic planning into the dynamic realm of strategic management. Imagine the difference, in terms of management, between still photographs and motion pictures.

The MIT Management in the 1990s research found that effective implementation matters more than a clever strategy. A consistent and focused program of implementation can make almost any strategy a huge success, while even the most novel strategy will fail if processes, plans and organizational behavior are not aligned. In the turbulent business environment expected in the 1990s, establishing the true effectiveness of even the most persuasive paper plan will be more difficult and more critical.

The notion of strategic management also proposes an expanded role for information technology. This is best expressed in a direct quote from the landmark MIT study, Management in the 1990s;

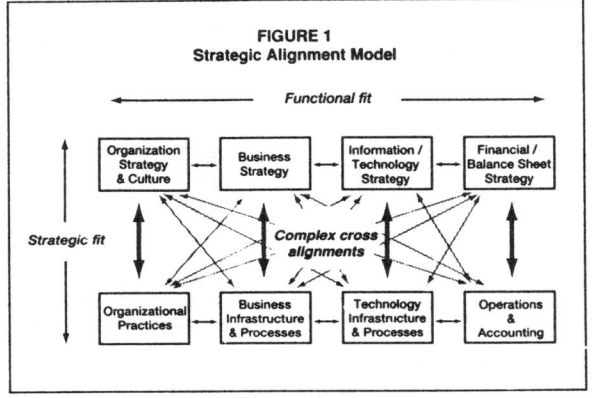

"New information technology is restructuring companies, industries and markets, creating winners and losers, now and in the years immediately ahead. It has a way of 'coming in from left field' and, within a short time, reworking the status quo beyond recognition. Corporate executives may be blindsided unless they

**FIGURE 1
Strategic Alignment Model**

understand its strategic impact, actively support it, and contribute creatively."[2]

Historically, information technology was only valued as a productivity or efficiency tool. Therefore, information technology strategy was, at best, a follow-on for general business strategy. Now it is becoming clear that information technology can open opportunities in all areas of business. One only need look as far as automated banking machines and online reservation systems to realize the pervasiveness of information technology as a strategic resource.

Strategic alignment elevates information technology to equal partnership with traditional areas of strategic planning. It shifts information technology from a supporting or reactive role to a proactive role. Furthermore, strategic alignment challenges the traditional cost/benefit assumptions that have always kept information technology behind the scenes.

One particularly interesting area of strategic alignment is the interrelationships of information technology and human resources. It was often feared that computers would "dehumanize" the workplace by isolating workers with their machines. On the contrary, however, office technology is enhancing lines of worker communication and creating informal, lateral relationships of support and cooperation. Local area networks, electronic mail and telecommunications are just a few of many technologies promoting this behavior.

Good management teams with strong track records will typically find their way to new levels of productivity and profitability through information technology,

> "In the turbulent business environment expected in the 1990s, establishing the true effectiveness of even the most persuasive paper plan will be more difficult and more critical."

while uncertain or mediocre management teams probably will not. In the 1990s, the penalties for flawed management of information technology will be very high.

Why Write About Strategic Alignment?

Although the examination of specific interrelationships is important to strategic alignment, the theory is more than just the sum of its parts. There are two broader reasons why we chose strategic alignment as the topic of our supplement to *Business Quarterly*.

First, strategic alignment has broad applicability; it is not just a manufacturing theory, or service model. As you will learn in articles to follow, strategic alignment can serve public sector organizations as well as private. It encompasses the full range of basic functional divisions within any organization, anywhere in the world. Furthermore, it is not tied to any particular system of national economic or public policies; in other words, it is transferable between countries. This quality make strategic alignment very useful for multinational and global organizations.

This last point strikes at the heart of why we chose to spotlight strategic alignment. Despite the fact that the words "globalization" and "competitiveness" have become buzzwords, they retain meaning. Competitors throughout the world will steadily increase their pressure on Canadian companies to produce faster, cheaper and better, whether the "product" be goods or services. These competitors are paring down the organizational obstacles to their success. They are shattering a long-held, cynical principle of North American organizational behavior – that complexity and inefficiency must rise in proportion to the size and scope of an organization. Strategic alignment provides a basis on which to compete with any organization in the world.

The Experiences of Our Contributing Authors

We are extraordinarily pleased to have attracted some leading figures from business, public service and academia to contribute to our supplement. We asked our academic contributors to write about the evolution and development of Strategic Alignment. We asked the authors from industry and government to write about their own experiences, in many cases, their response to a major change in the operating environment. Since all the articles deal with strategic planning and/or strategic management, I will now attempt to build a bridge between their experiences and the Strategic Alignment Model.

Don Lander, President and CEO, Canada Post Corporation
Canada Post Corporation was transformed from a government agency to a crown corporation in 1981, with a mandate to improve service (business strategy), labor relations (organization strategy and culture) and profitability (financial/balance sheet strategy). Instantly, one can recognize the involvement of at least three

> **"Managing the organization for functional fit and strategic fit is strategic management."**

categories from the Strategic Alignment Model. Ten years later, Canada Post has improved noticeably. How did they do it?

As Lander points out, Canada Post did not even have a bank account prior to 1981. Its first task was to create a corporate financial infrastructure, which became the linchpin to which all other elements would align. The need for revenues to fuel the infrastructure, and the imperative to become profitable, pulled a business strategy into alignment – short-term rate increases yielding to long-term business growth.

But Lander confesses the toughest challenge was aligning the corporate culture – the transformation of a public service environment to a profit-conscious corporate environment. Management was flattened and restructured, and changes were made to labor relations.

Facing a future of increasing telecommunication and competitive challenge from private carriers, Canada Post sees information technology strategy alignment as a key to success. This is a prime example where, as **Phil Pyburn** points out in his article, information technology can exceed its traditional role as productivity tool and adopt true market relevance.

Vic Stoughton, President and CEO, The Toronto Hospital
In 1986, Toronto General Hospital surprised many people by announcing a merger with cross-town Toronto Western Hospital. It was a bold and unusual move.

The merger was a unique alignment of financial and business strategies. It was an attempt to create economies of scale (financial strategy) to free up funds for improved patient service (business strategy). The idea arose from a prior crisis management decision that consolidated the two hospitals' obstetrical programs and achieved noticeable improvements.

The merger discussions initially flushed out a misalignment between public interest (business strategy) and institutional competition (organizational culture). This misalignment was especially complicated by structures, practices and even laws

> **"In the 1990s the fit or alignment between functional areas and structures will become as important to success as the functions themselves."**

peculiar to the medical profession. It was the benefits of the financial strategy that ultimately convinced the medical staff leadership, and moved the organizations rather unwillingly into a merger.

The alignment between organizational strategy, financial strategy and business strategy has continued throughout the four years since the merger. Nevertheless, the merged institution is realizing much of the cost savings it projected.

John Edwards, Manager, Public Service 2000, Government of Canada
In December, 1989, the Prime Minister announced an initiative called Public Service 2000. In the words of John Edwards, Manager of Public Service 2000, "The aim of

PS 2000 is nothing short of a complete transformation of the corporate culture of the public service."

Edwards explains that public expectations are changing and pressuring a shift in business strategy from one of regulation and control to one of client service. Public service organizational structures and practices, however, are strongly oriented toward regulations and controls. Adding to the difficulties, a financial strategy of restraint has been tightening down for over a decade – and this financial strategy cannot be realistically challenged. In terms of strategic alignment, therefore, the public service must bring together its organizational and business strategies.

This seems to be where PS 2000 is aimed. The task forces of PS 2000 have recommended an organizational strategy that responds to the demands of the "market" (business strategy) and also operates within the framework of fiscal restraint (financial strategy). Edwards also states that, " . . . systems (information technology strategies) are key elements in the strategic alignment of the enterprise (organizational strategy) and the environment (business strategy)." In mentioning this, he invokes the fourth element of the strategic alignment model.

Although Edwards has perceived widespread support for PS 2000 within the public service, he calls for a "new contract" with the political level that acknowledges and protects the new way of doing things.

Rose Patten,
Senior Vice President,
Manulife Financial
Rose Patten, Senior VP, Corporate Human Resources and Organization Development for Manulife, says, "We have been undergoing major

"Competitors throughout the world will steadily increase their pressure on Canadian companies to produce faster, cheaper and better."

reassessment . . . of our entire strategic direction since 1987 . . . to (better) compete in the new highly-diversified financial services industry and . . . expand our businesses in the . . . global markets in which we operate." These market-driven objectives safely fall into the category of business strategy for purposes of strategic alignment.

Several new priorities came from a newly-appointed CEO in 1987. Although many of these new priorities were not alien to modern management thinking, they were considered "a dramatic departure from our traditional business practices." It became clear that Manulife would have to align its organizational/cultural strategy with the newly aggressive business strategy. The information technology strategy so important to financial services organizations was accorded its appropriate level of importance and developed in alignment with these other two. Among other implementation techniques, Manulife deployed a cross-functional management team at a very senior level.

Rose documents some of the difficulties of aligning an organizational strategy. "Without careful and persistent alignment," she says, "our strategies would have quickly been lost in. . .deeply-rooted traditions." Nevertheless, she perceives an enormous amount of progress.

Bill Harker, Managing Partner and Chief Operating Officer, Canadian Operations, Royal Trust
Bill begins his article by projecting a vision of Royal Trust's business strategy in 1999 – highly responsive to individual clients wherever located and well aligned with a technology strategy. He then contrasts this vision with the "traditional" financial services management mindset, which has valued centralized controls. Unlike John Edwards' description of "politically" motivated control management in the public service, it appears that control management in financial institutions has been driven by financial or balance sheet strategy.

Harker goes on to explain Royal Trust's solution to bridging the gap between past and future management. It takes the form of a unique organization strategy developed to align with the visionary business strategy. The organization strategy incorporates a simple, yet effective balance between centralized and decentralized management. It relies on the fact that a particular cultural and management tone, radiating from the centre, can guide the behavior of remote units without the need for imposing excessive regulation. Highly progressive organizational structures, policies and procedures with even more progressive names are woven through this management implementation concept. Another part of Royal Trust's future obviously lies in constant alignment of business and information technology strategies.

Donald Fullerton, Chairman and CEO, Canadian Imperial Bank of Commerce
Early in the 1980s, CIBC realized it could not count on stability in environmental operating conditions. It concluded it did not have sufficient flexibility to capitalize on changes that might come from any direction. At the same time, customers were becoming more demanding and other industry members were improving their strength. In 1983, the board of directors approved a plan that affected over 25 different areas and articulated a future vision for CIBC within the financial services industry.

Fullerton describes an alignment between business and organizational strategies that left the door open to opportunities change might bring. The financial services industry was, and still is, in a dynamic regulatory environment. The bank does not know, from year to year, what range of services it might be allowed to provide. With a business strategy so easily influenced by change, any organization strategy in alignment must be equally pliable. This is a bold undertaking in an organization of several thousand people.

> "Strategic alignment provides a basis on which to compete with any organization in the world."

In his article, Fullerton chose not to dwell on his company's information technology strategy, although most of us have witnessed the increasing market relevance of information technology in banking. CIBC will continue to put its stock in its organizational strategy, concentrating on alignment with the business strategy and its changes.

Onward and Upward
I have discussed the origins of strategic alignment, visited the concept itself, and attempted to describe its importance for the organization. Then, in vastly oversimplified fashion, I related strategic alignment theory to the experiences of our contributing authors from business and public service. In the articles that follow, these authors' detailed accounts of their own experiences should strike a chord of association with your own organization's management issues. Articles by our other contributors, **John Henderson, N. Venkatraman, Philip Pyburn** and **Roy Steel**, illuminate the theoretic and technical issues in a way only they could manage.

Strategic Alignment, as a management theory, has been evolving and developing in several places since the conclusion of the MIT Management in the 1990s research.[3] You will find therefore that each article in the supplement dealing with Strategic Alignment theory, including my own, reflects a somewhat individualized view. In some cases the differences will relate mostly to style of expression; in others to the evolution of the theory itself. That is as it should be. We believe the concepts described here are at the leading edge of management thinking and consequently, diversity is to be expected. After all, as the *Regina Leader Post* says, "Where all think alike, no one thinks very much."

I opened this piece with some fond memories of 1983. Economically, we are close to that threshold once again; attitudinally, I certainly hope we are. But technologically we may have left 1983 centuries ago and so we see our time loop stretch into a spiral. We can never really go back again.

I thank all our authors for their contributions, and I hope you, our readers, enjoy our examination of strategic alignment. BQ

References
[1] *The Landmark MIT Study: Management in the 1990s*, Arthur Young International, Boston, 1989.
[2] *Op. cit.*
[3] See Scott Morton, Michael, S. (Ed.), *The Corporation of the 1990s*, Oxford University Press, Oxford, 1991.

How Innovators Thwart New Entrants into Their Market

By Thomas S. Robertson
and Hubert Gatignon

Innovator companies need to rehearse a logical strategic defense before they're ambushed by a new competitor.

Early market entry is worth the hard charge to the finish line. Market pioneers or "first movers" usually achieve a larger sustainable market share than later entrants. The ratio of market share advantage is about 1.0 for the first entrant, 0.6 for early followers, and 0.4 for late followers. In other words, followers can expect, on average, to garner 40 to 60 percent less of the business than pioneers.

Nevertheless, market pioneers do not necessarily maintain their market leadership. Reversals do occur. The British firm, E.M.I., was the first market entrant in the CT scanner market, but General Electric assumed market leadership by quickly offering second generation technology. SmithKline's Tagamet was the market pioneer in ulcer therapy but sales of Glaxo's Zantac have surpassed it. Take the example of Emery, the delivery service industry pioneer, which quickly lost market leadership in the shipment of small packages to Federal Express and its innovative hub system. How can market leaders prevent such costly reversals of fortune?

The Best Defense

Defensive strategy involves designing a planning process that should take place before the firm is threatened by new competition (see Exhibit 1). The initial decision is whether any competitive response is appropriate. There may be conditions when the best strategy is not to actively react, especially if the threat posed by a new entry is minor. In general, reaction may not be appropriate if the potential entrant is small in scale or is likely to enter a niche in which the market pioneer is not strongly represented. Thus, until recently, IBM chose to ignore Cray as a competitor in supercomputers, due to the limited size of this niche relative to IBM's revenue objectives. However, over time, as the niche expanded in size, a response became necessary. The danger of this approach, however, is that the new competitor may use the niche as a wedge of access and then expand to threaten the existing competitor. U.S. firms have often ignored Japanese entry in niches only to discover later that the niches become the dominant part of the market — for instance in modular television receivers, compact cars, or small microwaves.

If reaction to a market entrant is appropriate — as is usually the case—the strategic response must be compatible with the nature of the threat. The aggressiveness of the reaction may be represented by one of three strategies.

- **An attack or retaliation strategy.** This is generally the market pioneer's first inclination—but it may not be optimal.
- **Cooperation or accommodation.** That is, recognize the potential of new competition and avoid head-to-head retaliation, especially on pricing.
- **An abandonment strategy if outclassed on product quality or resources.** This strategy is often neglected, but sometimes it may be optimal under certain specific conditions.

Finally, a firm must consider what marketing initiatives to take, including actions in pricing, positioning, channels, and communications.

EXHIBIT 1
Decision Model for Determining Response to a New Entrant

```
        Is a
     Response         No      Ignore the
    Appropriate?    ───────►  New Entrant
        │
       Yes
        │
         How
    Aggressive Should
    the Response
        Be?
   ┌────┬────┐
   │    │    │
Retaliate  Abandon    Accommodate the
Against    the        New Entrant.
the New    Market.
Entrant.
                │
             What
         Should Be the
           Domain of
          Response?
         ┌────┴────┐
    Respond in the   Respond in a
        Same          Different
   Product/Market.  Product/Market.
         └────┬────┘
         What Marketing
         Initiatives Should
            Be Taken?
          • Pricing?
          • Product
            Strategy?
          • Communication?
          • Distribution?
```

Thomas S. Robertson is the John & Laura Pomerantz Professor of Marketing at the Wharton School, University of Pennsylvania, and a Visiting Professor at the London Business School. Hubert Gatignon is Associate Professor of Marketing at Wharton.

How Aggressive Should the Response Be?

Given a decision to react to impending entry, the market pioneer must decide on the aggressiveness of that response: Whether to retaliate, accommodate, or abandon the market (see Exhibit 2, page 7). If a pioneer decides to retaliate, where should the counter-attack occur? Should the firm respond in the same product/market domain threatened by the potential entrant, or in a different one? In a recent retaliation strategy in the airline industry, for example, Northwest first responded to Midway in the initial market where the threat occurred. But then, in order to heighten the pressure on Midway, it expanded its price cutting into a new set of markets.

Retaliating Against the New Entrant. Retaliation is essentially a declaration of war. The market pioneer sends signals to the potential entrant and other competitors that it intends to fight back, for example, Pizza Hut's retaliation against McDonald's pizza entry (see box). The pioneer can then instigate a set of preemptive moves to prevent further market entry.

Successful retaliation requires:

- Holding a significant competitive advantage.
- Lower scale of entry of the new competitor, and
- Low-to-medium access to resources of the new competitor.

An assessment of competitive advantage should be made for the product/market under attack. Only after it acquired a portfolio of wine brands did Coca-Cola discover to its dismay that the market leader, Gallo, had substantial sustainable cost and distribution advantages. Eventually, Coca-Cola chose to withdraw from the wine market. While Phillip Morris has fared better in the beer market, it has nevertheless encountered stiff resistance from Anheuser-Busch, the leader, which has distribution and image/reputation advantages. The Budweiser name and other "intangible assets" were built over a long planning horizon and are not readily matched by Phillip Morris. Anheuser-Busch also matches any innovative move Miller takes (see box).

The scale of entry of the new competitor is another major factor in deciding how aggressively to respond. In general, response should be less vigorous if the new entrant's investment is high, thus signaling favorable costs and a long-run commitment. For scale or investment to play such a role, it must be both observable to rival firms and be non-recoverable. For example, a recent retaliation by Nutrasweet against new competitors shows its confidence based on greater scale and superior cost structure. In response to Nutrasweet's aggressive pricing, a number of competitors have left the market, alleging predatory pricing. Nutrasweet's CEO responds: "If they don't like the pricing, maybe the problem is their cost structure."

The decision to retaliate, however, must also take into account the new entrant's access to resources. Aggressive retaliation is most likely to succeed if new entrants have limited available resources, as in the trunk airlines' responses to the now-defunct People Express. However, retaliation against competitors with deep pockets may lead to a great deal of bloodletting, unless the market pioneer is confident that the new competitor isn't planning to make substantial investment.

Executive Overview

Innovation can be a source of substantial competitive differentiation for a firm. However, innovative advantage is often short-lived. Very soon a competitor will imitate and improve on the original product, prices will fall, and advantage will be lost. One reason many headstarts last so briefly is that, while many executives are highly involved in the development and initial launch of innovative products, firms frequently fail to design advance strategies for the imitative entry which they will inevitably face.

What are the appropriate defense strategies for market pioneers? What constitutes an appropriate response to a "me too" entrant? Although the natural tendency is to retaliate, it sometimes is more advisable to accommodate the new entrant. For example, when your product is outclassed by the new entrant, the most logical strategy is to abandon the market.

The next question is: Where should you respond? Most competitive responses occur in the same product/market domain where the imitator's threat occurs. However, in some cases it may be more effective to respond in another market.

What marketing initiatives should be taken in response to a new entrant? When is aggressive pricing in order? Should a second brand be considered? Should changes be made in product positioning? Are there appropriate distribution initiatives to counter new entrants?

Companies need a logical strategic flow for designing defense strategies. The time to initiate defensive maneuvers is before a new entrant threatens the market pioneer's dominant position. The established leader generally has advance notice of an impending entry, ranging from a few weeks to as much as a year or more. In consumer packaged goods, for example, there may be only a few weeks warning based on intelligence efforts monitoring advertising placement or distribution authorization commitments. However, in the pharmaceutical industry, potential entrants may have to reveal their intentions a year or more in advance since they must seek government approval for their products.

EXHIBIT 2
How Aggressive Should the Response Be?

	Market Pioneer's Level of Competitive Advantage	New Entrant's Economies of Scale	New Entrant's Access to Resources
Retaliate Against the New Entrant When →	Pioneer enjoys a competitive advantage.	New entrant will have lower scale.	New entrant will have low or medium access to resources.
Accommodate the New Entrant When →	Pioneer has minimal or equivalent competitive advantage.	New entrant will have equivalent scale.	New entrant will have equivalent access to resources.
Abandon the Market When →	Pioneer is at a competitive disadvantage.	New entrant will have higher scale.	New entrant will have higher access to resources.

Accommodating the New Entrant. An accommodation strategy either recognizes that there is enough business for all competitors or that the pioneer may benefit from the new entrant's investment and end up with a smaller percentage, but a larger market. In either case, some cooperative behavior among the players would be in everyone's best interest. This approach could minimize declines in profits due to battles over entry. A possible danger, however, is that initial accommodation by the market pioneer might be interpreted as a signal inviting more competition.

The conditions favoring accommodation are:

- Lack of, or minimal, competitive advantage.
- Equivalent scale of the entrant.
- Equivalent accessibility to resources of the entrant.

In these cases it is desirable to avoid hostilities by showing a desire to cooperate in order to minimize the probability of declining prices.

Apple quite logically accommodated IBM's entry into personal computers, given the tremendous resource disparity between the two firms. A new entrant may also be of value to an existing competitor if it assumes some of the burden of market development. For example, IBM undertook a considerable amount of consumer education in personal computers, which substantially expanded the market for everyone.

For many market pioneers the motivation to accommodate is based on the recognition that the new competitor is putting in place substantial scale and investment. In the worldwide chemical industry, for example, aggressive reaction is inappropriate if a new entrant is committing to a $500 million plant. This represents a "credible commitment" to the market. Under such circumstances the new entrant can be expected to take strong countermoves against any aggressive behavior from the pioneer. Such reactions and counter-reactions are sure to escalate and thus lower the profitability of all players.

Abandoning the Market. The decision to exit the market reflects a firm's lack of competitive advantage over the new entrant. In some circumstances an entrant's superior product or depth of resources indicates that staying in the market (with or without fighting) would mean greater losses than a graceful exit. Examples of strategic exits are: AT&T's abandonment of the personal computer market, General Electric's retreat from the small appliance market, and Motorola's departure from the television receiver market when it was outclassed by Japanese technology.

In such cases, when the pioneer's product or marketing resources don't measure up to the entrant, there may be very little that can be done to preserve market leadership. A cutback in funding is appropriate. In addition, if the new competitor has committed, or has the potential to commit, substantial resources, then the pioneer's only option is to abandon the market.

Selecting the Domain of Response

After choosing a strategy of retaliation, the market pioneer must decide where to focus an aggressive response. Most often this is done in the market segment in which entry occurs. However, the most effective reaction strategy might not be a direct counter-attack. Suppose the new competitor in market X is vulnerable in market Y, and has not made commitments in that market which constitute exit barriers. It might be more effective to attack in market Y, forcing the newcomer to defend both X and Y markets.

Thus, the alternative retaliative strategies are:
- Retaliating in the product/market domain of the anticipated entry.
- Retaliating in a different product/market domain from the one in which entry is anticipated, but where the newcomer is already competing.

When is each of these alternatives appropriate? This decision depends on the relative strength of the pioneer in the product/market domain where the entry is anticipated as well as the relative strength in each of the other product/market domains where the entrant is engaged in business.

If the pioneer's strength is greatest in the product/market domain in which the entry is anticipated, retaliation in this market will be preferred. However, if the pioneer has a stronger competitive advantage in another domain, this is where retaliation should occur. Reaction should occur where the pioneer has the greatest impact on the entrant. If the strengths of the pioneer surpass those of the entrant in several markets, a multi-market reaction could send a strong signal to the entrant to reconsider further commitments.

Marketing Initiatives to Counter Entry

Market pioneers in successful product categories must ultimately expect competition. The challenges for the pioneer are:
- Delay competitive entry as long as possible.
- Limit the number of competitors if possible.
- Limit the investment of new entrants in the market.

Marketing approaches the pioneer must consider in order to limit entry (see Exhibit 3):

- **Pricing.** Should the pioneer lower prices aggressively? Under what conditions is lower pricing an advantageous response?
- **Product Strategy.** How does the firm maintain its innovative advantage? When should line extension be pursued? What is the appropriate positioning strategy? Under what conditions should a second brand or a "fighting" brand be introduced?
- **Communication Response.** Should advertising and sales force expenditures be increased? Should the ad campaign be redesigned? What can be done to limit the communication effectiveness of later entrants?
- **Distribution Response.** What initiatives can be taken to block the distribution access of later entrants? If it is not possible to block the distribution channel, what forms of distribution resistance are possible?

Pricing Response. Later entrants often use lower price as a means of market entry. A common scenario for later entrants is to match the pioneer's product benefits and to emphasize price advantage. Examples include Bristol Myer's entry of Datril in competition with Tylenol, the battles between various generic drugs versus established brands coming off patent, the various price imitators against Federal Express, and the computer clones or compatibles in competition with IBM in mainframes.

The question is, how aggressively should the market pioneer respond on pricing? A price decrease could reduce the pioneer's revenues or it could expand the market. However, the market pioneer often provides the price umbrella for later entrants. Followers may just keep cutting price regardless of the incumbent's reductions. An intriguing battle: MCI's premise for existence is that it has lower prices than AT&T. But will it keep lowering them? AT&T evidently doesn't think so because it has attacked with ads that suggest MCI's advantage amounts to pennies.

EXHIBIT 3
What Marketing Actions Should Be Taken by the Market Pioneer?

	Marketing Program	Conditions
Price Response	Should price be reduced?	• Market is price sensitive. • Cross-elasticity of demand is high. • Economies of scale and/or experience effects are strong.
Product Response	Should product enhancement or migration occur?	• The new entrant achieves product parity.
	Should the product be repositioned or the positioning extended?	• Consumer needs are heterogeneous. • It is necessary to subsume any salient product dimension that the new entrant offers.
	Should a second brand be considered?	• Market demand is extensive and growing. • Multiple segments exist. • Differentiation opportunities are available. • Price sensitivity is low. • Multiple distribution systems exist.
Communication Response	Media and personal communication expenditures	• Ability to differentiate product from entrant. • Communication expenditures of entrant are high. • Asymmetric communication advantage of pioneer.
Distribution Response	Should breadth of distribution be increased?	• Efficiency of broader channels as product life cycle advances. • Consumer needs dictate broader channels.
	Should new channels be utilized? What distribution tactics to use: discounts, building inventories, loyalty programs?	• Market growth is via emerging channels. • Initial new entrant sales can be blunted.

The conditions favoring aggressive pricing are:

- If the market is price sensitive.
- If cross elasticity of demand is high.
- If economies of scale and experience strongly affect profitability. If these conditions are not met, then the market pioneer should seek to maintain its existing price structure.

Price Sensitivity. If the market is highly price elastic, then it follows that aggressive pricing will be necessary and desirable. It will be untenable to maintain higher prices if consumers are susceptible to the lower priced product. Furthermore, if the market is price elastic, then total revenues will increase by pursuing low prices. There are two recent examples in the global telecommunications industry. When newly created International Telecom Japan entered the market at prices 23 percent lower than the established KDD, the latter cut its rates by 15 percent within a month. Similarly, when challenged by Mercury Communications, British Telecom has lowered its rates 17 percent over three years.

Of course, where the market is segmented, price sensitivity levels are likely to vary and the responses become more complex. Airline yield management models are excellent examples of pricing systems keyed to varying levels of price sensitivity. When a competitor enters the market, the prices are likely to fall differentially depending on the price sensitivity levels of the various classes or categories of travelers.

Elasticity of Demand. Aggressive price cutting may not work if the market is heterogeneous and new entrants can pursue a differentiation strategy rather than a price strategy. In such cases, product line responses are more appropriate. However, if the market is reasonably homogeneous, and customers don't see much difference among offerings, then the market pioneer will have to lower prices.

Scale and Experience Effects. Obviously, a dominant firm that achieves significant economies of scale can price its product to make make it unprofitable for a small company with higher costs to enter the market. To make this happen, however, the dominant firm must know the costs of the smaller potential competitor and have a sufficiently large cost advantage. A problem is that the additional supply provided by the new entrant could cause a market glut that weakens prices.

A firm fearing an entrant with a competitive cost structure could choose to increase its capacity to achieve additional economies of scale—forcing the newcomer to match or drop out. Or the market leader could cut its overhead, enabling it to slash costs.

There are conditions where the pricing approach will be ineffective; for example, when there is uncertainty about costs. If the potential entrant knows its own cost structure but must infer the incumbent firm's costs from its pricing behavior, then the incumbent firm should price low to signal how low their costs are. This would appear to be Nutrasweet's strategy in the low-calorie sweetener market. This deters entry, as the low prices give an indication of the expected post-entry prices in the market.

Product Line Strategy. Later entrants may pursue innovation and/or product differentiation rather than price to penetrate the market. The innovation scenario as a means of entry suggests that the market pioneer is not optimally fulfilling market needs—remember GE's entry against EMI in the CT scanner market, and Glaxo's entry against SmithKline in the ulcer market. The differentiation scenario assumes that market needs are heterogeneous and that differentiation and segmentation are possible. Examples include Lexus in the luxury car market, and Coke and Pepsi's new entries against Gatorade in the sports/beverage market.

Defense alternatives for the market pioneer include:

- Innovation via migration or enhancement.
- Extended positioning and repositioning.
- The introduction of a second brand.

Innovation. The market pioneer generally achieves this position based on innovation. Inevitably, the innovative advantage is dissipated as new entrants imitate and ultimately match or exceed the premise of the first firm's successful entry. The typical scenario in a competitive market is: Innovation yields supra-normal returns; these returns are highly visible and encourage competitive entry; this, in turn, lowers margins and overcomes the initial innovative advantage.

The inevitable challenge for the market pioneer is to re-innovate and to seek ongoing advantage based on migration or enhancement strategies. Migration seeks to reach a new technological plateau that makes the emerging competitor's product obsolete. This is a typical strategy in such technology-driven industries as computers and telecommunications. Enhancement seeks to add benefits that emerging competitors do not provide. Federal Express for example, offered earlier delivery (10:30 A.M.) when threatened by competitors. A process of continuous innovation has become critical in today's globally competitive markets.

Much of the strategy literature in the 1980s focused on maintaining competitive advantage by building structural barriers to entry. Although this is a valid approach, it can blind a firm to consumer needs and the advantages of innovation. A firm that is fixated on erecting entry barriers against new entrants may not be directing adequate resources to R&D and the design of new products. Market pioneers may use strategic alliances (or sometimes acquisitions) to gain access to new technology and to maintain innovative momentum, such as IBM's alliances with Steven Chen in supercomputers and with "Go" in

> **Anheuser Busch responded to Miller Genuine Draft introduced in 1985 with a copycat in 1990.**
>
> "The new brew is almost a dead ringer for Miller Genuine Draft, the highly successful premium-priced beer introduced in 1985 by Miller Brewing Co., a unit of Philip Morris Cos. 'It's Miller Genuine Draft in sheep's clothing,' says Emanuel Goldman, an analyst for Paine-Webber Inc. . . ."
>
> "There's no question that Busch Cold Filtered Draft is a copycat" says Beverly Jurkowski, a spokeswoman for Miller." (*Wall Street Journal*, May 1, 1990).

handwriting recognition computers. Indeed, an appropriate response to potential entrants may be cooperation through technology and marketing alliances rather than competition.

Extended Positioning and Repositioning. By positioning multiple product offerings, the market pioneer can cover the market so well that the potential entrant cannot generate enough demand from a specific segment to justify entry. This strategy works best when there are economies of scale or when there are large fixed costs in production or marketing. Otherwise, even a small untapped segment would attract an entrant. Of course, implementing an extended positioning strategy means that market needs must be heterogeneous.

When brand proliferation is possible, this strategy is more likely to deter entries than aggressive pricing. In fact, segmentation and differentiation are excellent methods of avoiding bloody price wars.

In addition, saturating the market with brands that satisfy a variety of customer needs reduces the likelihood that new entrants will break even. The synergies on the demand and cost sides of producing and marketing multiple (but somewhat similar) brands increase the market coverage and cost advantages of the existing competitor. In fact, the breadth of the market covered is a major indicator of a pioneer's high market share. Brand proliferation creates problems for distributors with limited space or selling time, so it's easier for them to deal with the established firm with a reputation supported by a demand/pull strategy. Finally, brand proliferation signals commitment to the market—a formidable message to a potential entrant. All in all, brand proliferation appears to offer numerous complementary benefits that add to a formidable deterrence strategy.

Repositioning may also be a necessary defense for the market pioneer. In principle, repositioning means adopting those product features that give the competitor a relative advantage. In the disposable diaper market, for example, Procter and Gamble was forced to reposition Pampers to emphasize how much more comfortable thinness is when Huggies was seizing the market initiative by focusing on fit.

Second Brand. An intriguing possibility as a strategic defense may be the introduction of a second brand. The factors favoring a second brand are:

- Market demand is extensive and growing. This correlates with the ability to achieve cost effectiveness with a second brand. Inevitably, multiple brands raise costs and this may well lower profits unless the demand is substantial.

- Multiple market segments exist. There is no need for a second brand if market needs are homogeneous and price is the driving force.

- Differentiation opportunities are available. The key is the opportunity to deliver differentiated products to a variety of market segments. Obviously it's important to minimize cannibalization of the primary brand or to achieve higher margins than the primary brand. For example, higher margins drive American Express' strategy of multiple brands of charge cards —Green, Gold, and Platinum.

- Price sensitivity is low. Differentiation strategy assumes that demand is not driven solely by price but rather by added value.

- Multiple distribution systems exist. Finally, a second brand may be necessary and desirable in order to be represented in multiple distribution systems. In the kitchen cabinet market manufacturers have added second brands because traditional specialty stores lose interest in the brand if it is represented in "home centers." It becomes necessary, therefore, to develop or acquire brands aimed at those centers. Merilat, the market leader, has done so by acquiring a second brand for the new channel.

The objectives for a second brand are to position it so that it takes sales away from the new entrant while minimizing cannibalization of the pioneering brand. Ideally, the second brand will expand the overall market. Many companies reject second brands because of expected cannibalization and higher costs. However, the decision should not be made without first examining the total projected revenue stream (assuming competition) with and without the potential second brand. It may be better to accept some cannibalization than to allow new entrants to steal market share.

An unusual use of a second brand strategy is to position it as a "fighting brand," or "spoiler brand." In some cases manufacturers introduce fighting brands simultaneously with the appearance of competitors. There may or may not be long-run commitment to the brand. Indeed, it may only be on the market for a limited period of time. Examples include Maxwell House Division's introduction of Horizon coffee simultaneously with Folger's expansion into new markets, and Coca-Cola's introduction of Mr. Pibb to blunt Dr. Pepper's advances.

The idea of a fighting brand is that some customers like to try out new brands. So why not split any trial and put a damper on the new competitor's results? The fighting brand also allows the manufacturer to try out new ideas and programs without risking injury to the reputation or sales of the pioneering brand.

A few years ago, spoiler brands were in a "war" over a new niche in the supermarket cookie business. The new entrant, Procter and Gamble, introduced Duncan Hines' "crisp and chewy" cookies, which achieved considerable test market success. Competitors (Nabisco and Keebler in particular) defended by introducing highly similar products and rolling them out nationally almost simultaneously with Duncan Hines. The effect was to split the available demand for this innovative type of product and to severely reduce Duncan Hines' market share.

This led to a patent infringement lawsuit, which was settled just before trial. Threats of litigation against interlopers may be an effective means of market defense, even where patent issues are not clearly in the pioneer's advantage. New entrants too often threaten litigation as a bargaining tool to win concessions from the market leaders.

Communication Response. Communication strategies can keep competitors at bay. Both advertising and sales force expenditures may serve to build substantial barriers to entry. In the pharmaceutical market, for example, the presence of a detailing force to provide direct contact with doctors seems to be a necessary requirement for market entry. However, it takes two to three years to hire and train such an organization. The alternative is to license or co-venture the marketing of drugs with established firms, which is what Japanese pharmaceutical companies are now doing in the U.S. market.

Advertising establishes entry barriers by increasing the capital required for getting the attention of the market. Firms that do not have the resources to invest in advertising have little hope of achieving a significant share of a large market, as in breakfast cereals. Advertising effects are also relatively long lasting, and this leads to consumer inertia and brand loyalty. Consequently, by advertising heavily, the market pioneer builds equity that a new competitor may be unable to overcome.

Indeed, new entrant strategy is sometimes to acquire brands with strong equity, thus slashing the time and investment required to develop new brands. Phillip Morris's acquisition of Kraft and General Foods was driven by the desire to add high equity brands to its portfolio.

Distribution Response. Control of distribution can effectively block other entrants. Indeed, this could be a

> **Pizza Hut's reaction to McDonald's testing pizza.**
> "Pizza Hut Inc., the top pie chain, plans a tough ad campaign to keep McDonald's out of its turf. Two years ago, Pizza Hut blasted the single-serving, frozen pizza product tested under the Golden Arches in Charlestown, N.C., and Salt Lake City. Pizza Hut's TV ads featured an icy McPizza thudding onto a store counter." (*Business Week*, August 7, 1989).

highly effective marketing mix variable for sustaining a long-term competitive advantage. The key is to appropriately manage the relationships with efficient distribution channels so that later entrants will be blocked from using them.

For example, later entrants in the personal computer market have found distribution to be their major roadblock. Value-added resellers (VARS) and computer stores rarely handle more than five brands. For the dozens of brands trying to gain late entry, it is exceedingly difficult to dislodge one of the pioneering brands, such as IBM or Apple, from the distribution system to make way for the new brand. An interesting example of a late entry creatively overcoming the distribution barrier is Dell, which built its own catalog/direct mail channel. Similarly, the Japanese television producers, such as Matsushita (Panasonic), initially had difficulty accessing the distribution system, which had allegiance to RCA, Zenith, and other U.S. brands. Matsushita acquired Motorola's TV business as a means of achieving access to retailers.

Distribution defense strategies may be thought of in terms of breadth and depth. Breadth strategies seek the broadest possible number of distribution channels, while depth strategies seek maximum commitment (such as shelf space or inventory) from each outlet. The two strategies tend to be in conflict: Breadth generally limits the level of depth that any one type of distributor will be willing to commit, while depth limits the number of sales outlets willing to commit. Whether expanded breadth or greater depth is more appropriate depends on the efficiency of current distribution channels, the product's life cycle position, and, most importantly, customer behavior patterns.

■ **Efficiency of current distribution channels.** The starting point in considering distribution channel defense strategy is examining the performance of current distribution channels. Extending breadth may not be appropriate if sales are maximized through the present structure and relationships. In such a case, further depth

Continued on page 48.

INNOVATORS, *From page 11.*

may be the logical means of defense. However, mass market distribution channels may have the advantage of lower margins and may reach more diffuse segments.

- **Life cycle position.** In general, as the product moves through its life cycle, it is usually desirable to switch to distribution channels that reach larger markets. As demand builds, and as consumer information needs decrease, it is often necessary to move beyond specialty outlets providing service (which may have been necessary due to their expertise at product introduction) to a portfolio of outlets.

- **Addressing consumer needs.** Ultimately, distribution channel design must be responsive to consumer needs. Broader distribution channels will only be appropriate if they are consistent with consumer buying patterns and provide the benefits sought by customers. High consumer information needs are usually reflected in specialty outlets, while low consumer information needs are reflected in mass market channels.

If the market leader is not sensitive to changing customer preferences in distribution outlets, competitors may be able to enter and grow as new distribution channels emerge. If the market leader is overly committed to present distribution channels, it may be difficult to move into emerging channels, although alternative models or second brands provide possible means to do so. In automobiles, for example, dealerships are moving from single-line/single-location to multi-line/multi-location dealerships, and to leasing as well as sales. Some experimentation is also occurring in separating auto sales and service, since consumer needs are quite different. One key issue is how far people are willing to travel to buy a car as compared with how far they'll go for service. Market pioneers can easily lose leadership positions if they are not represented in high-growth distribution channels.

Finally, at a tactical level, a number of distribution defense initiatives can be used effectively to limit the likely success of a new entrant. These include volume discounts and loyalty programs to maintain the customer's business. Another useful approach is to offer temporary trade discounts when competition is imminent. A basic tactical theory is to build inventory and to utilize distributors' credit lines to preclude competitor sales as much as possible. Since initial sales are important for new entrants in assessing likely future success, any efforts by the pioneer to limit these early sales will discourage the newcomers.

Maintaining Market Leadership

Wisely handled, the substantial advantages of a market pioneer can deter potential entrants. Generally, defense strategies tend to be more successful with more time for advance planning. This gives the market pioneer a chance to develop strategies to discourage entry up front. We believe that advance planning helps block entry and limits competitive inroads. Thus, a critical function of the market pioneer is to continuously monitor potential rivals to gauge the likelihood and timing of competitive entry. This is accomplished by monitoring competitors' advertising, requests for distribution authorization, investments in plant and equipment, and their patent applications. Reading these signals gives the pioneer time to design and implement an effective defense strategy before the competition hits the market.

There are times, however, when the best strategy is not to retaliate, especially when the newcomers are offering superior technology and can also achieve equal scale and access to resources. Under such conditions, the smart move may be to abandon the market. On the other hand, when the new entrant can match the pioneer's advantages and has viable scale and resources, the most successful response may be to make room for the newcomer.

However, when conditions favor retaliation, the market pioneer must chose the domain in which to react. If the pioneer has a stronger competitive advantage in a different market, reaction may sometimes be more successful there than where the new entry is taking place.

Finally, the pioneer must design a marketing defense program aimed primarily at thwarting entry. We have considered such questions as when to lower price, when to innovate, when to extend positioning, when to introduce a second brand, how to gain communication advantage, and how to gain channel advantage. At best, a well-thought-out defense program will discourage entry. But when this is not possible, it can limit the extent and aggressiveness of entry and thus maintain the market pioneer's leadership. □

Notes

1. The following articles document market pioneer advantages. W. T. Robinson and C. Fornell, "The Sources of Market Pioneer Advantages in Consumer Goods Industries," *Journal of Marketing Research.* 22, August 1985, 297-304; and W. T. Robinson, "Marketing Mix Reactions to Entry," *Marketing Science,* 7, Fall, 1988, 368-385; and G. L. Urban, T. Carter, S. Gaskin, and Z. Mucha, "Market Share Rewards to Pioneering Brands: An Empirical Analysis and Strategic Implications," *Management Science,* 32 June, 1986, 645-659.

2. Readers are undoubtedly familiar with the influential work of Michael Porter and his emphasis on entry barriers in *Competitive Strategy,* New York: The Free Press, 1980; and *Competitive Advantage,* New York: The Free Press, 1985.

3. J. Bains's classic work on the role of advertising as an entry barrier is: J. Bain, *Barriers to Competition,* Harvard University Press, Cambridge, Mass, 1956.

Strategy Search and Creativity: The Key to Corporate Renewal

SIMON MAJARO, *Visiting Professor of Marketing Strategy, Cranfield School of Management*

Simon Majaro's recent work focuses on injecting creativity into a company's strategy. A model of eight interrelated elements is described which top management should pursue to encourage creativity and innovation.

The author demonstrates the process of 'Strategy Search', structured group work using specially-devised techniques and aids to creative thinking — exploring many issues. Creative thinking at the top is necessary to move the whole organisation.

Finally, top management must view creativity and innovation holistically; although interrelated, they are just one approach, together with visioning, shared values and knowledge, to a single vital corporate aim — satisfying the customer.

Top management is often heard to exhort people in the organisation to become more creative. Some enlightened companies go as far as investing in the process of educating and training members of the organisation on how to become more creative. Yet very few leaders of industry and commerce actually indulge themselves in creative activities. Creativity is regarded as a very desirable pattern of behaviour for others to pursue. Those who have reached the top of the hierarchical ladder somehow believe that 'Creativity' is a concept that one can delegate to other members of the firm. A very illustrious captain of industry once told me, in unequivocal terms: 'I pay people high salaries to do their job and that includes being creative'.

There follows a little checklist for those belonging to the strategic level of the firm:

1. When did you last participate in a creative session designed to solve problems and/or explore new opportunities?   Yes   No
2. Have you taken part in a brainstorming session (or any other session utilising creative techniques) since you got to your top position?   Yes   No
3. Have you ever reflected upon the barriers that stand in the way of your firm's ability to improve its creativity and innovation?   Yes   No
4. When planning the future of your company, do you attempt to use creative methods in coalescing a vision of the future?   Yes   No
5. When developing the firm's Mission, do you:
   (a) Use creative methods to identify the most relevant statement within the firm's circumstances?   Yes   No
   (b) Insert a statement about creativity being part of the firm's culture?   Yes   No
6. Do you go out of your way to ensure that ideas flow from:
   (a) Personnel inside the firm?   Yes   No
   (b) From the international environment?   Yes   No
7. Do you take steps to motivate people to be creative?   Yes   No
8. Do you monitor the firm's level of creativity and innovation in a systematic way?   Yes   No

If senior managers respond to any of these questions with a 'No', they ought to reflect very seriously about their contribution to the firm's creative processes and identify the role which they propose to play in enhancing creativity and innovation in the organisation. The one point that top management should always remember is that they often represent a role model which managers at lower levels seek to emulate. The boss who stifles everybody's ideas cannot expect members of the organisation to behave differently. On the other hand, the chief operating officer who grasps every idea with open arms provides a powerful stimulant to the generation of ideas and their communication throughout the firm.

I have been involved in helping firms to become more creative and more innovative for many years, and in many parts of the world. During the last five years,

I and a number of colleagues from one of the leading business schools started applying the principles of creative thinking towards the search for company strategy and the development of corporate plans. In other words, we have been seeking to inject creativity at the strategic level of the firm. In common with most consultants/academics, we have had our share of successes and failures. Nonetheless, valuable lessons were learnt from both and in this paper I wish to summarise a few of these lessons.

Background Concepts

I always start my explorations in the field of creativity and innovation by defining my terms. Experience has taught me that although the two words 'creativity' and 'innovation' are being used in the business world with great frequency, communication is often hampered by the fact that different people ascribe different meanings to these two words. When I ask ten managers on a workshop to describe their understanding of these two terms, I usually receive ten different definitions.

I use the two terms in the following way:

'Creativity' is the thinking process which helps us to generate ideas;

'Innovation' is the application of an idea towards doing things better, cheaper, more aesthetically and/or more effectively.

An idea can be bizarre, outlandish, wild or even useless. On the other hand, an innovation has to be useful, results-orientated, profitable or effective. Why waste time on outlandish ideas? The reason is simple: without ideas one is unlikely to attain innovations. Moreover, history has shown that one needs many ideas to feed the innovation process. As many as 60 ideas are needed before a successful innovation is attained. In other words, a firm that deprives itself of the input generated by the creative process will find that it starves itself of the desirable task of innovating. Creativity *per se* does not amount to much. It is purely the 'input' which facilitates the attainment of innovation — the 'output'. We need people's creativity because without it we are not likely to achieve the level of innovation which makes our organisations more effective, more productive and more successful. Figure 1 illustrates the relationship between creativity and innovation in a diagrammatic form.

On the whole, top management understands this simple truth. However, there is normally a gap between what management believes in and what actually happens at lower levels. Top management, or as I prefer to call the people at the top, the Strategic Level, often prefer to exhort others to 'become more creative and more innovative', but do not want to become involved in the process of changing attitudes and leading the task of developing the kind of shared values that enhance the firm's creativity and innovation demands. Bosses who abdicate from this vital task cannot expect the organisation to become truly creative and ultimately innovative.

For those who recognise the importance of developing a more creative organisation, the integrated approach to creativity and innovation described in Figure 2 is a useful starting point. A number of elements must be in place if the whole process of innovation can be managed in a cohesive and well-structured manner. Eight elements are being shown and a brief description of each one of them will help to place this model in its proper context.

Climate

The climate for innovation is right when every person in the firm — senior or junior — 'thinks', 'talks', 'dreams'

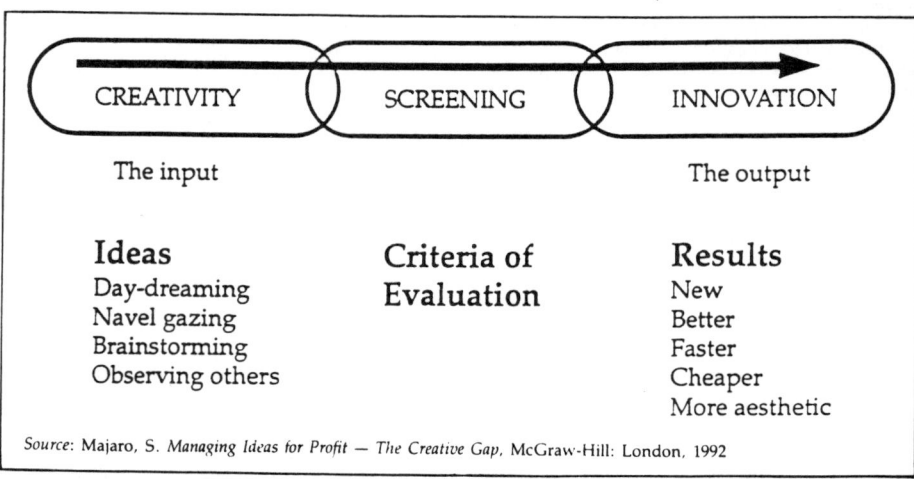

CREATIVITY → SCREENING → INNOVATION

The input   The output

Ideas   **Criteria of**   **Results**
Day-dreaming   **Evaluation**   New
Navel gazing   Better
Brainstorming   Faster
Observing others   Cheaper
                                                            More aesthetic

Source: Majaro, S. *Managing Ideas for Profit — The Creative Gap*, McGraw-Hill: London, 1992

Figure 1 The relationship between Creativity and Innovation

Strategic Planning Process

STRATEGY SEARCH AND CREATIVITY

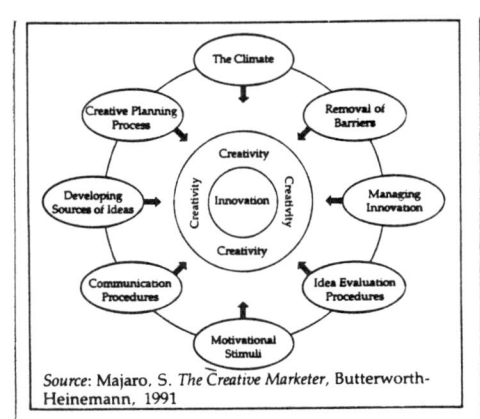

Source: Majaro, S. *The Creative Marketer*, Butterworth-Heinemann, 1991

Figure 2 Creativity and Innovation — an Integrated approach

and 'acts' creatively. In other words, it becomes an integral part of the firm's culture and *shared value*. An easy concept to talk about; a daunting task to achieve. It calls for a persistent and imaginative programme of work, masterminded from the top but implemented at all levels.

Creative Planning Process

As emphasised earlier, innovation must start at the top; the bosses must demonstrate their ability to develop an innovative vision and plan the future direction of the firm in a creative way. This particular element will form the main thrust of my paper.

Removal of Barriers

Every firm suffers from a number of barriers that impede the flow of ideas. These barriers differ from company to company although obstacles such as bureaucracy, the 'not invented here' syndrome and 'bean-counting' exist in many organisations. Top management of every company should 'audit' the specific barriers that interfere with the creativity of their respective organisations and seek to remove them. (For further details, see Majaro, 1992.)

Developing Sources of Ideas

Ideas can be tapped from inside the firm (e.g. through suggestion schemes or the use of idea-generation techniques) and from outside sources (e.g. customers, consultants, competitors, different industries). The options are multifarious, but active steps must be undertaken to develop a systematic approach to harnessing them. (See Von Hippel, 1988.)

Communication Procedures

People in any organisation have ideas or observe interesting innovations in the external environment. A system must be established to ensure that every member of the organisation knows how and to whom to convey such ideas. Communication procedures do not happen by themselves. This is particularly true in the context of multinational organisations. Companies operating in a number of countries have an opportunity to benefit from the cross-fertilisation of ideas emanating from different environments and cultures. Failure to exploit such a rich seam of ideas almost negates the value of being multinational. Figure 3 illustrates the two ways in which ideas can flow in a multinational context. Clearly, the systematic way described in the second model is the one that a company should strive to develop. (See Majaro, 1988.)

Motivational Stimuli

Members of the organisation can easily become more creative when they know that their input is appreciated. Such stimuli need not be of financial or material nature. A symbol of recognition can often have a more potent impact than a monetary reward.

Idea Evaluation Procedures

Let us assume that the firm has organised itself to tap people's ideas and/or generate a myriad of ideas through the many techniques that exist for that purpose. The ability to screen and evaluate such ideas promptly and efficiently is a most powerful tool in the whole process. One of the killers of creativity is the inability to convert ideas to reality in a systematic fashion.

Managing Innovation

The innovative company must establish a system for monitoring and controlling the level of innovation that has been achieved during a given period. The best stimulus to creativity is the knowledge that ideas are being implemented from time to time. Moreover, the system should highlight the lessons learnt from recent successes and failures.

Figure 4 provides one example of the kind of controlling procedures which I have been inviting my clients to maintain in this regard. Many other monitoring procedures can be developed in response to the specific needs of each organisation.

In summary, there are eight highly interrelated elements which must be developed and put in place by top management if the firm is to become more creative and, in turn, increase its ability to become more innovative. They are all important and they must all be pursued with steadfastness and imagination. Nevertheless, for the purpose of this paper I want to dwell on the 'Creative Planning Process', as it was in this area we discovered rich pickings.

Strategy Search and Creativity

Top management of most companies realise that their businesses operate in an environment which is more

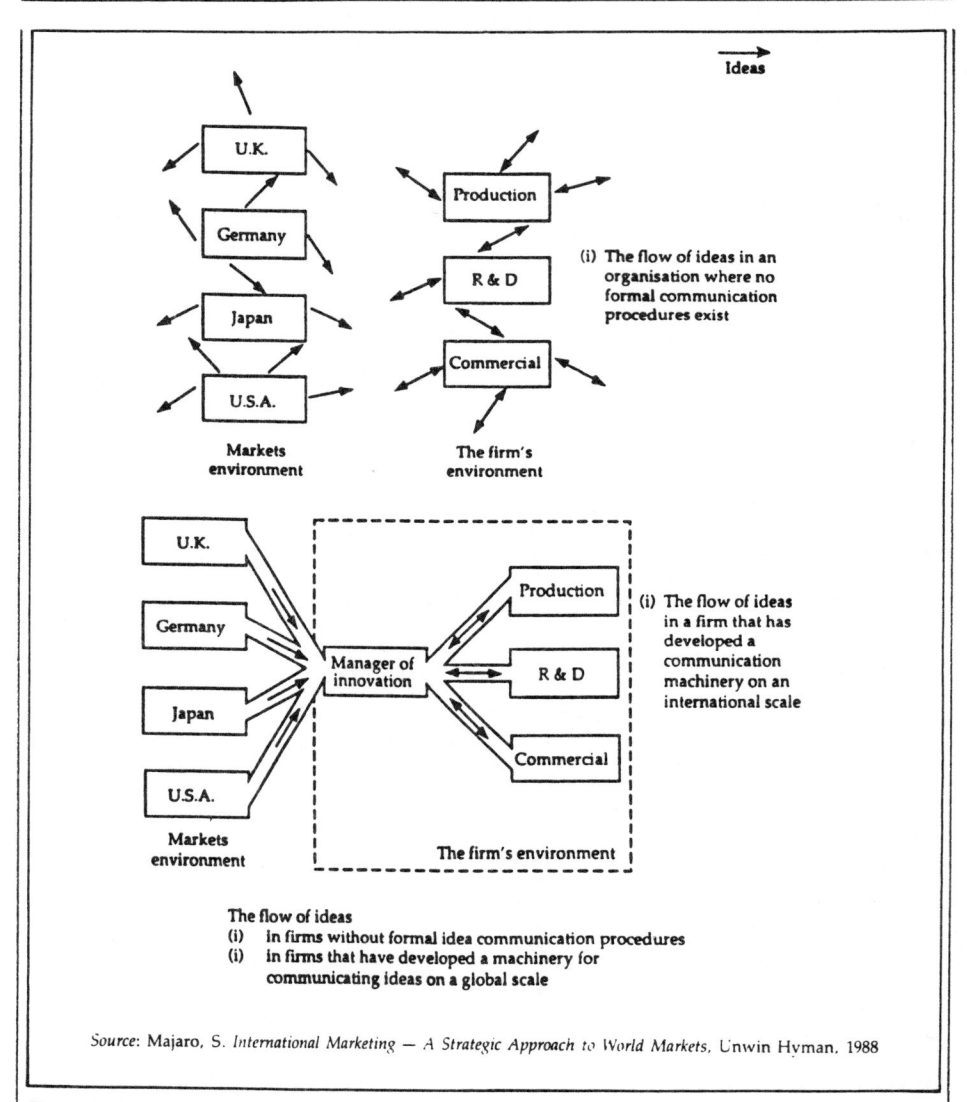

Figure 3 Systematic flow of ideas in a multinational context

complex, more dynamic and more hostile than ever. Competitive pressures have increased, technology is shortening product life cycles and customer requirements are becoming more sophisticated. The challenge is how to manage such an environment within the context of existing corporate resources in a more creative way. Moreover, how can we move towards a management style which anticipates these changes rather than reacts to them? To use the language of the modern planner — how can we become proactive rather than reactive in our corporate behaviour. Clearly, being proactive also calls for a measure of creative thinking.

Together with a number of colleagues at my business school, we developed a structured approach to the search for strategies. We call the process 'Strategy Search'. It is a systematic step-by-step process aimed at identifying the alternative options facing the company in its search for the most appropriate future direction. It is an informal gathering of senior managers and deci-

STRATEGY SEARCH AND CREATIVITY

Innovation number	Description of Innovation	Date implemented	Benefits attained (over period to be specified)	Further work needed	Lessons learned

Source: Majaro, S. *The Creative Marketer*, Butterworth-Heinemann, 1991

Figure 4 Innovation analysis worksheet

sion makers (usually no more than a dozen) from one organisation, in a pleasant environment, in which major strategic issues can be ventilated. During a short period of two or three days, and away from the normal workplace, the group explores and evaluates, together with two independent and experienced strategic thinkers, the most viable and innovative route which the company could pursue.

Through the use of a number of specially-devised techniques and aids to creative thinking, the participants are encouraged to appraise objectively the threats and opportunities that their organisation is facing and to recognise the company's most significant strengths and weaknesses. The outcome of this analysis provides the starting point for the development of successful product/market strategies.

Our facilitators who run the 'Strategy Search' meetings are all experienced in providing unobtrusive direction to the discussions. They are also well-versed in the use of methods and techniques associated with the management of creativity. By bringing senior managers together in an informal environment, and by following a number of well-tried processes, our approach can yield good results in a short period of time.

The kind of topics that fall within the orbit of a 'Strategy Search' programme are as follows.

1 Developing a Vision

The role of the strategic planning process is to lead the firm towards the future. This requires long-term perspectives. Short-term orientation does not lead to competitive advantage and continual self-renewal. The process of developing a vision helps management to gain a deeper awareness of its values, and that in turn helps to hone a set of values which are empathic towards the needs of the future. When vision and values are in harmony, a compelling desire to act is aroused. Thus, if the vision points at a 'greener' world, it forces us to reflect upon our role in such an environment and respond to the challenges prescribed by such a world.

The tool we use for this activity is a well-structured exercise in 'scenario daydreaming'. Unlike 'scenario writing', the visioning process takes place verbally. It is like a brainstorming session but relates to the group's imaging of the world at a given date in the future, say year 2000. Each individual is allocated a factor for exploration such as economic trends, politics and geopolitics, ecology, cost of commodities. Topics for exploration are often allocated in accordance with people's specific knowledge and/or expertise. The important thing is that the discussions are centred around the concept that 'today is January 2000 and this is what is happening in the world around us ...'. The use of the future tense must be avoided. A scribe records the main issues that emerge and through an iterative process the vision is refined and the implications for the company explored in some depth. Clearly, the collective knowledge of those present can enrich the value of the deliberations.

If one remembers that the most important point about planning is the process itself rather than the outcome, this vision development exercise can be a most potent generator of ideas for further reflection and analysis.

2 Developing a Mission

'What is the purpose of our firm?' Defining the mission of the firm is a popular pastime. Many firms feel that without an elegant mission statement they have not earned their spurs. Once again, it is worth remembering that it is not the elegance of the mission statement which guarantees corporate excellence. It is the quality of knowledge and intellectual input which has gone into the process which provides the company with its cutting edge on the competitive scene. In this connection, we always emphasise the fact that a sound mission statement should avoid encompassing too many fancy and meaningless phrases. It should fulfil a number of basic and logical dimensions:

(a) be specific enough to have an impact upon the behaviour of individuals throughout the business,
(b) be focused more on customer need−satisfaction,
(c) be based on an objective recognition of the company's strengths and weaknesses,
(d) recognise the opportunities and threats in the competitive environment,
(e) be realistic and attainable,
(f) be flexible.

(For more details see Majaro, 1989.)

A good mission statement is the banner under which the firm will be operating. If carefully defined and refined, it inevitably projects the firm's set of shared values. These in turn reflect the firm's climate and culture.

During the search for a suitable mission we use techniques like brainstorming, trigger sessions, metaphorical analogy and brain patterns. More recently, we started using IdeaFisher, one of the computer software packages designed to augment one's idea-generation activities.

3 Identifying and Developing 'Shared Values'

We have learnt during the last decade how important it is for a company to articulate a set of 'values' which are universally known among the company personnel and wholeheartedly shared. Once the vision and the mission have been coalesced, the key 'values' which may be instrumental for the attainment of excellence should be highlighted and built into the firm's ethos, code of behaviour and management development plans. These are the 'shared values' that distinguish an outstanding company from the rest.

Our favoured technique in this regard is metaphorical analogy or synectics. The ability to draw inspiration from analogous successes from other areas of human endeavour worldwide and from history can be of great help.

4 Managing Change

At this stage, top management often realises that managing change is becoming a major task. A Vision leads to a Mission and a Mission helps to highlight the Shared Values that could be instrumental for future success. Clearly, this involves the firm in cultural changes which demand a creative input from both top management and those responsible for management development and training.

Once again we find that the use of metaphorical analogy can be a powerful stimulant to the process of planning for and managing change. Through freewheeling sessions we seek to identify organisations, from any sphere of human activity, including religious creeds and political bodies, that have succeeded in indoctrinating a large number of people in the value of their beliefs. Changing an organisation from a production-orientated mode to a marketing-orientated creed bears some similarity with the way the early Christians have propagated their beliefs. Successes and failures of this nature can provide a powerful stimulus to the creative thinking of the participants.

5 Developing a 'Sustainable Competitive Advantage'

Sooner or later, the Board of Directors must address itself to the task of attempting to develop a sustainable competitive advantage for the firm and its products and services. There is no need to stress here the importance of this activity. We all know that the winners of the 1990s will be those companies that manage to differentiate their offerings from their competitors. In marketing terms, innovation often entails differentiation and differentiation requires creative leaps. In this context, we use the 'strategic leap' method specifically devised for the purpose, and also such techniques as 'Attribute Listing' and brainstorming.

6 New Product Exploration and/or Development

This is a logical culmination of the 'Strategy Search' cycle. Having started with vision development, one is bound to reach a point at which the participants want to consider practical ways in which to enrich the product portfolio for the future. A plethora of fun techniques exist to assist the group in exploring potential new products or product enhancements. Morphological Analysis, Attribute Listing and Brain Patterns are useful methods in this connection. (For details of the techniques mentioned see Majaro, 1991.)

These are some of the issues that are explored during 'Strategy Search' workshops. The important point to remember is that top management must tackle issues and problems relating to strategy, business direction and proactive anticipation of events. All these can benefit from creative thinking as much as any other operational problem can.

So far this does not represent a major breakthrough in the field of creativity and innovation. All that I have tried

STRATEGY SEARCH AND CREATIVITY

to highlight is the importance of applying well-tried techniques and methods that we all associate with problem solving and exploratory creativity towards assisting the company's top management in charting a course to the future.

Major Lessons Learned

'Strategy Search' as a Spur to Creativity Throughout the Firm

The important revelation that we stumbled across almost 'by serendipity' is the fact that when a Board of Directors agrees to undertake a 'Strategy Search' session, they provide a most powerful spur to creativity throughout the firm. The news that the bosses are 'playing the creative game' in the pursuit of an innovative vision, mission and strategy is more potent than a massive programme of management development designed to enhance a climate in which creativity can spawn.

With this thought in mind, we have started to reverse the process: when top management ask us to help to stimulate creativity in the firm, we recommend that they, the people at the top, agree to participate in a well-publicised 'Strategy Search' creativity-orientated workshop. When I say 'well-publicised', I do not mean that the details of the deliberation should be communicated. It is the style of the programme, the method used and the aims sought which ought to be communicated. People lower down the organisation are bound to decode the message in an unequivocal way: 'If the bosses are playing the creative game we ought to do the same'. The impetus for learning about the creative processes which starts at the top becomes all-pervasive and translates itself into a bottom-up pressure for a sustained effort at promulgating a more creative climate. We all tend to model ourselves on the way our leaders behave. A chairman of one of my client companies has recently started to arrive at work on a mountain bike. It is fascinating to watch the growth in number of such bikes in the firm's car park! Similarly, if the strategic level indulges in creative sessions, it does not take long for the rank and file to pursue similar activities. In other words, what has started as an exercise designed to help the firm to formulate strategies has proved to have much wider developmental spin-offs, albeit by association rather than by design.

The Need for a Holistic Approach to Strategy

The most significant lesson that we learnt from this experience is the importance for top management to look at 'Creativity and Innovation' as one component in a complex framework of interrelated elements. Stimulating creativity out of context is unlikely to turn a poor enterprise into an excellent one. It may simply help the firm to 'do the wrong things better'. This is the subtle difference between efficiency and effectiveness. Creativity should be the tool that helps the firm to become more effective and not just more efficient. A *holistic* approach is required if the input of creative thinking is to play a contributing role in the pursuit of long-term success. This is a vital point which is often missed by top management. The myth still persists that all one needs to do is exhort people to be more creative or train them in idea-generation techniques and all will be well with the world.

Business gurus' books attempt to tell us about the panaceas for corporate excellence. Michael Porter has taught us about the value of *Competitive Advantage*; Gifford Pinchot in *Intrapreneuring* has attempted to explain why big business, despite spending most of the world's R&D money, has a grossly disproportionate share of major innovations. In the highly fashionable field of quality, people like Demming, Crosby *et al.* tell us all about the importance of getting the quality right, almost to the exclusion of everything else; Peters and Waterman, in their *In Search of Excellence*, have attempted to view excellence from a holistic vantage point, but unfortunately the book has too much pretence to balanced research. The one guru who always appears to view businesses in a holistic fashion is Peter Drucker. This is probably the main reason his books have survived the test of time.

In spite of all my research into the literature on the subject of creativity and innovation, I have not found any definitive paradigm that can guide us towards a better understanding of the exact role that top management can play in promulgating more innovative and more successful enterprises. My own proposition is based on empirical observation of company strategists during 'Strategy Search' workshops and an attempt at getting back to basics.

The proposition is based on a very simple axiom: *the success of any business depends on its ability to satisfy the customer*. Companies that fail to satisy their customers are not likely to survive. The whole panoply of the marketing function is designed to assist us in fulfilling this fundamental task. 'Come close to the customer' is one of the prescriptions of Peters and Waterman in their book *In Search of Excellence*. So far so good, but the whole concept begs many questions:

1. *Who is the customer and what exactly are his needs?*
2. *Are we talking about today's customers or those of the future?*
   Clearly looking at the firm from the vantage point of the strategic level, one has to accept that the future may be different from the present in many respects. To that extent, developing a vision, mission and strategy is an essential part of good top management.
3. *Who is responsible for satisfying the customer?*
   Is this purely the job of marketing personnel or should this be a company-wide process? The obvious answer is that it must be part of the total firm's ethos and shared values. Once again, top management must be a prime mover in inculcating such a creed.
4. *What 'knowledge' do we require to understand what*

would satisfy the customer now and in the future?
It is almost a cliché to say that we live in an era in which 'knowledge' is one of the prime assets of any organisation. According to a story attributed to Einstein, he was once asked how he would spend his final hour in the face of a mortal danger. His answer was: 90% of that hour would be spent on collecting information; 5% on weighing up alternative courses of action; the final 5% taking a decision. The whole world of information technology is at management's disposal. Is top management spending enough time exploring its value to the firm? One must remember that the essence of information is 'knowing what one needs to know'. Information *per se* is of limited value.

5. *Do the customers value our creativity?*
The answer must be a loud 'yes' if our creativity leads to an innovation which provides the customers with a better and/or less costly and/or more aesthetic benefit or utility. Rare would be the customer who would not bless 3M for its development of 'Post-it' or Glaxo for its Zantac innovation. Both are successful and few would dispute the fact that creativity and innovation were major factors in that success.

Figure 5 summarises this holistic approach to an effective and creative top management philosophy. It aims to highlight the role that creativity and innovation can play in the whole process. The model described represents the main tasks of top management. They do not have to 'run' each of the activities encompassed in the satellites shown, but they certainly must reflect upon and initiate and mastermind the appropriate developmental programmes of work envisaged by each of them.

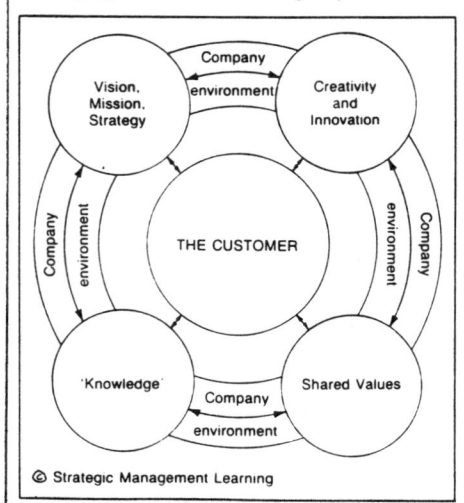

Figure 5 Satisfying the customer: the company's 'input' — a holistic approach

If 'the Customer is King', the four satellites shown must work in total harmony within the company's environment, present and future, with the view of promulgating all the appropriate 'satisfiers' that would keep him or her happy and such happiness should maintain the enterprise's overall success.

It is hoped that the model shown in Figure 5 is capable in itself of providing the reader with a framework for reflection and analysis pertaining to his or her business environment. It must be recalled that my aim is to highlight the strategic context within which 'creativity and innovation' can act as a powerful spur to a longer term excellence. Two important points must be emphasised:

1. The model described is only relevant in the context of firms that have accepted the validity of being marketing-orientated. Obviously, companies that are still resisting the 'marketing concept' are fighting gravity and are not likely to achieve corporate renewal. All the evidence gleaned during our 'Strategy Search' workshops has reinforced our long-held conviction that companies that refuse to move towards a customer-led or marketing-led mode are gambling with their future. Market conditions are such that the punishment for those who refuse to grapple with change is likely to be severe.

2. The four elements shown must be viewed as an integrated assemblage. They interact, enrich and fertilise each other. Creativity enhances visioning and visioning, in turn, stimulates creativity. A shared vision has the potential of being an integrating force in the organisation culminating in a set of shared values to which people can feel fully committed.

Creativity and innovation must become part of the firm's shared values if they are to become part of the organisation's cutting edge. When 3M talk about the '25% Rule' they invite all managers to analyse their product portfolio and ensure that, at all times, at least 25% of the products under their control are less than five years old! The message is clear: 'you must invest time in creativity in order to innovate'. This in turn becomes an integral part of the firm's shared values. Members of the organisation 'talk', 'think' and 'act' innovation. It is part of the firm's creed.

'Knowledge' is another powerful catalyst that can enrich the company's input towards satisfying the customer. (See Oliff and Marchand, 1991.) It is outside the scope of this paper to enumerate all the areas in which effective knowledge management or information management can provide the company with a powerful competitive advantage. Suffice it to emphasise within the paradigm described in Figure 5 that a company that acquires more accurate, more comprehensive and more anticipatory knowledge than its own customers possess is in a pretty strong position in the competitive world we live in. Customers will gravitate towards such a supplier!

STRATEGY SEARCH AND CREATIVITY

'Knowledge' can enrich the vision, mission and strategy development processes. All can gain enormously from the support of a team that adheres to a cohesive and unified set of values. All three can be spurred by creativity. A firm that manages to slot creativity into such a holistic framework will be the winner of the 1990s. Obviously, this can only be achieved at the instigation of the firm's top leadership.

References

Adams, J.D. (ed.), *Transforming Leadership: From Vision to Results*, Alexandria, VA: Miles River Press, 1986.

Christopher C., Majaro, S. and McDonald, M., *Strategy Search*, Gower Publishing, 1987.

Lamb, R.B., *Competitive Strategic Management*, Englewood Cliffs, NJ: Prentice Hall, 1984.

Leavitt, H.J., *Corporate Pathfinders. Building Vision and Values into Organizations*, Homewood, IL: Dow Jones-Irwin, 1986.

Majaro, Simon, *International Marketing — A Strategic Approach to World Markets*, Unwin Hyman, 1988.

Majaro, Simon, *Managing Ideas for Profit — The Creative Gap*, London: McGraw Hill, 1992.

Majaro, Simon, *The Creative Marketer*, Oxford: Butterworth-Heinemann, 1991.

Moss Kanter, R., *The Changemasters*, Simon & Schuster, 1983.

Oliff, M.C. and Marchand, D.A., Strategic Information Management in Global Manufacturing, *European Management Journal*, Vol. 9, No. 4, December 1991.

Parker, Marjorie, *Creating Shared Vision*, Dialog International Ltd, 1990.

Porter, M.E., *Competitive Advantage — Creating and Sustaining Superior Performance*, The Free Press, 1985.

Quinn, J.B., *Strategies for Change: Logical Incrementation*, Homewood, IL: Irwin Inc., 1980.

Taylor, Robert S., *Value Added Processes in Information Systems*, Norwood, NJ: Ablex Publishing Corp., 1986.

Von Hippel, E., *The Sources of Innovation*, Oxford University Press, 1988.

Zuboff, Shoshana, *In the Age of the Smart Machine*, New York: Basic Books Inc., 1988.

[14]

The Myths of Strategic Planning

Commentary

Strategic planning has had a painful coming of age. In some companies, its value was lost in mountains of paper. In others institutionalized 'systems' of strategic planning actually blocked sound strategic thinking. Yet as **Walter Schaffir**, president of **Growth Dynamics**, and **David Moore**, president of **Interchem** point out, having been formalized, criticized, reshaped, misunderstood, oversold, redefined, misapplied, discarded and revitalized, strategic planning is alive and well today in the real world of business. To make it acceptable as a practical, everyday management tool, practictioners had first to demolish several myths.

Myth No. 1: Having a sound strategic plan is tantamount to having a successful business. Wrong. A strategic plan can point you in the right direction. It can help sell the right product to the right customer while facing strategy-conscious competitors. But nothing happens in business without a sale. Good strategy is only a start in generating good business.

Myth No. 2: A sound strategic plan must be developed bottom-up, because only that way can all organizational levels be involved. Wrong. Bottom-up strategic planning can create a chasm between the CEO's corporate vision and the operating units' narrower view of their business. Strategy is best developed in top-down/bottom-up iterative cycles that join top-level vision, insight and perspective with the competitive/market familiarity of the operating units.

Myth No. 3: A sound strategic plan is best developed by planning staff specialists. Wrong. Strategic planning is such an integral part of managing the business that the CEO himself or the general manager of an operating unit must in effect be the chief planner. Only if the plan is shaped and its underlying issues resolved by the chief and his executive team, will strategies be owned up to by those who must implement them.

Myth No. 4: Because planning must be primarily a line responsibility, there is no longer a need for planning staff. Wrong. Staff are needed to support planning decisions with information, provide uniform methodologies, consolidate unit plans into a corporate overview, advise on trade-offs and other issues. Most importantly, staff must teach and coach executive teams at various levels – a role yet to be fully realized.

Myth No. 5: There is a clear distinction between strategy and tactics. Wrong. The tactic of one level becomes the strategy of the level below; its strategy translates into tactics that become the strategies of the next tier down. Understanding this helps getting out of a semantic box.

Myth No. 6: The primary objective of planning is to develop a plan. Wrong. The primary objective of strategic planning is to get something done. The plan is a by-product of this process, not its objective. The plan is useful for summarizing decisions, communicating direction, gaining approval, and serving as the basis for implementing action. But by itself it does not move the action forward.

But dismantling the myths is not enough. To change a burdensome planning process into a dynamic and managerially useful discipline, three interacting elements must be put in place. Strategic thinking as an on-going, day-to-day activity cannot exist without any one of them.

Firstly, a uniform methodology allowing ready comparisons. Without it, one business unit may characterize its 3% market growth as 'explosive', while another thinks of it as 'level'. The CEO must then interpret what each unit is telling him.

Secondly, communication of key information in easily digestible form. In a $3 billion chemical company with 72 strategic business units, the consolidated corporate plan comprised 1,400 pages plus an extensive summary and staff commentary. Sounds familiar? You can guess what the CEO read. The executive summary plus some favorite SBU excerpts – followed by a sigh of relief that that job's over for another year.

A better idea is to level evaluative methodology at the business unit level. Then, ask each business team to write a two to four-page strategic direction paper (SDP) describing: the few major issues facing the business; the alternatives evaluated to resolve each issue; the alternative chosen; the program(s) including capital and manpower requirements; and the likely range of results for three or five years.

Thirdly, focused dialog between corporate and business unit managements. The SDPs prepare for the third, most important phase – the dialog between corporate management and business teams, where insight and judgement meet information and analysis. The purpose of these sessions is to test the plan and end up with agreement. The test questions are: Why are these the major issues? Why was the particular alternative chosen? How confident are you the program can be implemented with stated resources? And that it will produce anticipated results? If the chosen direction doesn't make sense or doesn't seem worth the effort, it may be necessary to refer to source data. Otherwise, the business unit team proceeds in accordance with the agreed-upon plan until the next review. Should circumstances change, another dialog session is held regardless of when this occurs in the 'normal' planning cycle.

The advantages of this disciplined, sharply focused approach are easily understood. But what about the cynic who is skeptical of any kind of strategic thinking? Schaffir and Moore advise avoiding arguments about abstractions such as 'strategy' and 'planning'. Instead, focus on practical, unavoidable questions such as: What is likely to upset your expectations? What are your competitors doing differently? What opportunities are you currently foregoing?

SBU STRATEGIES, CORPORATE-SBU RELATIONS, AND SBU EFFECTIVENESS IN STRATEGY IMPLEMENTATION

ANIL K. GUPTA
University of Maryland at College Park

In a departure from earlier studies focusing only on the effects of corporate strategies, this study examined the effects of strategic business units' (SBUs') strategies on the utility of various states of corporate-SBU relations. For SBUs trying to build market share or to pursue differentiation as a competitive strategy, openness in corporate-SBU relations and subjectivity in performance assessment were found to be positively associated with effectiveness; for SBUs trying to maximize short-term earnings or to pursue low cost as a competitive strategy, the corresponding associations were found to be negative. In contrast, corporate-SBU decentralization emerged as positively associated with SBUs' effectiveness irrespective of their strategic contexts; although SBUs' competitive strategies moderated the magnitude of that association, their strategic missions did not.

Perhaps the most salient topic in analyses of how multibusiness firms should be managed has been relations between corporations and their strategic business units (SBUs). The topic was certainly of primary concern to executives as diverse as Alfred Sloan of General Motors, Ralph Cordiner of General Electric, and Harold Geneen of ITT (Cordiner, 1956; Geneen, 1985; Sloan, 1964). Importantly, it also has been the primary issue examined in some prominent studies in business history (Chandler, 1962), organization theory (Lorsch & Allen, 1973; Ouchi, 1984), strategic management (Rumelt, 1974), management control (Vancil, 1980), and even institutional economics (Williamson, 1970).

It is curious that, despite the sheer number and the generally outstanding quality of the studies, this stream of research continues to suffer from a major limitation: although it has examined the effects of strategic context at a corporate level on the management of corporate-SBU relations, it has completely overlooked the impact that SBU-level strategic context might also have on those relations. SBUs' own strategic contexts are important because competitive battles are fought primarily at the SBU rather than the corporate level (Anderson & Zeithaml, 1984; Hambrick, 1983; Porter, 1980). Further, as

---

N. Venkatraman and V. Ramanujam provided helpful comments on earlier drafts of this paper. The Human Resources Policy Institute, based at Boston University, provided financial support.

this study suggests, there exist theoretical grounds for expecting SBUs' strategic contexts to affect the management of relations between parent corporations and their SBUs.

To help redress this deficiency, the present study examined the effects of two dimensions of SBUs' strategic contexts—strategic mission and competitive strategy—on the performance implications of three aspects of corporate-SBU relations. The three aspects are (1) the openness of the relationship between an SBU's general manager and his or her superior, (2) corporate use of subjectivity in assessments of the performance of SBU managers, and (3) corporate-SBU decentralization.

THEORETICAL BACKGROUND

Although several reasons exist for expecting SBUs' strategic contexts to influence the utility of various states of corporate-SBU relations, the dominant rationale derives from the information-processing perspective on organization design (Duncan, 1973; Egelhoff, 1982; Galbraith, 1973; Tushman & Nadler, 1978). Building on March and Simon (1958), advocates of this perspective have argued that unless an organization's information-processing capacity adequately meets its need for information processing, the decisions that emerge will be flawed or late, thereby resulting in suboptimal performance.

Every SBU must explicitly or implicitly make a series of ongoing decisions along many dimensions pertaining to inputs (labor, raw materials, capital), throughputs (technology, capacity, quality), and outputs (marketing, distribution, service). Further, since managers are neither omniscient nor omnipotent, many decisions must be modified in whole or in part as events unfold over time and new information is generated. The underlying premise of this study was that the need for such mid-course modifications will differ systematically across different SBU-level strategic contexts. More specifically, I expected that some strategic contexts would be associated with greater task uncertainty than others and that SBUs in such contexts would thereby require more frequent mid-course modifications.

It is obvious that the greater the need for mid-course modifications in strategic decisions, the greater is the need for internal information-processing capacity within an SBU. However, because SBUs within corporations are not freestanding entities, modifications in their strategic decisions would also require interaction with corporate management for these reasons: (1) A decision may imply a modification in the amount, the timing, or both, of the allocation of financial and other resources by an SBU's parent corporation. (2) Because of interdependence among SBUs, a business may need to factor in the secondary implications for other units when modifying decisions that superficially pertain only to itself. Finally, (3) modification of a decision may require renegotiation of the specific goals to be accomplished by an SBU as well as the specific timing of those accomplishments. Accordingly, for SBUs requiring more frequent mid-course modifications in strategic decisions, the quality and timing of modifications is likely to be better when the information-processing capacity of the corporate-SBU dyad is high than when it is low.

Corporate-SBU Relations: Dimensions of Interest

Although no previous study has examined corporate-SBU relations in the context of SBU-level strategy, literature on the subject rooted in strategy at the corporate level can nonetheless serve as a useful guide for selecting the relational dimensions to address. The results of this stream of research can be summarized as follows: a high level of corporate diversification is associated with (1) divisional, rather than functional, structures (Chandler, 1962; Grinyer, Yasai-Ardekani, & Al-Bazzaz, 1980; Rumelt, 1974), (2) more formal mutual coordination of decisions between corporate and SBU managers (Bower, 1970; Lorsch & Allen, 1973), (3) formula-based and strictly financial performance-oriented incentive systems for SBUs' managers (Kerr, 1985; Pitts, 1974; Salter, 1973), and (4) high decentralization, with functional authority largely in the hands of SBUs' managers (Vancil, 1980). Of the four dimensions, the present study focused on aspects of only the last three—mutual coordination, incentive systems, and decentralization. Since all SBUs in this study came from firms with divisional structures, there was no variance in corporate-SBU relations along the first dimension. For the other three dimensions, the specific aspects chosen for study were: openness in corporate-SBU relations (mutual coordination), corporate use of subjectivity in assessments of an SBU manager's performance for the purposes of bonus determination (incentive systems), and extent of decentralization of strategic decisions to an SBU (decentralization). I expected that the information-processing capacity of corporate-SBU dyads would be high when corporate-SBU relations are open, when subjectivity in performance assessment is high, and when decentralization is high.

Openness in corporate-SBU relations refers to the degree to which relations between SBUs' managers and their corporate superiors are open and informal and allow for spontaneous and open exchange of information and ideas. True, mutual coordination of strategic decisions also depends on the features of a corporation's strategic planning system. However, the primary utility of formal planning systems lies in forcing strategic reviews at prespecified intervals—once every year, for example—and not in enabling ongoing adjustments during the course of the year (Lorange & Vancil, 1978). Since the impetus for ongoing adjustments would come generally from unexpected environmental events, their appropriateness depends primarily on openness and informality in relations between a corporation and an SBU, not on a formal planning system. Further, since a major objective of formal planning systems is to compare various SBUs for resource allocation (Lorange & Vancil, 1978), such systems are unlikely to differ across SBUs in the same corporation. What would differ across SBUs is how a planning system actually works, which is a function of the extent of openness and informality between an SBU's general manager and the corporate superior.

The second variable, subjectivity in performance assessment, derives from the empirical findings of Lorsch and Allen (1973) and Pitts (1974). Essentially, a bonus award for any SBU's general manager can be determined on the basis of either a strict formula, such as a certain percentage of the SBU's operating profits, or a purely subjective assessment by corporate superiors, or some combination of the two. Objective formulas have the merit of precision and detailed a priori specification, but they suffer from an inability to tie rewards to difficult-to-quantify, yet important, performance dimensions like research and development or human resource management. Since subjective approaches for bonus determination have exactly the opposite qualities, an appropriate combination of the two is generally likely to be superior to a formula-based approach alone. The present study focused on subjectivity in performance assessment because high subjectivity would almost always imply and occur simultaneously with high corporate involvement in and understanding of ongoing events, decisions, and actions of an SBU. Compared to involvement limited to assessment of quarterly or year-end outcomes, such a high level of involvement in effect increases the information-processing capacity of corporate-SBU dyads.

Finally, the variable decentralization refers to the degree of influence that an SBU's general manager has on the major decisions pertaining to the focal SBU relative to the influence of corporate superiors. The importance of the variable for the present study derives from the anticipation that decentralization increases information-processing capacity by pushing the locus of responsibility down towards an SBU, thereby helping prevent an overloading of a corporate-SBU dyad; thus, to the extent that different strategies imply different information-processing needs, the utility of decentralization is likely to vary across SBUs' strategic contexts.

SBUs' Strategic Contexts: Dimensions of Interest

This study focused on two very different dimensions of strategic context at the level of SBUs: (1) an SBU's *strategic mission* in a corporate portfolio (Henderson, 1970) and (2) its *competitive strategy* vis-à-vis other firms in its industry (Porter, 1980). These dimensions not only have been of major interest to researchers as well as practitioners but also appear important on logical grounds.

Strategic mission. All businesses compete for customers in an external product-market environment. However, unlike the context of freestanding single-business firms, the strategic context of an SBU within a diversified firm is also substantially influenced by the role the business is intended to play in the corporate portfolio (Hambrick, MacMillan, & Day, 1982; Henderson, 1970; Hofer & Schendel, 1978; Larreche & Srinivasan, 1982), that is, its strategic mission. Because the markets in which different SBUs compete are often differentially attractive, and because different SBUs possess different competitive strengths, SBUs are rarely equally attractive candidates for either long-term market-share building or short-term maximization of profits and cash flow (Abell & Hammond, 1979). Thus, multibusiness corporations must decide explicitly or implicitly what strategic mission each SBU will pursue. I describe the strategic extremes open to ongoing businesses as "build" and "harvest" missions. A build strategic mission implies a goal of increased market share, even at the expense of short-term earnings and cash flow. Such a mission, which typically also implies net capital investment into an SBU, is likely in the case of businesses with weak competitive positions in markets that are otherwise very attractive (Abell & Hammond, 1979). At the other extreme, a harvest strategic mission implies a goal of maximizing short-term earnings and cash flow, even at the expense of market share. Such a mission, which typically also implies net capital disinvestment from an SBU, is likely in the case of businesses with strong competitive positions in markets that have otherwise become unattractive (Abell & Hammond, 1979). True, growth in market share need not always imply reduction in short-term earnings and cash flow, or vice versa (Hambrick et al., 1982; Zeithaml & Fry, 1984); however, such trade-offs often do need to be made (Buzzell & Wiersema, 1981; Zeithaml & Fry, 1984: 851). For identifying an SBU's strategic mission, what is critical is the type of trade-off that would be made if one were necessary.

Competitive strategy. Consistent with Porter's (1980) conceptualization, in this study competitive strategy signifies an SBU's intended basis for achieving a competitive advantage over other firms in an external product-market. According to Porter's conceptualization, which Dess and Davis (1984) and Hambrick (1983) supported empirically, the two generic bases for achieving competitive advantages are "differentiation" and "low cost." A strategy of differentiation, exemplified by Mercedes Benz in automobiles and Sony in television sets, implies "creating something that is perceived industrywide as being unique . . . . [Such a] strategy does not allow the firm to ignore costs, but rather they are not the primary strategic target" (Porter, 1980: 37). In contrast, a strategy of low cost, exemplified by Chevrolet in automobiles and Emerson in television sets, implies that "low cost relative to competitors becomes the running theme through the entire strategy, though quality, service, and other areas cannot be ignored" (Porter, 1980: 35). As with strategic mission, trade-offs along this dimension may not always have to be made. The critical aspect for defining the competitive strategy of an SBU is the type of trade-off that it would make if one were necessary.

Given their totally different conceptualizations, strategic mission and competitive strategy are regarded here as orthogonal dimensions. As will be seen, actual data support the premise. The next two subsections argue, for quite different reasons, that SBUs located at different points along each of the two strategic dimensions may face differing degrees of task uncertainty, and thereby have differing needs for information-processing capacity; accordingly, the utility of different states of corporate-SBU relations is hypothesized to vary across different SBUs' strategic contexts. It should be noted that the relationship between SBUs' strategies and the information-processing capacity of a corporate-SBU dyad is almost certainly more complex than what this study describes and discusses. Although information-processing capacity influences the effectiveness and efficiency with which strategies are implemented, it is conceivable that choice of strategies may itself be in part a function of information-processing capacity.

Strategic Mission and Corporate-SBU Relations

My specific expectation is that SBUs on build strategic missions face greater task uncertainty than those on harvest missions; following Galbraith (1973: 5), I use task uncertainty to signify the relative amount of information that must be acquired during task performance. Three arguments support this expectation. First, by definition, a build mission signifies a desire to increase market share, whereas a harvest mission signifies at best an indifference towards it. Because the total market share of all firms in an industry would always be 100 percent, making the battle for market share a zero-sum game, a build mission pits an SBU into greater conflict with its competitors than a harvest mission does. As Pfeffer and Salancik (1978: 68) argued, the greater the degree of conflict between an organization and actors in its external environment, the greater the uncertainty it confronts. Second, it is also clear that the decision to increase market share makes an SBU engaged in a build mission more dependent on the decisions and actions of customers and competitors than an SBU that is harvesting. To increase market share, it is not sufficient to increase the demand for products; a firm must also increase the input of resources and the volume of production by corresponding amounts. Thus, even on the input side, a manager who is building faces greater external dependencies than does a manager who is harvesting. As Pfeffer and Salancik (1978: 68) and Thompson (1967: 29) argued, given a nondeterministic world, the greater the external dependencies facing an organization, the greater the uncertainty it confronts. Third, businesses are more likely to undertake build strategies in the early, rather than later, stages of a product's life cycle (Hofer, 1975). Given the relative unpredictability of market demand and the instability of the rules of the game for most industries in the early stages of a life cycle (Porter, 1980), on this account as well, task uncertainty is likely to be greater for SBUs pursuing build, rather than harvest, missions.

As was discussed, the greater the uncertainty in a task environment, the greater is an organization's need for information-processing capacity (Duncan, 1973; Galbraith, 1973; Tushman & Nadler, 1978). Accordingly, for effective implementation, build missions should call for greater organizational information-processing capacity than harvest missions. Combining that expectation with the earlier discussion on the information-processing capacities of various states of corporate-SBU relations yields:

> Hypothesis 1: Openness in corporate-SBU relations will make a positive contribution to an SBU's effectiveness at the build end of the strategic-mission spectrum; in contrast, towards the harvest end, its contribution will be either less strongly positive, or negative.

Hypothesis 2: Subjectivity in performance assessment will make a positive contribution to an SBU's effectiveness at the build end of the strategic-mission spectrum; in contrast, towards the harvest end, its contribution will be either less strongly positive, or negative.

Hypothesis 3: Corporate-SBU decentralization will make a positive contribution to an SBU's effectiveness at the build end of the strategic-mission spectrum; in contrast, towards the harvest end, its contribution will be either less strongly positive, or negative.

Arguments not premised on task uncertainty further support the hypotheses. First, because SBUs that are on build missions are generally newer than SBUs on harvest missions, corporate executives are likely to have less direct personal experience in and intuitive knowledge of the first type. Yet the need to make ongoing capital investments into the building SBUs requires that corporate understanding of such SBUs' competitive contexts be high. Thus, administrative mechanisms, such as open and informal corporate-SBU relations, that can help corporate executives become more knowledgeable about an SBU are likely to be particularly beneficial for SBUs engaged in building. Second, because of their orientation toward increasing long-term market share, SBUs that are building generally need to place greater emphasis than SBUs that are harvesting on many difficult-to-quantify performance dimensions like product-market development and human resource development. A reliance on subjective, rather than formula-based, approaches to performance assessment is more likely to encourage that emphasis and thus is likely to prove more beneficial for SBUs that are building than for those that are harvesting. Finally, because of their goal of winning a competitive battle for market share, general managers of SBUs that are building need to focus more on customers and their market than on intracorporate issues; the reverse would be true for SBUs engaged in harvesting. Accordingly, corporate SBU decentralization is also likely to be more beneficial for the first type of SBU.

Competitive Strategy and Corporate-SBU Relations

The choice of a strategy of differentiation rather than low cost would also increase uncertainty in an SBU's task environment. The primary concern of SBUs pursuing cost leadership is likely to be maximizing their throughput efficiency, which generally implies having narrow product lines so that they can keep inventory-carrying and distribution costs low and maximally realize the cost advantages of mass production (Hambrick, 1983). In contrast, success at implementing the differentiation strategy is likely to require primary attention to the unique identification of unfilled customer needs and the design and production of unique products to meet those needs. Since there are usually many ways to achieve uniqueness, and achieving differentiation requires creating "a perception of exclusivity" (Porter, 1980: 38), the product lines of SBUs pursuing differentiation would generally be broader than those of SBUs pursuing low cost (Hambrick, 1983). Such breadth implies that SBUs pursuing differentiation rather than low cost are likely to face greater uncertainties in their task environments. Given their preference for cost minimization, SBUs with low cost as their strategy are also likely to keep their product offerings stable over time. In contrast, for SBUs pursuing differentiation, sustaining uniqueness is almost always more important than low cost. Thus, they are also likely to exhibit greater product innovation and greater dynamism, or changes over time, in product mix than will SBUs pursuing cost leadership (Dess & Davis, 1984). Again, SBUs pursuing differentiation are predicted to face more uncertain task environments than those pursuing low cost.

As discussed earlier, the greater environmental uncertainty faced by SBUs pursuing differentiation implies a need for greater information-processing capacity. Combining that expectation with expectations concerning the differing information-processing capacities of different states of corporate-SBU relations yields:

> Hypothesis 4: Openness in corporate-SBU relations will make a positive contribution to an SBU's effectiveness at the differentiation end of the competitive-strategy spectrum; in contrast, towards the low-cost end, its contribution will be either less strongly positive, or negative.
>
> Hypothesis 5: Subjectivity in performance assessment will make a positive contribution to an SBU's effectiveness at the differentiation end of the competitive-strategy spectrum; in contrast, towards the low-cost end, its contribution will be either less strongly positive, or negative.
>
> Hypothesis 6: Corporate-SBU decentralization will make a positive contribution to an SBU's effectiveness at the differentiation end of the competitive-strategy spectrum; in contrast, towards the low-cost end, its contribution will be either less strongly positive, or negative.

Further arguments not premised on task uncertainty support Hypotheses 4–6. Creating and sustaining differentiation requires incurring discretionary expenditures in several areas—improvement of quality and speed of delivery, advertising to build an image, research and development, and so forth. In contrast, a low-cost strategy implies economies in all forms of discretionary expenditures. Cost savings are easy to measure, but the potential differentiating benefits of high discretionary expenditures are not. Accordingly, implementing differentiation strategies is likely to require decision making by intuitive judgment to a greater extent than will implementing low-cost strategies. It follows that SBUs pursuing differentiation need greater corporate-SBU openness, informality, and subjective approaches to performance assessment than do those pursuing low cost if those intuitive decisions are to be made and assessed correctly. Additionally, because SBUs pursuing low cost as a strategy have greater need for scale economies, they are likely to benefit from and engage in inter-SBU resource sharing more than those pursuing differentiation (Gupta & Govindarajan, 1986). Because corporate-SBU centralization can help provide the needed coordination among SBUs, decentralization is likely to be less beneficial for businesses pursuing low cost.

METHODS

I collected data for this study from the general managers of 58 SBUs within eight diversified *Fortune* 500 firms headquartered in the northeastern United States. Using Rumelt's (1974) criteria, I classified six of the firms as related-diversified and two as unrelated-diversified. Although limitations on obtaining access to firms and constraints of time and funding prevented the use of a random sample from the entire *Fortune* 500, the range of sizes in terms of sales ($500 million to $10 billion in 1981) as well as the diversity of industries in which the firms operate[1] indicated no prima facie reason to expect any systematic bias in the findings from their business units. Nonetheless, given the variations in corporate diversification strategies as well as in corporate size, I tested the hypotheses both before and after controlling for the possible confounding effects of those two contextual variables.

Within each firm, I interviewed one or more corporate senior executives and persuaded them to send copies of a questionnaire to four or more general managers of SBUs with a request that this distribution cover a mix of strategically diverse businesses. A cover letter accompanying the questionnaire guaranteed respondents' anonymity and assured them that only aggregate data from multiple business units would be published. Of the 70 questionnaires distributed by corporate executives, I received 58 usable responses, 48 from the six related- and 10 from the two unrelated-diversified firms. Because of the high response rate, no tests for response bias seemed necessary.

Measurements

The Appendix gives details on how the variables of interest—strategic mission, competitive strategy, openness of corporate-SBU relationship, subjectivity in performance assessment, corporate-SBU decentralization, and SBU's effectiveness—were measured; also included therein are test results supporting the reliability and the validity of measures. Table 1 provides both summary statistics and zero-order correlation coefficients for all variables. Those data lend support to statements made earlier in this paper regarding the orthogonality of the two dimensions of SBU-level strategic context under consideration.

Since an SBU's effectiveness is the dependent variable in all six of the predicted hypotheses, a brief elaboration on my approach to measuring that key variable might be useful here. Given corporations' desire for confidentiality, objective data on the financial performance of individual SBUs that

---

[1] The group studied included producers of consumer as well as industrial products in both mature and high-growth industries.

TABLE 1
Summary Statistics and Zero-Order Correlation Coefficients for All Variables[a]

Variables	Range	Means	s.d.	1	2	3	4	5
1. SBU's effectiveness	1.46–4.80	3.21	0.74					
2. Strategic mission	−1.00–1.00	−0.03	0.51	.13				
3. Competitive strategy	5.00–10.00	7.79	1.24	.02	−.07			
4. Openness of relationship	1.75–4.00	3.15	0.60	.13	.26*	.30*		
5. Subjectivity in performance assessment	0.00–100.00	26.81	32.89	.11	.25*	−.17	.13	
6. Decentralization	0.60–4.38	1.86	0.75	.25*	.12	.13	.08	.08

[a] $N = 58$.
* $p < .05$, one-tailed test.

reveal organizational identities are virtually impossible to obtain.[2] Lawrence and Lorsch (1967) also faced that constraint. Further, I expected that the absolute financial performance of any business unit would depend not just on the effectiveness with which it implements its chosen strategies but also on the state of the economy, industry characteristics, and the choices of strategies themselves (Lenz, 1981). Thus, even if objective financial data could somehow be obtained, they would be meaningless from the perspective of this study unless the effects of economy, industry, and strategic choice were first factored out—yet another virtually impossible task. In light of these considerations and the fact that managers' a priori expectations of performance are likely to take into account the expected effects of industry- and strategy-related factors, I measured SBUs' performance in the form of a comparison between actual performance and a priori expectations rather than on an absolute scale. In the interest of increasing validity, I also decided (1) to assess performance along several dimensions rather than on any single dimension and (2) to weight the various performance dimensions in terms of their relative importance for an SBU. Such a multivariate approach with criterion weights is consistent with Steers's (1975) advice and seemed particularly appropriate for taking into account the differing priorities implied by different strategic contexts. As the data in Table 1 show, the resulting index of effectiveness does not correlate with either strategic mission or competitive strategy, indicating that the research design appears to have adequately controlled for the effects of strategic context on performance.

---

[2] Data in the Profit Impact of Market Strategies (PIMS) data base do not, for instance, include organizational identities.

Controlling for Corporate Diversity and Size

Given the potential for a corporation's diversification strategy and size to influence corporate-SBU relations, it seemed important to control for the possible confounding effects of those two contextual variables. For computational purposes, I made corporate diversification strategy (U) a binary variable, assigning the 48 SBUs from the six related-diversified firms the value $U = 0$, and assigning the other 10 SBUs from the two unrelated-diversified firms the value $U = 1$. I measured corporate size (Z) in terms of total corporate revenue in billions of dollars; given the extreme variability in size, I decided to use the natural logarithms of revenues rather than absolute figures.

Analysis

Hypotheses 1 through 6 are all of the following form: the effect of X_1 (e.g., openness) on Y (SBU's effectiveness) will be positive when X_2 (e.g., strategic mission) is high; however, when X_2 is low, that effect will be either less strongly positive, or negative. Mathematically, that specification implies that $\partial Y/\partial X_1$ will be a function of X_2:

$$\frac{\partial Y}{\partial X_1} = a_1 + bX_2 ,$$

where b is predicted to be positive. In order to control for any potential confounding effects of corporate diversification strategy (U) and corporate size (Z), I modified the equation to:

$$\frac{\partial Y}{\partial X_1} = a_1 + (b_1 + b_2U + b_3Z)X_2 .$$

With that modification, b_1 provided the exact test for each hypothesis after effects of corporate context had been controlled, b_2 captured any marginal effects of corporate diversification strategy, and b_3 captured any marginal effects of corporate size. For statistical purposes, I then integrated the equation over X_1 and rewrote it as:

$$Y = c + a_1X_1 + a_2X_2 + b_1X_1X_2 + b_2UX_1X_2 + b_3ZX_1X_2 .$$

Following that equation as the general model, I computed three multiple regressions for each of the six hypotheses, the first with just X_1 and X_2, the second with X_1, X_2, and X_1X_2, and the third with X_1, X_2, X_1X_2, UX_1X_2, and ZX_1X_2. Mathematically, for any independent variable in a multiple regression equation, the significance of the regression coefficient (computed through a two tailed t-test) always equals the significance of the increase in R^2 (computed through an F-test) that is due to the introduction of the particular variable into the equation. Thus, in my general equation, a significant value for b_1 also implies that the introduction of the term X_1X_2 added significantly to the variance explained over and beyond that explained by the other four independent variables. Argote (1982), Brownell (1981), and Schoonhoven (1981) used this specific model of contingency relationships, and Southwood (1978) discussed and supported the mathematical properties of the model at length.

RESULTS

Effects of Strategic Mission

Table 2 presents the results of the multiple regression analyses undertaken to test Hypotheses 1, 2, and 3.[3]

Openness in corporate-SBU relations. For Hypothesis 1, dealing with the effect of strategic mission (M) on the utility of openness in corporate-SBU relations (R), the results are clearly supportive. As Equations 2 and 3 indicate, the coefficient of the interaction term, MR, is positive and significant both before ($p < .01$) and after ($p < .05$) potential confounding effects of corporate diversity and size are controlled. To determine exactly how the beneficial effects of openness in corporate-SBU relations vary across different strategic missions, I conducted a further analysis, employing this partial derivative of Equation 2:

$$\frac{\partial E}{\partial R} = .216 + .694M.$$

Over the observed range of the strategic-mission variable (−1.000 to 1.000; see Table 1), it can be calculated that $\partial E/\partial R$ is positive for $1.000 > M > -.311$ and negative for $-.311 > M > -1.000$. To sum up, for SBUs at the build end of the strategic-mission spectrum, the effect of openness on effectiveness is positive; however, at the harvest end, its effect is negative. Thus, results support both the first and the second parts of Hypothesis 1.

Subjectivity in performance assessment. For Hypothesis 2, dealing with the effect of strategic mission (M) on the utility of subjectivity in performance assessment (S), the results are again strongly supportive. As Equations 5 and 6 indicate, the coefficient of the interaction term, MS, is positive and significant ($p < .01$) both before and after the potential confounding effects of corporate diversity and size are controlled. This partial derivative of Equation 5 yields further analysis of the results:

$$\frac{\partial E}{\partial S} = -.001 + .015M.$$

---

[3] Both Tables 2 and 3 report unstandardized regression coefficients. That decision was based upon Southwood's (1978) mathematical analysis, which I crosschecked empirically. The analysis indicated that if the points of origin of X_1 and X_2 are changed, the values, as well as the significance levels, of both standardized and unstandardized regression coefficients of the variables X_1 and X_2 will also change. However, for the cross-product term X_1X_2, the value of the unstandardized, but not the standardized, regression coefficient; its standard error; and its level of significance are always independent of the points of origin of X_1 and X_2. Since virtually all variables in this study are interval-scale variables, their points of origin are arbitrary, rendering the standardized—but not the unstandardized—regression coefficients essentially meaningless.

TABLE 2
Results of Multiple Regression Analyses of Strategic Mission and Corporate-SBU Relations on SBU Effectiveness[a]

Results of Equations[b, c]	Eq.	R^2	F^d	ΔR^2	F^d
Hypothesis 1					
$E = 2.759 + 0.076M + 0.138R$	1	.02	0.50		
$\quad\quad\quad\;\;(.206)\quad\;\;(.172)$			(2,55)		
$E = 2.460 - 2.098M^* + 0.216R + 0.694MR^{**}$	2	.14	2.85*	.12	7.41**
$\quad\quad\quad\;\;(.822)\quad\;\;(.165)\quad\;\;(.255)$			(3,54)		(1,54)
$E = 2.532 - 2.044M^* + 0.193R + 0.675MR^* - 0.264UMR + 0.156ZMR$	3	.17	2.02†	.03	0.85
$\quad\quad\quad\;\;(.826)\quad\;\;(.166)\quad\;\;(.257)\quad\;\;(.248)\quad\;\;(.158)$			(5,52)		(2,52)
Hypothesis 2					
$E = 3.179 + 0.308M + 0.001S$	4	.06	1.46		
$\quad\quad\quad\;\;(.204)\quad\;\;(.003)$			(2,55)		
$E = 3.173 - 0.079M - 0.001S + 0.015MS^{**}$	5	.18	3.48*	.12	7.17**
$\quad\quad\quad\;\;(.241)\quad\;\;(.003)\quad\;\;(.006)$			(3,54)		(1,54)
$E = 3.151 - 0.123M + 0.001S + 0.018MS^{**} - 0.027UMS - 0.010ZMS$	6	.22	2.54*	.04	1.25
$\quad\quad\quad\;\;(.244)\quad\;\;(.003)\quad\;\;(.006)\quad\;\;(.024)\quad\;\;(.012)$			(5,52)		(2,52)
Hypothesis 3					
$E = 2.767 + 0.133M + 0.232D^†$	7	.07	2.03		
$\quad\quad\quad\;\;(.189)\quad\;\;(.129)$			(2,55)		
$E = 2.773 + 0.304M + 0.231D^† - 0.089MD$	8	.07	1.38	.00	0.15
$\quad\quad\quad\;\;(.481)\quad\;\;(.131)\quad\;\;(.229)$			(3,54)		(1,54)
$E = 2.797 + 0.361M + 0.209D - 0.099MD - 0.250UMD - 0.065ZMD$	9	.09	0.94	.02	0.34
$\quad\quad\quad\;\;(.541)\quad\;\;(.137)\quad\;\;(.264)\quad\;\;(.408)\quad\;\;(.242)$			(5,52)		(2,52)

[a] $N = 58$. Unstandardized regression coefficients are reported.
[b] Figures in parentheses represent standard errors.
[c] E = SBU's effectiveness, M = SBU's strategic mission, U = corporate diversification strategy, Z = corporate size, R = openness of relationship, S = subjectivity in performance assessment, and D = decentralization.
[d] Figures in parentheses represent degrees of freedom.

† $p < .10$, two-tailed t-test.
* $p < .05$, two-tailed t-test.
** $p < .01$, two-tailed t-test.

Over the observed range of the strategic-mission variable, it can be calculated that $\partial E/\partial S$ is positive for $1.000 > M > .067$ and negative for $.067 > M > -1.000$. Thus, at the build end of the spectrum of strategic missions, the effect of subjectivity on effectiveness is positive; however, at the harvest end, it is negative. Thus, results support both the first and the second parts of Hypothesis 2.

Decentralization. For Hypothesis 3, dealing with the effect of strategic mission (M) on the utility of corporate-SBU decentralization (D), the results are not supportive. As Equations 8 and 9 indicate, the coefficient of the interaction term, MD, is not significantly different from zero either before or after the potential confounding effects of corporate diversity and size are controlled.

To shed more light on what, if any, relationship exists between corporate-SBU decentralization and an SBU's effectiveness, I conducted a further analysis with this partial derivative of Equation 8:

$$\frac{\partial E}{\partial D} = .231 - .089M .$$

As can be calculated, $\partial E/\partial D$ is positive over the entire observed range of the strategic-mission variable, $1.000 > M > -1.000$. Further, the value of $\partial E/\partial D$ is somewhat greater for SBUs engaged in a harvesting strategy than for those engaged in building. Thus, the data are consistent with the first part of Hypothesis 3 but not with the second part.

Effects of Competitive Strategy

Table 3 presents the results of multiple regression analyses undertaken to test Hypotheses 4, 5, and 6.

Openness in corporate-SBU relations. For Hypothesis 4, dealing with the effect of competitive strategy (C) on the utility of openness in corporate-SBU relations (R), the results are clearly supportive. As Equations 11 and 12 indicate, the coefficient of the interaction term, CR, was positive and significant both before ($p < .01$) and after ($p < .05$) I controlled for the potential confounding effects of corporate diversity and size.

A further analysis of the results, intended to determine exactly how the beneficial effects of openness in corporate-SBU relationship vary across different competitive strategies, employed this partial derivative of Equation 11:

$$\frac{\partial E}{\partial R} = -2.469 + .339C .$$

Over the observed range of the competitive-strategy variable (5.000 to 10.000; see Table 1), it can be calculated that $\partial E/\partial R$ is positive for $10.000 > C > 7.283$ and negative for $7.283 > C > 5.000$. To sum up, for SBUs pursuing a competitive strategy of differentiation, the effect of openness on effectiveness is

TABLE 3
Results of Multiple Regression Analyses of Competitive Strategy and Corporate-SBU Relations on SBU Effectiveness[a]

Results of Equations[b, c]	Eq.	R^2	F[d]	ΔR^2	F[d]
Hypothesis 4					
$E = 2.943 - 0.042C + 0.181R$	10	.02	0.55		
(.086) (.174)			(2,55)		
$E = 11.109 - 1.096C^{**} + 2.469R^* + 0.339CR^{**}$	11	.15	3.03*	.13	7.86**
(.385) (.959) (.121)			(3,54)		(1,54)
$E = 10.665 - 1.041C^* + 2.302R^* + 0.319CR^* - 0.009UCR + 0.006ZCR$	12	.16	1.92	.01	0.37
(.396) (.994) (.125) (.011) (.009)			(5,52)		(2,52)
Hypothesis 5					
$E = 2.695 + 0.055C + 0.003S$	13	.02	0.50		
(.087) (.003)			(2,55)		
$E = 3.538 - 0.052C - 0.030S + 0.004CS^\dagger$	14	.08	1.38	.06	3.09†
(.104) (.019) (.002)			(3,54)		(1,54)
$E = 3.575 - 0.056C - 0.035S + 0.005CS^\dagger + 0.000UCS + 0.000ZCS$	15	.08	0.81	.00	0.05
(.108) (.025) (.003) (.001) (.001)			(5,52)		(2,52)
Hypothesis 6					
$E = 2.578 + 0.022C + 0.238D^\dagger$	16	.06	1.81		
(.083) (.130)			(2,55)		
$E = 4.545 - 0.227C - 0.823D + 0.133CD$	17	.09	1.81	.03	1.78
(.204) (.806) (.100)			(3,54)		(1,54)
$E = 5.405 - 0.369C^\dagger - 1.180D + 0.200CD^* - 0.044UCD^* + 0.029ZCD^\dagger$	18	.18	2.15†	.09	2.60†
(.208) (.800) (.100) (.020) (.016)			(5,52)		(2,52)

[a] $N = 58$. Unstandardized regression coefficients are reported.
[b] Figures in parentheses represent standard errors.
[c] E = SBU's effectiveness, C = SBU's competitive strategy, U = corporate diversification strategy, Z = corporate size, R = openness of relationship, S = subjectivity in performance assessment, and D = decentralization.
[d] Figures in parentheses represent degrees of freedom.
$^\dagger p < .10$, two-tailed t-test.
$^* p < .05$, two-tailed t-test.
$^{**} p < .01$, two-tailed t-test.

positive; however, for those whose strategy is to keep costs low, that effect is negative. Thus, results supported both the first and the second parts of Hypothesis 4.

Subjectivity in performance assessment. For Hypothesis 5, dealing with the effect of competitive strategy (C) on the utility of subjectivity in performance assessment (S), the results are again supportive, although less strongly so than for Hypothesis 4. As Equations 14 and 15 indicate, the coefficient of the interaction term, CS, was positive and significant ($p < .10$) both before and after I controlled for the potential confounding effects of corporate diversity and size.

This partial derivative of Equation 14 yields further analysis of the results:

$$\frac{\partial E}{\partial S} = -.030 + .004C.$$

Over the observed range of the competitive-strategy variable, it can be calculated that $\partial E/\partial S$ is positive for $10.000 > C > 7.500$ and negative for $7.500 > C > 5.000$. To sum up, at the differentiation end of the spectrum of competitive strategies, the effect of subjectivity on effectiveness is positive; however, at the low-cost end, the effect is negative. Thus, results support both the first and the second parts of Hypothesis 5.

Decentralization. For Hypothesis 6, dealing with the effect of competitive strategy (C) on utility of corporate-SBU decentralization (D), the results are again supportive, although only after the effects of corporate diversity and size are controlled. As Equations 17 and 18 indicate, the coefficient of the interaction term, CD, is positive and significant ($p < .05$) after, but not before, my controlling for the potential confounding effects of corporate diversity and size.

This partial derivative of Equation 17 yields further analysis of the results:

$$\frac{\partial E}{\partial D} = -.823 + .133C.$$

Over the observed range of the competitive-strategy variable, it can be calculated that $\partial E/\partial D$ is positive for $10.000 > C > 6.188$ and negative for $6.188 > C > 5.000$. Thus, results support both the first and the second parts of Hypothesis 6.

INTERPRETATION OF THE RESULTS

Although the results reported are fully sufficient for testing the hypotheses, for purposes of interpretation I decided to go one step further in examining the data. Specifically, I split the data twice, once by strategic mission and once by competitive strategy. In the first case, I termed the top third of the cases the build subgroup and the bottom third the harvest subgroup and discarded the middle third. Similarly, for the second split, I termed the top third of the cases the differentiation subgroup and the bottom third the low-cost subgroup, again discarding the middle third. Figure 1 graphs the ordinary-least-squares regression lines between each corporate-SBU relationship variable and SBU effectiveness for all cases and for the subgroups.

As expected, the results presented in Figure 1 are fully consistent with those presented earlier; the objective of graphing the data was not to retest the hypotheses. In any case, the analysis shown in Figure 1 is inferior to that shown in Tables 2 and 3 for testing the hypotheses on at least these two grounds: The creation of nominal strategic subgroups out of continuous variables—in addition to the discarding of a third of the data—results in a significant loss of information; as Dubofsky and Varadarajan (1987) also argued and illustrated, it is almost always preferable to test for the effects of strategies on organizational outcomes using continuous rather than subgroup or nominal measures of strategies. Second, the analysis in Figure 1 does not permit control for any confounding effects of variables related to corporate context. Essentially, the incremental utility of that analysis lies in making the results of this study more intelligible both to practicing managers and to those who must advise or train them. Besides the moderating effects of SBU-level strategic context, perhaps the most useful conclusion to emerge from the graphs is that each of the three corporate-SBU relational variables appears to have a unique relationship with performance.

An examination of Figures 1a and 1b indicates that although the beneficial effect of openness in corporate-SBU relations on effectiveness is quite strong in the case of SBUs pursuing build and differentiation strategies, the detrimental effect of openness of effectiveness is almost insignificant for SBUs pursuing harvest and low-cost strategies. In other words, despite the moderating effect of an SBU's strategic context, the upside benefits of a high level of openness in some strategic contexts are much greater than the downside negative effects of openness in other strategic contexts. Accordingly, a practical implication of this study would seem to be the following: if corporate executives find it difficult to fine-tune their degree of openness across SBUs to fit specific SBUs' strategic contexts, it should be preferable to opt for more, not less, openness across the board. Such a conclusion also implies that, on the dimension of openness in relations, the proponents of universalistic (Argyris, 1964; Peters & Waterman, 1982) as well as contingency (Galbraith, 1973) perspectives might both be partially correct.

The conclusions regarding subjectivity in performance assessment appear to be different. For some strategic contexts, high subjectivity seems to be strongly desirable (Figure 1d); however, in some other strategic contexts subjectivity seems to be strongly undesirable (Figure 1c). Thus, there appears to be strong justification for fine-tuning the mix of formula-based versus subjective approaches in assessments of SBU managers' performance for the purposes of bonus determination. Specifically, for build and differentiation strategies, subjective approaches seem to be more desirable, but for

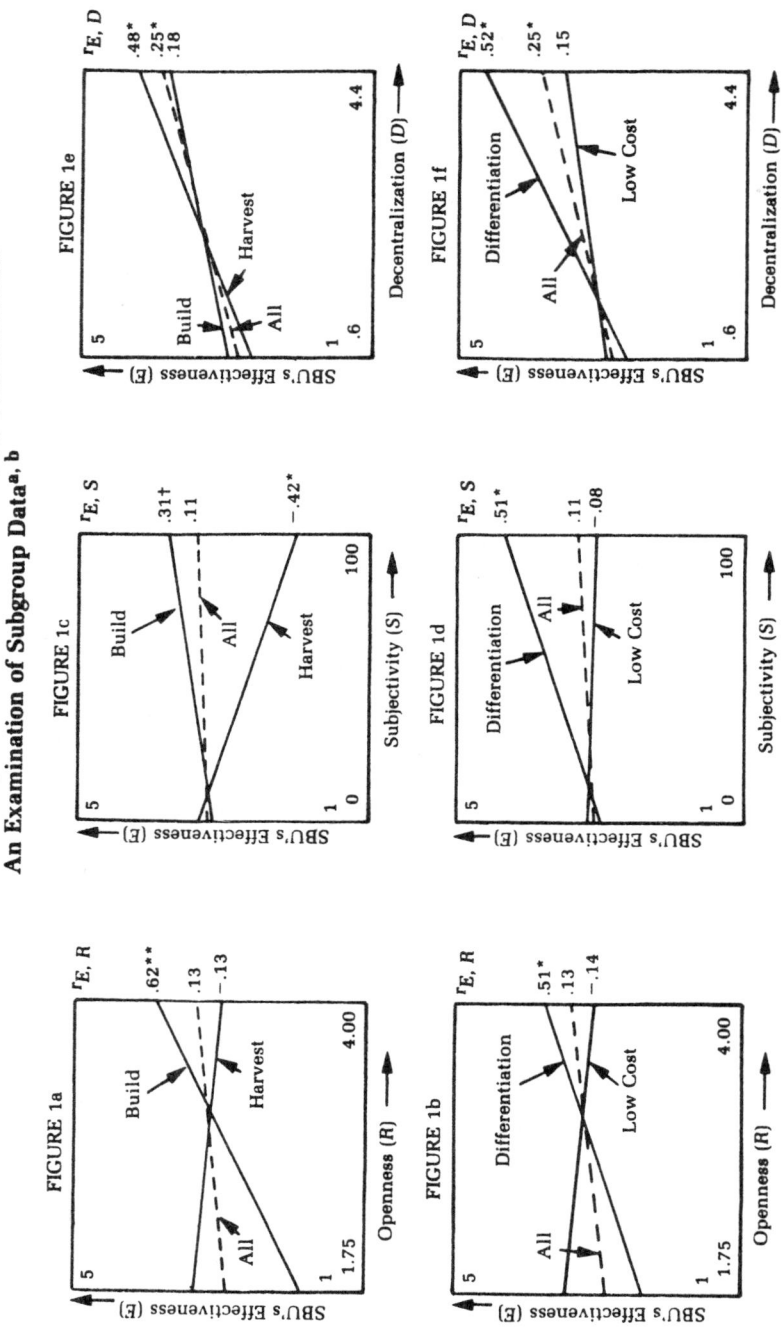

FIGURE 1
Associations Between Corporate-SBU Relations and SBU's Performance: An Examination of Subgroup Data[a,b]

[Figure 1a: SBU's Effectiveness (E) vs. Openness (R), showing Build, All, and Harvest lines; $r_{E,R}$: .62**, .13, -.13]

[Figure 1b: SBU's Effectiveness (E) vs. Openness (R), showing Differentiation, All, and Low Cost lines; $r_{E,R}$: .51*, .13, -.14]

[Figure 1c: SBU's Effectiveness (E) vs. Subjectivity (S), showing Build, All, and Harvest lines; $r_{E,S}$: .31†, .11, -.42*]

[Figure 1d: SBU's Effectiveness (E) vs. Subjectivity (S), showing Differentiation, All, and Low Cost lines; $r_{E,S}$: .51*, .11, -.08]

[Figure 1e: SBU's Effectiveness (E) vs. Decentralization (D), showing Build, All, and Harvest lines; $r_{E,D}$: .48*, .25*, .18]

[Figure 1f: SBU's Effectiveness (E) vs. Decentralization (D), showing Differentiation, All, and Low Cost lines; $r_{E,D}$: .52*, .25*, .15]

[a] The build and harvest subgroups respectively represent the top and the bottom thirds of cases on the strategic-mission variable. Similarly, the differentiation and the low-cost subgroups represent the top and the bottom thirds on the competitive-strategy variable.
[b] The graphs represent least-square regression lines plotted over the entire observed ranges of the corporate-SBU relationship variables (R, S, and D).

† $p < .10$, one-tailed test; * $p < .05$, one-tailed test; ** $p < .01$, one-tailed test.

harvest and low-cost strategies, formula-based approaches seem to be more desirable.

As for the effect of corporate-SBU decentralization on effectiveness, Figures 1e and 1f seem to suggest that greater decentralization should always be preferred, regardless of an SBU's strategic context, and that the benefits of decentralization would be particularly salient in the case of SBUs pursuing differentiation rather than low cost strategies. Such a conclusion is also consistent with the overall positive correlation between decentralization and effectiveness ($r = .25, p < .05$; see Table 1). However, another interpretation is equally plausible. Decentralization might be primarily an outcome rather than a strategy-dependent design variable. It is conceivable that rather than opting for more or less decentralization in order to optimize an SBU's effectiveness, corporate executives might actually be opting for more or less intervention as a response to a current actual level of performance. Although the results of this study do not permit differentiation between those two interpretations, anecdotal evidence cited by Lorsch and Allen (1973) does seem to support the decentralization-as-outcome interpretation: "One division general manager . . . summarized [his view] as follows: 'A high profit contribution does give you a considerable "go to hell factor" in dealing with the headquarters people. But when you are losing, it's a whole new ball game. In fact, I'll say that the amount of supervision that a division receives is directly proportional to the trouble it's in' " (1973: 68). On the basis of a study of 291 manufacturing companies, Vancil (1980) similarly concluded that when an SBU's performance fell below expectations, one or more corporate managers would offer to "help where we can" and that the SBU manager's freedom to take action without prior corporate approval would tend to be sharply curtailed. Although the choice between those two alternative interpretations must await further research, it would seem that at least this conclusion emerges from this study's results: from the perspective of SBU-level strategic context, decentralization is not a highly salient design variable, and the choice of more or less decentralization seems to depend on factors other than strategic context.

CONCLUSIONS

The results of this study indicate that SBUs' strategic contexts do significantly moderate the utility of various states of corporate-SBU relations. Accordingly, this study as well as others like it (Gupta & Govindarajan, 1984), lends impetus to examinations of how SBU-level strategic contexts influence the management of multibusiness firms. Given this study's focus on corporate-SBU relations, it is particularly relevant to note that in focusing on the effects of corporate strategic context, previous research has tended to completely overlook the implications of different SBU-level strategic contexts. That observation is particularly important because although corporate strategy may influence SBUs' strategies, it does not determine them. As Montgomery put it: "Corporate leaders would do well to remember that diversified firms must ultimately compete in a series of individual markets" (1985: 795). Her observation is also consistent with Burgelman's (1983) conclusion that the same multibusiness firm can easily engage in many strategic choices and that strategic choice at the SBU-level can have major implications for the management of corporate-SBU relations. A recent study by Lamont and Anderson (1985) is also relevant. After finding that mixed approaches to corporate diversification are quite prevalent and that the performance of firms pursuing mixed approaches is not statistically different from that of purely internal or the purely acquisitive diversifiers, they concluded: "Unfortunately, or fortunately, the findings reported here raise more questions that they answer. What structures do mixed diversifiers use? Does structure contribute to performance?" (1985: 933). If "structure" refers to the overall context of corporate-SBU relations, the present study would seem to help address some of Lamont and Anderson's queries.

These appear to be among the more productive directions for future research in this area: (1) an examination of other aspects of corporate-SBU relations, such as management information system, (2) an examination of the effects of other dimensions of SBU-level strategic contexts, such as consumer versus industrial goods or fragmented versus concentrated industry environments, (3) an examination of the joint effect of corporate and SBU-level strategic contexts, and (4) an examination of the effects of various states of corporate-SBU relations on other outcome variables like job satisfaction and turnover among key SBU managers—a major problem in some industries, notably electronics.

Future research should also benefit from a clear identification of some of the major limitations of the present study. Perhaps the most obvious is the self-report nature of the data; although I believe that the results of the reported tests of reliability and validity lend sufficient support to the measures to justify their use, a similar study employing multi-rater measurement approaches would increase confidence in the validity of the proposed theoretical framework. Similarly, a study using larger and more representative samples would increase confidence in the generalizability of the framework. Another limitation of this study is its reliance on cross-sectional data. Although the theoretical discussion preceding the hypotheses implies a specific causality in each case, the snapshot-like quality of the data prevented any tests for such causality; as might be recalled, causality emerged as a particularly intriguing question regarding the association between decentralization and performance. Longitudinal studies would seem to be a more appropriate methodological route for the examination of specific causal linkages.

REFERENCES

Abell, D.F., & Hammond, J. S. 1979. *Strategic market planning.* Englewood Cliffs, N. J.: Prentice-Hall.

Anderson, C.R., & Zeithaml, C. P. 1984. Stage of the product life cycle, business strategy, and business performance. *Academy of Management Journal*, 27: 5–24.

Argote, L. 1982. Input uncertainty and organizational coordination in hospital emergency units. *Administrative Science Quarterly*, 27: 420-434.

Argyris, C. 1964. *Integrating the individual and the organization.* New York: John Wiley & Sons.

Bower, J. L. 1970. *Managing the resource allocation process.* Boston: Division of Research, Harvard Graduate School of Business Administration.

Brownell, P. 1981. Participation in budgeting, locus of control, and organizational effectiveness. *Accounting Review*, 56: 844-860.

Burgelman, R. A. 1983. A process model of internal corporate venturing. *Administrative Science Quarterly*, 28: 223-244.

Buzzell, R. D., & Wiersema, F. D. 1981, Modelling changes in market share: A cross-sectional analysis. *Strategic Management Journal*, 2: 27-42.

Chandler, A. D., Jr. 1962. *Strategy and structure: Chapters in the history of the industrial enterprise.* Cambridge, Mass.: MIT Press.

Cordiner, R. J. 1956. *New frontiers for professional managers.* New York: McGraw-Hill Book Co.

Dess, G. G., & Davis, P. S. 1984. Porter's (1980) generic strategies as determinants of strategic group membership and organizational performance. *Academy of Management Journal*, 27: 467-488.

Dubofsy, P., & Varadarajan, P. R. 1987. Diversification and measures of performance: Additional empirical evidence. *Academy of Management Journal*, 30: 597-608.

Duncan, R. B. 1973. Multiple decision-making structures in adapting to environmental uncertainty: The impact on organizational effectiveness. *Human Relations*, 26: 273-291.

Egelhoff, W. G. 1982. Strategy and structure in multinational corporations: An information processing approach. *Administrative Science Quarterly*, 27: 435-458.

Galbraith, J. R. 1973. *Designing complex organizations.* Reading, Mass.: Addison-Wesley.

Geneen, H. 1985. *Managing.* New York: Doubleday & Co.

Grinyer, P.H., Yasai-Ardekani, M., & Al-Bazzaz, S. 1980. Strategy, structure, the environment, and financial performance in 48 United Kingdom companies. *Academy of Management Journal*, 23: 193-220.

Gupta, A. K., & Govindarajan, V. 1984. Business unit strategy, managerial characteristics, and business unit effectiveness at strategy implementation. *Academy of Management Journal*, 27: 25-41.

Gupta, A. K., & Govindarajan, V. 1986. Resource sharing among SBUs: Strategic antecedents and administrative implications. *Academy of Management Journal*, 29: 695-714.

Hambrick, D. C. 1983. High profit strategies in mature capital goods industries. *Academy of Management Journal*, 26: 687-707.

Hambrick, D. C., MacMillan, I. C., & Day, D. L. 1982. Strategic attributes and performance in the BCG matrix: A PIMS-based analysis of industrial product business. *Academy of Management Journal*, 25: 510-531.

Henderson, B. D. 1970. *Perspectives on the product portfolio.* Boston: Boston Consulting Group.

Heneman, H. G. 1974. Comparisons of self- and superior ratings of managerial performance. *Journal of Applied Psychology*, 59: 638-642.

Hofer, C. W. 1975. Toward a contingency theory of business strategy. *Academy of Management Journal*, 18: 784-810.

Hofer, C. W., & Schendel, D. E. 1978. *Strategy formulation: Analytical concepts.* St. Paul, Minn.: West Publishing Co.

Kerr, J. L. 1985. Diversification strategies and managerial rewards: An empirical study. *Academy of Management Journal*, 28: 155-179.

Lamont, B. T., & Anderson, C. R. 1985. Mode of economic diversification and economic performance. *Academy of Management Journal*, 28: 926-933.

Larreche, J., & Srinivasan, V. 1982. Stratport: A model for the evaluation and formulation of business portfolio strategies. *Management Science*, 28: 979-1001.

Lawrence, P. R., & Lorsch, J. W. 1967. *Organization and environment*. Boston: Division of Research, Harvard Graduate School of Business Administration.

Lenz, R. T. 1981. "Determinants" of organizational performance. *Strategic Management Journal*, 2: 131-154.

Lorange, P., & Vancil, R. F. 1978. *Strategic planning systems*. Englewood Cliffs, N. J.: Prentice-Hall.

Lorsch, J. W., & Allen, S. A., III. 1973. *Managing diversity and interdependence*. Boston: Division of Research, Harvard Graduate School of Business Administration.

March, J. G., & Simon, H. A. 1958. *Organizations*. New York: John Wiley & Sons.

Montgomery, C. A. 1985. Product-market diversification and market power. *Academy of Management Journal*, 28: 789-798.

Ouchi, W. G. 1984. *The M-Form society*. Reading, Mass.: Addison-Wesley.

Peters, T. J., & Waterman, R. H., Jr. 1982. *In search of excellence*. New York: Harper & Row Publishers.

Pfeffer, J., & Salancik, G. R. 1978. *The external control of organizations*. New York: Harper & Row Publishers.

Pitts, R. A. 1974. Incentive compensation and organization design. *Personnel Journal*, 53: 338-344.

Porter, M. E. 1980. *Competitive strategy*. New York: Free Press.

Rumelt, R. P. 1974. *Strategy, structure, and economic performance*. Boston: Division of Research, Harvard Graduate School of Business Administration.

Salter, M. S. 1973. Tailor incentive compensation to strategy. *Harvard Business Review*, 49 (2): 94-102.

Schoonhoven, C. B. 1981. Problems with contingency theory: Testing assumptions hidden within the language of contingency "theory." *Administrative Science Quarterly*, 26: 349-377.

Sloan, A. P., Jr. 1964. *My years with General Motors*. New York: Doubleday & Co.

Southwood, K. E. 1978. Substantive theory and statistical interaction: Five models. *American Journal of Sociology*, 83: 1154-1203.

Steers, R. M. 1975. Problems in the measurement of organizational effectiveness. *Administrative Science Quarterly*, 20: 546-558.

Tannenbaum, A. S. 1968. Control in organizations: Individual adjustment and organizational performance. *Administrative Science Quarterly*, 7: 236-257.

Thompson, J. D. 1967. *Organizations in action*. New York: McGraw-Hill Book Co.

Tushman, M. L., & Nadler, D. A. 1978. Information processing as an integrating concept in organizational design. *Academy of Management Review*, 3: 613-624.

Vancil, R. F. 1980. *Decentralization: Managerial ambiquity by design*. New York: Financial Executives Research Foundation.

Williamson, O. E. 1970. *Corporate control and business behavior*. Englewood Cliffs, N. J.: Prentice-Hall.

Zeithaml, C. P., & Fry, L. W. 1984. Contextual and strategic differences among mature businesses in four dynamic performance situations. *Academy of Management Journal*, 4: 841-860.

APPENDIX A

Strategic mission. Since SBUs usually have several closely related products or product lines, the strategic mission for each SBU was measured by aggregating the differing strategic missions of its various products. Specifically, each general manager was asked to indicate the percentage of an SBU's current total sales accounted for by activities in pursuit of these missions: (1) increase sales and market share, be willing to accept low returns on investment in the short-to-medium term if necessary, (2) maintain market share and obtain reasonable return on investment, (3) maximize profitability and cash flow in the short-to-medium term, be willing to sacrifice market share if necessary, (4) prepare for sale or liquidation, and (5) none of the above. All respondents entered 0 under category 5. The other four items were coded as +1, 0, −1, and −2, respectively. I then used the percentage breakdown provided by the SBUs' managers for each item to derive a weighted average measure of strategic mission, with low values indicating a harvest mission and high values indicating a build mission.

The construct validity of this measure was assessed by asking each respondent to provide data on the current market share of an SBU's principal products, a factual rather than perceptual item of information; as anticipated, the strategic-mission index correlated negatively with current market share (Pearson $r = -.23$, $p < .05$ one-tailed test). In addition, each respondent was asked to indicate the degree of importance attached by superiors to SBU performance on each of 12 performance dimensions on a 5-point Likert-type scale ranging from of little importance to extremely important. Responses were again consistent with expectations. Strategic mission correlated positively with the importance of sales growth (.57, $p < .001$), market share (.29, $p < .05$), new product development (.24, $p < .05$), and market development (.30, $p < .01$) but negatively with the importance of operating profits ($-.23$, $p < .05$).

To test for response consistency (a surrogate for internal reliability), I asked respondents to indicate whether they expected the market share of their SBUs' principal products to decline rapidly (=1), decline slowly (=2), remain at the current level (=3), increase slowly (=4), or increase rapidly (=5). As anticipated, the strategic-mission index correlated positively with expectations of an increase in market share ($r = .49$, $p < .001$).

Competitive strategy. Using a 5-point scale ranging from significantly lower to significantly higher, respondents were asked to position their products relative to industry competitors in terms of performance and price. The sum of responses provided a measure of each SBU's competitive strategy with high values indicating differentiation and low values indicating low cost ($\alpha = .61$). Tested for construct validity, the competitive-strategy index correlated positively with the importance of new product development (.24, $p < .05$), market development (.32, $p < .01$), and research and development (.24, $p < .05$) but negatively with the importance of cost reduction programs ($-.17$, $p < .10$).

Openness in corporate-SBU relations. The variable was measured with a 4-item scale for the following items: (1) I would characterize my relationship with my boss as quite informal, (2) I feel quite free to call my boss when and as often as I like, (3) I never let my hair down in front of my boss, and (4) my boss and I have an open relationship. Respondents indicated whether they definitely agreed (=1), were inclined to agree (=2), were inclined to disagree (=3), or definitely disagreed (=4). The measure was a straight average of the responses to the four statements, with item 3 reverse-scored; high values indicated an open relationship. Values ranged from 1.75 to 4.00, with a mean of 3.15 ($\alpha = .76$).

Subjectivity in performance assessment. Respondents indicated whether superiors relied totally on a formula-based or a subjective approach, or on a combination approach, indicating, in the last case, the percentage of total bonus determined via a subjective approach. Values ranged from 0 (totally formula-based) to 100 (totally subjective), with a mean of 26.81.

Corporate-SBU decentralization. This variable was measured through two questions both patterned after Tannenbaum (1968). The first concerned the influence of SBUs' managers and their corporate superiors, both line and staff, on the formulation of business units' long-range strategic plans; the second sought similar data for the formulation of business units' annual operating budgets. For each question, I divided an SBU manager's influence by superiors' influence and averaged the ratios; high values indicated greater decentralization. Values ranged from 0.60 to 4.38, with a mean of 1.86 (α = .77).

SBU's effectiveness. Data were collected on sales growth rate, market share, operating profits, profit to sales ratio, cash flow from operations, return on investment, new product development, market development, R&D activities, cost reduction programs, personnel development, and political/public affairs. Respondents rated an SBU's performance on each dimension relative to superiors' expectations on a 5-point scale ranging from not at all satisfactory to outstanding. Using the data on dimensional importance—obtained earlier for validating the strategic-context variables—as weights, I obtained a weighted-average effectiveness index for each SBU. Values ranged from 1.46 to 4.80, with a mean of 3.21, indicating that as a group respondents appear not to have inflated their reported performance. Heneman (1974) reported very high correlations between superiors and self-ratings when subordinates are guaranteed anonymity and understand that the objective of data collection is scientific and not evaluative, conditions that were met fully in this study.

Anil K. Gupta earned his D.B.A. degree at Harvard University. He is on the faculty of the College of Business and Management of the University of Maryland at College Park. His current research projects explore the implementation of business units' strategies within diversified firms and the strategic implications of corporate executives' backgrounds.

Part III
Implementation Processes and Strategic Planning

Avoid the Breakdowns Between Planning and Implementation

William Sandy

There are eight areas in a business plan where energy is often wasted. Here's how to spot the gaps that prevent plans from being put into action.

The payoff from planning is what people actually do to convert ideas into performance. The most important partnership in organizations is between the planner and those who must make the plan work. It's important to recognize and act on the patterns of successful and unsuccessful handoffs.

Frustration is the common cold of organizational life. Planners can become frustrated because bold initiatives often remain lifeless prisoners in plan books that are rapidly filed away. Those who receive the plans can become frustrated because they don't perceive the initiatives as relevant to their real-world issues. Such perception might be flawed, but we live in a world in which perception is reality.

How do you break this cycle of frustration that, if uncorrected, can keep repeating itself as new initiatives are begun with great fanfare and then slowly die, never to be heard from again? The business landscape is littered with rallying slogans and themes that live on as empty labels, without resources, leadership, or commitment, testimony to just one more intention gone awry.

Eight Planning Breakdowns

Where do the breakdowns occur? What causes them? What can be done about it? It is important to recognize the patterns that prevent plans from being implemented. Here are eight places where energy leaks out at the seams of organizational intentions.

Underestimating the Voice of the Customer

Just about every plan today has a preface about customer satisfaction, increasing market share, etc. But it's vital to go beyond generalities.

The customer is the one who pays for everybody and everything in your organization. Most entities today are resource-constrained and so, spoken or unspoken, resources and energies are going to move toward what matters to customers.

How do you make that connection? How do you organize your recommendations so they are tightly connected to how customers start to consider their choices, how customers make their ultimate decisions, how customers are satisfied or left unsatisfied, how

William Sandy is Chairman and CEO of Sandy Corporation, a Troy, Michigan, performance improvement organization. He is the author of Forging the Productivity Partnership (McGraw-Hill, 1990).

customers decide to buy again, and most important, recommend to others? Have you charted this decision flow? Have you put your initiatives into this real-world context?

Customer focus also means internal customers as well as external customers. Diagram the chain of action in your organization—who hands off work to whom—(e.g., sales to the office, engineering to manufacturing, etc.). These are the seams of the organization, and seams are where the energy leaks out. Pay attention to the handoffs from function to function, to the differences in language and perspectives.

In some visionary franchise organizations, particularly the automobile industry, planning with dealers is taking on new systemic seriousness. Automobile dealers represent the epitome of the American entrepreneurial culture. Their business has become complex and challenging enough to require sophisticated planning.

Automobile dealerships today are crammed with computers, satellite television receiving stations, and other contemporary tools for reaching sound decisions. But the human element must be factored into the process of converting plans into decisions, decisions into actions, and actions into results.

As independent businessmen and businesswomen (sometimes very independent) who at times are distant from the manufacturer both geographically and in outlook, dealers will do only what they conclude is in their self-interest to do. The good news is that manufacturers are looking at their dealers as customers rather than as extensions of factory policy, reversing the planning flow to build manufacturer strategy from the base of dealer input (not the other way around).

This is just one example of customer perspectives becoming the driving force of the planning process—not just one more input, but the mainstream propellant of what gets attention. This reverse flow of planning can cause a draining clash of viewpoints—unless all the participants become accustomed to supporting their perspectives.

Information Is Not Organized for Action

We are drowning in data. Some complain that "we can't find what we know." As the plan seeks to persuade others to action, there can be a tendency to increase the weight of factual support. And yet the key today is to crystallize information to its essence.

Information can be organized for the convenience of the collector or the usability of the user. The best way to gear your plan for easy conversion to implementation is to organize the logic of the plan in a way that fits the organization of the implementation work to be done. When you follow that logic, information is available to users in the way that they think and work.

Diagram the flow of work that will result from your plan. Anticipate where the problems and the barriers to change will be. Then, at those exact juncture points, intersperse the information that not only supports your initiatives, but that gives practical assistance to those who are following the road that you have laid out.

Looking at the nature of work today and the information required to do that work—together, simultaneously—can trigger innovations.

For example, consider the computerized data that salespeople use to sell various products and services. Planners might organize the information one way for the purposes of a plan but structure the information very differently if the perspective is shifted to how those on the receiving end will apply the information.

How can information be reduced to its crystallized essence? When do you

PLANNING BREAKDOWNS

decide what information goes into the mind as concepts and building blocks—and what can remain at the fingertips for retrieval when needed? These concepts of "just-in-time learning" become very important at the implementation stage. So the planner who organizes the plan and its documentation for the user will produce plans that are far more implementation-ready.

The Process of Reaching Conclusions Does Not Involve the Right People

We have all been involved in global challenge and recession long enough so that the easy incremental improvements were planned and implemented long ago. So now we are at the frontiers, where human skepticism and fear play a part. It isn't enough to have the right answers. The planning dialogue needs to be truly interactive, with all of the stakeholders, so that they move through a discovery process.

If telling were the same as teaching, the world would be a much smarter place. The planner today needs skills of leadership and tutoring to bring people along, at their own pace, so that they move from understanding to belief to commitment to a zest for action.

Asking those who must implement plans how they see their world is a very direct way to find out what stands in the way of the actions you need.

When major changes that depend on people don't happen, there can be many reasons. But most of the time, it is one of these three:

- People don't know what you expect or why you expect it, which depends on the clarity of your plan;
- They don't know how to do it, which depends on education;
- They don't believe the effort is worth the gain, which is why motivation is part of successful planning.

Fragmented, Piecemeal, or Insufficient Solutions

Not only must the plan be solid, but people you are counting on must believe it. They sense the difference between a crusade and a charade and commit their energies accordingly.

Good planning must combine scope and simplicity. If you scope the issues out with confusing or intimidating thoroughness, you will produce paralysis. On the other hand, the world is filled with people who solve one small piece of a problem and proclaim that as the total answer, which leads to diminished credibility and repetitive failure. The planning process should be a dynamic process that moves from the widest possible consideration of bold alternatives to a disciplined set of actionable choices.

No Champions and Few Reasons to Take on That Role

Someone must decide who is in charge of the change process. No matter how powerful your plan, rarely will more be accomplished than the leader expects.

Strategic planners can't always pick and choose who the baton gets handed to for implementation. But the planning process can and should address constraints, and it is legitimate for the plan to consider such structural, organizational hindrances to leadership as the following:

- Organization charts that vaguely define roles rather than the tasks to be accomplished;
- Overlapping charters that leave two or more people vaguely accountable for results, with little individual accountability;
- Convoluted decision paths, with too many deciders;
- Authority not commensurate with responsibility; rewards not commensurate with risk;

"Strategic planners can't always pick and choose who the baton gets handed to for implementation. But the planning process can and should address constraints."

- Praise for activity rather than for results;
- Financial procedures that discourage innovation by easily approving past expenditures with precedents, but fiercely challenge new solutions because "we've done okay without them";
- Innovation without the special nurturing that untried ideas must have.

People You Count On Don't Understand How to Succeed

The key here is the word "how." Too many plans concentrate on *what* you want, without moving to the next logical consideration of how you will achieve that.

A business plan is not complete unless it is extended into a human performance plan, factoring in the knowledge, skill, and beliefs of those you are counting on and committing to fill in the gaps.

Nobody Keeps Score

Every improvement in your plan will be cloaked in vagueness if you do not have the will and the skill to analyze results. Measuring performance is at the very heart of getting commitment from others.

Playing a sport loses intensity and focus if you don't keep score. Wandering in the woods can be dangerous if you don't have a compass. By the same token, people do not make major commitments and do not sublimate their differences unless there is evidence that the direction is clear and a consequence system is in place (e.g., good things like raises or promotions will follow success, and adverse consequences will follow preventable failure).

All participants must understand where they are, where they are going, how they are going to get there, how they are progressing, and how it pays off for the total organization and for individual contributors.

Good measurement begins at the beginning, illuminates what is important, is consistent and fair, and converts into action. Keeping score is not simply the difference between what is and what was. It is an integral, dynamic part of the plan that lays out a path between what is and what can be.

Measurement is a tool of motivation as well as a tool for decision making. Most importantly, dynamic and continuing measurement is a way to continually adjust the plan to meet changing circumstances.

Nothing Happens When You Win

Bold moves forward need the reinforcement of small victories. Celebrating accomplishment provides powerful propulsion for organizational change. The way to start generating momentum (over and above the joy you give people when you recognize their accomplishments) is by remembering what you have asked for and rewarding promptly when you achieve it.

Momentum in many organizations is the precious missing element. Many companies and individuals who have figured out the right direction to move stay in the same place because there is little energy or intensity behind their intentions.

These days, it isn't enough to have better ideas. Those ideas must take on a fast-to-market pace. Of all the forces that can spark momentum, nothing is more powerful than recognizing the right people for the right reasons at the right time.

At every step of massive change and significant improvement, you as a planner and those who you count on to implement the plan are at a juncture point. At each point, decisions and actions can result in pitfalls or they can mobilize power within the organization. ■

The Role of Systems In Implementing Strategy

R Malcolm Schwartz
Frank A. Petro

Mr. Schwartz is a senior vice president of Booz-Allen and the firm's chief financial officer.

Mr. Petro is a vice president of Booz-Allen based in San Francisco.

Have you ever called a meeting to resolve a problem, and watched it degenerate into an argument about whose numbers were right? With your financial reviews showing profit below plan, have you ever been told that a special study would have to be undertaken to determine what really caused the variance? Have you been surprised to find that you were rewarding a function manager for achieving an objective that was suboptimal from the firmwide standpoint?

Arguments over "the numbers," an inability to determine what is going wrong when a shortfall is reported, and rewards for performance inconsistent with corporate goals are all symptoms of a basic lack of integration of a company's systems with its strategy and organization design. Such events should serve as warning signals, alerting top management to the need to revisit the roles played by systems.

By "systems," we mean more than information technology and its applications; we use the term in the sense of management systems, which include any of the purposefully organized, established procedures that pervade a business. These systems may be automated or manual.

To sort through the fundamental influences and effects of systems, consider the following three categories (see Exhibit 1):

Execution systems focus directly on the basic processes for conducting the firm's business. They include systems that enable products to be designed, or supplies to be ordered, or production scheduled, or goods shipped, or cash applied, or employees paid.

Monitoring systems are any procedures that measure and assess the basic processes. They can be designed to gather information in different ways to serve a number of internal or external reporting purposes—to meet SEC or other regulatory requirements, for budgetary control, for taxes, and, as we shall see, to serve the strategic and organizational intent of the company.

Control systems are the means through which processes are made to conform or are kept within tolerable limits. At the broadest level, they include separation of duties, authority limits, product inspection, and plan submittals.

As can be seen from this brief description, systems pervade the conduct of business. For that very reason, systems provide ample opportunity for strategy to fail.

Beyond Electronic Systems Intensity

Some businesses are so dependent on information technology that one might assume their management systems were sophisticated. Banks are one example, given the transaction intensity of their business. Airline companies are another, with their reservation and route systems. Telephone companies are a third, with their reliance on their networks for effective routing, diagnostics, and call supervision.

But the systems savvy that exists in these industries mostly operates at the execution level; until recently, managers in many of such companies were shortsighted about using monitoring and control systems to derive strategic advantage. Banks are just starting to link transactions to products and to account management; airlines are learning to manage maintenance, fares, and interline settlements; and telephone companies are just beginning to array costs toward services, as they move to become more competitive.

In other words, mere intensity of information-technology systems in a firm does not guarantee that those systems are properly monitored and controlled. In fact, the extreme importance of maintaining the execution systems in such cases might be a reason why management pays too little attention to monitoring and control systems.

Creating systems that support the strategic and organizational intent requires top management to include not just execution but monitoring and control systems in strategic thinking; and to focus on systems in strategy implementation. It means, as part of the strategic planning, answering such key questions as: What are the critical success factors, and how do they translate into operational performance? How should that operational performance be measured and motivated, and how should information about financial performance be derived? What business cycles are important, and how should systems support them? What is the role of financial controls and measures? Where should control of information reside? How should strategic objectives and organizational performance be monitored—and modified, as necessary? How should internal and external information be linked?

In short, integrating all systems with strategy requires a rare commodity—the ability to see the firm as an organic whole. Unfortunately, too many systems managers lack the vision or the clout, and too many executives lack the understanding or the inclination to make this happen.

Understanding the Gap Between Systems and Strategy

As we shall see, there are a number of ways that a gap can arise between a company's systems and top management's strategic and organizational intent: First, management might rely too heavily on financial statistics for strategic purposes, not realizing that monitoring systems can be designed to report operational performance measures such as market share and operations efficiency directly as well as to report financial information derived from that performance. Second, the company might lack a common framework for information gathering; such a framework is necessary if management is to track the underlying causes of shortfalls in performance, not just within a function or business unit, but through all the value-adding stages of the business. Third, management might understand the need to review all systems and make them support strategy but have false expectations that the task will become easier to do at some point in the future. Finally, there is the issue of information "ownership," or emotionalism about the uses to which information will be put, which tends to bog down efforts to link systems strategically.

Problem #1: Financial Indicators and Operational Performance

Strategy cannot be effectively implemented without monitoring and control systems that specifically support the strategic and organizational intent. As the feedback loop (again, we use this term in its broadest sense) on the execution of strategic and organizational objectives, monitoring systems should provide the information that management needs to redirect operations and refine strategy—and, if they are designed and installed correctly, monitoring systems will enable management to do precisely that.

Historically, however, most monitoring systems used financial indicators to measure performance. Where there were links to strategy, the links were usually budget related—showing how a division performed against plan, from a budgetary perspective. Such indicators were frequently derived in a way that masked the causes of variations in operating performance and thus obscured factors that were and are important for management feedback and control.

Exhibit 1
The Roles of Systems

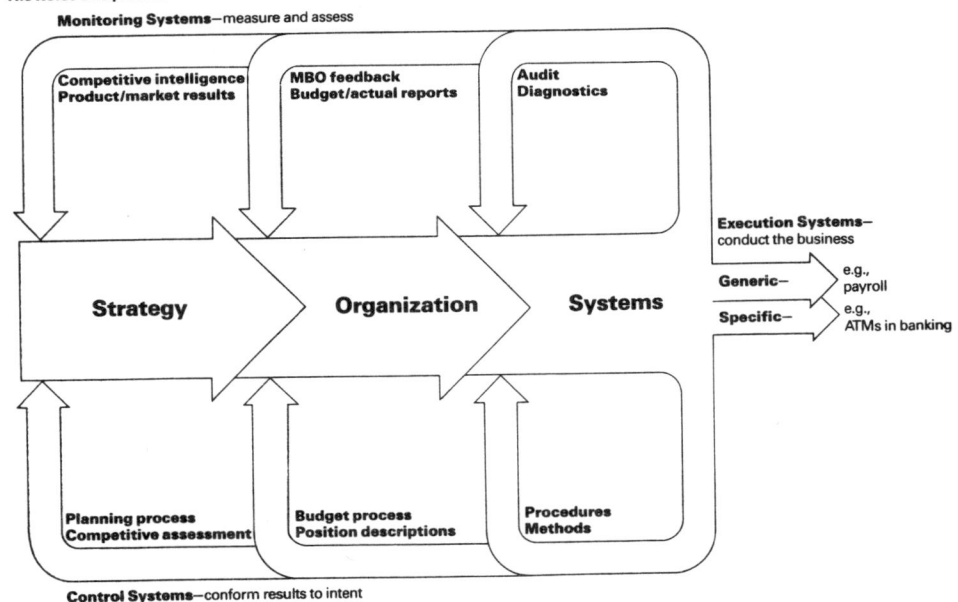

Monitoring Systems—measure and assess

- Competitive intelligence
- Product/market results
- MBO feedback
- Budget/actual reports
- Audit
- Diagnostics

Strategy → Organization → Systems

Execution Systems—conduct the business
- Generic— e.g., payroll
- Specific— e.g., ATMs in banking

- Planning process
- Competitive assessment
- Budget process
- Position descriptions
- Procedures
- Methods

Control Systems—conform results to intent

48 Linking Organization, Systems, and Compensation

Inventory provides the classic example of a summary financial indicator that masks both operating factors and functional differences. From the perspective of the financial function, "inventory" is a monetary amount derived from receipts from suppliers, additions of standard costs through manufacturing processes, relief of accounts for the value of invoiced shipments, and reserves. From the perspective of operations, "inventory" is built up from quantities, translated into standard costs. These two measurements of inventory are equally valid—but they serve different functional purposes and seldom yield the same monetary value.

The CEO of a prominent producer of consumer products told us how, in one major product-line division, differences in inventory valuation became such that marketing, operations, and financial management often could not agree on the size of an inventory problem—or even if there was one. The reports and analyses that each function manager provided were suspect in the eyes of the others. As time passed, planning and forecasting suffered—and inventory investment both grew and became more unbalanced. Service deteriorated. In one attempt to solve the problem, distribution channels were changed, but to no avail. The company's competitive position worsened. The CEO eventually was forced to sell the operation at less than book value.

A similar disconnect can exist between "the numbers" at the operating levels and overall corporate performance. Income statements, balance sheets, and cash flow are a means of accumulating and translating a myriad of actions across a range of functions into a common set of measures. These statistics show whether or not a profit is being made. Most function managers, however, do not make a profit; they spend their time minimizing scrap, improving labor productivity, increasing the success rate of sales calls, or increasing the earnings on available funds. Their actions enable profits to be made.

Top management needs to know whether or not a profit is being made, but it also needs to know that that profit is the result of the desired performance—and that the combined performance of all function managers is converging on overall strategic goals.

If systems are to support strategy, they will focus on what is important to the business. Instead of trying to measure performance in uniform financial terms, they will allow differentiated measures to be derived from the company's performance with regard to its critical success factors. Performance measurement systems (see sidebar) provide an example. With performance measurement, management will have a means of keeping score. The score will be good or bad depending on what causes the unit to be able to perform effectively, and when—that is, depending on cycles that are inherent to its business and not on accounting cycles.

Problem #2: A Common Framework

To provide a common framework, monitoring systems must include linkages among functions, geographies, product lines, and other business segments. If goods or services (or information) are transferred from one unit to another, or if costs derived from a common source must be distributed, vertical and horizontal links should relate internal buying and selling activities to the value-added chain of vertical integration.

The CEO of a chemicals company, wanting his strategic business unit (SBU) general managers to "take ownership," had delegated to each the responsibility for his unit's systems strategy. The CEO intended inter-SBU transactions (such as the transfer of domestically manufactured products to the offshore distributing SBU) and the management of resource sharing (such as two SBUs sharing a common manufacturing facility) to continue, but failed to realize the need for a common systems framework to support these activities. The corporate systems director, faced with conflicting managerial practices, was unable to sustain systems for any shared strategic imperatives. Instead, he led the corporate systems development effort away from strategic management and toward administrative support.

As the ability to consolidate firmwide results deteriorated, the CEO became more and more frustrated about each SBU's performance—yet found himself less and less able to redirect the SBU's efforts. Eventually, the CEO recognized the need to reintegrate key and common aspects of the systems effort.

The creation of a vertically linked systems framework requires a clear understanding of the hierarchy of factors that cause performance to vary within each business unit: that these factors be related to the critical success factors of the business; and that performance indicators be consistent with organizational function and level. Given such reporting systems, top management can backtrack through derived results to causative factors.

For example, assume that an office products company aims to be the low-cost provider for its market, but the reports received by management show that the company's selling expense is high relative to that of competitors. The problem could be in the product (for example, in price or product mix) or it could be in the selling effort (compensation, duties, call focus, or support). If the company's systems do not provide linkages of causative measures (see Exhibit 2), the company is forced to rely on time-consuming special studies—or judgment, hunch, and anecdote—to attempt to achieve its strategic objectives.

In situations in which linkages among SBUs are important to strategy and organization, systems must be designed so that operational information can be transferred easily. Central design, firmwide codes, and common data bases are important features.

Problem #3: False Expectations

False expectations arise in many guises. Some managers look to technological breakthroughs in information systems to provide an easy way to integrate systems with their strategic and organizational thrusts. For example, some thought that distributed processing would in some magical way do the trick but found that the need to direct systems toward strategic consistency is as urgent for distributed systems as it is for large, mainframe systems. Given distributed processing and minicomputers, sophisticated users often create planning models that, over time, come to bear little relationship to the operating details of a business; keeping them synchronized can often be a nightmarish problem.

This was the case with one supplier of nationwide network communications services: With simplifying algorithms and rather casual maintenance, the company's planning models (developed and operated in a distributed, functionally oriented environment) came to have less and less consistency with the underlying technologies, costs, and service parameters of the network itself. The various planning models even started to disagree with each other, playing havoc with pricing and strategic analysis.

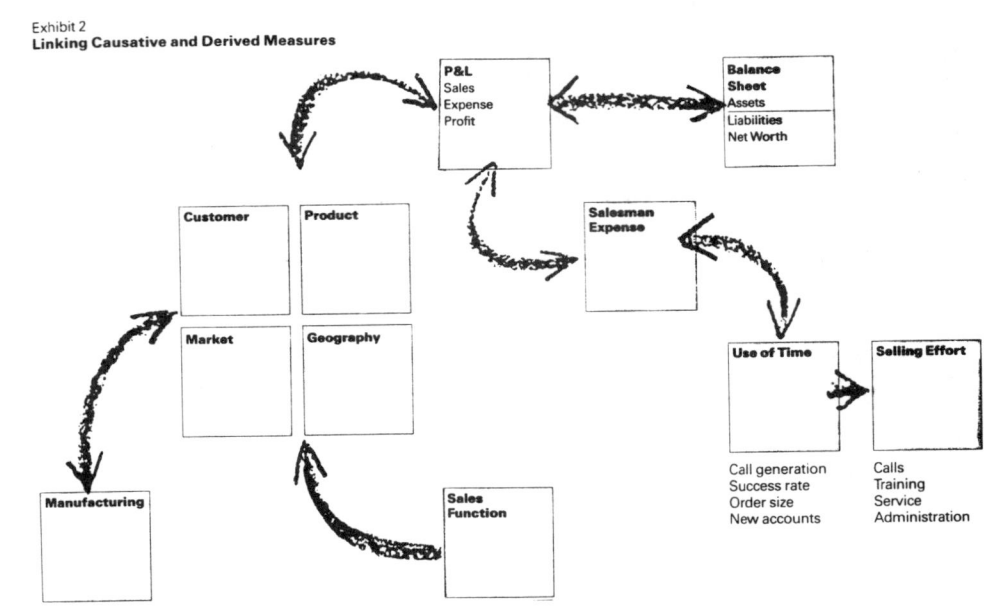

Exhibit 2
Linking Causative and Derived Measures

```
                           ┌──────────┐              ┌──────────┐
                           │ P&L      │              │ Balance  │
                           │ Sales    │ ◄──────►     │ Sheet    │
                           │ Expense  │              │ Assets   │
                           │ Profit   │              │ Liabilities│
                           └──────────┘              │ Net Worth│
                                                     └──────────┘
     ┌──────────┐  ┌──────────┐    ┌──────────┐
     │ Customer │  │ Product  │    │ Salesman │
     │          │  │          │    │ Expense  │
     └──────────┘  └──────────┘    └──────────┘

     ┌──────────┐  ┌──────────┐             ┌──────────┐  ┌──────────┐
     │ Market   │  │ Geography│             │Use of Time│ │Selling Effort│
     │          │  │          │             │          │  │          │
     └──────────┘  └──────────┘             └──────────┘  └──────────┘
                                            Call generation  Calls
                                            Success rate     Training
                                            Order size       Service
     ┌──────────┐                ┌──────────┐ New accounts   Administration
     │Manufacturing│             │ Sales    │
     │          │                │ Function │
     └──────────┘                └──────────┘
```

Some companies look not to a new architecture, but to a new generation of computer-literate middle managers to ensure systems consistent with strategic objectives. They will be disappointed. A company might employ sophisticated users of computers, but if organization roles and priorities are not well communicated, such users might put their capabilities to work ineffectively. For example, a long-range planning staff might use a microcomputer to consider and rank a number of options for growth; but if staff members do not realize that the strategic imperative is low-cost operations, they might analyze and rank opportunities that add incremental costs as well as revenue, as opposed to seeking revenue opportunities from the current cost base.

Problem #4: Information Intent
It might appear that, once all the management homework has been done, creating systems that support the strategic and organizational intent is largely a matter of design; however, the ability to create the appropriate design is not enough to ensure success. Systems development often falls prey to emotionally charged questions such as: Which function owns the information? Who is in charge of it? Who controls its usage? Is it correct?

Emotionalism about the use of the information—and the distrust that causes organizational conflicts—can be minimized. That was the lesson learned by the chief executive of a high-technology business-equipment producer, who had wanted his business to develop a common culture. To that end, sales information was formally used only for summary financial results. Sales reports by product, market, organization, or function (service expense related to service contracts, as an example) were not allowed, "to avoid a profit center approach."

The result? An inability to analyze segments of the business, and little sense of responsibility for such discrete segments as small business and national accounts. Eventually, the chief executive realized that sales information had to be used for different purposes; and that, so long as the sources of the information were consistent, it could be used for different purposes to support—not destroy—organization intent and common goals.

Executives must be wise enough to use information to accomplish strategic objectives and should not allow the precision of information gathering—particularly for financial controls—to get in the way. Systems tend to force precision in terms of the data and the transactions. Managers should create ambiguity in the information assembled from data when it is useful to do so. Transfer prices provide an example: To accomplish corporate objectives, it might be useful for the system to show goods sold internally at market prices and those bought internally at cost. As another example, it might be useful to credit certain sales to more than one market category, as opposed to enforcing precise definitions that cause territorial and organizational disputes.

Techniques for Systems Design
As we mentioned earlier, the creation of systems that support strategic and organizational intent requires top management to include systems in strategic thinking and to focus on systems in strategy implementation. Once the critical success factors have been identified and translated into operational measurements, good system-design techniques are needed to ensure that those factors and measurements are appropriately accommodated by all systems. Some guidelines for good systems design are:

1. *Design an effective information-capture procedure.* Data should be captured close to the source, and source documents should be linked. For example, at one company, data

Linking Organization, Systems, and Compensation

Performance Measurement Systems (PMS)

Performance measurement is a key component of the monitoring systems that support business strategy. Performance measurement as a management reporting system differs from traditional financial reporting systems by using: *Both strategic and financial indicators*—performance measurement highlights such areas as markets and operations efficiency as well as financial results. *Exception based reporting*—instead of producing long, voluminous reports, performance measurement provides summary-level analysis with fast access to follow-up information. *Differentiated rather than uniform measures*—traditional reporting approaches show the same information for each unit, but performance measurement is designed to provide the 10-15 critical performance factors based on the unit's strategy. And, *both profit and cash flow*—traditional systems emphasize profit reporting, performance measurement reports cash flow for the unit because of its influence on overall performance.

Implementation of performance measurement calls for analysis of each unit's strategy and then the identification of the factors needed to evaluate progress in meeting the strategy. For example, a strategy for a marketing unit might involve one of several options, such as developing new products for existing markets, developing new-to-the-world products, expanding market share, or developing new markets for current products. The first option—new products for existing markets—would increase product development costs as a percentage of sales, depending on the number and effectiveness of new development projects. Another option, one for greater market share, would most likely emphasize advertising and promotion; in pursuing this option, management would expect an increase in sales expenses (advertising, direct selling, promotions).

The matrix in Exhibit A summarizes possible relationships between each of these four marketing options and specific performance measures. This illustration should not be viewed as a list of generic performance measures that should be applied to these strategic options. Rather, it is one example of strategic options available to a corporation and of some performance measures that might be used for these options. Naturally, these measures would vary, depending on the strategy, and on the segment—geographic, functional, product, market, or expense category—being measured. The targets for the measurements would also vary with the business cycle. A similar matrix can be created for each strategic alternative and related performance measures. The strategic options associated with, for example, production, overseas expansion, or financing can be determined and each one evaluated to identify the appropriate performance measures.

Exhibit A
Relationship between Strategic Options and Performance Measures

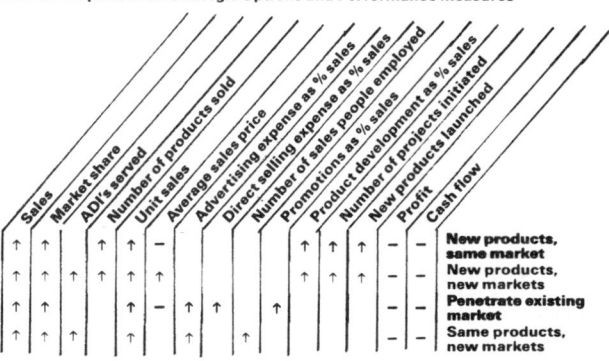

	Sales	Market share	ADI's served	Number of products sold	Unit sales	Average sales price	Advertising expense as % sales	Direct selling expense as % sales	Number of sales people employed	Promotions as % sales	Product development as % sales	Number of projects initiated	New products launched	Profit	Cash flow	
	↑	↑		↑	↑	—				↑	↑	↑	—	—		New products, same market
	↑	↑	↑	↑	↑	↑				↑	↑	↑	—	—		New products, new markets
	↑	↑		↑	—	↑	↑		↑				—	—		Penetrate existing market
	↑	↑		↑		↑	↑		↑				—	—		Same products, new markets

This type of analysis sharpens the distinctions within a function by strategy option and can result in a matrix with 10 or more strategy options and 75 to 80 performance measures for each option. These relationships then form the basis for understanding how to integrate a unit's strategic direction, what factors are critical to success, and how to establish pertinent reporting and monitoring.

To illustrate this point, look at the PMS report for the computer-aided-design products division of a major electronics manufacturer (see Exhibit B). This division is the parent company's entry in an embryonic, fast-changing market; participants must invest heavily in product development to keep abreast of competitors. However, as this exhibit shows, the division increased its profitability by cutting back on product development. This action would have been less visible in traditional reporting approaches, which are based on profit and report only financial results. The performance measurement report, on the other hand, highlights the implication of this action. It shows a reduction in the number of product introductions and in product development expenditures as a percentage of sales.

Exhibit B
Sample of a Performance Measurement Report
Computer-Aided-Design Products Division

	This Month Actual	Plan	Last Year
Financial Indicators ($000s)			
Sales	$ 3,412	$ 3,171	$ 2,124
Less:			
Cost of Goods Sold	$ 1,461	$ 1,200	$ 967
Sales and Administration	1,961	1,700	860
Profit (Loss) Contribution	$ (10)	$ 271	$ 297
Less:			
Inventory Addition	$ 159	$ 125	$ 222
Capital Projects	597	638	310
Product Development	681	1,345	370
Other	61	53	52
Fund Flow to (from) Corporation	$(1,508)	$(1,890)	$ (657)
Strategic Indicators			
Development Projects Initiated	1	3	1
New Features Introduced	1	0	0
Number of Salespersons	20	21	17
Development/Marketing Costs (% Sales)			
Product Development	19%	40%	21%
Advertising	6	6	5
Sales Compensation	7	7	5
Sales Support	2	2	1
Total Marketing	16	15	11
Market Indicators			
Key Industry Sales			
Secondary Schools	$ 400	$ 395	$ 281
College	1,141	725	340
Professional	1,426	1,671	1,322
Technical	445	380	181
Total Sales	$ 3,412	$ 3,171	$ 2,124

(Shading indicates information not provided in traditional reports)

processing personnel collected information on raw material from receiving reports two days after delivery and entered that information into purchasing control and inventory management systems. Another two days later, accounting gathered information on the same delivery from invoices, this time entering it into accounting systems. The failure to link source documents led to apparent inventory discrepancies. The operating processes focused on inventory codes and quantities; the accounting process dealt with accounting codes and monetary amounts, available only at the end of the month.

The problems required a threefold solution: the placement of terminals at the receiving dock, where receiving clerks could enter operating information; the use of internal linkages to accounting codes; and a reconciliation proof and entry of quantity and amount as invoices were received.

It is also important to decide what characteristics have to be described when information is captured. For example, when sales information is accumulated, a number of other characteristics can be attached—such as type of customer, type of product, and geographic market. If done effectively, "sales" can have a number of meanings, all derived from a consistent element of information.

2. *Manage commonly used data elements for firmwide accessibility and control.* If a multidivisional firm allows each unit to code inventory discretely, stock that is commonly used cannot be traded and rebalanced. Traditionally, auto dealers maintained independent inventory controls. By contrast, Ford Motor Company has worked to keep its inventory records consistent, and thus accessible to dealers, so that imbalances at one location can lead to opportunities for another.

Today, with the potential of transmitting data among locations (as Ford recognized with its dealers), common code structures are as important as compatible software and hardware. Systems designers should consider from the onset not just who "needs to know," but also who has a "value in knowing." By starting with the assumption of broad and quick accessibility, decisions about security will become more obvious—and technical roadblocks will not be carelessly designed into the systems.

3. *Decide which applications are common and which tolerate distributed processing.* Typical considerations here include pinpointing the need to share data, determining the availability of hardware and software offerings that make a distributed approach feasible, and investigating the effect of geographical distance. Once a particular application or function is judged appropriate for a distributed approach, it must be integrated into an information network.

4. *Manage information, not reports.* Often, systems are developed with the end reports in mind—with a focus on output and not content. If needs change, or if developers and users misunderstand each other, the results of such an approach can lead to frustration at best, or the inability to modify the output at worst. When the development focus is on the content—on the information that has been strategically identified as critical to success—then users can tailor the output presentation to their purposes. For example, in one company with a well-constructed receivables data base, one manager has chosen to compare cash collections to target amounts, another uses days outstanding, and a third uses turnover ratios.

5. *Mind your cost effectiveness.* Questioning the value of a system—and of the work required to support it—is healthy. Delegation of systems responsibility is no answer to the problem of "administrivia" if it just causes someone else to do useless work. Procter & Gamble, to escape merely chipping away at existing processes through cost reduction, developed its Elimination Approach, which is based on the key "if" question: If it were not for this (reason), this (cost) would be eliminated.

A similar approach can be applied to systems and to the procedures that surround them, such as: assigning costs to a function or department that cannot control them, preparing reports that people do not use, undertaking special studies when "the back of the envelope" would provide reasonable discrimination to the analysis, or spending time resolving who should bear what portion of a variance when the cost is not changed and the results are not improved. Justifying one more administrative step because "the system requires it" is senseless—it is people who cause "the system" in the first place.

Questioning any system undertaking that does not produce short-run and continual benefits is also important. Systems projects often disappear into the development back-office for months. The progress reports boil down to, "We're working on it." And backlog lists are a way of life. There is a different approach. Identifying the overall outcome in a strategic framework is the first step, followed by segmenting the work into small projects—one or two people, and one or two months—that will enable quick and visible results. If users are involved early on, they can work with partial deliverables and get a sense of the value of the system. The strategy stays constant, but task priorities change as the internal "market" takes shape. The result: more satisfied users who are taking ownership, and a sense of tangible accomplishment on the part of the developers.

Strategy: Systems Make It Happen

Designing and maintaining systems that focus on the strategic intent and assess performance in terms of that intent are crucial to the success of a strategy. In fact, a lack of integration between systems and strategy is an important reason why sound strategic and organizational concepts get bogged down in implementation and do not achieve the results that their creators intended. Soundly designed and managed systems do not happen casually, but only with top-management involvement and a clear vision of the importance of systems to strategic outcomes.

Building Successful Strategic Alliances

Peter Lorange, Johan Roos and Peggy Simcic Brønn

In this paper we will discuss (1) why a firm would want to go into a strategic alliance, (2) the different types of alliances, and (3) guidelines to follow when forming an alliance.

Thinking of a strategic alliance as a parental relationship is not a new idea, but it works. Two firms come together to give birth to an idea, a product, another firm, or research that embodies the best characteristics of each parent. And, just as in human parental relationships, the firms have varying levels of responsibilities toward their 'child'. At one end of the spectrum a firm may wish to develop a product, and needs another firm for its expertise, but they do not necessarily want any long-term commitment from the relationship.

The opposite end of the spectrum is the classical parental relationship where both partners take full responsibility. In the business world, this is known as the full-blown joint venture. Both firms have supplied resources towards the alliance and both have a stake in its success as an 'adult'. An excellent example of this type of relationship is the alliance between Fuji Films and Rank Xerox in Japan to create Fuji Xerox, now one of the world's largest copy machine manufacturers.[1]

Regardless of which approach is chosen, the decisions by firms to co-operate are not taken lightly and once made must be handled with great care. And because individuals are involved, there will always be differences of opinion and in the way that things are seen. But, usually, if there is not *too* much difference, common ground can be found and fruitful relationships can be built.

Peter Lorange is President, Johan Roos is Assistant Professor, and Peggy Simcic Brønn is a Researcher at the Norwegian School of Management, Elias Smithsvei 15, Postboks 580, N-1301 Sandvika, Norway.

Why the Strategic Alliance Solution?

Let's start from 'ground zero', and talk about the very first decision that has to be made; the decision to form an alliance. For the parent firms, there are a variety of reasons for wanting a strategic alliance including access to technology or access to a market. We find that there are four generic motives for forming alliances: as a defence, to catch up, to remain or to restructure. This can be understood by focusing on two strategy dimensions; the strategic importance of the business segment within the firm's portfolio and the market position of the business segment.

Defence

A defensive position is normal when the offspring, or product/idea/research/business, is core or of primary importance to a firm's family portfolio and where the firm is a leader in this particular business. At first glance it might be difficult to find any reason for such firms to consider an alliance. But the reasons are sensible; the firm may want additional access to new competencies, to markets, to technology or to specific resources in order to sustain its competitive advantage over time. Some examples of this are IBMs numerous strategic alliances with key customers for developing specialized software, the Swedish ball bearing firm SKF's alliance with the French firm SDM to develop electromagnetic

		Business' Market Position	
		Leader	Follower
Strategic Importance in Parent's Portfolio	Core	Defend	Catch Up
	Peripheral	Remain	Restructure

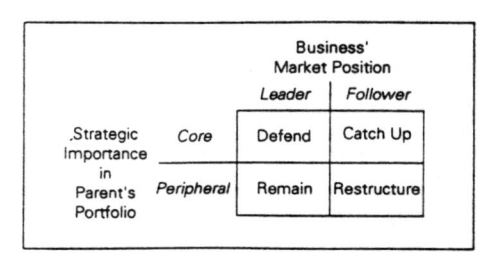

Figure 1. Generic motives for strategic alliances

bearings, Japanese alliances penetrating Viet Nam, and so on. The main thing is that these firms use alliances to build and develop their firm's specialties through learning new technologies or accessing difficult markets.

Catch Up
Another motive for an alliance is to catch up. This occurs in a situation where the business is still core in the firm's portfolio, but where it is more of a follower in the business segment. The use of a strategic alliance in this case should strengthen a firm's competitive position; helping it move toward becoming a leader. An example of this situation could be SAAB Automobile's alliance with General Motors in 1990. From SAAB's perspective, without the alliance they very well may have had to give up the automotive business.

Remain
When the business plays a peripheral role in the portfolio of a firm, but where the firm is a leader in its business segment, the main motive for forming an alliance is to remain in the business. The alliance could even be used as a way of getting the maximum efficiency out of a firm's position, given the limited corporate attention a peripheral business can get. Ericsson's 1989 strategic alliance with General Electric in the cellular radio field is an example of this. This business was more peripheral to GE's portfolio than to Ericsson's, but this $1bn a year strategic alliance still made sense because it created more value to GE than if the business had been unloaded. For Ericsson this was a unique opportunity, because of the firm's relative leadership, to remain in this business segment and to create a stronger competitive advantage within the segment, particularly in the U.S.A.

Restructure
If a firm is a follower in the business area and if the particular business plays a peripheral role in its portfolio, the main motive for a strategic alliance often is to restructure the business. In this case restructuring could also mean going to the point of actually exiting a business. An example from Sweden of using joint ownership to restructure a business is the case of Bulten AB, a member of the Kanthal Hóganás Group.

While an important member of the Kanthal business portfolio, Bulten, a manufacturer of fasteners, only provided a fraction to Kanthal's overall profitability and in the early 1980s the situation was getting worse. In order to overcome unfavourable market conditions, to strengthen market share, and to streamline manufacturing, as well as to infuse the firm with needed capital, Kanthal, through various partners and share ownerships with other Scandinavian producers, put the firm back on solid ground. Subsequently, and very importantly, Kanthal was able to purchase the firm in its entirety in the late 1980s and operate it as a wholly-owned subsidiary.

Alliance Types

An over-riding consideration driving the formation of a strategic alliance is the *type* of relationship that the parent firms are going to have. This has to do with resources—physical, organizational and human.

As discussed, resource input may be minimal or it may be abundant. But we must also talk about output. What happens to all of the output being generated by the alliance? How will the partners split them? How do they influence the alliance?

The parents' desires regarding input and output resources are the basic determinants of the type of strategic alliance a firm is going to enter into. For example, two firms may wish to put in a minimum set of complementary resources, perhaps on a temporary basis, and all of the output (learning, know-how, equipment, profit, etc.) is given to the parents. This is an *ad hoc* strategic alliance, and examples can often be seen in agreements among ship owners to trade their ships in a common pattern for a certain time charter arrangement.

In a consortium alliance the parents are willing to put in more resources than in the *ad hoc* case, but the output is still disbursed back to the parents. This can be found in situations where two firms pursue common research and development. Each partner puts in their best technologies, scientists, etc., but the benefits go back to each of the parents after the scientific discoveries (hopefully) have been made.

Moving along the continuum, we have the joint operations strategic alliance where the parents are still only contributing a minimum set of input resources into a common organization, but the main output resources are now retained in the alliance. The only output resources fed back to the parents are in the form of financial results, such as dividends or royalties. Firms that create strategic alliances to facilitate entry into foreign markets often use this type of alliance, or it can be seen in an oil platform construction project which has well-defined, short-term and predictable tasks.

The opposite end of the spectrum from the *ad hoc* pool is the full-blown joint venture. In this case,

		Parents' Input of Resources Sufficient for	
		Short-term Operation	Long-term Adaptation
Parents' Retrieval of Output	To Parents	Ad hoc Pool	Consortium
	Retain	Project-based Joint Venture	Full-blown Joint Venture

Figure 2. Types of strategic alliances

resources are supplied in abundance and most of the outputs are ploughed back to the alliance itself. An example of this is the long-term co-operation between partners to develop an entirely new business operation, as in the case of the Swedish firms, AGA and ESAB, which pooled each other's resources in the welding industry in order to produce and market *gas* welding equipment in the new firm of GCE, thus benefiting from increased scale and scope economies.

The Formation Process

There are two phases in the formation process of a strategic alliance; an initial phase and a more intensive phase. Both phases deal with political and analytical considerations of different types that must be handled at distinct times in the process.

The Analysis

Initial

The initial analytical phase of forming a strategic alliance deals with assessing the match, along several dimensions, between the prospective partners when it comes to overall strategic potentials for co-operation. The analysis should also yield answers to questions such as:

☆ What are the broad, readily apparent benefits from this strategic alliance for each partner?

☆ How can the two parties complement each other to create common strengths from which both can benefit?

☆ Do the partners combine in an offensive manner, or is this a case of the 'sick joining the sick'?

☆ What learning can take place between firms?

☆ What is the managerial capacity of the firms?

Sometimes it is important to place oneself in the partner's position and assess one's own situation from the other's point of view.

Taken together, the above questions should answer whether or not there is, in our favourite expression, an obvious win-win match between the two partners. If an apparent win-win is not obvious, the chances for success of the alliance are low regardless of how good the venture is. Even if a good match is apparent, further reflection on whether or not to proceed is still necessary.

An example of establishing a clear win-win perspective is the strategic alliance between Yokogawa Electric and General Electric Medical Systems which resulted in Yokogawa Medical Systems. This alliance emerged from a successful sales agent agreement in the early 1970s when General Electric Medical Systems planned to make available its latest technology for medical scanners. By the early 1980s, Yokogawa had learned so much about GEs technology that the firm suggested the development of a more cost-efficient and customer-adapted generation of products, for example smaller and more compact CT-scanners for the Japanese market. Following new negotiations, the two firms agreed to form a 50/50 full-blown joint venture company in 1982 that would develop, manufacture, market, distribute and service this new line of CT-scanners. The new product line was extremely successful, not only in Japan, and the operations grew rapidly.

The strategic match between these two firms was such that both firms gained tremendous advantages in the market place with financial benefits to all, but it is the internal analysis that is important here. The win-win strategic match issues received a great deal of attention not only during the initial formation period but also during the move from one evolutionary phase to the next when the alliance went through 're-formation' processes. The complementary benefits of continued co-operation for both partners were carefully reassessed at each phase. A meaningful continuation of a win-win posture led to a modification of each party's role, including the ownership split.

Intensive

As we move into the more intensive phase of the formation process the analysis must become truly in-depth and thorough. More detailed information gathering is necessary at this point, and the two

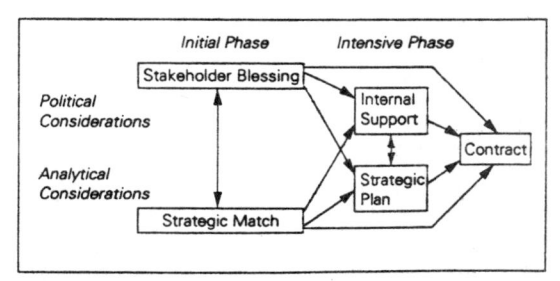

Figure 3. The formation process

prospective partners should be working closely together to answer the following questions:

☆ How do we each view the market potential?

☆ Whom do we view as key competitors, and how will the alliance want to compete with them?

☆ What is the worst-case scenario, particularly as applied to planned revenue levels?

☆ What are the sustainable competitive advantages of the strategic alliance?

☆ In short, how variable is the strategic alliance idea when translated into a business plan?

The *joint* capabilities and strengths of the two prospective parents must be used to produce synergies that benefit both partners. The combination of forces should enable both partners to experience our now quite familiar win-win situation.

There are numerous configurations that can result from combining various characteristics of parent firms. For instance, two firms can join R & D efforts in order to achieve a more critical size together. Or, firms can co-ordinate distribution systems, develop joint sales force activities, or combine product lines. Combinations can be upstream or downstream. The bottom line, however, must be that each parent's strategic intent is satisfied, and that the alliance is producing benefits to each parent.

Political Considerations

Of course, relationships and alliances are not created in a vacuum. When raising a child, decisions do not affect only single individuals within the family. So, too, with strategic alliances. What looks like a sound idea to the CEO may be seen as a threat by the stockholders. Or CEOs may hesitate to pursue an alliance if they feel that their discretionary powers are being diminished. Even further down the line, employees may fear restructuring, potential loss of jobs or additional cultural stresses. These considerations all have to do with the politics of forming alliances.

Internal Stakeholders

Foremost in this stage is lining up the support of *internal* stakeholders early on.[2] These are the people within the firm who are truly in positions that can make or break the alliance. Identifying these key stakeholders can be as simple as merely going to department heads, personnel representatives or even keeping an ear to the grapevine. Winning their support is another matter. Here, organizational management know-how and an understanding of human nature in group and individual decision making is of dominant importance. By understanding internal stakeholders' behaviours and methods and having a grasp of how to handle internal coalitions, management can begin the process accurately and give the alliance a proper start in life.

External Stakeholders

External stakeholders are as equally important to consider early on as are the internal ones. Indeed, this group can put enough pressure on an organization to actually stop the alliance. Critical external stakeholders can be owners, board members, banks, unions or the government. Some relevant questions to be addressed to this group are:

☆ What will be the effect on one's reputation and the response of the stock market from this alliance?

☆ Are relevant ownership groups convinced that the venture will be desirable from their stockholder viewpoint?

☆ How will customers, suppliers, existing alliance partners, financiers and competitors react?

Obviously, a great deal of energy must be expended to insure that major stakeholders (internally and externally) accept and promote the idea of a particular co-operative strategy. The task is often easier, however, if previous positive experiences, old contacts and good reputations exist. But the main purpose of a firm's efforts at this stage is to ensure that key individuals and groups see that the alliance makes good sense. If these stakeholders, at least tacitly, bless the venture at an early stage the chances for smooth implementation increase. Conversely, if there is active resistance to the project at this early stage, it is probably wise to call off the alliance idea and avoid the waste of a great deal of time and energy.

A good example of a strategic alliance where both parties very early established such a broad stakeholder blessing is the FiatGeotech-Hitachi Construction Machinery joint venture in hydraulic excavators. This alliance represents a joining of two major international firms, Fiat S.p.A. of Italy and Hitachi Construction Machinery of Japan, in a business with heavy competition.[3] The success of the venture is very definitely tied to the fact that the alliance idea was bought into at a very early stage by the top management of both firms. In fact, a major external stakeholder, Sumitomo Corporation, acted as an early catalyst in helping the parties to see the major aspects of the strategic alliance idea in a positive light.

More Politics

As in the initial phase, the intensive phase has its own set of political considerations that must be dealt with. Has it been made sufficiently clear *who* is to do *what* and by *when*? At this point we need to ensure that even broader internal stakeholders have 'bought into' and are committed to, and even enthusiastic about, the alliance.

Managers and other people, like researchers in the various operational functions, who might be particularly active in the strategic alliance are the key people to consider at this stage. Questions to ask are:

☆ Has the venture idea been sufficiently explained and clearly motivated throughout the organization?

☆ Has it been presented with sufficient detail to ensure that everyone sees the tasks ahead and can focus on them as opportunities?

☆ Has it been plausibly documented how combinations of activities are to be executed so that job security issues are addressed, and so that the strategic alliance will not be seen as a threat?

☆ Are relevant specialists motivated to carry out their specific tasks in a co-operative mode?

☆ Do the operational staffs have sufficient complementary styles to simplify their working contacts between the partner organizations?

In order for the entire organization to be prepared to move quickly on certain tasks during the venture's implementation, everyone must be 'sold' on the concept relatively early on. This can diminish the possibility of rejection later when power and territory builders can do their most damage if they feel that they have been left out.

An interesting aside is that in a study conducted recently on U.S.–Japanese alliances, it was found that the Japanese partners often were more forthright and effective when informing and bringing along members of their own organizations at an early stage in the strategic alliance formation process.[4] Perhaps this can be attributed to the much-discussed Japanese consensus process of 'nemawashi', which literally means watering the roots.

Of course, confidentiality considerations about a business deal may create problems if too many people are told too early. In certain cases it simply may not be possible to disseminate the venture plans to a broad range of people before they are already a fait accompli. The 1987 mega-alliance between the Swedish firm ASEA and the Swiss firm Brown Boveri, resulting in ABB, is a typical example of where it was not possible to inform too many people. Only a handful of the top executives initiated and implemented the entire deal due to a fear of insider trading in the two firms' stocks.

Undoubtedly, this secrecy created post-organizational integration challenges that might, to some extent, have been eased in the face of a more gradual and broader dissemination of information to the two organizations. It is our experience, however, that early and gradual information dissemination is done more readily in those strategic alliance negotiations where stock market disclosure constraints are of little direct concern.

The Business Plan

It is of the utmost importance that both parties identify and agree on how to co-ordinate and adapt their activities that are particularly critical to the alliance. This should be translated into a specific business plan that outlines how the alliance can become competitive. For instance, if a strategic alliance is meant to support joint R & D development, the two top management teams must ensure that operational integration takes place within the *two* R & D functions. This must be manifested in the joint plan. Scale, scope and market power synergies do not take place automatically, they require explicit endorsement and guidelines. We might inject here a seemingly obvious fact that the business plan must make sense to both parties. Leaving one partner with a partial understanding of events could lead to insular behaviour that will be detrimental to the alliance.

Some key questions that can be answered by paying attention to detail when developing the business plan are:

☆ What are each partner's relevant and available resources over the short- and long-term?

☆ What are the partners' attitudes toward long-term co-operation?

☆ How can this co-operation evolve harmoniously over time without conflicting with other strategic concerns of either partner?

Realistically assessing these issues can usually result in facilitating the implementation of the alliance.

Nippon Steel exemplifies a firm that emphasized the analytical considerations before it entered into the seemingly rather odd match with IBM. Due to the steel industry decline in the early 1980s, the firm made a strategic decision to diversify into several new business areas, one of which was the up and coming information systems industry. This bold decision resulted in the formation of numerous alliances, all announced in late 1988, one of which was NS & I, a relatively small venture with IBM. Nippon Steel contacted IBM directly with an invitation to form this strategic alliance, but during the year prior to the invitation, Nippon Steel had conducted very thorough assessments regarding strategic match and operations. As of this date, the implementation of this joint venture seems to be going well.

The Team

Let us get back to our considerations of the support needed at this stage and the question of *who* is doing these jobs. This can be the most important area of the alliance negotiations. A firm contemplating a strategic alliance must carefully consider the human resource aspects when putting together a team of people who are assigned to the formation tasks. The team must reflect the particular strategic intent that the alliance is meant to meet, or what a firm wants to get out of the alliance. It has been shown that six different categories of principal actors typically are involved in the formation team: The venture champions, the decision makers, the deal killers, the technocrats, the liaisons and the implementers.[5] While pretty much self explanatory, the categories are important to understand because these people can exert a strong influence on the success of the alliance.

To some extent this was seen in a study of Scandinavian strategic alliances. If the purpose of the alliance was to expand geographical operations, the management team included a balance of people representing a mixture of entrepreneurial, analytical and political competencies, focused on understanding the business plan behind the venture. On the other hand, if the purpose was to link up with a 'winning partner' the management team reflected more unilaterally entrepreneurial and political competencies.[6]

One of the main things to remember in the formation phase is that the management of the people and their competencies in multicultural and multinational settings will have a large impact on the overall long-term operations and effectiveness of the alliance and the parent firms. The success of alliances is shaped by people, choosing individuals for key positions is a vital step in alliance planning. It is clear that the human resource is a strategic resource that should be managed in an explicit, proactive manner. People represent critical competencies which need to be identified and cultivated.[7] The management functions regarding the strategic human resource must be co-ordinated and a common communication system established in order for the alliance to be successful. This involves assigning and motivating people so that the value creation within the strategic alliance is insured, as well as managing people in order to sustain and enhance their own competencies. While, as Ohmae points out, there is not much literature available on intercompany relationships,[8] there are many, many sources available for understanding the management of people in strategic alliances.

Our best advice in dealing with people, cross-company-wise, and a general good tip for the alliance, is to remain flexible. This is especially true for firms wishing to access the now open, unstable, Eastern European markets.[9] While there is a need for strong commitment, there is an obvious danger of becoming locked into networks that can become irrelevant over night as a result of political changes. Monitoring the environment while in the formation process is a major challenge to the prospective alliance as it attempts to put together a plan that will be as relevant in the end as it was in the beginning.

Be Fair

Some additional advice that should be followed during these negotiation phases includes insuring that equal attention is paid to the various issues. Heavy emphasis on analytical considerations without a consideration of the political issues can lead to unrealistic conclusions. An example where the political considerations were emphasized and the more detailed work neglected is the 1973 strategic alliance between Joseph Seagrams & Sons and Kirin Brewery Co. for the manufacture and distribution of spirits in Japan. This alliance was the result of, on the one hand, Seagrams' wish to enter the promising Japanese market and, on the other hand, Kirin's wish to link up with a well-known and reputable foreign partner with complementary products. Both partners had their relevant stakeholders' blessings for the alliance and made thorough, broad assessments of the strategic match. However, they appeared to have put relatively less emphasis on a detailed analysis of the market, particularly the distribution system required, during the formation phase. Difficulties subsequently occurred, including less than expected sales. One reason was that the alliance's main products, spirits, turned out to be very difficult to market through Kirin's existing distribution network for beer. Over the last few years, however, sales have improved significantly after a separate distribution plan was developed and today the venture generates a substantial profit, with new products being added to the assortment.

The Best Laid Plans...

We have offered our prescription for creating a strategic alliance. Of course, while we recommend that by following this outline the outcome of an alliance stands a greater chance of succeeding, it certainly does not guarantee success. There are numerous obstacles that can be thrown into the way of the alliance at any time during the formation process.

It is possible to identify 10 major challenges or obstacles that can play a key role in the success or failure of a strategic alliance (see Figure 4).

- Autonomy
- Forward Momentum
- Focus on the External Environment
- Politicking
- Change and Innovation
- Learning
- People
- 'Black Box'
- Culture
- Cooperation

Figure 4. Ten challenges to strategic alliances

The following is a brief discussion of each of these challenges.

Giving up autonomy over strategic resources and/or core competencies can be one of the hardest things for a partner to contemplate. Partners must share these resources with their new partner and are no longer as free to make decisions on how to use what was once exclusively their own.

Often it is difficult to actually get the alliance going. Individuals in the parent firms must *move* to get things done! It is crucial that the formation team is able to transfer their energy and enthusiasm into becoming an implementation team.

Management often tends to view the strategic alliance as being a set of internal co-operation problems. While they spend their time discussing various parts of the network and how the alliance is going to work, they lose their concentration on the customer and competitors move ahead. Keeping an eye on the external environment therefore is of utmost importance.

A primary consideration for the success of a strategic alliance, as stated previously, is insuring that the external and internal stakeholders see and sponsor the idea of the alliance. Failure to consider these groups and their political importance can mean disastrous results for an alliance.

Being open to new challenges, embracing changes and modifying operations are necessary for an alliance to grow and evolve. The inability of management to behave in this manner can hinder a venture's ability to maintain strong performance over time. A strategic alliance never, or seldom, represents a stable entity in itself, it is virtually always in transition.

When partners are unwilling to learn from each other they can risk the success of the alliance. They must develop and increase their willingness to learn in order to make sure that the overall competence of the alliance is consistent and that there is value created from the venture.

Firms need to be cautious in seeing that they do not become dependent on a single individual or groups of individuals who might be the driving force behind the success of a product, idea or strategic alliance. This includes being aware of managers who become overly fond of their role to the point that they unconsciously reject the participation and involvement of other members of the organization. It is the responsibility of senior management at the partner firms to see that no one person monopolizes any part of the strategic alliance.

When entering into a strategic alliance, partner firms must give up something. This can be technologies, markets, etc. Because the possibility of failure exists, most management analysts will recommend that firms create what is referred to as a 'black box'. This black box contains tangibles and intangibles that keep a firm in a stronger bargaining position or insure that a firm will not be totally stranded and out of business should the alliance not work.

Cross-cultural differences play a vital role in the formation and management of strategic alliances, and they should not be allowed to get in the way of the purpose of the strategic alliance. While one should always be sensitive to the differences in cultures, they should be seen as supporting the intent of the alliance and not hindering it.

Strategic alliances *must* be seen as co-operative efforts. If an alliance cannot be seen in this light, then the venture is doomed. Questions that arise here might be:

☆ Are you and your partner seriously motivated to co-operate?

☆ Can you and your partner afford to co-operate?

☆ Do you and your partner trust each other?

☆ Have you taken pre-alliance steps to ensure shared value between you and your partner's policies?

The key words here are trust and commitment, and while not sufficient conditions for long-term co-operation, they are certainly necessary conditions.

Conclusion

The formation process does not end here. The partly rational, partly political approaches discussed and recommended in this article must be seen as ongoing processes. The formation process model in Figure 3. in many senses, illustrates and synthesizes an 'ideal' internal management approach to an alliance. Perhaps the true dynamic approach is the one where these considerations are only the first phase of an ongoing reinvestigation of the political and analytical fundaments of a co-operative approach as it evolves.

Mixed up in this whole process is the concept of learning. The more alliances a firm executes the better it becomes at forming and implementing them. Some of the management teams in parent firms of successful alliances emphasize ongoing assessments of stakeholder blessing, strategic match, internal support, and the business concept as such. A good example of this is the joint venture between Mölnlycke Consumer Products of Sweden and Scott Paper (UK) Ltd. Scott Paper International's change of global focus, from paper tissue toward personal health care, coupled with the Swedish firm's acquisition of the French firm Peaudouce, resulted in changes in stakeholders' attitudes, internal support in both firms and the business rationale.

It takes more than luck to have a successful alliance. We can recommend the good advice of the heads of Ford and Mazda when they were asked to list their success criteria:[10]

(1) Ensure that top management is involved.
(2) Meet often and informally.
(3) Use a third party advisor.
(4) Keep your independence.
(5) Do not permit any project where one of the parties is scarified.
(6) Use a steering committee that continuously supervises the alliance.
(7) Assume that there are cultural differences.

Even the best planned strategic alliance can never succeed if the strategy it pursues turns out to be wrong. The basic match between partners, the attention paid to creating the alliance team, selling the alliance to all important parties, internally and externally, and developing a sound business plan are all critical factors in an alliance's ongoing success.

This article is based on the book *Strategic Alliances: Formation, Implementation and Evolution*, by Peter Lorange and Johan Roos, Basil Blackwell, Oxford (1992).
The research referred to includes: a 1989 survey of 67 Swedish and Norwegian firms' alliance strategies, and a 1989 survey of 7 Japanese and 10 US firms' alliance formation processes.

References

(1) G. Jacobson and J. Hillkirk, *Xerox, American Samurai*, Macmillan Publishing Co., New York (1986).

(2) L-G. MacMillan and P. E. Jones, *Strategy Formulation: Political, Power and Politics (2nd edn)*, West Publishing, St. Paul, MN (1987).

(3) For a further discussion of this example see Lorange and Roos, Basil Blackwell (1992).

(4) P. Lorange and J. Roos, Formation of US-Japanese Strategic Alliances: Differences in Management Approaches, Presented at the International Symposium on Pacific Asian Business, Honolulu, Hawaii (January 1990).

(5) J. M. Geringer and C. A. Frayne, Joint Venture Partner Selection: Key Actors in the Process, prepared for the Conference on Strategic Processes: Learning, Adaptation and Innovation, Oslo, Norway (19–22 June 1991).

(6) P. Lorange and J. Roos, Formation of Cooperative Ventures: Competence Mix of the Management Teams, *Management International Review*, 30, 69–86 (1990).

(7) G. Hamel and C. K. Prahalad, Strategic Intent, *Harvard Business Review*, 67 (3), 63–67 (1989).

(8) K. Ohmae, The Global Logic of Strategic Alliances, *Harvard Business Review*, 67 (2), 143–154 (1989).

(9) J. Roos, E. Veie and L. S. Welch, A Case Study of Equipment Purchasing in Czechoslovakia, *Industrial Marketing Management*, Spring (1992).

(10) *Business Week*, 2 February, p. 40 (1992).

Successful innovation and implementation of new processes

Chris Voss

When we talk of innovation we tend to think of new products, but successful innovation of processes can also lead to a company gaining significant competitive advantage. A good example is to be found in the recent book, The Machine that Changed the World, by Womak et al (1990). The machine in question is process technology and the book's argument is that process innovations which they aggregate as 'lean production' are responsible for the level of performance of the Japanese car industry. On the other hand many expensive investments in the latest Flexible Manufacturing Systems have worked, but have sometimes been less flexible than the processes that they replaced! Why is it that one firm can adopt a new production process and gain real benefits, and another can adopt the same new process; invest heavily in equipment and installation, yet not be able to achieve any benefit? This important question has been addressed in a series of recent research programmes undertaken at London Business School. This article examines some of what we and others have learnt about the successful and unsuccessful use of new process technologies. In addition it will argue that management of innovation of processes must cover the whole life cycle of its innovation and adoption, and in particular should include implementation.

Innovation and Implementation

The assumption of much of the innovation and engineering literature is that once successfully developed, a new process innovation will work in all subsequent uses. Research on success and failure has been confined to the success and failure of products, focusing on the development and marketing of the innovation. The diffusion literature also assumes that the once a product works it will work in all subsequent uses. In other words, implementation by each user is always successful. These assumptions break down when one considers complex innovations, in particular new processes. However, frequently a *new process* innovation can succeed in one attempt at adoption and fail in another. Once a new process technology has been developed with its first successful use, success or failure in subsequent in applications can be considered as *implementation* success or failure.

Unlike new product innovation, many of the activities and conditions that influence implementation success take place in the *adopting* organisation rather than the innovating organisation. Indeed the study of implementation might be called more precisely the study of the way in which innovations are adopted.

How is successful implementation defined?

A necessary precursor to discussion of implementation is the definition of what constitutes success (or failure). Typically, success is seen in technical terms; it works, it meets specification, productivity has been improved etc. Even when there are business objectives, rarely is success measured in terms of meeting these objectives. Organisations (and researchers) usually believe that they have successfully implemented new operating technology when two conditions are met. First, when all the bugs have been ironed out and it is working technically. Second, when the operation is working reliably and there is little down time, and/or the new technology has a high utilisation rate. One can put forward the proposition that in getting the technology to work, only half the battle has been won. If we take the example of Advanced Manufacturing Technology (AMT), the prime motivation for installing AMT must be to increase the competitiveness of the organisation. The increasing importance of manufacturing-led competition is being stressed by many authors (see, e.g. Hayes at al, (1984) and Rosenbloom et al (1983)). The improvements in competitiveness promised by Advanced Manufacturing Technology come not just from increased labour and machine productivity, but increased responsiveness, quality, flexibility and reduced inventories, lead time etc.

Full success can only be considered to have been realised if the benefits being looked for are realised, and ideally realised in the market place through increased competitiveness. Technical success is a necessary but not sufficient condition for realising the full benefits of advanced manufacturing technology. We can propose two levels of success in implementation:

(1) technical success, and

(2) realisation of benefits (business success)

The process of implementation

Implementation of innovations can be defined as:
"the process that leads to the successful adoption of an innovation of new technology". A commonly held view of implementation is that it encompasses the actions from purchase and installation through to the successful use of the technology. This is a narrow view of the process of implementation. For example, it can be argued that many important determinants of implementation success are actions and conditions prior to purchase or installation, such as strategic planning, technical planning, and workforce consultation (Voss 1988b). In addition one can postulate that the antecedents, for example, the context of the firm, its skills, existing technology, managerial attitudes etc., will have a significant impact on the process of implementation. The process of implementation has its roots in the firm's background and history, and includes both pre-installation and post-installation factors.

It is possible to postulate a simple life-cycle model of the process of implementation, in terms of a sequential process consisting of three phases. This model is represented diagrammatically in figure 1. The first phase comprises those factors prior to installations that may have a positive or negative impact on the final outcome. This phase can be called pre-installation. It finishes with the evaluation and go ahead. (If there is no go ahead, then there is no implementation). The second phase is that of installation and commissioning. This can be said to be complete when the new production process is working successfully; that is when the technical and utilisation targets are being met consistently. The third phase is consolidation. In this phase further technical improvement is likely to take place as will further activities needed to move beyond technical success to business success. The dividing line between

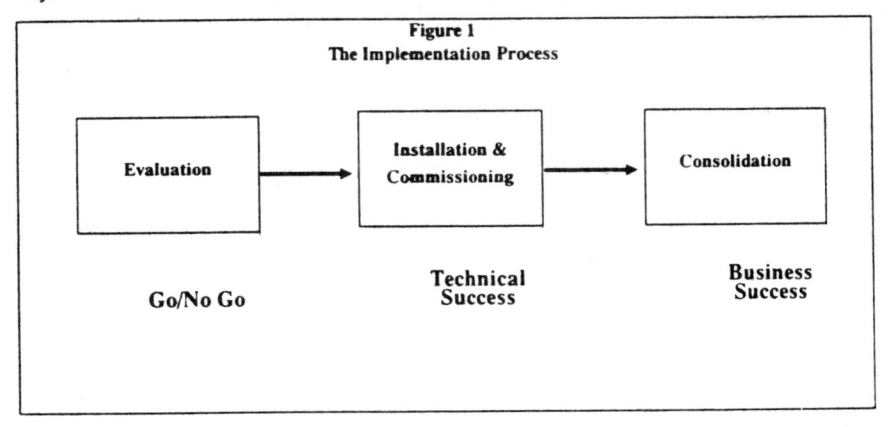

Figure 1
The Implementation Process

Evaluation → Installation & Commissioning → Consolidation

Go/No Go — Technical Success — Business Success

phases 2 and 3 is diffuse. as is the end of phase 3. It could be argued that phase 3 should not end as an effective company should be continually seeking ways of improving its production process.

Research at London Business School

Over the past few years, London Business School has been studying the use of new production technology, and in particular its implementation. We have conducted a longitudinal study over a three year period of fifteen companies implementing advanced manufacturing technologies. A case based approach was used, gathering data through interviews with a range of people in each firm. Using a structured research instrument, data was gathered on the context of the innovation; the choice of technology; the manufacturing strategy; the organisation, management, critical events and concerns during each stage of the implementation process; and finally the outcome of the implementation process. In the subsequent sections of this article, we examine each stage of the implementation process. drawing on the results of this research and on the results of others.

Success and Failure

There is considerable empirical evidence that the innovation of processes does not necessarily lead to success. In a study of a sample of 17 identical innovations of computer application software, we found that 11 reached successful use, while 6 failed to do so, (Voss (1984)). This pattern may seem obvious, though current innovation and diffusion theory implicity assumes otherwise. Of greater importance are the findings of various studies, that although having achieved technical success, many innovations of processes fail to reach business success. In a further study of success and failure, this time focusing on advanced manufacturing technology, we examined the degree to which new processes were successful against different definitions of success (Voss (1988b)). We found the pattern shown in figure 2.

Another example is a study of flexible manufacturing systems by Jaikumar (1986). He studied 35 systems in the US. and 60 in Japan. Flexible manufacturing systems are installed to deliver flexibility. He concluded that US systems "show an astonishing lack of flexibility, and in many cases perform worse than the technology that they replace". His indicators of flexibility included those shown in figure 3.

Figure 2
Patterns of Success

Measure of Success	Successful Firms (%)
Technical	
Technically successful	100
Business	
Productivity increases	86
Other benefits realised e.g. flexibility, responsiveness, design to manufacture lead-time	57
Competitiveness improved	14
	n = 14

Source: Voss (1988b)

Figure 3
Flexibility in Japan and US

	Japan	US
No of parts produced per system	93	10
No of new parts per year	22	1

Source: Jaikumar (1986).

A study by Tidd (1991) of robot assembly, comparing Japanese against UK practice, found a similar pattern to Jaikumar.

We can conclude that innovations of processes are not always successful in conventional, technical terms, and even when successful on this basis, often fail to achieve the capability and wider ranging benefits required of them: business success.

Some evidence on implementation

We will next examine some evidence of why this may occur. This will be done in the context of each of the three phases of the implementation model in figure 1.

The Pre-installation Phase

The first phase, pre-installation takes place prior to the decision to purchase. It includes many activities that are crucial to the subsequent success of the process technology.

Strategy

"robots installed in the UK were more complex and technically sophisticated than those in Japan. However, despite this seeming technical advantage, the performance of robot assembly lines was far superior in Japan"

Most writers on manufacturing strategy argue that choice of type of production process and process technology should be consistent with both the characteristics of the products to be produced, and the competitive priorities of the firm, (see for example Hill (1984), Hayes and Wheelwright (1985) and Voss (1986)). The impact of this on innovation of processes can be illustrated by the work of Tidd (1991). He studied the adoption of assembly robots in Japan and the UK. He found, in contrast to prior expectations about Japanese technology, that the robots installed in the UK were more complex and technically sophisticated than those in Japan. However, despite this seeming technical advantage, the performance of robot assembly lines was far superior in Japan than in the UK. He identified a very different pattern of managerial activities at the pre-installation phase; these are listed in figure 4. These differing strategies would seem to have had a major influence on the relative success of the UK and Japan in implementing assembly robots.

This is a remarkably similar set of conclusions to those of Jaikumar (1986) in his study of flexible manufacturing systems. He too found that the technology choice in the west was more sophisticated but less effective. US innovations of processes were highly sophisticated, but because of their complexity, were very difficult to implement effectively. In addition the pressure to start up the systems on time resulted in the systems in use not using their potential capability. In contrast, the Japanese systems were designed more simply, as a result they were more reliable. Despite their relative simplicity, they were managed more flexibly. Indeed their simplicity gave greater reliability, and enabled the maximum potential of the systems to be realised. As a result, the Japanese systems were both more flexible and achieved a higher utilisation than their US counterparts. What can we learn from this research? First, it is clear, that even within a single area of innovation of a production process, technology choice is a vital decision.

Figure 4
Assembly Robots in UK and Japan

	UK	Japan
Primary motives for development and adoption	to increase productivity and improve quality through the elimination of direct labour	to improve flexibility of production but continue to reduce costs through the elimination of waste
Technological trajectory pursued	Complex, sophisticated technology consistent with long-term goal of 'CIM', a computer systems approach	Relatively simple proven technology with continued reliance on operators, essentially a production engineering approach
Manufacturing	Reduction in diversity of production to facilitate further automation and computer integration	Flexible, but low cost production
Source of most significant developments	Specialist suppliers essentially 'technology push'	Major uses essentially 'demand pull'

Source: Tidd (1991)

Technology led approaches alone as embodied in the robot and flexible manufacturing system examples would seem to run a number of risks. Technology can be adopted that requires greater knowledge and embodied learning to implement, than many companies have. Second, that objectives based on technical vision, such as 'achieving Computer Integrated Manufacture' are insufficient to guide innovation, and indeed may misdirect as it may force loss of sight of the business objectives and the fit with the product. Third, objectives such as getting rid of direct labour may not be consistent with business needs. It is interesting to note that if this was the main objective in the UK, then simple robots rather than complex ones may have been the more appropriate response. In contrast, including business led approaches would seem to lead to more effective choice of technology and innovation.

"objectives based on technical vision, such as 'achieving Computer Integrated Manufacture' are insufficient to guide innovation, and indeed may misdirect"

Evaluation

The LBS studies found that despite common technology across cases, applicability and ease of use of new processes was very context dependent, with these dependencies not being known to the firms at the time of evaluation. Evaluation was being undertaken in a complex technical environment, both with much choice and with a rapidly changing technical capability, which resulted in many of the initial choices becoming obsolete before the end of the study. Many of the companies had repeated this phase of the implementation process, one was on its third evaluation process; and four had discarded their current system and adopted a different one. In addition, the research looked at the organisation for evaluation. It yielded a very rich set of data about how companies evaluated new technology and the issues faced at this stage. Most companies adopted some form of task force. Their patterns of actions were similar, but the re-evaluators tended to pay more attention to links with other business systems. Examination of the re-evaluators showed strong organisational learning.

In most cases, even at this early stage, there was an 'implementation champion' who could be credited with pushing the implementation through. The early adopters tended to evaluate on a narrow basis such as drawing office productivity. However later adopters used a much wider, more business driven set of criteria.

One of the key things to emerge through the longitudinal nature of this study is the existence of both strong industry and firm dynamics at the evaluation stage of the implementation process, reflecting technological development and diffusion of information and organisational learning.

> "A fundamental problem is the complexity and systemic nature of many innovations of processes. This makes it difficult to evaluate an individual investment in isolation."

There has been much written on the way in which current financial evaluation systems hinder innovation of processes and the adoption of new process technologies. However the evidence for this is thin. That discounted cash flow techniques impede the adoption of new technologies, is as much a function of high cost of money leading to high discount rates, as the inability of the technique to take in all factors. In addition, there is no evidence to suggest that the Japanese investments do not have very high expectations of financial payback, and indeed do achieve this. Conversations with Japanese managers indicate that they are expecting one to two year paybacks. Our problem may be that we cannot get as high a payback from the same investment.

A more fundamental problem is the complexity and systemic nature of many innovations of processes. This makes it difficult to evaluate an individual investment in isolation. For example Lindberg (1990) in studying manufacturing innovations in Sweden, concluded that 'in order to fully integrate the subsystems in manufacturing, a continuous and parallel development must take place'. To effectively deal with this problem in the evaluation stage, the full set of innovations and investments in a manufacturing system must be evaluated together, and investment appraisal must focus on alternative manufacturing systems.

The LBS implementation studies found that to manage the installation most companies tended to rely on the members of the task force who had done the initial groundwork. The project management styles were characterised by either participative or technocratic approaches. A number of factors influenced the way and the ease with which this phase was managed. These included information load, resource scarcity, the size of the system and the speed of the implementation. The evidence from the cases was that the participative approach only emerged when the information load was high, and in addition size and speed were large.

The Installation and Commissioning Phase

There are a wide range of factors associated with successful installation and commissioning.

Training

For example, Tidd (1991) found that the organisational context in UK companies was characterised by poorly trained, low skilled operators; little communication between design manufacturing and sales functions; distant relationships with suppliers and customers. On the other hand, the Japanese context was: highly skilled operators; good communication between design, manufacturing and sales; and close relationships between suppliers and customers.

Organisation

The use of cross functional teams has been seen as a particular requirement for successful installation (and implementation in general). Many innovations involve a number of different technologies, have to be implemented in an existing production environment and draw upon the expertise of various equipment suppliers.

Relationships with Suppliers

In studying implementation of CAD/CAM in UK companies we found many examples of poorly managed relationships with technology suppliers (Russell (1991)). There were widely contrasting patterns of relations with system vendors. One particular vendor was singled out for many of the major concerns. Users reporting poor relationships also reported poor technical performance from suppliers. The causal relationship between these two factors seems complex and difficult to unravel. There was found to be turbulence amongst systems suppliers making it additionally difficult for them to build consistent relationships. Finally, suppliers of integrated systems tended to be from the design and computer end of the market. As result, they were felt by users to have insufficient knowledge of manufacturing and to emphasise a sequential implementation strategy starting with CAD, whereas many users already had CAM and wanted implementation strategies that started with CAM and were more concurrent.

Industrial Relations

On the industrial relations side, while there have been frequent assertions that trade unions, or at least their members, are in some sense resistant to change, there was little evidence that this was the case in our sample companies. Not that there were no issues. There were problems of salary structure, double shift working, additional pay for using the system, and job reductions. These in some cases resulted in delays of up to two years.

The Consolidation Phase

The consolidation phase encompasses all activities that take place after the new process is installed and operating to specification. In characterising the implementation strategies of Japanese companies in comparison with US installers of Flexible Manufacturing Systems, Jaikumar (1986) found many of the major differences took place post-installation. In US companies, once the system was up and running, the installation team was disbanded and left to work on other projects. In Japanese companies, they remained in place and *after* installation. Even after installation, they continually made changes and as a result learning was maximised. This learning was translated into mastery of processes and productivity enhancement. It is the author's contention, that the post-installation phase is too often neglected, yet it is a vital part of the innovation and implementation process. This has been recognised by a number of authors, such as Ettlie (1984) who identified 'administrative innovations' required for successful implementation of processes, and Rogers, who used (inappropriately), the term re-invention for the same phenomenon. We can identify a number of areas in the consolidation phase which contribute to success or failure in the use of technology.

"the post-installation phase is too often neglected, yet it is a vital part of the innovation and implementation process."

Organisation

In a study of implementation of processes, Voss (1988b) observed that those companies who had made some form of matching organisational change had achieved some element of business success, and those who had not done so had not moved beyond technical success.

The need to adapt organisations can be illustrated well by the case of innovations of integrated processes in engineering and manufacturing.

The neglect of organisational issues in the implementation process has been identified as one of the reason for underachievement of the anticipated benefits from such technologies. This finding is, perhaps not surprising, given that managers are often faced with short deadlines in which to prove satisfactorily the investment in technologies. However, unlike many technologies that are isolated in their operation (what Kaplinsky (1984) terms intra-activity technologies), the new integrated technologies are having a more widespread area of effect on the organisation and therefore, consideration is required of parallel changes management of the technology, if benefits are to be realised. Figure 5 reflects this need; typically, technologies are implemented with a disproportional emphasis placed on technical integration (along line A-T); however, attention should now be directed towards organisation issues (a shift to the right).

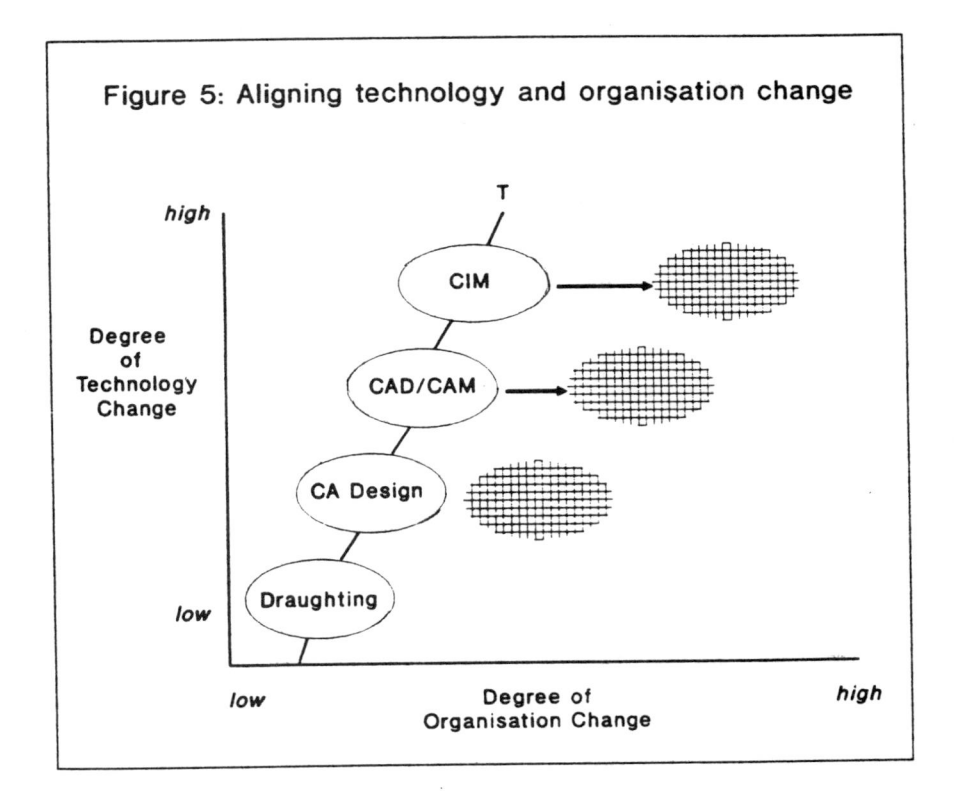

Figure 5: Aligning technology and organisation change

> "There are a wide range of options for organising so as to facilitate integration."

There are a wide range of options for organising so as to facilitate integration. The most important options can be divided into two groups. The first is composed of those options that provide integration across a whole range of functions and are involved in taking new projects from market concept, through design, manufacturing and finally to the customer. The second group is composed of those that provide integration between individual functions.

These mechanisms are outlined in figure 6. The order in each group is in approximate degree of difficulty. The earlier ones require little fundamental changes and can usually be implemented easily; the later ones require more changes and consequently, can provide greater integration, but can be more difficult to implement.

Figure 6
Ranked order of integration mechanisms used by companies to support computer integrated manufacture

Integration across the whole organisation	Integration between functions
Direct contact	-
-	Physical proximity
-	Decisions rules in software
-	Electronic mail
-	Liaison role
-	Secondment
-	Task force
Project team	-
-	Role combination
-	Integrator function
-	Combined department
Matrix organisation	-

Note: Mechanisms are ranked in order of increasing difficulty. The ranking should not be seen to imply increasing integration effectiveness.

Managerial Control

Kaplan (1983) has argued strongly that management control systems no longer recognise the priorities and needs of manufacturing systems. This is particularly true as we move from innovations whose sole objectives are cost reduction and maximisation of output. Innovations in processes has lead to the development of manufacturing systems whose objectives include flexibility, cycle time reduction and quality. These considerations are valid in the context of innovation of processes.

In the LBS study the performance of CAD/CAM systems tended to be bound up in the departments that used it. Usually these were cost centres. This led to a tension between manufacturing and engineering, and extra effort was needed in engineering to gain benefits in manufacturing, but engineering would not be rewarded on these. This could be a barrier to achievement of business benefits across the company. The environment of the company was found to play an important role in this phase with activities such as collaborative ventures and takeovers changing policies and objectives during implementation. In addition increasing pressures for reduced product lead times and smaller batch sizes also changed the requirements for the systems during their implementation.

In Jaikumar's (1984) research on Flexible Manufacturing System, he identified a mismatch between the objectives of the technology and the managerial control systems as a major reason behind the problems with gaining effective innovation. For example, in one case, studied separately by both Jaikumar and Voss (1986), a system installed to maximise medium term product change flexibility, had made no product changes whatsoever, and was also being managed to minimise short term flexibility. On close examination, this was found to be due to managerial control systems emphasising up-time and output. The only way up-time could be maximised was to minimise the flexibility of the flexible manufacturing system. Voss (1988b) identified a similar case in CAD/CAM, where a system has been installed to reduce design to delivery leadtimes. The managerial control system emphasised return on investment. He found:

"emphasising getting maximum throughput and minimising costs led to failure to realise some of CAD's major advantages."

> "To maximise return on investment, the CAD system was run on two shifts with the third being used for overnight processing of data and drawings. To achieve high utilisation..., large amounts of work were channelled through the CAD system. The results were two fold. First, because of the volume of work, a significant backlog of work developed, at one point there was a four month leadtime. Second there was little short term flexibility. As a result, emphasising getting maximum throughput and minimising costs led to failure to realise some of CAD's major advantages."

Conclusions, towards successful processes

This article has set out to develop a framework for looking at innovation and implementation of processes. It has illustrated this with data from a wide variety of sources which are summarised in figure 7. Any such

Figure 7
Factors Influencing Success and Failure in Implementing Process Technology

Implementation Phase	Pre-Installation	Installation and Commissioning	Consolidation
Success Measure		Technical	Business
Factors influencing success and failure of process implementation	Identifying and forecasting capabilities of the technology	Broadly based project teams	Keeping teams in place after commissioning
	Strategy - Business *and* technical objectives for process technology	Effective support from the supplier	Mutual adaptation of organisation and technology
	Broadly based evaluation team and implementation champion	Implementation champion	Appropriate managerial control
		Managing industrial relations	
	Matching complexity of technology to the firm's ability to handle it	Training and availability of skills	
	Long-term evaluation of the full system, not short-term evaluation of parts of it		

framework has limited use if it cannot be used to help companies manage new process technology. Part of the research described above is being adapted for use by practitioners through a workbook on managing organisation integration. (Twigg and Voss (1991)). In reviewing the above a number of guidelines and practical steps emerge. As above, these are listed in the sequence of the three stage model used earlier.

Pre-installation

Important considerations at the installation phase include:
- Innovation of processes should not just be technically led, but to be most effective should support both the organisation's strategic direction and the characteristics of the products to be produced.

- The complexity, uncertainty etc. of the technology should match the knowledge and capability of the firm to handle it, as well as the business needs.
- evaluation should be based on the full system to be developed, not parts of it.

Installation and commissioning

Installation requirements include:
- effective interaction with suppliers.
- the use of appropriately composed cross-functional teams.
- appropriate labour skills and availability.

Consolidation

Innovation and implementation does not stop at installation. Effective management of the post-installation consolidation phase can be crucial in obtaining success.
- Technical and user environment adaptations and modifications should be actively sought out.
- The implementation team should stay with the innovation until the main adaptations and learning have taken place.
- Appropriate organisation change should be actively sought out. Change should reflect the impact of the innovation on roles, communications flows and tasks.
- Performance measurements for those implementing and managing processes should match the objectives of the innovation.

"the ability to implement that process well; to get the best out of it, to continually learn and improve and above all to realise the full business benefits will gain competitive advantage for a company."

The successful innovation of new processes is critical for continued success of companies. Even when process technology is available off the shelf, the ability to implement that process well; to get the best out of it, to continually learn and improve and above all to realise the full business benefits will gain competitive advantage for a company. Managing the innovation and implementation of new processes is increasingly a key task for companies.

Chris Voss is BT Professor of Total Quality Management at London Business School. The support of the SERC and the ESRC/SERC joint committee who funded the LBS research quoted in this article are aknowledged.

References

R Hayes and S C Wheelwright, *Restoring Our Competitive Edge, Competing through Manufacturing* ,Wiley, 1984

T Hill, *'Manufacturing Strategy'*, London Macmillan, 1985

R Jaikumar, *Flexible Manufacturing Systems: a Managerial Perspective*, Working Paper, Harvard Business School, January 1984

R Jaikumar, Postindustrial Manufacturing, *'Harvard Business Review'*, Nov-Dec 1986, 69-76

R S Kaplan, Measuring Manufacturing Performance: A New Challenge for Accounting Research, *The Accounting Review* ,LVII (4). 1983

R Kaplinsky, *Automation*, Harlow, Longman, 1984

S R Rosenbloom and H Vossaghi, *Factory Automation in the US*, Research Report Series, Manufacturing Roundtable, Boston University School of Management, March 1983

V Russell, unpublished research documents, London Business School, 1991

J Tidd, *'Flexible Manufacturing Technologies and International Competitiveness'*; London, Pinter, 1991

C A Voss, Multiple Independent Invention and the Process of Technological Innovations, *Technovation 2* 1984 169-184

C A Voss, 'Implementing Manufacturing Technology, a manufacturing Strategy Approach' *International Journal for Operations and Production Management*, 1986, 6,4,16-26

C A Voss, 'Implementing, a key issue in Manufacturing technology, the need for a field of study', *Research Policy*, 17, 1988a, 53-63

C A Voss, Success and Failure in Advanced Manufacturing Technology, *International Journal of Technology Management*, vol 3 no 3, 1988b, 285-297

J P Womak, D Jones, D Roos, *The Machine That Changed the World*, Macmillan, 1990

[20]

Making Strategy Work:
The TEAM Approach

*Steven J. Heyer,
Daniel H. Marcus,
and Reginald Van Lee*

Portfolio strategies. Market-driven strategies. Technology-inspired strategies. The past decades have seen no lack of slogans coined to catch the strategic imagination of top management. And they're not just slogans. To be fair, some of these concepts represent significant advances in strategic thinking.

Despite these advances, we find more and more CEOs are increasingly frustrated with the strategies they have adopted. Even the most inspired plans, they have found, contain an incipient flaw: They have to be implemented effectively or they won't work.

When organizations don't achieve desired performance, it's rarely because people don't work hard enough or are unwilling to change. Rather, it often reflects a growing gap between business strategies and their implementation infrastructures: While the former have gained in complexity, the latter have grown relatively immature. The "Age of Strategic Management" has tantalized us with visions of what can be done, but has not empowered those who must implement the visions with a clear understanding of how to do it.

Corporate visionaries, armed only with rigorous analyses, can do little to transform entire organizations. And traditional reflex approaches to implementation, which interpret the strategy in terms meant for organization structure and functions, fall far short of the mark.

To realize a new strategy, management needs a more innovative and integrated "tool kit," with techniques to link individual accomplishment and collective goals.

In concert with clients determined to overcome institutional inertia, we have developed and refined new management techniques for the implementation of strategy. Taken together, they form what we call the TEAM approach.

We should note at the outset that the TEAM approach is not one that CEOs can simply delegate to their staffs. Given the revolutionary changes it entails—in the way a company, as a business, looks at itself, in the way employees come to view their roles, in the creation and communication of new measurement and reward systems, and in the ways a company monitors its own results —only CEOs can provide the necessary leadership.

TEAM comprises four steps: *translating* a strategy into concrete objectives for specific transaction groups (a term we'll explain shortly), *enlisting* the commitment of all the people on whom the execution of that strategy depends, *activating* the behavioral changes that will allow implementation to happen, and *monitoring* and reinforcing that behavior until it is embedded culturally within the organization. To make strategies happen, managers must create and empower TEAM effectiveness (Exhibit 1).

Exhibit 1
The CEO Toolkit

Objective	Tool	Output
Translate	• Business strategy and direction • Demystification of underlying economics • Organization blueprint/transaction flow	• What is important? • Why is it important? • What is controllable?
Enlist	• TEAM creation and definition • Key performance indices and objectives	• How do I fit in? • Who owns the problem? • Who is my support team?
Activate	• Measurement system • Reward system • Decision support system	• Are pay and performance linked? • Is personal optimization in synch with corporate optimization?
Monitor/ reinforce	• TEAM enfranchisement • TEAM meetings • Communication program • Education and training	• Are organization actions and culture consistent with team concept? • How will team performance be recognized?

Source: Booz • Allen & Hamilton

Translating a Strategy

Translating a strategy into the right goals is the cornerstone of TEAM effectiveness and strategy implementation. To put that cornerstone in place, management must learn to describe its own objectives in terms that pertain to the value-added transaction stages of the business, rather than to organization functions or units.

When we work with clients on this step, we begin by creating a value-added model, which segments a business into the discrete economic activities that reflect how the business really works and capture the key elements of long-term profitability. These value-added stages might progress, for example, from product planning and development through manufacturing (sourcing through quality control), marketing, selling, distribution, and finally to service. These stages might then be further segmented by product, market, or geography. When the model is complete, we are ready to translate strategy into the appropriate goals.

Service businesses, with their highly interdependent organizational groups, provide a prime example of the need to translate strategies by value-added parameters rather than traditional organization lines. Consider the case of a technology-intensive service provider that faced escalating costs and significant customer complaints on service quality.

Despite a clear commitment from the CEO and division presidents to a strategy that emphasized both reductions in cost and improvements in service, the company could not seem to turn itself around.

In our work with this company we found several discrepancies between the value-added interpretation of the strategy and the traditional interpretation. One problem emerged in the way the marketing and customer-service departments interacted with customers. Together, these departments were responsible for a key step—customer acquisition—in the company's value-added chain. Each department, however, worked towards its goal in isolation: Success for the marketing group meant significant revenue growth, while success for the customer-service group meant cost effectiveness and efficiency.

As a result, while marketing incurred heavy costs in identifying market needs and positioning the company for revenue growth, customer service focused on acquiring the most customers in the shortest time. Customers, meanwhile, felt pressured to purchase by the marketing department only to be rushed through the purchasing process by customer service.

In this case, the CEO's strategy had fallen short of expectations primarily because top management had translated the company's objectives into organizational-function goals. Value-added stages were ignored; functional units worked toward conflicting objectives. An effective translation of the company's strategic direction would have recognized customer acquisition as the broader focus of both departments, and balanced the conflicting objectives.

As this case shows, a real understanding of value-added stages sees beyond organization structure. It recognizes a different blueprint of the business. It identifies shared resource requirements and highlights organizational interdependencies. In short, it asks: What's important? Who makes it happen? How does it happen?

Once management answers these questions and decodes strategies across these transaction stages, the first implementation step is complete. Exhibit 2 shows how a multinational manufacturer used a value-added model of the business to articulate integration requirements and identify real roles and responsibilities. This construct was critical to enlisting commitment that would activate behavioral change—the next step in the TEAM approach.

Enlisting Commitment

Organization structures maintain control and focus expertise; they cannot, however, fully capture the intricate processes, transactions, and interdependent activities that make a business work. For example, even the most flexible structure cannot accommodate the complex interactions and the allocation of responsibilities that occur when products and services are distributed across multiple customer bases, and distribution facilities, technologies, support systems, and even people are shared across organizational boundaries.

To get their business done, all companies inevitably rely on informal, ad hoc structures—steering committees, task forces, unofficial alliances—which the formal organization structure does not recognize. If management wants to effect change, it must first clearly define its goals and then assign accountability to appropriate portions of this broader "executional network."

To enlist the commitment of these front-line people—the true implementers of any strategy—management must establish teams that parallel the value-added chain described above, define clear accountability, and articulate their shared measures and objectives. Defining the right teams and the right measures is a crucial step for encouraging enlistment and commitment.

These teams—the "transaction groups"—are paradigmatic of critical relationships in the value-added chain; they perform real and distinct activities, unrestricted by organizational boxes. Management's recognition of these teams in no way subverts the formal reporting structure; rather, it legitimizes informal and ad hoc structures.

Exhibit 2
Cross-Geographic Integration Needs

⟶ indicates cross-integration requirements

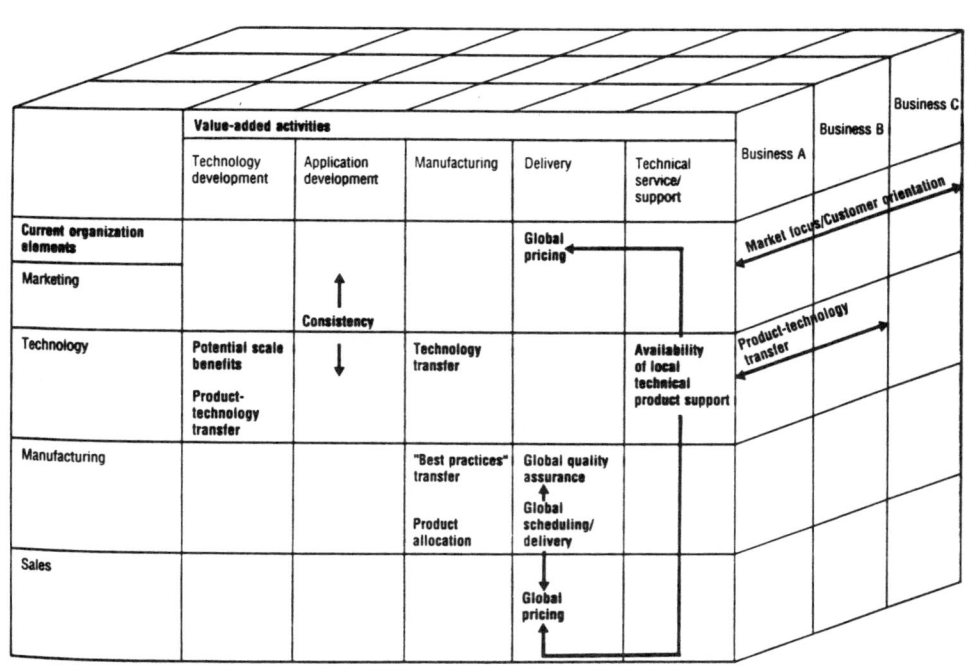

Source: Booz•Allen & Hamilton

Exhibit 3
Team Definition and Disaggregation

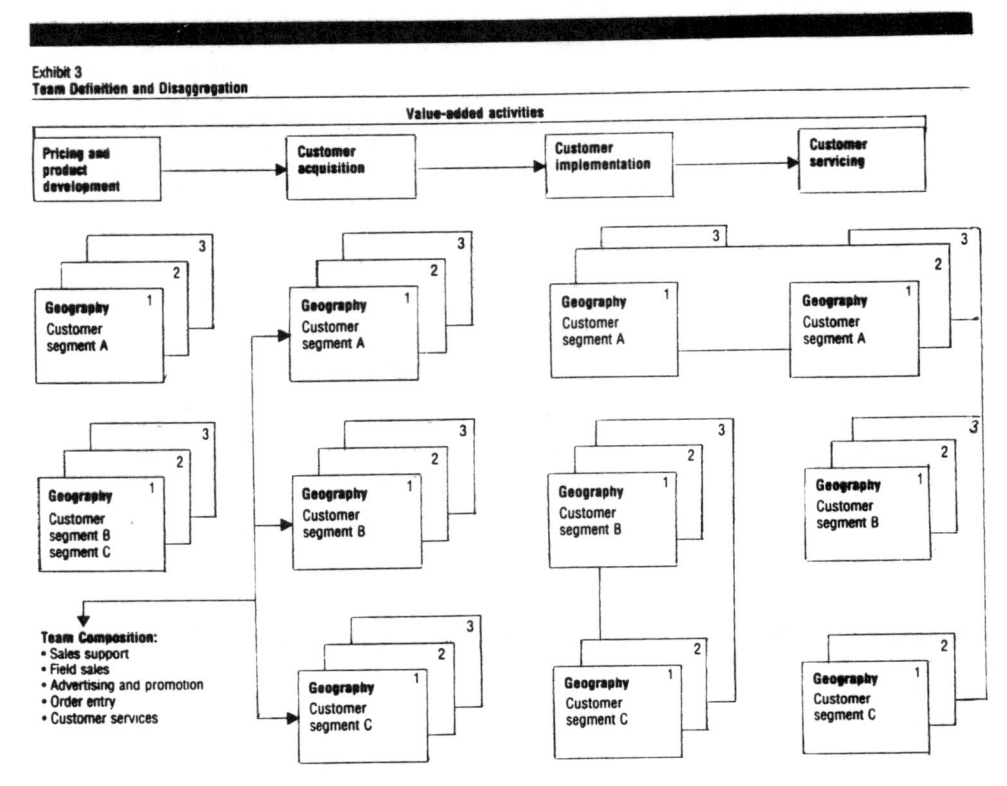

Value-added activities: Pricing and product development → Customer acquisition → Customer implementation → Customer servicing

Each stage broken down by Geography, Customer segment A, B, C (levels 1, 2, 3).

Team Composition:
- Sales support
- Field sales
- Advertising and promotion
- Order entry
- Customer services

Source: Booz·Allen & Hamilton

Understanding, defining, and assessing the real contribution of a team or individual is not a simple task. Many managers are inclined to throw up their hands and simply measure the bottom line, without asking "Whose bottom line?" or "What's important above the bottom line?" The result: personal optimization and corporate sub-optimization.

Remember the service business we mentioned whose marketing and sales people were working at cross purposes? Once the company defined its value-added stages, it was ready to create the transaction teams—the cross-function working groups that are legitimate vehicles for running the business.

To address this need, this company created "customer acquisition" teams—comprising people in sales support, field sales, advertising and promotion, order entry and customer services—for each market segment and, within most market segments, for each geographic territory (Exhibit 3). Management assigned objectives for customer satisfaction, revenue, productivity, and customer-contact duration for each team.

As soon as management created these teams, it started to reap some TEAM benefits: Interdepartment coordination and problem solving were significantly enhanced. More followed, with the implementation of other steps.

The benefits to be derived from a better understanding of teams—how they crystallize and can be deployed within a business—are not restricted to service companies or industries. Consider three more examples:

A multinational technology company needing to balance global product lines with local market requirements found that short-term, reactive local marketing decisions threatened long-term global technology positions. By defining the critical value-added dimensions and activities, and creating teams around them, the company was able to bridge the gap between marketing and technology, ensure that all voices were heard, and set priorities appropriately.

A retailer facing continual battles and lack of coordination between store managers and home-office merchandising managers was able to reinforce coordination and maximize returns on net assets by designing teams and performance objectives around major merchandising groups.

A thrift, suffering from both deteriorating volume and a narrow market image, developed teams of product specialists within individual branches, which enhanced the thrift's image as a "full service" provider. Moreover, management was able to increase cross-sell ratios dramatically by paying bonuses according to team performance—which brings us to our next point.

Exhibit 4
Balancing Measurement Systems and Business Complexity

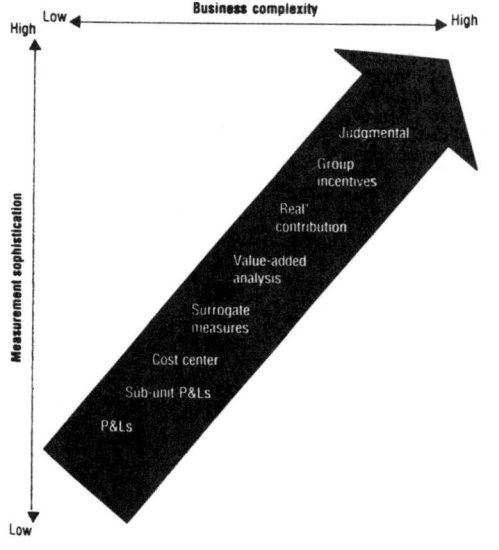

Source: Booz•Allen & Hamilton

Activating Behavioral Change

The next step in the TEAM approach is to make the new team and performance indices tangible to the individual. To activate the right behavior, management must measure performance correctly and link it explicitly to pay.

Performance-measurement systems should aid decision making at every level. Most current performance-measurement systems, however, are insensitive to the increasing complexities of strategies and organizations. They tend to either oversimplify or overmeasure a business, and not recognize the complexity of the business or team being measured (Exhibit 4).

In the network-television business, for example, program ratings are the ultimate measure of success. Is a low rating, however, the result of poor program development, lack of affiliate interest, low ratings of the lead-in show, poor scheduling, or poor transmission?

High ratings are the desired goal. A single measure of success, however, may not be totally appropriate for all individual managers or teams. Measures capable of isolating the discrete factors that influence ratings—an "adjusted" ratings index, for instance, designed to measure only program-development performance—would more closely parallel the workings of the business.

A measurement system, however, can only measure what is measurable. Customer profitability, for example, may be the desired gauge of a sales force's effectiveness, but the data may be insufficient to fully capture that profitability. A better approximation unbundles the performance criteria into representative "proxies," such as type of account, size of account, and product profitability. This approach captures the key drivers of customer profitability and links them to controllable, measurable elements.

Measurement systems alone do not ensure the right behavior. Linking performance to pay is crucial. All companies have formal and

Exhibit 5
Monitoring Change

Institutionalized monitoring	Ad hoc monitoring
• Install and maintain a tracking system to monitor and reward performance	• Promote self-motivated team meetings to plan, coordinate, and evaluate
• Develop ongoing corporate communications (publications, manuals, videotapes, etc.) to reinforce change	• Motivate informal cost, quality, and revenue reviews for self-monitoring of performance
• Create in-house training and development programs to institutionalize change	• Encourage the sharing of information across team boundaries, as appropriate
• Establish periodic reviews of each team's plans and performance with the CEO	• Encourage senior management to lead by example, by communicating and operating cross-functionally

Source: Booz•Allen & Hamilton

informal reward systems that include merit pay, incentives, and equity plans, as well as nonmonetary rewards, such as career-pathing. Viewing compensation as simply a pay-delivery vehicle—a view engendered by tradition and internal equity requirements—lessens its power as a motivational force.

With TEAM, a reward system is a logical extension of the executional network. Once management understands how strategies are translated into goals for value-added stages and how transaction groups are developed, it can integrate decisions on rewards. It can design pay opportunities to reflect both market requirements and the potential for incremental performance improvements. Plan participation levels and pay mix (fixed versus variable, short versus long term) flow from the value-added model of the business and reflect both individual and team accountability. The ability to capture, measure, and articulate both team and individual contributions drives pay differentiation.

Monitoring Change

Building teams that transcend the confines of traditional organization structures often involves a substantive change in attitude and culture. Most organizations accept change slowly. Getting individuals to believe in and accept a new system, to coordinate their efforts, and work together in non-traditional ways, is an iterative and dynamic process.

Successful execution and team building depend upon a monitoring infrastructure that can communicate and reinforce the new culture in both institutionalized and informal ways. On the institutional side, integrated data bases that transfer information across functions, industries and geographies can ease this communication. A tracking system to measure and assess team performance provides a degree of corporate control, as do training programs for team interaction.

Making Strategy Work

The CEO's Role in Making TEAM Work

To ensure success, the CEO must provide leadership and demonstrate his commitment throughout the process. His role is fourfold:

1. *Get the board and top management to buy into the process.*
Given the sweeping changes that the TEAM approach may entail, the CEO must communicate the need for change and explain what TEAM will accomplish.

2. *Inspire the troops.*
A successful kickoff is crucial. The CEO must convince employees that the TEAM approach is not just a slogan; it is a program that requires broad-based employee involvement and commitment.

3. *Arbitrate high-level disputes.*
The CEO must be prepared to resolve internal conflicts over benefit trade-offs and resource allocations.

4. *Stay the course.*
The CEO must demonstrate continued commitment—for example, by marking milestones achieved in internal communications programs, by asking for periodic comments from people who report directly to him, and most important, by meeting regularly with the transaction groups. One CEO puts aside three to four days every quarter for this purpose.

Ad hoc methods of monitoring are also crucial to inculcate behavioral change, since they enfranchise the individual and team and engender a sense of ownership. Self-motivated team meetings, for example, allow for the spontaneity in problem-solving that encourages creativity and innovation (Exhibit 5). The broader the basis for involvement, the greater the chance for an execution that successfully harmonizes the organization's structure, culture, and value-added activities.

One major service company that employed the full TEAM approach quickly realized the importance of effectively monitoring team building. Management directly supported teams through performance-tracking systems and training programs to provide timely information and to educate employees on this new way of thinking about the business. Most important, this process began with a full commitment from the CEO, who demonstrated his commitment through periodic reviews of team plans and performance.

Both the CEO and the teams realized critical benefits from these meetings. From the CEO's perspective, a clearer view of the business, conveyed in team presentations (rather than functional V.P. reviews), provided better information for better decisions. From the teams' perspective, the interest and insights of the CEO were a keen and undeniable source of motivation and support.

TEAM: A Powerful Management Tool

Every CEO has the tools to energize an organization. And the benefits of a TEAM approach to implementing strategy are considerable. Employees respond to goals described for value-added stages. Recognition of the transaction groups they participate in enlists their support. With a more personal understanding of the business, managers at all levels focus on complementary objectives. An appropriate measurement and reward system stimulates the desired performance. Monitoring ensures a smooth transition from planning to execution to results. Perhaps most important, when it comes to turning a CEO's strategic vision into reality, TEAM works.

Organizations that work

Why teams matter

An excerpt from *The Wisdom of Teams: Creating the High-Performance Organization*

Effective teams, not abstract commitments to teamwork or empowerment, are the real drivers of top-flight organizational performance

Jon R. Katzenbach and Douglas K. Smith

In their private lives, managers know that real teams can produce extraordinary performance results – results way beyond the reach of separate individuals or less cohesive groups. At work, however, turning this private knowledge to the advantage of their organizations has often proven difficult. It is not always clear when to use teams or how best to support them. Nor is it clear what, precisely, it is that makes a team a team. Drawn both from the authors' long experience working with organizations to improve their performance and from a detailed study of some 50 or so different teams of executives in 30 different companies, this excerpt from The Wisdom of Teams *describes in close detail what teams are, which attributes set them apart from other kinds of groups, and – most important – why they are the essential organizational units for achieving performance results as well as accelerating personal growth.*

SAVVY MANAGERS have always known that real teams – not just groups of people with a label attached – will invariably outperform the same set of individuals operating in a non-team mode, particularly where multiple skills, experiences, and judgments determine performance. Being more flexible than larger organizational groupings, they can be more quickly and effectively assembled, deployed, refocused, and disbanded. And being

---

This article is excerpted from *The Wisdom of Teams* by Jon R. Katzenbach and Douglas K. Smith, to be published in December by Harvard Business School Press, Boston. Reprinted by special permission of the publisher. Copyright © 1992 by McKinsey & Company, Inc. All rights reserved.

more firmly and mutually committed to tangible performance results, they can more readily leverage their combined skills to achieve objectives beyond the reach of less tightly-bound collections of individuals.

None of this is new. Ancient generals understood the wisdom of teams no less than do modern corporate leaders. What makes that wisdom of such importance now – and so worth the urgent attention of top management – is not novelty but the proven link between teams, individual behavioral change, and high-performance. Building organizations that consistently outperform their competitors, as well as the expectations of their key constituencies (customers, shareholders, and employees), over an extended period of time requires lasting behavioral change. And experience shows that the same team dynamics that boost performance also enable such change – and do so far more effectively than can larger organizational units or individuals left to their own devices.

Change has always been a top management challenge. But until recently, when executives spoke of managing change, they usually referred to normal change – that is, adapting to new circumstances where demands fall well within the scope of existing management approaches. Today, however, these demands often extend to "major" change, which requires people at all levels of a company to become very good at behaviors and skills they are not very good at now. As Jack Welch, Lawrence Bossidy, and Edward Hood of General Electric note, "Every effort of every man and woman in the company is focused on satisfying customers' needs. Internal functions begin to blur. Customer service? It's not somebody's job. It's everybody's job."

> *There is a proven link between teams, individual behavioral change, and high-performance*

This is, of course, a much more difficult challenge – one that cannot be met solely through top-down, command-and-control organizational responses. Change on this scale depends *on* teams because behavioral change occurs more readily *in* teams. Their collective commitment keeps members from being as threatened by change as individuals left to fend for themselves. Their flexibility offers members more room for growth. And their focus on performance motivates, challenges, rewards, and supports members who try to alter the way they do things.

WHY TEAMS MATTER

The lesson seems clear: only teams can make hierarchy responsive without weakening it, energize processes across organizational boundaries without distorting them, and bring multiple capabilities to bear on difficult issues without undermining them.

In fact, most models of the so-called "organization of the future" that we have heard about – "networked," "clustered," "non-hierarchical," "horizontal," and the like – are premised on teams surpassing individuals as the primary unit of performance. When managers seek faster, better ways to match resources with customer need or competitive challenge, the critical building block is – and will increasingly be – at the team, not the individual, level.

When do groups become teams?

If teams provide such a critical lever of performance, why is it that so many managers remain confused about what – exactly – they are? Some mentally lump them together with taskforces, committees, departments, and other forms of groups. Others think of them not in organizational terms but as the embodiment of values such as teamwork or cooperation or empowerment. Still others believe that merely calling a group a team makes it one. It does not.

There is a threshold below which an extremely dedicated group of people working together to accomplish something of great importance to themselves remains just that – an extremely dedicated *group* of people. It has not crossed the threshold. A team, a real team, is something different.

Based on our and our colleagues' work with both corporate and other kinds of organizations in all parts of the world, we have come to think of a team more precisely as *a small number of people with complementary skills who are committed to a common purpose, performance goals, and approach for which they hold themselves mutually accountable.*

Each part of this definition – or, better, this essential mode of organizational discipline – is worth closer attention:

...A small number of people

Virtually all the real teams we have met, read, heard about, or been members of, have ranged between two and twenty-five people. Most numbered less than ten. Size, of course, differs from the other key attributes of teams – meaningful purpose, specific performance goals, common approach, complementary skills, and mutual accountability – in that *they* are absolute necessities. "Small number" is more of a pragmatic guide. A larger number of people, say 50 or more, can theoretically become a team, but groups of such size usually break into subteams rather than function as a single unit.

Why? Because large numbers of people – by virtue of their size – have trouble interacting constructively as a group, much less agreeing on specific, actionable tasks. Ten people are far more likely than 50 to work successfully through their individual, functional, and hierarchical differences toward a common plan – or to hold themselves jointly accountable for the results.

When managers seek faster, better ways to match resources with customer need or competitive challenge, the critical building block is – and will increasingly be – at the team, not the individual, level

Large groups face not only logistical issues like finding enough physical space and time to meet together. They also face more complex constraints, like "crowd" or "herd" behaviors, that prevent the open, intense sharing of viewpoints needed to build a team. As a result, such groups tend to settle for fuzzy statements of purpose, which usually get set by the hierarchical leaders, and some vague reliance on the value of teamwork as their working approach. Thus, when purpose or approach breaks down, it is easy for the groups to revert to formal hierarchy, structure, policies, and procedures.

...*Complementary skills*

Real teams develop the right mix of complementary skills necessary to do the team's job. These requirements fall into three categories:

1. ***Technical or functional expertise.*** It would make little sense for a group of doctors to litigate an employment discrimination case in a court of law. Yet teams of doctors and lawyers often try medical malpractice or personal injury cases. Likewise, product development groups that include only marketers or only

engineers are less likely to succeed than those with the complementary skills of both.

2. ***Problem-solving and decision-making skills.*** Teams must be able to identify the problems and opportunities they face, evaluate the options they have for moving forward, and then make the necessary tradeoffs and decisions about how to proceed.

3. ***Interpersonal skills.*** Common understanding and purpose cannot arise without effective communication and constructive conflict. These, in turn, depend on such interpersonal skills as risk taking, helpful criticism, objectivity. active listening, giving the benefit of the doubt, support, and recognizing the interests and achievements of others.

Common sense tells us that it is a mistake to ignore the mix of skills when selecting a team. No team can get started without some minimum complement of skills. Nor can it achieve its purpose without developing all the skills required. Still, it is surprising how many people assemble teams primarily on the basis of personal compatibility or formal position in an organization.

...Commitment to common purpose and performance goals

A team's purpose and performance goals go together. Indeed. we have yet to find a real team without both. If near-term goals do not relate directly to overall purpose. team members become confused, pull apart, and revert to mediocre performance behaviors.

There are several reasons for this. First, working to shape *common, meaningful purpose sets the tone and aspiration* by which teams develop direction, momentum, and commitment. Building ownership and commitment to purpose, however, is not incompatible with taking initial direction from outside the team. The often-asserted view that a team cannot "own" its purpose unless top management keeps their hands completely off is seriously misleading. It is the exceptional case – true entrepreneurial situations, for example – when a team actually creates a purpose entirely on its own.

Direction from top management helps teams get started by broadly framing some kind of "team charter" within the performance requirements of the company. This is what Bob Waterman and Tom Peters in *In Search of Excellence* call defining a "solution space" – that is, defining the boundaries and scope of authority clearly enough to indicate direction, but flexibly enough to allow the modification required for commitment to develop.*

Exhibit 1 is one of the best illustrations we know of such a charter or set of management guidelines for teams. Developed at Procter & Gamble during their impressive major change and performance turnaround between 1985 and 1991, it makes clear the charter, the rationale, and the performance challenge for the team, but leaves plenty of solution space for the choice of specific goals, timing, and approach.

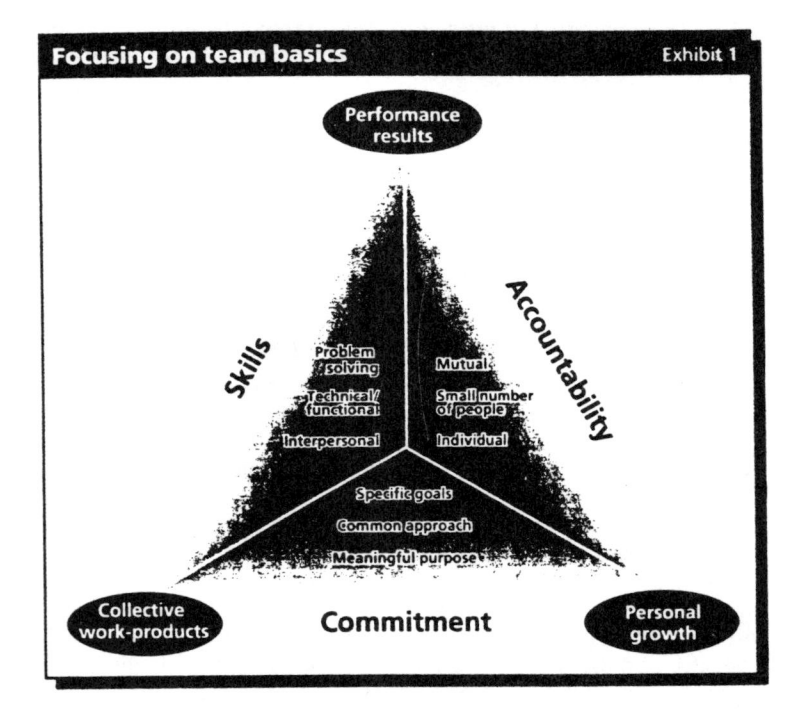

Focusing on team basics — Exhibit 1

Performance results

Skills
- Problem solving
- Technical/functional
- Interpersonal

Accountability
- Mutual
- Small number of people
- Individual

- Specific goals
- Common approach
- Meaningful purpose

Collective work-products

Commitment

Personal growth

The best teams invest a tremendous amount of time and effort exploring, shaping, and agreeing on a purpose that belongs to them both collectively and individually. In fact, real teams never stop this "purposing" activity because of its value in clarifying the aspirations of, and in providing a fundamental reason for, their extra effort.

---
* Thomas J. Peters and Robert H. Waterman Jr., *In Search of Excellence*. New York, HarperCollins, 1982.

WHY TEAMS MATTER

Second, *specific performance goals are an integral part of a team's purpose.* Transforming broad directives into concrete, measurable performance goals is the surest first step in a team's shaping of a common purpose that is meaningful to its members. Specific goals – like getting a new product to market in less than half the normal time, responding to all customers within 24 hours, or achieving a zero defect rate while simultaneously cutting costs by 40 percent – provide clear and tangible footholds.

Moreover, such goals define a team work-product that is different from both an organization-wide mission and the summation of individual job objectives. To be effective, these work-products must require roughly equivalent contributions from all team members to make something specific happen that, in and of itself, will add real value to company results.

The specificity of performance objectives has another benefit: facilitating clear communications and constructive conflict within the team. For example, one plant-level team at Sealed Air Corporation, a high-performing producer of packaging materials and systems, set a goal of averaging two hours for machine changeover. The clarity of that goal forced the team to concentrate on what it would take to achieve it – or, alternatively, on whether the goal should be changed. When goals are clear, team discussions can focus on how, exactly, to pursue them or whether to change them. When they are ambiguous or nonexistent, no such focus is possible.

> *The often-asserted view that a team cannot "own" its purpose unless top management keeps their hands completely off is seriously misleading*

A third reason for linking purpose with specific performance goals is that the latter help teams *concentrate on getting results.* A product-development team at Eli Lilly's Peripheral Systems Division set definite yardsticks for the market introduction of an ultrasonic probe, which would help doctors locate clogged arteries in patients. The probe had to have an audible signal through a specified depth of tissue, be manufacturable at a rate of 100 per day, have a unit cost less than a pre-established amount, and get developed in less than half the time the Lilly division usually took.

Because each of these objectives was attainable *and* measurable, the team always knew where it stood. At any given moment, it was achieving its goals or it was not. Until it did, there was no question where energy and attention had to focus. Moreover, the specificity of the goals allowed the team to achieve small wins along the way, which were invaluable in building its members' commitment and determination to overcome the inevitable obstacles they faced.

> *The best teams invest a tremendous amount of time and effort exploring, shaping, and agreeing on a purpose that belongs to them both collectively and individually*

Still another reason, as Outward Bound and other team-building programs illustrate, specific objectives have a *leveling effect conducive to effective team behavior*. When a small group of people challenge themselves to get over a wall or up a mountain or through a desert – or to reduce cycle time by 50 percent – their respective titles, perks, and other "stripes" fade into the background. The teams that succeed evaluate what and how each individual can best contribute to the general goal. More importantly, they do so in terms of the performance objective itself, rather than any individual's status or personality.

Performance goals are compelling. They provide drama, urgency, and a healthy fear of failure. They challenge the people on a team to commit themselves, as a team, to make a difference. At Lilly, all members of the medical probe team put their pride on the line when they actually committed to getting the new product to market in record time. No one beyond the team could make it happen. It was *their* challenge.

...Commitment to a common working approach

Teams also need to develop a common approach to how they will work together to accomplish their purpose. Crafting such an approach takes just as large an investment of time and effort as the shaping of purpose. It must include economic and administrative, as well as social, dimensions. Every member of a team must do equivalent amounts of real work. And everyone must agree on who will do which jobs, how schedules will be set and adhered to, which skills need to be developed, how continuing membership is to be earned, and how the group will make and modify decisions.

An approach that confines all real work to a few members (or staff outsiders) and allocates joint effort only to review and dis-

WHY TEAMS MATTER

cussion meetings cannot achieve team levels of performance. This is, in large measure, because there is no collective work-product to supplement individual performance. Moreover, this approach treats the social aspect of work as unrelated to performance. Effective teams, however, always have team members who, over time, assume important social as well as leadership roles, challenging, interpreting, supporting, integrating, remembering, and summarizing the work of others. These roles help promote the mutual trust and constructive conflict necessary to success but they are always an integral part of performance efforts, not ends in themselves.

> *When a small group of people challenge themselves to get over a wall or up a mountain or through a desert – or to reduce cycle time by 50 percent – their respective titles, perks, and other "stripes" fade into the background*

Because, in the best teams, each member assumes different social roles depending on the situation, each team develops its own unique processes for energizing and supporting one another and for keeping each other honest and on track. These roles evolve over time to meet performance needs. It is a troublesome, though common, mistake to go down some generic checklist of useful social roles, as a way of assembling a team that, at the beginning, has "all the right parts."

...Mutual accountability

No group ever becomes a team until it can hold itself accountable as a team. This is a demanding test. Think, for example, of the subtle but critical difference between "The boss holds me accountable" and "We hold ourselves accountable." The first case can lead to the second; but without the second, there can be no team.

At its core, team accountability has to do with the sincere promises we make to ourselves and to others, promises that underpin two critical aspects of teams: commitment and trust. By promising to hold ourselves accountable to the team's goals, we each earn the right to express our own views about all aspects of the team's effort and to have our views receive a fair and constructive hearing. By following through on such promises, we preserve and extend the trust on which any real team must be built.

Most of us enter a potential team situation cautiously; ingrained individualism discourages us from putting our fates too easily in the hands of others. Teams do not succeed by ignoring or wishing away such behavior. Mutual accountability cannot be coerced any more than people can be made to trust one another. But trust does tend to grow as a natural counterpart to the development of common team purpose, performance goals, and approach.

> *No group ever becomes a team until it can hold itself accountable as a team*

Accountability arises from – and reinforces – the time, energy, and action invested in figuring out what a team is trying to accomplish and how best to get it done. When a group of people all do real work together toward a common objective, trust and commitment follow. Consequently, teams enjoying a strong common purpose and approach inevitably hold themselves, individually and collectively, responsible for the whole team's performance.

Despite the fact that most of us are familiar with teams, we are often imprecise in thinking about them. That is why gaining a clear understanding of what a team is and is not – and, particularly, of how teams and performance depend on each other – can provide useful insights about how to strengthen group performance.

Imprecise or ambiguous talk, however, pales in comparison with the lack of discipline most of us bring to potential team situations. Teams do not spring up by magic. Nor does personal chemistry matter as much as most people believe. Focusing on performance and accountability – not chemistry or teamwork or good communications or good feelings – is what makes teams happen.

The team performance curve

The discipline of this multipart definition is what top managers need to understand and enforce if they are to capture the potential of real team performance at critical spots in their organizations. First, however, they must give equally disciplined attention to the question of whether – and when – real teams are appropriate. There are tradeoffs between relying on individuals, working groups, and teams. In what circumstances are teams the right answer?

WHY TEAMS MATTER

Consider, for example, the situation of the Cosmo Products executive group who were perceived by employees as not being enough of a team:

"Those kinds of comments are pretty hard to ignore. Obviously, the people in this company don't think we're a very cohesive team. I guess we don't work together as well as we might. But I didn't realize it was of that much concern to the rest of the organization. What should we do about it?"

The president of Cosmo was talking informally with his top executive group. They had just finished listening to disguised excerpts from taped interviews with more than one hundred employees, who had been asked for their views about the progress of a recently-launched change effort — a major undertaking aimed at changing the behaviors of literally thousands of people throughout the company.

Most of us enter a potential team situation cautiously; ingrained individualism discourages us from putting our fates too easily in the hands of others. Teams do not succeed by ignoring or wishing away such behavior

Many of the comments were to be expected. The employees understood that Cosmo Products' strategy and performance had declined significantly during the previous five years. The company no longer consistently beat the competition to market with the right products at the right time. Nor did its salesforce perform as well as it once had.

There were many explanations: product proliferation, quality problems, shifting consumer preferences, more aggressive competitors, demographic changes in the salesforce. And there was deep concern: the overall market had leveled, sales and share were down, and profits had fallen so much that analysts and the business press openly criticized the company. Morale and confidence were clearly shaken, and everyone knew that a great deal of change was required.

So it was not surprising to Cosmo's executives, although it was painful, to hear their employees recount the top group's earlier failures to correct the situation. They knew the current effort had better be different. Yes, the employees understood and agreed with the company's new vision. Yes, they shared its sense of urgency. And yes, they were ready to participate in the various efforts being mounted in key functions and operating units.

But something had to be different this time. This time, the taped comments insisted over and over, the top group *had* to become a real team. The message was inescapably clear: "You guys are all pulling in different directions. If you don't get your act together, nothing will change."

The critical choice

In our terms, Cosmo's top executives had to decide whether to concentrate on improving their effectiveness as a de facto working group or to try to become a real team. In the eyes of their employees, they were, as a group, working at cross purposes. Simply clarifying direction and role did not require them to become a team. Indeed, in many situations, particularly at the top of multibusiness companies, a structured working group makes the best sense. All too often, however, the choice between working group and team is neither recognized nor consciously made.

The basic distinction here turns on performance. A working group relies primarily on the sum total of the individual contributions of its members to boost group performance; a team multiplies the impact of individuals by requiring collective work-products. The choice depends largely on whether the aggregation of individual achievements can meet overall performance aspirations, or whether truly collective efforts, skills, work-products, and mutual accountability are needed.

Working groups tend to thrive in those hierarchical structures where individual accountability counts the most. The best of them come together to share information, perspectives, and insights, to make decisions that help each person do his or her own job better, and to reinforce each other's individual performance standards. But their focus is always on individual performance goals and accountabilities.

An effective working group, like a team, benefits from a clear purpose and common understanding of how performance will be evaluated. (The Cosmo executives had neither.) Unlike a team, however, a working group uses its purpose solely to delineate individual roles, tasks, and responsibilities, which typically match up quite well with formal organizational positions.

WHY TEAMS MATTER

To get their assigned tasks done, working group members, especially at senior levels, usually delegate the real work to others beyond the group. This is consistent with their paying attention only to individual outcomes and results. True, members may compete with one another in their pursuit of individual performance targets. They may even provide counsel and insights to each other and become concerned when any among them falters. But they do not take responsibility for results other than their own. Nor do they try to develop performance contributions requiring the combined, real work of two or more group members.

Teams are different. They require both individual *and* mutual accountability. They rely on more than group discussion, debate, and decision; on more than sharing information and best practice perspectives; on more than a mutual reinforcing of performance standards. What they produce they produce jointly. The performance they contribute is more than the sum of its parts.

These higher performance levels carry with them, of course, greater risk. The deep-seated values of individualism and the natural reluctance to trust one's fate to the performance of others make commitment to a team a leap of faith. Even the most rugged individuals – and there are many, especially at the top – cannot contribute to real team performance without taking responsibility for their peers and letting their peers assume responsibility for them. But there are people who instinctively believe that "if you want a job done right, do it yourself." It is against their nature to rely on others for the really important tasks in life.

A working group relies primarily on the sum total of individual contributions; a team multiplies them

The price of faking this leap of faith is also high. When teams fail, members get diverted from their individual goals, what they produce does not add significant value, costs outweigh benefits, and people resent the imposition on their time and priorities. By contrast, working groups present fewer risks. They need waste little time in shaping their purpose, objectives, and approach since the leader usually establishes them. Meetings are run against well-prioritized agendas and are efficient in the use of members' time. Decisions get implemented through specific, individual assignments and accountabilities.

Most of the time, therefore, if cumulative performance aspirations can be met simply by enabling individuals to do their respective jobs well, the working group approach is more comfortable, less risky, and less disruptive than stretching to reach the higher performance levels of real teams. Indeed, if there is no strict performance need that teams alone can satisfy, efforts to improve the effectiveness of a working group make much more sense than does floundering around trying to become a team.

From group to team

To help managers understand the choice facing such groups as the executives of Cosmo Products, as well as the risks and performance potential involved in that choice, we find it useful to refer to a simple framework we call the "performance curve" (*see* Exhibit 2). There are five key points along the curve:

1. **Working group.** This is a collection of individuals for whom there is no significant incremental performance need or opportunity requiring their mutual transformation into a team. Members interact primarily to share information, best practices, or perspectives and to make decisions that help each individual perform well within his or her own area of responsibility. But there is no deep common purpose nor any general wish for one, no common "stretch" performance goals, and no common work-products that call for collective skills and mutual accountability.

2. **Pseudo team.** This is a collection of individuals for whom there could be a significant performance need or opportunity, but who have not focused on collective performance and are not really trying to achieve it. There is no group interest in shaping a common purpose or set of performance goals, even though the group may call itself – or think of itself as – a team. They are concerned about togetherness, not performance.

Pseudo teams are the weakest arrangements of all in terms of performance impact. They almost always contribute less to a company's performance needs than do working groups because their interactions detract from each member's individual performance without delivering any joint benefit. On pseudo teams, the whole is less than the sum of the potential of the individual parts.

3. **Potential team.** This is a collection of individuals for whom there is a clear, significant performance need – and who really are trying to improve their performance impact. Typically, however,

they lack clarity about purpose, goals, or joint work-products, as well as the discipline to hammer out a common working approach. Nor have they established mutual accountability.

Our experience suggests that potential teams abound in organizations. This should be of concern to managers because the greatest possibility for improved performance anywhere on the curve usually comes between potential teams and real teams.

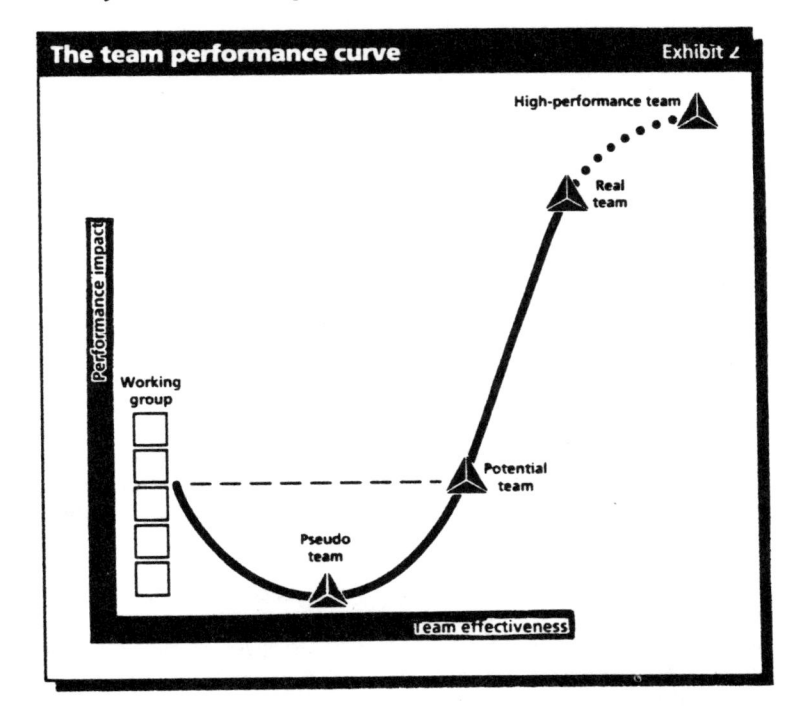

The team performance curve — Exhibit 2

(Chart: Performance impact vs. Team effectiveness, showing Working group, Pseudo team, Potential team, Real team, and High-performance team)

4. **Real team.** This, as we have already argued, is *a small number of people with complementary skills* who are equally committed to a common purpose, goals, and working approach for which they hold themselves mutually accountable.

5. **High-performance team.** This is a group that meets all the conditions of real teams – and whose members are also deeply committed, even beyond the team setting, to one another's personal growth and success. The high-performance team significantly outperforms not only all other teams but also all reasonable expectations, given its membership.

Why Cosmo failed

Cosmo's senior managers certainly had the potential to become the kind of team their employees hoped for. The performance challenge they faced called for a team. They were a small number of people with the right skill mix. Given the problems they faced, it should have been possible for them to establish a common purpose, performance goals, and approach for which they held themselves mutually accountable.

Prior to listening to the interview tapes, however, these managers did not even constitute a good working group. Instead, they were only a pseudo team – that is, they referred to themselves as a team but made no serious effort to establish collective purpose, performance goals, or approach. As they worked together, considerations of politics almost always overshadowed those of performance.

What Cosmo's president called the "pretty hard to ignore" message of the tapes spurred the group to want to move from pseudo team to real team. Indeed, they decided that becoming a team was, in and of itself, critically important if they were to have any chance of leading a transformation at Cosmo. What they, as many groups like them, did *not* do was to give serious consideration to the alternative goal of becoming a more effective working group. Nor did they look beyond the self-imposed task of becoming a team to focus on the real heart of the challenge facing them: boosting company performance beyond the results achievable in their roles as individuals.

Most of the group's meetings were marked by the candor necessary to team building – and by diligent efforts to grapple with the issues critical to managing the kind of broad-based change they thought was necessary. "The vision is too abstract," they told themselves, for example, "We've got to be clearer on what we want our vision to mean to employees and customers. Everything has become a priority around here. We have to find a way to get things into better focus before we create a system overload."

And they recognized the consequences if they failed: "Our people don't really understand what is expected of them. We need to communicate specifically what and how we want them to change, and then get them working on it." At the heart of the problem, however, was their mutual acknowledgment that "We still don't really trust one another. We need to keep having these meetings,

WHY TEAMS MATTER

maybe even a special retreat, to work on that issue." They were focused on togetherness, not performance.

Discussions like these went on sporadically for a few months after the employee feedback session. Out of them, the group emerged with a stronger sense of vision and purpose for the company, a better understanding of how to set company priorities, an intention to communicate more clearly with employees, and a firmer basis for trust among themselves. There was, however, no clarification of purpose or vision for the group itself, nor any agreement on specific performance goals to pursue *as a team*.

Such objectives were possible. As both the employees and executives knew, for example, Cosmo Products was introducing far too many products of varying quality every year. The senior executives could have taken on the challenge, as a team, to cut the number of new offerings by 50 percent while simultaneously designing a process to get them to market on time and within established quality standards. Or they might have committed themselves, as a team, to strengthen the account relationship skills of the traditionally part-time salesforce. Had the group defined such goals, it would have had something concrete and measurable to do as a team.

People throughout an organization always recognize pseudo teams for the sham they are. The net result is always the same: discomfort, disunity, and dysfunction

But without any mutually agreed-on performance objectives, the senior executives found no way to engage as a team in pursuit of their nobler aspirations. They did discuss and debate at length the urgency of the situation they faced as well as their desire to do something about it. But because they never translated this desire into specific team goals, these team-building sessions deteriorated into nothing more than frustrated and frustrating talk.

Three years after the launch of its major change program, Cosmo Products still had not developed the fundamentally different skills, values, and behaviors required for future competitive success. Instead, the company endured continuing financial disappointments, major takeover battles, key business divestitures, disturbing top management changes, and wrenching cost-cutting drives. The employee warnings had been right: the performance potential of the top managers becoming a real team was as enormous as their ultimate failure was disastrous – that is, their failure both to choose, explicitly, between being a working group and being a team and to support either choice with a rugged, disciplined eye on performance.

Companies with a weak performance ethic obscure or even destroy team performance

Most of us have belonged, at one time or another, to pseudo teams like the one at Cosmo Products. They exist in many parts and levels of most organizations. And most of us have experienced their confusion over purpose, their reluctance to focus, their inability to handle personal animosity or ambition, and their reliance on hierarchical ritual to avoid, rather than engage, one another. Worse, people throughout an organization always recognize these pseudo teams for the sham they are. The net result is always the same: discomfort, disunity, and dysfunction – and ultimately disrespect.

The cycle of reenforcement at Motorola

As experience at all points along the performance curve attests, significant performance challenges – the demands, say, of customer service or total quality or continuous improvement or innovation – do more than anything else to foster the development of real teams. The issue is not whether such challenges exist; every organization faces them. It is whether established managerial values and behaviors – what we call a company's "performance ethic" – help or harm the team-inducing effects of these performance challenges.

We see a mutually reenforcing relationship between the strength of a company's performance ethic and the number and performance of its teams. Companies that have a commanding performance ethic actively seek out the kinds of performance challenges that favor teams, which, in turn, deliver results that help sustain the overall performance ethic. The decisions, actions, and events that mark any group's evolution toward the status of real team will more likely occur inside a strongly performance-oriented company.

The reverse is also true. Companies with a weak performance ethic obscure or even destroy team performance opportunities in

WHY TEAMS MATTER

the endless shuffle of turf, politics, "not invented here," and "business as usual." And these lost opportunities, especially the more visible ones, further weaken the performance ethic.

The "Connectors" team at Motorola grew out of an effort by the company's Government Equipment Group (GEG) to partner more effectively with suppliers. This followed a 1989 decision to shift supply management from a decentralized, functional organization, dependent on the expertise and performance of individuals, to a centralized, process-oriented organization that depended primarily on teams.

The performance goal in this strongly performance-oriented company was to get both external and internal customers the supplies and materials they needed when they needed them at the lowest total cost. To do this, GEG's leadership team knew it had to move away from an organization emphasizing individual and functional accountability to one that focused on developing teams that began with suppliers and finished with customers.

GEG's formal designation of teams in late 1989 was just that – namely, the creation of organization units that were called teams but were not. Two years later, many of these potential teams had become real teams – thanks, in large measure, to the reenforcing effects of the company's strong performance culture.

Starting the cycle

Like the other potential teams in GEG, the Connectors team was charged with the general goal of boosting customer satisfaction. It was also expected to measure itself against five specific criteria: reject rate, number of corrective actions, cycle time, late deliveries, and number of suppliers. When members of the group first got together in January 1990, they agreed on a number of concrete performance goals – for example, reducing the percentage of defective components from 3.5 percent to 1 percent by the end of the year. They also discussed how to overcome the conflict between the two sets of experts involved in purchasing: engineers and purchasers.

Several of the engineers, who were responsible for specifying and inspecting products, believed that purchasers did little more than read catalogs and call suppliers. The purchasers, who selected, ordered, and paid for products, thought engineers had tunnel vision and routinely created unnecessary obstacles that prevented efficient purchasing. Not surprisingly, purchasers and engineers differed in their respective views of how best to improve the function's performance.

This conflict dominated the Connectors group as it struggled to set priorities, figure out how to work together, and build confidence in one another. Throughout this period, the group's leader, Sandy Hopkins, kept it focused on improving quality, cycle time, and cost. But she refused to make all decisions herself, and instead actively involved others in attacking and resolving problems. She also regularly held team meetings and tried to build camaraderie through pizza lunches, cocktail hours, and parties that included families. She did not, however, focus on team building exercises per se.

Reassessment

By October, engineers and purchasers were at least working together, and overall performance had improved. Yet, the Connectors team was still not a real team. It had clear performance goals and had begun to develop common aspirations, particularly around its own empowerment and skill development. But it still had not developed the common team approach or the full sense of mutual accountability that lead to real commitment.

> *Significant performance challenges do more than anything else to foster the development of real teams*

Furthermore, discontent was growing due to a gap between talk about empowerment and the nonempowering roles of two key managerial positions: the engineering manager and the purchasing manager. In effect, the group's members were still feeling each other out to discover how serious they all were about achieving their joint goals.

To break this logjam, Sandy asked the group to reassess its goals and objectives, decide how the work effort should be organized, and lay out a fair and effective approach for evaluating both team and individual performance. This turned out to be a key event in the group's emergence as a team. As a result of these discussions and analyses, the team members rededicated themselves to specific performance goals in improving quality, cycle time, and cost.

For example, they committed themselves to halving the defective component rate to 0.5 percent by the end of 1991. But they also began to articulate among themselves a broader, more meaningful sense of shared purpose. "We were the pilot for the team concept in the new supply management organization, and we wanted to achieve results," said one team member. "Other teams at Motorola were in the production area, and there was a feeling going around that teams wouldn't work in a service area like supply. We had something to prove."

A common approach

The team made several decisions that solidified its common approach and sense of mutual accountability. First, it set some rules. Everyone on the team had to identify two others who could serve as backups during vacation periods and sick days. To eradicate the attitude of "it's not my job," it was agreed that whenever anyone needed help, the person asked had to respond even if the activity was not in his or her area of expertise. The team also agreed on a peer appraisal system that gave everyone the opportunity to evaluate everyone else and, through Sandy, feed the results back to the person being evaluated.

Second, the team eliminated the two managerial positions that had limited empowerment. This effectively modified the membership of the team because only one of the two managers whose jobs were eliminated chose to stay. The other believed he could not take a perceived demotion and left. By January 1991, the Connectors team was a dramatically more effective group of people than it had been on its formation a year earlier.

New aspirations

Energy and enthusiasm reached still higher levels as the team started pushing itself harder and in more innovative ways. One of the engineers, for example, decided to become completely qualified as a purchaser as well. Instead of being threatened, the purchasers on the team worked hard to teach her the basics of the job. Moreover, the peer review approach worked so well that the team agreed on the additional – and, for many teams, difficult – step of directly providing each other feedback instead of relying on the team leader for this task.

The team then challenged a longstanding GEG policy by recommending that suppliers be trusted to do their own inspections, arguing that both quality and cycle time would improve dramatically if suppliers were made full partners in meeting the team's specific performance goals. The team asked management to allow it to qualify certain suppliers for self-inspection. Management said no, it was too risky.

The team did not give up. It worked hard to address management's concerns, brought the recommendation back for a second hearing, and was rewarded with approval. The fact that the team was able to regroup and overcome its initial "defeat" only added to its growth and level of commitment. By mid-1991, it had developed all the earmarks of real team performance – significant performance impacts, increasing personal commitment to one another, multiple skill development, dedication to purpose and goals, and shared leadership roles. The strong performance culture at Motorola nurtured the development of the Connectors team in a number of specific ways:

- Because everyone knew that performance comes first at Motorola, the team instinctively set clear goals at the beginning and never lost sight of them. In many organizations, when potential teams first gather, they lack a clear idea about which objectives matter the most. This was not so here.

When reorganizing the supply management activity, the leaders of GEG had pinpointed the importance of reject rates, on-time deliveries, number of corrections, cycle-time reduction, and number of suppliers. The critical nature of these objectives was, in turn, reenforced by such corporate-wide initiatives as "Six Sigma Quality" and "Total Cycle-Time Reduction." Accordingly, the Connectors team was able to move quickly beyond agreeing on common goals to tackling how its members would work together to accomplish them.

A strong performance ethic gives people both the confidence and the capability to figure out for themselves the best way to go after specific performance opportunities

- Because Motorola and GEG practised values of cooperation and involvement – a "constant respect for people" and "becoming best in class in people" – the team leader instinctively involved all members in establishing the team's purpose, per-

WHY TEAMS MATTER

formance goals, and approach. Moreover, several GEG leaders personified these values through their own actions. The head of GEG, for example, made it clear that he wanted, needed, and expected people throughout the Group to help the division become "the best." As a result, Sandy Hopkins had many reassuring role models for sharing solution space with the people who reported to her and could, with confidence, involve all of them in decision making.

- Because GEG's own management team had taken a bold step in streamlining the Group's supply management structure, the Connectors team had a strong precedent and example to follow when it acted to eliminate the two managerial positions it believed were retarding team performance. During the streamlining process, GEG's leaders had reduced the number of levels in the hierarchy from seven to four in order to improve both the speed and effectiveness of decision making. In doing so, they demonstrated that performance and contribution to performance were the critical yardsticks by which any managerial position should be evaluated. They also demonstrated their deep belief that teams were to be the basic unit of performance.

- Because Motorola encouraged open challenges to established policy in the service of achieving better performance, the team was not – and was not perceived to be – "out of line" in questioning GEG's longstanding policy against supplier self-inspection. GEG's reorganization of the supply-management activity explicitly addressed the link between the division's performance and the performance of its suppliers. Indeed, its vision of "transforming the contributions of suppliers into the satisfaction of customers" grew out of a desire to replace adversarial relations with partner-like relations. Although the idea of self-inspection might have taken a bit of getting used to, it was perfectly in keeping with established values and aspirations that are the core of Motorola's "performance ethic."

Each of the separate decisions, approaches, and events that helped move the Connectors group from a potential team to a real team could happen in a company with a less robust performance ethic. But they are less likely to happen there. When mediocre performance is accepted and tolerated, groups are less likely to establish clear performance goals, managers appointed as team leaders are less likely to share decision-making control, groups are less likely to restructure themselves by removing jobs, and established policies on "the way we do things around here" are less likely to get challenged.

A place to begin

Concrete performance results – that's what teams are all about. When the goals of a team do not define specific results that are important to overall company goals, team accomplishments will rarely be very powerful. After all, performance challenges are what create real teams to begin with. If a strong performance ethic is lacking or if a company's overall goals are unclear or confused, teams either will not form or, if they do, will fall significantly short of their potential. In organizations like Motorola, it is the existence of a strong performance ethic that gives people both the confidence and the capability to figure out for themselves the best way to go after specific performance opportunities – and to convince themselves that results matter more than politics.

The opportunity to make a difference does that to people: it keeps them coming back for more even when experience cautions them to do otherwise

By contrast, potential teams in companies with a weak performance ethic will be much less certain about, or even indifferent to, performance. They will have far more difficulty agreeing on team basics and will be far less likely to pursue their tasks with confidence. Instead of looking squarely ahead at a job to get done, they will constantly be looking over their shoulders.

When real teams do emerge in such environments, the need to overcome strong obstacles tends to make them more resilient, more conspicuous – even more heroic. As a result, they can have a disproportionately positive influence on a company's performance ethic and on the environment for teams that follow them. Such teams are among the brightest hopes those organizations have for pulling themselves out of their stagnation.

Leaders even in companies like Cosmo can often make a major difference simply by identifying a few key performance challenges and getting potential teams to pursue them. Time and again, we have found that, despite the effects of a weak performance ethic, there are often plenty of unsung heros around who, if asked, will suspend their disbelief and try again. The opportunity to make a

WHY TEAMS MATTER

difference does that to people: it keeps them coming back for more even when experience cautions them to do otherwise.

But if leaders do not demand – and then relentlessly support – a fearless pursuit of performance by their teams, such efforts will produce nothing except more cynicism, more frustration, more risk aversion, and more "playing it safe." But if only one of these teams succeeds, the fact of its triumph can help an indifferent or confused company begin to clarify its direction and recover its sense of performance. For successful companies, as well as for those in trouble, this is why teams matter. Q

Jon Katzenbach, a Director in the New York office, works with companies in a broad range of industries on issues of top management leadership, organization, and management process, with a special focus on institutional performance and major change. *Doug Smith*, a Principal in the New York office, also works with companies in a variety of industries on organizational issues, especially as they relate to major change.

Part IV
The Human Resource Dimension in Strategic Planning Implementation

Mental Models

By Peter M. Senge

The discipline of managing mental models — surfacing, testing, and improving our internal pictures of how the world works — promises to be a major breakthrough for building learning organizations.

Experienced managers know that many of the best ideas never get put into practice. Brilliant strategies fail to get translated into action. Systemic insights never find their way into operating policies. A pilot experiment may prove to everyone's satisfaction that a new approach leads to better results, but widespread adoption of the approach never occurs.

I am increasingly convinced that this lack of implementation is not the result of poor management. Rather, the process of adoption fails because the new ideas are at such variance with mental models currently accepted by the organization. More specifically, new insights fail to get put into practice because they conflict with deeply held internal images of how the world works, images that limit us to familiar ways of thinking and acting. That is why the discipline of managing mental models—surfacing, testing, and improving our internal pictures of how the world works—promises to be a major breakthrough for building learning organizations.

None of us can carry all the complex details of our world in our minds. What we keep in our heads are images, assumptions, and stories. "The Emperor's New Clothes" is a classic story, not about fatuous people, but about people bound by mental models. Their image of the monarch's dignity kept them from seeing his naked figure as it was.

Mental models can be simple generalizations, such as "people are untrustworthy," or they can be complex theories. But what is most important to grasp is that mental models shape how we act. If we believe people are untrustworthy, we act differently from the way we would if we believed they were trustworthy.

Why do mental models so powerfully affect what we do? In part, this is because they affect what we see. Two people with different mental models can observe the same event and describe it differently because they've noticed different details.

The way mental models shape our perceptions is no less important in management. For decades, the Big Three of Detroit believed that people bought automobiles on the basis of styling, not for quality or reliability. Judging by the evidence they gathered, the auto makers were right. Surveys and buying habits consistently suggested that American consumers cared about styling much more than quality. These preferences gradually changed, however, as German and Japanese auto makers slowly educated American consumers to the benefits of both quality and style—and increased their share of the U.S. market from near zero in 1965 to 38 percent by 1986. According to management consultant Ian Mitroff, these beliefs about styling were part of a pervasive set of assumptions for success at General Motors:

• GM is in the business of making money, not cars.

• Cars are primarily status symbols; therefore, styling is more important than quality.

• The American car market is isolated from the rest of the world.

• Workers do not have an important impact on productivity or product quality.

• Everyone connected with the system has no need for more than a fragmented, compartmentalized understanding of the business.

As Mitroff pointed out, these principles had served the industry well for many years. But the auto industry treated these principles as "a magic formula for success for all time, when all it had found was a particular set of conditions . . . that were good for a limited time."

The problems with mental models lie not in whether they are right or wrong—by definition, all models are simplifications. The problems with mental models arise when the models are tacit—when they exist below the level of awareness. The Detroit auto makers didn't say, "We have a mental model that all people care about is styling." They said, "All people care about is styling." Because they remained unaware of their mental models, the models remained unexamined. Because they were unexamined, the models remained unchanged. As the world changed, a gap widened between Detroit's mental models and reality, leading to increasingly counterproductive actions.

As the Detroit auto makers demonstrated, entire industries can develop chronic misfits between mental models and reality. In some ways, close-knit industries are especially vulnerable because all the member companies look to each other for standards of best practice. Such outdated reinforcement of mental models occurred in many basic U.S. manufacturing industries, not just automobiles, throughout the 1960s and 1970s. Today, similar outdated mental models dominate many service industries, which still provide mediocre quality in the name of controlling costs.

Failure to appreciate mental models has undermined many efforts to foster systems thinking. In the late 1960s, a leading American industrial goods manufacturer—the largest in its industry—found itself losing market share. Hoping to analyze their situation, top executives sought help from an MIT team of "systems dynamics" specialists. Based on computer models, the team concluded that the firm's problems stemmed from the way its executives managed inventories and production. Because it cost so much to store its bulky, expensive products, production managers held inventories as low as possible and aggressively cut back production whenever orders turned down. The result was

---

Peter M. Senge is Director of the Systems Thinking and Organizational Learning Program at MIT's Sloan School of Management, and a founding partner of Innovation Associates in Framingham, Massachusetts. This article was adapted from Chapter 10 of his book, The Fifth Discipline: The Art and Practice of the Learning Organization *(New York: Doubleday/Currency, 1990).*

slow and unreliable delivery, even when production capacity was adequate. In fact, the team's computer simulations predicted that deliveries would lag further during business downturns than during booms—a prediction that ran counter to conventional wisdom, but which turned out to be true.

Impressed, the firm's top executives put into effect a new policy based on the analysts' recommendations. From now on, when orders fell, they would maintain production rates and try to improve delivery performance. During the 1970 recession, the experiment worked. Thanks to prompt deliveries and more repeat buying from satisfied customers, the firm's market share increased. The managers were so pleased that they set up their own systems group. But the new policies were never taken to heart, and the improvement proved temporary. During the ensuing business recovery, the managers stopped worrying about delivery service. Four years later, when the more severe OPEC-induced recession came, they went back to their original policy of dramatic production cutbacks.

Why discard such a successful experiment? The reason was the mental models deeply embedded in the firm's management traditions. Every production manager knew in his heart that there was no more sure-fire way to destroy his career than to be held responsible for stockpiling unsold goods in the warehouse. Generations of top management had preached the gospel of commitment to inventory control. Despite the new experiment, the old mental model was still alive and well.

The inertia of deeply entrenched models can overwhelm even the best systemic insights. This has been a bitter lesson for many a purveyor of new management tools, as well as for systems thinking advocates.

But if mental models can impede learning—freezing companies and industries in outmoded practices—why can't they also help accelerate learning? As it happens, several organizations, largely operating independently, have given serious attention to this question in recent years.

Incubating a New Business Worldview

Perhaps the first large corporation to discover the potential power of mental models in learning was Royal Dutch/Shell. Managing a highly decentralized company through the turbulence of the world oil business in the 1970s, Shell found that, by helping managers clarify their assumptions, uncover internal contradictions in those assumptions, and think through new strategies based on new assumptions, they gained a unique source of competitive advantage.

Shell is unique in several ways that have made it a natural environment for experimenting with mental models. It is truly multicultural, formed originally in 1907 from a "gentlemen's agreement" between Royal Dutch Petroleum and the London-based Shell Transport and Trading Company. Royal Dutch/Shell now has more than a hundred operating companies around the world, led by managers from almost as many different cultures.

The operating companies enjoy a high degree of autonomy and local independence. From the beginning, Shell managers had to learn to operate by consensus, because there was no way these "gentlemen" from different countries and cultures would be able to tell each other what to do. As Shell grew and became more global and more multicultural, its needs for building consensus across vast gulfs of style and understanding grew.

In the turbulent early 1970s, Shell's tradition of consensus management was stretched to the breaking point. What emerged was a new understanding of the underpinnings of real consensus—an understanding of shared mental models. "Unless we influenced the mental image, the picture of reality held by critical decision makers, our scenarios would be like water on a stone," recalled Shell's former senior planner

> *"In the 1970s Shell discovered that, by helping managers clarify their assumptions, discover internal contradictions in those assumptions, and think through new strategies based on new assumptions, they gained a unique source of competitive advantage."*

Pierre Wack, in his seminal *Harvard Business Review* articles about the firm's mental models. Wack had come to this realization in 1972, as he and his colleagues desperately faced their failure to convey to Shell's managers the "discontinuities" they foresaw in the world oil market. That was the year before OPEC and the onset of the energy crisis.

In principle, as the central planning department responsible for coordinating planning activities in operating companies worldwide, Shell's "Group Planning" staff was in an ideal position to disseminate insights about the changes ahead. At the time, Group Planning was developing a new technique called "scenario planning," a method for summarizing alternative future trends. However, as they began to build the coming discontinuities into their scenarios, their audience of Shell managers found these new scenarios so contradictory to their years of experience with predictable growth that they paid them little attention.

Wack and his colleagues now realized that they had fundamentally misperceived their task. Wack wrote that, from that moment, "We no longer saw our task as producing a documented view of the future.... Our real target was the 'microcosms' [Wack's term for mental models] of our decision makers.... We now wanted to design scenarios so that managers would question their own model of reality and change it when necessary." If the planners had once thought their job was delivering information to the decision makers, it was now clear that their task was to help managers rethink their world view. In particular, the Group Planners developed a new set of scenarios in January-February of 1973 that forced Shell's managers to identify all of the assumptions that had to be true in order for the managers' "trouble-free" future to occur. In the process, the managers realized that they were holding on to a set of assumptions only slightly more likely to come true than a fairy tale.

Group Planning now began building a new set of scenarios, carefully designed to take off from the current mental models of Shell managers. These scenarios demonstrated how the prevailing view that "the oil business would continue as usual" was based on outdated assumptions about the nature of global geopolitics and the oil industry. The scenarios next led the managers to a clear understanding that these assumptions could not possibly hold in the future that was coming.

The planners then helped the managers begin the process of constructing a new mental model by helping them think through how they would have to manage in this new world. For example, exploration for oil would have to expand to new countries, while refinery building would have to expand to new countries, while refinery building would have to slow down because of higher prices and consequently slower demand growth. Also, with greater instability, nations would respond differently. Some, with free-market traditions, would let the price rise freely; others with controlled-market policies, would try to keep it low. Thus, more control would have to be given to Shell's locally based operating companies to enable them to adapt to local conditions.

Although many Shell managers remained skeptical, they took the new scenarios seriously because they began to see that their present views were untenable. The scenario exercises had begun to unfreeze the managers' mental models, and this, in turn, allowed them to begin to incubate a new world view.

When the OPEC oil embargo suddenly became a reality in the winter of 1973-74, Shell responded differently from the other oil companies. They slowed down their investments in refineries, and redesigned refineries to adapt to whatever type of crude oil was available. They produced forecasts of energy demands consistently showing lower levels than their competitors did—and consistently more accurately. In addition, they quickly accelerated development of oil fields outside OPEC.

While competitors reined in their divisions and further centralized their control—a common response to the crisis—Shell did the opposite. This gave their operating companies more room to maneuver, while their competitors had less.

Shell's managers saw themselves entering a new era of supply shortages, lower growth, and price instability. Because they had come to expect the 1970s to be a decade of turbulence (Wack called it the decade of "the rapids"), they responded to the turbulence effectively. Shell had discovered the power of managing mental models.

The net result of Shell's efforts was nothing short of spectacular. In 1970, Shell had been considered the weakest of the seven largest oil companies. *Forbes* called it the "Ugly Sister" of the "Seven Sisters." By 1979, it was perhaps the strongest. Certainly Shell and Exxon were in a class by themselves. By the early 1980s, articulating managers' mental models had become an important part of the planning process at Shell. Six months before the collapse of oil prices in 1986, Shell's Group Planning, under the direction of coordinator Arie de Geus, produced a fictitious Harvard Business School-style case study of an oil company coping with a sudden world oil glut. Managers had to critique the oil company's decisions. Thus, once again, they prepared themselves mentally for a reality that the planners suspected they might have to face.

The Discipline of Mental Models

Developing an organization's capacity to work with mental models involves both learning new skills and implementing institutional innovations that help bring these skills into regular practice. First, key assumptions about important business issues must be defined. This goal, predominant at Shell, is vital to any company, because the most crucial mental models in any organization are those shared by key decision makers. Those models, if unexamined, limit an organization's range of actions to what is familiar and comfortable. Second, Shell had to develop face-to-face learning skills.

Both sides of the discipline—business skills and interpersonal issues—are crucial. On the one hand, managers are inherently pragmatic. They are most motivated to learn what they need to learn in their business context. Training them in mental modeling, or "balancing inquiry and advocacy" with no connection to pressing business issues, will often be rejected. Or, it will lead to people's acquiring "academic" skills they have no reason to use. On the other hand, without the interpersonal skills, learning is still fundamentally adaptive, not generative. Generative learning, in my experience, requires managers with reflection and inquiry skills, not just consultants and planners. Only then will people at all levels of a business be able to surface and challenge their mental models before external circumstances compel rethinking, which can often be too little, too late.

As more companies adopt these techniques, these two aspects of mental modeling will become increasingly integrated. In the meantime, based on the experience of Shell and other companies, we can begin to piece together the elements of an emerging discipline.

Managing Mental Models Throughout an Organization

Institutionalizing the process of reflecting on and surfacing mental models requires the development of mechanisms that make these practices unavoidable. Two emerging approaches involve recasting traditional planning as a learning mode by establishing "internal boards of directors" that bring senior management and local management together regularly to challenge and expand the thinking behind local decision making.

Once Shell's planners had recognized the importance of articulating mental models, they had to develop ways to foster that articulation in over a hundred independent operating companies. The need for global reach is one factor behind Shell's unique approach to mental models, which involves developing and testing a variety of different tools in Group Planning in London, then disseminating them. Eventually, local planners master these tools for use with local company operating managers.

Scenarios, the first tool Shell adapted in pursuit of mental models, force managers to consider how they would manage under different alternative paths into the future. This offsets the tendency for managers to implicitly assume a single future. When groups of managers share a range of alternative futures in their mental models, they become more perceptive of changes in the business environment and more responsive to those changes. These are exactly the advantages that Shell enjoyed over its competitors during the post-OPEC era.

Shell has institutionalized managing models through its planning process. Shell managers still generate traditional budget and control plans. But Arie de Geus and his colleagues have begun rethinking the role of planning in large institutions. It is less important, they have concluded, to produce perfect plans than to use planning to accelerate learning as a whole. Long-term success, according to De Geus, depends on "the process whereby management teams change their shared mental models of their company, their markets, and their competitors. For this reason we think of planning as learning, and of corporate planning as institutional learning." De Geus goes on to say that the critical question in planning is, "Can we accelerate institutional learning?"

Reflection and Inquiry Skills: Managing Mental Models at Personal and Interpersonal Levels

The learning skills needed to develop and manipulate mental models fall into two broad classes: Skills of reflection and skills of inquiry. Skills of reflection concern slowing down our own thinking processes so that we can become more aware of how we form our mental models and the ways they influence our actions. Inquiry skills concern how we operate in face-to-face interactions with others, especially in dealing with complex issues that could lead to conflict.

Skills of reflection begin with recognizing "leaps of abstraction."

Leaps of Abstraction. Our minds literally move at lightning speed. Ironically, this often slows our learning, because we immediately "leap" to generalizations so quickly that we never think to test them. The proverbial "castles in the sky" describes our own thinking far more often than we realize.

Leaps of abstraction are common with business issues. At one firm, many top managers were convinced that "Customers buy products based on price. The quality of service isn't a factor." And it's no wonder they felt that way—customers continually pressed for deeper discounts, and competitors were continually attracting customers away with price promotions. When one marketer who was new to the company urged his superiors to invest in improving service, he was turned down kindly but firmly. The senior leaders never tested the idea because their leap of abstraction—that customers don't care about service, they buy based on price"—had become a "fact." As a result, they sat and watched while their leading competitor steadily increased its market share by providing a level of service quality that customers had never experienced and had therefore never thought to ask for.

Among high-tech companies there is a common belief that being first to market is the key to success. While this generalization is often based on concrete experience, it can also be misleading. Released in 1982, the Apple III computer (an improved version of the Apple II) was an innovative product. However, it had so many bugs it turned off would-be customers, and the product turned out to be one of Apple's biggest disappointments. Yet, other computer manufacturers continue to rush products to market that were, if anything, even less ready. And some of those products were big winners, such as the Sun-3 workstation.

So, why does the generalization "first to market" stand up in some instances but not in others? Because the Sun-3's customers were sophisticated engineers who forgave bugs—in part because they could fix them themselves. The Apple III's largest market, consumers and business people, was much more unforgiving. They needed the new system to work the first time out and were easily intimidated by a power machine that had the reputation of unreliability—even though the bugs were fixed within a few months of being discovered.

How do you spot leaps of abstraction? First, by asking yourself what you believe about the way the world works—the nature of business, people in general, and specific individuals. First, ask: "What is the data on which this generalization is based?" Then ask yourself: "Am I willing to consider that this generalization may be inaccurate or misleading?" It's important to ask this last question consciously because, if the answer is no, there's no point in proceeding.

RECOGNIZING DISCONTINUITY

After analyzing long-term trends of oil production and consumption, Pierre Wack, former senior planner at Shell, concluded that the stable, predictable world familiar to Shell's managers was about to change. Europe, Japan, and the U.S. were becoming increasingly dependent on oil imports. Oil-exporting nations such as Iran, Iraq, Libya, and Venezuela were becoming increasingly concerned with falling reserves. Others, such as Saudi Arabia, were reaching the limits of their ability to productively invest oil revenues.

These trends meant that the historical, smooth growth in oil demand and supply would eventually give way to chronic supply shortfalls, excess demand, and a "seller's market" controlled by the oil-exporting nations. While Shell's planners didn't quite predict the emergence of OPEC, they did foresee the types of changes that an OPEC would eventually bring about. Yet, despite attempts to impress upon Shell's managers the likelihood of radical shifts ahead, "no more than a third of Shell's critical decision centers" acted upon the new insights.

If you're willing to question a generalization, your next step is to explicitly separate it from the data that led to its formation. For example, you might say: "Paul Smith, the purchaser for Bailey's Shoes, and several other customers have told me they won't buy our product unless we lower the price 10 percent. Thus, I conclude that our customers don't care about service quality." This puts all your cards on the table and gives you, and others, a better opportunity to consider alternative interpretations and courses of action.

Where possible, test the generalizations directly. This will often lead to inquiring into the reasons behind your own and other people's actions.

Balancing Inquiry and Advocacy. Most managers are trained to be advocates. In fact, in many companies, what it means to be a competent manager is the ability to solve problems—figuring out what needs to be done, and enlisting whatever support is needed to get it done. Individuals often become successful in part because of their abilities to debate forcefully and thus influence others. Meanwhile, inquiry skills go unrecognized and unrewarded.

But as managers rise to senior positions, they find themselves confronted with issues more complex and diverse than their personal experience has yet prepared them for. Suddenly, they need to tap the insights of other people. They find that they need to learn. Suddenly, the advocacy skills we developed as managers have become counterproductive. They can actually close us off from learning from one another. What is needed now is the flexibility to blend advocacy with inquiry in order to promote collaborative learning.

Even when two advocates meet for an open, candid exchange of views, quite often there is little learning taking place. While they may be genuinely interested in each other's views, the habit of pure advocacy lends a different type of structure to the conversation. For example:

"I appreciate your sincerity, but my experience and judgment lead me to some different conclusions. Let me tell you why your proposal won't work...."

As each side reasonably and calmly advocates his viewpoint just a bit more strongly, positions become more and more rigid. Advocacy without inquiry begets more advocacy. In fact, there is a systems archetype that describes what happens next. It's called "escalation," and it's exactly the same structure that fuels an arms race.

The more vehemently A argues, the greater the threat to B. Thus, B argues more fiercely. Then A counter argues even more fiercely. And so on. Managers often find escalations so grueling that, thereafter, they avoid stating any differences publicly. "It causes too much grief," they'll tell you.

The snowball effect of reinforcing advocacy can be stopped by beginning to ask a few simple questions, such as: "What is it that leads you to that position?" and "Can you illustrate your point for me?" [In other words, can you provide some data or experience in support of it?] This approach can interject an element of inquiry into what began as an advocacy proceeding.

We often tape record meetings of management teams with whom we are working to develop learning skills. One indicator that a team is in trouble is when few, if any, questions emerge during the course of a several hour meeting. This may seem amazing, but I have seen meetings that went for three hours without a single question being asked! You don't have to be an "action science" expert to know there's not a lot of inquiry going on in such meetings.

But pure inquiry is also limited. Questioning can be crucial for breaking the spiral of reinforcing advocacy, but until a team or an individual learns to combine and integrate both inquiry and advocacy skills, learning is very limited. One reason that pure inquiry is limited is that we almost always do have a view, regardless of whether or not we believe that our view is the only correct one. Thus, simply asking lots of questions can be a way of avoiding learning by hiding our own view behind a wall of incessant questioning.

The most productive learning usually occurs when managers combine skills in advocacy and inquiry. Another way to say this is "reciprocal inquiry." By this we mean that everyone makes his or her thinking explicit and subject to public examination. This creates an atmosphere of genuine vulnerability. No one is hiding the evidence or reasoning behind his views —advancing them without making them open to scrutiny. For example, when inquiry and advocacy are balanced, I would not only be inquiring into the reasoning behind others' views. I would also be stating my views in a way that both revealed my own assumptions and reasoning and invited others to inquire into them. For instance, I might say: "Here's what I think, and here's how I have arrived at it. How does it sound to you?"

When operating in pure advocacy, the goal is to win the argument. When inquiry and advocacy are combined, the goal is no longer winning, but rather finding the best argument. This balanced goal is reflected in how we use data, and in how we reveal the reasoning behind abstractions. For example, when we operate in pure advocacy, we tend to use data selectively, presenting only the data that confirm our position. When we explain the reasoning behind our position, we expose only enough of our reasoning to "make our case," avoiding areas where we feel it might be weak. By

> "What has become obvious on repeated occasions is that, when genuine inquiry and advocacy are present, creative outcomes are much more likely."

contrast, when both advocacy and inquiry are high, we are open to disconfirming data as well as confirming data—because we are genuinely interested in finding flaws in our views. Likewise, we expose our reasoning and look for flaws in it, and we try to understand others' reasoning.

The ideal of combining inquiry and advocacy is challenging. It can be especially difficult if you work in a highly political organization that is not open to genuine inquiry. Speaking as a veteran advocate, I can say that I have found patience and perseverance are needed to move toward a more balanced approach. Progress comes in stages. For me, the first stage was learning how to inquire into others' views when I found I didn't agree with them. My habitual response to such disagreements was to advocate my view harder. Usually, this was done not with malice but in the genuine belief that I had thought things through and had a valid position. Unfortunately, it often had the consequence of polarizing or terminating discussions, and left me without the sense of partnership I truly wanted. Now, very often I respond to differences of view by asking other people to say more about how they came to this view, or to expand further on it. (I'm only just beginning to get to the second stage where I'm able to state my views in such a way that I invite others to inquire into them as well.)

Though I'm still a novice in the discipline of balancing inquiry and advocacy, the rewards have been gratifying. What has become obvious on repeated occasions is that, when genuine inquiry and advocacy are present, creative outcomes are much more likely. In a sense, when two people operate in pure advocacy, the outcomes are predetermined. Either person A will win, or person B will win, or both will simply retain their views. But when there is inquiry and advocacy, these limitations dissolve. By being open to inquire into their own views, A and B create an atmosphere in which it is possible to blend views and even to come up with completely new views.

While mastering the discipline of balancing inquiry and advocacy, I've found that it helps to keep the following guidelines in mind:

When advocating your view:
- Make your own reasoning explicit (that is, say how you arrived at your view and the data upon which it is based).
- Encourage others to explore your view (for example, "Do you see gaps in my reasoning?")
- Encourage others to provide different views ("Do you have either different data or different conclusions, or both?")
- Actively inquire into others' views that differ from your own ("What are your views?" "How did you arrive at your view?" "Are you taking into account data that are different from what I have considered? If so, could you tell me what they are?")

When inquiring into others' views:
- If you are making assumptions about others' views, state your assumptions clearly and acknowledge that they are assumptions.
- State the data upon which your assumptions are based.
- Don't bother asking questions if you're not genuinely interested in the others' response (that is, if you're only trying to be polite or to show the other person up).

When you arrive at an impasse (other people no longer appear to be open to inquiring into their own views):
- Ask what data or logic might change their views.
- Ask if there is any way that together you might be able to design an experiment (or some other inquiry) that could provide new information.

When you or others are hesitant to express your views or to experiment with alternative ideas:
- Encourage others (or yourself) to think out loud about what might be causing the difficulties ("What is it about this situation, and/or about me or others, that is making open exchange difficult?")
- If there is mutual desire to do so, work with others to design innovative ways of overcoming these barriers.

The point is not to follow such guidelines slavishly, but to use them to keep in mind the spirit of balancing inquiry and advocacy. Like any formula for starting on one of the learning disciplines, they should be used as "training wheels" on your first bicycle. They help to get you started, and to give you a feel for what it's like to ride—to practice inquiry with advocacy. As you gain skill, these formulas can and probably should be discarded. But it's nice to be able to come back
Continued on page 44.

MENTAL MODELS, *from page 10.*

to them periodically when you encounter some rough terrain.

However, it is important to keep in mind that guidelines will be of little use if you are not genuinely curious and willing to change your mental model of a situation. In other words, the true practice of inquiry and advocacy means being willing to expose the limitations in your own thinking—the willingness to be wrong. Nothing less will make it safe for others to do likewise.

Espoused Theory Versus Theory-in-Use. Learning eventually results in changes in action, not just taking in new information and forming new ideas." That's why recognizing the gap between our espoused theories (what we say) and our "theories-in-use" (the theories that underlie our actions) is vital. Otherwise, we may believe we've learned something because we've got the new language or concepts to use, although our behavior may be completely unchanged.

For example, I may profess a view (an espoused theory) that people are basically trustworthy. On the other hand, in my daily life I may never lend friends money, and jealously guard all my possessions. Obviously, my theory-in-use—my deeper mental model—differs from my espoused theory.

While gaps between espoused theories and theories-in-use might be cause for discouragement, or even cynicism, they needn't be. Often they arise as a consequence of vision, not hypocrisy. For example, it may be truly part of my vision to trust people. If so, the gap between this aspect of my vision and my current behavior holds the potential for creative change. The problem lies not in the gap but in failing to recognize and tell the truth about the gap. Until the gap between my espoused theory and my current behavior surfaces consciously, no learning can occur.

So the first question to pose when facing a gap between espoused theory and theory-in-use is: "Do I really value the espoused theory?" "Is it really part of my vision?" If there is no commitment to the espoused theory, then the gap does not represent a tension between reality and my vision. Rather, it may be a view I simply say I espouse, perhaps because of how it will make me look to others.

Because it's so hard to see theories-in-use, we often need the help of another person—a "ruthlessly compassionate" partner. In the quest to develop skills in reflection, we are each others' greatest assets. ☐

[23]

The Leader's New Work: Building Learning Organizations

Peter M. Senge   MIT Sloan School of Management

OVER THE PAST two years, business academics and senior managers have begun talking about the notion of the learning organization. Ray Stata of Analog Devices put the idea succinctly in these pages last spring: "The rate at which organizations learn may become the only sustainable source of competitive advantage." And in late May of this year, at an MIT-sponsored conference entitled "Transforming Organizations," two questions arose again and again: *How can we build organizations in which continuous learning occurs?* and, *What kind of person can best lead the learning organization?* This article, based on Senge's recently published book, *The Fifth Discipline: The Art and Practice of the Learning Organization*, begins to chart this new territory, describing new roles, skills, and tools for leaders who wish to develop learning organizations.

Sloan Management Review

Fall 1990

HUMAN BEINGS are designed for learning. No one has to teach an infant to walk, or talk, or master the spatial relationships needed to stack eight building blocks that don't topple. Children come fully equipped with an insatiable drive to explore and experiment. Unfortunately, the primary institutions of our society are oriented predominantly toward controlling rather than learning, rewarding individuals for performing for others rather than for cultivating their natural curiosity and impulse to learn. The young child entering school discovers quickly that the name of the game is getting the right answer and avoiding mistakes – a mandate no less compelling for the aspiring manager.

"Our prevailing system of management has destroyed our people," writes W. Edwards Deming, leader in the quality movement.[1] "People are born with intrinsic motivation, self-esteem, dignity, curiosity to learn, joy in learning. The forces of destruction begin with toddlers – a prize for the best Halloween costume, grades in school, gold stars, and on up through the university. On the job, people, teams, divisions are ranked – reward for the one at the top, punishment at the bottom. MBO, quotas, incentive pay, business plans, put together separately, division by division, cause further loss, unknown and unknowable."

Peter M. Senge is Director of the Systems Thinking and Organizational Learning program at the MIT Sloan School of Management.

Ironically, by focusing on performing for someone else's approval, corporations create the very conditions that predestine them to mediocre performance. Over the long run, superior performance depends on superior learning. A Shell study showed that, according to former planning director Arie de Geus, "a full one-third of the Fortune '500' industrials listed in 1970 had vanished by 1983."[2] Today, the average lifetime of the largest industrial enterprises is probably less than *half* the average lifetime of a person in an industrial society. On the other hand, de Geus and his colleagues at Shell also found a small number of companies that survived for seventy-five years or longer. Interestingly, the key to their survival was the ability to run "experiments in the margin," to continually explore new business and organizational opportunities that create potential new sources of growth.

If anything, the need for understanding how organizations learn and accelerating that learning is greater today than ever before. The old days when a Henry Ford, Alfred Sloan, or Tom Watson *learned for the organization* are gone. In an increasingly dynamic, interdependent, and unpredictable world, it is simply no longer possible for anyone to "figure it all out at the top." The old model, "the top thinks and the local acts," must now give way to integrating thinking and acting at all levels. While the challenge is great, so is the potential payoff. "The person who figures out how to harness the collective genius of the people in his or her organization," according to former Citibank CEO Walter Wriston, "is going to blow the competition away."

Adaptive Learning and Generative Learning

The prevailing view of learning organizations emphasizes increased adaptability. Given the accelerating pace of change, or so the standard view goes, "the most successful corporation of the 1990s," according to *Fortune* magazine, "will be something called a learning organization, a consummately adaptive enterprise."[3] As the Shell study shows, examples of traditional authoritarian bureaucracies that responded too slowly to survive in changing business environments are legion.

But increasing adaptiveness is only the first stage in moving toward learning organizations. The impulse to learn in children goes deeper than desires to respond and adapt more effectively to environmental change. The impulse to learn, at its heart, is an impulse to be generative, to expand our capability. This is why leading corporations are focusing on *generative* learning, which is about creating, as well as *adaptive* learning, which is about coping.[4]

The total quality movement in Japan illustrates the evolution from adaptive to generative learning. With its emphasis on continuous experimentation and feedback, the total quality movement has been the first wave in building learning organizations. But Japanese firms' view of serving the customer has evolved. In the early years of total quality, the focus was on "fitness to standard," making a product reliably so that it would do what its designers intended it to do and what the firm told its customers it would do. Then came a focus on "fitness to need," understanding better what the customer wanted and then providing products that reliably met those needs. Today, leading edge firms seek to understand and meet the "latent need" of the customer — what customers might truly value but have never experienced or would never think to ask for. As one Detroit executive commented recently, "You could never produce the Mazda Miata solely from market research. It required a leap of imagination to see what the customer *might* want."[5]

Generative learning, unlike adaptive learning, requires new ways of looking at the world, whether in understanding customers or in understanding how to better manage a business. For years, U.S. manufacturers sought competitive advantage in aggressive controls on inventories, incentives against overproduction, and rigid adherence to production forecasts. Despite these incentives, their performance was eventually eclipsed by Japanese firms who saw the challenges of manufacturing differently. They realized that eliminating delays in the production process was the key to reducing instability and improving cost, productivity, and service. They worked to build networks of relationships with trusted suppliers and to redesign physical production processes so as to reduce delays in materials procurement, production set up, and in-process inventory — a much higher-leverage approach to improving both cost and customer loyalty.

As Boston Consulting Group's George Stalk has observed, the Japanese saw the significance of delays because they saw the process of order entry, production scheduling, materials procurement, production, and distribution *as an integrated system*. "What distorts the system so badly is time," observed Stalk — the multiple delays between events and responses. "These distortions reverberate throughout the system, producing disruptions, waste, and inefficiency."[6] Generative learning requires seeing the systems that control events. When we fail to grasp the systemic source of problems, we are left to "push on" symptoms rather than eliminate underlying causes. The best we can ever do is adaptive learning.

The Leader's New Work

"I talk with people all over the country about learning organizations, and the response is always very positive," says William O'Brien, CEO of the Hanover Insurance companies. "If this type of organization is so widely preferred, why don't people create such organizations? I think the answer is leadership. People have no real comprehension of the type of commitment it requires to build such an organization."[7]

Our traditional view of leaders — as special people who set the direction, make the key decisions, and energize the troops — is deeply rooted in an individualistic and nonsystemic worldview. Especially in the West, leaders are *heroes* — great men (and occasionally women) who rise to the fore in times of crisis. So long as such myths prevail, they reinforce a focus on short-term events and charismatic heroes rather than on systemic forces and collective learning.

Leadership in learning organizations centers on subtler and ultimately more important work. In a learning organization, leaders' roles differ dramatically from that of the charismatic decision maker. Leaders are designers, teachers, and stewards. These roles require new skills: the ability to build shared vision, to bring to the surface and challenge prevailing mental models, and to foster more systemic patterns of thinking. In short, leaders in learning organizations are responsible for *building organizations* where people are continually expanding their capabilities to shape their future—that is, leaders are responsible for learning.

Creative Tension: The Integrating Principle

Leadership in a learning organization starts with the principle of creative tension.[8] Creative tension comes from seeing clearly where we want to be, our "vision," and telling the truth about where we are, our "current reality." The gap between the two generates a natural tension (see Figure 1).

Creative tension can be resolved in two basic ways: by raising current reality toward the vision, or by lowering the vision toward current reality. Individuals, groups, and organizations who learn how to work with creative tension learn how to use the energy it generates to move reality more reliably toward their visions.

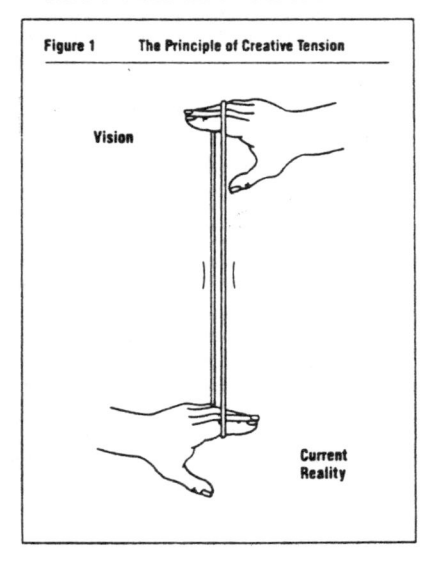

The principle of creative tension has long been recognized by leaders. Martin Luther King, Jr., once said, "Just as Socrates felt that it was necessary to create a tension in the mind, so that individuals could rise from the bondage of myths and half truths ... so must we ... create the kind of tension in society that will help men rise from the dark depths of prejudice and racism."[9]

Without vision there is no creative tension. Creative tension cannot be generated from current reality alone. All the analysis in the world will never generate a vision. Many who are otherwise qualified to lead fail to do so because they try to substitute analysis for vision. They believe that, if only people understood current reality, they would surely feel the motivation to change. They are then disappointed to discover that people "resist" the personal and organizational changes that must be made to alter reality. What they never grasp is that the natural energy for changing reality comes from holding a picture of what might be that is more important to people than what is.

But creative tension cannot be generated from vision alone; it demands an accurate picture of current reality as well. Just as King had a dream, so too did he continually strive to "dramatize the shameful conditions" of racism and prejudice so that they could no longer be ignored. Vision without an understanding of current reality will more likely foster cynicism than creativity. The principle of creative tension teaches that *an accurate picture of current reality is just as important as a compelling picture of a desired future*.

Leading through creative tension is different than solving problems. In problem solving, the energy for change comes from attempting to get away from an aspect of current reality that is undesirable. With creative tension, the energy for change comes from the vision, from what we want to create, juxtaposed with current reality. While the distinction may seem small, the consequences are not. Many people and organizations find themselves motivated to change only when their problems are bad enough to cause them to change. This works for a while, but the change process runs out of steam as soon

Figure 1   The Principle of Creative Tension

Vision

Current Reality

Sloan Management Review

9

Fall 1990

as the problems driving the change become less pressing. With problem solving, the motivation for change is extrinsic. With creative tension, the motivation is intrinsic. This distinction mirrors the distinction between adaptive and generative learning.

New Roles

The traditional authoritarian image of the leader as "the boss calling the shots" has been recognized as oversimplified and inadequate for some time. According to Edgar Schein, "Leadership is intertwined with culture formation." Building an organization's culture and shaping its evolution is the "unique and essential function" of leadership.[10] In a learning organization, the critical roles of leadership—designer, teacher, and steward—have antecedents in the ways leaders have contributed to building organizations in the past. But each role takes on new meaning in the learning organization and, as will be seen in the following sections, demands new skills and tools.

Leader as Designer

Imagine that your organization is an ocean liner and that you are "the leader." What is your role?

I have asked this question of groups of managers many times. The most common answer, not surprisingly, is "the captain." Others say, "The navigator, setting the direction." Still others say, "The helmsman, actually controlling the direction," or, "The engineer down there stoking the fire, providing energy," or, "The social director, making sure everybody's enrolled, involved, and communicating." While these are legitimate leadership roles, there is another which, in many ways, eclipses them all in importance. Yet rarely does anyone mention it.

The neglected leadership role is the *designer* of the ship. No one has a more sweeping influence than the designer. What good does it do for the captain to say, "Turn starboard 30 degrees," when the designer has built a rudder that will only turn to port, or which takes six hours to turn to starboard? It's fruitless to be the leader in an organization that is poorly designed.

The functions of design, or what some have called "social architecture," are rarely visible; they take place behind the scenes. The consequences that appear today are the result of work done long in the past, and work today will show its benefits far in the future. Those who aspire to lead out of a desire to control, or gain fame, or simply to be at the center of the action, will find little to attract them to the quiet design work of leadership.

But what, specifically, is involved in organizational design? "Organization design is widely misconstrued as moving around boxes and lines," says Hanover's O'Brien. "The first task of organization design concerns designing the governing ideas of purpose, vision, and core values by which people will live." Few acts of leadership have a more enduring impact on an organization than building a foundation of purpose and core values.

In 1982, Johnson & Johnson found itself facing a corporate nightmare when bottles of its best-selling Tylenol were tampered with, resulting in several deaths. The corporation's immediate response was to pull all Tylenol off the shelves of retail outlets. Thirty-one million capsules were destroyed, even though they were tested and found safe. Although the immediate cost was significant, no other action was possible given the firm's credo. Authored almost forty years earlier by president Robert Wood Johnson, Johnson & Johnson's credo states that permanent success is possible only when modern industry realizes that:

- service to its customers comes first;
- service to its employees and management comes second;
- service to the community comes third; and
- service to its stockholders, last.

Such statements might seem like motherhood and apple pie to those who have not seen the way a clear sense of purpose and values can affect key business decisions. Johnson & Johnson's crisis management in this case was based on that credo. It was simple, it was right, and it worked.

If governing ideas constitute the first design task of leadership, the second design task involves the policies, strategies, and structures that translate guiding ideas into business decisions. Leadership theorist Philip Selznick calls policy and structure the "institutional embodiment of purpose."[11] "Policy making (the rules that guide decisions) ought to be separated from decision making," says Jay Forrester.[12] "Otherwise, short-term pressures will usurp time from policy creation."

Traditionally, writers like Selznick and Forrester have tended to see policy making and implementation as the work of a small number of senior managers. But that view is changing. Both the dynamic business environment and the mandate of the learning organization to engage people at all levels now make it clear that this second design task is more subtle. Henry Mintzberg has argued that strategy is less a rational plan arrived at in the abstract and implemented throughout the organization than an "emergent phenomenon." Successful organizations "craft strategy" according to Mintzberg, as they continually learn about shifting business conditions and balance what is desired and what is possible.[13] The key is not getting the right strategy but fostering strategic thinking. "The choice of individual action is only part of . . . the policymaker's need," according to Mason and Mitroff.[14] "More important is the need to achieve insight into the nature of the complexity and to formulate concepts and world views for coping with it."

Behind appropriate policies, strategies, and structures are effective learning processes; their creation is the third key design responsibility in learning organizations. This does not absolve senior managers of their strategic responsibilities. Actually, it deepens and extends those responsibilities. Now, they are not only responsible for ensuring that an organization have well-developed strategies and policies, but also for ensuring that processes exist whereby these are continually improved.

In the early 1970s, Shell was the weakest of the big seven oil companies. Today, Shell and Exxon are arguably the strongest, both in size and financial health. Shell's ascendance began with frustration. Around 1971 members of Shell's "Group Planning" in London began to foresee dramatic change and unpredictability in world oil markets. However, it proved impossible to persuade managers that the stable world of steady growth in oil demand and supply they had known for twenty years was about to change. Despite brilliant analysis and artful presentation, Shell's planners realized, in the words of Pierre Wack, that they "had failed to change behavior in much of the Shell organization."[15] Progress would probably have ended there, had the frustration not given way to a radically new view of corporate planning.

As they pondered this failure, the planners' view of their basic task shifted: "We no longer saw our task as producing a documented view of the future business environment five or ten years ahead. Our real target was the microcosm (the 'mental model') of our decision makers." Only when the planners reconceptualized their basic task as fostering learning rather than devising plans did their insights begin to have an impact. The initial tool used was "scenario analysis," through which planners encouraged operating managers to think through how they would manage in the future under different possible scenarios. It mattered not that the managers believed the planners' scenarios absolutely, only that they became engaged in ferreting out the implications. In this way, Shell's planners conditioned managers to be mentally prepared for a shift from low prices to high prices and from stability to instability. The results were significant. When OPEC became a reality, Shell quickly responded by increasing local operating company control (to enhance maneuverability in the new political environment), building buffer stocks, and accelerating development of non-OPEC sources—actions that its competitors took much more slowly or not at all.

Somewhat inadvertently, Shell planners had discovered the leverage of designing institutional learning processes, whereby, in the words of former planning director de Geus, "Management teams change their shared mental models of their company, their markets, and their competitors."[16] Since then, "planning as learning" has become a byword at Shell, and Group Planning has continually sought out new learning tools that can be integrated into the planning process. Some of these are described below.

Leader as Teacher

"The first responsibility of a leader," writes retired Herman Miller CEO Max de Pree, "is to define reality."[17] Much of the leverage leaders can actually exert lies in helping people achieve more accurate, more insightful, and more *empowering* views of reality.

Leader as teacher does *not* mean leader as authoritarian expert whose job it is to teach people the "correct" view of reality. Rather, it is about helping everyone in the organization, oneself included, to gain more insightful views of current reality. This is in line with a popular emerging view of leaders as coaches, guides, or facilitators.[18] In learning organizations, this teaching role is developed further by virtue of explicit attention to people's mental models and by the influence of the systems perspective.

The role of leader as teacher starts with bringing to the surface people's mental models of important issues. No one carries an organization, a market, or a state of technology in his or her head.

Sloan Management Review

11

Fall 1990

Learning Organizations

12

Senge

What we carry in our heads are assumptions. These mental pictures of how the world works have a significant influence on how we perceive problems and opportunities, identify courses of action, and make choices.

One reason that mental models are so deeply entrenched is that they are largely tacit. Ian Mitroff, in his study of General Motors, argues that an assumption that prevailed for years was that, in the United States, "Cars are status symbols. Styling is therefore more important than quality."[19] The Detroit automakers didn't say, "We have a *mental model* that all people care about is styling." Few actual managers would even say publicly that all people care about is styling. So long as the view remained unexpressed, there was little possibility of challenging its validity or forming more accurate assumptions.

But working with mental models goes beyond revealing hidden assumptions. "Reality," as perceived by most people in most organizations, means pressures that must be borne, crises that must be reacted to, and limitations that must be accepted. Leaders as teachers help people *restructure their views of reality* to see beyond the superficial conditions and events into the underlying causes of problems—and therefore to see new possibilities for shaping the future.

Specifically, leaders can influence people to view reality at three distinct levels: events, patterns of behavior, and systemic structure.

Systemic Structure
(Generative)
↓
Patterns of Behavior
(Responsive)
↓
Events
(Reactive)

The key question becomes *where do leaders predominantly focus their own and their organization's attention?*

Contemporary society focuses predominantly on events. The media reinforces this perspective, with almost exclusive attention to short-term, dramatic events. This focus leads naturally to explaining what happens in terms of those events: "The Dow Jones average went up sixteen points because high fourth-quarter profits were announced yesterday."

Pattern-of-behavior explanations are rarer, in contemporary culture, than event explanations, but they do occur. "Trend analysis" is an example of seeing patterns of behavior. A good editorial that interprets a set of current events in the context of long-term historical changes is another example. Systemic, structural explanations go even further by addressing the question, "What causes the patterns of behavior?"

In some sense, all three levels of explanation are equally true. But their usefulness is quite different. Event explanations—who did what to whom—doom their holders to a reactive stance toward change. Pattern-of-behavior explanations focus on identifying long-term trends and assessing their implications. They at least suggest how, over time, we can respond to shifting conditions. Structural explanations are the most powerful. Only they address the underlying causes of behavior at a level such that patterns of behavior can be changed.

By and large, leaders of our current institutions focus their attention on events and patterns of behavior, and, under their influence, their organizations do likewise. That is why contemporary organizations are predominantly reactive, or at best responsive—rarely generative. On the other hand, leaders in learning organizations pay attention to all three levels, but focus especially on systemic structure; largely by example, they teach people throughout the organization to do likewise.

Leader as Steward

This is the subtlest role of leadership. Unlike the roles of designer and teacher, it is almost solely a matter of attitude. It is an attitude critical to learning organizations.

While stewardship has long been recognized as an aspect of leadership, its source is still not widely understood. I believe Robert Greenleaf came closest to explaining real stewardship, in his seminal book *Servant Leadership*.[20] There, Greenleaf argues that "The servant leader *is* servant first. . . . It begins with the natural feeling that one wants to serve, to serve *first*. This conscious choice brings one to aspire to lead. That person is sharply different from one who is leader first, perhaps because of the need to assuage an unusual power drive or to acquire material possessions."

Leaders' sense of stewardship operates on two levels: stewardship for the people they lead and stewardship for the larger purpose or mission that underlies the enterprise. The first type arises from a keen appreciation of the impact one's leadership can have on others. People can suffer economically, emotionally, and spiritually under inept leadership. If anything, people in a learning organization are more vulnerable because of their commitment and sense of shared ownership. Appreciating this naturally instills a sense of responsibility in leaders. The second type of stewardship arises from a leader's sense of personal purpose and commitment to the organization's larger mission. People's natural impulse to learn is unleashed when they are engaged in an endeavor they consider worthy of their fullest commitment. Or, as Lawrence Miller puts it, "Achieving return on equity does not, as a goal, mobilize the most noble forces of our soul."[21]

Leaders engaged in building learning organizations naturally feel part of a larger purpose that goes beyond their organization. They are part of changing the way businesses operate, not from a vague philanthropic urge, but from a conviction that their efforts will produce more productive organizations, capable of achieving higher levels of organizational success and personal satisfaction than more traditional organizations. Their sense of stewardship was succinctly captured by George Bernard Shaw when he said,

> This is the true joy in life, the being used for a purpose you consider a mighty one, the being a force of nature rather than a feverish, selfish clod of ailments and grievances complaining that the world will not devote itself to making you happy.

New Skills

New leadership roles require new leadership skills. These skills can only be developed, in my judgment, through a lifelong commitment. It is not enough for one or two individuals to develop these skills. They must be distributed widely throughout the organization. This is one reason that understanding the *disciplines* of a learning organization is so important. These disciplines embody the principles and practices that can widely foster leadership development.

Three critical areas of skills (disciplines) are building shared vision, surfacing and challenging mental models, and engaging in systems thinking.[22]

Building Shared Vision

How do individual visions come together to create shared visions? A useful metaphor is the hologram, the three-dimensional image created by interacting light sources.

If you cut a photograph in half, each half shows only part of the whole image. But if you divide a hologram, each part, no matter how small, shows the whole image intact. Likewise, when a group of people come to share a vision for an organization, each person sees an individual picture of the organization at its best. Each shares responsibility for the whole, not just for one piece. But the component pieces of the hologram are not identical. Each represents the whole image from a different point of view. It's something like poking holes in a window shade; each hole offers a unique angle for viewing the whole image. So, too, is each individual's vision unique.

When you add up the pieces of a hologram, something interesting happens. The image becomes more intense, more lifelike. When more people come to share a vision, the vision becomes more real in the sense of a mental reality that people can truly imagine achieving. They now have partners, co-creators; the vision no longer rests on their shoulders alone. Early on, when they are nurturing an individual vision, people may say it is "my vision." But, as the shared vision develops, it becomes both "my vision" and "our vision."

The skills involved in building shared vision include the following:
- **Encouraging Personal Vision.** Shared visions emerge from personal visions. It is not that people only care about their own self-interest—in fact, people's values usually include dimensions that concern family, organization, community, and even the world. Rather, it is that people's capacity for caring is *personal*.
- **Communicating and Asking for Support.** Leaders must be willing to continually share their own vision, rather than being the official representative of the corporate vision. They also must be prepared to ask, "Is this vision worthy of your commitment?" This can be difficult for a person used to setting goals and presuming compliance.
- **Visioning as an Ongoing Process.** Building shared vision is a never-ending process. At any one point there will be a particular image of the future that is predominant, but that image will evolve. Today, too many managers want to dispense with the "vision business" by going off and writing the Official Vision Statement. Such statements almost always lack the vitality, freshness, and excitement

of a genuine vision that comes from people asking, "What do we really want to achieve?"

- **Blending Extrinsic and Intrinsic Visions.** Many energizing visions are extrinsic—that is, they focus on achieving something relative to an outsider, such as a competitor. But a goal that is limited to defeating an opponent can, once the vision is achieved, easily become a defensive posture. In contrast, intrinsic goals like creating a new type of product, taking an established product to a new level, or setting a new standard for customer satisfaction can call forth a new level of creativity and innovation. Intrinsic and extrinsic visions need to coexist; a vision solely predicated on defeating an adversary will eventually weaken an organization.
- **Distinguishing Positive from Negative Visions.** Many organizations only truly pull together when their survival is threatened. Similarly, most social movements aim at eliminating what people don't want: for example, anti-drugs, anti-smoking, or anti-nuclear arms movements. Negative visions carry a subtle message of powerlessness: people will only pull together when there is sufficient threat. Negative visions also tend to be short term. Two fundamental sources of energy can motivate organizations: fear and aspiration. Fear, the energy source behind negative visions, can produce extraordinary changes in short periods, but aspiration endures as a continuing source of learning and growth.

Surfacing and Testing Mental Models

Many of the best ideas in organizations never get put into practice. One reason is that new insights and initiatives often conflict with established mental models. The leadership task of challenging assumptions without invoking defensiveness requires reflection and inquiry skills possessed by few leaders in traditional controlling organizations.[23]

- **Seeing Leaps of Abstraction.** Our minds literally move at lightning speed. Ironically, this often slows our learning, because we leap to generalizations so quickly that we never think to test them. We then confuse our generalizations with the observable data upon which they are based, treating the generalizations *as if they were data*. The frustrated sales rep reports to the home office that "customers don't really care about quality, price is what matters," when what actually happened was that three consecutive large customers refused to place an order unless a larger discount was offered. The sales rep treats her generalization, "customers care only about price," as if it were absolute fact rather than an assumption (very likely an assumption reflecting her own views of customers and the market). This thwarts future learning because she starts to focus on how to offer attractive discounts rather than probing behind the customers' statements. For example, the customers may have been so disgruntled with the firm's delivery or customer service that they are unwilling to purchase again without larger discounts.
- **Balancing Inquiry and Advocacy.** Most managers are skilled at articulating their views and presenting them persuasively. While important, advocacy skills can become counterproductive as managers rise in responsibility and confront increasingly complex issues that require collaborative learning among different, equally knowledgeable people. Leaders in learning organizations need to have both inquiry *and* advocacy skills.[24]

Specifically, when advocating a view, they need to be able to:

—explain the reasoning and data that led to their view;

—encourage others to test their view (e.g., Do you see gaps in my reasoning? Do you disagree with the data upon which my view is based?); and

—encourage others to provide different views (e.g., Do you have either different data, different conclusions, or both?).

When inquiring into another's views, they need to:

—actively seek to understand the other's view, rather than simply restating their own view and how it differs from the other's view; and

—make their attributions about the other and the other's view explicit (e.g., Based on your statement that . . . ; I am assuming that you believe . . . ; Am I representing your views fairly?).

If they reach an impasse (others no longer appear open to inquiry), they need to:

—ask what data or logic might unfreeze the impasse, or if an experiment (or some other inquiry) might be designed to provide new information.

- **Distinguishing Espoused Theory from Theory in Use.** We all like to think that we hold certain views, but often our actions reveal deeper views. For example, I may proclaim that people are trustworthy, but never lend friends money and jealously guard my possessions. Obviously, my deeper mental model (my theory in use), differs from my espoused theory. Recognizing gaps between espoused views and theories in use (which often requires the help of others) can be pivotal to deeper learning.

• **Recognizing and Defusing Defensive Routines.** As one CEO in our research program puts it, "Nobody ever talks about an issue at the 8:00 business meeting exactly the same way they talk about it at home that evening or over drinks at the end of the day." The reason is what Chris Argyris calls "defensive routines," entrenched habits used to protect ourselves from the embarrassment and threat that come with exposing our thinking. For most of us, such defenses began to build early in life in response to pressures to have the right answers in school or at home. Organizations add new levels of performance anxiety and thereby amplify and exacerbate this defensiveness. Ironically, this makes it even more difficult to expose hidden mental models, and thereby lessens learning.

The first challenge is to recognize defensive routines, then to inquire into their operation. Those who are best at revealing and defusing defensive routines operate with a high degree of self-disclosure regarding their own defensiveness (e.g., I notice that I am feeling uneasy about how this conversation is going. Perhaps I don't understand it or it is threatening to me in ways I don't yet see. Can you help me see this better?)

Systems Thinking

We all know that leaders should help people see the big picture. But the actual skills whereby leaders are supposed to achieve this are not well understood. In my experience, successful leaders often *are* "systems thinkers" to a considerable extent. They focus less on day-to-day events and more on underlying trends and forces of change. But they do this almost completely intuitively. The consequence is that they are often unable to explain their intuitions to others and feel frustrated that others cannot see the world the way they do.

One of the most significant developments in management science today is the gradual coalescence of managerial systems thinking as a field of study and practice. This field suggests some key skills for future leaders:

• **Seeing Interrelationships, Not Things, and Processes, Not Snapshots.** Most of us have been conditioned throughout our lives to focus on things and to see the world in static images. This leads us to linear explanations of systemic phenomenon. For instance, in an arms race each party is convinced that the other is *the cause* of problems. They react to each new move as an isolated event, not as part of a process. So long as they fail to see the interrelationships of these actions, they are trapped.

• **Moving beyond Blame.** We tend to blame each other or outside circumstances for our problems. But it is poorly designed systems, not incompetent or unmotivated individuals, that cause most organizational problems. Systems thinking shows us that there is no outside – that you and the cause of your problems are part of a single system.

• **Distinguishing Detail Complexity from Dynamic Complexity.** Some types of complexity are more important strategically than others. Detail complexity arises when there are many variables. Dynamic complexity arises when cause and effect are distant in time and space, and when the consequences over time of interventions are subtle and not obvious to many participants in the system. The leverage in most management situations lies in understanding dynamic complexity, not detail complexity.

• **Focusing on Areas of High Leverage.** Some have called systems thinking the "new dismal science" because it teaches that most obvious solutions don't work – at best, they improve matters in the short run, only to make things worse in the long run. But there is another side to the story. Systems thinking also shows that small, well-focused actions can produce significant, enduring improvements, if they are in the right place. Systems thinkers refer to this idea as the principle of "leverage." Tackling a difficult problem is often a matter of seeing where the high leverage lies, where a change – with a minimum of effort – would lead to lasting, significant improvement.

• **Avoiding Symptomatic Solutions.** The pressures to intervene in management systems that are going awry can be overwhelming. Unfortunately, given the linear thinking that predominates in most organizations, interventions usually focus on symptomatic fixes, not underlying causes. This results in only temporary relief, and it tends to create still more pressures later on for further, low-leverage intervention. If leaders acquiesce to these pressures, they can be sucked into an endless spiral of increasing intervention. Sometimes the most difficult leadership acts are to refrain from intervening through popular quick fixes and to keep the pressure on everyone to identify more enduring solutions.

While leaders who can articulate systemic ex-

Learning Organizations

16

Senge

planations are rare, those who *can* will leave their stamp on an organization. One person who had this gift was Bill Gore, the founder and long-time CEO of W.L. Gore and Associates (makers of Gore-Tex and other synthetic fiber products). Bill Gore was adept at telling stories that showed how the organization's core values of freedom and individual responsibility required particular operating policies. He was proud of his egalitarian organization, in which there were (and still are) no "employees," only "associates," all of whom own shares in the company and participate in its management. At one talk, he explained the company's policy of controlled growth: "Our limitation is not financial resources. Our limitation is the rate at which we can bring in new associates. Our experience has been that if we try to bring in more than a 25 percent per year increase, we begin to bog down. Twenty-five percent per year growth is a real limitation; you can do much better than that with an authoritarian organization." As Gore tells the story, one of the associates, Esther Baum, went home after this talk and reported the limitation to her husband. As it happened, he was an astronomer and mathematician at Lowell Observatory. He said, "That's a very interesting figure." He took out a pencil and paper and calculated and said, "Do you realize that in only fifty-seven and a half years, everyone in the world will be working for Gore?"

Through this story, Gore explains the systemic rationale behind a key policy, limited growth rate—a policy that undoubtedly caused a lot of stress in the organization. He suggests that, at larger rates of growth, the adverse effects of attempting to integrate too many new people too rapidly would begin to dominate. (This is the "limits to growth" systems archetype explained below.) The story also reaffirms the organization's commitment to creating a unique environment for its associates and illustrates the types of sacrifices that the firm is prepared to make in order to remain true to its vision. The last part of the story shows that, despite the self-imposed limit, the company is still very much a growth company.

The consequences of leaders who lack systems thinking skills can be devastating. Many charismatic leaders manage almost exclusively at the level of events. They deal in visions and in crises, and little in between. Under their leadership, an organization hurtles from crisis to crisis. Eventually, the worldview of people in the organization becomes dominated by events and reactiveness. Many, especially those who are deeply commited, become burned out. Eventually, cynicism comes to pervade the organization. People have no control over their time, let alone their destiny.

Similar problems arise with the "visionary strategist," the leader with vision who sees both patterns of change and events. This leader is better prepared to manage change. He or she can explain strategies in terms of emerging trends, and thereby foster a climate that is less reactive. But such leaders still impart a responsive orientation rather than a generative one.

Many talented leaders have rich, highly systemic intuitions but cannot explain those intuitions to others. Ironically, they often end up being authoritarian leaders, even if they don't want to, because only they see the decisions that need to be made. They are unable to conceptualize their strategic insights so that these can become public knowledge, open to challenge and further improvement.

New Tools

Developing the skills described above requires new tools—tools that will enhance leaders' conceptual abilities and foster communication and collaborative inquiry. What follows is a sampling of tools starting to find use in learning organizations.

Systems Archetypes

One of the insights of the budding, managerial systems-thinking field is that certain types of systemic structures recur again and again. Countless systems grow for a period, then encounter problems and cease to grow (or even collapse) well before they have reached intrinsic limits to growth. Many other systems get locked in runaway vicious spirals where every actor has to run faster and faster to stay in the same place. Still others lure individual actors into doing what seems right locally, yet which eventually causes suffering for all.[25]

Some of the system archetypes that have the broadest relevance include:

• **Balancing Process with Delay.** In this archetype, decision makers fail to appreciate the time delays involved as they move toward a goal. As a result, they overshoot the goal and may even produce recurring cycles. Classic example: Real estate developers who keep starting new projects until the market has gone soft, by which time an eventual glut is guaranteed by the properties still under construction.

- **Limits to Growth.** A reinforcing cycle of growth grinds to a halt, and may even reverse itself, as limits are approached. The limits can be resource constraints, or external or internal responses to growth. Classic examples: Product life cycles that peak prematurely due to poor quality or service, the growth and decline of communication in a management team, and the spread of a new movement.
- **Shifting the Burden.** A short-term "solution" is used to correct a problem, with seemingly happy immediate results. As this correction is used more and more, fundamental long-term corrective measures are used less. Over time, the mechanisms of the fundamental solution may atrophy or become disabled, leading to even greater reliance on the symptomatic solution. Classic example: Using corporate human resource staff to solve local personnel problems, thereby keeping managers from developing their own interpersonal skills.
- **Eroding Goals.** When all else fails, lower your standards. This is like "shifting the burden," except that the short-term solution involves letting a fundamental goal, such as quality standards or employee morale standards, atrophy. Classic example: A company that responds to delivery problems by continually upping its quoted delivery times.
- **Escalation.** Two people or two organizations, who each see their welfare as depending on a relative advantage over the other, continually react to the other's advances. Whenever one side gets ahead, the other is threatened, leading it to act more aggressively to reestablish its advantage, which threatens the first, and so on. Classic examples: Arms race, gang warfare, price wars.
- **Tragedy of the Commons.**[26] Individuals keep intensifying their use of a commonly available but limited resource until all individuals start to experience severely diminishing returns. Classic examples: Sheepherders who keep increasing their flocks until they overgraze the common pasture; divisions in a firm that share a common salesforce and compete for the use of sales reps by upping their sales targets, until the salesforce burns out from overextension.
- **Growth and Underinvestment.** Rapid growth approaches a limit that could be eliminated or pushed into the future, but only by aggressive investment in physical and human capacity. Eroding goals or standards cause investment that is too weak, or too slow, and customers get increasingly unhappy, slowing demand growth and thereby making the needed investment (apparently) unnecessary or impossible. Classic example: Countless once-successful growth firms that allowed product or service quality to erode, and were unable to generate enough revenues to invest in remedies.

The Archetype template is a specific tool that is helping managers identify archetypes operating in their own strategic areas (see Figure 2).[27] The template shows the basic structural form of the archetype but lets managers fill in the variables of their own situation. For example, the shifting the burden template involves two balancing processes ("B") that compete for control of a problem symptom. The upper, symptomatic solution provides a short-term fix that will make the problem symptom go away for a while. The lower, fundamental solution provides a more enduring solution. The side effect feedback ("R") around the outside of the diagram identifies unintended exacerbating effects of the symptomatic solution, which, over time, make it more and more difficult to invoke the fundamental solution.

Several years ago, a team of managers from a leading consumer goods producer used the shifting the burden archetype in a revealing way. The problem they focused on was financial stress, which

Sloan
Management
Review

17

Fall 1990

Figure 2   "Shifting the Burden" Archetype Template

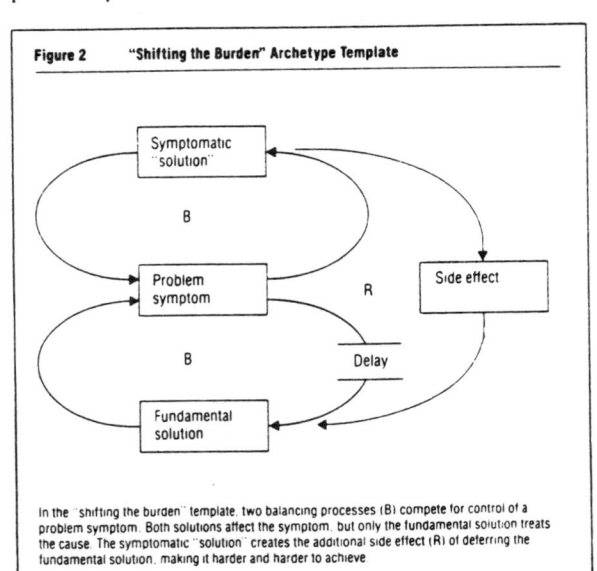

In the "shifting the burden" template, two balancing processes (B) compete for control of a problem symptom. Both solutions affect the symptom, but only the fundamental solution treats the cause. The symptomatic "solution" creates the additional side effect (R) of deferring the fundamental solution, making it harder and harder to achieve.

could be dealt with in two different ways: by running marketing promotions (the symptomatic solution) or by product innovation (the fundamental solution). Marketing promotions were fast. The company was expert in their design and implementation. The results were highly predictable. Product innovation was slow and much less predictable, and the company had a history over the past ten years of product-innovation mismanagement. Yet only through innovation could they retain a leadership position in their industry, which had slid over the past ten to twenty years. What the managers saw clearly was that the more skillful they became at promotions, the more they shifted the burden away from product innovation. But what really struck home was when one member identified the unintended side effect: the last three CEOs had all come from advertising function, which had become the politically dominant function in the corporation, thereby institutionalizing the symptomatic solution. Unless the political values shifted back toward product and process innovation, the managers realized, the firm's decline would accelerate—which is just the shift that has happened over the past several years.

Charting Strategic Dilemmas

Management teams typically come unglued when confronted with core dilemmas. A classic example was the way U.S. manufacturers faced the low cost-high quality choice. For years, most assumed that it was necessary to choose between the two. Not surprisingly, given the short-term pressures perceived by most managements, the prevailing choice was low cost. Firms that chose high quality usually perceived themselves as aiming exclusively for a high quality, high price market niche. The consequences of this perceived either-or choice have been disastrous, even fatal, as U.S. manufacturers have encountered increasing international competition from firms that have chosen to consistently improve quality *and* cost.

In a recent book, Charles Hampden-Turner presented a variety of tools for helping management teams confront strategic dilemmas creatively.[28] He summarizes the process in seven steps:

- **Eliciting the Dilemmas.** Identifying the opposed values that form the "horns" of the dilemma, for example, cost as opposed to quality, or local initiative as opposed to central coordination and control. Hampden-Turner suggests that humor can be a distinct asset in this process since "the admission that dilemmas even exist tends to be difficult for some companies."
- **Mapping.** Locating the opposing values as two axes and helping managers identify where they see themselves, or their organization, along the axes.
- **Processing.** Getting rid of nouns to describe the axes of the dilemma. Present participles formed by adding "ing" convert rigid nouns into processes that imply movement. For example, central control versus local control becomes "strengthening national office" and "growing local initiatives." This loosens the bond of implied opposition between the two values. For example, it becomes possible to think of "strengthening national services from which local branches can benefit."
- **Framing/Contextualizing.** Further softening the adversarial structure among different values by letting "each side in turn be the frame or context for the other." This shifting of the "figure-ground" relationship undermines any implicit attempts to hold one value as intrinsically superior to the other, and thereby to become mentally closed to creative strategies for continuous improvement of both.
- **Sequencing.** Breaking the hold of static thinking. Very often, values like low cost and high quality appear to be in opposition because we think in terms of a point in time, not in terms of an ongoing process. For example, a strategy of investing in new process technology and developing a new production-floor culture of worker responsibility may take time and money in the near term, yet reap significant long-term financial rewards.
- **Waving/Cycling.** Sometimes the strategic path toward improving both values involves cycles where both values will get "worse" for a time. Yet, at a deeper level, learning is occurring that will cause the next cycle to be at a higher plateau for both values.
- **Synergizing.** Achieving synergy where significant improvement is occurring along all axes of all relevant dilemmas. (This is the ultimate goal, of course.) Synergy, as Hampden-Turner points out, is a uniquely systemic notion, coming from the Greek *syn-ergo* or "work together."

"The Left-Hand Column": Surfacing Mental Models

The idea that mental models can dominate business decisions and that these models are often tacit and even contradictory to what people espouse can be very threatening to managers who pride themselves on rationality and judicious decision making. It is important to have tools to help managers discover for themselves how their mental models operate to undermine their own intentions.

One tool that has worked consistently to help managers see their own mental models in action is the "left-hand column" exercise developed by Chris Argyris and his colleagues. This tool is especially helpful in showing how we leap from data to generalization without testing the validity of our generalizations.

When working with managers, I start this exercise by selecting a specific situation in which I am interacting with other people in a way that is not working, that is not producing the learning that is needed. I write out a sample of the exchange, with the script on the right-hand side of the page. On the left-hand side, I write what I am thinking but not saying at each stage in the exchange (see sidebar).

The left-hand column exercise not only brings hidden assumptions to the surface, it shows how they influence behavior. In the example, I make two key assumptions about Bill: he lacks confidence and he lacks initiative. Neither may be literally true, but both are evident in my internal dialogue, and both influence the way I handle the situation. Believing that he lacks confidence, I skirt the fact that I've heard the presentation was a bomb. I'm afraid that if I say it directly, he will lose what little confidence he has, or he will see me as unsupportive. So I bring up the subject of the presentation obliquely. When I ask Bill what we should do next, he gives no specific course of action. Believing he lacks initiative, I take this as evidence of his laziness; he is content to do nothing when action is definitely required. I conclude that I will have to manufacture some form of pressure to motivate him, or else I will simply have to take matters into my own hands.

The exercise reveals the elaborate webs of assumptions we weave, within which we become our own victims. Rather than dealing directly with my assumptions about Bill and the situation, we talk around the subject. The reasons for my avoidance are self-evident: I assume that if I raised my doubts, I would provoke a defensive reaction that would only make matters worse. But the price of avoiding the issue is high. Instead of determining how to move forward to resolve our problems, we end our exchange with no clear course of action. My assumptions about Bill's limitations have been reinforced. I resort to a manipulative strategy to move things forward.

The exercise not only reveals the need for skills in surfacing assumptions, but that we are the ones most in need of help. There is no one right way to handle difficult situations like my exchange with Bill, but any productive strategy revolves around a high level of self-disclosure and willingness to have my views challenged. I need to recognize my own leaps of abstraction regarding Bill, share the events

---

The Left-Hand Column: An Exercise

Imagine my exchange with a colleague, Bill, after he made a big presentation to our boss on a project we are doing together. I had to miss the presentation, but I've heard that it was poorly received.
Me: How did the presentation go?
Bill: Well, I don't know. It's really too early to say. Besides, we're breaking new ground here.
Me: Well, what do you think we should do? I believe that the issues you were raising are important.
Bill: I'm not so sure. Let's just wait and see what happens.
Me: You may be right, but I think we may need to do more than just wait.

Now, here is what the exchange looks like with my "left-hand column":

What I'm Thinking	What Is Said
Everyone says the presentation was a bomb.	*Me:* How did the presentation go?
Does he really not know how bad it was? Or is he not willing to face up to it?	*Bill:* Well, I don't know. It's too early to say. Besides, we're breaking new ground here.
	Me: Well, what do you think we should do? I believe that the issues you were raising are important.
He really is afraid to see the truth. If he only had more confidence, he could probably learn from a situation like this.	*Bill:* I'm not so sure. Let's just wait and see what happens.
I can't believe he doesn't realize how disastrous that presentation was to our moving ahead.	*Me:* You may be right, but I think we may need to do more than just wait.
I've got to find some way to light a fire under the guy.	

Learning Organizations

20

Senge

Learning at Hanover Insurance

Hanover Insurance has gone from the bottom of the property and liability industry to a position among the top 25 percent of U.S. insurance companies over the past twenty years, largely through the efforts of CEO William O'Brien and his predecessor, Jack Adam. The following comments are excerpted from a series of interviews Senge conducted with O'Brien as background for his book.

Senge: Why do you think there is so much change occurring in management and organizations today? Is it primarily because of increased competitive pressures?

O'Brien: That's a factor, but not the most significant factor. The ferment in management will continue until we find models that are more congruent with human nature.

One of the great insights of modern psychology is the hierarchy of human needs. As Maslow expressed this idea, the most basic needs are food and shelter. Then comes belonging. Once these three basic needs are satisfied, people begin to aspire toward self-respect and esteem, and toward self-actualization—the fourth- and fifth-order needs.

Our traditional hierarchical organizations are designed to provide for the first three levels, but not the fourth and fifth. These first three levels are now widely available to members of industrial society, but our organizations do not offer people sufficient opportunities for growth.

Senge: How would you assess Hanover's progress to date?

O'Brien: We have been on a long journey away from a traditional hierarchical culture. The journey began with everyone understanding some guiding ideas about purpose, vision, and values as a basis for participative management. This is a better way to begin building a participative culture than by simply "letting people in on decision making." Before there can be meaningful participation, people must share certain values and pictures about where we are trying to go. We discovered that people have a real need to feel that they're part of an enobling mission. But developing shared visions and values is not the end, only the beginning.

Next we had to get beyond mechanical, linear thinking. The essence of our jobs as managers is to deal with "divergent" problems—problems that have no simple answer. "Convergent" problems—problems that have a "right" answer—should be solved locally. Yet we are deeply conditioned to see the world in terms of convergent problems. Most managers try to force-fit simplistic solutions and undermine the potential for learning when divergent problems arise. Since everyone handles the linear issues fairly well, companies that learn how to handle divergent issues will have a great advantage.

The next basic stage in our progression was coming to understand inquiry and advocacy. We learned that real openness is rooted in people's ability to continually inquire into their own thinking. This requires exposing yourself to being wrong—not something that most managers are rewarded for. But learning is very difficult if you cannot look for errors or incompleteness in your own ideas.

What all this builds to is the capability throughout an organization to manage mental models. In a locally controlled organization, you have the fundamental challenge of learning how to help people make good decisions without coercing them into making *particular* decisions. By managing mental models, we create "self-concluding" decisions—decisions that people come to themselves—which will result in deeper conviction, better implementation, and the ability to make better adjustments when the situation changes.

Senge: What concrete steps can top managers take to begin moving toward learning organizations?

O'Brien: Look at the signals you send through the organization. For example, one critical signal is how you spend your time. It's hard to build a learning organization if people are unable to take the time to think

> through important matters. I rarely set up an appointment for less than one hour. If the subject is not worth an hour, it shouldn't be on my calendar.
> **Senge**: Why is this so hard for so many managers?
> **O'Brien**: It comes back to what you believe about the nature of your work. The authoritarian manager has a "chain gang" mental model: "The speed of the boss is the speed of the gang. I've got to keep things moving fast, because I've got to keep people working." In a learning organization, the manager shoulders an almost sacred responsibility: to create conditions that enable people to have happy and productive lives. If you understand the effects the ideas we are discussing can have on the lives of people in your organization, you will take the time.
> ∎

and reasoning that are leading to my concern over the project, and be open to Bill's views on both. The skills to carry on such conversations without invoking defensiveness take time to develop. But if both parties in a learning impasse start by doing their own left-hand column exercise and sharing them with each other, it is remarkable how quickly everyone recognizes their contribution to the impasse and progress starts to be made.

Learning Laboratories: Practice Fields for Management Teams

One of the most promising new tools is the learning laboratory or "microworld": constructed microcosms of real-life settings in which management teams can learn how to learn together.

The rationale behind learning laboratories can best be explained by analogy. Although most management teams have great difficulty learning (enhancing their collective intelligence and capacity to create), in other domains team learning is the norm rather than the exception — team sports and the performing arts, for example. Great basketball teams do not start off great. They learn. But the process by which these teams learn is, by and large, absent from modern organizations. The process is a continual movement between practice and performance.

The vision guiding current research in management learning laboratories is to design and construct effective practice fields for management teams. Much remains to be done, but the broad outlines are emerging.

First, since team learning in organizations is an individual-to-individual and individual-to-system phenomenon, learning laboratories must combine meaningful business issues with meaningful interpersonal dynamics. Either alone is incomplete.

Second, the factors that thwart learning about complex business issues must be eliminated in the learning lab. Chief among these is the inability to experience the long-term, systemic consequences of key strategic decisions. We all learn best from experience, but we are unable to experience the consequences of many important organizational decisions. Learning laboratories remove this constraint through system dynamics simulation games that compress time and space.

Third, new learning skills must be developed. One constraint on learning is the inability of managers to reflect insightfully on their assumptions, and to inquire effectively into each other's assumptions. Both skills can be enhanced in a learning laboratory, where people can practice surfacing assumptions in a low-risk setting. A note of caution: It is far easier to design an entertaining learning laboratory than it is to have an impact on real management practices and firm traditions outside the learning lab. Research on management simulations has shown that they often have greater entertainment value than educational value. One of the reasons appears to be that many simulations do not offer deep insights into systemic structures causing business problems. Another reason is that they do not foster new learning skills. Also, there is no connection between experiments in the learning lab and real life experiments. These are significant problems that research on learning laboratory design is now addressing.

Developing Leaders and Learning Organizations

In a recently published retrospective on organization development in the 1980s, Marshall Sashkin and N. Warner Burke observe the return of an emphasis on developing leaders who can develop organizations.[29] They also note Schein's critique that most top executives are not qualified for the task of developing culture.[30] Learning organizations represent a potentially significant evolution of organizational culture. So it should come as no surprise that such organizations will remain a distant vision until the leadership capabilities they demand are developed. "The 1990s may be the period," suggest Sashkin and Burke, "during which organization development and (a new sort of) management development are reconnected."

I believe that this new sort of management development will focus on the roles, skills, and tools for leadership in learning organizations. Undoubtedly, the ideas offered above are only a rough approximation of this new territory. The sooner we begin seriously exploring the territory, the sooner the initial map can be improved – and the sooner we will realize an age-old vision of leadership:

> The wicked leader is he who the people despise.
> The good leader is he who the people revere.
> The great leader is he who the people say, "We did it ourselves."
>
> – Lao Tsu ■

References

1
P. Senge, *The Fifth Discipline: The Art and Practice of the Learning Organization* (New York: Doubleday/Currency, 1990).

2
A.P. de Geus, "Planning as Learning," *Harvard Business Review*, March-April 1988, pp. 70-74.

3
B. Domain, *Fortune*, 3 July 1989, pp. 48-62.

4
The distinction between adaptive and generative learning has its roots in the distinction between what Argyris and Schon have called their "single-loop" learning, in which individuals or groups adjust their behavior relative to fixed goals, norms, and assumptions, and "double-loop" learning, in which goals, norms, and assumptions, as well as behavior, are open to change (e.g., see C. Argyris and D. Schon, *Organizational Learning: A Theory-in-Action Perspective* (Reading, Massachusetts: Addison-Wesley, 1978)).

5
All unattributed quotes are from personal communications with the author.

6
G. Stalk, Jr., "Time: The Next Source of Competitive Advantage," *Harvard Business Review*, July-August 1988, pp. 41-51.

7
Senge (1990).

8
The principle of creative tension comes from Robert Fritz' work on creativity. See R. Fritz, *The Path of Least Resistance* (New York: Ballantine, 1989) and *Creating* (New York: Ballantine, 1990).

9
M.L. King, Jr., "Letter from Birmingham Jail," *American Visions*, January-February 1986, pp. 52-59.

10
E. Schein, *Organizational Culture and Leadership* (San Francisco: Jossey-Bass, 1985).
Similar views have been expressed by many leadership theorists. For example, see:
P. Selznick, *Leadership in Administration* (New York: Harper & Row, 1957);
W. Bennis and B. Nanus, *Leaders* (New York: Harper & Row, 1985); and
N.M. Tichy and M.A. Devanna, *The Transformational Leader* (New York: John Wiley & Sons, 1986).

11
Selznick (1957).

12
J.W. Forrester, "A New Corporate Design," *Sloan Management Review* (formerly *Industrial Management Review*), Fall 1965, pp. 5-17.

13
See, for example, H. Mintzberg, "Crafting Strategy," *Harvard Business Review*, July-August 1987, pp. 66-75.

14
R. Mason and I. Mitroff, *Challenging Strategic Planning Assumptions* (New York: John Wiley & Sons, 1981), p. 16.

15
P. Wack, "Scenarios: Uncharted Waters Ahead," *Harvard Business Review*, September-October 1985, pp. 73-89.

16
de Geus (1988).

17
M. de Pree, *Leadership Is an Art* (New York: Doubleday, 1989) p. 9.

18
For example, see T. Peters and N. Austin, *A Passion for Excellence* (New York: Random House, 1985) and
J.M. Kouzes and B.Z. Posner, *The Leadership Challenge* (San Francisco: Jossey-Bass, 1987).

19
I. Mitroff, *Break-Away Thinking* (New York: John Wiley & Sons, 1988), pp. 66-67.

20
R.K. Greenleaf, *Servant Leadership: A Journey into the Nature of Legitimate Power and Greatness* (New York: Paulist Press, 1977).

21
L. Miller, *American Spirit: Visions of a New Corporate Culture* (New York: William Morrow, 1984), p. 15.

22
These points are condensed from the practices of the five disciplines examined in Senge (1990).

23
The ideas below are based to a considerable extent on the work of Chris Argyris, Donald Schon, and their Action Science colleagues:
C. Argyris and D. Schon, *Organizational Learning: A Theory-in-Action Perspective* (Reading, Massachusetts: Addison-Wesley, 1978);
C. Argyris, R. Putnam, and D. Smith, *Action Science* (San Francisco: Jossey-Bass, 1985);
C. Argyris, *Strategy, Change, and Defensive Routines* (Boston: Pitman, 1985); and
C. Argyris, *Overcoming Organizational Defenses* (Englewood Cliffs, New Jersey: Prentice-Hall, 1990).

24
I am indebted to Diana Smith for the summary points below.

25
The system archetypes are one of several systems diagraming and communication tools. See D.H. Kim, "Toward Learning Organizations: Integrating Total Quality Control and Systems Thinking" (Cambridge, Massachusetts: MIT Sloan School of Management, Working Paper No. 3037-89-BPS, June 1989).

26
This archetype is closely associated with the work of ecologist Garrett Hardin, who coined its label: G. Hardin, "The Tragedy of the Commons," *Science*, 13 December 1968.

27
These templates were originally developed by Jennifer Kemeny, Charles Kiefer, and Michael Goodman of Innovation Associates, Inc., Framingham, Massachusetts.

28
C. Hampden-Turner, *Charting the Corporate Mind* (New York: The Free Press, 1990).

29
M. Sashkin and W.W. Burke, "Organization Development in the 1980s" and "An End-of-the-Eighties Retrospective," in *Advances in Organization Development*, ed. F. Masarik (Norwood, New Jersey: Ablex, 1990).

30
E. Schein (1985).

Reprint 3211

Knowledge Workers: The Last Bastion of Competitive Advantage

By Kathryn Rudie Harrigan and Gaurav Dalmia

Who are your knowledge workers? Do they know things that you don't?

"To share an asset, usually it must first be divided. But knowledge is one of the few assets that multiplies as it is shared."

--Indian Proverb

In the Nineties, most industries will become increasingly competitive and customers will grow ever more demanding. The pace of innovation has accelerated and companies that can't keep up will quickly find themselves in trouble. Frequently the only source of sustainable competitive advantage firms possess in such settings is their talented employees and the management systems that empower them. Unfortunately many managers do not understand how to identify and harness the power of their firms' talent.

Savvy managers, however, are learning how to train and empower their "knowledge workers"—their firm's international repositories of problem-solving skills—to implement competitive maneuvers faster. The process by which they identify people with critical knowledge and authorize them to act is shaking up old ideas, especially those about managing international strategy. The result of these changes has been dramatic:

- Products have been introduced faster.
- Corporate cultures have grown stronger.
- Value creation by knowledge workers has become more critical to firms' success.

What are knowledge workers? Let's define them as key employees who create intangible value-added assets (and often transport those assets in their heads when they change employers). Knowledge workers are most common in high-tech innovation centers like Silicon Valley. But they also reside inside mature organizations—often in places where the managerial hierarchy seldom thinks to look.

How can organizations maximize the contribution of their knowledge workers? For a start, formal and informal organizational changes are needed to enhance strategic information sharing among knowledge workers. But managing knowledge workers also requires top management to make philosophical changes. By learning to see the future from the perspective of the knowledge worker, a visionary leader can successfully harness these key employees as a source of competitive advantage.

Kathryn Rudie Harrigan is a Professor of Strategic Management and Director of the Strategy Research Center at Columbia University. Gaurav Dalmia is Vice President, Strategic Planning, Orissa Cement, Limited, in New Delhi, India. The names of most of the firms described in the examples could not be used because the authors made their observations while working as consultants.

Knowledge Workers In Global Markets

Global Markets Require Information Sharing. Knowledge workers often possess the critical information needed for effective global marketing and logistics. With such information, managers could pursue successful preemptive strategies. Without it, firms would be perpetuating products, policies, and practices that are inadequate for the needs of a changing marketplace.

A giant British assembler of engines and light machinery with problems in its newly opened German subsidiary found that its traditional approach to serving customers did not cater well to the highly sophisticated buyers it was now encountering. The British parent had not considered customer differences when it transferred technical knowledge and work practices to its German subsidiary. When these differences started surfacing, they were ignored—both by the British parent and local German executives—because their information systems (and subsequent reward systems) did not tell them what really mattered to customers. While the local managers earnestly tried to implement directives handed down from headquarters, the British parent blamed the local German marketing managers and sales force for ineffective handling of their products. The most knowledgeable sales representatives and service personnel took jobs elsewhere.

After three years of poor performance, the British parent finally realized that fundamental product changes were indeed needed to sell its products in Germany and that allowing these changes to occur would also initiate other improvements on the shop floor. Two years after headquarters let local managers upgrade and broaden their product line, change its positioning, and modify their distribution and sales incentive system to accommodate differences in the German marketplace, the firm was finally able to penetrate the German market and recover their investment. However, the firm was less successful in recruiting back the knowledge workers who jumped ship.

Shared Information Should Transcend Narrow Boundaries.

Even when managers adopt programs to share information, they often limit them to specific product, market, or technological topics instead of recognizing the need to disseminate strategic information. Frequently, managers cannot anticipate critical events because their firm's method of organizing information flows isolates the knowledge workers who should be sharing experiences and insights. Instead of facilitating the creation of knowledge pools, some firms' management systems drive knowledge workers into ivory towers of specialization.

The Learning Process Is as Important as the Knowledge Shared. The process by which knowledge workers solve problems and make decisions that contribute to their companies' success is critical in developing logistical excellence. It is more than just sharing hard facts. To be effective, it must encompass the sharing of their ideas and experiences throughout the diverse parts of an international firm. If firms can induce their knowledge workers to share information effectively, they gain strategic flexibility. This, in turn, allows them to implement strategies faster and gives them the organizational tools for bringing the right products to market sooner.

In highly competitive industries where the product life cycles grow ever shorter and few technologies remain proprietary for long, almost everything that makes a product successfully distinctive can be easily copied. Some firms discover too late that the only way to distinguish themselves from the pack is through improving service or response time. However, the logistical skills needed to excel in those areas necessitates knowledge workers sharing information on a wide range of subjects.

The six global subsidiaries of *a Fortune* 100-sized metal fabrication firm shared information about new products and process technologies adequately but they did not share information about customers well enough. This was unfortunate because substitute products were eroding the firm's market position, even though the firm was a technological leader in its field. Analysis showed that this industry trend had been readily apparent in some countries for at least eight to ten years, and that some regional subsidiaries had modified products in their respective countries to serve newer applications. Unfortunately, these forward-looking divisions had failed to communicate to the others that this trend was occurring and how they were responding to it.

Problem: Global Customers Have Individual Needs. There are still enough important differences among customers throughout the world to merit recognizing their distinct needs. Having the flexibility to serve local needs is often more important than the ability to deliver large volumes of homogeneous products for global distribution. Firms can nurture this flexibility by recognizing that their knowledge workers already know or know how to learn the differences in customer sophistication, availability of infrastructure, and other critical factors. The largest markets are still composed of customers who do not fit any global profiles.

Problem: Simple Idea Transplants Aren't Sufficient. Marketing specialists are once again earning their paychecks by advising firms how customers differ in each marketplace. But ideas may not cross borders well. Recognizing the worldwide fragmentation of markets is a problem for firms that are only willing to serve the needs of familiar customers. Their management systems do not permit knowledge workers to adapt to local differences in operations.

Problem: Global Value Chains Can Suffer from Centralization. Top management often copes with the complexity of international operations by dividing their firms into strategic business units (SBUs). While they hope to simplify intra-firm relationships, they frequently complicate them instead. It is often impossible to segment a company into SBUs that will be equally appropriate in terms of products, markets, and technologies. The danger is that SBUs placed inside the same division exchange information more readily than SBUs in different divisions.

Problem: Divisions Don't Share Similar Strategic Intents. Differences in the strategic focus of different subsidiaries cause problems for effective information sharing. A division that focuses on being a low-cost producer may not have any interest in sharing information with a sister unit that focuses on product innovation or one that operates in a more dynamic geographic environment. Regional differences may also be asymmetrical. For example, North American and European subsidiaries may position themselves at the high end with a broad line of customized products and excellent service, while South American subsidiaries must play a missionary role to build up generic demand for their products. When sister divisions have different orientations, it is difficult for them to learn from each other's experiences—even if they once faced similar problems.

Misunderstandings can be as simple as cost differences arising from resources being readily available to some subsidiaries but very scarce elsewhere. For example, in countries where manpower costs are low—even for high-level managers—the perceived cost of flying managers around the globe for face-to-face meetings is much higher than in countries where manpower costs are higher. Lower wage divisions may be reluctant to spend their scarce resources to participate in such meetings even though they have much to share if they attended.

When different divisions are organized as profit centers, their mutual inclination is to compete for corporate resources. Divisions often have little incentive to coordinate, especially if it is unclear who will reap the benefits. These concerns are well founded if their firm has no explicit reward system for information exchange and coordinated action. This is particularly true at the lower corporate levels, where day-to-day information sharing is the most effective.

Problem: Often Strategic Alliances Don't Facilitate Knowledge Sharing. Joint ventures and other forms of strategic alliance suffer from special informa-

> "Knowledge workers understand critical success factors better than managers they report to."

tion-sharing problems. Just as the transfer of knowledge is usually from headquarters to subsidiary as firms expand internationally, it begins from parent to child in strategic alliances. Later—when one might expect two-way information flows to develop—strategic alliances are in danger of becoming derailed, especially where there is no clear understanding of the roles and capabilities of the participating firms.

The international divisions of a major U.S. factory automation firm had shared information very well in Asia. But then it hit problems with cross-divisional communications involving three divisions that were not wholly owned subsidiaries of the firm. (All three were joint ventures with local companies that had been in existence for quite a while.) There was little interaction because headquarters had failed to establish links between the respective employee groups when they formed the alliance. Without this foundation for sharing information and coordinating activities, no communications were occurring in activities that needed substantial coordination to meet developmental deadlines.

To improve the situation, key executives were rotated from each of the ventures to the divisions to give them a broader corporate perspective and to allow them to build personal working relationships. Divisional knowledge workers were sent to the ventures. Within three years, international project activity had become more effective, the problem of not meeting deadlines was almost eliminated, and more accurate information was being provided on customer requirements and competitor activities.

How To Improve the Management of Knowledge Workers

Problem: Knowledge Workers Don't Feel Part of Corporate Family. Old ideas about managing human resources were fine when capital assets provided greater sources of competitive advantage than human assets. But now that knowledge workers have risen in importance in many international firms, the old wisdom about organizational design has been turned on its head.

Knowledge workers often have a better understanding of critical success factors than the managers they report to. However, because they believe that bureaucracies slow them down, they often try to take organizational shortcuts to get their jobs done. Chafing under centralized coordination, they prefer to be organized like hospital physicians or college faculties. Because knowledge workers crave access to specialized knowledge and peer recognition, all too frequently they focus only on their own jobs—not their firm's global situation. Still, they cannot be forced to share the knowledge stored in their heads; sharing must be voluntary.

Appeals to corporate teamwork rarely inspire knowledge workers because they feel they are an elite. They often overtly resent authority and reject hierarchical organization designs. This attitude makes it difficult for managers to share decision-making power with these upstarts without losing face.

But this may be a self-limiting problem. The difference between manager and non-manager is fast deteriorating as technology makes hierarchical notions of work groups hopelessly obsolete. Increasingly, there must be direct contact between the sources of information and the users in order to speed decision making and increase responsiveness to customer needs.

One of the most common responses to managing knowledge workers has been to rotate them around the organization so they will build a wide network of working relationships. This also gives them the chance to meet the key people who are repositories of desired information. And, yet, the true solution to the problem of knowledge sharing often means restructuring an entire organization.

The local managers of a European telecommunications firm operating in Korea had developed an intelligent data-collection system that was more sophisticated than the one used by headquarters. Because the Korean managers felt the head office wouldn't be interested in this development, they didn't share information about it. On the other hand, because headquarters didn't actively solicit information from its Korean subsidiary, it was not aware of the development and its significance.

When the corporate vice president for new product development saw this technology during one of her visits to Korea, she was understandably surprised to learn that information about this development had not been made available to the international marketing group at the head office. She saw to it that overseas assignments were given to key knowledge workers from this subsidiary—not only to share this specific information but also to send signals to the entire organization regarding the importance of knowledge sharing. Thereafter, engineering personnel in regional offices were rewarded for soliciting information from each other in an effort to encourage the cross-fertilization of ideas. Special efforts were made to overcome the barriers that prevented the divisions from sharing information throughout the firm.

Problem: To Be Motivated, Knowledge Workers Need Special Rewards. Traditional monetary appeals do not always motivate knowledge workers. Some are willing to sacrifice, or at least defer, monetary rewards in order to satisfy their personal needs. This is why fast-track personnel in some countries choose government jobs over higher paying corporate jobs, while others leave to open their own businesses.

Because knowledge workers are motivated by professional recognition, they want to work with the right teams—ones that will enhance their résumés. Sales and service personnel, for example, want to represent the products of only the best firms. Knowledge workers are also motivated by opportunities to learn and increase their own specialized knowledge. Two good examples: Cray Research's links to Seymour Cray's expertise and their state-of-the-art research labs attract top computer scientists. And Warren Buffet's expertise attracts fast-track financial managers to Berkshire Hathaway like moths to a flame.

Because knowledge workers want to be part of the action and enjoy creating value, they are likely to split their loyalty between their profession and peers on one hand, and their employing organization on the other. They stay committed to particular firms as long as those firms provide them with the needed resources for working on interesting projects. If this isn't forthcoming, knowledge workers will swiftly trade up to bigger sandboxes.

Redesigning Global Organizations to Gain Competitive Advantage from Knowledge Workers

How can international firms integrate knowledge workers into their international strategy? What cultural and management system changes are needed to attain an appropriate balance between the laissez-faire environment that knowledge workers crave and the centrally coordinated system necessary to achieve operating synergies? The solution could be to align knowledge workers' needs with corporate strategy needs. This would require developing a different view of international operations and the systems that coordinate them.

One Solution: Partial Integration of Vendors. Some international firms obtain the benefits of vertical and horizontal integration through very close relationships with suppliers, distributors, and competitors (quasi-integration). By using this kind of strategic alliance, firms can draw from the expertise of a broader base of people without necessarily employing them.

Unfortunately, the closely coupled work among vendors and customers on technical and marketing matters that is key to fast responses to competitive challenges only works if firms realize that each division working for the corporate good is also pursuing its own competitive marketing strategies. Unless the mission of a particular business unit is explicitly geared to support the other profit-generating businesses in the family, it must be assumed that sister business units will share resources with or help each other only when it is convenient, or profitable, to do so. The trick is getting knowledge workers to want to share information with their counterparts.

Problems seem to arise when sister organizations are direct competitors, have a vendor-distributor relationship, or are generally contemptuous of each other's capabilities and performance. Sometimes their better knowledge of each other's activities and resources makes managers more critical of in-house suppliers and distributors than they are of outsiders. Where knowledge workers are involved, managers must sell their ideas by appealing to logic and intellect to elicit the commitment and cooperation they seek.

The managers of the world's largest Japanese electrical firm had attained U.S. dominance in electronic products and refused to allow its American sales representatives to call or write up orders from what appeared to be (from their Tokyo vantage point) fledgling firms. Tokyo-based plants would ship products only to well-established U.S. firms such as IBM, AT&T, or General Electric. After U.S. managers tried valiantly (but unsuccessfully) to persuade their parent firm to broaden their list of acceptable customers, their sales force's access to those innovative "fledgling" clients was cut off. The smaller firms refused to discuss ideas with the electronic firm's personnel. Without a continuing stream of information about cutting-edge innovations to inform the firm's investment strategies, the Japanese firm was relegated to the position of manufacturing low-margin products. Even that temporary advantage, which was based on lowest cost production technologies, was soon challenged by firms with even lower operating costs.

New Ideas About the Role of Knowledge Workers

To be effective, knowledge workers need to bond with their employing firms. In the United States, a major Japanese auto maker recruited people who had never before worked in an automobile assembly plant and sent many of them to Japan for training. This information exchange process worked well because expectations and work habits were shaped among the assemblers from the beginning. But when marketing, engineering, and other knowledge workers were hired away from other auto makers, they were not similarly indoctrinated. They dragged their heels on accepting their new employer's problem-solving methodologies, and soon, the transfer of ideas from Japan to the United States became very difficult.

The tasks of the knowledge workers in this example were erroneously viewed differently than that of hourly employees. In spite of the advanced training and critical experiences of the knowledge workers, they also needed the experience of being key parts of a new team. Knowledge workers must be recognized as the linchpins that hold operating units together and make timely logistics possible.

In companies with international operations, the roles and responsibilities of knowledge workers have become broader and more interrelated. Yesterday, knowledge workers may have been working for the plastics division in the Middle East. Today, they may be in the aerospace division in Japan. Tomorrow, they may be loaned out to value-added resellers to develop self-monitoring hospital beds. Everywhere they go, cross-fertilization of knowledge should be occurring. To attain this level of performance, firms must give knowledge workers the freedom to break away from the pack and push exciting ideas through to completion. While they are limited to operating on a project-by-project basis, formal reporting relationships become hazy at best. To elicit their cooperation, knowledge workers must become members of a cadre of innovators.

A very special relationship existed between Honda's body fabrication division and its composite materials division. The two divisions worked very closely to bond composites to steel in making automobile frames. However, this kind of close working relationship did not develop between the same body fabrication division and a structural design division because of elitist attitudes among the design engineers. They didn't feel that turning the body fabrication division's suggestions into workable prototypes was worthy of their attention. The difference lay in how knowledge workers thought of their work.

Having special knowledge gives workers the potential to create change, but a corporation must encourage their leadership skills. Knowledge workers must not believe that their responsibility to transfer technology ends once they pass on information to their sister units. To be effective, the receiving end of the transfer must be taught to assimilate and use the knowledge provided. Instead of allowing divisions to hoard power by withholding information, knowledge workers must learn to see their jobs as part of a corporate-wide communications process.

A European electrical engine manufacturer created vertical relationships between divisions to share information about the future of costs, technologies, and market. But the strategy was undermined because divisions tried to operate as autarchies—self-sufficient units. They took the information provided by sister divisions for granted or ignored it because they wanted no transactions with other parts of their firm. Although the divisions had been created to monitor and improve upon outside vendors' designs, costs, and quality, they did not realize that performing these tasks for sister business units was an important part of their mission. The engine manufacturer did not realize the strategic potential of the vertical relationships it fostered until they were made an explicit part of each job description.

In another case, BBC ASEA found that employees in the Airbus division did not exchange information with other divisions. Management began making special efforts to communicate to its employees the role of that division in the firm's overall strategy. They next designed a program to make certain that entering engineers built relationships with members of the design staff in other divisions. Within two years, the Airbus division saw remarkable improvement in the information-exchange process, evidenced by greater and faster standardization, an increased number of cross-developed technologies, and a lower bill for materials for newer products.

New Management Systems for Knowledge Workers

To persuade knowledge workers to see their jobs differently, managers must be creative about designing incentives. These should take into consideration the unique motivations of these employees, their decision-making processes and career paths, and the role of knowledge workers in pursuing international strategies. Only team players should be fully rewarded with opportunities for international travel, peer recognition, and opportunities to work with cutting-edge innovators.

Effective information sharing requires the forging of internal company alliances that will appeal to the unique attitudes of knowledge workers. For example, establishing formal devices that determine whether managers communicate through a product-division structure, matrix organization, or country-by-country functional bases. Also, less formal devices could also be used, such as teams of temporary management organizations (TMOs), sharing rallies, and skillful use of symbolism. All of these techniques have proved useful at encouraging knowledge workers to enhance international operations.

Decision-Making Processes. Knowledge workers favor evolutionary, consensual decision-making processes in which they consult other professionals whose opinions they value. When they are supervised by managers who lack their own technical training, progress must be assessed primarily through the knowledge workers' own judgments. *Continued on page 48.*

KNOWLEDGE WORKERS, *Continued from page 9.*

Leadership Style. Knowledge workers need visionary leadership, not rules and cumbersome management systems. They need guidance from leaders they respect—people who grasp corporate strategy needs and can lobby effectively for resources that will enable knowledge workers to achieve their goals. Because their organizational acumen tends to be limited, knowledge workers also need protection and advice from their team leaders. Each leadership need could be satisfied by a different type of manager:

- An integrating genius could inspire the visionary leadership.
- Skillful "handlers" could become the negotiators who balance the needs of knowledge workers for operating autonomy with the organization's international strategy needs.

Career Paths. Because effective international strategies must have a feel for the "hot news" from different parts of the firm, a network of information-sharing relationships—formal and informal, internal and external—must be developed and maintained. This means moving knowledge workers around and rewarding them for applying the ideas they developed by observing practices inside sister business units around the world.

It also means showing knowledge workers how other firms—suppliers, customers, venture partners, or even competitors—do things. Aircraft engine manufacturers, Pratt and Whitney often lend some of their engineers to customers while continuing to pay their salaries. Daewoo both trains its suppliers' personnel and donates key Daewoo employees to them. Semiconductor manufacturers build their gossamer information-gathering networks through alliances in which their engineers work with counterparts employed by competitors to develop and commercialize key technologies.

A petrochemical firm found that the effectiveness of its information-sharing process varied considerably among its different divisions worldwide. When a well-known consulting firm investigated the causes, it found that key engineers and other knowledge workers had informally played a significant role in shaping the information-sharing process as they accompanied key division managers through assignment rotations. As these managers were rotated, they carried their unique mind-sets with them. And when division managers moved from one division to another, communication patterns in the new divisions they entered had to adapt to their ways of doing things.

To improve the interdivisional communications process, as well as the mind-sets of divisions with histories of communication breakdowns, the petrochemical firm created an internal program of team rotations whenever they found appropriate knowledge workers who could produce this desirable result. Thereafter, division managers were not the only successful employees rewarded with overseas assignments—critically skilled employees also traveled.

Rewards. Rewards for knowledge workers need to reflect their desires for recognition and personal skills development; access to world-class superstars, or even membership on their respective teams; and a sense of ownership. When knowledge workers feel the broader sense of responsibility that ownership provides, they become more loyal to their employers. They are eager to run that extra mile to deliver the goods.

Role in International Strategy. To foster the knowledge sharing that is so important in information-intensive businesses, expectations of reciprocity must be created. Knowledge workers who do not cooperate by sharing germane information are then cut off from the insider's pipeline. They lose their membership in the international meritocracy. Because many of the challenges that knowledge workers want to tackle are too big and costly to undertake alone, they must be shown that playing their appropriate role in international operations is the price of access to the equipment, supplies, and colleagues they value.

A Global Network of Knowledge Workers

The vision of a network of knowledge workers seems attractive for international firms because of the significant advantages that would result from sharing information across structural and geographic barriers. Problems arise, however, when middle managers are reluctant to give up power to the joint decision making outcomes implicit in such information-sharing arrangements. Ways must be found to prevent managers from losing face when they are implicitly demoted. This is especially true if they have always used access to information to indicate status. It is difficult to give up this perk and adjusting to the new reality that knowledge workers control an ever larger portion of the critical information.

Our research has suggested several ways of developing logistical excellence by asking the knowledge workers themselves to develop innovative methods of organizational information sharing. These include both formal and informal mechanisms for attaining strategic flexibility as managers reposition their firms in a market, deliver products appropriate to their customers' evolving needs, and change their firms' game plans in arenas where technological change accelerates the pace of operational innovations. Recognizing these changes—and their implications for implementation of international strategies—is necessary to empower the people who can provide firms with a sustainable competitive advantage in a world where few other sources of advantage remain.

Chapter 8

The Two Logics Behind Human Resource Management

Paul Evans and Peter Lorange

Multinational corporations (MNCs) often operate in many different product-market segments. The employees in their far flung geographic operations represent very different social cultures. The policies and practices for human resource management that are effective in managing one product-market may not be the most appropriate for another; those that work well in one cultural setting will not necessarily function in another.

How can a firm operating in different product-markets and diverse socio-cultural environments effectively establish human resource policies? What principles should guide corporate management of the complex MNC in the management of its human resources? In assessing the orientation of human resource management in the corporation, we believe that it is necessary to examine the implications of these two logics both separately and together. These are the issues discussed in this chapter.

PRODUCT-MARKET AND SOCIO-CULTURAL DIVERSITY

Most multinational enterprises administer a portfolio of products, some of which may serve multiple markets. Some of their operations may be in mature business segments while others are in growth settings.

The first complexity for the MNC is that these different product-markets require appropriately adapted approaches to human resource management (Fombrun, Tichy and Devanna, 1984; Lorange and Murphy, 1983; Gupta,

1986). Subsidiaries with products at different stages of the product life cycle may require very different types of general managers to run them, and correspondingly different approaches to personnel management. Mature business typically depend upon efficient cost-conscious management; general managers require strong integrative skills, while appraisals and rewards may be linked to operating targets. In contrast, emerging businesses require more adaptive entrepreneurial capacities on the part of general managers, and rewards that provide a stake in business growth. The orientation of personnel management is likely to vary in these businesses. Recruitment may be a critical success factor in one setting, management development in another, while labor relations may be the key personnel problem in a third. An important aspect of strategy implementation is adapting HRM to specific product-market requirements.

The second complexity for the MNC is that the social, legislative, and cultural environment varies from one country of its operations to another. Differences in labor legislation are obvious. Going further, Hofstede (1980a) has established that strong cultural differences exist between nations, criticizing American management theories and personnel practices as being too culture bound. Laurent (1986) shows that the concept of management and organization may vary significantly from one national culture to another, even among employees within the same MNC. Germans, for instance, tend to have a concept of management based on competence, Latins a more social conception, while an instrumental notion of management typically prevails in the United States (see Chapter 5). Both he and Hofstede argue that management methods may succeed in one culture but backfire in another. For example, management-by-objectives and pay-for-performance are quite natural in the United States and Germany, but they have been widely rejected in France and other Latin cultures.

What principles should guide the formulation of human resource policies in a multiproduct-market, multinational enterprise? One set of principles can be induced from research and practice based on applying product-market reasoning, the logic of business dynamics. Another set of principles follow from the logic of socio–cultural analysis. Let's take a look at these two logics in turn.

HRM Based on Product-market Logic

The multidivisional organization has emerged to cope with the challenge of managing a complex firm which operates in different product-market environments. In such a firm, one can distinguish between three levels of policy making:

1. the *corporate level*, concerned with the strategic management of a portfolio of enterprises and the integration of these firms;

2. the *divisional level*, where strategic and operational concerns meet in a family of enterprises with common product-market characteristics; and
3. the *business unit* level, where operational plans for each product-market are translated into functional policies and practices to achieve them (Lorange, 1980).

Within this structure, human resource management should be largely decentralized to the divisional and business unit levels. Human resource policy is typically general and non-contingent at the corporate level, progressively becoming more specific and operational as one descends to the business unit level. Indeed, the major challenge is to obtain a better matching of the strategic and operational plans of the division and business unit with the human resource practices to implement them.

From this business perspective, human resource management and the personnel function has not traditionally been regarded either as a strategic task or a critical corporate domain. However, there are at least three important tasks for corporate and divisional human resource management, the importance of which is reinforced by increasing needs for corporate integration.

The first task is human resource allocation, *key executive appointments and succession planning*, which is analogous to investment and other resource allocation decisions. Strategic decisions are in part implemented through decisions on general manager appointments, as well as through selecting people for key functional positions. The appointee should have a profile that matches the desired strategic development and the product-market logic in the business unit concerned – be it an entrepreneurial person, someone with desired functional competencies in marketing or engineering, an integrative generalist, or someone with experience in the rationalization of a declining business, as the case may be.

The second task is the *design and management of appropriate incentive systems*, intended to align managerial rewards with the strategic tasks of these individuals. The incentive package for managing a mature product-market setting may thus emphasize efficient, result-oriented management, while the incentives for managing a more entrepreneurial growth business may stress building business strength for future payoff rather than the "bottom line".

The third task is that of fostering the *cross-fertilization of functional and business experiences*, so that important lessons of experience in particular subsidiaries and divisions are communicated rapidly to others, as are relevant developments outside the corporation. The principle tools here are management education and training, as well as the organization of functional meetings for the sharing of experiences.

Increasing Needs for Corporate Integration

While the principle of decentralization of HRM applies to all but the most simple of firms, many industries have witnessed product-market trends leading to a heightened need for corporate integration, particularly since the late 70s. We might highlight three such trends. The first is the globalization of industries such as chemicals, many types of industrial equipment, computers, and pharmaceuticals. The driving forces behind this are increased economies of scale in production and R & D, decreasing costs of transport and communication, and intensified international competition, as well as a progressive homogenization of markets. Even traditionally country-based, consumer-type industries, such as retailing and food products, are beginning to feel the pressure to develop global strategies (Levitt, 1983; Bartlett and Ghoshal, 1987).

The second trend is an increasing interdependence in certain industries between subsidiaries and even divisions, particularly where marketing imperatives dictate the provision of a system type service to client. Consumer electronics, computer and telecommunication industries are notable examples.

The third trend is a need for increased flexibility in the deployment of resources, especially where product life cycles are shortening and competitor reactions sharpening.

How can this integration be provided in an effective manner? In the early 70s there was a search for structural matrix solutions involving dual or multiple direct reporting relationships. However, the costs of communication and ambiguity often outweighed the benefits of such complex structures.

The alternative was to provide integration through an overlay of management processes – and notably strategic management processes (Lorange, 1980). Strategic objectives need to be established and reconciled. These are translated into strategic programs at corporate, divisional and functional levels, programs to realize the objectives (acquisition, negotiation of joint-ventures, new business development, cost reduction, development of a stronger market orientation, quality improvement, and so forth). These strategic programs then need to be concretized as action plans and strategic budgets. Reconciling the objectives, programs and budgets at the levels of the corporate portfolio, the divisional business family, and the business unit levels requires an interactive and iterative process, such as the one illustrated in Figure 8.1 – a top-down and bottom-up process of negotiation and tradeoff between different perspectives.

In recent years, we have discovered that one of the major constraints in the functioning of these strategic management processes is human. Three human resource factors begin to act as constraints:

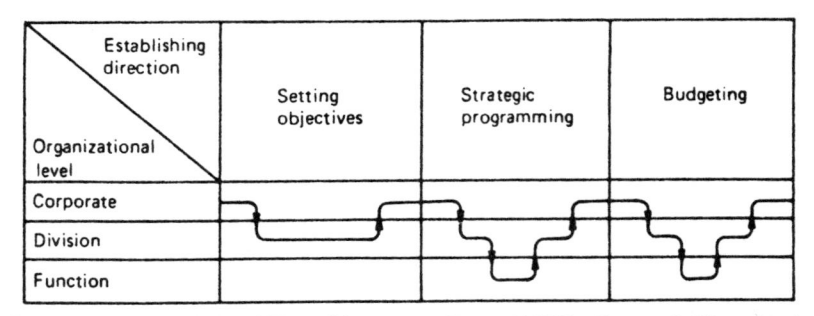

Organizational level \ Establishing direction	Setting objectives	Strategic programming	Budgeting
Corporate			
Division			
Function			

Source: Vancil, Richard F. and Lorange, Peter (1975) "Strategic Planning in Diversified Companies", *Harvard Business Review* (January–February) 81–90.

FIGURE 8–1
Strategic Management as an Interactive Process to Develop Both a Corporate-wide Plan and a Business Plan

1. the lack of strategic human resources effectively to implement global strategic objectives and programs;
2. weakness in terms of the strategic capabilities of managers in the firm (which is often particularly difficult for such managers open-mindedly to acknowledge); and
3. the loss of flexibility that stems from otherwise necessary differences in personnel systems between divisions and operations.

A recent Conference Board survey of 277 chief executives from multinational corporations in different regions of the world showed that the first two of these issues were their top human resource management priority (Shaeffer, 1985). Consequently, human resource management is today often becoming a strategic priority of the corporate management team, providing a new focus for the corporate and divisional personnel functions. Let us briefly discuss these three emerging management challenges.

Developing strategic human resources

Any implementation decision ultimately boils down to a question of staffing: the effectiveness of implementation depends on having the right people in the right place at the right time. The limits to strategy implementation are thus largely set by the resource pool of key strategic human resources.[1] To overcome this limit, the corporate concern with executive appointments and succession leads to a wider concern for the development of strategic human resources (as discussed in Chapter 7).

A strategic resource, human or otherwise, is a resource that can be transferred from one business strategy application to another (Lorange,

1980). For people to constitute strategic resources, their talents must be transferable to other business settings. Flexibility and mobility (in an inter-functional, inter-divisional and geographic sense) are thus essential criteria.

Strategic human resources are therefore associated with some concept of "generalism" – although this is a misleading term since it denotes general managers, who constitute only one type of strategic human resource. "Generalist managers" is the label used by Philips, "executive resources" by IBM, "corporate property" by Citibank and other firms. They are the occupants of key strategic positions (most general management roles, and key functional or staff roles), as well as the people deemed to have the potential to occupy such positions. Employees with such capacities are known as "high potentials".

The transferable expertise that characterizes strategic human resources is proven and honed above all through managed experience in different functions, in strategically important businesses, in different geographic regions, in headquarters and operating roles, complemented by management training and project assignments.

The forum for taking these development and mobility decisions is typically a *management review*, as described in Chapter 7. In large MNCs a cascading series of interlocking review committees may exist at corporate, divisional, and major business element levels. The "inputs" into the review are the needs of the organization based on its strategic and operating plans, together with the inventory of strategic human resources or high potentials. The outputs are assignment and developmental decisions, though the review process may lead to discussion of changes in human resource policy or organizational design. This review process can in fact become an intrinsic element of strategic management, constituting an arena for a general management dialogue on the tailoring of strategic and human resource management.

It is important that this management review process be driven and chaired by senior line management, supported though not usurped by the personnel department. It is in this resource allocation process that important strategic tradeoffs are made, decisions that can be made only by the line: decisions to assign key people to certain divisions rather than others, tradeoffs between the strategic needs and the operating needs, and between the different geographic areas of operations. This leads us to the second strategic challenge for HRM.

Development of strategic management capabilities

One of the lessons of the 70s was that strategic management is the responsibility of line management, be it corporate, divisional or business unit level of the firm. It cannot be entrusted to corporate staff – strategic planners, marketing co-ordinators, human resource managers, and the like. Nor can one expect any CEO in situations short of turnaround crisis singlehandedly to direct the process of strategic management. As described earlier, strategic management is an interactive process involving dialogue and negotiation on complex tradeoffs, so that a broadly shared sense of strategic direction can emerge among the management team.

This requires capabilities that few line managers, with their predominantly operational orientations, traditionally possess. First, it requires a capacity to think strategically, analytically to size up a business situation with its threats and its opportunities, all with a sense for competitive, market, and technological dynamics. Second, it requires the ability to adopt perspectives other than one's own – the perspectives of other functions, higher corporate levels, and perhaps even other divisional areas. Strategic management programs often involve working in ad hoc teams with a deliberately diverse set of managers, calling for open-mindedness, give-and-take, and tolerance. Without a high degree of teamwork, the process of strategic negotiation breaks down. And third, it requires the ability to work in two different attitudinal modes – a strategic mode (oriented toward change, adaptation and development), and an operating mode (oriented toward realizing the operating budget of the particular business unit). This ability to wear two hats is not easily understood or developed.

Pierre Borgeaud, the CEO of Sulzer (one of Switzerland's leading industrial firms), talked about this challenge in an interview with Paul Evans:

> We have to tackle the task of preparing the firm for its longer term future in different ways. Long-range planning has lost its credibility in an uncertain world. Will we see open trade or a return to global protectionism, recession or growth? What about inflation and exchange rates? Will the Gorbachev revolution in Russia continue or not? What about competitor reactions? There are too many uncertainties to permit anything but the planning of broad scenarios.
>
> And yet preparing Sulzer for the 1990s is one of my major responsibilities as CEO. What this implies is that its leaders and managers and its organization must be prepared to face whatever business and economic circumstances we turn out to confront ten years in the future.
>
> This is going to require a significant change in way of thinking and behavior on the part of our executives. We have managers who are excellent at running their business and delivering today's operating results. That's vital, but they have also to be capable of preparing their businesses to deal with the changes and shifts that we know lie ahead.

The process of executive development should assist managers to develop these strategic capabilities. Exposure to different jobs within the MNC is likely to foster an analytic perspective, while establishing necessary personal communication networks and developing a broad feel for the corporation as a whole. Although management development decisions are typically made in order to staff jobs and develop individual potential, the development of strategic capabilities appears to be an important "hidden" benefit (Edstrom and Galbraith, 1977).

The development of strategic capabilities may be supported by management training. One such example is ICL, discussed in Chapter 3. After a successful turnaround in the early 80s, the CEO realized that the future of the firm would depend on the capacity of executives to manage a constant process of strategic change. A successful series of executive training programs were organized in order to sensitize senior management to this reality, which for many of them turned out to be an eye-opening experience.

Increasing human resource flexibility

The necessary differences in human resource management policies and practices from business unit to another can create major obstacles to mobility and flexibility. The managers who constitute strategic human resources will therefore typically be governed by a separate corporate compensation and employee management program. Ensuring that the mobility of key managers is not constrained by locally favorable conditions is a complex specialist domain of personnel management.

Where strategic developments require great flexibility, one may see further corporate centralization of human resource policies and practices. IBM certainly seems to believe in this, with the corporate-level attention it pays to personnel management. As described later in Chapter 11, the fact that their successful independent venture unit in personal computers was not allowed much autonomy in the area of personnel policy and practice facilitated the ultimate integration of this unit into the mainstream business, where it was needed to satisfy the market for network systems. IBM also has a corporate policy that managers should spend no more than three to four years in a particular job, a policy which also facilitates flexibility in the strategic deployment of human resources.

Overall, while most operational human resource practices are being decentralized to divisions and business units, the pressures of global integration and the related challenge of making strategic management processes work more effectively are leading corporate human resource management to an important strategic role in the domain of executive management and development. Let's now change perspective, moving on the implications of socio–cultural diversity.

HUMAN RESOURCE MANAGEMENT BASED ON SOCIO–CULTURAL LOGIC

The business units of the multinational enterprise are typically based in geographic subsidiaries, and the firm also has to contend with another source of diversity, that of managing employees from different social and cultural environments. As mentioned earlier, there are two strategies for adapting to socio–cultural differences between subsidiaries: the global and polycentric approaches to human resource management respectively.[2]

1. The *global enterprise* typically manages its global workforce in a relatively centralized, co-ordinated way. Corporate policy on human resource management tends to be quite specific and influential – there are numerous guidelines, procedures, principles, and guiding corporate values. Examples of such procedures are worldwide policies regarding recruitment and promotion criteria; "single status" policies; a uniform stance toward unions; standardized procedures for performance evaluation; global compensation policies; uniform monitoring of human resource management through opinion surveys; a code of corporate values guiding the indoctrination of newly hired recruits. It goes without saying that corporate and divisional personnel officers typically have powerful roles in global enterprises. Such firms are also seen as having "strong" organizational cultures.

   IBM is perhaps the most well-known global enterprise, as are Hewlett-Packard, Procter & Gamble, and Unilever. Many of the companies upon whom the book *In Search of Excellence* (Peters and Waterman, 1982) is based are indeed such firms, and the global approach to human resource management (building the strong worldwide culture) is currently much publicized.

2. The *polycentric enterprise*, on the other hand, decentralizes the management of human resources to its subsidiaries. Corporate co-ordination, to the extent that it exists, tends to be loose and informal. There are few guidelines, policies are typically quite vague, and there is little specification of desired practice – all of these tasks are left to the subsidiary or business unit general manager and his or her personnel staff. The role of the headquarters staff is limited to tasks such as executive recruitment and advice on key appointments, and the organization of occasional meetings of subsidiary executives to exchange lessons of experience. Examples of polycentric enterprises are Holderbank (a Swiss firm that is the world's largest cement company), American Express, Britain's GEC, Sweden's AGA, Schlumberger, and Nestlé.

Two Strategies for Socio-cultural Adaptation

These two approaches constitute different adaptive strategies for coping with the heterogeneous social, legislative, and cultural environment of a complex multinational firm.

One theoretical model for organizational adaptation is known as the variation–selection–retention model, loosely based on Darwinian theory of natural evolution and applied by a branch of organizational theory called "population ecology". The argument is that among the natural *variation* of any phenomenon, environmental forces will favor the *selection* of certain types, leading these to be retained or to become success models (i.e. subsequent *retention*) until environmental forces change. Population ecologists have applied this to analyze how old forms of organization die when the environment changes, while new organizational forms come into prominence. Let us apply this model in a different way to explain how the global organization copes with its heterogeneous socio–cultural environment.

The global organization, with its centralized or co-ordinated policies and practices, selects and retains those people in any given country who most closely fit with its own cultural values. It adapts to different local environments by controlling selection; indeed, recruitment (complemented by socialization and management development) becomes a core function of such a firm.

This represents one way of adapting to socio–cultural differences. Deep differences in values, attitudes, and conceptions of management do exist between cultures, as researchers such as Hofstede and Laurent have established. But those differences are stereotypes, statistical differences in means between the normal curve distribution of values and attitudes in any given national population. Certainly, Germans are different from Americans who are different from the French. But *some* Germans are very American in their attitudes, and *some* French are more similar to the "average" German than to their own compatriots. When a globally-oriented company, for example Hewlett–Packard, is recruiting a German manager for a career at their plant near Munich, they are not simply seeking any technically qualified German manager; they are looking for a German whose personality matches Hewlett–Packard's cultural values. Global enterprises adapt through selection. In turn, those persons who are promoted into positions of power are individuals who most closely conform to these core values (i.e., further internal selection).

Polycentric enterprises, on the other hand, adapt in a more direct way. As pointed out, adaptation to local socio–cultural circumstances is the task of the local subsidiary, at best loosely circumscribed by corporate guidelines. Thus, the German subsidiary is likely to have markedly stereotypical German properties, the United States subsidiary different American characteristics, and so on. Socio–cultural adaptation is the task of local management, rather than that of the corporation.

The Importance of Internal Consistency

Leaving product-market logic aside, neither adaptation strategy is intrinsically superior to the other. Effectiveness in adaptation to socio-cultural differences appears to be largely a function of the internal consistency of human resource management policy and practice. Inconsistent policies and practices can lead to disruptive uncertainties about the rules of the corporate game, typically perceived as disconcerting swings in the centralization-decentralization pendulum. Inconsistencies mean that the energy of managers and other employees are drained away by internal politics rather than channeled into the market place. Indeed, in complex organizations it is advisable to keep the basic ground rules simple and coherent - the importance of simple form in a complex firm.

Internal consistency of policy and practice is easier to ensure in the polycentric enterprise. It implies a slim corporate staff with the limited role of ensuring executive succession and the cross-fertilization of experience. Divisional staff may have a co-ordination role, but real power lies in the hands of subsidiary line and staff executives. Inconsistencies arise if, for example, a strong-willing corporate vice president is appointed, armed with a mission to co-ordinate tightly policies and practices throughout the subsidiaries. This message is likely to be ignored or defeated by local subsidiary managers, entailing disruptive political infighting.

Internal consistency is more difficult to attain in the global firm. The attention paid to selection has to be complemented by retention policies, by socialization and management development practices to build corporate as well as national loyalty. IBM could perhaps be taken as an example, not because of the widely discussed content of its approach to human resource management, but rather because a high degree of internal consistency has developed over the decades. Even in its recent headcount reductions, IBM has taken pains to try to preserve that consistency.

In firms like IBM, individuals are rigorously and selectively recruited in national labor markets for careers, not jobs. The early career years are marked by indoctrination experiences to test the loyalty of the individual. The young manager is guided by a transparent code of corporate values and conduct. Such firms may have relatively high turnover rates among their graduate recruits during the first two years of socialization; these individuals discover that their own values and needs do not match those of the firm, and they quit - a desirable result for both the firm and the individual. After the early career years, a variety of policies exist to ensure the retention of these carefully groomed employees, so as to obtain a payoff from this investment in human capital: salaries well above the industry average; close attention to welfare policies; safety valve and grievance procedures such as an open door policy, and morale monitoring in the shape of opinion surveys; and a policy of transfer to new positions every few years, ensuring that individuals develop firm-specific rather than labor-market competencies.

Perhaps the most frequently cited and enduring example of a global organization is the Catholic Church, whose recruitment and indoctrination procedures for the priesthood (i.e., selection and retention), and whose rigorous adherence to an "organizational" credo of values will soon pass the two-thousand year test of adaptability.

In contrast, other firms espousing global philosophies have less consistent policies and practices. Selection procedures are less rigorous, socialization is neglected, less attention is paid to retention management. The external labor market often steals the capable individuals at the time in their careers when the firm's investment in human capital is beginning to pay off. The company is saddled with the investment costs of aiming to be global but without the benefits. It may then be obliged to recruit local talent into senior positions from the outside labor market, individuals who, however technically competent, do not necessarily share the values and attitudes of the global corporation. Consistency is further compromised since disruptive clashes can break out with these newcomers.

The *costs and benefits* of these two adaptive strategies also differ. The global firm gains in terms of corporate integration, but the price is the heavy cost of selection and retention. The polycentric firm gains in terms of lower overhead costs (relatively little time and energy devoted to human resource management; salaries linked more closely to local labor market rates), though it typically loses out in corporate integration.

Modifications to the Extremes

In a highly competitive environment, companies are obliged to minimize the disadvantages of the chosen strategy. But how can the firm do this in such a way as not to compromise the necessary internal consistency? Our observation is that effective firms do this with "subtle" management processes; in contrast, less effective firms tend to use overt management actions that disruptively compromise consistency.

Examples of disruptively overt management actions in the polycentric firm are new centralized corporate guidelines, closely monitored corporate programs, and the appointment of mother country nationals with little foreign experience to subsidiary general manager positions. Disruptively overt management actions in the global firm are sudden cut-backs in corporate or divisional human resource budgets, corporate programs saying "drop everything except the bottom-line results", and forced and rapid nationalization of the managerial workforce in a developing country.

Subtle management processes, to use the term of Doz and Prahalad (1981), can achieve the same ends without compromising internal consistency. Let us provide some examples of subtle countervailing mechanisms in the polycentric and global enterprises respectively.

A major problem for polycentric firms is how to introduce a degree of corporate integration into the otherwise decentralized firm. Doz and

Prahalad have mapped out mechanisms for this, which they call data management, conflict management (e.g., ad hoc task forces), and manager management. Limiting ourselves to the latter, manager management involves above all paying careful attention to the development of key managers for subsidiaries or business units (see Chapter 7). Other devices exist. Both Holderbank (the Swiss-based cement corporation) and the French multinational Generale de Biscuits make use of corporate "troubleshooters", members of the executive committee who take over troubled or rampantly independent subsidiaries until they have been realigned. There are the periodic "jamborees" and meetings where subsidiary and corporate executives get together to discuss policy, problems and experiences. Corporate worldwide executive training programs have become an important integrative tool for many polycentric firms.

Turning to the global enterprise, the heavy costs of selection and retention cannot be radically cut with ease. However, over time, corporate and divisional staff can usually be thinned, as has occurred at IBM. Line management, socialized through their own experience into the global corporate norms, can gradually take over the responsibility for selection and retention. A global culture probably takes at least one or two decades to create, though gradually more freedom can be given to subsidiary line managers without compromising globalism. However, a major risk for the global enterprise is that of "cloning", as discussed in Chapter 7.

BALANCING PRODUCT-MARKET AND SOCIO–CULTURAL LOGICS

Human resource management is all too often guided by black-and-white generalizations or fashions, by the imitation of competitors or today's "excellent companies". We believe that human resource policies should instead be guided by two logics: the business logic of products and markets and the socio–cultural logic of geographic spheres of operations. But although we have presented them separately, these two logics are of course *not* independent (see Figure 8.2). Whereas the dictates of product-market strategy may sometimes be consistent with the chosen socio–cultural adaptive strategy, in many instances there may be serious friction between the two logics.

Compatible Strategies

For some firms, product-market logic and the chosen socio-cultural adaptation strategy may be quite compatible (cells 2 and 4 in Figure 8.2). The current concern with product-market integration has, in particular, led firms with global adaptation strategies (cell 4) to be much in the limelight –

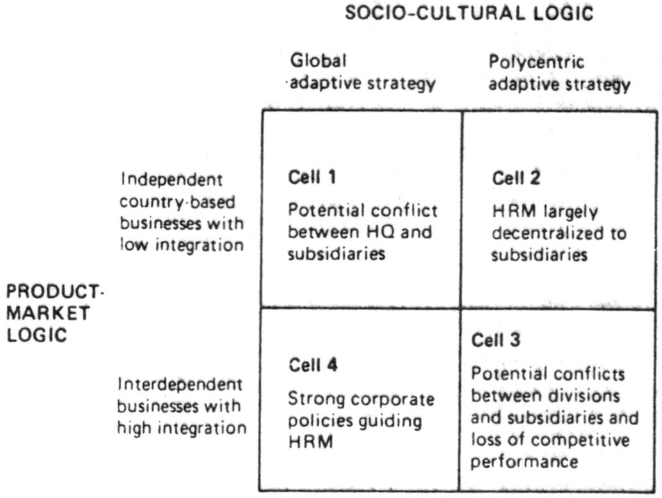

Paul Evans and Peter Lorange

SOCIO-CULTURAL LOGIC

	Global adaptive strategy	Polycentric adaptive strategy
PRODUCT-MARKET LOGIC — Independent country-based businesses with low integration	**Cell 1** Potential conflict between HQ and subsidiaries	**Cell 2** HRM largely decentralized to subsidiaries
Interdependent businesses with high integration	**Cell 4** Strong corporate policies guiding HRM	**Cell 3** Potential conflicts between divisions and subsidiaries and loss of competitive performance

FIGURE 8-2
The Relationship Between Product-market Logic and Socio-cultural Logic in Determining the Orientation of Human Resource Management in the International Firm

the human resource systems of companies like IBM and Hewlett–Packard have frequently been upheld as models.

Many firms have in fact developed *mixed human resource management strategies* in the sense that human resource management is global and centralized for senior executives and those with such potential (as discussed in Chapter 7), though for all other employees the human resource management approach is polycentric, decentralized, and country-based. In such firms, the decision to label someone as having "potential" constitutes the critical selection decision that was discussed earlier. This trend to dual human resource cultures seems to be developing into the typical pattern; it is also consistent with the emerging strategic integration forces that were discussed when considering product-market problems above.

Incompatible Strategies

In other firms, human resource management can be a more problematic domain (cells 1 and 3), with unresolved tensions between the forces of centralization and decentralization. The competitive evolution in a particular industry may argue for closer integration between product-markets units or divisions, which clashes with their polycentrism. This is the case for certain firms which had a technological speciality in a particular niche (of electronics, for example), and which expanded their international sales rapidly by setting up polycentric subsidiaries. Local entrepreneurs were hired, sales agencies were bought up, and the autonomy given to these subsidiaries indeed stimulated rapid growth in the early stages of market development. Today, however, competitive pressures and technology shifts necessitate closer product-market integration, which is resisted by the managers of now established local fiefdoms.

Conversely, product-market decentralization is important in industries based primarily on differentiation rather than integration (e.g., retailing, food products, and consumer durables), which would clash with a global adaptive strategy. For example, Marks & Spencer has a tradition of global-type employee management which has been outstandingly successful in Britain, and which they regarded as one of their distinctive strategic assets (Evans and Wittenberg, 1986). This was applied abroad when they opened stores in France and Canada, partly accounting for the disappointing results of their internationalization (see p. 39 for details).

The subtle management mechanisms described earlier may be employed to combat these problems, either providing more diversity within globalism or providing a measure of integration to the polycentrism. But these subtle mechanisms take time to have any visible effect – five to ten years is a good rule of thumb – and this may be too long to ensure survival if competitors are moving fast or if the industry structure is changing rapidly. In this case, the firm logically has one of two choices: either to modify its approach to human resource management, or to modify its product-market strategy. At first sight, the former seems to be the obvious choice, though experience suggests that it is difficult to achieve in a short time frame. Typically, it is only via the trauma of turnaround that one can change the basic approach to human resource management since this involves the deep transformation of organizational culture that was described in Chapters 3 and 4. Companies will naturally avoid this unless crisis forces it upon them.

The aphorism "stick to your knitting" may well be the appropriate guide for firms with global management philosophies. Such enterprises should restrict their strategic development to related businesses that share a similar product-market logic, rather than engaging in strategic diversification, however appealing that diversification may be. While there is little empirical data to substantiate this, our experience is that global corporations find it difficult to manage diversified product-markets, where the global human resource philosophy clashes with the need for differentiated approaches to human resource management in these product-markets.

Examples of this dilemma are Hewlett-Packard, Ciba-Geigy, and IBM, all corporations with global management philosophies. By origin an instruments business, Hewlett-Packard ventured into computers during the 70s. For a while, this led to a widespread loss of identity, internal confusion, and a clash between different cultures in a firm noted for its single value system. The choice was either to compromise those values or to get out of computers, and Hewlett-Packard has chosen a variant of the latter. Symbolized by changes in top management as well as in business strategy, the firm is resetting its path as a global instruments company, with computers as a strategic support to the mainstream business.

Ciba-Geigy, the Swiss pharmaceutical and chemical multinational, has had a similar experience. It ventured into consumer products with the acquisition of its Airwick division. After a decade of clashes and conflicts, Ciba-Geigy's top management concluded that they may never understand the values and dynamics of such a business, leading to the sale of the division. Furthermore, IBM diversified into telecommunications, but has recently decided to sell off its Rolm acquisition in a partnership deal with Siemens. For the global firm, it may be that strategically necessary competencies can be best obtained via joint-ventures and strategic partnerships rather than through outright acquisition or internal diversification. Research on the difficulties in acquisition integration provides at least indirect support for this view (Haspeslagh, 1983).

Polycentric enterprises, on the other hand, have more strategic flexibility; they do not have to stick to their knitting. It is easier for them to acquire businesses in new product-markets or to develop them internally. Their difficulty is in exploiting the synergies between these businesses, or in building on the interdependencies between businesses that may develop with the evolution of product-markets. Diversified polycentric firms are well advised to introduce a measure of integration by focusing attention on international executive development, particularly in newly-created divisions of interdependent companies. However, as noted, this takes time: where the cultures of competitors are better equipped to exploit these synergies rapidly, the polycentric firm may be forced into selling off businesses that it acquired.

The Longer-term Perspective

This analysis of balancing product-market logic and socio-cultural logic is admittedly tentative, based on our observations of a limited number of companies. But it does lead us to a provocative conclusion.

Intuitively, most businessmen will say that product-market logic is far more important than socio-cultural logic, and that it should drive strategic decisions in the firm. Classic strategic management theory and practice has also tended to draw uniquely on product-market reasoning. In the short term, where most attention is focused, this may be true. However, the above observations suggest that socio-cultural logic constrains strategic development more than most people believe when it comes to the long term.

The choice of a basic socio-cultural adaptive strategy (global or polycentric) is typically taken on the basis of managerial values and the perception of product-markets at a particular stage in the evolution of the firm. If we assume that this choice, while perhaps not irrevocable, takes at least a generation to modify (global organizations cannot easily become polycentric or vice versa), then the firm is implicitly deciding on its long-term way of adapting to a competitive environment that *will* inevitably change. This implies that while product-market logic may indeed be the important consideration behind short-term competitive strategy, socio–cultural logic is the more important consideration framing the choice of long-term strategic arenas.

Let's return to an insight provided by the population ecologists. The polycentric firm can be viewed as a "population" of loosely integrated entities. Over time, some are likely to die and others are likely to expand. Some will be sold off, and others brought up. If a film of the polycentric firm is speeded up to show decades in minutes, it will be seen to be constantly changing boundary, shape, and form. The "organization" loses its identity.

The global organization, on the other hand, is more likely to endure as an organization with relatively stable boundaries, precisely because of the attention paid to selection and retention of its human resources. Over the decades it will certainly change markets and products, it will go through good times and bad times, but as an "organization" it is more likely to retain its basic identity.

Borrowing from the perspective of a sociologist, one might point out that product-markets are essentially ephemeral. Markets shift and products change with increasing rapidity. Though varying from industry to industry, market forces argued for centralization in the 60s, decentralization in the 70s, integration in the 80s . . . and the catchword of the 90s may be some variant on deintegration, or global niches facilitated by new technologies.

However, social cultures do not change so quickly – quite to the contrary. It takes decades, if not centuries, to achieve even small changes in the deep fabric of society; similarly organizational cultures change slowly and painfully – such was the message of Part II of this book. Thus in choosing one socio–cultural adaptation strategy or the other, a decision that perhaps was arbitrarily based on product-market logic at a particular point in time, the firm may have fundamentally determined how it will adapt to currently unknown forces in the future. From the long-term perspective, as many have suspected, what is ultimately important is a cultural choice reflected in a basic stance on human resource management.

Notes

1. It is worth pointing out that this is one of the central arguments of a classic work in microeconomics, Edith Penrose's *The Theory of the Growth of the Firm* (1959). In analyzing what limits the growth of an organization, Penrose concludes that the limits on the growth of a firm are set not by factors such as

technological diseconomies of scale: "the capacities of the *existing* managerial personnel of the firm necessarily set a limit to the expansion of that firm in any given period of time, for it is self-evident that such management cannot be hired in the market-place" (Penrose, 1959, pp. 45–6).
2. The "global" and "polycentric" concepts are based on the pioneering work of Perlmutter (Heenan and Perlmutter, 1979). What we call "global enterprises" may, in his terms, be either ethnocentric or geocentric (respectively, policy centralized from the home country, or developed on a worldwide basis). The term "polycentric" is taken directly from Perlmutter, though such firms may be regiocentric (co-ordinated at a regional rather than at the subsidiary level). However, for the purposes of this chapter, Perlmutter's distinctions between ethno- and geo-centric, and between poly- and regio-centric, are left aside.

[26]

Implementing Corporate Strategy: Using Management Education and Training

D. E. Hussey, *Managing Director, Harbridge Consulting Group Ltd., London*

This article surveys a wide area—all of it relevant to the chief executive and the corporate planner—in linking management training and education to corporate strategy. Some companies are well aware of the benefits of using training as a means of implementing strategy. Unfortunately the management of many firms does not seem to be aware that the option exists and they are not able to use training this way because of their organizational and control systems. Training is a powerful weapon for implementing strategy. All the evidence suggests that it works, so who can afford to ignore it?

In an article published in this journal in 1984,[1] I suggested that one cause of strategic failure in many British companies was that generations of managers defined their industry and markets in an inappropriate way. The 'perceptual boundaries' to their situation forced them into strategies which were only logical for as long as the perception was close to reality. Once a gap opened between perception and reality there might be no *real* basis of logic to a strategy based on the perception. Part of my argument was that firms needed to take specific actions to test their perceptual boundaries, and I postulated that one value of using new techniques of analysis was that they changed the interpretation of information, revealing new patterns, and often forcing a re-assessment of the perceptual boundaries.

The thoughts in that article arose from my experience in planning and consultancy, and by my reading in the planning field. My thoughts were shaped also by some research that my own organization was undertaking into management training and education and in this article I should

---

The author is Managing Director of Harbridge Consulting Group Ltd., 3 Hanover Square, London W1.

like to explore a related contention, that too few companies link management training and education to corporate strategy.

Strategy and Structure

The case for considering structure in the content of strategy has been well made, beginning with Chandler's[2] famous study and the massive research contribution from the Harvard Business School which followed,[3] to which must be added the contributions of behaviouralists such as Lawrence and Lorsch[4] (whose contingency theory of organization has had a far-reaching impact on thinking). Even without the background of the research, few readers would have difficulty in accepting the premise that strategy can be frustrated if the structure is not compatible with the requirements of the strategy, and that when this happens either the structure or the strategy has to change. Structures exist for the implementation of strategies, even when the strategies are implicitly rather than explicitly defined. Those who wish to follow the research findings in greater depth are referred to Galbraith and Nathanson,[5] whose book provides an excellent summary of the most important research findings.

Structure is only a part of what we call 'the organization', and the most common image the word organization conjures up is the organogram. In reality an organization is much more than this, and consists of several inter-related variables of which structure is one, but others such as the tasks that have to be filled, the nature and skills of the people, the decision processes and the information processes are equally important. Again most managers will accept the reasonableness of the statement that a change in any one of these variables

73

has the potential to change any one of the others. We are all familiar with the situation where tasks have to be redefined and the structure changed, because people with the preferred skills cannot be hired and the job has to be changed to fit the available people. We have all seen how a new technology, such as the word processor, can change skill requirements, structure and the way information flows. Reward systems can affect the manner in which tasks are performed and therefore numbers of people needed, the structure and the information requirements.

The ideas expressed here and in Figures 1 and 2 were derived from a variety of sources. I believe that the original concepts were developed by Leavitt,[6] Galbraith and Nathanson[5] have an expanded variant, and my figures are variations on this theme.

This diagram, in Figure 1, implies that most organizational changes are fired by the interaction of changes in the variables, and could happen despite the company's strategy. This is only partly true, and Figure 2 adds the ideas that the organization should be driven by the strategy to achieve actions/results, and that both the strategy and the organization can be affected by the environment in which it operates.

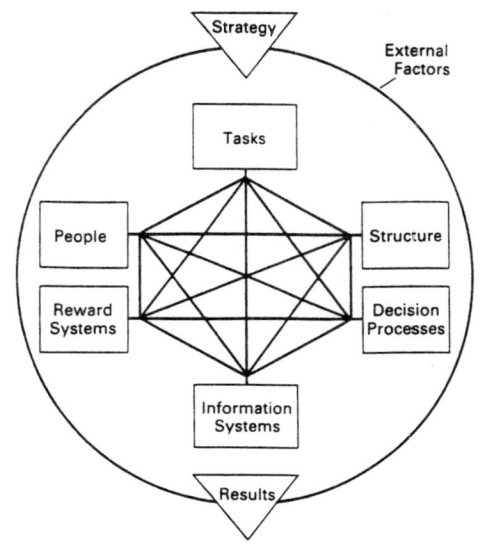

Figure 2. Strategy, environment and organizational variables

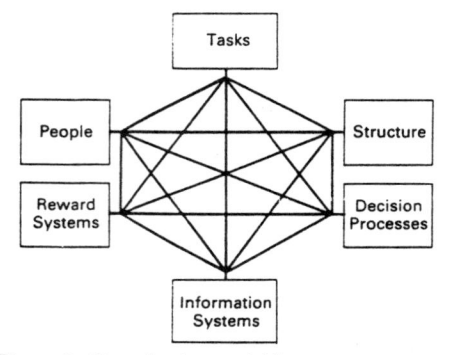

Figure 1. Organization variables

In my view, Figure 2 provides a useful model with many practical applications. It serves to illustrate that a new strategy must be considered in the context of organization, if it is to be effectively implemented. Failure here often results in strategies that do not work as management intended, and in extreme cases the lack of an appropriate organization may prevent the strategy from being implemented at all. I have heard more than one management complaining that their inability to find certain key people has frustrated a major initiative.

This clear link between strategy and organization, and the relationship between the variables, leads me to two basic premises on which to build my argument.

(1) Because the management education/training activity of the firm can be used to alter the variables, it should be positioned in the context of strategy.

(2) Because management education/training has the power to make a positive contribution to the implementation of strategy, the training objectives and initiatives should be periodically reviewed by top management, and specifically when a major switch in strategic emphasis is planned.

Unfortunately the research evidence is that few managing directors appear to accept either point.

The Research Background

This article draws on two surveys undertaken by my organization. The first,[7] researched in late 1982, drew a sample of 80 companies from the 150 largest U.K. business organizations. These can only claim to represent what is happening in the larger companies, although it is a reasonable assumption based on contact with many firms that the larger companies are able to devote the most effort to management training (although not necessarily the greatest expenditure per employee). This survey provided some comparative data which were widely used in the government discussion paper on qualifications for civil servants.[8]

Our second piece of research was conducted in 1984, into the MBA degree and British Industry.[9] This study had three sample bases: MBA students at four business schools; the business schools themselves; and 50 firms mainly drawn from the larger organizations but deliberately biased by the inclusion of a few smaller firms (e.g. consultants) known to be heavy recruiters of new MBAs and to have an influence on MBA starting salaries.

Unless there is a need to make reference to a particular study I will refer to findings from both studies under the term 'our research'. Both reports are published for those who wish to follow up the matter, and they cover a much wider scope than the few issues mentioned in this article.

In addition we have some further findings, unpublished, on graduate/MBA recruitment and career progression in a number of large companies.

Other recent research findings which will be referenced specifically include a postal survey of U.K. training practices by an organization called ODI[10] (1982) and a survey by the British Institute of Management[11] (1984).

It is difficult to separate the terms training and education, when applied to company internal or sponsored activities. The BIM Survey[11] suggested two definitions in common usage. One was that long courses were education, short ones were training. The other was that education is to improve knowledge, training to improve skills. Rather than try to find the point when training becomes education I will use the words synonymously for the purpose of this article. If there is a difference it is for me that management education signifies breadth, and management training suggests depth, but in the context of the link with strategy such subtle differences are of little importance. Management development is a term that is wider than training and education, and includes other methods of developing people, including projects and job rotation.

Some Research Findings

Our research asked respondents to describe the aims and objectives of their management training activity. It was encouraging to find that some companies felt that their need was for training that could be directly tied to the achievement of corporate objectives, but disappointing that this direct link was seen by only one third. A greater percentage (39 per cent) believed that training objectives should follow a general pattern of specific skill training for managers at each level while all managers should be taught a general business background. A large minority (19 per cent) argued that training objectives should be related to individual rather than corporate needs, with the main function being to remedy defects. Some 10 per cent made their training objectives the preparation of people for promotion.

The respondents who related training to corporate objectives gave their answers in a general rather than a specific sense and a much smaller number linked their activities with strategy.

It would be unfair to argue that the two-thirds, who do *not* explicitly relate training objectives to corporate strategy, are all ignoring corporate needs. Certain types of training may be difficult to relate to the strategy, and this does not mean that such training has no value. My argument is that all firms should start with the strategy and make the training plan in relation to it. The individual's annual training needs assessment, or the residential assessment centre findings, may still provide vital information in the formulation of the training plan, but will not be the only input as it is with many of the companies in our sample. We found that a majority of companies, regardless of their philosophy on training objectives, rely on the annual training appraisal for assessing training needs. The BIM survey[11] also found this to be the majority method. This grass roots approach has many strengths, but is not always in touch with shifts in strategy and has many critics as will be discussed later. The following examples are of situations where we have been concerned in training that relates more directly to company strategy.

★ *Case 1.* L'Oreal's U.K. operation decided on a major shift in strategy in an attempt to attain a higher brand share in their sector of the toiletries market. To effect the strategy meant achieving some changes in the channels of distribution which they used. In order to meet the changed channel priorities it was necessary to reorganize the sales force and the tasks of many of the representatives. Top management realized that they had a better chance of succeeding with this strategy if they gained the commitment of the sales force, and equipped them with the necessary knowledge needed to deal with different types of wholesaler and retailer. As a deliberate part of the strategy we constructed a short course where, by using a case study based on real market data, the representatives were able to discover the reason for the new strategy, and where specific training was given to help them over the situations they would confront once the change went 'live'. The point of this example is that the annual training needs assessment could not have revealed the gap except in retrospect, by which time the implementation of the strategy might have been threatened.

★ *Case 2.* One of the world's largest multinational companies, always seen as one of the best managed, identified that more attention had to be placed on competitor analysis both at top level and in the development of marketing plans by each operating unit. This was after careful self-analysis had revealed that much of the company's growth was without profit, because of weaknesses in the market place where competitors were proving more aggressive than the assumptions on which past plans had been based. Many companies would have issued an edict that in future strategies were to be formulated after more competitor analysis, and many would have failed to cause any changes whatsoever. In this company the chief executive personally directed a worldwide educational initiative to bring the new thinking into life. He led top managers in a week-long introduction to the theme of 'what about competition', and insisted that several hundred senior people should spend 2 weeks on a strategic planning workshop. He also introduced an 8-hour audio-visual presentation to thousands more managers as a basis for discussion of and coommitment to real strategic thinking. Many implementation workshops have been held throughout the world with practical training in competitor analysis, leading to the implementation of more realistic strategies.

★ *Case 3*. British Petroleum in 1978 worried over the problem of how to ensure that it could meet the challenge of the future. The environment had changed, and would continue to change; the concept of the integrated oil company was under challenge; diversification would increase. Yet the senior managers who would have to cope with the future results of strategies now being implemented were probably already employed in middle management. The identified need was to give hundreds of managers a business-school type education to help them cope with the challenges that could be foreseen, and to begin to change the corporate culture. An in-house, 10 × 1 week modular programme was designed around BP's priorities and needs. The breaking down of the programme into modules meant that individuals could spread their attendance over several years, if necessary. There is a regular updating programme to keep the modules relevant, and sessions are held in three centres in the world. The programme was independently reviewed against its objectives by a British university, and the courses have also been critiqued by professors from leading business schools. The impact on the company has been considerable, very much as expected by the instigators of this project. Such a massive educational effort could only arise from a perception of corporate strategic needs, and indeed did not figure in the routine training needs assessments which tended to throw up individual skill deficiencies.

Supporting Research Findings

If training were always closely related to strategy, one would expect a measure of turbulence in companies' training programmes. Few firms emerged from the recession with the same strategy with which they entered it. Yet our research found a great deal of lethargy. Outsiders used on internal training are rarely re-evaluated. The BIM survey[11] found that 'previous experience with the provider' was the most important factor in the use of outsiders: such a phenomenon occurs in other consultancy purchase decisions.

In fact we found that many trainers judged the success of training by its very stability. 'With the exception of trainers who operate courses on a commercial basis, few respondents were able to indicate the criteria by which programme success is measured. Some appeared to be embarrassed by the question; others referred to the demand for particular courses or the number of years their programmes had been running.'

However, our research also found that in the minority of companies where top management did take an interest in training activities, 'spending is substantial and revision of training programmes relatively frequent'.

'The majority of training courses we came across remain relatively stable from one year to the next.' We found that any major changes that did take place tended to happen when top management got involved.

In most companies they did not get involved. There are enormous variations in the way the training function is organized, and in the standing and seniority of its head. In a few companies his or her stature was such that the chief executive would be likely to involve him/her in the implementation of strategies. In other organizations we found training managers who were little more than clerks booking places on outside courses and who would never get near the chief executive, let alone his strategy. Whatever the organization of training, most firms gave policy responsibility to the Personnel Director. The fact that few appear to relate the policies to corporate strategy has already been demonstrated. My hypothesis is that almost all managing directors will get involved in structure, because this is seen as a top management thing to do; very few see training policy as an issue for them, and in this they are greatly mistaken.

Lest I am considered to be reflecting no more than my own biases, I should also refer to some recent U.S. research on overcoming problems in strategy implementation by Alexander.[12] Of the ten most frequent problems which he encountered, the top six may be directly related to training (Table 1).

Table 1. The six most frequent strategy implementation problems. Alexander's findings[12]

	Problem	Percentage of firms	My comments
(1)	Implementation took more time than originally allocated.	76	This does not necessarily relate to training, but it can do. The sort of programme L'Oreal used cuts down the time required.
(2)	Major problems surfaced during implementation which had not been identified beforehand.	74	Again training is not the universal answer. However, the right sort of course can be used to identify and remove problems.
(3)	Co-ordination of implementation activities not effective enough.	66	Potentially, but not necessarily, helped by training.
(4)	Competing activities and crises distracted management from implementing this decision.	64	The second of my examples quoted earlier was a company that used a training initiative to ensure the priority of the new policy.
(5)	Capabilities of employees involved were not sufficient.	63	May be a training or a recruitment problem.
(6)	Training and instructions given to lower level employees were not adequate.	62	A straight training problem.

Among Alexander's recommended solutions are communication and involvement. Strategy-related training, creatively designed, can be a way of providing both. It would be hard for any manager anywhere in the world in the second of my examples quoted earlier to be ignorant of the chief executive's policy, or to remain un-involved in its implementation. To avoid attending one of the courses would have required a dedicated effort by the manager: his alibis would have to be perfect.

Leading on from U.S. research I believe that U.S. companies are more likely to relate training to strategy than British companies. Company courses designed to improve some aspect of corporate business performance seem to occur more frequently in the U.S.A. than in the U.K. and they require a different sort of consultancy skill to that generally purchased by British trainers. Few companies have the ability to run objective training of this type from internal resources.

Assessing Training Costs and Benefits

In the late 1960s the concept of total physical distribution was in vogue. Many companies made improvements by taking a total view of distribution and its costs, whereas previously responsibility, and costs, had been spread across numerous managers. The decision to use air services to supply an overseas market became different when associated reductions in inventory and warehouse costs were brought into the picture. Economic sense did not come from just comparing sea and air freight rates without looking at other costs which would be affected, including the extra financing charges of inventory while on a long journey.

Our research showed that, in the U.K., training decisions are related to an erroneous economic perception very much akin to the misperceptions which used to pervade physical distribution.

Although we found wide variations in budgeting practice, with a minority of trainers having to sell their courses on an internal company market, and a majority operating as a free service, almost nobody ever looked at the full cost of training. Typically the training manager's budget will cover only the professional services (lecturing and course development), his own overheads and the training centre/hotel costs. Travel to a course normally falls on the budget of those people attending, as does the largest item: the salaries of those on a course. The British Institute of Management[11] survey found that only 66 per cent of respondents included course participants' travel and subsistence expenses in the budget and only 24 per cent included the salaries of participants while on the course.

Because of this traditional approach to budgeting, few companies know the full cost of training to them. The management pressure is on the training manager to do well against his budget, which means his motivation is to hold down or reduce those costs for which he is accountable. A much better economic decision would be a trade-off in terms of costs of a course and its effectiveness: in other words, trying to maximize the return on the sacrifice of the opportunity cost, instead of aiming to minimize the out-of-pocket expenses.

The British Institute of Management survey[11] found that most of the 40 per cent of companies which had a cross charging system for training services did not make a charge for overheads. 'This being so, a rational decision, on the grounds of costs, as to whether to "buy out" management training or to use internal resources must be difficult. The dice can be loaded against the external provider.'

Comparatively little is spent per head on training. ODI[10] reported minimal figures: the BIM survey found the figures to be £36–£40 per head. However, the true figures, although small, would be somewhat larger because of the omissions discussed earlier.

My hypothesis is that there are three reasons for the economic distortions found around training costs and training decisions, and they all contribute to a degree of disinterest by top management teams.

(1) Few top managements appear to see the desirable link between corporate objectives, strategy and training initiatives, which means that they rarely see a need to become involved in training policy and training strategy.

(2) Our survey found that few companies attempt serious evaluation of the benefits of training, which means that almost all training is an act of faith rather than a reasoned economic decision.

(3) Many firms are unaware of the true range of training options available to them.

The predominant use of the annual training needs appraisal as the only source of information on which to build training initiatives tends to reinforce prejudices in a company. It is a factor which prevents training from being one of the mechanisms by which a company can question its 'perceptual boundaries', to return to the phrase with which I began this article.

These issues will be expanded later when I suggest some remedies to the present situation. Before I reach this point I should like to focus on what for many is seen as the pinnacle in management education, the Master of Business Administration degree.

The MBA

The MBA qualification has two different roles in relation to the diagram in Figure 2. Firstly, companies may sponsor employees, using the MBA course as an element in management development. Secondly, the MBA may be a desirable qualification for new recruits. In theory, the MBA graduate should be well equipped to help companies to probe their perceptual boundaries, and to play a major role in the development and implementation of strategy.

Our research shows a very mixed reaction to the MBA in British industry. The survey was in three parts:

★ 20 business schools;

★ students at four business schools (sample 126; 40 per cent response rate to postal questionnaire);

★ companies (interviews with 50 companies mainly selected from the larger organizations but biased by the inclusion of a few smaller companies known to be heavy recruiters of MBAs). Much of the research is not relevant to the theme of this article, but there are a few points worth mentioning.

(1) The number of MBA graduates produced every year is small relative to the size of the employment market and to the number of MBAs qualifying in the U.S.A. British business schools produce only about 1500 MBA graduates per year and it would take them roughly 40 years to equal the *annual* MBA output of the U.S.A. At least 25 per cent of those graduating from British business schools are foreign students who will not enter the U.K. labour market.

(2) Only 16 per cent of companies were fully committed to sponsoring their employees for MBAs, and this included some firms who would not recruit a raw MBA. Some firms sponsored an occasional employee but 40 per cent refused to consider this and preferred either the short business school courses or in-house training.

(3) As far as the recruitment of new MBAs is concerned, we found that 20 per cent of our sample had a strong bias against MBAs, while 40 per cent were regular recruiters. The remaining 40 per cent have no specific policy on MBAs and do not recruit them on a regular basis, although they may occasionally recruit them. This means that some 60 per cent of the larger firms do not accept the benefits of a *regular* intake of qualified new MBAs. Prejudice against MBAs is strongest in the manufacturing industries, with the possible exception of electronics. Some consultancy and financial services firms have a bias the other way and specifically seek MBAs. Indeed we found that 28 per cent of the 1282 persons who graduated over the period 1974–1983 *and* were also members of the Business Graduates Association were employed in banking or consulting. Other evidence suggests that this proportion is typical for all new MBA graduates.

(4) There was a unanimous feeling among the business students that British companies rarely understand or appreciate the MBA. 'Companies prefer the "university of life"' (Bradford student). 'Companies view it as an unsuitable U.S. panacea to U.K. problems' (Manchester student). The companies which rejected the MBA as a new recruit gave reasons such as:

★ prefer school leavers and graduates;
★ interested in individual not degree;
★ MBA unsuited to company culture;
★ no need for MBA expertise;
★ prefer sponsorship;
★ good in-house training sufficient;
★ bad experience of MBAs.

(5) We found a common misconception among some companies that the MBA is a homogenous product. The reality is that there is a wide difference between the degrees offered by the various business schools, and between the individuals who take those degrees.

The position of the MBA in industry is a fascinating field for study, and since publishing our report we have been able to continue our research with an indepth study of graduate and MBA recruitment and career development in several companies. For the purposes of this article, the main conclusion I would draw is that if firms are deliberately not making use of MBAs it becomes all the more important for them to see that their internal training is providing the right sort of strategic stimulus. For those that do recruit MBAs there remains the question of using them effectively and, again through training, bringing other parts of the organization into some degree of compatability with them.

Some Suggested Improvements

There are a number of clear lessons which emerge from the foregoing analysis, and several areas where attention would be beneficial to most companies.

(1) *Closer Integration of Training to Company Objectives and Strategies*
This requires new action from the top, essentially an initiative that should be taken by the chief executive, and is an area where the corporate planner might also be expected to play a key role. There are three specific aspects which would repay attention, and all require *a mental shift from the common idea that training should be for the improvement of the individual because this will benefit the firm, to the concept that training should be for the benefit of the firm and this will benefit the individual*. This change of emphasis is more than a play on words.

It is often overlooked that a course can be used for more than the stimulation of learning. It can, as in the L'Oreal example given earlier, create an understanding of the reasons for as well as the existence of a new corporate strategy. It can ensure that the strategy is communicated effectively through the organization. It can create an involvement in implementation and a genuine commitment to action. The three situations where there is a specific value in using training as part of the implementation of strategy are to:

★ *help implement a new strategy;*
★ *seek business improvement;*
★ *stretch corporate thinking to challenge the 'perceptual boundaries'.*

Examples have been given of the first. The second may be made clearer by reference to another real situation.

> A multinational firm of mechanical engineers began using a training initiative as a means of improving business results. Objectives of the 2-week course began with the need to improve results, and worked through the various issues including market analysis, competition, understanding management accounting and people management. The teaching material was written around the firm and was relevant to the central theme of the course. Individual weaknesses in these topics might have been identified through the annual appraisal, but it is unlikely that initiatives developed from this would have achieved a drive from the top or be integrated around such an important, practical theme that all would perceive as highly relevant. Much of the course is in a workshop mode, but there is also some education. The initiative started in the U.S.A. domestic division and is now going world-wide. The course may not deal with every facet of the topic which could have been identified in a needs appraisal. What it does do is deal with a corporate issue and those facets which are relevant to it.

Developing the ability to challenge the perceptual boundaries is only partly a function of training, and depends on other factors also. I have already mentioned the use of different analytical approaches during the formulation of strategy. For the highest levels of management a workshop approach is usually most relevant, when the educational element is thoroughly wrapped up in work. For middle management the answer may lie in the broadening experience of the tailored substitute for the business school course given in the British Petroleum example.

(2) *Select the Appropriate Training Option for the Course Objectives*
Top managers in many companies need to become more aware of the training options open to them and to ensure that internal systems do not rule out the most appropriate option. Because of the budgeting approach discussed earlier, the common failure to evaluate any training initiatives, the basis on which training needs are assessed and a fairly widespread disinterest by top management, many firms make training decisions which are not cost-effective.

The research points to the popularity of internal course, particularly up to middle-management level. External courses tend to be the most popular choice for senior managers. The internal course can offer a multitude of options many of which are never explored by the training function. This may be because of the way training is organized and controlled, because top management is not demanding enough, or because many company trainers feel personally threatened by some of the options.

Some of the possible options for internal courses are:

(a) *The course is designed and taught by the training staff.* This particularly occurs with basic subjects such as interpersonal skills, communication, health and safety at work, industrial relations, interviewing and the like. It is interesting that more than half of the training subject areas identified in the BIM Survey[11] were of this type. One is tempted to ask whether this is because of a true specification of corporate need, or because most trainers feel competent to run courses on these subjects.

(b) *An off-the-shelf course presented by outsiders in-house.* The main advantage of an internal course over sending managers on the same course outside the organization is that the cost per head is likely to be less. In all but a few situations lack of relevance means that this is not a very effective use of a participant's time.

(c) *The 'slanted' off-the-shelf course.* This is similar to (b) except that the provider of the course spends a little time on cosmetics, so that company language is used and a few company examples are given. It is a little more expensive and a little more effective than (b).

(d) *The multi-lecture course.* Here the outline is usually put together by the trainers, and speakers from inside and outside the company are invited to teach parts of the proceedings. This sort of format often has value in providing a 'how we do it' familiarization from line managers, or in exposing senior managers to a host of new ideas. It is also frequently misused as a cheap way of putting together a course, without regard for the teaching objectives. This sort of approach can also be expensive when top-ranking speakers are flown in from all parts of the world.

(e) *The true tailored course.* This is the only way to tackle strategy-related training. It costs more than some of the other options, but it is very effective and enables participants to optimize the use of their time. The actual cost of teaching a course may be similar to that of other options using external lectures and the main cost difference comes in the development. Figure 3 shows the main tasks in developing such a course. On average at least 10 days of development time are needed for each day of the course. As Figure 3 shows, some of this time is spent researching the priorities and understanding the participants, and most of it in the design of teaching material, such as case studies. Typical skills required are consultancy, creative course design, writing teaching materials and teaching. Few individuals in industrial training possess all these skills. It is possible for a company to develop a tailor-made course from internal resources, but it is more likely to be externally provided.

Research evidence is lacking, but my impression is that the tailored course is more widely used in the U.S.A. than in the U.K., while the U.K. is ahead of many other countries. In all countries, too many firms deny themselves the power of this option.

(3) Assessment of Training Needs

The linking of training to corporate strategy changes the emphasis of the annual training needs appraisal, since the key initiative starts with the strategy and subordinates individual needs to this. Of course not *every* training initiative should be related to strategy and there will always be some needs which should be given attention although their link with strategy would be tenuous. However, I believe this should become the bottom third of the training activity, and the remaining two-thirds should deal with those needs which are related to strategy.

Although the annual appraisal is the most popular approach, all the evidence is that it does not work. Leavitt[13] states that he knows of no organization which is pleased with its appraisal system. Handy[14] argues that the normal objectives of appraisal systems are not psychologically compatible, and some are 'difficult to do well, even in isolation'. Some firms try to overcome the problems by separating the training appraisal from the performance appraisal.

In a study which we undertook for a large public undertaking in the U.K. we found little correlation between the training needs of the organization and the information coming out of the appraisal system: because top management suspected this they took outside advice.

In another company for which I once worked I was appalled at the standard of letter writing, a mixture of Agatha Christie style police reports and Edwardian English. A high proportion of the letters which I examined were barely intelligible, and most were considerably longer than was desirable. Yet this need was not identified through the extensive training needs appraisal system, simply because neither the subordinates nor their managers were aware that their letters were badly written. The whole company, with the exception of a few directors, wrote in the same old-fashioned style, and did not know any better.

Many individual needs can be picked up by beginning with corporate objectives and strategies, and this should be the starting point. However, this by itself is not enough and companies which rely on the needs appraisal should consider either setting up assessment centres, or supplementing the appraisal with a separate studies. This can be done from either

Strategic Planning Process

Implementing Corporate Strategy — Using Management Education and Training

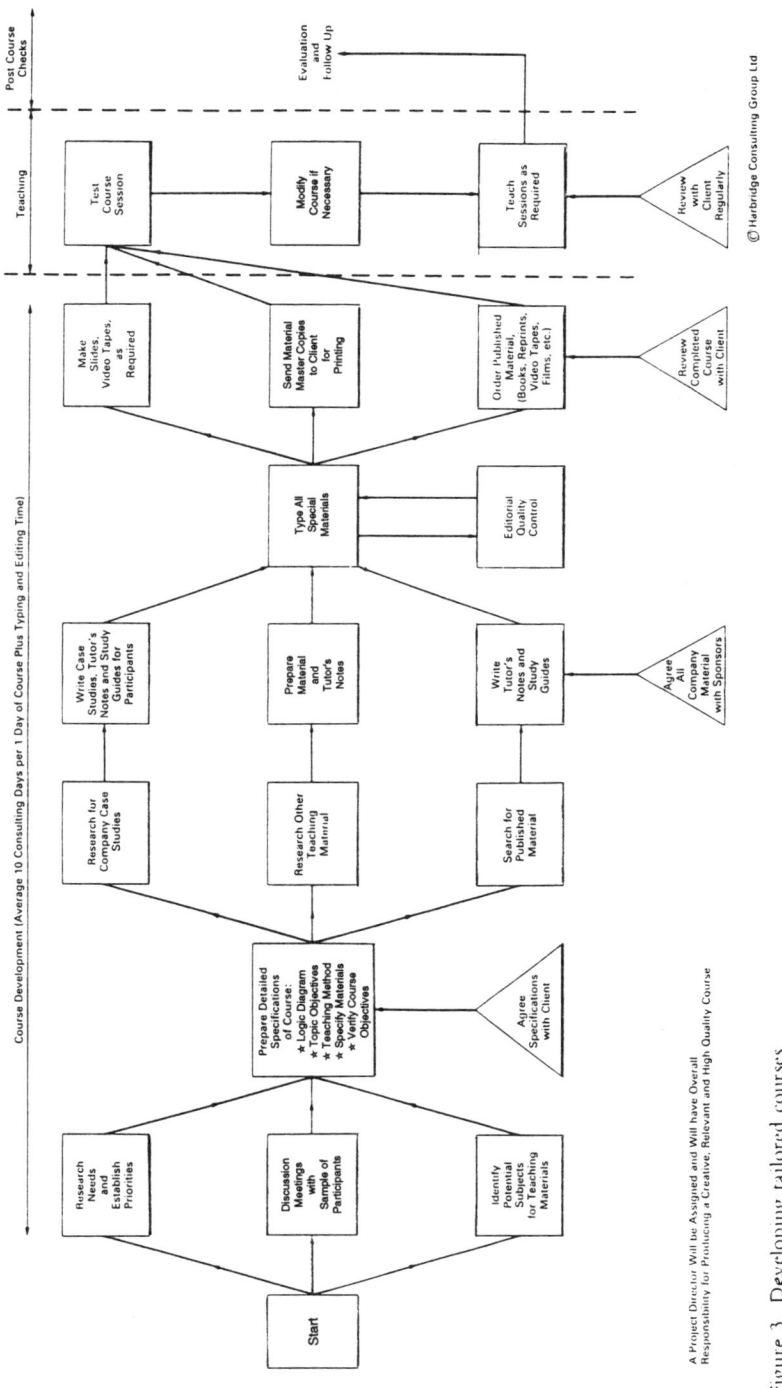

Figure 3. Developing tailored courses

82 Strategic Planning for Human Resources

internal or external resources, but obviously requires certain skills and an objective approach.

(4) Evaluation

The evaluation of training is unusual. Neither our survey nor that of the BIM found many firms which attempted an evaluation. Obviously there are times when money spent on evaluation is wasted: for example, a unique event which is not to be repeated when any information gathered would be like closing the door after the horse has bolted. However, when courses are organized regularly companies should make an effort to determine whether they are achieving their objectives.

The ability to evaluate in a practical way is very often tied to the degree of clarity in the course objectives. Although it may be difficult to be truly scientific and eliminate all the other variables, it is often possible to make reasonable business assumptions about the impact of the course. L'Oreal management,[15] for example, felt sufficiently confident to claim publicly that their training initiative had been a major factor in the achievement of their market objectives. If more courses were designed to help *the company* achieve something specific, more managing directors might be willing to give a greater personal commitment to training.

At the individual level, too, more can be done to evaluate the effect of training initiatives, and some methods such as post-course interviews with participants can also increase the value of the training to the individual. Unfortunately, the low level of interest in training prevents many companies from doing this. With a fixed budget, more follow-up and evaluation mean less money for courses. Therefore training tends to remain an act of faith when it need not be.

References

(1) D. E. Hussey, Strategic management—lessons from success and failure, *Long Range Planning*, **17** (1), 43–53 (1984).

(2) A. D. Chandler, *Strategy and Structure*, MIT Press, Cambridge, MA (1962).

(3) Some examples are: (a) B. R. Scott, *Stages of Corporate Development*, Harvard Business School (1971); (b) R. Rumelt, *Strategy, Structure and Economic Performance*, Harvard Business School (1974); (c) D. Channon, *Strategy and Structure of British Enterprise*, Macmillan, London (1973).

(4) P. Lawrence and J. Lorsch, *Organisation and Environment*, Harvard Business School (1967).

(5) J. R. Galbraith and D. A. Nathanson, *Strategy Implementation—The Role of Structure and Process*, West Publishing (1978).

(6) H. J. Leavitt, Applied organisation change in industry—structural, technical and human approaches in *New Perspectives in Organisational Research*, Wiley, New York (1964). Abridged version in Vroom and Deci (Eds.) *Management and Motivation*, Penguin, Middlesex (1970).

(7) K. Ascher, *Management Training in Large U.K. Organisations—A Survey*, Harbridge House, London (1983).

(8) I. Nisbet, *Qualifications: A Discussion Document*, Management and Personnel Office, Cabinet Office (1983).

(9) K. Ascher, *Masters of Business? The MBA in British Industry*, Harbridge House, London (1984).

(10) *ODI 1982 Management Training Survey*, ODI—Summary (1982).

(11) M. Peel, *Management Development and Training: A Survey of Current Policy and Practice*, British Institute of Management (1984).

(12) L. Alexander, Successfully implementing strategic decisions, *Long Range Planning*, **18** (3), 91–97 (1985).

(13) H. J. Leavitt, *Managerial Psychology*, 4th edn, University of Chicago Press (1978).

(14) C. B. Handy, *Understanding Organisations*, 2nd edn., Penguin, Middlesex (1981).

(15) L. Wilson, 'How l'Oreal learned to accept change', *Marketing*, March (1979).

Executive Development as a Business Strategy

Morgan W. McCall, Jr.

The author argues that companies should take an energetic role in sponsoring activities to develop executive leadership; such a program will develop leadership abilities at the broadest level.

The only legitimate reason to put in place an executive development program is that it is integral to the business strategy. Any other reason will result, at best, in a series of interesting training programs tangentially related to the business or, at worst, in a variety of expensive activities conveying irrelevant or contradictory messages. The only way to sustain the necessary commitment of time, passion, and resources to executive development is through a bedrock belief that leadership is a critical source of competitive advantage and that leadership can be developed through systematic attention to development.

One of the general truths of business strategy is that there can be only a few real priorities; if not, everyone becomes bogged down in a confusing array of possibilities. A second truth is that those priorities must be maintained with some consistency if they are to be taken seriously.

In this regard, executive development begins with two serious disadvantages. First, no corporation I've ever worked with has placed developing people as its first priority; second, it's difficult to make a good case that development should be a first priority. With no shot at top priority, development must still compete with other compelling issues even to make the priority list.

From global marketing to technological innovation to total quality, legitimate sources of competitive advantage clamor for berths on the priority list. And should development make the list against the odds, it is still possible that higher-ranked priorities will take precedence over lower-ranked development activities. If legitimate squabbling over the relative priority of development weren't enough, the perception of executive development as a series of training programs, educational activities, and succession systems run by the human resources staff can be the final blow. Development defined in this way is overhead, and overhead is the first victim of the business cycle.

I propose that development of leadership talent must be one of the top five corporate priorities, that developing talent requires just as intensive a commitment of organizational effort as any other top priority, and that training pro-

Morgan W. McCall, Jr., is professor of Clinical Management and Organization and a senior research scientist with the Center for Effective Organizations at the University of Southern California. He is the co-author of several books, including The Lessons of Experience *(Lexington MA: Lexington Books, 1988), with Michael M. Lombardo and Ann M. Morrison.*

EXECUTIVE DEVELOPMENT

> **As compelling as belief in organizational Darwinism can be, there is ample evidence that leadership skills are learned.**

grams and human resource systems (though important) are not at the heart of the process.

Traditional sources of competitive advantage are losing their edge. Control over raw materials, technology, and capital, which used to provide strategic leverage for US corporations, is increasingly difficult in the face of global competition. Leadership, on the other hand, is a potentially renewable resource that is not easily copied or stolen by other corporations. Further, it might be argued that it is only through effective leadership that a firm can identify and take advantage of other sources of potential competitive advantage, thus staying ahead of competitors in a rapidly changing environment.

The obvious central role of effective leadership would still not make developing it a top priority if effective leaders were easily replaceable as well as available. In accepting this premise, most strategic planning models ignore leadership altogether, leaving the people who concoct and conduct the strategy out of the equation. Available evidence suggests that far from being interchangeable and abundant, effective leaders are relatively rare; in addition, hiring them from outside the organization at senior levels is risky. Knowledge of the business and knowledge of the people involved in the business are crucial components of effective leadership, and people who successfully lead a particular organization in a specific industry usually have spent significant time in it.

Organizational Darwinism

Even if leaders were pivotal to effective use of sources of competitive advantage and even if leaders were not easily interchangeable in the external market, leadership development still might not be a worthy priority. If leadership qualities were innate and if people with those abilities automatically rose to the top, expending resources on developing leaders would not make sense. However, both assumptions are widely believed by executives, many of whom attribute their own success to their personal qualities and to their success in the face of tough assignments. As compelling as belief in organizational Darwinism can be, there is ample evidence that leadership skills are learned.

Negotiating trade agreements with China, designing a quality program, or motivating a demoralized group are but a few examples of skills unlikely to have genetic origins. Even learning skeptics might pause before accepting a Darwinian process that produces an end product that has evolved to fit a particular environment. Organizations and their environments are changing too fast for Darwinian evolution; having survived the trials of the 1960s and 1970s hardly ensures being fittest for the world at the turn of the century.

Even the most hard-bitten executive will admit that things other than cream rise in the organization and that there is room for improving whatever process produces the leadership of the organization. In fact, a compelling argument can be made that natural organizational forces act to produce middle and even senior managers who are parochial and possess a relatively narrow range of leadership skills. Acting rationally, organizations plan leadership succession on the basis of demonstrated skill. Therefore, a typical replacement table will list candidates who are "ready now," "ready in two years," etc., with the explicit goal of having backup managers who are fully qualified for the next job.

As sensible as this may be, development of new skills requires that a person not already possess the skills required for the job (or, in other words, that the person be stretched). Ironically, to the extent that so-called rational succession decisions are made, leaders are simultaneously rewarded for what they already know how to do and denied the

EXECUTIVE DEVELOPMENT

opportunity to develop new skills that might serve them well. It is only because the perfect candidate is hardly ever available that opportunities for growth occur.

A logical conclusion is that the development and implementation of strategic choice (whatever the particular source of advantage might be) depends on effective leadership; that effective leaders are not easily found, replaced, or substituted; and that effective leaders do not necessarily emerge naturally. It therefore follows that a corporation must include in its top priorities the development of leadership talent and that it is irrational to expect that without leadership, other priorities can be achieved and sustained.

But how is it possible to choose among multitudes of possible priorities like total quality, winning the Baldrige award, globalization, technological innovation, service to the customer, managing cultural diversity, or any of the other panaceas that promise restoration of competitiveness and positioning for the new order of the 20th century? Each has a compelling logic, and some have a potential link to the immediate bottom line. Unfortunately for many firms, the pivotal importance of having a large reservoir of leadership talent is not apparent until a shortage of it precipitates a major crisis.

Such crises sometimes occur in cycles of rapid growth when an organization begins to miss opportunities because it lacks sufficient leadership talent to exploit them. They can also occur after dramatic downsizing, when the new organization emerges only to discover that it lacks the leaders needed to take it in a new direction. Whatever the source of the realization, there is no quick fix to a leadership problem. The evidence is that it takes 10 to 20 years to develop general managerial skills.[1] Although people can be promoted faster than that, they can't learn the skills any faster. For this reason, organizations that consider leadership development a priority and maintain the necessary developmental infrastructure will have a long-term business advantage.

If leadership development were just a human resources program, its effectiveness could be measured by the thickness of a company's training catalog. Nothing could be more misleading, however. Firms that do a good job of developing managerial talent focus on a broad range of activities (including training) but emphasize on-the-job experience as the primary vehicle for development.[2]

Paradoxically, even executives who think of executive development in terms of human resource programs readily accept that they learned most of their managerial skills on the job. They also readily translate that personal experience into a model for others, as expressed by one executive who observed:

> Of course we believe in developing leadership. When I find someone I think has some talent, I put them in the toughest assignment I can find to develop them. If they do well, I know I made the right choice.

This straightforward description of leadership development underscores the four fundamental issues that must be addressed for any developmental program to work:

☐ "When I find someone I think has some talent" raises the question of what *potential* means, how to identify it, and who should assess it. What does it mean to have "some talent"?

☐ "The toughest assignment I can find" raises questions about what kinds of experiences can teach what kinds of things. Is toughness the key attribute? What does a tough assignment teach?

☐ "I put them in" suggests that the primary vehicle for matching talent to a developmental opportunity is the immediate manager, raising questions about how an organization can best manage

66 The pivotal importance of having a large reservoir of leadership talent is not apparent until a shortage of it precipitates a major crisis. 99

---
[1] J.P. Kotter, *The General Managers* (New York: Free Press, 1982).
[2] J.P. Kotter, *The Leadership Factor* (New York: Free Press, 1988).

EXECUTIVE DEVELOPMENT

EXHIBIT 1
A Framework for Development

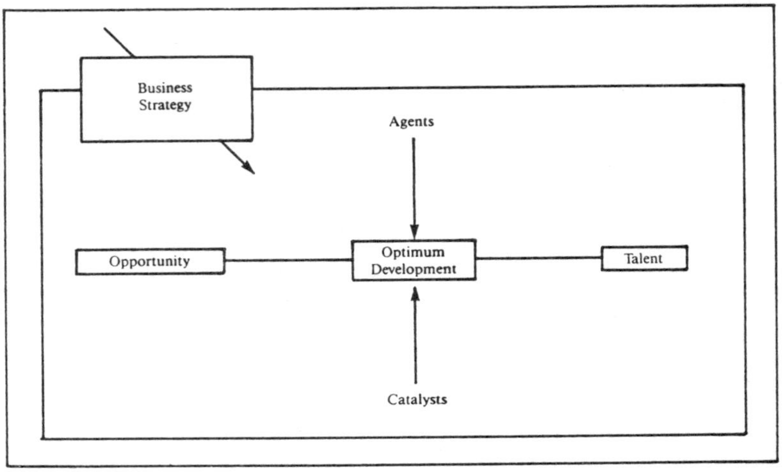

[Diagram: Business Strategy box connects to Optimum Development, which links horizontally to Opportunity and Talent, with Agents arrow from above and Catalysts arrow from below]

its strategic human assets. Is the immediate manager in the best position to make developmental decisions?

☐ Finally, "if they do well" brings up the issue of learning—notably, who is responsible for it and what, if anything, might be done to facilitate it.

These four elements, represented in Exhibit 1, constitute the backbone of a development strategy. The final outcome can be no stronger than the weakest link. If we don't know what *potential* means, we have no way to select people for developmental opportunities. If we don't understand the types of experiences that can teach specific lessons, we have no way of identifying the opportunities that would allow talented people to reach their potential.

If we have no mechanisms for getting people with specific developmental needs into the appropriate developmental opportunities (called agents in the exhibit), no growth can occur. And if we have no means of helping a person make the most of the experiences they have (called catalysts in the exhibit), potentially we've done all of this for nothing.

Each of these four elements is a domain in its own right; effectively integrating them is the core of a leadership development strategy. This does not necessarily mean developing extensive bureaucratic procedures and volumes of forms. Because development is central to the business strategy, responsibility for it properly resides in the hands of line management. The procedures will be more useful (and more used) if they are simple, efficient, and effective.

Identifying Talent

The easiest thing to believe about leadership is that we know it when we see it. Spotting executive or leadership talent is no exception, and the illusion of omniscience persists in the face of overwhelming evidence that we are flawed judges. But even if we were accurate

EXECUTIVE DEVELOPMENT

perceivers and assessors, the list of potentially important qualities that might lead to senior executive effectiveness is seemingly endless. From action orientation to zeal, few virtues would not be handy in the executive suite.

The fact that research has begun to narrow in on the sine qua non of leadership[3] reduces the sheer magnitude of possibilities, but it also highlights a crucial feature of potential: whatever the list of qualities one might desire in a leader, they are end states. That is, if one believes in development, the qualities represent what is to be developed rather than what already exists. In identifying potential, then, the focus must be on those abilities that would enable someone to acquire the end-state qualities through a series of developmental experiences. To focus on the end states themselves implies an underlying belief that desired leadership qualities are innate—or at lease residing in a person waiting to be discovered rather than awaiting development.

The suggestion, then, is that identifying talent is not simply assessing such things as the ability to set direction, align critical constituencies, and create and act within acceptable values, because these are the qualities that successful leaders have. Rather, development requires identifying people who can learn to do those things, not who necessarily do them now. Instead, one might look for such things as awareness of strengths and weaknesses, ability to seek out and use feedback, recognition of limits, ability to learn from experience, a passion for learning, demonstrated growth, and related abilities. The bottom line: identifying potential means assessing progress toward meaningful end states, but it also means assessing a person's underlying ability to learn from experience.

The executive quoted earlier in this article seemed to believe that the key to a developmental assignment was its toughness. That's not far from wrong; research on developmental experiences has documented that adversity drives growth. What is also clear is that adversity comes in many forms, that all experiences are not equal (nor do they teach the same things), and that adversity is not an unqualified blessing. In short, identifying, creating, and using experience for developmental purposes is not as simple as it seems.[4]

In spite of the commonly shared belief that tough assignments are what develop leadership, the single most common tool for on-the-job development is rotation—across functions, divisions, departments, or most recently, countries. This practice is based on the assumption that learning from experience comes primarily from exposure to something new. Conversations about developmental moves almost always contain some variation on the theme of "he needs to see how they do it in marketing" or "she needs some foreign experience" or "he needs some exposure to the R&D lab."

Research has shown that it's what a person has to do, not what he or she is exposed to, that generates crucial learning. It is simply not the same to be exposed to customers as to have to deal directly with an irate customer who has just taken his business elsewhere. It is not the same to spend six months in a plant as it is to run the plant. As obvious as this seems, the single biggest waste of learning opportunities results from a failure to specify what it is that one hopes is learned from an experience—specifically, what leadership-relevant skills are potentially taught. Exposure will happen, but it is the activities that people must engage in that can teach these skills.

The bottom line for developmental opportunities is to recognize that dif-

> **"The single most common tool for on-the-job development is rotation—across functions, divisions, departments, or most recently, countries."**

---

[3] See, for example, W. Bennis, *On Becoming a Leader* (Reading MA: Addison-Wesley, 1989); W. Bennis and B. Nanus, *Leaders: Strategies for Taking Charge* (New York: Harper & Row, 1985); and J.M. Kouzes and B.Z. Posner, *The Leadership Challenge* (San Francisco: Josey-Bass, 1987).

[4] M.W. McCall, M.M. Lombardo, and A.M. Morrison, *The Lessons of Experience* (Lexington MA: Lexington Books, 1988); and C. McCauley, "Developmental Experiences in Managerial Work," Technical Report No. 26 (Greensboro NC; Center for Creative Leadership, 1986).

EXECUTIVE DEVELOPMENT

ferent kinds of experiences (e.g., start-ups, turnarounds, staff assignments, and projects) have the potential to teach quite different things. The crucial development component lies in what a person must learn to do in order to succeed in the experience (i.e., what crucial challenges will stretch a given individual). In that sense, moving through the chairs or simple rotational assignments reveal little about the developmental potential of the experiences.

Matching Talent and Opportunity

Exhibit 1 uses the term *agent* to indicate that some mechanism is necessary to ensure that people identified as having the talent necessary to develop leadership skills actually get the opportunity to do so. In most cases, the most common agent in organizations is the immediate manager of the talented person. Immediate supervisors, however, are questionable judges of subordinate performance even in the current job.[5] Yet they are asked to evaluate another person's potential (not demonstrated performance) for a job the manager may never have had and then to make a decision against his or her best interest (which could result in losing a talented person by initiating a developmental move).

The second fatal flaw of using only the immediate manager as the agent to develop leadership skills is that keeping track of talented people over time is problematic. Each hand-off to a new manager is an independent event; any continuity of development over time would require an unlikely acceptance of personal responsibility or an unheard-of level of cooperation among disparate managers within the firm. More likely, development becomes a game of Russian roulette for the talented manager who progresses until he or she runs across a boss who, because of insecurity, bad judgment, or lack of interest, puts a stop to it.

To offset these inherent problems, sophisticated organizations develop systems that involve more than a single manager's judgment of potential and developmental needs and that provide for tracking talented people over time. These more sophisticated agents may include succession planning systems, high-potential pools overseen by a special executive development staff, or executive review committees that regularly monitor progress and development of the high-potential talent.

These mechanisms require time and commitment from line management, underlining the fact that development is primarily their responsibility. In the best-run systems, the executive resources staff guides and documents the process, serving as a resource to the line managers responsible for achieving the desired results.

Crucial Catalysts

The best practice in executive development pays careful attention to assessing potential, systematically uses experience for developmental purposes, and employs effective agents to track and champion the process of getting talented people into the developmental loop and providing them with the opportunities they need. Doing this much sets an organization apart from most others and might be sufficient if learning from experience were automatic. Unfortunately, it is not.

Many people have experiences but learn nothing or learn the wrong things. A developmentally oriented firm doesn't just throw talented people into fires; it commits itself to doing whatever it can to help them succeed in learning from the experiences they have. Whether a person is successful in performance terms may be unrelated to his or her

> **Whether a person is successful in performance terms may be unrelated to his or her success in growth terms.**

[5] See, for example, M. Sorcher, *Predicting Executive Success* (New York: Wiley, 1985).

EXECUTIVE DEVELOPMENT

EXHIBIT 2
Examples of Developmental Practices

Talent
Assessment of potential for development of executive leadership skills:

- Assess progress against leadership model
- Assess known potential flaws
- Assess previous experience
- Assess ability to learn from experience

Agents
Mechanisms for matching talent with opportunity:

- Succession planning
- Executive review committees
- Managed high-potential pool
- Immediate manager makes the decision
- Use of policy and rewards

Opportunities
Experiences that might develop leadership skills:

- Special assignments
- Adding responsibility to jobs
- Leading a start-up or turnaround
- Increased scope
- Project and task forces
- Staff assignments
- Diversity of bosses

Catalysts
Actions that facilitate learning from experience:

- Coaching
- Targeted training
- Accountability
- Feedback on development
- Contingency rewards

success in growth terms. Helping people learn requires knowing what it is that they can learn in a given experience, then setting meaningful developmental goals, establishing accountability for attaining them, and providing necessary resources.

These activities are illustrated in Exhibit 1 by the term *catalysts,* used in the sense that they precipitate or increase the rate of reaction. In this case, the goal is to produce useful learning from a mixture of talent and opportunity.

The most frequently missing ingredients in corporate development activities are catalysts that support individual learning and growth. Although performance goals are almost always specified, learning is left to chance.

In addition to developmental objectives and accountability for growth, a variety of practices can provide this catalytic function. These include coaching or teaching aimed at increasing learning, using measurement and rewards (monetary or otherwise) to encourage growth or to encourage managers to develop their staffs, providing training at crucial junctures, finding ways to provide regular and substantive feedback on developmental progress, and designing experiences so that developmental opportunity is maximized.

Developing Executive Talent

The only reason to go to all this trouble is that developing leadership talent is crucial to the business strategy. If senior management believes that leadership is not a critical source of competitive advantage, that the current supply of leadership is adequate for present and future needs, that executive and leadership ability cannot be developed, or that the cream rises without any help, then executive development will end up as a showpiece rather than a strategic tool. Even with strategic commitment, effective development systems still depend on line management's taking responsibility for all four of the necessary components shown in Exhibit 1.

Exhibit 2 summarizes some of the suggestions for identifying and assessing talent, providing meaningful developmental experiences, establishing agents to move talent into developmental opportunities, and providing catalysts to enhance the learning that takes place. Like any other serious strategic thrust, developing executive leadership requires time, resources, commitment, and risk. By making it integral to the business strategy, it can become a natural and ongoing part of running the corporation.

The other option—leaving leadership to chance—is ultimately the greater risk. ■

Part V
Appendix
Strategic Planning Techniques: Summary Articles

[28]

Designing product and business portfolios

Steps leading to construction of a portfolio model for planning strategy

Yoram Wind and
Vijay Mahajan

As an outgrowth of the diversification trend in U.S. corporations, in which companies are expanding their product lines and entering new businesses, portfolio models have gained wider acceptance. General Electric is perhaps the best-known exponent of the portfolio approach. The models fall into two general categories—the standardized approaches, which usually concentrate on growth and share of market, and the tailor-made varieties, which offer more flexibility in the dimensions along which the products or business lines are measured. This article outlines seven steps to follow in evaluating an existing portfolio model or in designing an idiosyncratic approach.

Mr. Wind is professor of marketing and director of the Center for International Management Studies at the Wharton School, University of Pennsylvania. He is also editor of the *Journal of Marketing*.

Addison-Wesley will soon publish his latest book, *Product Policy: Concepts, Methods and Strategy.* For HBR he has collaborated on an article on conjoint analysis, "New Way to Measure Consumers' Judgments" (July-August 1975). Mr. Mahajan is associate professor of marketing and director of the Center for Strategic Marketing Research at Wharton. He has written extensively on product diffusion and marketing strategy. In 1981 Addison-Wesley will also publish a book by the two authors on portfolio analysis and strategy.

In our complex business environment, companies big and small continually assess the compatibility of their strategy for each product or service—existing or planned—with the needs, resources, and objectives of the organization. Should we be in this business? Should we add a new business? How can we win and hold a substantial share of the market?

In seeking answers to such probing questions, many companies view product mix decisions as portfolio decisions. A company offers a variety of product lines, each requiring a certain investment and promising a certain return on that investment. In this view of operations, top management's role is to determine the products (or businesses) that will comprise the portfolio and to allot funds to them on some rational basis.

A number of product portfolio models have appeared over the past several years to assist management in this task. Examples are the growth/share matrix, the business profile matrix, the business assessment array, and the directional policy matrix. *Exhibit I* classifies these four models as well as five others that have also gained acceptance. Conceptually the models differ in three ways:

> Whether the model offers a general prescriptive framework or a framework tailored to that particular company's needs and its top officers' preferences.

> The dimensions used to construct the model.

> The degree to which the model imposes rules for allocating resources among products.

Exhibit II compares the nine illustrative portfolio approaches according to these three characteristics.

The question facing management is which approach, if any, to select. To the extent that the models yield the same results (strategic guidelines), the choice may not matter much. Recently, however,

Exhibit I
Selected product portfolio models and approaches

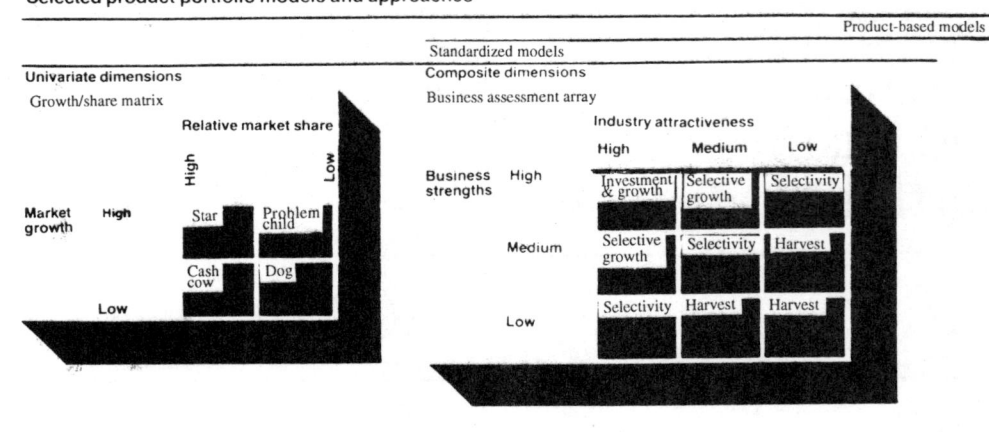

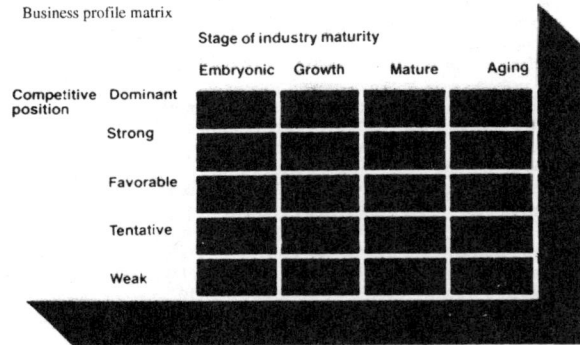

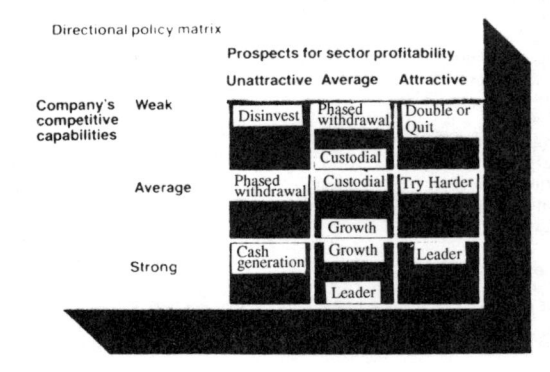

Product-based models

Standardized models

Univariate dimensions — Growth/share matrix

Relative market share / Market growth:
- High share, High growth: Star
- Low share, High growth: Problem child
- High share, Low growth: Cash cow
- Low share, Low growth: Dog

Composite dimensions — Business assessment array

Industry attractiveness (High / Medium / Low) × Business strengths (High / Medium / Low):

Business strengths \ Industry attractiveness	High	Medium	Low
High	Investment & growth	Selective growth	Selectivity
Medium	Selective growth	Selectivity	Harvest
Low	Selectivity	Harvest	Harvest

Business profile matrix

Stage of industry maturity (Embryonic / Growth / Mature / Aging) × Competitive position (Dominant / Strong / Favorable / Tentative / Weak)

Directional policy matrix

Prospects for sector profitability (Unattractive / Average / Attractive) × Company's competitive capabilities (Weak / Average / Strong):

	Unattractive	Average	Attractive
Weak	Disinvest	Phased withdrawal / Custodial	Double or Quit
Average	Phased withdrawal	Custodial / Growth	Try Harder
Strong	Cash generation	Growth / Leader	Leader

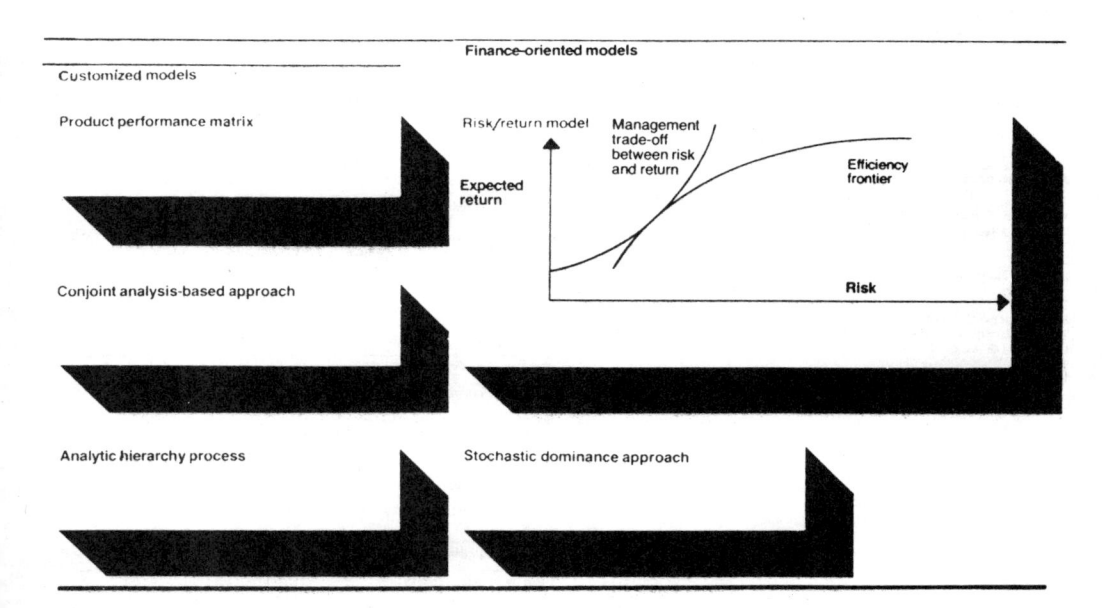

Customized models
- Product performance matrix
- Conjoint analysis-based approach
- Analytic hierarchy process

Finance-oriented models
- Risk/return model
  - Expected return / Risk
  - Management trade-off between risk and return
  - Efficiency frontier
- Stochastic dominance approach

one of us compared three of these models and found that a set of products can be classified quite differently depending on the model adopted. And, more disturbing, product classification can also depend on the measures a model uses to construct the dimensions and evaluate the products.

The importance of the measurement aspect of portfolio analysis is evident even from a cursory examination of the diverse dimensions and definitions various approaches use. But surprisingly, most of the literature on portfolios has focused not on the fundamental issues of definition and measurement but on the selling of one approach or another and on the strategic implications of, for example, the "dog" or "cash cow" status of a certain product.

We contend that, in selecting a portfolio approach or evaluating a model already in place, management should pay more attention to the construction of the model and the likely sensitivity of the results (and hence the strategic conclusions) to the dimensions employed and their measures. The selection of the correct dimensions (and a careful evaluation of their measures) is a critical matter.

Framework for design

Analysis of a product portfolio requires seven major steps:

1. Establishing the level and unit of analysis and determining what links connect them.
2. Identifying the relevant dimensions, including single-variable and composite.
3. Determining the relative importance of the dimensions.
4. To the extent that two or more dimensions are viewed as dominant, constructing a matrix based on them.
5. Locating the products or businesses on the relevant portfolio dimensions.
6. Projecting the likely position of each product or business on the dimensions if (a) no changes are expected in environmental conditions, competitive activities, or the company's strategies and if (b) changes *are* expected.
7. Selecting the desired position for each existing and new product (as a basis for developing alternative strategies to close the gap between the current and new portfolios) and deciding how resources might best be allocated among these products.

Exhibit II
Key characteristics of the nine portfolio models

Growth/share matrix

Degree of adaptability

None; a rigid framework.

Dimensions

1. Relative market share (cash generation).
2. Market growth (cash use).

Allocation rules

1. Allocation of resources among the four categories (move cash to problem child).
2. Consideration for product deletion (e.g., dogs).
3. No explicit portfolio recommendations (as to the optimal mix of stars, cows, and dogs, etc.) except with respect to the balance of cash flows.

Comments

Widely used but conceptually questionable given the forcing of two dimensions, the unique operational definition, and lack of rules for determining a portfolio of dogs, stars, and so forth. No consideration of risk. No weighting of dimensions.

Business assessment array

Degree of adaptability

More flexible than growth/share matrix but limited to two composite dimensions.

Dimensions

1. Industry attractiveness.
2. Business strengths.

Each of the dimensions is a composite of a number of variables.

Allocation rules

In its basic use, it offers slightly greater precision than the growth/share matrix. (Nine cells versus four; better definition of dimensions.) In its more sophisticated uses (as by GE), classification of products on these two dimensions is used only as input to an explicit resource allocation model.

Comments

Forcing of two dimensions that might not be the appropriate ones. Empirical determination of the correlates of the two dimensions is superior to the growth/share matrix. Yet, given the tailoring of factors to each industry, comparability across industries is difficult. No consideration of risk.

Business profile matrix

Degree of adaptability

Same as business assessment array.

Dimensions

1. Competitive market position.
2. Industry maturity.

Allocation rules

Same as business assessment array.

Comments

Same as business assessment array.

Directional policy matrix

Degree of adaptability

Same as business assessment array.

Dimensions

1. Profitability of market segment.
2. Competitive position in the segment.

Allocation rules

Same as business assessment array.

Comments

Same as business assessment array.

Not present, the reader will notice, is the strategy recommendations step. Despite their attractiveness as a ready cure for any ailment, standardized guidelines such as "all-out push for share" and "hold position" are very dangerous. If a prescription ignores any relevant dimensions or the projected position of the business under alternative scenarios, it will be quite misleading. Portfolio analysis can be an effective vehicle for analyzing and evaluating strategic options only if it exploits management's creativity and imagination—instead of conforming to some general prescription.

Establishment of the level & unit

At what level of the organization should the analysis be conducted? Ideally, at all the strategic business levels. And at the lowest level it should include each product (by its positioning, if possible) by market segment. Such thoroughness, however, takes much management time and requires huge quantities of data.

On the other hand, the aggregation of product-market segments may mean that they fall into a misleading "average" position in the portfolio, which, in turn, may cause inappropriate strategy designation. Consider the case of a manufacturer of (among other products) shampoo, shaving cream, bath soap, toothpaste, and other personal care items for which a single strategic business unit (SBU) is responsible. The company has constructed a growth/share matrix designating this SBU as a cash cow. Now, clearly this designation may be inappropriate for each line in the product mix and, further, for each item in the line. So aggregation may lead to erroneous positioning in the portfolio matrix as

Product performance matrix		Analytic hierarchy process	
Degree of adaptability	**Dimensions**	**Degree of adaptability**	**Dimensions**
Considerable; the specific dimensions are selected by management.	No general dimensions; International Harvester, for example, has used four dimensions: 1. Industry sales. 2. Product sales. 3. Market share. 4. Profitability. The data are calculated and analyzed by market segment.	Fully adaptable to management needs.	As with conjoint analysis, dimensions are determined by management.
		Allocation rules	**Comments**
		Optimal allocation among all items of the portfolio (e.g., products, market segments) is determined algorithmically.	Conceptually and mathematically very appealing, but not widely used. Allows management to evaluate strategic assumptions and allocate resources across products, market segments, and distribution networks under different scenarios. Weighting of dimensions considered.
Allocation rules	**Comments**		
Same as growth/share matrix but based on *projected* results in response to alternative marketing strategies.	Applications are limited; offers the conceptual advantage of management-determined performance dimensions and allocation of resources based on projected rather than historical performance. No weighting of dimensions.	**Risk/return model**	
		Degree of adaptability	**Dimensions**
		Limited. It is a theory-derived model.	1. Expected return (mean). 2. Risk (variance).
Conjoint analysis-based approach		**Allocation rules**	**Comments**
Degree of adaptability	**Dimensions**	Determination of optimal portfolio.	Conceptually the most defensible, yet difficult to make operational for the product-portfolio decision. Limited real-world applications.
Fully adaptable to management needs.	No general dimensions; they and their relative importance are determined by management.		
		Stochastic dominance	
Allocation rules	**Comments**	**Degree of adaptability**	**Dimensions**
Based on computer simulation which incorporates management utility functions and product performance data (supplemented by management judgment on the performance of current and new products and businesses). No optimal allocation is offered, but any portfolio can be evaluated on the basis of performance on all dimensions.	Limited applications; also time consuming. The approach is analogous to consumer choice of new products based on the relative importance of the key attributes and perception of the product's performance on these attributes.	Same as risk/return model.	The entire distribution of return.
		Allocation rules	**Comments**
		Same as risk/return.	Same as risk/return.

well as to poor resource allocation and strategy recommendations.

A hierarchical structure of portfolios would start at the level of the product line (or product group or division), proceed through the product mix of one SBU to the mix of several SBUs, and culminate at the corporate level, which would, of course, include all lower-level portfolios. This would permit evaluation of relevant strategies at the different levels of analysis and assist in designation and allocation of resources to SBUs and product lines. General Electric has a five-level portfolio approach: product, product line, market segment, SBU, and business sector.

Whereas such a hierarchy represents a considerable improvement over a single portfolio for the entire company, the complexities of modern business, particularly with respect to competition among large corporations (increasingly on a global basis), suggest the need for development of a dual hierarchy—a domestic hierarchy plus a worldwide one. Furthermore, both hierarchies should be examined not only according to patterns of competition among brands and businesses but also according to potential cooperation. That is, the company should ask itself: Which companies or businesses should we consider as candidates for merger or acquisition?

Related to the analysis level is the desired extent of market segmentation and product positioning. Portfolio analysis should be undertaken first in every relevant market segment and product position, then at higher levels across the positionings of the various product-market segments, and finally—if the company is multinational—across countries and modes of entry (such as export, licensing, and joint ventures).

The issue here is: When does it become meaningful to divide the total market into segments? And when to divide the products into specific positionings? The answers become complicated when the market boundaries cannot be identified easily. The risk of aggregating market segments and product positionings is high. Detailed positioning/segment-level portfolio analysis is necessary for higher-level portfolio examination. Without it, the value of recommendations for corporate-level portfolios is questionable, especially when the units are heterogeneous with respect to their perceived positioning and intended market segments.

According to one authority, segmentation should be limited to grouping those buyers who share strategically relevant situational or behavioral characteristics. (In such cases the company must use different marketing mixes to serve the identified segments, which will result in different cost and price structures.) Other manifestations of a strategically important segment boundary are a discontinuity in growth rates, share patterns, distribution patterns, and so forth.[1]

The marketer must take into account consumers' perceptions, their preference for and usage of the various products, their desire for variety, their inventorying activity (for example, hoarding when they expect a price increase), and the multiperson nature of consumption in most households. Traditional approaches to portfolio analysis tend to ignore the consumer and concentrate on product performance. The two focuses of analysis are not alternatives but complementary diagnostic tools.

After adding the second dimension of investigation—markets—to its portfolio analysis, management should evaluate and then settle on the most attractive combination of products and markets. Identification of a product-market portfolio and subsequent selection of the target markets and products are consistent with the concept and findings of market segmentation, which suggest that the demand for any product varies by segment. Resource allocation decisions should not be limited, therefore, only to allocation among products; they should also take into account the trade-offs of investing in various market segments.

In cases where the distribution system figures importantly in the company's marketing mix, management can extend the analysis to include distribution as a third dimension. Of course, acquisition or development of new distribution outlets is often used to improve a company's portfolio.

As a rule, the portfolio should be constructed to include all major options management has for using its resources. The company, however, may not be organized in terms of resource allocation units. If it isn't, it should consider reorganizing so that resource allocation needs will match portfolio levels and units.

Identification of the dimensions

The most common portfolio approach is based on the dimensions of market share and market growth. In contrast, the directional policy matrix is based on sector profitability and competitive position, while the product performance matrix allows selection of other dimensions as management deems appropriate.

The four standardized portfolio models rely on a matrix in which one axis represents the strength of the product or business in terms of market share or some broader characteristic while the other represents industry or market attractiveness. These models use two approaches to measure the axes: one relying on a single measurable criterion along each axis (for example, relative market share and market growth), the other using composite measures consisting of a number of objective and subjective factors to label each axis (for example, business strengths and industry attractiveness).

The factors defining the composite dimensions naturally vary among companies and even (though not often) among different businesses of the same company. Furthermore, the factors can change over time. In 1980 GE reduced its original 40 factors to 15. Six of these factors define industry attractiveness—market size, growth, profitability, cyclicality, ability to recover from inflation, and world scope—while nine define business strengths. Business strengths, in turn, have two components: market position (domestic market share, world share, share growth, and share compared with the leading competing brand) and competitive strength, defined according to leadership in five respects (quality, technology, cost, marketing, and relative profitability).

The members of top management who select the portfolio dimensions naturally assume that they

---

1. See George S. Day, "Diagnosing the Product Portfolio," *Journal of Marketing*, April 1977, p. 29.
2. Sidney Schoeffler, Robert D. Buzzell, and Donald F. Heany, "Impact of Strategic Planning on Profit Performance," HBR March-April 1974, p. 137.
3. Dan E. Schendel and G. Richard Patton, "A Simultaneous Equation Model of Corporate Strategy," *Management Science*, November 1978, p. 1611; and Jean-Claude Larréché, "On Limitations of Positive Market Share-Profitability Relationships: The Case of the French Banking Industry," *1980 Educators' Conference Proceedings* (Chicago: American Marketing Association, 1980), p. 209.

are choosing dimensions related to their corporate (and hence portfolio) objectives. Unfortunately, justification for this assumption is often unconvincing or hard to document.

Consider the market share dimension. Its inclusion in product portfolio models reflects the general acceptance of the relationship of share with competitive strength, with profitability, and with the market response function. Indeed, research for the PIMS (profit impact of market strategy) project, which examines the correlates of profitability in the modern corporation, found businesses with large market shares to be more profitable than those with small shares.[2]

This correlation is not perfect, however, and its causes are not completely understood. Is it due to the benefits of the learning curve, with respect to both product and marketing economies of scale for large-share businesses, or due to the fact that many large-share products compete on a nonprice basis and hence command higher margins and profits?

Moreover, studies of industries—for example, brewers and banks—have contradicted the positive relationship between share and profitability found by PIMS.[3] Also, a number of banks that reduced their unprofitable segments thereby boosted their profitability. Whatever the relationship between market share and profit, it is important to examine not only the relationship between share (and its measures) and profitability but also the relationship between a change in share (that is, investment in share) and a change in the resulting profitability.

The connection between market share and the product's market response function is even less understood. Supposedly, a dollar increase in the marketing effort for a low-share brand will yield a smaller return than that achieved by a dollar increase in the marketing effort for a large-share brand.

This supposed relationship, illustrated in *Exhibit III*, assumes that the low-share brand will have lower sales at zero incremental marketing effort, a lower saturation level, and probably also a less effective marketing effort (a gentler slope of the response function). Why? Because a larger-share brand can achieve greater economies of scale and because the advertising and other marketing efforts of well-known, high-share brands often spill over to benefit less-familiar brands.

If this relationship does exist, the marketer of a low-share brand must work harder to differentiate that brand. This relationship further suggests the importance of assessing the response elasticities of the company's various brands and, if it is not closely correlated with another portfolio dimension, adopting elasticity as one of the portfolio dimensions.

Operational definitions

Before settling on an existing product portfolio model or designing a new one, management must define the dimensions selected. The importance of operational definitions for the chosen dimensions, both single-variable and composite, should not be underestimated. They could significantly alter results.

Single-variable dimensions: Take account of a relative share measure, such as the one employed in the growth/share matrix (the most notable example of measurement of single-variable dimensions), and then compare it with other possible share measures based on:

1. Different units of measurement, such as dollar sales, unit sales, units purchased, or users.

2. Product definition (product lines and brands in various sizes, forms, and positionings).

3. Definition of the served market that defines the competitive arena (competitors, customers, and technology) within which the product is sold, including markets defined in terms of geography, channel, customer segment, or usage occasion.

4. The time horizon involved.

5. The nature of the denominator in the share calculation. Usually the definition of the denominator is based on either: (a) all the brands in the particular market, whether defined by the product category or preferably the perceived position of the brand; or (b) a selected number of brands—an option that includes all brands within a subcategory (like national brands), the leading competitor, or the leading two or three competitors. A third approach, less popular but conceptually more defensible, defines the denominator on the basis of all products serving the same consumer need or solving the same problem.

Clearly a marketer must make some critical decisions before selecting a definition of market share. Similar complexity faces him with the definition of any dimension. Think of product sales, of which there are at least four measures: absolute level, rate of growth, level by industry or by product class, and industry or product class rate of growth.

Whatever measure is used, it is necessary to establish the relevant instrument in terms of units (such as dollar sales or unit sales), necessary adjustments (such as per capita sales), time (such as quarterly or

Exhibit III
Hypothesized relationship between market share and market response function for competing brands

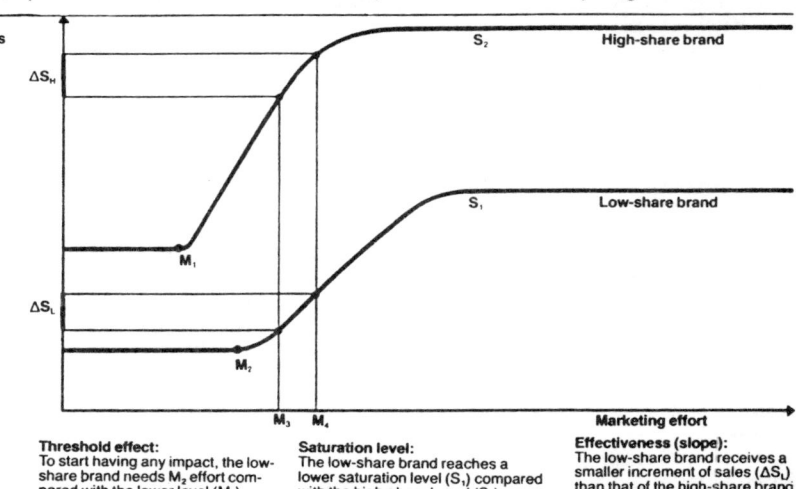

Threshold effect:
To start having any impact, the low-share brand needs M_2 effort compared with the lower level (M_1) required by the high-share brand.

Saturation level:
The low-share brand reaches a lower saturation level (S_1) compared with the high-share brand (S_2).

Effectiveness (slope):
The low-share brand receives a smaller increment of sales (ΔS_L) than that of the high-share brand (ΔS_H) for each one-unit increase in marketing effort (a move from M_3 to M_4).

---

annually), and data sources used (such as company shipments, wholesale and retail audits, or consumer diaries and reports).

Different yardsticks can, of course, produce different results. A pharmaceutical manufacturer found that sales generated by a promotion varied from success to failure depending on the data used—company shipments, physician panel, drugstore survey, and third-party payments. It is essential, therefore, that top management understand the selected measures and their properties.

Composite dimensions: Several portfolio models use composite dimensions to designate the matrix axes. The business assessment array, for example, labels one axis "business strengths" and the other "industry attractiveness." Each is a composite of a number of objective and subjective factors. The rationale is that the factors and their relative importance depend mainly on customer behavior, the nature of the product, the industry, the characteristics of the company, and the preference of its management.

Unlike the growth/share matrix approach, portfolio models using composite dimensions rely heavily on managerial judgment to identify the relevant factors and determine their relative importance. Identifying those factors requires assumptions about the relationships among them and how they will change over time. This process has the healthy result of nurturing strategic thinking, but unlike the growth/share matrix framework, it makes considerable demands on management's time.

Composite-dimension models have other limitations:

☐ They may mask important differences among products. Suppose a manufacturer evaluates three products on a composite dimension (say, business strengths) consisting of two factors. The scale is 1 (low) to 10 (high). The results might be like those in Exhibit IV. Obviously the performance characteristics differ markedly. Yet on this particular composite dimension (assuming equal weight for the two factors) the products would be assigned identical positions in the portfolio matrix.

☐ The subjective evaluation that is to an extent necessary raises questions as to who the respondents should be or how any discrepancy in their evaluations should be treated. Should we seek consensus, as in a Delphi approach? Or would any lack of consensus suggest the need to weight the judges' views according to their expertise or importance? Should we even exclude the disputed factor from the analysis?

☐ A weighting system that does not take into account close correlations among factors can produce a misleading product classification. This will hold true even if no weights are used to obtain the composite score. In this case, if the company employs five measures of sales and one measure of product technology to define business strengths, the relative weight of the two factors is not equal but 5 to 1.

☐ If the weights of the factors that are combined to develop a composite measure are to be determined empirically, based on the historical relationships among the factors, the calculation imposes heavy data requirements because of the type of statistical analysis required—like multiple regression analysis (if a dependent variable can be identified) or factor analysis.

Determination of relative importance

Most portfolio matrices, like the growth/share approach, assume equal weight for the dimensions. As we said, in composite dimensions the factors are often weighted, but rarely are differential weights placed on the two major dimensions that constitute the matrix.

In contrast, most customized portfolio models, the analytic hierarchy process (AHP) for one, allow for management's assessment of weights. Conjoint analysis has been used in the design of other customized portfolio models as a way of assessing weights assigned to the risk/return dimensions and other relevant dimensions.

To the extent that weighting calls for subjective evaluation, management must decide who the evaluators will be and how conflict among them will be resolved. These decisions cannot be left to staff members involved in the construction or implementation of the portfolio.

Construction of the portfolio matrix

Portfolio models differ in the degree to which they offer a general, rigid, and normative framework or a flexible format reflecting the user's characteristics. The growth/share framework is the most rigid, followed by the risk/return model (which takes into account differences in managers' trade-offs between risk and return). Both the directional policy matrix and the product performance matrix are flexible—the former in the factors determining the dimensions and the latter in the number and definition of the dimensions.

The simplicity of a 2x2 or 3x3 matrix makes it very attractive. It is easy to communicate and it is

Exhibit IV
Two-factor rating of three products

	Market share rating	Product technology rating	Composite dimension score
Product A	9	1	10
Product B	1	9	10
Product C	5	5	10

typically accompanied by some generalized strategic guidelines. But it becomes simplistic and misleading if (a) it ignores major dimensions and the conditions under which the recommended strategy is most likely to be effective or if (b) the grouping of continuous variables, like market share or growth, into two or three categories leads to loss of pertinent information.

Limitations like these make portfolio models not in matrix form attractive. The AHP, the most recently developed model, uses a hierarchical structure and permits complete flexibility in selecting dimensions. The risk-return approach relies on generation of efficient frontiers graphically or mathematically.

Location in the portfolio

In any portfolio analysis, the most time-consuming task is the collection of data on the products or other items in the portfolio and on their performance in terms of the selected dimensions. This evaluation requires hard data from company records (for instance, on sales and profitability) and from outside sources (for instance, market share, industry growth, and perceived positioning). And of course there is the key element of management's judgment.

Care should be given to collecting valid data. If the company uses consumer surveys, it should examine the projectability of the sample and the accuracy of the measurement instruments. Naturally, obtaining data and measures from several sources will help safeguard the reliability of the data.

Projection of the product position

In analysis of the positions of products in the portfolio, should the dimensions be measured only on the basis of historical data or should they also reflect projected positions? Most product portfolio models rely on historical data.

Measuring, say, the sales growth rate in terms of the historical growth rate in the past x years is satis-

For further exploration

Readers interested in learning more about the methodological and technical underpinnings of the portfolio models and approaches discussed in this article are referred to the following published and unpublished material.

Growth/share matrix
Bruce D. Henderson, *Perspectives on the Product Portfolio* (Boston: Boston Consulting Group, 1970); and Bruce D. Henderson, *Henderson on Corporate Strategy* (Cambridge, Mass.: Abt Books, 1979).

Business assessment array
Stanley H. Hoch, "Strategic Management in General Electric," mimeographed, February 1980; and Michael G. Allen, "Diagramming G.E.'s Planning for What's WATT," in Robert J. Allio and Malcolm W. Pennington, editors, *Corporate Planning: Techniques and Applications* (New York: AMACOM, 1979).

Business profile matrix
Robert V.L. Wright, "A System for Managing Diversity," in Stuart Henderson Britt and Harper W. Boyd Jr., editors, *Marketing Management and Administrative Action* (New York: McGraw-Hill, 1978).

Directional policy matrix
The Directional Policy Matrix: A New Aid to Corporate Planning (Royal Dutch Shell Company, 1975).

Product performance matrix
Yoram Wind and Henry Claycamp, "Planning Product Line Strategy: A Matrix Approach," *Journal of Marketing*, January 1976, p. 20.

Conjoint analysis-based approach
Yoram Wind, *Product Policy: Concepts, Methods, and Strategy* (Reading, Mass.: Addison-Wesley, forthcoming).

Analytic hierarchy process
Yoram Wind and Thomas Saaty, "Marketing Applications of the Analytic Hierarchy Process," *Management Science*, July 1980, p. 641.

Risk-return model
Yoram Wind, "Product Portfolio: A New Approach to the Product Mix Decision," in Ronald C. Curhan, editor, *Proceedings of the August 1974 American Marketing Association Conference*, p. 460; and Richard Cardozo and Yoram Wind, "Portfolio Analysis for Strategic Product-Market Planning," Wharton School working paper, 1980.

Stochastic dominance approach
Vijay Mahajan, Yoram Wind, and John Bradford, "Stochastic Dominance Rules for Product Portfolio Analysis," *Management Science*, special issue of TIMS Studies on Marketing Planning Models, Andy Zoltners, editor, forthcoming in 1981.

---

factory if that growth rate is expected to continue. If, however, the company anticipates deviation from it, the historical data should be supplemented with projected performance and, where possible, conditional forecasts. Such forecasts—also used in the product performance matrix approach—consist of, for example, a series of projections conditional on certain marketing activities.

A corporation can also forecast performance for a number of environmental scenarios. The analysis should include at least three scenarios: (1) continuation of the current trend, (2) a scenario in which all environmental, market, and competitive conditions are favorable, and (3) a disaster scenario. Sensitivity analyses for both the short and long term can ascertain the sensitivity of results to these (and perhaps other) scenarios. General Electric, Monsanto, Shell Oil, and Atlantic Richfield, among other companies, use scenarios in strategy formulation.[4]

A variety of econometric forecasting procedures are in use for projecting the performance of existing products. Simulated test market is one of the new-product forecasting models available.

At this stage, management evaluates the projection procedure and the likely future scenarios. As evaluators, the executives should be asking such questions as: Do the assumptions of the approach make sense? Do the projections meet our expectations? As devil's advocates, they can help those designing the portfolio to make sense out of the approach and the projections.

Selection of the desired portfolio

It goes without saying that the most critical aspect in portfolio analysis is a decision on what changes, if any, are necessary. Unfortunately, most of the standard portfolio models do not offer explicit guidelines for establishing an optimal portfolio. For example, classifying certain products as dogs, problem children, cash cows, and stars does not help determine their optimal mix.

Obviously management wants many stars and no dogs. Yet in many cases the cash cows, not the stars, provide the funds necessary to fuel growth and yield profits. Furthermore, at times dogs may be essential as insurance against the risk of certain contingencies. A multinational may cherish its foreign dogs as hedges against currency fluctuations, likely government restrictions, or materials shortages.

The standardized portfolio models are useful primarily for analyzing the relationships among business units and products. They do not offer answers to questions like: When should a cash cow be milked of its cash? When should a dog be disposed of? Which stars should be selected for investment and which de-emphasized? At the same time, by suggesting simple strategies such as "harvesting," the standard models may constrain management's motivation to try alternative solutions like repositioning products or developing new domestic or international market segments.

Furthermore, most of the current portfolio models, designed to accommodate existing product-market relationships, lack guidelines to deal with corporate directional changes. These models do not answer such questions as: How can we convert a problem child to a star? How can we find new stars? What characteristics should a new product line have to balance the company's portfolio?

---

[4] For a description of how GE uses environmental scenarios for this purpose, see Ian H. Wilson, "Reforming the Strategic Planning Process: Integration of Social and Business Needs," *Long Range Planning*, October 1974, p. 2.

[5] See Derek F. Channon, "Commentary on Strategy Formulation," in Dan E. Schendel and Charles W. Hofer, eds., *Strategic Management* (Boston: Little, Brown, 1979).

Sometimes the way the portfolio model is constructed suggests an unwise change. Conceivably, for example, a low-market share business in a low-growth market may be very attractive in cash flow terms if it is also low in capital intensity. Since the growth/share matrix does not explicitly consider capital intensity, a dog may be inappropriately considered a candidate for divestment.[5] Similarly, a business identified as high in market attractiveness that also has a strong position in the business assessment array could produce a good ROI but not a good cash flow.

In shaping the portfolio, top officers should not leave the generation of strategy options to the staff. Often top managers prefer to position themselves as evaluators, but their involvement in the creative process is critical to the enterprise. The staff members who develop the portfolio should incorporate a resource allocation procedure to guide management in apportioning financial and material resources among the existing and new portfolio parts.

In a portfolio context there are two approaches to resource allocation:

> General Electric's approach, which uses GE's business assessment array as a product classification device. The company combines information from this process with other data to build a resource allocation model.

> The analytic hierarchy model, which includes a resource allotment algorithm in the portfolio model.

What kind of approach?

Since its emergence in the early 1970s, the portfolio technique—along with related concepts like the SBU and the experience curve—has become the framework for strategic planning in many diversified companies. Now the art has advanced enough to give a diversified company a variety of approaches when it is considering installing such a system or substituting one that evidently meets its needs better than the current portfolio.

Conceptually, we think, the tailor-made approaches are superior because they:

> Permit inclusion of the conceptually desirable dimensions of risk and return, plus any other idiosyncratic elements viewed by management as important.

> Stimulate creativity by forcing management's involvement in developing strategic options.

> Help to gain an advantage over competitors, who are ignorant of the company's portfolio framework and so cannot "read" it with the aim of anticipating the company's strategic moves.

> Can offer explicit guidelines for resource allocation among the portfolio items.

But a tailor-made system costs more, mainly in data requirements and management time. Even if top management decides not to implement an idiosyncratic approach (based on a cost-benefit analysis), an evaluation of currently used portfolio models, using the seven steps we have described, should add to the value of the portfolio analysis and the quality of the strategies designed to build a new portfolio.⊽

Not what they seem...

"You see, this has got to be learned; there isn't any getting around it. A clear starlit night throws such heavy shadows that if you didn't know the shape of a shore perfectly you would claw away from every bunch of timber, because you would take the black shadow of it for a solid cape; and you see you would be getting scared to death every fifteen minutes by the watch. You would be fifty yards from shore all the time when you ought to be within fifty feet of it. You can't see a snag in one of those shadows, but you know exactly where it is, and the shape of the river tells you when you are coming to it. Then there's your pitch-dark night; the river is a very different shape on a pitch-dark night from what it is on a starlit night. All shores seem to be straight lines, then, and mighty dim ones, too; and you'd run them for straight lines only you know better."

From
Mark Twain, *Life on the Mississippi* (New York: the New American Library), p. 58.

12

Strategic Decision Processes

AN INTEGRATIVE FRAMEWORK AND FUTURE DIRECTIONS[1]

Nandini Rajagopalan, Abdul M. A. Rasheed and Deepak K. Datta

Research in the area of strategic management has been characterized by a dichotomy between 'content' and 'process' issues. However, content issues such as portfolio management through mergers, acquisitions or divestments, product-market choice, and the alignment of firm strategies with environmental characteristics have dominated the research agenda. Models proposed by Ansoff (1965), Andrews (1971), Grant and King (1980), and others, as well as Porter's (1980) work on generic strategies, have provided content researchers with a common vocabulary and a reasonable level of consensus on underlying theoretical and research questions. To some extent, this has led to the building of cumulative knowledge. On the other hand, there has been less theory-building and empirical research directed at process issues, which focus on the political, informational, and temporal dimensions by which strategic decisions are made and implemented. However, currently there is renewed interest in process research, as well as increased awareness of the critical interrelationships between content and process issues (Huff and Reger, 1987). As suggested by Mintzberg and Waters (1985:269): 'More research is required on the process of strategy formation to complement the extensive work currently taking place on the content of strategies; indeed, we believe that research on the former can significantly influence the direction taken by research on the latter (and vice versa)'.

In order to provide meaningful direction to strategic decision processes research, it is important to identify the crucial patterns and contradictions in extant research. Considerable diversity in the findings of past studies has often made it difficult to arrive at generalizable conclusions. For example, the performance implications of comprehensiveness in decision processes is still not clear, with studies finding both negative (e.g., Fredrickson and Mitchell, 1984) as well as positive (e.g., Eisenhardt, 1989) performance effects of comprehensive decision processes in rapidly changing environments.

The objectives of this paper are threefold. First, to review and synthesize past research on strategic decision processes. Unlike the exhaustive review of the entire body of stategic process research undertaken by Huff and Reger (1987), the focus of our review is strictly limited to empirical research on strategic decision processes. In order to do the review in a systematic manner, we develop a parsimonious integrative framework which identifies critical relationships among key antecedent and outcome variables. This framework seeks to clarify our understanding of the determinants and outcomes of strategic decision processes. Second, the paper uses the framework to identify gaps in the body of research, i.e., areas in which past research has been limited. Finally, based on a review of the literature, the paper suggests several useful directions for future research. These suggestions address theoretical, methodological, and managerial issues.

Theoretical Overview and Integrative Framework

Following Mintzberg, Raisinghani and Theoret (1976) and Schilit and Paine (1987), strategic decisions can be defined as those that utilize an organization's threats and opportunities to enhance its long-term prospects. By their very nature, strategic decision problems are more complicated and ill-defined than other problems (Lyles, 1987). They are also characterized by interconnectedness to other problems, complexity with recursive feedback, uncertainty in a dynamic environment, ambiguity dependent upon viewpoint, and conflicting trade-offs associated with alternative solutions (Mason and Mitroff, 1981). A number of theoretical models of strategic decision processes have been proposed. In the following paragraphs we briefly compare the major models and identify key variables and sets of relationships which form the basis for our integrative model of strategic decision processes.

Strategic decision process models: a comparison

Models that attempt to explain the process of strategic decision making reflect different conceptions of organizations. They range from 'rational' models that present the image of an integrated, well co-ordinated decision making body, making reasoned choices from clearly defined alternatives (e.g., Andrews, 1971; Ansoff, 1965) to political/behavioural models in which decisions are viewed as an outcome of bargaining and negotiations among individuals and organizational subunits with conflicting perceptions, personal stakes and unequal power (Narayanan and Fahey, 1982; Pettigrew, 1973; Tushman, 1977). Different classificatory schemes of strategic decision process models have been suggested by Allison (1971), Chaffee (1985), Mintzberg (1973) and Lyles and Thomas (1988). These models differ substantially in terms of their underlying assumptions, biases, and performance outcomes. This is not surprising, given the models' underlying theoretical grounding in diverse disciplines such as social psychology, and group decision-making (Janis, 1982) on the one hand and political/governmental processes (Lindblom, 1959) on the other.

While a detailed review of the various strategic decision process models is beyond the scope of this paper, we can classify those models under the following four broad categories: (1) rational/analytical; (2) political/power-behavioural; (3) organizational process/bureaucratic; and (4) organizational adaptation/adaptive models. These categories reflect different assumptions about the decision context and different characteristics of the decision process itself. A comparison of the assumptions and characteristics underlying each category is provided in table 12.1. While the table highlights differences across categories, considerable diversity exists even within categories, especially in the conceptualizations used by various authors. For example, while 'logical incrementalism' (Quinn, 1980) and 'disjointed incrementalism' (Braybrooke and Lindblom, 1970) both fall into the category of adaptive models, the former emphasizes the existence of a visionary leader while the latter describes a situation which lacks a central, co-ordinating vision.

The classificatory scheme presented in table 12.1 is by no means exhaustive. Moreover, the paper does not advocate the use of a single model of the strategic decision making process to the exclusion of other models for either normative or descriptive purposes. In fact, much of the richness of process research emanates from the use of multiple conceptualization of the same organizational event (e.g., Allison, 1971; Johnson, 1988). Rather, what is needed is a clarification of the assumptions and attributes of each of the models. In this way, empirical investigations of organizational processes can be guided by a clearer understanding of the model employed and its methodological imperatives, rather than an ad hoc examination of relationships among variables belonging to radically different models.

Strategic decision processes: an integrative framework

Table 12.1 allows us to draw certain broad conclusions. First, strategic decisions are made in the context of two sets of factors: (1) an organization's environment, in terms of its complexity and volatility; and (2) organizational conditions such as the internal power structure, past performance, past strategies, and the extent of organizational slack. Since both sets of factors vary from one organization to another even within the same industry, strategic decisions are likely to follow different patterns in different organizations. Second, even within a single organization, the process varies across decisions. This is due to differences in the impetus for the decision, the urgency associated with the decision, the degree of outcome uncertainty, and the extent of resource commitment. Thus, environmental and organizational factors as well as decision-specific factors determine a wide range of decision process characteristics, such as the duration of the process, the degree of rationality and comprehensiveness, the amount of political activity, and the extent of individual/subunit involvement in the decision process. The decision process, in turn, translates itself into certain process outcomes, namely, the timeliness/speed of the decision (Eisenhardt, 1989), the level of commitment from individual and organizational units (Carter, 1971), and the extent of organizational learning (Dutton and Duncan, 1987). Process characteristics as well as process outcomes in turn influence economic outcomes such as ROI/ROA and sales or profit growth (Eisenhardt and Bourgeois, 1988; Fredrickson and Mitchell, 1984). The interrelationships identified above can be depicted in the form of an integrative strategic decision process framework (figure 12.1). In addition to helping integrate the various perspectives, it serves as an analytical review scheme to summarize past empirical research on strategic decision processes. As noted by Ginsberg and Venkatraman (1985:422), '... an analytic review scheme is necessary for systematically discerning patterns from a widely differing set of studies and evaluating the contributions of a given body of research'. Such a framework also constitutes a broader, more completely specified model which can form the basis for identifying issues for future research.

This framework identifies primary links (I–VI) and secondary links (represented by dotted lines). We shall focus on the primary links since these links directly explore relationships between decision process characteristics, their antecedents, and their outcomes.

Figure 12.1 identifies six primary linkages, with the central role played by strategic decision process characteristics. This framework identifies three sets of antecedent relationships: environmental factors (Link I), organizational factors (Link II), and decision specific factors (Link III) and two sets of outcome relationships: process outcomes (Link IV), and economic outcomes (Link V). It also postulates relationships between process and economic outcomes (Link VI). These six sets of relationships are directly relevant for understanding the antecedents and outcomes of different types of strategic decision processes. It is important to note that our definition of the strategic decision process subsumes all the different steps involved in making strategic decisions, i.e., problem/issue identification,

Table 12.1 Comparison of strategic decision making processes models

Characteristics	Rational/analytical	Political/power/behavioral	Organizational processes/bureaucratic	Organizational adaptation/adaptive
Classification examples	Allison (1971: Model I) Chaffee (1985: Linear) Mintzberg (1973: Planning) Lorange & Vancil (1977) Andrews (1965) Ansoff (1965), etc.	Allison (1971: Model III) Tushman (1977) Pettigrew (1973) Narayanan & Fahey (1982)	Allison (1971: Model II) Mazzolini (1981)	Chaffee (1985: Adaptive) Mintzberg (1973: Adaptive) Quinn (1980) Braybrooke & Lindblom (1970) Miles, Snow, Meyer & Coleman (1977), Summer (1980)
Environment of the organization	Closed, certain and relatively predictable	Complex and unpredictable	Largely routine; predictable for sub-units	Complex, relatively unpredictable
Internal power structure	Centralized, integrated power structure	Dispersed bases of power. Existence of groups with conflicting priorities and perceptions	Loosely allied sub-units with parochial priorities. Fractionated power without strong leadership	Less centralized and integrated
Organizational norms and traditions	Not vital to strategy formulation. Could be a criterion in alternative evaluation	May/may not exist. Used as a bargaining/negotiating tool	Well established procedures and practices. Rules govern actions	Constitute a constraint in decision making.
Role of top management/leadership	Opportunity/problem identification, co-ordination and communication of alternatives	Coalition management, building commitment, keeping political exposure low and forcing decisions	Initiating force in problem identification, managing the structural context to influence behaviour. Providing approval/commitment to a course of action	problem/opportunity identification. Gearing internal organization to achieve alignment. Building awareness

Continued overleaf

Time horizon	Brief and timely	Many interruptions, delayed	Quick for routine decisions. Delayed for complex decisions spanning many sub-units	Varies from one decision to another
Focus of decision making	Achievement of predetermined goals	Choice of acceptable/workable alternative	Sequential problem solving as per standard operating procedures	Organization-environment alignments. Achievement of organizational goals
Nature of organizational goals	Predetermined and explicit	Determined by conflict/compromise between coalitions	Constraints that limit the choice of alternatives	Changing goals that reflect demands of the environment
Impetus for change	Problem/opportunity	Individual/group initiative	Problem/top management's initiative	Environmental opportunity/threat, internal performance standards, performance failure
Decision process	Linear. Formulation precedes implementation	Iterative. Commitment built prior to choice of alternative	Centralized formulation. Implementation as per standard operating procedures	Co-evolving goals and means for implementation

280   Designing Strategic Systems

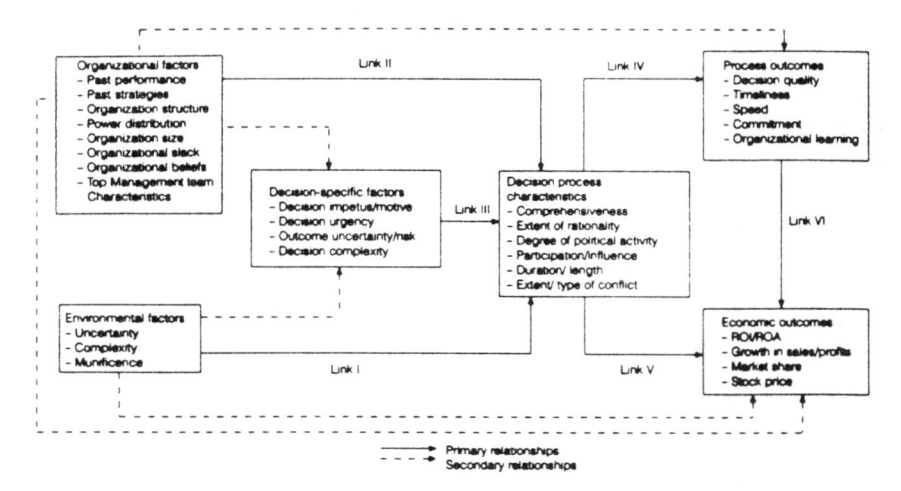

Figure 12.1 Strategic decision processes: an integrative framework

alternative generation, evaluation, and selection (Fredrickson, 1984). While a few studies have examined how strategic decision process characteristics differ across different phases (Fahey, 1981; Nees, 1983; Schilit, 1987) the focus has not been on the strategic decision process as a whole. Moreover, these studies do not identify any consistent or significant pattern in the differences among the various phases. This suggests that there is limited utility in distinguishing among these phases.

Link I in the framework pertains to the relationship between environmental factors and strategic decision process characteristics. The key issue addressed in research related to this link is how environmental factors (e.g., environmental complexity or uncertainty) influence strategic decision process characteristics (e.g., the extent of rationality and comprehensiveness). On the other hand, Link II research has primarily examined how organizational factors such as organizational size, past strategies and performance, structure, top management team characteristics, beliefs, and organizational slack influence decision process characteristics. Research on Link III has examined the relationships between decision-specific factors such as decision urgency, decision impetus, decision complexity, and outcome uncertainty, and process characteristics. Finally, Links IV, V and VI focus on outcomes and attempt to establish some prescriptive relevance for research on strategic decision making by relating it to either process outcomes (IV) or economic outcomes (V) or both (VI). The following section reviews key studies in each linkage as well as emerging patterns and contradictions.

Review of Past Empirical Literature

A systematic search[2] was undertaken to identify empirical studies which examined at least one of the six linkages identified in figure 12.1. Each study was then classified by one of the authors along six key theoretical and methodological dimensions: the underlying theoretical bases of the paper, sample, data sources/methods, measures of key variables (including the controls used), analytic methods and major findings. The classification was independently verified by co-authors for the purpose of validity and consistency. The results of our review are presented in table 12.2. The table is organized in terms of studies which examined a single linkage, followed by studies which examined multiple linkages.

Link I: Relationships between environmental factors and decision process characteristics

As seen in table 12.2, studies pertaining to Link I have focused primarily on one environmental dimension, namely, the extent of environmental uncertainty defined in terms of stability (e.g., Fredrickson, 1984, Fredrickson, 1985, Fredrickson and Iaquinto, 1989) or velocity (e.g., Eisenhardt and Bourgeois, 1988; Eisenhardt, 1989). The findings of studies belonging to this stream are, however, somewhat contradictory. For example, studies conducted by Fredrickson and his colleagues indicate that comprehensive strategic decision processes are associated with superior economic performance in stable environments and inferior performance in unstable environments. In contrast, Eisenhardt's studies found that effective strategic decisions in high velocity environments, though made within a short time duration, are characterized by comprehensiveness. This contradiction may be partly attributable to organizational factors, such as power distribution and information processing systems, which were included in Eisenhardt's studies, but not in Fredrickson's. In addition, Fredrickson and Iaquinto (1989) found significant differences in the levels and types of comprehensiveness across industries, which suggests that industry factors play a crucial moderating role in the relationship considered in Link I. These studies also indicate that there may be important interaction effects between environmental and organizational factors when we consider the performance effects of decision processes. Thus, not only do different combinations of environment and strategic decision process characteristics have different performance effects, but also within a given environment, different combinations of decision processes and organizational contexts may give rise to different performance implications.

Review of Link I studies also revealed certain major gaps in the literature. For example, the effects of two important aspects of the environment,

Table 12.2 Summary of empirical studies on strategic decision processes

Study/links	Theoretical bases	Sample	Data sources/methods	Measures	Analytic methods	Major findings
Welsh & Slusher (1986) Link II	Contingency theory and political models of decision making	40 professional colleges (decision about selection of a dean)	Questionnaires and interviews	*Organizational factors* Task specialization, faculty heterogeneity, centralization, consensus, interdependence *Decision process characteristic* Political activity	Correlations Hierarchical regression	When interdependence is low, increasing consensus leads to more political activity among faculty members.
Duhaime & Baird (1987) Link II	Divestment theory	91 divested units in mail study, 56 personal interviews in Fortune 500 firms	Mail survey, personal interviews	*Organizational factor* Unit sales as a percentage of total firm sales (measure of unit size) *Process characteristic* Unit manager's involvement	Chi-square	Managers of smaller units generally had greater involvement in the decision process than did managers of larger units. Business unit size is an important issue in divestment decision-making.
Langley (1990) Link II	Contingency theory	In-depth analysis at senior levels in three organizations, eight/ten recent strategic issues	80 interviews with senior managers, analysts, professionals and line managers	*Organizational factors* Three structural types (machine bureaucracy, professional bureaucracy, 'adhocracy') *Decision process characteristic* Formal analysis	Content analysis Kruskal-Wallis test Chi-square	Patterns in decision making processes and the use of formal analysis related to organizational structure, leadership style and the nature of issues faced by the organization.

Continued overleaf

Schilit (1987) Link III	Rational decision models, socio-political decision models	60 middle-level managers, 329 strategic decisions	Questionnaires, participant records, single informant	*Decision-specific factor* Riskiness/return *Decision process characteristic* Upward influence *Controls* Stage of the process, type and size of organization	Frequencies Tests for proportion differences Multiple regressions	Upward influence activity more likely in i) low risk/return decisions than high risk/return decisions ii) implementation than formulation iii) private organizations than in public organizations.
Schwenk (1984) Link IV	Group decision making	80 undergraduate students	Laboratory experiment, questionnaires	*Decision process characteristics* Decision making approach – Dialectical inquiry, devil's advocacy or consensus *Process outcomes* Number of strategic alternatives, number of functional area alternatives, satisfaction with the process	ANOVA	Subjects using DA & DI reported higher satisfaction than those using expert approach. DI worked better with video presentation and DA with written aids.

(continued)

Study/links	Theoretical bases	Sample	Data sources/methods	Measures	Analytic methods	Major findings
Schweiger, Sandberg & Ragan (1986) Link IV	Group decision making	120 MBA students	Laboratory experiment, questionnaires	*Decision making characteristics* Decision making approach – DI, DA or consensus *Process outcomes* Number of assumptions, quality of assumptions and recommendations, satisfaction and desire to continue to work in group, acceptance of group decisions	MANOVA, ANOVA	Quality of recommendations DI & DA > C Quality of assumptions surfaced DI > DA Satisfaction with decision and desire to continue to work in group C > DI & DA
Schweiger, Sandberg & Rechner (1989) Link IV	Group decision making	120 middle and upper-middle level managers from three divisions of a Fortune 500 company	Laboratory experiment, questionnaires	*Decision process characteristics* Decision making approach – DI, DA or consensus *Process outcomes* Number, validity, and importance of assumptions, quality of recommendations, satisfaction and desire to continue to work with group, acceptance of group decision, critical evaluation, meeting duration	MANOVA, ANOVA Correlations	Quality of decisions: DI = DA > C Acceptance of decisions: C > DI = DA Experience in using DI, DA & C reduced time required to reach decision and improved decision quality, critical re-evaluation levels and reactions of group members

Continued overleaf

Schweiger & Sandberg (1989) Link IV	Group decision making	120 MBA students	Laboratory experiment, questionnaires	*Decision process characteristics* Decision making approach – DI, DA or consensus *Process outcomes* Number, validity and importance of assumptions: quality of recommendations *Other* Utilization of individual capabilities	Construct validity & reliability tests MANOVA, ANOVA	Quality of recommendations DI & DA > C Quality of assumptions DI > DA, C DI yields better group performance on all measures, but does not differ substantially from DA in utilization of individual members' capabilities
Schwenk (1990) Link IV	Group decision making	42 executive MBA students from business and not-for-profit organizations	Questionnaires	*Decision process characteristics* Decision making approach – DI, DA or consensus *Process outcomes* Quality of decision: overall quality, clarity, assertiveness	Factor analysis Correlations	High conflict is associated with high quality in not-for-profit organizations but with low quality in for-profit organizations
Dess (1987) Link V	Organization theory	74 members of the top management team of 19 privately held firms in the paints and allied products industry	On-site interviews and mail questionnaires	*Decision Process characteristics* Consensus on competitive methods *Performance* Sales growth, after tax return on assets, overall firm performance *Controls* Sales	Correlational analysis ANOVA	Consensus on methods/strategies is positively related to organizational performance

(continued)

Study/links	Theoretical bases	Sample	Data sources/methods	Measures	Analytic methods	Major findings
Bourgeois (1980) Link V	Political and behavioural models of decision making	CEO's of 12 non-diversified public corporations plus 67 members of their top management teams	On-site interviews, questionnaires	*Decision process characteristics* Consensus on industry relevant competitive weapons *Performance* Factor score of ROA, growth in capital, growth in net earnings, growth in EPS, improvement in ROS	Analysis of variance	Consensus on means leads to higher performance
Fahey (1989) Links II & III	Rational decision models, behavioural/political decision models	Six multi-divisional firms in diverse industries, strategic energy management decisions in each firm, key executives at corporate and divisional levels	Structured questionnaires interviews, multiple informants	No a priori constructs/measures: decision process characteristics derived from observations/descriptions	Inductive/descriptive theory building No statistical tests	Strategic decision processes are characterised by both rational and behavioural/political processes: phases in the process are interrelated, interactive, and often characterized by considerable political activity. Also influenced by degree of criticalness, impetus and frequency of occurrence.

Continued overleaf

Jemison (1981) Links I & II	Strategic contingency theories of intra-organizational power	124 senior executives from 15 firms in 3 industries	Survey questionnaires, multiple respondents	*Organizational factors* 3 types of power bases *Environmental factors* 3 boundary spanning roles *Decision process characteristic* Departmental influence *Controls* Industry type	Construct reliability tests ANOVA Correlation analysis	Environmentally derived sources of strategic decision making have a greater association with departmental influence than organizationally derived sources
Astley, Axelsson, Butler, Hickson & Wilson (1982) Links II & III	Political models of decision making	150 decision topics analysed in 30 organizations	Rating of cases by researchers	*Organizational factor* Cleavage *Decision specific factor* Complexity *Decision process characteristics* Scrutiny, negotiation, discontinuity, centralization, duration *Process outcome* Synopticism, anticipation and acceptability	Generalization based on case studies Cross tabulation of data	Centralization is high when complexity and political cleavage is high. When decision is simple and without cleavage, decision making process is fast. Negotiation is high when political cleavage is high.
Fredrickson & Mitchell (1984) Links I, V	Synoptic and incremental decision making	109 executives in 27 firms	Structured interviews, questionnaires utilizing decision scenarios	*Decision process characteristic* Comprehensiveness *Performance* ROA, % of sales growth	Partial correlations	Negative relationship between comprehensiveness and performance. Relationship holds for both measures of performance.

(continued)

Study/links	Theoretical bases	Sample	Data sources/methods	Measures	Analytic methods	Major findings
Fredrickson (1984) Links I, V	Synoptic and incremental decision making	152 executives in 38 firms	Structured interviews, questionnaires utilizing decision scenarios	*Decision process characteristic* Comprehensiveness *Performance* ROA, % of sales growth	Partial correlations	Positive relationship between comprehensiveness and performance (ROA) in a stable environment. However, no significant relationship is observed when performance is operationalized as sales growth.
Fredrickson (1985) Links I, II, III	Organizational decision making	321 MBA students and 116 upper-middle level executives	Laboratory study, questionnaires	*Organizational factors* Past performance *Environmental factors* Opportunity, threat *Decision process characteristic* Comprehensiveness	MANOVA, ANOVA	MBA students were more comprehensive when recommending actions in response to environmental threats and poor performance than to environmental opportunities and excellent performance. Similar results were not observed in the case of executives.

Continued overleaf

Shrivastava & Grant (1985) Links I, II, III, IV	Organizational information processing, organizational learning, adaptive decision making models	61 senior executives from 31 firms in diverse industries, computerization decisions	Interviews, organizational records	No a priori measures; several constructs; organizational, environmental and process characteristics derived from post-facto analysis	Grounded theory and historical analyses Within-case and cross-case comparisons Thematic analyses Frequencies & descriptive statistics	Four models of strategic decision making can be identified: managerial autocracy, systemic bureaucracy, adaptive planning, and political expediency. Each is characterized by different organizational and environmental conditions, process characteristics, and outcomes.
Bourgeois (1985) Links I, II, V	Group decision making	20 nondiversified firms, 99 responses (multiple respondents from each firm including CEO)	Interviews, questionnaires, secondary sources	*Environmental factors* Volatility, perceived environmental uncertainty (PEU) *Decision process characteristic* consensus *Economic outcomes* ROTA, growth in net earnings, EPS, return on sales and capital	Correlations Factor analysis	Consensus on PEU and goals together lead to poor economic performance. Congruence between PEU and volatility is positively related to performance. Diversity in environmental perceptions and goals related positively to performance, but only when it occurs in conjunction with congruence between PEU and volatility.

(continued)

Study/links	Theoretical bases	Sample	Data sources/methods	Measures	Analytic methods	Major findings
Pinfield (1986) Links II, III	Structured and anarchic decision making	A Canadian governmental bureaucratic organization	Participant observation, archival data, interviews	*Decision specific factor* Decision urgency *Decision process characteristic* Participation *Organizational factors* Structural arrangements, organizational goals	Case study/ Qualitative methodology	A partial synthesis of the structured and anarchic decision models can link changes in participation and external variables to decision process.
Miller (1987) Links II, V	Contingency theory	CEOs, VPs or general managers of 97 firms (multiple respondents)	Questionnaires	*Organizational factors* Structure: integration, decentralization, complexity *Process characteristics* Rationality, assertiveness, interaction *Performance* Self reported scores on relative profits, growth in income & ROI	Principal components analysis Multiple regression	Organizational structures and strategy-making processes must be complementary to ensure good performance. Formal integration was found to be positively related to rationality and interaction in strategy making. Decentralization showed a weak positive association with interaction and assertiveness.

Continued overleaf

Schilit & Paine (1987) Links III & IV	Rational decision models, group decision making, socio-political models	60 middle-level managers, 329 strategic decisions	Questionnaires, participant records, interviews, single informant	*Decision-specific factors* Information source, riskiness, return *Decision process characteristics* Duration, coalition activity, conflict, rationality *Process outcomes* Speed *Controls* Stage of process, functional background	Factor analysis Chi-square tests	Higher the riskiness/return, greater is the duration of the process, the use of collaborative and incremental techniques, and the level of coalition activity and negotiation.
Segev (1987) Links II, V	Contingency theory, strategic typologies	133 MBA students	Laboratory experiment, questionnaires	*Organizational factors* Strategic type: prospectors, analysers, defenders and reactors *Decision process characteristics* Strategy making mode: entrepreneurial adaptive and planning *Economic outcomes* Market shares, profitability measures	MANOVA, ANOVA Correlations Fisher Exact tests Cronbach Alphas for reliabilities	Strong associations between strategic types and strategy making modes. Fit between strategic type and mode associated with higher market share for prospectors.

(continued)

Study/links	Theoretical bases	Sample	Data sources/methods	Measures	Analytic methods	Major findings
Bourgeois & Eisenhardt (1988) Links I, V	Rational, political and incremental models of decision making	4 decisions in 4 microcomputer firms (multiple informants)	Interviews and questionnaires	*Decision process characteristics* Comprehensiveness, newness of alternatives tried *Process outcomes* Decision speed *Economic outcomes* Market acceptance of product, sales and profitability	Embedded multiple case design	In high velocity environments, successful firms do comprehensive analysis but make quick decisions, have powerful CEOs & TMTs, and seek risk and innovation but execute safe, incremental implementation.
Eisenhardt and Bourgeois (1988) Links I, II, IV, V, VI	Political models of decision making	8 firms in microcomputer industry (multiple informants)	Interviews, questionnaires, secondary sources	*Organizational factor* Centralization of power *Decision process characteristics* Political behaviour, conflict, stability of alliances *Process outcomes* Decision speed *Economic outcomes* CEO's ranking relative to other firms in industry, sales growth, return on sales	Grounded theory and historical analyses Within-case and cross-case comparisons Thematic analyses Frequencies and descriptive statistics	Politics arises from power centralization. Politics is organized into stable coalitions based on demographic characteristics. Politics within top management teams are associated with poor firm performance (both in economic and process outcomes).

Continued overleaf

Miller, Droge, Toulouse (1988) Links I, II	Contingency theory	CEOs, VPs or general managers in 77 firms (multiple respondents)	Questionnaires	*Organizational factors* Structure: integration, formalization, centralization, CEO need for achievement *Environmental factor* Uncertainty *Decision process characteristic* Analysis, interaction	LISREL	Extent of analysis and interaction in strategic processes are positively influenced by CEO need for achievement, structural formalization and integration.
Eisenhardt (1989) Links I, II, IV, VI	Synoptic and incremental processes, political model of decision making	8 firms in microcomputer industry (multiple respondents)	CEO interviews, semistructured interviews with each member of a firm's top management team, questionnaires, and secondary sources.	*Decision process characteristics* Consensus, real-time information, multiple simultaneous alternatives, two-tier advice process *Process outcomes* Decision speed, number of alternatives considered, integration among decisions, commitment to decisions *Economic outcomes* Sales growth and profits, CEO self reports	Grounded theory and historical analyses Within-case and cross-case comparisons Thematic analyses Frequencies and descriptive statistics	Fast decision makers in high velocity environments use more information, consider more alternatives, use counsellors, and pursue active conflict resolution strategies. Decisions based on this pattern of behaviours lead to superior performance.

(continued)

Study/links	Theoretical bases	Sample	Data sources/methods	Measures	Analytic methods	Major findings
Fredrickson, Iaquinto (1989) Links I, II, V	Synoptic and incremental decision making, group decision making	45 firms from 2 industries, 159 executives including CEOs (multiple respondents)	Interviews, questionnaires utilizing decision scenarios	*Environmental factor* Stability/instability *Organizational factors* Change in size, change in executive team intrafirm tenure, executive team continuity *Decision process characteristics* Comprehensiveness, change in comprehensiveness *Economic outcomes* Average after tax return on assets adjusted for extraordinary items	Correlations Multiple regression Analysis of variance	Relationships found in the two 1984 studies continue to hold. Changes in organizational size, executive team tenure, and level of team continuity were positively associated with changes in comprehensiveness. Comprehensiveness exhibited considerable inertia. Also, significant across-industry differences were found in comprehensiveness.
Wooldridge & Floyd (1990) Links IV, V, VI	Organizational processes, group decision making	11 banks and 9 manufacturing organizations	Semi-structured interviews with CEOs and questionnaires from middle-level managers	*Decision process characteristics* Participation involvement *Process outcomes* Commitment and understanding of strategy *Economic outcomes* competitive position, ROA, efficiency, growth rate	Correlations	Involvement by middle level management in the formation of strategy leads to greater understanding by them and improved economic performance.

Continued overleaf

Cray, Mallory, Butler, Hickson & Wilson (1988) No specific links examined	Information processing, political models of decision making, group decision making	30 firms from diverse industries, 150 strategic decisions	Interviews with multiple key executives in each firm, company documents	*Decision process characteristics* Scrutiny, interactions, duration, centrality, gestation time, process time	Content analysis Clustering Discriminant analysis	Three types of decision making processes capture a wide range of decision processes – i) Sporadic: discontinuous, prolonged, highly politicized ii) Fluid: continuous, rational, shorter duration iii) Constricted: procedure-dominated, low involvement and interaction, single/few decision makers.
Nees (1983) No specific links examined	Strategic decision making, divestment decision making	Two separate groups of 25 European middle- to senior-level managers in a management development programme	Simulation experiment with three business cases: observations and video taping	*Decision process characteristics* Time allotted to different stages in the decision process; total time for arriving at decision; number and characteristics of different phases in decision process	No statistical tests *except* for percentages	The divestment process consists of four phases: identification, solution development, selection and implementation; more time spent on solution development and selection than implementation; groups with *more* experience develop *faster* solutions.

namely, complexity and munificence (Dess and Beard, 1984) on decision process characteristics have not been examined. The degree of environmental complexity in a firm's operating environment directly impacts the amount and nature of information that has to be processed by decision makers (Schwenk, 1984; Thomas, 1984). This, in turn, affects strategic decision process characteristics such as comprehensiveness, rationality, and duration. Research on cognitive processes (Schwenk, 1984; Schwenk, 1988) suggests that high environmental complexity may lead to greater use of cognitive simplification processes such as selective perception, heuristics and biases, and the use of analogies. These cognitive simplification processes, in turn, affect the strategic decision process by potentially restricting the range of strategic alternatives considered and the information used to evaluate alternatives. Techniques developed in social and cognitive psychology such as cognitive mapping (Axelrod, 1976), may help researchers understand how decision makers assess interrelationships among environmental factors, which factors they consider important, and how they arrive at particular choices.

In addition to environmental complexity, munificence should also influence strategic decision processes. Munificence refers to an environment's capacity to provide resources which support the organization. Organizations are less likely to be penalized for poor or suboptimal decisions in munificent than in non-munificent environments. Thus, decision processes suited to munificent environments may be inappropriate for less munificent ones. However, past research has failed to address these questions, in spite of the fact that findings would have important normative implications for managers who must formulate strategic decisions in a variety of environmental contexts.

Link II: Relationships between organizational factors and decision process characteristics

Studies pertaining to this link have mostly focused on two sets of organizational factors: power distributions within the decision-making group (Eisenhardt, 1989; Jemison, 1981; Shrivastava and Grant, 1985) and structural aspects such as formalization, integration, and decentralization (Miller, Droge, and Toulouse, 1988). Several theoretical arguments have been made which indicate how these two organizational factors influence strategic decision processes. Provan (1989) argues that managerial perceptions and enactment of the environment are heavily influenced by power distribution within an organization. Powerful individuals and departments are likely to determine the identification of problems and issues (Dutton and Jackson, 1987), the type and extent of information used, and the criteria used to evaluate alternatives (Shrivastava and Grant, 1985). Similarly, organizational structure can influence information flow (Bower, 1970; Fahey, 1981), as well as the extent of analysis and interaction at different organizational levels (Miller, Droge, and Toulouse, 1988).

While a number of empirical studies have been undertaken on relationships identified by Link II, consistent patterns with meaningful implications for practitioners are lacking. For example, Shrivastava and Grant (1985) suggest that formal structures and power centralization are associated with rationality in decision making processes, lower degree of political activity and subunit involvement, and quicker decisions. Similarly, Miller, Droge and Toulouse (1988) and Miller (1987) found positive relationship between structural formalization and integration and also between the extent of rationality and integration in strategic decision processes. In contrast, Eisenhardt (1989) and Eisenhardt and Bourgeois (1988) found that in rapidly changing environments, power centralization is associated with a higher degree of political activity within the top management team and poorer economic performance. As noted earlier in our discussion of Link I studies, this suggests crucial interactions between organizational and environmental factors in the relationship between strategic decision processes and performance. In other words, alternative power distributions and structures may affect strategic decision processes differently in different environments and the outcome effects of different structure/power and strategic decision process combinations may also vary across different environments.

Research relating other organizational factors (identified in figure 12.1) to strategic decision processes is limited. Exceptions include studies by Fredrickson (1984), which examined the role of past performance and Fredrickson and Iaquinto (1989) which examined the effects of changes in organizational size and top management team characteristics on decision process comprehensiveness. In other studies exploring this link, Fahey (1981) and Shrivastava and Grant (1985) examined a wide range of organizational factors through case studies but did not identify the specific effects of these factors except in terms of general propositions. Segev (1987), using laboratory and field experiments, found significant associations between a firm's strategic orientation and strategy making modes. However, because of the small number of studies which examine these relationships, it is difficult to draw any generalizable conclusions or identify consistent patterns.

The review of Link II studies also points to several organizational factors which, though theoretically meaningful, have received little or no attention in past research. These include the role of organizational slack, belief structures, top management team characteristics, and past strategies and performance. Also, our review indicates that past research in this link has predominantly used contingency theories to study relationships. This is appropriate since these studies primarily focus on structure and power. However, other theoretical arguments may be needed to explore the role of the neglected organizational factors in the future. In particular, theories of group decision making and cognition which emanate from a social psychological perspective of decision making are relevant. Bateman and Zeithaml (1989) used the psychology literature on escalation and decision framing to study the effects of past performance and organizational slack on the divestment decision. While their study focused on the content rather than the process of decision making, interesting parallels can be drawn. For example, favourable past performance and high organizational slack can create positive decision frames, and high levels of decision maker confidence which, in turn, can lead to a limited examination of new alternatives, limited information search, and less comprehensive, but faster decision processes. Past strategies can have similar effects on strategic decision processes according to theories of escalating commitment. Cognitive simplification processes such as illusion of control and selective perception, which can restrict the range of strategic alternatives considered, may be associated with favourable past perfomance and the presence of organizational slack. Research into the effects of top management team (TMT) characteristics (such as size, tenure and demography) on strategic decision processes can draw upon theories of group decision making such as polarization (Lamm and Myers, 1978; McGrath, 1984), social comparison (Jellison and Arkin, 1977), and persuasive argumentation (Vinokur and Burnstein, 1974). These theories of intra-group decision processes can constitute relevant theoretical bases for understanding the effects of TMT characteristics on strategic decision processes. For example, the study by Gladstein and Reilly (1985), on group decision making has useful implications for TMT decision making as well.

With regard to methodological perspectives, most studies belonging to this link have utilized field surveys and case studies. Given the number of confounding factors in such settings and the wide variety of factors examined, there are serious concerns of internal validity. In order to improve future theory building, researchers may need to make greater use of laboratory and carefully controlled field settings. These research designs permit the researcher to identify specific effects of each organizational factor while controlling for other factors, as well as possible two-way and three-way interactions (e.g. Bateman and Zeithaml, 1989). Relationships identified in such controlled settings can then be tested among a wide variety of organizations using techniques of stratified sampling which control for one set of factors while varying the others (Harrigan, 1983).

Link III: Relationships between decision-specific factors and decision process characteristics

Our review of the literature indicates that relationships between decision specific factors and decision process characteristics have received very limited attention in past research. Only seven out of the thirty-one studies reviewed in table 12.2 examined Link III. Five of these tested specific hypotheses with the remaining two being case studies. In addition, the available body of research is also fragmented. Given the variety in the types of strategic decisions that managers make, there clearly is a need to examine the influence of decision context on process characteristics. Carter's (1971) pioneering study indicated that decision context, defined in terms of level of technical uncertainty, degree of outcome uncertainty, and criticalness to decision makers, has an important influence on process characteristics. In a more recent study of strategic energy management decisions, Fahey (1981) found that the process characteristics were influenced by factors such as degree of criticalness, impetus, and frequency of occurrence. Also, Schilit's (1987) findings suggest that the risk/return characteristics of a decision impact the extent of upward influence exercised by middle level managers. Other decision specific factors that have been identified as having influence on process characteristics include decision complexity (Astley *et al.* 1982), decision urgency (Pinfield, 1986), decision motive (Frederickson, 1985; Shrivastava and Grant, 1985), information source (Schilit and Paine, 1987), and problem classification (Volkema, 1986). Further empirical evidence supporting the impact of problem characterization on decision processes and outcomes is available in studies by Cowan (1988) and Dutton and Duncan (1987).

In summary, two factors limit our ability to draw generalizable conclusions about the relationship between various decision specific factors and process characteristics. First, little consensus exists regarding the definition and operationalization of important decision specific factors, leading to loose and inconsistent definitions of key constructs. Further, terms such as decision criticalness, decision urgency, and outcome uncertainty have been used in several studies with little or no attempt to satisfy the requirements of construct validity and reliability. Only one out of the seven studies in this link (Frederickson, 1985) provided tests for construct validity and reliability. Second, very few studies in Link III have simultaneously examined or controlled for the influence of environmental and organizational factors. This clearly limits our ability to draw strong inferences regarding this link or to build theory cumulatively. Perhaps the major contribution of studies in this link is a heightened awareness of the need for closer examination of the interrelationships between decision specific factors and process characteristics.

300 Designing Strategic Systems

Links IV, V, & VI: Relationships among decision process characteristics and process/economic outcomes

As Venkatraman and Ramanujam (1986) point out, performance improvement is at the heart of strategic management. Therefore, it is not surprising that a number of empirical studies have examined the relationship between process characteristics and performance outcomes. However, most studies have focused on Links IV (process characteristics and process outcomes) and V (process characteristics and economic outcomes), leaving Link VI (process outcomes and economic outcomes) as the most underresearched link in our model. Of the nineteen studies which examined strategic decision process outcomes, ten studied Link IV, eleven studied Link V, but only three examined Link VI.

Studies in Link V have attempted to establish some prescriptive relevance for strategic decision making research by investigating the relationship between decision process characteristics and economic outcomes. These include studies by Fredrickson (1984) and Fredrickson and Mitchell (1984) which found a positive relationship between decision process comprehensiveness and superior performance in stable environments, and a negative relationship in unstable environments. In a longitudinal extension, it was found that these relationships hold even after several years (Fredrickson and Iaquinto, 1989). However, conflicting results have been reported by Eisenhardt (1989) who found a positive relationship between comprehensiveness and performance in high-velocity environments. This lack of consensus on the relationship between comprehensiveness and performance is very similar to the contradictions encountered in the research on formal planning systems and financial performance (Pearce, Freeman, and Robinson, 1987), since the formality of the planning system may often be indicative of the comprehensiveness of the planning process.

A number of studies belonging to Link V have also investigated the relationship between TMT consensus and economic performance. (See Dess and Origer [1987] for a comprehensive review of these studies.) As with the relationship between the comprehensiveness of the decision process and economic performance, empirical results in this area are conflicting. While Bourgeois (1980), and Dess (1987) found a positive relationships between consensus and firm performance, Bourgeois (1985) and Grinyer and Norburn (1975) found the relationship to be negative. Priem (1990) suggests that a direct relationship between consensus and performance may be too simplistic and that environmental change may strongly moderate such a relationship. Further, he argues that consensus itself may be the outcome of organizational factors or more specifically TMT characteristics such as homogeneity and group structure.

While the impact of decision process characteristics on economic outcomes has been of considerable interest to both researchers and practitioners, it must be recognized that several organizational and environmental factors also affect economic performance. As a result, cause-effect relationships are difficult to establish. Because of the model underspecification which characterizes many of these studies, reported relationships are likely to be confounded by factors extraneous to the research question under investigation.

In contrast, the relationships between process characteristics and process outcomes (Link IV) are more direct and are less likely to be confounded by extraneous factors. Timeliness, speed of decision making, acceptability to organizational members, adaptiveness to change, and the extent of organizational learning appear to be useful indicators of strategic decision process outcomes (Quinn and Rohrbaugh, 1983). Studies belonging to this link include Eisenhardt (1989), who found that speed of decision making is positively related to comprehensiveness and extent of analysis, and Langley (1990), whose study indicated that formal analysis in strategic decisions ensures convergence towards action.

A stream of research that has focused on Link IV relationships consists of several laboratory studies on the relative effectiveness of Dialectical Inquiry (DI) and Devil's Advocacy (DA) on decision performance. Both of these methods are based on inducing cognitive conflict in the decision making process. While these studies provide some evidence that cognitive conflict generally leads to better quality decisions (e.g., Schweiger, Sandberg, and Rechner, 1989; Schweiger, Sandberg, and Ragan, 1986), they do not provide any conclusive evidence as to whether one method is superior to another (Schwenk, 1989). Further, if a broader definition of outcome is adopted, incorporating such factors as satisfaction with the decision and desire to continue to work in the group, the results become even more confusing.

Lastly, empirical studies pertaining to Link VI, i.e., the relationship between process outcomes and economic outcomes, are scarce. Our research identified only three such studies (Eisenhardt, 1989; Eisenhardt and Bourgeois, 1988; Wooldridge and Floyd, 1990). Eisenhardt (1989) found a positive relationship between decision speed and performance. Wooldridge and Floyd (1990) found that involvement and commitment by middle-level managers lead to better performance.

Our review of Link's IV, V, and VI suggests that a number of important questions have remained unanswered. For example, are there patterns in the relationships between different strategic decision making process characteristics and the extent/type of organizational learning that takes place as a consequence of these processes? Also, what are the performance/

outcome implications of these relationships? Since learning is an ongoing process in organizations an important issue is whether we should view it as an outcome variable at all. In other words, while the knowledge base resulting from organizational learning is a process outcome, learning itself could be viewed as a continuous organizational process. Shrivastava and Grant (1985) suggest that different types of organizational learning systems support different types of strategic decision making models. For example, formal learning systems such as strategic planning systems and management information systems support adaptive strategic decision making processes. But do different strategic decision making processes contribute differentially to organizational learning? Mintzberg and Waters (1985) argue that comprehensive, deliberate strategic decision making can often hinder strategic learning since messages from the environment tend to get blocked out. On the other hand, strategies which are characterized by emergent/evolutionary processes may keep the organization open, flexible, and responsive.

Conclusions and Implications for Future Research

Based on the preceding review of empirical research on strategic decision processes, several conclusions and implications for future research can be identified. These are discussed in the following paragraphs grouped along theoretical, methodological, and managerial dimensions.

Theoretical implications

Need for more theory testing

Strategic decision process research to date is based on a very rich and diverse theoretical base. Empirical studies have often used more than one theoretical model to study strategic decision processes, resulting in a much richer description of the process than would have occurred with simpler theoretical models. In particular, the use of both rational and political/behavioural models has been far more prevalent in process research than in content research. However, our review does indicate the importance of utilizing multiple theories in order to develop more testable hypotheses. Given the rich descriptions of the strategic decision process and multiple models used to analyse it, the development of additional descriptive models is likely to result in only limited benefits. More useful would be studies which attempt to test the normative and predictive usefulness of existing models. Such studies would not only permit the identification of the nature of causal relationships but also result in greater cumulation of research findings.

Greater use of cognitive/psychological theories

Past empirical research on strategic decision processes has been dominated by theoretical models which adopt an organizational/macro perspective rather than an individual/micro perspective. This is evident in the number of studies which have utilized contingency theories, rational, sociopolitical, and organizational process models of decision making. Twenty-one out of the thirty-one studies in our review utilized macro/organizational theoretical perspectives, as opposed to only six studies which adopted a more micro view of the decision process. The latter set of studies typically utilized group decision making theories. Only four studies (Cray *et al.* 1988; Fredrickson and Iaquinto, 1989; Schilit and Paine, 1987; Wooldridge and Floyd, 1990) reflect a combination of the micro and macro perspectives in studying this topic. While a macro perspective is both necessary and useful, the role of the individuals and groups involved in the strategic decision process needs to be acknowledged to a greater extent in future research. In this regard, cognitive psychological theories of decision making (e.g., Axelrod, 1976; Bateman and Zeithaml, 1989: Kahneman and Tversky, 1984) and theories of group decision making (Gladstein and Reilly, 1985) can certainly contribute to a better understanding of the impact of factors such as individual backgrounds, experiences, biases, group composition, and tenure on the strategic decision process. We believe that combining the macro and the micro views of strategic decision making should be particularly important in both future theory building and theory testing. Several specific research questions which can be explored from a micro perspective were identified earlier in our discussion of Links I and II.

Multiple theoretical specifications

Boal and Bryson (1987) identify four underlying theoretical models to represent interrelationships between contextual, process, and outcome variables: independent, intervening, moderating, and interaction effects models. In the intervening effects model, contextual factors (such as environment, organization, and decision-specific factors) impact outcomes through their effects on process-related variables. In the independent effects model, contextual and process variables have independent effects on outcomes. In the moderating effects model, context moderates the effect of process on outcomes. Finally, in the interaction model, context and process jointly determine outcomes. Knowing which theoretical model best describes each link in figure 12.1 could have a number of significant implications for theory testing, as well as for managerial practice. The choice of a model, in itself, raises a number of questions. First, should managers focus on context or process or both? Second, can they influence strategic decision processes in such a way as to realize desired outcomes?

304 Designing Strategic Systems

Third, where in the causal sequence should top managers intervene? While a detailed discussion of these models is beyond the scope of this paper (see Boal and Bryson [1987] for a detailed treatment), our review indicates the dominance of the independent/intervening effects models in past research. Although this is appropriate for Link I, II, and III studies, studies examining the outcome-oriented links IV, V, and VI are more likely to benefit from utilizing the moderating/interaction effects models since these specifications will enable researchers to include contextual variables in the process-outcome linkage.

Methodological implications

Research on strategic decision processes reveals rich theory development. However, far less attention has been paid to methodological rigour. Undoubtedly, the complexity of the topic complicates both data collection and analysis. Our review suggests several useful directions and guidelines regarding research methods for future research. These are discussed in the following paragraphs.

Operationalization and measurement of research constructs

As noted earlier in our review of Link III studies, empirical studies have often been plagued by a plethora of definitions and operationalizations, especially in the context of decision-specific antecedent factors and strategic decision process characteristics. More importantly, very little attention has been paid to issues of construct validity and reliability. Utilization of single-item measures in field studies and surveys, and post-facto description of measures by the researcher not only reduce the comparability across studies but also raise questions about the internal validity of the findings. Very few studies in our review made use of multi-item measures, and provided tests for scale reliability and validity. This is a shortcoming which needs to be addressed in future research.

Data sources and data collection methods

Several studies in the past have used survey questionnaires and single respondents for data collection. There are several problems to be noted in this respect. First, questionnaires are subject to respondents' varying interpretations and cognitive orientations and do not establish whether the context is strategic (Fredrickson, 1986). Second, the perceptions of a single individual, notwithstanding the person's organizational status, may not reflect organizational reality. Wolfe and Jackson's (1987) study, for example, found a severe lack of agreement among participants about the nature and details of their own strategic decisions. In their study, subjects disagreed more than half the time on even the most basic elements of their strategic decisions. This suggests that data obtained through survey questionnaires needs to be validated using other data sources (Huber and Power, 1985). Content analyses of transcripts of actual processes, cross-check of recall data, and multiple concurrent self reports can be used in conjunction with survey questionnaires to overcome problems of respondent bias and distortions (Wolfe and Jackson, 1987).

The use of decision scenarios as a research methodology also holds considerable promise (Fredrickson, 1986). Scenarios enable researchers to adopt a decision-based perspective which assumes that strategic decision processes are patterns of behaviour that develop in organizations, with individual decisions being made and integrated into an overall strategy (Mintzberg and Waters, 1985). As demonstrated in studies by Fredrickson and his colleagues, scenarios based on detailed industry knowledge allow the creation of strategic contexts, while providing respondents with standardized stimulus. Scenarios can be tailored to different industry contexts. Moreover, multiple scenarios, when used in a single study, can enable researchers to achieve internal validity as well as generalizability. Scenarios also permit the use of multiple respondents, multi-item indicators of research constructs, and construct development techniques which maximize both agreement within firms and between-firm variance (Fredrickson, 1986). Finally, scenarios can also be used to assess cross-sectional and temporal variances by administering them to the same set of respondents at different points in time and thereby assessing causal patterns of relationships over time. Scenarios appear to combine some of the advantages of controlled laboratory studies (i.e., high internal validity through controlled stimulus) with those of field studies (i.e., realism and generalizability). For this reason, they offer a promising data collection method for future studies.

Greater utilization of longitudinal research designs

Field studies, commonly used in past research on strategic decision processes, have been largely cross-sectional. They pool strategic decisions and respondents from multiple industries and environmental contexts without incorporating adequate controls. Thus, if we are to more fully understand the causal relationships (and their directions) between the antecedent factors and process characteristics and also their impact on outcomes, it is important that longitudinal research designs are emphasized. Van de Ven's (1980 a, b) work in programme planning provides an excellent illustration of how longitudinal studies can explain the relationships among context, process, and outcomes over time. Fredrickson's various studies in the paint and forest products industries reviewed earlier also indicate the usefulness of a longitudinal approach in determining whether certain synoptic/incremental modes of strategic decision making persist over time and their performance implications. While it has been argued that cross-sectional studies permit greater generalizability, longitudinal studies have the advantage that they help eliminate the possibility of reverse causalities among a study's variables, an unavoidable problem associated with cross-sectional studies.

Several options are available, with respect to data collection and analysis, which combine both generalizability and accuracy within certain limits. Samples of firms and industries can be chosen to permit maximum variation on one set of antecedent variables while controlling the others (Harrigan, 1983). For each member within this sample, data on process characteristics and various outcome variables can be collected at different points in time. The effects of cross-sectional variations and temporal effects can then be assessed simultaneously by employing data analytic methods suited for pooled cross-sectional time series data.

Causal modelling and multivariate analysis methods

The most commonly used statistical methods in past empirical studies are bivariate, zero-order, and partial correlations and also analysis of variance techniques which assess main effects and simple interactions. Although these methods are both appropriate and useful in assessing relationships within independent/intervening effects models (Boal and Bryson, 1987), more complex analytic methods will be needed to assess multivariate relationships within moderating/interaction effects models. Moderated regression analysis and subgroup regression analysis are particularly useful for this purpose (Arnold, 1982). Second generation multivariate models such as LISREL could be very useful in testing interaction effects models. Moreover, the model depicted in figure 12.1 suggests the need to examine direct as well as indirect effects through causal modelling techniques such as path analysis (Wright, 1960). For example, path analysis can be used to assess whether process characteristics have a direct impact on economic outcomes or whether the effect is indirect through their effects on process outcomes. Such analysis would also expose the relative strength of these direct and indirect effects.

Managerial implications

Need for greater outcome orientation

Nineteen out of the thirty-one studies in our review included either economic or process outcomes or both. In spite of the large number of studies which have examined the outcomes of strategic decision processes, little by way of useful advice to practising managers can be drawn from these. Two general conclusions seem to emerge from our review. First, the performance effects of strategic decision processes are context specific. Environmental and organizational factors have independent as well as interaction effects, but unequivocal patterns are hard to establish. Second, processes which induce intra-group cognitive conflict appear to improve decision quality, but whether such processes also improve other process outcomes such as decision speed, commitment etc. is unclear. These conclusions point to a rather serious limitation of strategic decision process research, namely, limited prescriptive relevance. Strategic process research should aspire to descriptive accuracy as well as prescriptive relevance. Research to date has been very productive in terms of describing how and why decision process characteristics vary between different contexts. However, it tells us little about whether one set of characteristics is more effective than another and the conditions under which such effectiveness can be realized. It also fails to tell us whether decision processes account for significant variance in performance, economic or otherwise. As suggested by Bateman and Zeithaml (1989), research needs to identify and explicate relationships which are not obvious to managers. To the extent that the outcome effects of strategic decision processes are both non-obvious and extremely complex, studies which examine these links are likely to have considerable practical significance.

Defining relevant outcomes

Variables used to capture outcomes in the strategic decision process research, to a large extent, reflect the economic orientation of content researchers. This research emphasis raises the interesting question as to whether economic measures of performance are the only legitimate outcome variables or whether they reflect the biases imposed by the researcher's cognitive framework (Reger, 1988) and data availability. A broader conceptualization of process effectiveness is needed which incorporates both process-related as well as economic-performance-related measures (Venkatraman and Ramanujam, 1986). Cause-effect relationships are much harder to assess in the study of economic performance outcomes than in the study of process outcomes, because of the variety of organizational and environmental influences on economic performance (as indicated by the secondary links in figure 12.1). Future researchers must also ask themselves whether research is focusing on outcomes which are considered desirable and valuable by top managers and other decision makers. Other topics of relevance to managers are the possibility of trade-offs among different outcomes, their potential benefits, and their long-term and short-term effects. These and several other related questions reflect greater attention to performance implications of strategic decision processes and are likely to be very meaningful from the point of view of practising managers.

In conclusion, while considerable research has been undertaken on strategic decision processes in the last decade by scholars in strategic management, the research has remained fragmented and non-cumulative. Our evaluation of the empirical literature suggests that there are a number of gaps and inconsistencies in past research. It is our hope that the framework proposed in this paper, which is based on a careful assessment of the existing theoretical and empirical literature, will be of help in addressing the many unresolved research issues relating to strategic decision processes. It also suggests several useful directions for future research. As discussed in the preceding paragraphs, we expect such research to not only enhance our understanding of the complexities surrounding strategic decision processes, but also provide meaningful guidance to managers in the making of effective strategic decisions.

Notes

1 The authors wish to thank Anthony Daboub, Gregory G. Dess, Peter Lorange, Johan Roos and V.K. Narayanan for their helpful comments on earlier drafts of this paper.
2 Our review covered empirical work published in Academy of Management Journal, Administrative Science Quarterly, Strategic Management Journal, Journal of Management, Journal of Management Studies, Management Science, Organization Science, and Organization Studies during the period 1981–90.

References

Allison, G. T. 1971: *Essence of decision*, Little, Brown and Co.: Boston, MA.
Andrews, K. R. 1971: *The concept of corporate strategy*. Irwin: Homewood, IL.
Ansoff, H. I. 1965: *Corporate strategy*, McGraw-Hill: New York.
Arnold, H. J. 1982: Moderator variables: A clarification of conceptual, analytic, and psychometric properties, *Organizational Behavior and Human Performance*, 29, pp. 143–174.
Astley, W. G., Axelsson, R., Butler, R. J., Hickson, D. J. and Wilson, D. C. 1982: Complexity and cleavage: Dual explanations of strategic decision-making. *Journal of Management Studies*, 19, pp. 357–375.
Axelrod, R. (Ed.) 1976: *Structure of decision: The cognitive maps of political elites*. Princeton University Press: Princeton, New Jersey.
Bateman, T. S. and Zeithaml, C. P. 1989: The psychological context of strategic decisions: A model and convergent experimental findings. *Strategic Management Journal*, 10, pp. 59–74.
Boal, K. B. and Bryson, J. M. 1987: Representation, testing, and policy implications of planning processes. *Strategic Management Journal*, 8, pp. 211–231.
Bourgeois, L. J. 1980: Performance and consensus. *Strategic Management Journal*, 1, pp. 227–248.

Bourgeois, L. J. 1985: Strategic goals, perceived uncertainty and economic performance. *Academy of Management Journal*, 28, pp. 548-573.

Bourgeois, L. J. and Eisenhardt, K. M. 1988: Strategic decision processes in high velocity environments: Four cases in microcomputer industry. *Management Science*, 34, pp. 816-835.

Bower, J. 1970: *Managing the resource allocation process*. Graduate School of Business Administration, Harvard University Press: Boston.

Braybrooke, D. and Lindblom, C. E. 1970: *A strategy of decisions: Policy evaluation as a social process*, Free Press: New York.

Carter, E. 1971: The behavioral theory of the firm and top level corporate decisions. *Administrative Science Quarterly*, 16, pp. 413-428.

Chaffee, E. E. 1985: Three models of strategy. *Academy of Management Review*, 10, pp. 89-98.

Cowan, D. A. 1988: Executive knowledge of organizational problem types: Applying a contingency perspective. *Journal of Management*, 14, pp. 513-527.

Cray, D., Mallory, G. R., Butler, R. J., Hickson, D. J. and Wilson, D. C. 1988: Sporadic, fluid and constricted processes: Three types of strategic decision making in organizations. *Journal of Management Studies*, 25, pp. 13-39.

Dess, G. G. 1987: Consensus on strategy formulation and organizational performance: Competitors in a fragmented industry. *Strategic Management Journal*, 8, pp. 259-277.

Dess, G. G. and Beard, D. W. 1984: Dimensions of organizational task environments. *Administrative Science Quarterly*, 29, pp. 52-73.

Dess. G. G. and Origer, N. K. 1987: Environment, structure and consensus in strategy formulation: A conceptual integration. *Academy of Management Review*, 12, pp. 313-330.

Dutton, J. E. and Duncan, R. B. 1987: The creation of momentum for change through the process of strategic issue diagnosis. *Strategic Management Journal*, 8, pp. 279-295.

Dutton, J. E. and Jackson, S. 1987: Categorizing strategic issues: Links to organizational action. *Academy of Management Review*, 12, pp. 76-90.

Eisenhardt, K. M. 1989: Making fast strategic decisions in high-velocity environments. *Academy of Management Journal*, 32, pp. 543-576.

Eisenhardt, K. M. and Bourgeois, L. J. 1988: Politics of strategic decision making in high-velocity environments: Toward a midrange theory. *Academy of Management Journal*, 31, pp. 737-770.

Fahey, L. 1981: On strategic management decision processes. *Strategic Management Journal*, 2, pp. 43-60.

Fredrickson, J. W. 1984: The comprehensiveness of strategic decision processes: Extensions, observations, future directions. *Academy of Management Journal*, 27, pp. 445-466.

Fredrickson, J. W. 1985: Effects of decision motive and organizational performance level on strategic decision processes. *Academy of Management Journal*, 28, pp. 821-843.

Fredrickson, J. W. 1986: An exploratory approach to measuring perceptions of strategic decision process constructs, *Strategic Management Journal*, 7, pp. 473-483.

310   Designing Strategic Systems

Fredrickson, J. W. and Iaquinto, A. L. 1989: Inertia and creeping rationality in strategic decision processes. *Academy of Management Journal*, 32, pp. 543-576.

Fredrickson, J. W. and Mitchell, T. R. 1984: Strategic decision processes: Comprehensiveness and performance in an industry with an unstable environment. *Academy of Management Journal*, 27, pp. 399-423.

Ginsberg, A. and Venkatraman, N. 1985: Contingency perspectives of organizational strategy: A critical review of the empirical research. *Academy of Management Review*, 10, pp. 421-434.

Gladstein, D. L. and Reilly, N. P. 1985: Group decision making under threat: The tycoon game. *Academy of Management Journal*, 28, pp. 613-627.

Grant, J. H. and King, W. R. 1980: *The logic of strategic planning*. Little, Brown & Co.: Boston.

Grinyer, P. and Norburn D. 1975: Planning for existing markets: Perceptions of executives. *Journal of the Royal Statistical Society*, 138 (1), pp. 70-97.

Harrigan, K. R. 1983: Research methodologies for contingency approaches to business strategy. *Academy of Management Review*, 8, pp. 398-405.

Huber, G. P. and Power, D. J. 1985: Retrospective reports of strategic-level managers: guidelines for increasing their accuracy. *Stategic Management Journal*, 6, pp. 171-180.

Huff A. S. and Reger, R. K. 1987: A review of strategic process research. *Journal of Management*, 13, pp. 211-236.

Janis, I. L. 1982: *Victims of Groupthink*, Houghton-Mifflin: Boston, MA.

Jellison, J. and Arkin, R. 1977: Social comparison of abilities: A self-presentation approach to decision-making in groups. In J. Suls and R. Miller (eds.), *Social comparison processes: Theoretical and empirical processes*, Hemisphere Press. Washington, D. C.

Jemison, D. B. 1981: Organizational versus environmental sources of influence in strategic decision making. *Strategic Management Journal*, 2, pp. 77-89.

Johnson, G. 1988: Rethinking incrementalism. *Strategic Management Journal*, 9, pp. 75-91.

Kahneman, D. and Tversky, A. 1984: Choices, values, and frames. *American Psychologist*, 39, pp. 341-350.

Langley, A. 1990: Patterns in the use of formal analysis in strategic decisions. *Organization Studies*, 11, pp. 17-45.

Lamm, H. and Myers, D. G. 1978: Group induced polarization of attitudes and behavior. In L. Berkowitz (ed.), *Advances in experimental social psychology*, 11, pp. 145-195.

Lindblom, C. E. 1959: The science of muddling through. *Public Administration Review*, 19, pp. 79-88.

Lyles, M. A. 1987: Defining strategic problems: Subjective criteria of executives. *Organization Studies*, 8, pp. 263-279.

Lyles, M. A. and Thomas, H. 1988: Strategic problem formulation. *Journal of Management Studies*, 25, pp. 131-146.

Mason, R. O. and Mitroff, I. I. 1981: *Challenging strategic planning assumptions*. Wiley: New York.

McGrath, J. E. 1984: *Groups: Interaction and performance*, Prentice Hall. New Jersey.

Miller, D. 1987: Strategy making and structure: Analysis and implications for performance. *Academy of Management Journal*, 30, pp. 7-32.

Miller, D., Droge, C. and Toulouse, J. M. 1988: Strategic process and content as mediators between organizational context and structure. *Academy of Management Journal*, 31, pp. 544-569.

Mintzberg, H. 1973: Strategy-making in three modes. *California Management Review*, 16, pp. 44-53.

Mintzberg, H. and Waters, J. A. 1985: Of strategies, deliberate and emergent. *Strategic Management Journal*, 6, pp. 257-272.

Mintzberg, H., Raisinghani, D. and Theoret, A. 1976: The structure of 'unstructured' decision processes. *Administrative Science Quarterly*, 21, pp. 246-75.

Narayanan, V. K. and Fahey, L. 1982: The micro-politics of strategy formulation. *Academy of Management Review*, 7, pp. 25-34.

Nees, D. B. 1983: Simulation: A complementary method for research on strategic decision-making processes. *Strategic Management Journal*, 4, pp. 175-185.

Pearce. J. A. Freeman, E. B. and Robinson, R. B. 1987: The tenuous link between formal strategic planning and financial performance. *Academy of Management Review*, 12, pp. 658-675.

Pettigrew, A. 1973: *The politics of organizational decision making*. London: Tavistock.

Pinfield, L. T. 1986: A field evaluation of perspectives on organizational decision making. *Administrative Science Quarterly*, 31, pp. 365-388.

Porter, M. E. 1980: *Competitive strategy*. Free Press: New York.

Priem, R. L. 1990: Top management team group factors, consensus, and firm performance. *Strategic Management Journal*, 11, pp. 469-478.

Provan, K. G. 1989: Environment, department power, and strategic decision making in organizations: A proposed integration. *Journal of Management*, 15, pp. 21-34.

Quinn, J. B. 1980: *Strategies for change*. Dow-Jones Irwin: Homewood, IL.

Quinn, R. E. and Rohrbaugh, J. 1983: A spatial model for effectiveness criteria: Towards a competing values approach to organizational analysis. *Management Science*, 29, pp. 363-377.

Reger, R. K. 1988: *Competitive positioning in the Chicago banking market: Mapping the mind of the strategists*, Unpublished doctoral dissertation, University of Illinois, Urbana-Champaign.

Schilit, W. K. 1987: An examination of the influence of middle level managers in formulating and implementing strategic decisions. *Journal of Management Studies*, 24, pp. 271-293.

Schilit, W. K. and Paine, F. T. 1987: An examination of the underlying dynamics of strategic decisions subject to upward influence activity. *Journal of Management Studies*, 24, pp. 161-187.

Schweiger, D. M., Sandberg, W. R. and Ragan, J. W. 1988: Group approaches for improving strategic decision making: A comparative analysis of dialectical inquiry, devil's advocacy and consensus. *Academy of Management Journal*, 29, pp. 51-71.

Schweiger, D. M., Sandberg, W. R. and Rechner, P. L. 1989: Experiential effects of dialectical inquiry, devil's advocacy and consensus approaches to strategic

312 Designing Strategic Systems

decision making. *Academy of Management Journal*, 32, pp. 745-772.

Schweiger, D. M. and Sandberg, W. R. 1989: The utilization of individual capabilities in group approaches to strategic decision-making. *Strategic Management Journal*, 10, pp. 31-43.

Schwenk, C. R. 1984: Effects of planning aids and representation media on performance and affective responses in strategic decision making. *Management Science*, 30, pp. 263-271.

Schwenk, C. R. 1988: Cognitive simplification processes in strategic decision-making. *Strategic Management Journal*, 9, pp. 111-128.

Schwenk, C. R. 1989: A meta-analysis on the comparative effectiveness of devil's advocacy and dialectical inquiry. *Strategic Management Journal*, 10, pp. 303-306.

Schwenk, C. R. 1990: Conflict in organizational decision making: An exploratory study of its effects in for-profit and not-for-profit organizations. *Management Science*, 36, pp. 436-447.

Segev, E. 1987: Strategy, strategy making, and performance in a business game. *Strategic Management Journal*, 8, pp. 565-577.

Shrivastava, P. and Grant, J. H. 1985: Empirically derived models of strategic decision-making processes. *Strategic Management Journal*, 6, pp. 97-113.

Thomas, H. 1984: Strategic decision analysis: Applied decision analysis and its role in the strategic management process. *Strategic Management Journal*, 5, pp. 139-156.

Tushman, M. L. 1977: A political approach to organizations: A review and rationale. *Academy of Management Review*, 2, pp. 206-216.

Van de Ven, A. H. 1980a: Problem solving, planning, and innovation. Part I. Test of the program planning model. *Human Relations*, 33, pp. 711-740.

Van de Ven, A. H. 1980b: Problem solving, planning, and innovation. Part II. Speculations for theory and practice. *Human Relations*, 33, pp. 757-779.

Venkatraman, N. and Ramanujam, V. 1986: Measurement of business performance in strategy research: A comparison of approaches. *Academy of Management Review*, 11, pp. 801-814.

Vinokur, A. and Burnstein, E. 1974: Effects of partially shared persuasive arguments on group induced shifts: A group problem solving approach. *Journal of Personality and Social Psychology*, 29, pp. 305-315.

Volkema, R. J. 1986: Problem formulation as a purposive activity. *Strategic Management Journal*, 7, pp. 267-279.

Wolfe, J. and Jackson, C. 1987: Creating models of the strategic decision making process via participant recall: A free simulation examination. *Journal of Management*, 13, pp. 123-134.

Wooldridge, B. and Floyd, S. W. 1990: Strategy process, middle management involvement and organizational performance. *Strategic Management Journal*, 11, pp. 231-242.

Welsh, M. A. and Slusher, E. A. 1986: Organizational design as a context for political activity. *Administrative Science Quarterly*, 31, pp. 389-402.

Wright, S. 1960: Path coefficients and path regression: alternative or complementary concepts? *Biometrika*, 47, pp. 189-202.

[30]

FAR Contest Winner

The Manager's Guide to Strategic Planning Tools and Techniques

By James L. Webster, William E. Reif, and Jeffrey S. Bracker

As more line managers are given primary responsibility for planning, there is an urgent need to acquaint them with the spectrum of potent tools and techniques for developing and focusing strategy. This guide evaluates 30 established planning tools in terms of potential benefits and logistical requirements.

Strategic planning in most companies has not contributed to strategic thinking. The answer, however, is not to abandon planning. The need for strategic thinking has never been greater. Instead, strategic planning needs to be rethought and recast. While some companies have taken the first steps in doing so, few have transformed strategic planning into the vital management discipline it needs to be.

—Michael Porter, "Corporate Strategy"
The Economist May 23, 1987.

In an era when more line managers are responsible for doing their own planning, the value of techniques and tools has been downplayed. But familiarizing implementers with powerful tools could potentiate their planning abilities.

As strategic planning evolves, most practitioners and academics would agree with Michael Porter's proposition that few companies have transformed planning into a vital management discipline. We would like to offer a radical hypothesis: A more effective use of strategic planning tools and techniques could integrate strategic planning into the core management process. To fully appreciate the current state of strategic planning, and the role that these techniques can play in refining the strategic thinking process, we need a brief overview of the history of strategic planning.

An Historical View of Strategic Planning

Inception. Strategic planning was born in the mid 1950s. The forerunners of this process—such as the planning, programming and budgeting systems (PPBS)—introduced in the 1940s and early 1950s were being practiced on a very limited basis by managers in business and government. Project management techniques were being used because of their ability to improve the planning and controlling of large, complex endeavors. In Peter Drucker's work, *The Practice of Management*, he makes a strong case for what we know today as strategic management. Soon, leading firms, such as General Electric, were not only practicing strategic planning, but were actively promoting its merits in the business press. The focus of attention during this initial period was on answering the basic questions: What is strategic planning? What are its benefits? How does a firm develop and implement strategic plans?

Growth. The 1960s and 1970s represented a major growth stage for strategic planning. As corporations burgeoned in size, scope, and complexity, two pressing needs emerged. First, it was imperative to develop a more systematic approach to managing the various business units. And second, it was clearly necessary to extend the planning and budgeting horizon beyond the traditional twelve-month operating period. Managers also had a heightened awareness that financial planning alone was not a sufficient management framework—that planning, organizing, and controlling growth-oriented companies required a more comprehensive, "strategic," approach. During the growth stage, the emphasis was on the process of strategic planning, and high-performing companies began to pay a great deal of attention to strategy implementation as well as strategy formulation.

Maturity. As strategic planning moved into the 1980s, the euphoria that typically accompanies a fast ride through the growth stage was over. Business writers began to critique the applications of strategic planning, and cases of failures appeared alongside the successes. It was not unusual for companies to have tried several approaches to strategic planning, none of which totally met their expectations.

As strategic planning came under closer scrutiny, there was general agreement that while there were no fatal flaws in the concept itself, the majority of unsatisfactory experiences resulted from:

- Less than full commitment from top management.
- Too little emphasis on building the data base.
- The misconception that once objectives are set, they will take care of themselves.
- The failure to integrate planning and budgeting.
- And a lack of attention to implementation strategies.

From Process to Technique. In the late 1980s there has been a shift in the emphasis from process to technique. Although the strategic planning process varies somewhat from company to company, the basic steps are:

1. Defining the business—including a concept of mission, corporate goals, and key business values.
2. Conducting a situational analysis, which usually includes both external (environmental/competitive) analysis and internal (organizational) analysis.
3. Establishing planning assumptions or premises.
4. Setting objectives and priorities.
5. Developing implementation strategies and/or action plans.
6. Designing a control system to assist managers in "managing by the plan."

James L. Webster is president of Webster & Associates, a management consulting firm in Fayetteville, Arkansas; William E. Reif is professor of management at Arizona State University in Tempe, Arizona; and Jeffrey S. Bracker is associate professor of management at George Mason University in Fairfax, Virginia. This First Place Winner in the 1988 Foundation for Academic Research (FAR)/The Planning Forum contest was revised over the past year by the authors to include additional tools and techniques in their inventory.

On the one hand, most practitioners of strategic planning recognize the value of the process as a means of disciplining their planning activities and applying critical thinking to their business situation. On the other hand, there is a sense that the process has taken us about as far as it can. Future value added will come from the more extensive use of available tools and techniques that are capable of increasing managers' analytical and diagnostic skills. But our reading of the current situation is that strategic planning in most companies has not contributed to strategic thinking. The solution lies in the application of appropriate tools and techniques to the strategic planning process.

The Status of Strategic Planning Tools and Techniques

During the last three years we conducted comprehensive interviews with over 100 chief executive officers and other senior managers; corporate planners and other staff specialists; and functional, product, and business level managers. Based upon our findings, and those of other researchers, we compiled a list of twelve frequently used strategic planning techniques and where they are typically used in the strategic planning process (see Exhibit 1).

We found that most companies utilize only a limited number of techniques, most of which are used to build data bases (for example, situational, competitive, and market opportunity analysis), or to help them develop operating budgets (financial and forecasting/trend analysis). The gap between strategic management theory and practice appears to be fostered by—it can be argued—a lack of familiarity with tools and techniques. And one of the primary reasons line managers do not take greater advantage of these techniques is that they have little working knowledge of what's available, and thus little expertise in evaluating the cost and benefits associated with their use.

The Manager's Guide

"The Manager's Guide," presented in Exhibit 2, offers managers a framework for evaluating the potential of thirty strategic planning tools and techniques, and is the end product of a three-step process. Our research initially produced the set of twelve techniques. To broaden the scope of our inquiry, we next conducted an exhaustive review of the literature over the last ten years. A total of 347 articles were abstracted from 14 leading business management journals.

This netted another 37 techniques. We then weeded through our collection, which now totaled 49, and reduced our list to 30. The criteria used to pick the winners were:
- The frequency with which the technique appears to be used (the assumption being there is a correlation between frequency of use and perceived value).
- The ability of the tool or technique to be applied without adding unduly to the complexity of the strategic planning process (in terms of training time, need for specialists, computer and facilities requirements, and access to proprietary materials).
- The tool or technique's potential for increasing the effectiveness of the strategic planning process.

How to Use the Guide

The Manager's Guide is designed to help strategic planners examine the relative merits of the thirty most useful techniques. These are listed as column headings, numbered 1 to 30. The Manager's Guide also evaluates each tool or technique in terms of output (what it contributes to the strategic planning process); and data inputs and resource requirements (human, financial, specialized skills, and computer support). These evaluation dimensions are listed on the left in Exhibit 2 as row headings A to I.

The most useful thing to do when first using the Manager's Guide is to become familiar with all thirty techniques by reviewing Exhibit 3, which provides a brief description of each technique, and a reference that the user may want to consult for more detailed information.

EXHIBIT 1
Twelve Frequently Used Strategic Planning Tools and Techniques

Tool or Technique	MS	EA	OA	PA	OP	AP	CS
Nominal Group Technique	X	X	X	X			
Driving Force	X	X	X	X	X		
Forecasting Trend Analysis	X	X		X			
Market Opportunities Analysis		X		X			
Critical Factors/Strategic Issues Analysis		X	X	X	X	X	
Product/Market Matrix		X	X	X			
Situational Analysis (SWOT or TOWS)		X	X	X			
Competitive Analysis (Porter)		X		X			
Portfolio Analysis		X	X	X			
Financial Analysis				X	X	X	
Operating Budgets					X	X	X
Management by Objectives (MBO)	X	X	X	X	X	X	X

Abbreviations for Steps in the Strategic Planning Process:
MS = Mission Statement.
EA = Environmental/Competitive Analysis.
OA = Organizational Analysis.
PA = Planning Assumptions.
OP = Objectives and Priorities.
AP = Action Plans.
CS = Control Systems.

The next thing to do is to see where each technique generally fits in the planning process by scanning the bottom seven rows of the Guide. An "X" indicates that the technique can be used in conjunction with that planning phase. For example, number 2, Nominal Group Technique (a group idea-generation process), may be applied to several phases of strategy formulation, from shaping a mission statement to developing planning assumptions. On the other hand, number 26, McKinsey & Company's 7-S Framework, is used as part of strategy implementation to develop action plans and design control systems.

The Output Dimension. Rows A and B define the techniques' major contributions to the planning process. Row A, Output Content, evaluates each technique on the basis of the information or analysis it generates. Row B, Output Form, indicates whether the output is usually presented in a quantitative or qualitative format. For example, number 27, Operating Budgets, are quantitative measures consisting of revenues and cost forecasts.

Input Dimension. This guideline looks at each technique in terms of Input Content (Row C) and Input Form (Row D). Content refers to the data needed to apply the technique, and Form indicates whether the data is usually expressed in narrative statements or quantitative measures. If a particular technique has not been used before, managers may find that the required input data is not readily available. For example in number 21, if Competitive Analysis is not used, it's unlikely that current competitor profiles will be available. A possible exception is that an alternative technique has been used—such as number 9, Market Opportunity Analysis, which also includes competitor profiles as part of its diagnostic procedure.

The Time Dimension. Row E gives the user an estimate of the time required to apply each technique—a qualifying statement is included for some techniques. For example, the time required to apply number 1, Dialectic Inquiry, is "extensive"—with the qualifier, "limited time may compromise quality." This means that taking short cuts—such as little or no research or preparation time on the part of participants—may seriously limit the benefits the technique is designed to provide.

The actual time spent on the application of a particular technique may vary from one organization to the next, depending on the relationship between time (cost) and the perceived value of the output (benefit). To illustrate, some managers prefer to take an incremental approach to budgeting by applying a percentage increase to last year's numbers, while other managers choose forecasting techniques and a more "zero-based" approach. In the latter case, the time required is greater, but the managers who use it contend that benefits far outweigh costs.

Many factors affect the time required to apply a particular technique. Examples are, the breadth of the search process (calling your best customer and getting some feedback, versus conducting a survey of your entire active customer base); the degree of detail required (the depth of knowledge about a specific issue); and the choice between primary and secondary sources of information. For example, number 9, Market Opportunity Analysis, lists the time required as "extensive." However, the actual time to complete a Market Opportunity Analysis may range from an armchair analysis with very little empirical research, to an extensive five-year industry forecast with a detailed analysis for each product/market niche.

If time is a primary concern for the manager, the appropriate techniques may be those that have limited or moderate time requirements. The outputs may not be as comprehensive or detailed as those generated by other techniques, but they may serve the purpose.

Other Resource Requirements. These are listed in rows F through I. Human Resources (Row F) indicates which management levels are likely to be involved in applying the technique. Establishing guidelines for this dimension proved to be quite difficult. The decision to involve middle managers (functional, product, and business unit) as well as lower level managers is often based more on management style and an organization's culture than whether it's a criterion for successfully applying the technique. If there is a trend, however, it is probably to involve more people in the process, and to take advantage of in-house expertise regardless of where it may be located within the organization.

Financial requirements (Row G) provides a guideline for assessing the costs associated with each technique. In the majority of cases, salaries, the primary expense, is a function of the participants' time and the opportunity costs assigned to competing demands. In terms of hard dollars, the major factors are data collection, computer analysis, and use of strategic management consultants.

Skills requirements (Row H) are classified as qualitative and, quantitative. Given the strong process orientation of strategic planning, it is not surprising that many of the techniques rely heavily upon qualitative analysis or "good judgment" skills. Quantitative skills are most commonly needed in simulation and modeling techniques, and in forecasting, financial analysis, and budgeting.

Computer requirements are addressed in Row I. While the majority of the techniques listed are not computer dependent, there are a number of techniques that are routinely supported by computer-based models and data analysis.

Continued on page 12.

Benefits of Using the Guide

Building the Data Base. The Manager's guide shows that the majority of strategic planning tools and techniques have several characteristics in common. The Guide's dominant feature may well be the number of techniques designed to improve the quality of the data base. This is done: by forcing search activities to discover the facts; by requiring planners to take the next step and analyze data; and by using analytical frameworks or models to classify data, set priorities, and encourage comparative analysis. In fact, many techniques emphasize the importance of good empirical business research, which is consistent with the adage that there is a high correlation between the quality of the data base and the quality of the strategic plan.

Output and Input Content. A review of the Output dimension reveals that current strategic planning seems to rely more heavily on qualitative analysis than on mathematical models, computer-based simulations, or other forms of quantitative analysis. While one should not underplay the importance of quantitative analysis in improving the quality of strategic decisions, at the same time, given the condition of uncertainty that characterizes such decision making, qualitative analysis is just as appropriate for improving strategic thinking skills.

For techniques with qualitative outputs, it follows that data inputs would be narrative in form. For example, inputs for techniques such as number 12, Situational Analysis, number 4, Focus Groups, and number 15, Product/Market Analysis, usually consist of sets of descriptive data. These, in turn, are subjected to critical analysis and converted into outputs in the form of ranked lists of priorities, detailed support for alternative strategies, and recommendations for gaining and sustaining competitive advantage.

Resource Requirements. Applying tools and techniques to the strategic planning process can be both time-consuming and expensive. The most time consuming techniques are those requiring substantial research and data collection (such as number 4, Focus Groups, number 9, Market Opportunity Analysis, and number 16, Future Studies), and/or extensive group participation to reach agreement on strategic issues, alternatives, and/or recommended courses of action. These include number 7, Dialectic Inquiry, number 3, the Delphi Technique, and number 28, MBO.

Skill requirements for strategic planning include functional expertise, such as marketing and sales, service, operations, R&D, finance, human resources, and IS (information systems). IS in particular is becoming a critical resource for strategic planners. Good strategic decisions are dependent upon specific, relevant, and timely information about an organization and its operating environment. Information systems must be capable of scanning the environment and receiving feedback on a regular basis from customers, suppliers, major competitors, and other stakeholders who are in a position to influence strategic decisions.

Many organizations use the services of a management consultant to help facilitate the strategic planning process and add business or technique-related knowledge. Consultants should be evaluated on the basis of their process skills, knowledge of tools and techniques, and ability to translate their broad-based business experience into guidelines and suggestions that add value to the client's strategic planning efforts.

The Linkage Between Tools & Techniques & Strategic Thinking

In the quote introducing this article, Michael Porter contends that strategic planning in most organizations has not contributed to strategic thinking. It would be presumptuous of us to suggest that greater use of tools and techniques is the only answer to this problem. However, they are clearly capable of raising the level of strategic thinking in both individuals and companies. We base our opinion on the demonstrated benefits of incorporating carefully selected techniques into the planning process. While no list can be all inclusive, some of the most important are:

- **Techniques force critical thinking.** They urge managers to look at both the pros and cons; to present and analyze opposing views; and to prepare well-reasoned arguments in support of their recommendations.

- **Techniques encourage managers to concentrate on the facts** ("I know" versus "I think," "I feel," "I believe"). They turn managers into data-based decision makers who are knowledgeable about both the organization and its operating environment.

- **Techniques call for managers not just to describe situations but to understand them as well.** Asking "Why?" requires both quantitative and qualitative analysis. This, in turn, produces insights derived from observations and empirical data rather than intuition and experience alone.

- **Techniques provide a more disciplined, rigorous approach** to problem solving and opportunity seeking—the cornerstones of strategic planning. Peter Drucker warned us years ago that what we need are fewer problem solvers and more opportunity seekers. His concern was based on the observation that while many managers develop decent problem-solving skills, the majority lack the ability to define and exploit opportunities systematically. Process alone does not develop opportunity-seeking skills. Tools and techniques do.

- **Techniques emphasize the need to develop and**

apply decision criteria when analyzing alternatives and choosing courses of action. Criteria help reduce the influence of personality and personal biases and assure that the same standards are used to judge the merits of alternative strategies.

- **Techniques promote a "be prepared" attitude.** Within a strategic planning context, it is not unusual for two or more issues or alternatives to be considered equally cost effective and capable of providing a "good fit" between strategic requirements and organizational capabilities. Under these circumstances, the relative merit of competing arguments usually prevails. Strong arguments are based upon facts, critical analyses, and well-designed output or presentation formats. In other words, being prepared is a natural outcome of the proper use of tools and techniques.

Strategic Rewards: We believe The Manager's Guide serves as a useful framework for evaluating the costs and benefits of recommended tools and techniques. The Manager's Guide is not designed to assess which technique is best, but it does provide the means for making informed decisions about techniques that fit an organization's approach to strategic planning. And, if these techniques are then applied in a conscientious manner, they should increase both the levels of thinking, and the effectiveness of the strategic planning process. □

Name Index

Abell, D.F. 150, 151
Abernathy, W.J. 4
Adam, J. 264
Aguilar, F.J. 101
Al-Bazzaz, S. 149
Alexander, L. 298
Allen, S.A. 147, 149, 150, 165
Allison, G.T. 329, 331
Amara, R. 41
Anderson, C.R. 147, 166
Andrews, K.R. 327, 328, 331
Ansoff, H.I. 31, 327, 328, 331
Argote, L. 158
Argyris, C. 163, 263
Arkin, R. 351
Armstrong, J.S. 105
Arnold, H.J. 359
Astley, W.G. 340, 352
Athos, A.G. 6
Axelrod, R. 349, 356
Axelsson, R. 340

Baird 335
Baldridge, M. 51
Bartlett, C.A. 98, 280
Bateman, T.S. 351, 356, 360
Bateson, C. 34, 38
Baum, E. 260
Beard, D.W. 349
Boal, K.B. 356, 357, 359
Boe, A. 27
Borgeaud, P. 283
Bossidy, L. 216
Bourgeois, L.J. 330, 334, 339, 342, 345, 350, 353, 354
Bower, J.L. 5, 116, 149, 350
Bowman, E.H. 116
Bracker, J.S. xvii, 367–72
Brandt, S.C. 7
Braybrooke, D. 329, 331
Brønn, P.S. xvi, 183–90
Browne, P.C. 95
Brownell, P. 158
Bryson, J.M. 356, 357, 359
Bucy, J.F. 13
Burgelman, R.A. 166
Burke, N.W. 265

Burnstein, E. 351
Butler, R.J. 340, 348
Buzzell, R.D. 151, 372

Camillus, J.C. xv, 25–32, 101, 105
Carter, E. 330, 352
Chaffee, E.E. 329, 331
Chakravarthy, B.S. xv, xvi, 3–15, 87–99, 101–18
Chandler, A.D. jr 147, 149, 295
Christensen, C.R. 6, 101
Cleland, D.I. 101
Coleman 331
Colvin, G. 13
Cool, K. 90
Cooper, A.C. 88
Cordiner, R. 147
Cowan, D.A. 352
Craig, G.L. 372
Craig, T.G. 23
Cray, D. 348, 356
Crosby 141

Dalmia, G. xvii, 269–75
Datta, D.K. xv, xvii, 25–32, 327–65
Davis, P.S. 151
Davis, S. 13
Day, D.L. 150, 154
Deal, T.E. 14
de Bono, E. 41
de Geus, A. 35, 36, 39, 246, 247, 251, 255
Delbecq, A.L. 372
Deming, W.E. 141, 251
de Pree, M. 255
Dess, G.G. 151, 154, 338, 349, 353
Devanna, M.A. 277
Dierickx, I. 90
Doz 288, 289
Droge, C. 346, 349, 350
Drucker, P. 141, 368
Dubofsky, P. 163
Duhaim 335
Duncan, R.B. 148, 152, 330, 352
Dutton, J.E. 330, 349, 352

Edstrom 284
Edwards, J. 122–3
Egelhof, W.G. 148

Einstein, Albert 142
Eisenhardt, K.M. 35, 328, 330, 334, 345, 346, 349, 350, 353, 354
Ettlie 200
Evans, P. 277–94, 283, 291

Fahey, L. 101, 329, 331, 333, 339, 350, 352
Floyd, S.W. 347, 354, 356
Fombrun, C. 277
Ford, Henry 251
Forrester, J. 254
Fredrickson, J.W. 328, 330, 333, 334, 340, 341, 347, 350, 352, 353, 356, 357, 358
Freeman, E.B. 89, 353
Freeman, R.E. 372
Fry, L.W. 151
Fullerton, D. 124

Gaedeke, R.M. 115
Gage, G.H. 105
Galbraith, J.R. 101, 148, 152, 163, 284, 295
Galer, G. 38
Garvin, D.A. 23
Gatignon, H. xvi, 125–33
Geenan, H. 4, 147
Ghoshal 280
Ginsberg, A. 330
Gladstein, D.L. 351, 356
Gorbachev, Mikhail 283
Gore, W.L. 260
Govindarajan, V. 155, 165
Grant, J.H. 101, 327, 342, 349, 350, 352, 355
Greenleaf, R. 256
Grinyer, P.H. 149, 353
Gupta, A.K. 147–70, 277
Gustafson, D.H. 372

Hambrick, D.C. 147, 150, 151, 153, 154
Hamel, G. 88
Hamermesh, R.G. xv, 13, 17–23, 88, 105
Hammond, J.S. 150, 151
Hampden-Turner, C. 35, 262
Handy, C.B. 302
Harker, Bill 123
Harrigan, K.R. xvii, 269–75, 351, 359
Haspeslagh, P. 7, 292
Hax, A. 88, 101
Hayes, R.H. 4, 23, 26, 192, 196
Heaney, D.F. 372
Henderson, B.D. 6, 88, 104, 150
Henderson, J. 124
Heyer, S.J. 207–13
Hickson, D.J. 340, 348
Hill, T. 196

Hitt, M.A. 101
Hofer, C.W. 150, 152
Hofstede, G.H. 278
Hogg, C.A. 23
Hood, E. 216
Hopkins, S. 234, 237
House, R. 26
Hrebiniak, L.G. 101, 116
Huber, G.P. 358
Huff, A.S. 327, 328
Hunt, P. 6
Hurtt, C.B. 23
Hussey, D.E. xvii, 295–304

Iaquinto, A.L. 334, 347, 350, 353, 356
Ireland, R.A. 101

Jackall, R. 23
Jackson, C. 357, 358
Jackson, S. 349
Jaikumar, R. 194, 196, 200, 203
Janis, I.L. 329
Jellison, J. 351
Jemison, D.B. 340, 349
Jillings, G. 40
Johnson, G. 329
Johnson, R.W. 254
Johnston, D.L. 372

Kahneman, D. 356
Kanter, R.M. 23
Kaplan, R.S. 202
Kaplinsky, R. 201
Katzenbach, J.R. xvi, 215–39
Kazanjian, R.K. 101
Kennedy, A.A. 14
Kerr, J.L. 149
King, M. Luther 253
King, W.R. 31, 101, 105, 327
Krager, D.W. 26

Lamm, H. 351
Lamont, B.T. 166
Lander, D. 122
Landers, D.W. 372
Langley, A. 335, 354
Larreche, J. 150
Laurent, G. 278
Lawrence, P. 13, 156, 295
Leader, C.A. xv, 49–70
Leavitt, H.J. 296, 302
Levitt 280
Lindberg 198
Lindblom, C.E. 329, 331

Lipinski, A. 41
Lorange, P. xiii–xviii, 3–15, 87–99, 101, 102, 103, 104, 116, 149, 183–90, 277–94, 331
Lorsch, J.W. 147, 149, 150, 156, 165, 295
Lyles, M.A. 328, 329

McCall, M.W. jr 305–11
McClean, R.J. xv, 71–7
McGrath, J.E. 351
MacMillan, I.C. 150
Mahajan, V. xvii, 6, 103, 315–25
Majaro, S. 135–43
Majluf, N.S. 88, 101
Malik, F.A. 26
Mallory, G.R. 348
Mandel, T. 39
March, J.G. 148
Marchand, D.A. 142
Marcus, D.H. 207–13
Maslow, A.H. 264
Mason, R. 255, 372
Mazzolini 331
Mendleson, A.H. 372
Mennon, L.J. 372
Meyer, A. 331
Miles, R.E. 91, 92, 331
Miller, D. 343, 346, 349, 350
Miller, L. 257
Mintzberg, H. 36, 87, 255, 327, 328, 329, 331, 355, 358
Mitchell, T.R. 328, 330, 340, 353
Mitroff, I. 255, 256, 372
Montgomery, C.A. 165
Moore, D. xvi, 145–6
Murphy, K.J. 277
Myers, D.G. 351

Nadler, D.A. 148, 152
Narayanan, V.K. 329, 331
Nathanson, D.A. 101, 295, 296
Nees, D.B. 333, 348
Neubauer, F. 28
Newman, W.H. 101
Niblock, E.G. 101
Norburn, D. 353

O'Brien, W. 252, 254, 264–5 *passim*
O'Halloran, J.D. xv, 49–70
Oliff, M.C. 142
Origer, N.K. 353
Ouchi, W.G. 147

Paine, F.T. 328, 352, 356
Palia, K.A. 101

Pankratz, H. xvi, 119–24
Pascale, R.T. 6
Patten, R. 123
Pearce, J.A. 353
Peters, T.J. 14, 87, 141, 163, 219, 285
Petro, F.A. 177–82
Pettigrew, A. 329, 331
Pfeffer, J. 152
Pinchot, G. 141
Pinfield, L.T. 343, 352
Pitts, R.A. 149, 150
Porter, M.E. 22, 38, 88, 90, 97, 141, 147, 150, 151, 152, 153, 327, 367, 372
Power, D.J. 358
Prahalad, C.K. 88, 288, 289
Priem, R.L. 353
Provan, K.G. 349
Pyburn, P. 122, 124

Quinn, J.B. 329, 331, 354

Ragan, J.W. 337, 354
Raisinghani, D. 328
Rajagopalan, N. xvii, 327–65
Ramanujam, V. 101, 105, 353, 360
Rangan, U.S. 98
Rasheed, A.M.A. xvii, 327–65
Rechner, P.L. 337, 354
Reger, R.K. 327, 328, 360
Reif, W.E. xvii, 367–72
Reilly, N.P. 351, 356
Robertson, T.S. xvi, 125–33
Robinson, R.B. 353
Rogers, R. 200
Rohrbaugh, J. 354
Roos, J. xvi, 183–90
Rosenbloom, S.R. 192
Rothschild, W. 88
Rumelt, R.P. 104, 149, 155
Russell, V. 199

Salancik, G.R. 152
Salter, M.S. 149
Sandalls, W.T. 101
Sandberg, W.R. 337, 338, 354
Sander, W. 84
Sandy, W. 173–6
Santi-Flaherty, T. 23
Sashkin, M. 265–6
Schaffir, W. xvi, 145–6
Schein, E. 254, 266
Schendel, D.E. 150
Schilit, W.K. 328, 333, 336, 344, 352, 356
Schoeffler, S.R. 372

Schoemaker, P.J.H. 43–8
Schoonoven, C.B. 158
Schwartz, P. 34, 35, 36, 37, 42
Schwartz, R.M. 177–82
Schweiger, D.M. 337, 338, 354
Schwenk, C.R. 336, 338, 349, 354
Segev, E. 344, 350
Selznick, P. 254
Senge, P.M. xvii, 37, 38, 243–69
Shaeffer 281
Shank, J.K. 95, 101
Shaw, G. Bernard 257
Shephard, M. 13
Shobe, L. 84
Shrivastava, P. 342, 349, 350, 352, 355
Silverman, D. 372
Simon, H.A. 13, 148
Simpson, D.G. 33–42
Sloan, A.P. jr 147, 251
Slusher 335
Smith, D.K. xvi, 215–39
Snow, C.C. 91, 92, 101, 331
Solomon, N. 28
Southwood, K.E. 158
Srinivasan, V. 150
Stalk, G. 252
Steel, R. 124
Steers, R.M. 156
Steiner, G.A. xiv, 101, 105
Stoughton, V. 122

Theoret, A. 328
Thomas, H. 329, 349
Thune, S. 26
Tichy, N.M. 277
Tidd, J. 195, 196, 199
Tobia, P.M. 79–84
Tootelian, D.H. 115
Toulouse, J.M. 346, 349, 350
Tregoe, B.B. 79–84, 372
Tushman, M.L. 148, 152, 329, 331
Tversky, A. 356
Twain, Mark 315
Twigg 204

Uttal, B. 13

Vancil, R.F. 4, 8, 93, 94, 95, 101, 115, 147, 149, 165, 331
van der Heijden, C.A.J.M. 43–8
Van de Ven, A.H. 358, 372
Van Lee, R. 207–13
Varadarajan, P.R. 163
Venkatraman, N. 101, 105, 124, 330, 353, 360
Vinokur, A. 351
Volkema, R.J. 352
Von Hippel, E. 137
Voss, C. 191–206

Wack, P. 37, 39, 41, 245, 246, 248, 254
Walleck, A.S. xv, 49–70
Waterman, R.H. 14, 36, 87, 141, 163, 219, 285
Waters, J.A. 87, 327, 355, 358
Watson, T. 251
Webster, J.L. xvii, 367–72
Weihrich, H. 372
Welch, J. 216
Welsh 335
Wheelwright, S.C. 196
White, R.E. xv, 17–23
Wiersema, F.D. 151
Wilkinson, L. 37
William of Ockham 39
Williams, J. 23
Williamson, O.E. 147
Wilson, D.C. 340, 348
Wind, Y. xvii, 6, 103, 315–25
Wittenberg 291
Wolfe, J. 357, 358
Womak, J.P. 191
Woo, C.Y. 88
Wooldridge, B. 347, 354, 356
Wright, R.A. 6, 104
Wright, S. 359
Wriston, W. 252

Yasai-Ardekani, M. 149

Zaphiropoulos, R. 23
Zeithaml, C.P. 147, 151, 351, 356, 360
Zimmerman, J.W. 372